The Psychoanalytic Study
of the Child

VOLUME XXI

The Psychoanalytic Study

of the Child

VOLUME XXI

INTERNATIONAL UNIVERSITIES PRESS, INC.
New York   New York

CONTENTS

Normal and Pathological Development

Diagnostic Profiles

Pathobiography

A SHORT HISTORY OF CHILD ANALYSIS

ANNA FREUD, LL.D., D.Sc.

It seems realistic for psychoanalysts to begin a new venture with a historical survey since this acknowledges the part which past experience plays in present actions and in expectations for the future. For this reason I suggested to the Program Committee of this new Association that their first meeting should be opened by a look back to the beginnings of child analysis, however abbreviated such an introductory account may have to be under the circumstances.

THE WIDENING SCOPE OF PSYCHOANALYSIS IN THE 1920s

Child analysis as a subspecialty of psychoanalysis appeared on the scene approximately forty years ago. At the time this did not happen as an isolated new departure but as part and parcel of what we call in retrospect the "widening scope of psychoanalysis." While until then analytic therapy was confined in the main to young adults and the neuroses, from that era onward other ages as well as other categories of disturbance were included in its field of application. In Vienna, it was Siegfried Bernfeld who began with the analytic study and treatment of disturbed *adolescents;* August Aichhorn who pioneered in the field of *Wayward Youth;* Sadger who specialized in *perversions;* Paul Federn who experimented with the treatment of *psychotics.* In Berlin, Alexander and Staub turned to the study of *criminals.* In this extended area of work, child analysis occupied no more than a section, represented almost simultaneously by Hug-Hellmuth and after her me in Vienna; by Berta Bornstein, Melanie Klein, Ada Mueller-Braunschweig in Berlin; by Steff Bornstein in Prague and by Alice Balint in Budapest. Since this was at the time before formal psycho-

---

Presented at the first scientific meeting of the American Association for Child Psychoanalysis, in Topeka, Kansas, on April 9, 1966.

analytic training had come into being, none of the people named, except perhaps Hug-Hellmuth and Ada Mueller-Braunschweig, were in a teacher-pupil relationship to each other. Ideas as well as techniques developed individually and independently.

VIENNA: CHILD ANALYSIS IN SOCIETY AND INSTITUTE

It was a step forward in the line toward more systematic development when I was asked to talk on child analysis within the framework of the newly founded Vienna Institute of Psychoanalysis, a course of four lectures which appeared 1926/27 under the title of *Introduction to the Technique of Child Analysis*. As was the habit then, the Course was attended by most members of the Vienna Psychoanalytic Society, and it stimulated in some of them the wish in their turn to embark on experimental work in the newly opened field. It was followed therefore by a first Seminar on Child Analysis, a regular meeting in which cases were presented, technical innovations described, and theoretical conclusions put up for discussion.

It was in this seminar that Berta and Steff Bornstein, Editha Sterba, and Jenny Waelder Hall presented the child cases which became landmarks in the literature of child analysis. Other active participants, among them some founder members of this Association, joined earlier or later, in the late twenties and early thirties, as they completed their analytic training and entered the Vienna Psychoanalytic Society. To name only some, in alphabetical order: Dorothy Burlingham, Edith Buxbaum, Erik Homburger Erikson, Hedwig and Willie Hoffer, Anny Angel Katan, Marianne Kris, Anna Maenchen, Margaret Mahler, E. Menaker; and as psychoanalytic students from abroad: Marie Briehl, Julia Deming, Edith Entenman, Margaret Fries, Elisabeth Geleerd, Margaret Gerard, Mary O'Neil Hawkins, Rosetta Hurwitz, Edith Jackson, Estelle Levy, Marian Putnam, Margaret Ribble, Helen Ross.

I consider it in line with later developments that even in these early days the new venture into the area of childhood did not remain restricted to therapy but was carried further into the fields of application and prevention by means of a Course for Educators, founded by Willie Hoffer. Here, teachers from nursery schools, elementary schools, and high schools were introduced in careful, consistent, and painstaking manner to the principles of psychoanalytic child psychology and to their relevance for the understanding, upbringing, and teaching of children of all ages. The results of this instruction are open to view in many valuable articles published in the *Zeitschrift für psychoanalytische Pädagogik* of which Willie Hoffer soon became editor. The alumni of the Vienna Course for Educators can still be found in responsible positions in the children's field all over the world, and quite especially in the United States.

Two Schools of Child Analysis

It was not to the advantage of the development of child analysis that from the outset the new movement proceeded on two lines, distinct from each other. While the Vienna school of child analysis grew, on the whole connected with my name, the Berlin, later London, school developed simultaneously under the leadership of Melanie Klein. Differences which seemed to be confined at first to the area of technique spread increasingly to essential points of theory as publications followed each other.

So far as we were concerned, we explored above all the alterations in the classical technique as they seemed to us necessitated by the child's inability to use free association, by the immaturity of his ego, the dependency of his superego, and by his resultant incapacity to deal unaided with pressures from the id. We were impressed by the strength of the child's defenses and resistances and by the difficulty of interpreting transference, the impurity of which we ascribed to the use of a nonanalytic introductory period. This latter difficulty was removed later by Berta Bornstein's ingenious use of defense interpretation for creating a treatment alliance with the child patient. As regards the specific motivation for child analysis, we learned to see as our long-term aim the preventing of arrests and inhibitions, the undoing of crippling regressions and compromise formations, and, thereby, the setting free of the child's spontaneous energies directed toward the completion of progressive development.

In Melanie Klein's school of child analysis, no similar concerns about technique played a part since with them, from the outset, free play was seen as a full equivalent of free association and accepted as the basis for symbolic interpretations and as the vehicle of transference. The new theory of early development which emerged as the outcome of their findings concerned in the main the struggle between the life and death instincts at the beginning of life, the splitting of objects into good and bad, the role of projection and identification in the building up of the personality, the overwhelming importance of orality. In fact, according to this theory, it is the events of the oral, not of the phallic-oedipal, phase from which the main features of superego and character formation as well as the roots of mental illness have to be deduced.

THE TEACHING OF CHILD ANALYSIS

If there was one point, nevertheless, on which the two schools were in full agreement, it was the form in which instruction was offered to their candidates. Obviously, at that early date, no technique of child analysis could be more than an outcrop of the classical technique for adults, i.e., a variation and adaptation of the latter, developed from it by trial and error. Accordingly, no student of psychoanalysis was supposed to embark on such experimentation before he was sufficiently rooted in the adult technique. We had seen too much of the danger of "wild analysts" in the adult field to wish to produce a similar breed for the treatment of children.

On the basis of such considerations child analysis was—and is being—taught in the official Institutes strictly as an addition to the regular training course for adult analysis. In some places, candidates are permitted to treat a child after their first adult case, in others after their second or third cases. More often than not, adult training has to be completed altogether before training in child analysis is permitted to begin.

So far as teaching is concerned, it is therefore the most significant advance in recent years that we believe to have at last developed an independent approach to the analytic therapy of the child, and that we can now instruct people in this technique as an alternative to adult analysis, i.e., before, or simultaneously, or after their supervised adult cases. Or to put it differently: it does not matter as much any more at which end of the scale we initiate child training; just as child analysis can be acquired as an addition to adult training, so can adult training come in as a second period additional to child analysis (either, of course, based in the usual way on personal analysis plus course and seminar instruction).

An independent training course in child analysis was implemented for the first time in Hampstead after the Second World War, and has produced by now sixty-seven graduates who work actively in psychoanalytic child therapy and child study in England, in the United States, and in other continents and countries. A second course, built on the same lines, has opened more recently under Anny Katan and Robert Furman in Cleveland, Ohio. A third, devised by Teuns, is on the point of being opened in Leyden, Holland, with supervisory help given by the teaching staff of the Hampstead Course and Clinic. It is a significant point that this last-named training comes into being not only tolerated or sponsored by a Branch Society of the International Psycho-Analytical Association, but fully integrated with the teaching program of the Dutch Society and Institute of Psychoanalysis.

With this last step taken, child analysis has made an important move toward independent existence. Candidates are not trained directly anywhere for the analytic treatment of either psychotics, perverts, delinquents or criminals, and no technique, more or less equivalent to the classical technique, is taught anywhere for use with these categories of patients, as the child analytic technique can be taught at present. It is perhaps this unique status of child analysis among the other subspecialities of psychoanalysis which has culminated in the present venture: the formation of an independent American Association for Child Psychoanalysis.

CHILD ANALYSIS AS THE GATEWAY TO APPLICATION, OBSERVATION, AND RESEARCH

Application to the Children's Services

In line with similar developments in the adult field, child analysts in their turn moved from the therapy of disturbed children to the general study of children of all kinds, and from there to the application of the knowledge gained to the problems of educational and preventive work.

The Vienna Course for Educators mentioned above, far from being or remaining the only attempt of its kind, was preceded and followed by a whole host of similar ventures in which the principles of psychoanalytic child psychology not only were taught but actually put to the test in practical work with children. There is a direct line from Kinderheim Baumgarten, founded after the First World War by Siegfried Bernfeld and Willie Hoffer, by way of the Jackson Nursery (1937-38) to the Hampstead Nurseries in the Second World War (1940-45), and from there again to the Nursery Schools of the James Putnam Clinic in Boston, Mass., of the Child Study Center in Yale, New Haven, of the Child Development Center in New York, the therapeutic Nursery School in Cleveland, The Master's Nursery in New York, the School for Nursery Years in Los Angeles, the Orthogenic School in Chicago, the High Wick Hospital for Psychotic Children in Hertfordshire, England, and the Nursery Schools for Normal and for Blind Children in the Hampstead Clinic, London. There is also the untiring work done on the basis of psychoanalysis with well-baby clinics, with pediatricians and on pediatric wards, in short-stay and in long-stay hospitals, with residential institutions, foster parents, etc. Many of these tasks were, and still are, uphill ones since they are carried out in the face of opposition derived from ingrained traditional attitudes to teaching, nursing, medical or institutional routines; they are no less rewarding for this reason, of course. The indivisibility of body and mind in the first year of life, the close interaction between emotion and intellect, between object relatedness and stimulation, between the defensive and the adaptive processes were the main insights brought to bear on the problems of child care.

Direct Observation as a Source of Knowledge

Apart from the practical results achieved by means of these labors, there was considerable gain from them in the form of added knowledge as evidenced in a small number of books and a large number of articles published in *The Psychoanalytic Study of the Child*, in International Universities Press, and elsewhere. Nevertheless, in spite of many insights gained into essential processes of child development, into phase-adequate conflicts and behavior problems, into the interactions between children and their object world, etc., this method of exploration remained more or less haphazard and unsystematic until Ernst Kris set up a laboratory for himself in the Child

Study Center in Yale (appr. 1950) and opened up the possibilities for the systematic longitudinal study of young children. This was carried further after his death by Eleanor Pavenstedt in Boston, and in Yale by Marianne Kris, Seymour L. Lustman, Sally Provence, Samuel Ritvo, Albert Solnit. We do not forget that it is due to Ernst Kris if today we automatically link up areas which were deliberately kept separate before him, such as the microscopic and the macroscopic approach to child study; manifest surface behavior and unconscious id content; reconstruction of the past and prediction of the future; in short, that we owe it to his endeavors that the observation of children outside analysis is now accepted as a legitimate second source of knowledge for the analyst.

Margaret Ribble, Margaret Fries, René Spitz in the United States, John Bowlby, James Robertson in London are notable independent contributors to the same field.

Psychoanalytic Research

In line with the developments in adult analysis, and as Melanie Klein, D. W. Winnicott, and their followers had done from the outset, our child analysts also extended their interest gradually from abnormal to normal psychology. In our case this meant the move from a theory of childhood pathology to the recognition of a hypothetical norm in the processes of mental growth, and from there to the construction of a developmental metapsychology. With this new "widening of the scope," new tasks opened up for us and new responsibilities developed.

It is a basic fact for all analysts that the same technique serves both analytic therapy and analytic exploration. Nevertheless, the official psychoanalytic Institutes, following the tradition in which they were set up initially, train carefully in its former use and in comparison neglect the latter. Thus, candidates are guided how to extract the maximum information from transference, resistance, dreams, other id derivatives, or ego mechanisms; how to time their interpretations; in short, how to cure their patients. They receive no guidance in such important matters as how to record their material, or sift and summarize it, or verify their findings, or pool them with others; how to trace the history of psychoanalytic concepts, to inquire into their definitions and to clarify and unify their technical terms;

how to select specific area for their research interests or to become alerted to the gaps in our knowledge. Not that these latter activities are not pursued abundantly in the analytic community, as evidenced by the analytic journals and book publications. But they are left more or less completely to individual effort and individual ingenuity, or at best to postgraduate opportunities which exist in some localities and are lacking in others.

In fact, it was the wish to provide such missing facilities which led to the building up of the departments of the Hampstead Course and Clinic. At least so far as child analysis is concerned, the various facets of psychoanalysis are treated there as if they were on a par, and students are from the beginning of their training systematically introduced to psychoanalysis as a method of treatment; as a tool to use for exploration and study; as a theory in need of scrutiny and expansion; as a body of knowledge capable of application to a wide number of needs in the community. What is left to the individual candidate is the final selection of one or more of these part aspects of psychoanalysis for his future career.

I would like to think that this new Association, on the occasion of its first convention, is committing itself to a similar wide outlook on the subject and thereby will shape the future of child analysis in the United States so far as analytic child therapy, analytic child psychology, analytic child study, and analytic child services are concerned.

CONTRIBUTIONS TO PSYCHOANALYTIC THEORY

A NOTE ON TRAUMA, DREAM, ANXIETY, AND SCHIZOPHRENIA

K. R. EISSLER, M.D.

It has long been known that terrifying dreams may be the precursors of grave mental disorders.[1] Yet it would be wrong to conclude that in these instances the dreams themselves had traumatic effects, driving the subject into a psychosis. It is in line with psychoanalytic thinking rather to assume that, in this form of the seemingly traumatic dream, a latent disease made itself apparent during the night, causing dreams that were terrifying to the sleeper, who in his waking life had not yet been made aware of the disorder that was already germinating in him. After all, a comparable state of affairs has been observed in regard to physical disorders: symptoms of a physical disease that only later becomes manifest appear as elements in the manifest dream content, at a time when the subject feels himself to be in excellent physical health (see, for example, Sully, 1893).

Indeed, a psychoanalyst who is skilled in recognizing the import of such harbingers may—even if rarely—be able to save a patient's life, by suggesting a consultation with a specialist, the need for which has not yet made itself evident otherwise.

Moreover, if Freud's theory of dreams is accepted as valid, one must assume that no dream could ever itself constitute a trauma: events become traumatic only when the intensity of stimulation passes beyond a certain level; the anxiety signal would arouse the dreamer instantaneously when the total cathexis of dream elements came close to the traumatic level. It stands to reason that a subject's potential for the endurance of stimulation is limited, but in this respect the dreamer appears to be particularly well protected.

Clinical experience provides abundant confirmation of the fact

---

[1] Some writers (Sanctis, 1899) have thought that such dreams were the actual causes of the disorders. Freud discussed the relationship between dreams and mental disorders as early as 1900 (pp. 88-92). (See also Freud, 1933, p. 16.)

that it is precisely in the state of sleep that anxiety is regularly at hand to discontinue any situation that may grow into a threat to the integrity of the psychic apparatus.[2]

It is also to be remembered that, according to Freud, the anxiety dreams of patients who are suffering from traumatic neuroses serve the function of reducing the effect of trauma, and are thus stepping-stones toward health. In this respect, one may even regard the dream as an *anti*traumatic agent—a position that would be in accordance with Robert's theory of the healing power of dreams (Freud, 1900, p. 79).[3]

The dreamer is, with regard to traumatization, in a more favorable position than the waking person, who is exposed without warning to the accidental complexities with which external reality may suddenly impinge upon him. The following may serve as a typical clinical example:

A patient—a young man of eighteen—while sitting in the subway was seized by a severe attack of anxiety when a blind beggar, whose eye sockets were empty, entered the car and passed by. The patient was generally well protected against anxiety by a score of transitory but fairly well integrated compulsions, and it was no easy task during treatment to convince him of the extent to which many of his symptoms served as safeguards against anxiety.

The above-mentioned incident was one of the few during the early phase of his treatment when he found himself exposed to the

2 The sleeper has other defenses as well at his disposal, such as the judgment, "After all, this is only a dream." The conditions that determine whether this judgment is made or anxiety breaks out, have not yet been sufficiently differentiated. Freud thought that the judgment is made after the censorship has allowed the passing of a dream that should have been suppressed. The judgment would then serve the purpose of allaying the oncoming anxiety (1900, p. 489). (See also Freud, 1901, p. 680.) It is my impression that the dreamer's surprise at an unexpected turn in the manifest events of the dream sometimes has a similar function. The feeling of surprise may be one of the means of representation on the occasion when surprise itself is the content of a latent dream thought. But with the progress of analysis and increasing tolerance toward the repressed, the dreamer may respond with surprise where he would previously have awakened with anxiety. Surprise permits the recognition of an unwelcome harbinger of the repressed, under the cloak of incredulity; it stands for a protest, and its effect is milder than that of negation (see Freud, 1925).

3 According to Ferenczi (1934), every dream is an attempt to settle the unresolved consequences of a past trauma. Ferenczi's proposal of a traumatolytic function of dreams —a generalization of Freud's comments on the function of dreams in traumatic neuroses (1920)—was recently revived in a paper by Stein (1965). I shall later put forward a proposition in the same direction.

experience of anxiety without being able to rationalize it as reality danger. The meaning of the attack is almost obvious: it was a matter of castration anxiety. The sight of the empty eye sockets must have aroused the thought: after all, men are occasionally castrated—a thought which had been until then repressed. The patient's attack of anxiety was not brought on by subjects that stood at that time in the center of his treatment. His castration fears were alive enough, however, to be stimulated by any such gruesome sight, whenever he met it by chance.

The genetic foundation of his attack may have been brought into being either by an early trauma, upon perceiving the female genitals for the first time, or else by the fact that what had been an early fantasy was suddenly shown to occur in reality. In general, one does not, I think, make a firm distinction between these alternatives. The prevailing custom seems to be to conclude that such reactions in the adult always signify the repetition of an infantile trauma, even though it may quite often be a matter of a fantasy come true.

If we now transpose the equivalent situation into the sleep state, we encounter a different economic distribution. Should imagery having to do with the reality of castration become by any chance cathected, there are, for the dreamer, adequate escape routes on hand. Displacement, symbolic representation, or representation by the opposite may even lead to a pleasurable or emotionally neutral dream. If all these mechanisms should nevertheless prove inadequate, the anxiety signal or acute anxiety will then generally discontinue the phantasmagoria.

Here a question arises that warrants some general consideration. It is clinically known that some dreams do occur in children and adults that anxiety does not succeed in discontinuing. Recognition of that fact led to the distinction between the nightmare and the simple anxiety dream (cf. Jones, 1931). The characteristic feature of the former is the dreamer's long-lasting paralysis, while he is being exposed to grievous dangers and undergoing the most dreadful anxiety. In pavor nocturnus, the nightmare is continued even after the child rises and seeks refuge with his parents. Some writers, including Stern, attribute a traumatic effect to the nightmare and pavor nocturnus. Curiously enough, the analysis of a true nightmare is not to be found, as far as I know, anywhere in Freud's work. In his writings,

the arousal function is consistently assigned to—and fulfilled by—
anxiety in dreams. The dreamer's motor paralysis in the dream was
explained by Freud as the sensation of an inhibition of will ("approximating so closely to anxiety"), the representation of a vigorous
"no" (1900, pp. 335-338).

In view of Jones's interpretation of nightmares as caused by "the
guilt of the repressed incestuous wishes that are striving for imaginary gratification" (1931, p. 343), one may conclude that, in the
nightmare, highly forbidden impulses are particularly intensive and
for that reason require particularly severe punishment and a particularly vigorous "no." Yet this still does not answer the question
of whether or not anxiety itself can have a traumatic effect.

We can see that the formula that anxiety will awaken the dreamer
and in that way protect him against traumatization is too simple, in
view of the paralyzing nightmare. At this point, however, we must
leave the question open, particularly because of a regular finding
with regard to the classical phobic patient, who insists that his inhibitions started with an overpowering phobic attack. He will assure
us that he would feel free to go out alone, or take a plane, or engage
in whatever the activity may be that has been made impossible for
him by the enforced security measures—had he not suffered a devas-
tating attack of anxiety when he did expose himself to a situation of
that kind. Did not the anxiety attack in those instances traumatize
the patient?

We now turn to Freud's latest theory of anxiety of 1926 and its
slight modification in 1933. Freud's theory of anxiety has been
discussed so often and so profoundly that it does not need elaborate
presentation. What is called for, however, is concentration on a few
points that seem to me to be controversial or contradictory.

An adequate discussion of the contradictions and inconsistencies
that are to be found in the 1926 text (even though it did constitute
an enormous step forward in the theoretical understanding of anxiety, as well as in its technical handling on the clinical level) would
require altogether too much space. I shall therefore try to present
the problem in an abbreviated form.[4]

---

[4] For the same reason, a discussion of the contributions of Schur (1953, 1958) and
Stern (1951, 1953a, 1953b), with both of whose views on anxiety I do not agree in part,
has to be postponed.

My chief concern in this context is the distinction between trauma and danger, which is not only of theoretical, but also of practical importance.

Freud's publication of 1926 placed the function of anxiety as a signal at the center, and this part of the theory seems to have been generally accepted and integrated. Indeed, some of the unanswered questions in this area are of secondary importance only. The opinions of psychoanalysts seem to be divided, for example, with regard to the phenomenology of the anxiety signal: some consider it to be an element that is regularly conscious; others, myself included, assume that more often than not it does its work subliminally. It seems reasonable to postulate a spectrum that covers the full range of the anxiety attack, precipitating a phobia at one end, and at the other a subliminally functioning anxiety signal, by means of which the ego manipulates the distribution of cathexes automatically—that is, without distraction from its main pursuits by conscious arousal.

At one extreme, the signal function breaks down, in view of an overwhelming instinctual demand that threatens to break through from the repressed; extraordinary measures therefore have to be instituted, in order to banish extraordinary wishes. At the other extreme, the actual dangers are of a low order, so that the ego is able to rely on automatism in order to regulate the dangerous situations. I here follow Freud's inclination to rely on linguistic usage. It is significant how often the phrase "I am afraid that . . ." (in German: "*Ich habe Angst, dass . . .*") is used without the subject's actually feeling any anxiety. I do not see any well-founded objection to the assumption that in such situations a subliminal anxiety signal is given that automatically induces the activation of mechanisms or actions which serve the purpose of avoiding dangers or of neutralizing their consequences.

Another problem is the question of whether or not the anxiety signal is produced only after the danger has first found preconscious or conscious representation, at least in the form of derivatives of repressed contents. Here, too, the opinions seem to be divided; I myself incline toward the belief that anxiety may be produced without the repressed invading the ego's territory in any way.

Be that as it may, it is a different order of problems that one encounters with regard to the other form of anxiety, which is described as physiological or automatic, as "being freshly created out of the economic conditions of the situation" (Freud, 1926, p. 130) or "not aroused as a signal but . . . generated anew for a fresh reason" (Freud, 1933, p. 94). Freud gave, as his examples of this type of anxiety, birth anxiety and anxiety neurosis.[5]

Now then, we have, on the one hand, signal anxiety, produced by the ego, and serving the well-defined purpose of forestalling danger and consequent traumatization; on the other hand, automatic anxiety, which is imposed upon the psychic apparatus through economic conditions that have been brought about by an undue accretion or influx of stimulation, and which cannot be dealt with by ordinary means but renders ineffective the pleasure-unpleasure principle (1933, p. 94).

The inconsistency, in my opinion, arises out of the fact that Freud attributes the occurrence of anxiety at different times to danger and to trauma, whereas one position, which he stated in 1926 and repeated in 1933, rested on the conceptual differentiation between the two.

This inconsistency is adumbrated in Freud's terminology by his occasionally referring to birth as a trauma, and more often to birth as an act or event.[6] Yet what is at stake here is a factual matter. It is not theory alone but observation that can decide whether birth is a trauma or just a danger. Spitz (1965) objects strongly to the idea that birth is a traumatic event.[7] To be sure, it may lead to severe injury and even to death; it may leave the neonate in a state of shock, etc. But under conditions of birth that we may refer to as normal, average or optimal, one can observe a fact that, in my opinion, disproves the belief that in all instances birth is a traumatic event: regularly, the healthy neonate, as soon as he has been cleaned, dressed and put into the crib, starts mouthing. He starts to slide the tip of his tongue along his lips and, as far as can be determined experimentally (Eissler,

---

[5] At one point (1926, p. 135), Freud seems to intimate that all instances of "inexpedient" anxiety—which would therefore include the full-fledged attack that leads to phobia in the adult—belong to this type of anxiety. (See also 1926, p. 165.)

[6] It is significant that, in his *Introductory Lectures,* Freud never spoke of birth trauma.

[7] Early reviewers of Rank's book (1924) already expressed doubt that a traumatic effect can be assigned to birth as such (see Sachs, 1925, p. 108). For a discussion of the biological economy of birth, see Greenacre (1945). See also Winnicott (1949).

1938), the rhythm of these movements is characterized by an acme, whereas the movements of the sucking reflex proceed in a pattern that is rigidly structured in coequal oscillations.[8]

Although the objection that I am proceeding along adultomorphic lines is probably inescapable, I will assert, nevertheless, that mouthing is a pleasurable activity. It is hardly conceivable that an organization as tender, vulnerable, and sensitive as the newborn would turn to such activity immediately after having suffered something that can be in any way judged as a trauma.

Freud explained repeatedly why, under average conditions, birth does not become traumatic, by demonstrating the utility of birth anxiety, insofar as the "innervation, in being directed to the respiratory organs, is preparing the way for the activity of the lungs, and, in accelerating the heartbeat, is helping to keep the blood free from toxic substances" (1926, p. 134). It is precisely anxiety that *prevents* birth from becoming a trauma and thus proves, at its earliest occurrence, that its function is protection against traumatization. Moreover, Freud (1926) rightly stressed that anxiety, in contrast to pain and grief, is "a special state of unpleasure *with acts of discharge* along particular paths" (p. 133; my italics). Is it not this discharge function that, from the biological point of view, makes automatic anxiety in emergency situations a desirable, though often inadequate, last resort for combating danger in the service of heading off traumatization?

This assertion can also be made for anxiety neurosis, which was conceived by Freud as a toxic state, brought about by frustration or ineffectual discharge of libido.[9]

Freud himself describes the anxiety of actual neuroses as corresponding "to the earliest and original danger-situation" (1926, p. 141). To be sure, the utility of automatic anxiety is not as clear in

[8] It is quite remarkable that the mouthing of the newborn has not found its place in psychoanalytic theory formation. It disproves the current theory of anaclisis since, in the majority of instances, mouthing occurs prior to the sucking reflex. This is an action completely without any element of reflex. It seems to be the earliest spontaneous activity and should, therefore, have long since earned the particular attention of analysts who are doing research on the genesis of the ego. See, however, Wolff (1966).

[9] Psychoanalysts in general reject the existence of "actual" neuroses (yet see Reich, 1927; Nunberg, 1932; Fenichel, 1945). Even if this rejection is correct, it is suitable to use Freud's concept here for the purpose of discussing the theory of trauma and danger. Moreover, the anxiety of asthmatic and cardiac patients proves the justification of Freud's distinguishing between anxiety in psychoneuroses and in states based on the disturbance of homeostasis as a consequence of physical factors.

actual neurosis as it is in birth, yet the psychic apparatus would probably be damaged, perhaps even permanently, if it were to be continuously exposed to a physical urge which, for certain reasons, could not be gratified even when the necessary biological processes did occur. Here, I think, anxiety prevents traumatization (1) by serving a discharge function and (2) by protecting the psychic apparatus against constant irritation by a source of stimuli which remain alien to it.

The surprising inconsistency is that, toward the end of the text, Freud once again introduces the trauma as the source of automatic anxiety. "Anxiety is the original reaction to helplessness in the trauma" (1926, p. 166f.; see also, 1933, p. 94). In one passage, Freud even says about the traumatic neuroses that "anxiety is also being freshly created out of the economic conditions of the situation" (1926, p. 130)—meaning by this the breaking through of the protective shield and the impingement of excessive amounts of excitation upon the mental apparatus—although in 1920 he had demonstrated that it is the *absence* of anxiety that is the prerequisite of traumatization in traumatic neurosis.

Trauma is defined by Freud as the experience of helplessness, as the consequence of excessive stimulation (which cannot be reduced); danger, on the other hand, is defined as the expectation of such helplessness. Yet it is questionable whether, in the birth situation, at a time when the baby is exposed to excessive stimulation, anxiety—which automatically, by accelerated breathing and heartbeat, reduces the excitation—still leaves the newborn in a state of traumatic helplessness. Furthermore, I do not believe that Freud's definition of trauma is clinically tenable, though it is no doubt extremely helpful in the understanding of the early phases of development. Helplessness may be actively sought after for libidinal gratification; furthermore, not every situation of helplessness has the effect of a trauma.

Moreover, it can also happen that the carrying out of an act will lead to traumatization. I recall a patient who suffered a severe trauma in infancy when he pushed his shovel against his father and the father fainted. He probably did feel helpless when the father collapsed, yet the trauma was incurred not by his feeling but by the action and its consequence, both of which preceded and in fact gave rise to the feeling.

Finally, there is clinical evidence that traumatization may occur without the subject's even being aware of it. Freud himself presented this by drawing the model of the development of a traumatic neurosis: "a man who has experienced some frightful accident . . . leaves the scene of the event apparently uninjured. In the course of the next few weeks, however, he develops a number of severe psychical and motor symptoms which can only be traced to his shock, the concussion or whatever else it was. He now has a 'traumatic neurosis' " (1939, p. 67).

Here there is no reference to anxiety; the immediate response to the trauma is instead reported as fright. Indeed fright, stupor, paralysis, shock, and allied phenomena are the phenomenological indices of severe traumatization of the psychic apparatus.

When the phobic patient asserts that he was traumatized by the long-lasting and excessive, unbearable helplessness of his first anxiety attack; when patients maintain that they are suffering from insomnia because they have been traumatized by dreams of long-lasting paralysis in a state of excessive anxiety—these statements are, of course, subjectively correct.

Metapsychologically, one has to formulate, however, a different equation. If the phobic patient had not suffered the anxiety attack, he would have (or so at least maintains his unconscious) raped women on the street or jumped out of a plane he was traveling in, while the insomniac would have dreamed of consorting with his mother and killing his father. These would have been the traumata against which the two were protected by their anxiety; thus, in these two instances too, one sees that anxiety is the reaction to a dangerous situation and as such protects the individual against traumatization.

At one point, I believe, Freud describes trauma in the same terms: missing the mother is, for the infant, "a traumatic situation if the infant happens at the time to be feeling a need which its mother should be the one to satisfy" (1926, p. 170). That is to say, the exposure to an unsatisfied urge, wish or desire is traumatic; it is only when there is danger of repetition that anxiety sets in, yet the traumatic situation per se contained sensations other than anxiety. Anxiety, to be sure, does not always protect against traumatization. The influx of excitation may reach such proportions that despite anxiety the psychic apparatus suffers damage. But at that time, as far as I could determine from the observation of concentration camp victims, the production of anxiety comes to a halt and phenomena of a different order appear. The concentration camp situation was an exceptional one, far different from the "average expectable environment" (Hartmann, 1939), and the following generalization cannot therefore be applied to it. It seems to be a general feature of neuroses that a shift takes place from concern about danger to concern about anxiety. It may be one of the many differences between animal and man that the animal, because of the reliable working of its instincts, remains geared to danger, whereas man's relative freedom to detach himself from the exigencies of external reality and instead to serve the exigencies of his inner world permits him to focus on the subjective and to disregard the objectively real. The chief concern of the neurotic is to live in a state in which he is free of anxiety, as if the absence of anxiety also guaranteed absence of danger. (One gets the impression from a reading of history that, in this regard, mankind has at times followed the pattern of the neurotic.)

Anxiety cannot traumatize the psychic apparatus, any more than the defense mechanisms can. Both can interfere with a smooth functioning of the ego, they can even undermine the ego's solidity; yet the harm they are able to cause should be differentiated from that which is capable of being produced by trauma.[10]

The psychic apparatus can be traumatized only by an excessive influx of id stimuli or of external stimuli.[11]

By way of strengthening my thesis, I would like to cite a poem about an interesting situation, not too easy to disentangle psychologically:

A legend has found poetical representation in a famous German

[10] The argument that a subject may even die under the impact of anxiety can be raised in favor of the idea of the traumatic effect of anxiety. However, when anxiety does have a lethal effect, that fact is always a sign of cardiac disease. After all, the same thing can happen during intercourse, and yet no one would call intercourse, for that reason, a trauma.

[11] This definition of trauma is, of course, not sufficient, since traumatization depends also on the meaning of the stimuli. Yet there should be no difficulty in converting the quantitative definition into a qualitative one. Furthermore, consideration of the superego is purposely omitted.

ballad: *Der Reiter und der Bodensee.*[12] In the ballad, a horseman tries in wintertime to reach the shores of Lake Constance. He traverses a great plain without trees or human habitation, and at long last reaches a village. Upon inquiring where the lake is, he finds out that, without knowing it, he has just crossed the frozen lake on horseback. Upon learning this, he dies:

> His heart stops short, his hair stands on end,
> Close behind him still grins the grisly danger;
> His eye perceives nothing but the horrible abyss,
> His mind becomes submerged into the black bottom.
> In his ear there is thunder like cracking ice,
> Cold sweat trickles around him like a wave.
> Then he sighs; then he drops from his horse,
> And the shore becomes for him a dry grave.

> [Es stocket sein Herz, es sträubt sich sein Haar
>   dicht hinter ihm grinst noch die grause Gefahr
> Es sieht sein Blick nur den grässlichen Schlund,
>   sein Geist versinkt in den schwarzen Grund.
> Im Ohr ihm donnert's wie krachend Eis
>   wie die Well' umrieselt ihn kalter Schweiss.
> Da seuftzt er, da sinkt er vom Ross herab,
>   da ward ihm am Ufer ein trocken Grab.]
>   —Gustav Schwab

Here a man is stricken by death upon hearing of the magnitude of the dangers he has been exposed to, *but has, without knowing so at the time, successfully overcome.* According to the poet's intuition, the victim now experiences, in hallucinatory fashion, the trauma he would surely have experienced if things had gone their customary way. Again, we encounter the absence of anxiety, and instead meet with the overloading of the psychic apparatus by external stimuli— which, in this instance, are the result of projections. Another general problem crops up here. After all, the horseback rider might have responded, upon being apprised of his phenomenal feat, with a feeling of omnipotence. Survival in spite of danger and possible traumatization harbors, in principle, the possibility of an experience of triumph. This may be used therapeutically, as I myself chanced to observe.

12 Cf. Schur (1953, p. 18), who derives, however, a conclusion different from mine from this ballad.

A middle-aged, hysterical, somewhat primitive woman returned from her vacation in a shaken condition. On her way home, she was taking refreshments when her car, which she had left parked outside the restaurant, was demolished by a hit-and-run driver. Since that time, she had thought incessantly of what would have happened to her if she had been in the car at the time of the accident. She was by this time anxious, shaky, and extremely nervous. When her inter-locuter remarked, somewhat drily, "Strange, when something of that kind happens to me, I get the feeling that nothing can happen to me, that I am indestructible," she instantly quieted down and became free of her anxiety reaction.

The history of the concept of trauma in psychoanalysis has been admirably presented by Khan (1963). One obtains the impression that this concept is perhaps overemployed in psychoanalysis, and that the tendency has developed to regard all noxae that are not constitu-tional as traumatic. It seems hardly possible at present to arrive at a satisfactory definition of the concept of trauma. The matter is immeasurably complicated by the fact that traumata are not only unavoidable occurrences in the child's development, but that, if it were indeed possible to eliminate them, the child would not long survive. Trauma holds, in this respect, a position equivalent to in-fection in the child's physical upbringing. A child who grew up in a germ-free environment would, as an adult, be a victim before long of some deadly infection. Furthermore, we know of life histories that are replete with what must be described as the severest traumatiza-tion in infancy and childhood; yet as adults these same individuals produced the greatest achievements. Isaac Newton (see More, 1934) has always impressed me as the most striking example of this kind. I regret that space does not permit going into his life history. If the principle of psychic determinism has any general validity, one cannot help seeing some form of connection between traumatization and later greatness.[13]

One may be reminded here of Alexander's concept of "benign traumata" (Alexander and French, 1946, p. 164), but that term is a

[13] See Freud (1928). The autobiographical inclusions in Freud's own *Interpretation of Dreams* strongly suggest that Freud was aware of the productive role in his own life of certain traumata suffered in the relation to the father.

misnomer, inasmuch as the concept of trauma is indissolubly linked with damage.

More promising is Ernst Kris's reminder that "the further course of life seems to determine which experience may gain significance as a traumatic one" (1956, p. 73),[14] yet in such a case as Newton's the traumatic events in his infancy and youth were of such dramatic force that an instantaneous effect must be assumed—which, of course, does not gainsay the wholesome effect of later events. I would be inclined to assume that, in the early reaction to traumata, a fundamental pattern, which will dominate the subject's later life, can already be dimly perceived.

It seems that, in some subjects, traumatization is comparable to grafting. In order to force the stock to reproduce the scion, a severe trauma must first be produced. In the art of grafting, something is added to this injury to the stock that makes the original injury a "productive" trauma. Yet what it is in particular children that makes them regenerate what is for others their undoing, into actions of the highest degree of creativity, is as little understood as is the process of creativity itself.

The importance of trauma was re-emphasized in a clinical context by Freud in one of his later papers, in which he wrote: "There is no doubt that an aetiology of the traumatic sort offers by far the more favourable field for analysis" (1937, p. 220). It is not altogether clear why damage that has been brought about by trauma can be more easily undone than damage resulting from the strength of drives.

It may be that under optimal conditions the trauma has the effect of a roadblock—that is to say, an inhibiting effect on the further development of an ego function. Once it is removed, that function may then blossom out; by contrast, the ego functions that have developed under the impact of hardly tamed pregenital drives are poorly developed to begin with, and therefore cannot easily be restored to their originally potential optimum. Be that as it may, in view of the prognostic value Freud attributes here to the etiological factor, it is of clinical importance not to overextend the meaning of trauma until it has lost its clinical applicability altogether. There

[14] The outstanding example of this is to be observed in the reconstruction of the Wolf Man's infantile development, to which I shall later return.

are other accidental noxae of nontraumatic origin, such as, for example, the contents of identifications—particularly those of early vintage—which are of no less significance.[15]

In returning now to the original question of whether or not a dream can have a traumatic effect, we have to consider another factor. Freud's psychology of dreams rests on an assumption that has been confirmed by a huge number of observations, and which can be described in several different ways: (a) the manifest dream never contains more than its latent content; (b) the dream work can utilize only the givens as of when the subject falls asleep; (c) the elements of the manifest dream contain nothing more than has found psychic representation prior to the onset of the dream work, or is added in the form of internal or external stimuli; (d) the dream work cannot add anything of its own to the content of the dream; (e) the output (dream) is never larger than the input (day residues, previous experiences, and present excitations).

Thus, the dream is essentially lacking in originality in terms of producing truly new contents. Despite the seemingly original appearance of the manifest dream, analysis of a dream regularly demonstrates its content to be a composite of previously formed elements.[16]

If the dream is really thus bound to the past, in that the silent dream work cannot produce anything but a combination of elements already latently existing in the psychic apparatus, this in itself reduces the probability of a traumatic effect, since newness or surprise may be regarded as a formal quality frequently attached to stimuli

15 I wonder whether the breadth of clinical discussion would not be constructively enlarged by using the concept of viability in connection with the goals of therapy. The goal of psychoanalytic therapy is a change of ego structure. It is known that in some patients this cannot be achieved at all, or if so only to a limited degree. Yet the patient's viability may be achieved under certain circumstances without effecting a structural change. The effect of trauma in relation to psychoanalytic prognoses may be better understood when graduated in terms of what the therapy may achieve with regard to improving the patient's viability. Of course, it would be necessary first to explore the metapsychology of viability in comparison with that of a structural change.

16 Cf. Freud (1900): "the relation of the second agency towards dreams is of a *defensive* and not of a *creative* kind" (p. 146); or: "there are dreams in which the most complicated intellectual operations take place, statements are contradicted or confirmed, . . . just as they are in waking thought. . . . we find that the whole of this *is part of the material of the dream-thoughts and is not a representation of intellectual work performed during the dream itself*" (p. 313). Thus, the analysis of a dream regularly demonstrates that what may appear to be an original judgment, or another kind of original intellectual work, is in fact a composite of latent dream thoughts.

patterns that produce the effect of actual or potential traumata. Traumatic events, after all, have in most instances no antecedents in the subject's experience, at least according to the model devised by Freud in conjunction with war neuroses, in which the significant relation is expressed in quantitative terms.

It is, indeed, the lack of experience that makes the infant, and later on the child, particularly susceptible to traumatization. The more experienced a person is, the less likely it is that he will fall victim to a trauma (assuming that the psychic apparatus is not particularly handicapped).

Freud states that the dream does not create anything new, since all the dream elements can be referred to the latent dream thoughts; yet this does not hold true with regard to the perceptions that make up the manifest dream. To be sure, some perceptive elements can be traced back to antecedents—that is, to previous perceptions; but the final Gestalt, or the series of Gestalten that comprise the manifest dream, is new. All the images that are perceived in a kaleidoscope are made up of the same elements, yet each twist of the kaleidoscope creates a new Gestalt, essentially different from the preceding one, or the one to follow.

The procedure to which the perceptive material is subjected in dream work may be visualized in the following manner: Let us assume that a blindfolded man cuts up in an arbitrary manner the reproduction of a painting, after which he gathers the pieces, jumbles them up and then, still blindfolded, puts them together, again without following any principle. The outcome will be a new Gestalt and it is not impossible that such a new combination will look terrifying. Of course, dream work does not proceed in any such extreme and even barbaric fashion; yet the final dream Gestalt—for all that it is made up of previously existing perceptive elements—will be different from anything the dreamer has ever perceived or imagined. The exceptions are, of course, those rare cases in which the manifest dream is the exact reproduction of a previous experience. ". . . faithful and straight-forward reproductions of real scenes only rarely appear in dreams" (Freud, 1901, p. 659f.).

Freud was aware of the originality of the perceptive content of the manifest dream: "The process of condensation . . . explains certain constituents of the content of dreams which are peculiar to

them and are not found in waking ideation. What I have in mind
are 'collective' and 'composite figures' and the strange 'composite
structures', which are creations not unlike the composite animals
invented by the folk-imagination of the Orient. . . . in dreams fresh
composite forms are being perpetually constructed in an inexhaust-
ible variety" (1901, p. 650f.).[17]

One of the consequences of the originality of perceptions in
dreams can be found in the possibility that the image of a centaur—
as I am sure I am not the first to suggest—was initially perceived
in a dream. In his dreams, prehistoric man might easily have jumbled
up the image of human and animal bodies and, so to speak, by accident created a new image that proved its value in terms of man's
mythological thinking.[18]

The term accident is permissible here; Freud, in establishing the
laws that are followed by dream imagination, pointed out how dream
work makes use of accidental factors of a considerable variety. The
final form depends on accidental impressions that the dreamer has
absorbed—for the most part inadvertently—during the day. This
relative unselectivity of the dream work vis-à-vis the perceptions and
events of the dream day must not be confused with that supposed
absence of any recognizable law or regularity that most dream psychologists had been maintaining before 1900.

Once it is acknowledged that, in the form of the manifest dream,
something new—namely, a new Gestalt—is almost regularly produced, the idea that a dream can have a traumatic effect may appear
less improbable, despite the wish-fulfillment character of the dream
and the ease of anxiety arousal during sleep. As a matter of fact, one
finds in Freud's own work an example of a traumatic dream. At
least, one must draw that conclusion from several explanatory statements that Freud added to the Wolf Man's dream, to the effect that

17 It is only fair to concede also to the neologisms that are formed in dreams the same
quality of newness or originality, and to acknowledge that in most instances they have
not found representation prior to their occurrence in the dream. Cf. Freud (1900, p.
466): "it was only the *name* of the breakfast-ship that was newly constructed by the
dream. The *thing* had existed. . . ."

18 Of course, such a conclusion presupposes a stimulus-bound (eidetic) perceptive
system in primitive man. If one assumes a model of a quite different structure—
namely, that the primary process has had free access to the perceptive system—then the
first image of a centaur would probably have been the content of a hallucination produced by condensation in the system *Ucs*.

this dream served as a trauma for the four-year-old boy. Interestingly enough, this is also a dream (the only one, I believe, among those published and analyzed by Freud) in which the content of the manifest dream comprises *more than* the sum or the condensation of latent dream material.

The traumatic aspect comes to the fore in the very way in which Freud introduces the dream, when he considers the trauma that the patient suffered by his sister's seduction at the age of three and a quarter years as equipotential with the dream: "the event which makes this division [in the patient's history] possible was not an external trauma, but a dream, from which he awoke in a state of anxiety" (Freud, 1918, p. 28). Indeed, the dream did affect the child *as* a trauma, not just in a way that was *comparable to* a trauma. The child's behavior pattern changed from the aggressive type to the neurotic: he suffered from phobia, which later changed to a compulsive-obsessional neurosis.

But did the dream work or the dream per se also lead to something *"new"*? As is well known, the latent content of the Wolf Man's dream comprised the revival of an infantile recollection and the wish for a passive gratification by the father. "The strength of this wish made it possible to revive a long-forgotten trace in his memory of a scene which was able to show him what sexual satisfaction from his father was like; and the result was terror, horror of the fulfilment of the wish" (Freud, 1918, p. 35f.). It is this "result" that constitutes the new element, which cannot be included in the latent material.

Indeed, Freud specifically states: "During the dream he [the patient] had reached a new phase in his sexual organization. . . . He discovered the vagina and the biological significance of masculine and feminine" (p. 46f.); and further: "We have been driven to assume that *during the process of the dream* he understood that women are castrated" (p. 78; my italics). There is no doubt that, according to Freud's interpretation, the dream per se not only provided an insight that the child did not previously have, but also established a psychic organization that did not yet exist even as late as the time when the child fell asleep. "The process of the dream" in this instance produced something new, and had—not least for that reason—a profoundly traumatic effect. One may find here a contradiction to general statements by Freud, already referred to earlier, and best summarized in the statement that "the dream-work is not creative, . . . it develops no phantasies of its own, . . . it makes no judgements and draws no conclusions" (1901, p. 667).

The alleged lack of creativity of the dream is in contradiction also to what many creative people have reported. To be sure, one has to be cautious about accepting subjective testimonies concerning the creativity of dreams, since the dream is not regarded by most people, particularly the creative ones, as merely a psychological phenomenon, but is assigned "meanings" and surrounded by mystery. Thus, when Goethe reports that he woke up with perfectly formed poems, so that he had nothing else to do but write them down, an apparent refutation of that part of Freud's dream theory may be read into his assertion. Goethe's report may be interpreted, however, in at least three different ways: (1) The poet was trying to form in the reader a certain image of his self that was narcissistically cathected, and he therefore attributed to himself a trait that did not actually exist, or was at least not quite of the kind he sought to make us believe. (2) Goethe also reported that when he was free-associating, as we are likely to do when we are taking a walk, poems came to his mind effortlessly, just as daydreams do in such situations to the less gifted. That daydreams of this sort are important parts of the latent dream content, and may even be reproduced *en bloc* in the manifest dream, is well known. In that sense, Goethe's report of dreaming perfect poems would not pose any clinical problem: if such conditions are taken to be valid, the dream would only have reproduced contents that had been formed by the dreamer during the daytime, with or without his awareness. (3) It is conceivable that, in the hypercreative person, certain fundamental principles are different from their counterparts in the average person; that the genius, as the embodiment of creativity, does not succeed in keeping the creative function out of his dream life, and that for him the creative function cannot be decathected during sleep but continues to pervade even the dream work.

Many a genius has asserted that he was far from being in control of his own creativity: that as an adult he never acquired autonomy vis-à-vis his creative function or functions, but was an appendage to them, in a sense even enslaved by them. Thus it may happen in the case of a select few that dream and dream work are not bound by their biological function, but submit instead to the exclusive purpose to which the lives of these exceptional individuals seem to be destined.

I assume that the reader will choose one or the other of these three possibilities, in accordance with his own personal bent. Lewin has devoted two illuminating papers (1958, 1962) to this question, without stating whether or not he believes that the dream can create more than exists in its latent content. The clinical evidence he offers shows three types. Descartes' dream seems to pose the least difficulty to the analyst, in terms of fundamental principles, since the creative connotation lay in the effect that the dream had subsequently on the philosopher. Freud's basic assumptions about the process that brings about the dream are not in any way contravened by the awakened dreamer's ingenuity in using the manifest dream for his particular creative purposes.

As Lewin has convincingly demonstrated, the peculiarity of cathexis in dreams and their specific disturbances in Descartes' dreams had profound effects upon Descartes' philosophy, in terms of his separation of the universe into a *res cogitans* and *res extensa*. Creative people use almost every experience for their basic purposes, and thus the dream too becomes a source of creative stimulation.

A different situation is encountered with regard to Professor Hilprecht's dream. In this case, an authoritative figure tells him to put together three fragments among the treasures of the museum; when he does so, they really complement each other to form a correct whole, just as had been maintained by the dream figure. Had the dreamer's preconscious mentation perceived the connection between the fragments? Had he himself formed the fantasy that they might belong together? The twentieth-century reader will recoil from assuming a supernatural event. Did the dream work establish a connection between the disparate elements that had never been established preconsciously? This outcome would definitely go beyond Freud's theoretical framework.[19]

The third example in Dr. Lewin's papers is Kekulé's dream, which provided him with the solution to a puzzle that had been

---

[19] Newbold's examination (1896) of the dream also discloses that Hilprecht's dream did not contain more than was already in the dream thoughts.

haunting his mind—namely, the structural formula of the benzol ring. In this instance, we can accept that the dream work may actually have been creative, without any necessity for going outside of Freud's theoretical edifice in order to do so.

As has already been mentioned, on the perceptive level dream work almost regularly leads to the creating of new configurations. It is conceivable that, in the instance of Kekulé's dream, previous perceptive elements formed—by way of the array of mechanisms at the disposal of the dream work—a new arrangement that by accident provided the sought-for solution to an intellectual problem. According to this view, the manifest dream was psychologically not at all different from the common run of dreams, but its content supplied accidentally the "missing link" of a hypercathected chain of thought contents that had been part and parcel of the dreamer's waking mentation. The perceptive elements of the dream content were taken from the latent dream contents; they then went through the well-known process of breaking down and recombination until they resulted in a new configuration, which was more meaningful to the dreamer—only in terms of its specific significance—than the usual dream is.[20]

In the Wolf Man's dream, it is not a mere matter of rearrangement of the perceptive elements, although these were the agents that spread terror in the child's mind. The traumatic effect arose out of the meaning attached to the perceptive material. This new meaning was created by a simple process. The two psychic contents (the memory of parental intercourse and the libidinal wish for the father), which had never apparently been viewed in context, were drawn together during the dream work. In this instance, something had happened on the thought level that is quite commonly produced on the perceptive level, in the formation of collective and composite figures: two or more configurations were brought together, in a form

[20] Among the day's residues, there is also that large group of thought impulses that have not been carried to a conclusion, because of some "chance hindrance" (Freud, 1900, p. 554). This may help explain Tartini's dream, in which the devil ("with an inexpressible charm") played for him a sonata that he had struggled to compose the day before (Flammarion). Sleep may remove the "chance hindrances" of the day, and then all the Gestalten, the seeds of which have been sown during the day, may blossom forth unrestrainedly. I believe that this may be particularly true of acoustic Gestalten, such as tunes, which are already latently contained in the initial sounds.

that reminded Freud of Galton's technique of producing composite photographs (1900, pp. 293, 494).

The wish for the father and the previous observation of the parents' (or animals') intercourse were fused into a new image of receiving sexual gratification—at the cost of a highly cathected organ. This new picture, which was never explicated in the dream because of its terrible content, is equivalent to or identical with an insight that is summarily designated as the castration complex. It is important to keep in mind that the explanation of the Wolf Man's dream does not need the introduction of any hitherto overlooked mechanism: apparently the well-known mechanisms of dream work can, under rare circumstances, lead to an unusual result, unusual in that it passes beyond the orbit of latent dream thoughts.

Yet it should be emphasized that it was not anxiety that was the traumatic event, but the dream's latent content, and anxiety was mobilized against its becoming conscious.

The clinical problems that follow in the wake of infantile traumatic dreams are manifold. Have such dreams an enduring effect on the further course of ego formation, since the traumatization occurred at a time when the child's self—vulnerable in any case because of his being at the peak of the oedipus complex—was also at a particular disadvantage, owing to his being at sleep? Is the subsequent course of a neurosis different according to whether internal traumata serve as the causative agents during sleep or in the waking state? (See Stein, 1965.)

Here it is proper to remind the reader that the Wolf Man has been (in my opinion, wrongly) diagnosed at times as having suffered from a psychosis, referred to either as paranoia or as schizophrenia. To be sure, he did occasionally go through psychotic or psychoticlike states; yet the clinical evidence speaks against the actual presence of one of the major chronic psychoses. Still, the structure of his ego apparently had weak points that made him more vulnerable than was to be expected in terms of what we call vaguely the broad stream of normal psychopathology. Was this vulnerability caused by the fact that he had suffered a decisive trauma in his dream? Can traumata that are brought about by internal stimulation under such conditions (rare as they are) leave irreparable damage, at least in a circumscribed area of the psychic apparatus?

I would like now to discuss a chance observation that I owe to a friend of mine, which seems pertinent to our subject.

A few days after the Germans occupied Austria, he and his wife decided, suddenly, to leave Austria the same evening and to join friends in Italy. Travelers leaving the country were searched at the border for valuables: they were permitted to take with them only one suitcase containing daily essentials and money to the amount of approximately four dollars. While they were packing, his wife asked him whether she might take with her a gold ring, set with jewels, which was an heirloom of great sentimental value to her. Fearing trouble at the border, he strenuously objected. When they arrived at the border the following morning, the German frontier guards let them pass without inquiry or search; at the Italian frontier station, however, they were told that, since the previous night, entry had been prohibited to Jews, and that they would have to return. He then requested permission to pass through Italy in order to reach the Swiss border, instead of staying in Italy, as they had originally planned. After waiting for a long time, they were told that their request would be granted if they left Italy immediately by the other border. This required the purchase of new tickets and. since he did not have Italian money, the officer escorted him to the money-exchange counter. There he requested the exchange of the Swiss francs that he thought he had taken with him. Yet the teller returned his proffered coins, telling him that what he had taken were French francs, which at that time had little value, and not Swiss francs, for which the rate of exchange was far higher. Evidently he had, the previous evening, made the mistake of confusing the two currencies. Thereupon he offered the clerk some important documents as collateral for borrowing the comparatively small amount of liras that he needed. The teller, who at first seemed ready to accept these documents as collateral, changed his mind on the grounds that they had no commercial value.

He was at that moment objectively in a difficult situation: the officer in back of him threateningly pressing him on with repeated "avanti! avanti!" and the clerk in front of him adamantly refusing to go ahead with the deal. This situation was, however, unexpectedly resolved when his wife who, unnoticed by him, had followed, without a word slipped the heirloom—which he had forbidden her the previous evening to take along—onto the counter. This was of course gladly accepted as collateral, and the journey of the two refugees then went through without any further incident.

Yet despite the happy ending of the entire episode, which might easily have ended instead in tragedy, and even though he had not felt anxiety or any other untoward feeling during that crucial minute or so, it happened every so often during subsequent years that the whole scene returned to his mind in quite unpleasant vividness. He would then hear the *"avanti!"* of the officer at his back and feel, for a few seconds, a dolorous and stressful sensation, which endowed those moments with a quality of eeriness that was otherwise quite strange to him. Indeed, the later sensation seemed to him far more painful than the feelings he had experienced while the actual event was taking place. Finally, when the situation came back to his mind, he never carried it through in thought to the moment of the happy solution; instead the experience ended in the highly disconcerting question: What would I have done—what would have happened—if my wife had *not* taken the ring with her?

I may perhaps have described the aftereffect in too dramatic terms. The disagreeable recall of the past experience lasted only a few moments and never interfered with what he was doing. Yet the unusual quality of inner stress and eeriness was indisputable. Undoubtedly, during the short time when, for a few seconds, he was actually in the midst of serious danger without seeing any way out, he was traumatized. In the recurrence of the recollection, an equivalent may be seen to the anxiety dreams in traumatic neurosis.

The reason why I am reporting this incident in such detail, however, is the way in which this "traumatic neurosis" in miniature was brought to an end. One day, quite without warning, it came to the subject's mind that he could have given the suitcase that was standing beside him to the teller as collateral, since the value of even part of its contents would have been sufficient to balance the amount of money he needed. From the moment that this solution, which was quite reality-adequate, occurred to him, he was freed from the discomforting sensation that had until then haunted him sporadically. The memory of the event had been relieved of its mark.

This is a quite surprising turn of events. His belated finding of a viable solution did not change anything in the potential of danger to which he had been exposed, and to which he had been responding inadequately. Nor was he bothered by the question of why such an obvious solution had not occurred to him at a time when the reality situation required it urgently as a possibly life-saving device. Be that as it may, from then on he no longer felt disquieted by the danger in which he had found himself. The discovery—long after the events in question—that, even if the ring had not made its unexpected appearance on the teller's counter, he *could have* saved his wife and himself, undid the damage that the trauma had caused; that is to say, he responded as if the idea *had come to his mind* at the actual moment of danger.

Freud has called our attention to the fact that thinking stands for an experimental way of acting. This was meant, of course, with respect to future actions. The mind has the ability to anticipate future contingencies, and it stores up plans and schemes upon which the necessary actions can be built. In our example, however, an equivalent process took place, but *in reverse*. The subject acted as if his later coming upon a solution actually had a retroactive effect on an incident that had occurred years before.

From the behavioristic point of view, one would have to call this highly irrational; in view of the working of the psychic apparatus, it must be regarded as a highly salubrious process. This clinical observation impresses me as important. It demonstrates how a conscious inner process may undo a traumatic effect. In the psychoanalytic situation, in fact, our way of undoing traumatic effects is to bring the unconscious meaning of events to the subject's awareness.

In analysis, the meaning of this man's apraxia would probably have stood in the center. The masochism, the feelings of guilt for his flight, the aggression against his wife, and the self-destructive implication—all these would have been worked through. I do not know whether this would really have eliminated the awful sensation for, to a certain extent, he had incurred reality guilt by needlessly endangering his wife's and his own life.

Although the clinical example I have set forth is not likely to occur frequently, and cannot therefore be taken as typical, it is still striking that it occurred at all. The fact that there are apparently mental processes capable of undoing the damage that has been wrought by trauma, without having to resort to the activation of a defense mechanism (for the subject did not have to pay the price of denial, or of renewed repression, in order to rid himself of the traumatic effect), may make us look in search of areas in which the same effect is achieved in a way that is more typical than was shown in the foregoing example.

A broader approach to the problem should convince us that there must be some processes in which structure is destroyed. To be sure, the question that occupies most analysts is how structure is formed; yet the formation of a healthy personality also requires that, during the period of growth, structure be dissolved. Anna Freud (1961, p. 26f.), having demonstrated that the preserved recollection of a trauma actually covers a large number of similar events, speaks of "telescoped" experience. It is only one step further to assume that not all traumata maintain their significance. Freud's metaphor of the various Romes (1930, pp. 69-71), all of which remain preserved on the same spot—he employed this metaphor to allegorize a constituent element of the human mind—is probably not satisfactory, as is already adumbrated in his paper "The Dissolution of the Oedipus Complex" (1924).

The growth of the psychic apparatus must be visualized, like the growth of bone, as a process in which new structure is formed on the surface, and old structure is dissolved underneath. Repression is one of the mechanisms that remove to the unconscious debris which would otherwise interfere with an adequate growth process—but it may also hinder that process. Clinical evidence speaks in favor of the assumption that, although much of the past is stored in the repressed, not all of it is, and that part of the structures that have existed in the past is irremediably destroyed, in the same way as osteoclasts destroy part of the existing bone structure. We may then use the trabecular system, with its many empty spaces forming part of the inner space of the bone, as an analogy to the repressed; in this view, the repressed, even if it could be known in its totality, would still not contain a complete record of the past, but would instead show lacunae of nodal importance.[21]

21 Research to validate this view is feasible, although it would be extremely complicated. Subjects about whom longitudinal developmental studies, such as are now being carried out at various centers, are extant, would have to be subjected consistently, in later years, to deep hypnosis, in which state one could then examine which recollections had been preserved in the repressed, and which had not. Further, in old people,

It has become an accepted truism that the study of dreams is one of the principal sources in any endeavor to reconstruct the early phases of development. The fact that dreams are so easily forgotten has been explained as a result of resistance directed against the repressed (of which dreams contain so much, although in a distorted form). Recent experimental dream research, however, has ascertained that the nightly dream production is so rich and extensive that, if a patient were able to recall the full extent of his nightly dream productions, that in itself would make it well-nigh impossible for him to be analyzed, for the mere reporting of his dreams would take far more time than is allocated for the entire psychoanalytic session.

This, of course, does not disprove the belief that *some* dreams are forgotten as the result of resistance, but it can hardly be maintained any longer that in every instance it is resistance that is responsible for the forgetting of dreams. At this moment, the analyst's interest turns from the recalled to the forgotten dream, and the question arises: what takes place in those dreams that are forgotten, not because of resistance, but for other, as yet undetermined reasons?

We know now that Socrates, when he spoke in the *Apology* of the sleep "of him who is undisturbed even by dreams," was objectively wrong: there is no such sleep under natural conditions. Subjectively, however, he was right. There are mornings when the sleeper awakens, particularly refreshed and sprightly, with the feeling of having slept very soundly, undisturbed by dreams. Indeed, during those nights, dreams, even though they have taken place, have not in fact disturbed the sleeper. The memory of them has vanished, if a memory of them has been formed at all. There is something puzzling about the recollection of dreams; as far as I know, it has not yet found any explanation. There is no known instance in which psychoanalysis could have recovered the recollection of a dream that had actually taken place a long time before, unless the dream was recalled by the subject at least once shortly after it had been dreamed.

When Freud writes that a patient "may be able to remember a dream which he had dreamt three or four or even more days before and which had hitherto remained forgotten" (1900, p. 520), he is

---

particularly when they are developing dementia simplex, there is a tendency to recall early memories, so that here is another avenue that may make possible the designing of a comprehensive map of the repressed.

referring to the exception;[22] at the same time, he indicates that a dream, if it is not converted into conscious memory relatively soon after its occurrence, is irretrievably lost. This is quite different from the situation with regard to the recall of external events, or of any experience during the state of wakefulness, for that matter. Years after its occurrence, the recollection of a fantasy or of an external event may still suddenly return, even though this particular psychic event may have been repressed immediately after it took place, or may have occurred subliminally at the time without ever reaching consciousness thereafter.[23]

From all this I take it that dreams in general are not "meant" to be recalled, and that those that are actually recalled belong to a special group of dreams, which have not achieved the purpose for which the dream is really destined. I suggest that the fact that a dream is remembered may more often than not indicate that the function of providing the fulfillment of a wish has not operated satisfactorily.[24] This may be one of the reasons why it is generally not an easy matter to detect wish fulfillment in dreams.

Now one of the main trends in life, organic as well as psychological, is directed toward the undoing of traumatic damage, the restoring of psychobiological integrity. With increasing differentiation, this goal becomes more and more difficult to achieve, but that does not rule out an ever-active tendency toward it. If one looks at Freud's model of childhood dreams (of which we now know that it occurs rather rarely, because of the early onset of conflicts brought about by the differentiation of the psychic apparatus) (cf. Freud 1900, p. 131), one can observe that here the dream openly serves this very function.

[22] A patient of mine once insisted that a dream that he recalled for the first time during the session had been dreamed ten days earlier. I seriously doubt the correctness of such an assertion.

[23] To be sure, this is not true of all psychic contents that are formed consciously and then repressed, or which have been formed subliminally from the beginning. But that should not prevent acknowledgment of the principal difference between memories, with regard to their having their source in sleep or in wakefulness. The difference is perhaps also reflected in the psychoanalytic procedure, which aims at the reconstruction of a variety of psychic events relating to infancy and childhood, but never at the reconstruction of the dreams of that same period. The irrecoverable loss of the majority of dreams is perhaps the most potent argument against Freud's Rome metaphor.

[24] The discussion of orgastic dreams that are recalled frequently would lead us too far afield.

A girl of three years was disappointed by the little time it took for her to cross a lake by boat, the first time she did so. Next morning, she said: "Last night I went on the lake" (Freud, 1900, p. 129). This sample is particularly instructive because the child did not call her reported venture a dream, but presented it as an actual event. In childhood, frustrations are seeds of traumata, or they are actual traumata, depending on the quantitative factor. When this child awoke the following morning, the frustration of the previous day had been extinguished, reality had taken the desired course, and the trauma had been eliminated.

Two objections will likely be raised to this. In the light of my proposal, such a dream, to begin with, should not have been recalled at all. That may be quite true. Hypothetically, I would suggest that there may have been just a little tinge of fear mixed in with the dream, in which the dreamer did alone what she had done the day before under parental protection. Further, one may think of the aggressive implication of the dream and the ensuing shade of guilt. Both may have made the dream fall short of an ideal wish fulfillment.

It will probably also be asserted that the example is a simple instance of denial or repression, such as we are abundantly familiar with, from clinical experience. The recollection of the day's events will be denied or repressed by the infant and replaced by a more pleasing one. That may also be quite true in this instance. But my surmise is that such dreams occur quite frequently without their being remembered at all, from which it is only a small step to the assumption that the simultaneous occurrence, during sleep, of the unpleasant day's residue and the blissful event of the dream makes them neutralize each other, as positive and negative electrical charges do, so that both are in effect simply gone the next morning: the recollection of frustration, as well as the dream of bliss. In that sense, one structure has been quashed by the formation of a second; the latter, in turn, has exhausted itself in the process of nullifying the former.

On a quite different level, something similar took place when my subject's psychic apparatus lost its ability to produce the sensation of eeriness, once his saving idea came into his mind—that, after all, he *had* had the means of rescue at hand, in a past situation of indeterminate, although grave, danger.

I feel somewhat more certain about the possible correctness of my proposition, now that the changes with age in the percentage of REM sleep in total sleep are known (Roffwarg et al., 1966). In the neonate, REM sleep occupies 50 percent of total sleep; it falls off to 13.8 percent (or slightly more) in old age. Yet the older we grow, the less we are able to be traumatized. I have deliberately said, *able*, in that traumatization is a sign of life, and studies of old-age patients who are suffering from dementia simplex have convinced me that they can no longer suffer a trauma. Curiously enough, they lose at the same time the fear of death.[25]

When we learn that the percentage of REM sleep rises slightly in adolescence and early adulthood (from 18.5 to 22), this hardly serves to contravene my proposition; but the claim that REM sleep is abundant *in utero*,[26] where the fetus seems so well protected against traumatization (unless one regards growth as a traumatic process, which it might well be), does appear to be a formidable counterargument. Roffwarg et al. propose the ingenious theory that "the REM mechanism serves as an endogenous source of stimulation," that it assists "in structural maturation and differentiation of key sensory and motor areas within the central nervous system, partially preparing them to handle the enormous rush of stimulation provided by the postnatal milieu, as well as contributing to their further growth after birth."

The theory has not been proven, but let us assume its correctness. REM would then be a built-in source of stimulation *in utero* to growth of important brain areas. After birth, this stimulation is taken over by "the enormous rush of stimulation" from exogenous sources, and REM is left, as it were, "without a job." It would not be unusual, however, for a mechanism to change its function, in correspondence with a dynamic change of the total situation in which it is involved. In prenatal life, REM allegedly stimulates and prepares central areas for their later task of dealing with exogenous stimuli; postnatally,

---

[25] I wonder whether the examination of such patients may not show a reduction below 13.8 percent. At any rate, the curve published by Roffwarg et al. indicates that, if we were to live long enough, REM sleep might even disappear altogether.

[26] Prematurely born babies show a high percentage of REM sleep and this has given cause to the assumption that REM occurs already *in utero*. However, it would not be surprising if it were found that the first appearance of REM occurs after a massive stimulation of the cerebrum.

according to my view, it would protect the cerebrum against over-loading, thus continuing its salubrious effect in accordance with newly arising demands.[27]

One more argument may be presented in favor of my thesis. We sometimes forget that aging is not a straight-line process. We not only rise biologically younger in the morning than we were before falling asleep, but we also feel that way. In the light of Freud's suggestion that sleep is a regression to the womb, this is not surprising. After a good night's sleep, we say that we feel "newborn." This, however, occurs only after undisturbed sleep. Notwithstanding the physiological factors, can it be that the degree of rejuvenation we feel upon being aroused is correlated with the degree to which the dream has fulfilled its function—which, in this context, would mean the degree to which psychic structure was dissolved?[28]

I turn now to the last clinical problem I wish to discuss in this paper.

A woman who, since her early twenties, had been in treatment

[27] Another objection, which it may be premature to discuss, may be raised with regard to the fact that no manifest difference was observed between dreams that subjects reported, upon being awakened during an early REM period (these are usually forgotten), and those of late REM periods, occurring toward the morning hours (these are usually remembered much better by patients in psychoanalysis).

[28] Whether every dream is an attempt to settle an infantile trauma, as Ferenczi suggested in a posthumous paper (1934), seems questionable. The analyst may obtain this impression since, in the course of the analytic process, if it takes hold of the patient, the repressed memories of infantile traumata are acutely recathected. When Stein writes: "The dream has . . . an essential function in the adaptation to trauma" (1965, p. 73), he seems to follow Ferenczi. Yet he then accentuates the sleeper's reaction, when he is aroused from terror and responds: " 'It was only a dream—it's all imagination,' " at which point Stein finds "the deepest instinctual component of the dream" to be "the wish to restore omnipotence by the incorporation of the frightening event" (1965, p. 74). Two criticisms of this formulation seem warranted. (1) Strictly speaking, this would not be an instinctual component, if Freud's terminology is to be maintained, but rather the gratification of a highly libidinized component, attributable to the ego or self. (2) Notwithstanding the possibility that in atypical instances this narcissistic component may become the principal momentum of a dream, this interpretation has unfortunate overtones of a way of thinking that Freud allegorized when discussing the secondary gain of neurotic disease: "It would be equally true to say that a man who had lost his leg in the war had got it shot away so that he might thenceforward live on his pension without having to do any more work" (1926, p. 99). According to my proposition, some dreaming would have the effect of completely extinguishing the memories of some traumata. Those traumata whose memories have been preserved in the repressed and which have such a profound effect on later dreams, would be such as have withstood the traumatolytic effect of dreaming, either because of quantitative factors, or by force of particular circumstances inherent in the traumatic situation or the traumatized personality, or owing to a disturbance of the dream mechanism itself (see later).

with several psychoanalysts for a chronic schizophrenic disorder which was taking a relatively benign course, reported that, in her infancy, her mother had cut off her penis. The patient's disorder had never before led to the production of delusions and hallucinations. Furthermore, this alleged memory was mentioned in a way that did not sound like a paranoid or delusional production, but rather like the way in which a patient reports a screen memory, about which the listener knows that, because of its inner inconsistency, it could not possibly have happened. The fact that the patient did not recognize the impossibility of such a recollection was not the result of an intellectual deficit; her thinking was usually impeccable, and her intelligence above average.[29] I once told the patient that the event she "recalled" could not possibly have taken place, since castration is a serious crime: if her mother had committed it, there would certainly have been reports about it in the newspapers. This was quite aside from the fact that she was a woman, and not a castrated boy. The latter argument carried no conviction for her, but she did concede to the former as convincing proof that her memory must have been mistaken.

As a matter of fact, she never again asserted that the event had occurred. Her ambivalent feelings toward the mother, however, were in no way influenced by the proof that her chief "justification" for her fits of rage against her mother was in fact untenable. The course of her association productions did not change, either.

The fact that this highly intelligent person, who was an astute observer and usually recorded events in her environment correctly, reported the castration as a remembered fact, convinced me that she must have dreamed it as an infant, but had not been capable, at that time, of discriminating between dream and reality (cf. Piaget, 1927). As a matter of fact, mankind for the larger part of its history did not make a strict distinction between reality and dream, and it is still a question what makes it possible for us to do so.

The assumption that the child who leaves the latency period with a predisposition toward a schizophrenic disorder has suffered from a disturbance in the dream mechanism, of the kind I have outlined,

---

[29] This patient was close to the group of patients Stein (1965) described, aside from her being schizophrenic. She too had suffered in childhood from otitis media.

would help explain a few of the salient features that are shown by some patients suffering from the disorder.

The reader may recall my comparison of ego formation with the growth of bones. The formation of ego structure in the type of patient I have in mind may be compared to the pathology that leads to osteopetrosis ("marble bone disease"), a congenital disorder in which the bones are hard but fragile, dense and sclerotic, and form a mass throughout, without any inner space left free, as in healthy bone. For the purpose of analogy, let us say (though this is not quite correct) that, in this disorder, the osteoclasts have not done their work of resorption. Yet an equivalent process does take place in the schizophrenic. *All* past structures are preserved; when the individual reaches puberty, he is bogged down by the completely unmanageable load of his wholly unreduced past. His ego can no longer grow.[30]

In the case of the patient just mentioned, it was, indeed, observed that the manifest dream did in fact produce a severe trauma; but this happened in a child whose defenses had been malfunctioning since very early in life, so that one must describe it as exceptional. It is, after all, quite remarkable that the child did not evolve anxiety, or a pavor nocturnus, and was therefore not aroused, as would have happened with any other child in whom the dream function per se had not fallen victim to disease. In this child, the dream did not show anything of its "osteoclastic" function; quite the opposite, it *added* structure, so that we must not be astonished to learn that, at the end of puberty, the patient felt herself to be in an almost paralyzed state.[31]

I wonder to what extent the schizophrenic patient's delusions, his hostility to the world, his implacable accusations, go back to the dreams of his infancy and childhood. It may be that the child who later will suffer from this disease does not obtain relief from his REM sleep, that most of his dreams only injure his psychic apparatus anew.

[30] This description ought, of course, to be taken in its most general terms.

[31] Here, of course, one has to call to mind the dream theory of W. Robert of 1886, in which so much of the functional part of Freud's theory was anticipated, although the dream was for Robert principally a somatic process. Robert's theory has primarily nothing to do with trauma, but his claim that a subject who was deprived of dreaming would eventually become insane (Robert, 1868, p. 10; cf. Freud, 1900, p. 79) makes his work particularly interesting in view of recent experimental research (Fisher, 1965).

It is possible that psychopathology of clinical relevance is in general based on *disturbances of the dream mechanism*—that here, indeed, is the organic core that stands in its center. In view of the almost incredible strides modern research has made in the physiology and pathophysiology of the dream, there is reason to hope that, one day, these disturbances will be concretely demonstrated. Then, for the first time, psychiatry will also have at its disposal a reliable nosology, such as other branches of medicine have been able to obtain with the progress of pathological anatomy.

BIBLIOGRAPHY

Alexander, F., French, T. M., et al. (1946), *Psychoanalytic Therapy: Principles and Application*. New York: Ronald Press.
Eissler, K. R. (1938), Zur genaueren Kenntnis des Geschehens an der Mundzone Neugeborener. *Z. Kinderpsychiat.*, 5:81-85.
Fenichel, O. (1945), *The Psychoanalytic Theory of Neurosis*. New York: Norton.
Ferenczi, S. (1934), Gedanken über das Trauma. *Int. Z. Psa.*, 20:5-12.
Fisher, C. (1965), Psychoanalytic Implications of Recent Research on Sleep and Dreaming. *J. Amer. Psa. Assn.*, 13:197-303.
Flammarion, C. (1917), Dreams as "Reflected Impressions" of Waking Problems, from: L'Inconnu et les problèmes psychiques. In: *The World of Dreams*, ed. R. L. Woods. New York: Random House, 1947, pp. 522-524.
Freud, A. (1951), Observations on Child Development. *This Annual*, 6:18-30.
Freud, S. (1900), The Interpretation of Dreams. *Standard Edition*, 4 & 5. London: Hogarth Press, 1953.
—— (1901), On Dreams. *Standard Edition*, 5:629-686. London: Hogarth Press, 1953.
—— (1918), From the History of an Infantile Neurosis. *Standard Edition*, 17:7-122. London: Hogarth Press, 1955.
—— (1920), Beyond the Pleasure Principle. *Standard Edition*, 18:1-64. London: Hogarth Press, 1955.
—— (1924), The Dissolution of the Oedipus Complex. *Standard Edition*, 19:173-179. London: Hogarth Press, 1961.
—— (1925), Negation. *Standard Edition*, 19:235-239. London: Hogarth Press, 1961.
—— (1926), Inhibitions, Symptoms and Anxiety. *Standard Edition*, 20:87-172. London: Hogarth Press, 1959.
—— (1928), Dostoevsky and Parricide. *Standard Edition*, 21:177-194. London: Hogarth Press, 1961.
—— (1930), Civilization and Its Discontents. *Standard Edition*, 21:57-145. London: Hogarth Press, 1961.
—— (1933), New Introductory Lectures on Psycho-Analysis. *Standard Edition*, 22:3-182. London: Hogarth Press, 1964.
—— (1937), Analysis Terminable and Interminable. *Standard Edition*, 23:216-253. London: Hogarth Press, 1964.
—— (1939), Moses and Monotheism. *Standard Edition*, 23:7-137. London: Hogarth Press, 1964.
Greenacre, P. (1945), The Biological Economy of Birth. *This Annual*, 1:31-52.
Hartmann, H. (1939), *Ego Psychology and the Problem of Adaptation*. New York: International Universities Press, 1958.

Jones, E. (1931), *On the Nightmare*. London: Hogarth Press, 1949.

Khan, M. M. (1963), The Concept of Cumulative Trauma. *This Annual*, 18:286-306.

Kris, E. (1956), The Recovery of Childhood Memories in Psychoanalysis. *This Annual*, 11:54-88.

Lewin, B. D. (1958), *Dreams and the Use of Regression* [The Freud Anniversary Lecture Series]. New York: International Universities Press.

—— (1962), Knowledge and Dreams. *Bull. Phila. Assn. Psa.*, 12:97-111.

More, L. T. (1934), *Isaac Newton*. New York: Dover, 1962.

Newbold, W. R. (1896), A Dream Detective Solves Professor Hilprecht's Famous Dream. In: *The World of Dreams*, ed. R. L. Woods. New York: Random House, 1947, pp. 525-530.

Nunberg, H. (1932), *Principles of Psychoanalysis*. New York: International Universities Press, 1955.

Piaget, J. (1927), *The Child's Conception of the World*. New York: Harcourt, Brace, 1929.

Rank, O. (1924), *The Trauma of Birth*. New York: Harcourt, Brace, 1929.

Reich, W. (1927), *Die Funktion des Orgasmus*. Leipzig, Vienna, Zürich: Internationaler psychoanalytischer Verlag.

Robert, W. (1886), *Der Traum als Naturnotwendigkeit erklärt*. Hamburg: Hermann Seippel.

Roffwarg, H. P., Muzio, J. N., Dement, W. C. (1966), Ontogenetic Development of the Human Sleep-Dream Cycle. *Science*, 152:604-619.

Sachs, H. (1925), [Review of] Rank, O.: *Das Trauma der Geburt und seine Bedeutung für die Psychoanalyse*. *Int. Z. Psa.*, 11:106-113.

Sanctis, S. de (1899), *I sogni*. Turin: Spandre e Lazzari.

Schur, M. (1953), The Ego in Anxiety. In: *Drives, Affects, Behavior*, ed. R. M. Loewenstein. (New York: International Universities Press, 1:67-103.

—— (1958), The Ego and the Id in Anxiety. *This Annual*, 13:190-220.

Spitz, R. A. (1965), *The First Year of Life*. New York: International Universities Press.

Stein, M. H. (1965), States of Consciousness in the Analytic Situation: Including a Note on the Traumatic Dream. In: *Drives, Affects, Behavior*, ed. M. Schur. New York: International Universities Press, 2:60-86.

Stern, M. M. (1961), Anxiety, Trauma and Shock. *Psa. Quart.*, 20:179-203.

—— (1953a), Trauma, Projective Technique and Analytic Profile. *Psa. Quart.*, 22:221-252.

—— (1953b), Trauma and Symptom Formation. *Int. J. Psa.*, 34:202-218.

Sully, J. (1893), The Dream as a Revelation. *Fortnightly Rev.*, 53:354.

Winnicott, D. W. (1949), Birth Memories, Birth Trauma, and Anxiety. In: *Collected Papers*. New York: Basic Books, 1957, pp. 174-193.

Wolff, P. H. (1966), *The Causes, Controls, and Organization of Behavior in the Neonate* [*Psychol. Issues*, Monogr. 17]. New York: International Universities Press.

THE SUPEREGO AND MORAL DEVELOPMENT IN THE THEORIES OF FREUD AND PIAGET

MARTIN L. NASS, Ph.D.

The purpose of this paper is to present an exposition of the psychoanalytic conception of the superego, to show how the concept developed and became modified, and to compare it with an exposition of the theory of moral development of Jean Piaget. An attempt is made to define areas of common concern in both positions and to outline theoretical overlap.

What has come to be called the superego in psychoanalysis actually comprises several aspects of personality which are often grouped together. The conceptualization of these structures and functions has undergone changes with the evolution of psychoanalytic theory. The fact that some authors have at times distinguished between such terms as "superego," "ego ideal," and "conscience," and at other times used them interchangeably has served to make the dimensions of the superego unclear. In addition, the various elements which comprise the superego are modified during the course of the individual's development and these developmental considerations gave rise to the problem of dating the onset of the superego. Most writers reserve the term superego for the postoedipal period and refer to the earlier manifestations as superego precursors. This practice follows Freud's conception of the superego as the "heir of the oedipus complex" (1923, p. 36) and his statement that "We ought not to speak of a conscience until a super-ego is demonstrably present" (1930, p. 136).

It is one of the purposes of this paper to trace the development of these concepts through the history of psychoanalysis and then to

From the Postdoctoral Program, Graduate Department of Psychology, New York University.

The comments and helpful suggestions of Dr. Robert R. Holt who read an earlier version of this paper are gratefully acknowledged.

present the current thinking, particularly in terms of the overlap and lack of clarity in the conceptions of ego and superego.

THE EARLY PSYCHOANALYTIC CONCEPTION OF THE SUPEREGO

The term "superego" was first used in *The Ego and the Id*. However, the functions which Freud attributed to it were discussed a good deal earlier. In his paper "On Narcissism" (1914) he proposed the concept of ego ideal. In the course of ontogenesis, he wrote, the ego ideal is formed in order to help recapture the state of primary narcissism after the latter has been given up. The ego ideal is the mental agency onto which the narcissism is displaced and which "is the substitute for the lost narcissism of . . . childhood" (p. 94). The "conscience" acts as watchman, comparing the ego with the ego ideal; it arose from the critical influence of parents and, later, teachers and others who trained the child.

In 1917, in his paper on "Mourning and Melancholia," Freud made a further reference to the conscience, indicating that it is a part of the *ego*. He said, "We see how in him [the melancholic] one part of the ego sets itself over against the other, judges it critically, and, as it were, takes it as its object. . . . We shall really find grounds for distinguishing this agency from the rest of the ego. What we are here becoming acquainted with is the agency commonly called 'conscience' " (p. 247).

In *Group Psychology and the Analysis of the Ego* (1921), Freud used the term ego ideal differently. He then employed it to include the concept of conscience, previously (1914) differentiated from the ego ideal. He says, "some such agency develops in our ego which may cut itself off from the rest of the ego and come into conflict with it. We have called it the 'ego ideal,' and by way of functions we have ascribed to it self-observation, the moral conscience, the censorship of dreams, and the chief influence in repression" (pp. 109-110). Thus, he combined the two concepts and this combination remained throughout his later writings, with the exception of one brief return to the original 1914 formulation (Freud, 1933).

When Freud introduced the term "superego" in *The Ego and the Id* he presented it as "the super-ego (ego ideal)," thus cementing the unity of the concept.

Freud viewed the superego as a modification of the ego and as the main force in the resolution of the oedipal conflict. The superego develops as a result of identifications with the parents, by replacing object cathexes which are formed through the necessity of dealing with normal and inverse oedipal components. The superego is made up not only of identifications but also of reaction formations against them (1923, p. 34). The superego is the representative of the id, as the ego is the representative of the external world, and Freud viewed it as primarily unconscious. "If the ego has not succeeded in properly mastering the Oedipus complex, the energic cathexis of the latter, springing from the id, will come into operation once more in the reaction-formation of the ego ideal. The abundant communication between the ideal and these *Ucs.* instinctual impulses solves the puzzle of how it is that the ideal itself can to a great extent remain unconscious and inaccessible to the ego" (1923, p. 39).

For the most part, from this point on, Freud's conception of the superego remained unchanged. However, it has been pointed out that Freud frequently used the term *ego* where he appeared to mean *superego* alone or ego and superego simultaneously (Schafer, 1960). This fact contributes to the difficulty of conceptual clarity. Subsequent writers either have used superego as synonymous with "conscience" or "ego ideal," or did not attempt to clarify or define these terms. Specific functions of the superego were at times attributed to the ego and then again to the superego. However, some attempts to clarify the concepts were made and are discussed below.

THE MOVE TOWARD CONCEPTUAL CLARITY

From the literature on the superego in the past four years, one might get the impression that a development parallel to that which took place some fifteen years ago in the area of the ego is emerging with regard to the superego. By far the most comprehensive paper was written by Hartmann and Loewenstein (1962) in an attempt to define and conceptualize the scope and functions of the superego. In so doing, they subsume under the concept of superego both the ego ideal and conscience aspects, a classification with which several other theoreticians are not in agreement (e.g., Lampl-de Groot, 1962; Reich, 1954; Sandler, Holder, and Meers, 1963). Hartmann and Loewenstein suggest that some of the problems with this concept arise from a lack of clarity in differentiating between the developmental stages prior to the superego system and the functions of the completed superego. They regard the superego as a system in its own right with aims of its own. They do not regard it as having developed out of the ego, but see it as closely related to ego development yet dynamically independent. They believe that much confusion would be avoided if the term *superego* were reserved for the postoedipal period of development, with the earlier phases regarded as genetic determinants.

Hartmann and Loewenstein attempt to define the various functions and contents of the superego. To broaden the scope of this review, some aspects of this controversy and some of the disagreements will be considered.

Reality Testing

Freud (1914) originally assigned the function of reality testing to the superego. In *The Ego and the Id* he ascribed it to the ego. Hartmann and Loewenstein relate this shift to the development of ego psychology, and agree that reality testing is an ego function.

Inner Perception

Freud (1933) assigned the task of self-observation to the superego. Hartmann and Loewenstein indicate that it is rightfully an ego function but can come under the influence of the superego which may both stimulate and interfere with self-observation.

Self-Criticism

Self-criticism has consistently been regarded as a superego function. In fact, Jones (1926) cites it as the superego's only function. He says, "The function [of the superego] is to criticize the ego and to cause pain to the latter whenever it tends to accept impulses proceeding from the repressed part of the *id*" (p. 304). Compare this to the much greater scope attributed to the superego in current literature.

Ideal Function

Hartmann and Loewenstein feel that Freud's conception of the ego ideal as one aspect of the superego should be maintained. They use the analogy of attributing various functions to the ego, e.g., perception, thinking, defense, in a global fashion and argue that basic changes in the conception of the superego should not be made, just as no changes were made in the concept of the ego when its functions were spelled out and elaborated. They assert that contrasting tendencies can exist in the superego and can be compared to the intrapsychic conflicts of the ego.

This view is in sharp contrast to the position taken by Lampl-de Groot (1962). She regards the ego ideal as an agency of wish fulfillment which, by re-establishing narcissistic equilibrium, serves to provide pleasure and undo pain caused by frustrations. In his development, the child attributes omnipotence to his parents and partakes of it through identification. The ego ideal supports the ego in dealing with the disappointments and frustrations and is essentially an ego function. Lampl-de Groot sees it as a separate province *within the ego*. She conceives of the superego, on the other hand, as an agency of restriction and prohibition requiring the renunciation of wish fulfillments and the compliance with parental dictates. Both ego ideal and superego guide the ego in its dual task of allowing the individual sufficient drive satisfaction and capacity to live up to the demands of the external world; both work in harmony in normal development. Both institutions are marked by identification with parents and can be seen as special ego areas with their own functions. However, the critical difference elaborated by Lampl-de Groot is in their functions, the ego ideal wish fulfilling, the superego prohibiting.

Novey (1955) also regards the ego ideal as a distinct psychic institution which is, however, related to the ego and the superego.

Annie Reich (1954) makes a similar superego-ego ideal differentiation. While she does not consider them in relation to structures, she states that the "ego ideal expresses what one desires to be; the superego, what one ought to be." The ego ideal represents identifications with parental figures seen "in a glorified light" while the superego contains the identifications "resulting from the breakdown of the oedipus complex" (p. 218).

Part of the controversy and some of the reasons for the confusion are touched on by Hartmann and Loewenstein (1962) in their discussion of the functions and genesis of the superego. Most writers, when they deal only with structural considerations, indicate the overlap and integration of the two systems. When the origins are traced and compared, the rift becomes greater. Hartmann and Loewenstein (1962) feel that it is reasonable to view the *ego ideal aspect of the superego* in close relationship to other oedipal developments and to distinguish it from other earlier idealizations, which are not part of the superego. These ideals are transformed during and after the oedipal phase, merge with other aspects of the superego, and become a function of the superego. By setting up their formulation along functional lines, these authors avert many of the genetic difficulties.

Another part of the confusion is due to the shifting meaning of the same terminology appearing in Freudian and post-Freudian literature. This is clearly pointed out by Bronfenbrenner in a paper dealing with the concept of identification (1960): "When one finally views Freud's writings on this subject as a whole, it becomes abundantly clear that he often uses the same terms to refer to what are basically quite different concepts. [This] confusion becomes still further confounded in the later developments and modifications of Freud's theories by contemporary writers, who typically apply the same terminology in still other ways and introduce new names for concepts and processes discussed by Freud himself" (p. 15).

With respect to the ego ideal, Sandler, Holder, and Meers (1963) have culled the following meanings in the writings of Freud alone: "1. The superego in the sense of that specialized set of ego functions which we call the 'conscience.' 2. Certain ego functions which were at one time considered to be functions of the superego. . . . 3. The ideal of self-representation or ideal self-image. 4 Ideal parental introjects which serve as models for the self . . ." (pp. 149-150).

Thus, the term ego ideal has been used to refer to various constellations which include functions and contents belonging to both the ego and the superego and has shifted in meaning throughout psychoanalytic writings.

Relationship with the Ego

As indicated above, superego and ego functions have shifted their locus several times. The confusion is further compounded by the fact that superego functions are regulated by ego functions. For example, Beres (1958) points out that morality (a superego function) requires thought, memory, and affect. Reality testing and object relations are necessary ego factors which relate to superego operations. Identification is a process crucial to both ego and superego development (Bronfenbrenner, 1960; Kohlberg, 1963). Hartmann and Loewenstein (1962) discuss the growing autonomy of superego functions both from the objects and from the drives. They add, however, that it would be difficult to propose the superego's independence from the ego. "Not only does early superego development depend on ego development, but once the superego as a system is set up, its normal functioning is constantly bound to certain activities of the ego; and the further evolution of the superego does not diminish the developing ego's influence, but tends to increase it" (p. 65). They further suggest that the greater the ego's capacity for neutralization, the more rational is the superego, hypothesizing that cruel and over-punitive superego structures are related to impaired ego capacity for neutralization.

Freud (1921) originally assigned the function of repression to the superego. With the advent of ego psychology and the ego as locus of defense, this became an ego function (A. Freud, 1936). Similarly, the superego has evolved from being mostly unconscious (Freud, 1923; Jones, 1928) to "for the most part conscious" (A. Freud, 1936, p. 5).

Hartmann and Loewenstein believe that superego development, after beginning in latency, continues into adolescence; the mutual adjustment of ego and superego is gradually enhanced and promoted and results in a workable equilibrium. This is consistent with recent psychoanalytic writings on ego development (e.g., Erikson, 1959; Hammerman, 1965; Jacobson, 1964) and with the child development literature (Kohlberg, 1963).

It is apparent that part of the conceptual confusion has resulted from some of the changes in theory over the years, from varying meanings attributed to the superego concept, and from the somewhat unquestioning tradition of workers in the field to employ jargon which does not have a consistent meaning. The several attempts which have been made to gain conceptual clarity appear to be long overdue and should be pursued further in the direction of integrating the cognitive theory of moral development with psychoanalytic principles.

However, a further difficulty arises from the fact that attempts to clarify the conception of the superego do not deal with problems unique to the basic aspects of the tripartite model in Freud's structural theory. Thus, the issue of whether a certain behavior is primarily derived from an id impulse, an ego defense against the impulse, or a superego compromise may be argued in different ways. However, the arguments are based on the supposition that the use of the tripartite model furthers conceptual clarity. There are writers in psychoanalytic theory who believe otherwise. Thus, Gill (1963), in discussing the relationship between ego and id, points out that the introduction of the structural theory, while avoiding the problems of the topographic position, resulted in many difficulties and contradictions of its own, such as linking primary process with id and secondary process with ego while at the same time attributing some primary-process functions to the ego. He maintains that rather than using a sharp division of the structures of the mind, it would be advantageous to conceptualize the mental apparatus in terms of hierarchies and continuities. He proposes that id and ego be seen as a continuum of forms and structures existing at all levels. At the same time, he acknowledges that the position of the superego in this hierarchy is still unclear. Rubinstein (1965) also deals with the inadequacies of the id, ego, superego classification and particularly stresses the need to reformulate the theory in terms of current neurophysiological knowledge.

While these issues are not critical to the theme of this paper, they are areas which need to be clarified in psychoanalytic theory.

PIAGET'S WORK ON MORAL DEVELOPMENT

Working in a context independent of psychoanalysis, the Swiss psychologist Jean Piaget investigated the development of moral judgment in children. Piaget gathered his data through observations and interviews of children. His position on moral development, as expounded in *The Moral Judgment of the Child* (1932), is that there are two types of morality in the child. He refers to the first stage as "the morality of constraint" or "heteronomous morality," which is characteristic of the child up until the age of seven or eight years. This type of morality is a reflection of the child's egocentrism, a quality prevalent in the young child's thinking in all areas studied by Piaget. It is characterized by moral realism and contains the following elements: (1) objective responsibility; (2) unchangeability of rules; (3) absolutism of value; (4) transgression defined by punishment; (5) duty defined as obedience to authority; (6) ignoration of reciprocity; (7) expiative justice; (8) immanent justice; (9) collective responsibility (Kohlberg, 1963).

The older child, in interaction with peers, develops the "morality of cooperation," characterized by autonomy and mutual respect. Peer reciprocity develops through the give and take of social interaction rather than through the imposition of sanctions. The child must have the capacity for thought processes which are relatively free from egocentric influences. The autonomous level is characterized by (1) responsibility judged by intent; (2) flexibility of rules; (3) relativism of value; (4) moral judgments made independently of sanctions; (5) duty defined in terms of peer expectations; (6) reciprocity; (7) restitutive justice; (8) naturalistic causality; (9) individual responsibility (Kohlberg, 1963).

Piaget's theories have stimulated a good deal of empirical research since the emphasis is on behavior and the data are more readily available than Freud's. The studies on moral development are reviewed by Kohlberg (1963). For the most part they have substantiated the existence of stages of conscience development (e.g., Boehm and Nass, 1962). The critical nature of peer interaction reported by Piaget is not borne out by some data (Kohlberg, 1958) and the existence of two distinct moralities has also been questioned (MacRae, 1954; Kohlberg, 1958). There are also some open issues concerning the nature of the factors responsible for the development of more mature moral judgments. Kohlberg (1963) states that mature moral behavior should be seen as a product of the development of "broad social-cognitive capacities and values rather than of a 'superego' or of 'introjection of parental standards' " (p. 325). He suggests that moral judgment follows a continuous process and is a reaction to the whole social world rather than a product of a certain stage, concept, or social relationship.

While Kohlberg's last point is in close agreement with more recent data, it is not at variance with the "superego" position which he criticizes. Psychoanalysis conceives of the superego as greatly influenced by cognitive factors, and to postulate stages in the development of any function or structure is not to deny the existence of an overall broad process. The recent changes in the psychoanalytic concept of superego have not been incorporated into the current literature on moral judgment and conscience development. For example, Kohlberg (1963) states that "learning theorists interested in overt behavior, psychoanalysts interested in fantasy, and Piaget, interested in moral judgment have all assumed that the basic features of adult conscience have developed by early childhood (ages 5-8)" (p. 321). Contrast this view with the writing of Hartmann and Loewenstein (1962) who speak of modifications in the superego through experiences in adolescence. "With the setting up of the superego as a separate agency, its development has not come to an end. Later objects the person takes as his models and the value systems of his cultural environment leave their imprints on it. The further development of the ego tends to integrate the superego with the value systems of a person's cultural environment" (p. 76). And Jacobson (1964) stated: "During latency and adolescence the superego normally undergoes further maturation, which proceeds essentially along those very lines of building up a coherent system" (p. 127), a view she had earlier (1954) voiced without elaboration.

The attempts to test psychoanalytic hypotheses have often resulted in a tendency toward reductionism. This is further seen in the treatment of other key concepts in the field. For example, in his review, Kohlberg states that psychoanalysis assumes that guilt is inward aggression (pp. 288, 294) and then cites research studies which refute this assumption. However, the psychoanalytic model describes guilt as a form of anxiety, the anxiety of the ego toward the superego (Freud, 1930, p. 135), which may not be related to inward aggression. In fact, self-destructive and self-punishing behavior is not necessarily an indication of guilt or internalized superego activity (Beres, 1958). When Kohlberg cites as evidence of refuting the psychoanalytic position studies which indicate that children whose parents inhibit overt aggression display no more guilt than children treated otherwise, he misses a critical essence in the transformation of aggressive impulses and assumes that psychoanalysis maintains that only one alternative is available. Thus, in testing the "guilt as measured by inner-turned aggression" hypothesis, these studies do not provide an accurate statement of the psychoanalytic position. In attempting to measure the data by experimental means, crucial aspects of the theory are short-circuited.

The cognitive research on guilt and moral development as reviewed by Kohlberg (1963) in many instances seems to ignore the entire issue of the internal, projective structure of guilt and its pleasurable (masochistic) properties, although some reference is made to a variable need for punishment among children. Thus, he cites as "defiance of the 'pleasure principle'" studies in which children inflict psychic and physical pain upon themselves after transgression (Kohlberg, 1963, p. 288).

In general, the most striking features of researches designed to test the psychoanalytic model of superego are their lack of familiarity with current theoretical issues in the field and the current concept of superego in psychoanalysis, and the tendency to reduce concepts and distort basic phenomena in attempts to render them measurable.

Kohlberg is aware of the difficulty in evaluating the psychoanalytic model of superego development in terms of children's verbal responses to little stories (see also Nass, 1964), but he concludes that the theory is "inadequate to account for the social-developmental research observations on guilt and allied responses" (p. 295).

AN ATTEMPT AT INTEGRATION

One of the original purposes of this paper was to attempt to compare the positions of Freud and Piaget in the area of conscience development. While such a comparison was made by Wolff (1960) in the area of sensorimotor functioning, little work has been done in the area of conscience development and superego, the one exception being Peters's (1960) concise overview. Moreover, the relationship between moral judgment and superego is not clear. What is clear, however, is that the two theories in their overall approaches proceed from different points of view and collect different kinds of data, Piaget's approach using behavior (mostly verbal responses to situations) as the basis for the formation of judgments, and the Freudian approach using introspective reports, developmental reconstructions, and theoretical inferences. Piaget seems more concerned with the cognitive aspects of development, while Freud was involved with the affective side of behavior. However, in the area of sensorimotor functioning they seem to deal with processes that are not necessarily complementary. Anthony (1957) points out that attempts at a marriage of theories all too easily "result in a 'syncretic' and not a synthetic mixture" (p. 261).

An early attempt of this kind was made by Odier (1948), who used the concept of anxiety as a focus in integrating the two theories. Odier judged that Piaget and Freud were fundamentally concerned with the same object: the psychological evolution of the human being. "Comparing the evolution of the individual to a river, I should say that Freud and Piaget both ascended to its source—but each on his own bank. . . . I believe it is high time that we throw some bridges across the river joining the intellectual and affective banks" (p. 32).

The bridge which Odier used was, in essence, the fact that anxiety can break down cognitive and intellectual processes and thus cause more primitive, magical affective forces to come into focus. This approach seems rather artificial and does not deal with any of the basic concepts of either theory. Flavell (1963), commenting on the attempts to bring the systems together, states that "all the evidence suggests that Piaget himself has neither been profoundly influenced by Freud nor has tried to wed the two theories in any systematic way" (p. 5). The fact that Piaget was interested in psychoanalytic theory in the 1920s was noted by Anthony (1957) and by Flavell (1963), but this interest has not been continued in more recent years. In fact, Cobliner (1965), in a lucid exposition of Piaget's findings on cognitive development and the development of object permanency, indicates that Piaget moved away from psychoanalysis after 1933. Some of Piaget's recent criticisms were formulated against a theoretical position which antedated ego psychology.

Inhelder (1956) made an attempt to relate affective and cognitive functioning in children, although she did not deal with the problem solely on the basis of theory. In her view, both are aspects of mental development which form one unity; moreover, will plays a role in affective development analogous to that of thought operations in cognitive development (p. 264). Both Piaget and Inhelder state that affective and cognitive aspects of behavior develop together and create new structures simultaneously (Piaget, 1932; Piaget and Inhelder, 1959).

Psychoanalytic and cognitive theories of moral development are in many respects intertwined. Phenomena and objects of study overlap, are called by other names, are selected or ignored for further study, but generally are concerned with similar basic issues, viz., the development of moral and ethical values from a more heteronomous position to a more autonomous position. In this respect the field of moral development differs somewhat from the sensorimotor field, where Wolff (1960) found that the two theories do not deal with the same kinds of phenomena.

One of the major differences between the two approaches, aside from the methodological one, is that psychoanalytic theory started with the study of the drives and has more recently concerned itself with cognitive processes and the adaptive use of drives, whereas cognitive theory has not been concerned with drives or drive derivatives other than in their indirect manifestation. Psychoanalytic theory has attempted to relate its findings in studies of cognitive processes to the broader aspects of drive theory (e.g., Rapaport, 1951) and to formulate its concepts in relation to underlying structures and processes. Cognitive theory has tended to remain more at the descriptive level, rendering empirical research more feasible.

The parallels between the two theories as they apply to conscience development can be observed through Piaget's stages. Piaget's early morality of constraint, which is a reflection of the child's egocentrism, develops through dependency on the adult world and through the child's submissiveness and lack of autonomy. The child does not evaluate or test fantasies and magical beliefs but accepts them as fact. Piaget (1932) states, "Just as, if left to himself, the child believes every idea that enters his head instead of regarding it as a hypothesis to be verified, so the child who is submissive to the word of his parents believes without question everything he is told, instead of perceiving the element of uncertainty and search in adult thought. The self's good pleasure is simply replaced by the good pleasure of a supreme authority" (p. 409).

Although this statement has important implications in psychoanalytic theory—e.g., the perpetuation of magical beliefs through passivity, dependency, and lack of autonomy by relinquishing power to the authority—the major concern at this juncture is in the parallel phase in psychoanalytic theory in which the immature ego is unable to test reality. Thus, Jacobson (1964) states that the ability to build up superego identifications depends on the advancing maturation of the ego. The early form of the superego as conceptualized in psychoanalytic theory is cruel, harsh, and unyielding (Freud, 1923). Its pattern of values has been referred to as "sphincter morality" (Ferenczi, 1925), i.e., morality in strict response to pleasing the parent, as in the toilet-training phase. This is almost identical in form to Piaget's morality of constraint, in which rules are obeyed automatically and without question.

Between the autonomous and heteronomous stages there is an intermediate stage of moral development in which moral behavior is variable and responses are specific to the type of situation encountered (Boehm and Nass, 1962). The parallel in psychoanalytic theory can be found in Freud's early writings where he states that morality in children "does not set in simultaneously all along the line" (1900, p. 250). It can also be seen in the recent work in tracing the development of superego autonomy (e.g., Hartmann and Loewenstein, 1962; Jacobson, 1964) in which intrasystemic variations result in conflicting patterns of morality within the same individual. Thus, as Piaget (1932) speaks of an intermediary stage between the morality of cooperation and the morality of constraint, Hartmann and Loewenstein discuss its counterpart in psychoanalytic theory: "Contradictions between conscious and unconscious morality, between the demands of the ego ideal and the moral taboos, and between various parts of the individual value systems are frequent, and may be the rule. Contrasting tendencies in the superego do exist and can be compared to the intrasystemic conflicts in the ego" (p. 63).

The content of the mature adult conscience in both systems appears to be couched in similar terms. Thus, Hartmann and Loewenstein (1962) characterize superego autonomy as independence from drives on the one hand and objects on the other. Jacobson (1964) adds the autonomy from pressures caused by the superego's early precursors. The later superego is to a larger extent subject to influence by the ego and its maturation and thus helps to transform magic images and conceptions into internalized ideals, moral codes, and ethical standards (Jacobson, 1964). This is made possible only by the increased maturity of the ego as the individual moves into adolescence and adulthood with the concomitant remodeling of psychic structures.

Piaget (1932) describes the more mature stage of morality as being free from egocentric influences, i.e., from the kind of magical imagery which psychoanalytic theory characterizes as primary process and which is less subject to influence by the mature ego. In Piaget's view, the modifications in moral development come about through peer interaction and cooperation which create a phenomenon that is parallel to the ego's greater activity and maturity. He says, "it is also requisite that the mind should tend towards morality as to an autonomous good and should itself be capable of appreciating the value of the rules that are proposed to it" (p. 410). Also: "cooperation suppresses both egocentrism and moral realism, and thus achieves an interiorization of rules. A new morality follows upon that of pure duty" (p. 411). Piaget is describing the phenomenon analogous to that referred to by analytic theorists as the autonomous superego. However, the age at which this autonomy is attained—according to Piaget, eight to ten years—is in keeping neither with the psychoanalytic findings nor with the empirical findings of Kohlberg (1963).

The parallel between the two points of view can be seen through the growth of the *ego*, which becomes increasingly able to deal with the drives and the outside world on the one hand, and which helps to temper the irrational superego (heteronomous morality) on the other. Piaget's work has shown that magical thinking is dominant in the thought processes of children and helps them orient their actions to their limited world (Rapaport, 1960). As ego processes gain greater influence in the child, moral judgments become more autonomous and rational. The child, through his increased strength, is better able to evaluate, question, and reshape the content of his conscience. This process continues through adolescence and early adulthood and does not appear to be complete by eight to ten years, as Piaget has stated. It is more in keeping with Kohlberg's report (1963) of changes into preadolescence and adolescence. This summary position is most clearly formulated by Jacobson (1964) who says: "under the influence of its adjunct, the ego, the superego's operational methods become enriched and endowed with new individual features and with a variability and flexibility which the infantile superego lacks. . . . the growing harmony between the moral and ethical standards of the superego and the reality-directed goals of the ego will eventually facilitate the desirable, smooth, and intimate collaboration between the superego and corresponding ego functions" (p. 188).

The child's developing moral and ethical system can be viewed, from the standpoints of both psychoanalytic and cognitive theory, as passing through a series of developmental stages which relate closely to maturational factors. As cognitive processes mature they bring moral and ethical conceptions into greater accord with rationality. Psychoanalytic theory attempts to anchor moral development in a broader framework, citing its interrelationship with drives as well as cognitive apparatuses, whereas cognitive theory does not concern itself with these issues. The more recent work in psychoanalytic theory has brought it much closer to the findings of cognitive psychology.

BIBLIOGRAPHY

Allinsmith, W. (1957), Conscience and Conflict: The Moral Force in Personality. *Child Develpm.*, 28:469-476.
Anthony, E. J. (1956), The Significance of Jean Piaget for Child Psychiatry. *Brit. J. Med. Psychol.*, 29:20-34.
—— (1957), The System Makers: Piaget and Freud. *Brit. J. Med. Psychol.*, 30:255-269.
Beres, D. (1958), Vicissitudes of Superego Functions and Superego Precursors in Childhood. *This Annual*, 13:324-351.
Boehm, L. & Nass, M. L. (1962), Social Class Differences in Conscience Development. *Child Develpm.*, 33:565-574.
Brodbeck, A. J. (1954), Learning and Identification: IV. Oedipal Motivation as a Determinant of Conscience Development. *J. Genet. Psychol.*, 84:219-227.
Bronfenbrenner, U. (1960), Freudian Theories of Identification and Their Derivatives. *Child Develpm.*, 31:15-40.
Bychowski, G. (1943), On Relations between the Ego and the Superego in Psychoanalysis. *Psa. Rev.*, 30:313-325.
Cobliner, W. G. (1965), The Geneva School of Genetic Psychology and Psychoanalysis: Parallels and Counterparts. In: R. A. Spitz, *The First Year of Life*. New York: International Universities Press, pp. 301-356.
Erikson, E. H. (1959), *Identity and the Life Cycle* [*Psychological Issues*, Monogr. 1]. New York: International Universities Press.
Fenichel, O. (1935), The Scoptophilic Instinct and Identification. In: *Collected Papers*, 1:373-397. New York: Norton, 1953.
—— (1945), *The Psychoanalytic Theory of Neurosis*. New York: Norton.

Ferenczi, S. (1925), Psycho-Analysis of Sexual Habits. *Further Contributions to the Theory and Technique of Psycho-Analysis.* London: Hogarth Press, 1926, 159-297.

Flavell, J. H. (1963), *The Developmental Psychology of Jean Piaget.* Princeton, N.J.: Van Nostrand.

Freud, A. (1936), *The Ego and the Mechanisms of Defense.* New York: International Universities Press, 1946.

Freud, S. (1900), The Interpretation of Dreams. *Standard Edition,* 4 & 5. London: Hogarth Press, 1953.

—— (1914), On Narcissism: An Introduction. *Standard Edition,* 14:67-102. London: Hogarth Press, 1957.

—— (1917), Mourning and Melancholia. *Standard Edition,* 14:237-260. London: Hogarth Press, 1957.

—— (1921), Group Psychology and the Analysis of the Ego. *Standard Edition,* 18:67-143. London: Hogarth Press, 1955.

—— (1923), The Ego and the Id. *Standard Edition,* 19:3-66. London: Hogarth Press, 1961.

—— (1925), Some Psychical Consequences of the Anatomical Distinction Between the Sexes. *Standard Edition,* 19:243-258. London: Hogarth Press, 1961.

—— (1930), Civilization and Its Discontents. *Standard Edition,* 21:59-145. London: Hogarth Press, 1961.

—— (1933), New Introductory Lectures on Psycho-Analysis. *Standard Edition,* 22:3-182. London: Hogarth Press, 1964.

Gill, M. M. (1963), *Topography and Systems in Psychoanalytic Theory [Psychological Issues,* Monogr. 10]. New York: International Universities Press.

Greenacre, P. (1948), Anatomical Structure and Superego Development. *Amer. J. Orthopsychiat.,* 18:636-648.

Hammerman, S. (1965), Conceptions of Superego Development. *J. Amer. Psa. Assn.,* 13:320-355.

Hartmann, H. (1960), *Psychoanalysis and Moral Values.* New York: International Universities Press.

—— Kris, E., & Loewenstein, R. M. (1946), Comments on the Formation of Psychic Structure. *This Annual,* 2:11-38.

—— & Loewenstein, R. M. (1962), Notes on the Superego. *This Annual,* 17:42-81.

Hoffman, M. L. (1963), Childrearing Practices and Moral Development: Generalizations from Empirical Research. *Child Develpm.,* 34:295-318.

Inhelder, B. (1956), Die affektive und kognitive Entwicklung des Kindes. *Schweiz. Z. Psychol. & ihre Anwend.,* 15:251-268.

Jacobson, E. (1954), The Self and the Object World. *This Annual,* 9:75-127.

—— (1964), *The Self and the Object World.* New York: International Universities Press.

Jones, E. (1926), The Origin and Structure of the Super-ego. *Int. J. Psa.,* 7:303-311.

—— (1928), The Development of the Concept of the Super-ego. *J. Abnorm. Soc. Psychol.,* 23:276-285.

Klein, M. (1944), The Early Development of Conscience in the Child. In: *Psychoanalysis Today,* ed. S. Lorand. New York: International Universities Press, pp. 64-74.

Kohlberg, L. (1958), Moral Judgment in the Years Ten to Sixteen. Unpublished Doctoral Dissertation, University of Chicago.

—— (1963), Moral Development and Identification. *National Society for the Study of Education Yearbook,* 62, Part I:277-332.

Kramer, P. (1958), Note on One of the Preoedipal Roots of the Superego. *J. Amer. Psa. Assn.,* 6:38-46.

Lampl-de Groot, J. (1947), On the Development of Ego and Superego. *Int. J. Psa.,* 28:7-11.

—— (1962), Ego Ideal and Superego. *This Annual,* 17:94-106.

MacRae, D. (1954), A Test of Piaget's Theories of Moral Development. *J. Abnorm. Soc. Psychol.*, 49:14-18.

Miller, D. R. & Swanson, G. E., eds. (1960), *Inner Conflict and Defense*. New York: Holt-Dryden.

Morris, J. F. (1958), The Development of Adolescent Value-Judgments. *Brit. J. Educ. Psychol.*, 28:1-14.

Nass, M. L. (1964), The Development of Conscience: A Comparison of the Moral Judgments of Deaf and Hearing Children. *Child Develpm.*, 35:1073-1080.

Novey, S. (1955), The Rôle of the Superego and Ego-Ideal in Character Formation. *Int. J. Psa.*, 36:254-259.

Odier, C. (1948), *Anxiety and Magic Thinking*. New York: International Universities Press, 1956.

Peters, R. S. (1960), Freud's Theory of Moral Development in Relation to That of Piaget. *Brit. J. Educ. Psychol.*, 28:250-258.

Piaget, J. (1932), *The Moral Judgment of the Child*. New York: Harcourt.

—— & Inhelder, B. (1959), Die Psychologie der frühen Kindheit. In: *Handbuch der Psychologie*, ed. D. Katz. Basel, Stuttgart: Benno Schwabe, pp. 275-314.

Rapaport, D. (1951), The conceptual model of psychoanalysis. *J. Pers.*, 20:56-81.

—— (1960), Psychoanalysis as Developmental Psychology. In: *Perspectives in Psychological Theory*, ed. B. Kaplan & S. Wapner. New York: International Universities Press, pp. 209-255.

Reich, A. (1954), Early Identifications as Archaic Elements in the Superego. *J. Amer. Psa. Assn.*, 2:218-238.

Ritvo, S. & Solnit, A. J. (1958), Influences of Early Mother-Child Interaction on Identification Processes. *This Annual*, 13:64-85.

—— —— (1960), The Relationship of Early Ego Identifications to Superego Formation. *Int. J. Psa.*, 41:295-300.

Rubinstein, B. B. (1965), The Mind-Body Problem. In: *Psychoanalysis and Current Biological Thought*, ed. N. S. Greenfield & W. C. Lewis. Madison: University of Wisconsin Press, pp. 35-56.

Sandler, J. (1960), On the Concept of Superego. *This Annual*, 15:128-162.

—— Holder, A., & Meers, D. (1963), The Ego Ideal and the Ideal Self. *This Annual*, 18:139-158.

Schafer, R. (1960), The Loving and Beloved Superego in Freud's Structural Theory. *This Annual*, 15:163-188.

Wolff, P. H. (1960), *The Developmental Psychologies of Jean Piaget and Psychoanalysis* [*Psychological Issues*, Monogr. 5]. New York: International Universities Press.

Zilboorg, G. (1955), Derivation, Structure and Function of the Superego. In: *Ministry and Medicine*, ed. I. Galdston. New York: International Universities Press, pp. 100-118.

AFFECTS IN RELATION TO SELF AND OBJECT

A Model for the Derivation of Desire, Longing, Pain, Anxiety, Humiliation, and Shame

LEO A. SPIEGEL, M.D.

In this study I shall draw on the concepts of self and object presentation to investigate a number of disparate though related affects. My primary focus will be on pain; other affects—desire, longing, anxiety, humiliation, and shame—will be discussed in relation to it.

Throughout this paper the terms physical and mental pain are avoided because they foreclose two important questions: does the subjective experience of pain vary with its source, and do the processes underlying it likewise vary with its source? Instead, I shall use pain of physical and of mental origin, terms which do not imply any stand on this issue. The term pain is always used in the sense of a specific *affect*, corresponding to the German *Schmerz*. While pain is obviously painful, not every painful feeling can be classified as pain; for example, anxiety too is usually painful. To avoid misunderstanding, unpleasurable and unpleasure will usually be substituted for painful and painfulness. At this time no attempt will be made to discuss three important and relevant issues: pain of physical origin as sensation and as affect, the classification and structure of affects (Glover, 1939; Jacobson, 1953; Lewin, 1961; Schafer, 1964; and others), and the relation of the self to the ego.

NARCISSISTIC PHENOMENA AND AFFECTS

Some of the thoughts presented in this paper were stimulated by clinical experiences encountered in the analyses of highly "narcis-

This paper is a revised version of one presented at The Hampstead Child-Therapy Clinic, March, 1963; at The New York Psychoanalytic Society, October, 1963; and at The Baltimore Psychoanalytic Society, April, 1964.

sistic" patients.[1] An attempt to conceptualize the phenomena usually subsumed under the heading "narcissistic" led me to the conviction that much analytic material can be more systematically classified and more easily understood by relating it to pain of mental origin than by leaving it under the present heading of "narcissistic" alone.

Freud made a number of enlightening references to pain (1895, 1917, 1920, 1923) and treated the topic systematically in 1926. Only a few other analysts have studied pain (Ramzy and Wallerstein, 1958; Szasz, 1957; Joffe and Sandler, 1965). This scarcity may in part be related to the complexities of the subject, but a more likely reason can be found. The productions of our patients rarely contain explicit references to it. Therefore, lacking the overt clinical confrontation with pain, the analyst is not likely to think or to write about it. However, I shall attempt to demonstrate that narcissistic lesions are first cousins to pain of mental origin. Pain in this narcissistic guise is actually encountered daily in our analytic work and thus worthy of our attention.

As already mentioned, my own interest in pain gradually emerged in the course of analyzing a number of "narcissistic" patients. A small but important segment of an analytic session of such a patient will serve to illustrate the conceptual tangle which stimulated my wish to understand such material better and led me to a consideration of pain of mental origin as an ordering and clarifying principle.

This patient came into analysis because of severe anxiety attacks. In one of his previous analyses, his extraordinary obesity had come under discussion and he was given the interpretation or, if you will, the explanation that because he had received so little maternal love, his longing for love was satisfied by his eating a great deal. This very intelligent patient accepted this explanation but complained that it was mechanical. During one of his sessions with me he again began to rail about his mother's lack of attention, her lack of interest, how she never spent any time with him and so on. Then he proceeded, in his own mechanical way, to connect this lack of maternal interest with his overeating. I said to him at the time: "No matter how much you tried to interest your mother in you, no matter how much you exerted yourself, you were never successful in keeping her home with you and this was profoundly humiliating." This stress

[1] In an earlier paper (1954), I have considered the relation of narcissistic lesions to acting out.

on humiliation interested the patient, and for the first time his analysis took on a personal meaning.

From this episode we can infer an empirical rule that may be of value in dealing with certain patients. It is based on Freud's advice that when the patient talks about the present, we should talk about the past and vice versa. Similarly, when the patient talks about his love needs, perhaps we should turn our attention to certain narcissistic aspects; and when he talks about certain narcissistic aspects, turn our attention to his love needs.

The connection, made in the patient's earlier analysis, between his conscious desire for food and his unconscious wish for maternal love could have been correct only in an abstract and programmatic way. For it can be said of anyone that whatever activity he may be engaged in, this activity will in some way be related to basic needs such as a wish for maternal love. Specifically, however, only two data of subjective experience were available for interpretation: a well-recognized intense urge to eat and a more recently recognized affect of humiliation. The patient and I came to see that when he ate he *experienced* not a desire for maternal love but a need for a feeling of well-being, importance, and quasi-omnipotence. It became clear that his eating was in part a counterphobic measure against unpleasurable feelings of humiliation, and this affect could in turn be meaningfully connected with his memories of his mother. This and similar clinical experiences led to my desire for a crisper theoretical understanding of such "narcissistic" affects as humiliation, feelings of inferiority, shame.

How is this patient's affect of humiliation to be classified? Obviously it comes under the rubric of "narcissistic lesions"—and a narcissistic lesion is obviously a consequence of nonfulfillment of a narcissistic need; but what really is a "narcissistic need"? This term has been used without explicit definition of content. How is a narcissistic need related on the one hand to the needs of the id, sexual and aggressive, and on the other to narcissism? For example, is a narcissistic need to be equated with a drive need; does it work with raw, instinctual energy? Or is it an ego activity using neutral energy? I have been unable to find an explicit discussion of these clinically and theoretically significant questions except in Fenichel (1938), who·

stated: "what is characteristic for the 'unifying' tendency of the ego is the way in which it brings its various trends into harmony with one another. Among these trends one is particularly interesting because under certain circumstances it assumes an instinct-like character, which competes with the genuine instinctual aims of the id . . . I refer to the so-called 'narcissistic need' " (p. 78).

Regrettably, it can be seen that this time Fenichel does not help us. He answers neither question, leaving the same confusing dilemma by saying that on the one hand a narcissistic need is an ego activity and that on the other hand it is instinctlike. As a sign of the lack of clarity that pervades this area, it is worth noting that in the above quotation, the term "narcissistic need" is not only enclosed by quotation marks but is also preceded by the attenuating words, "so-called." How much meaning can attach to a term which has been thus doubly watered down? I believe that the term "narcissistic need" cannot be applied as an explanatory concept because it combines, but fails to harmonize, both ego and id aspects. (The way out of this dilemma is suggested by Hartmann's distinction between ego and self [1950] to which I shall return.)

In contrast, as a description of clinical phenomena, the term "narcissistic need" is quite clear. We immediately recognize the patient who is described as having an excessive need to be liked, who is easily hurt, sensitive, whose self-esteem is labile. Intuitively we "understand" the "meaning" of the phrase: he is dependent on "narcissistic supplies." Despite this intuitive understanding, the question poses itself whether we obtain any new insight by using terms such as narcissistic lesions, needs, and supplies? Is any more insight achieved than if the patient were described as sensitive, easily hurt, etc.? To ask the question is to answer it in the negative.

Why is the labeling of clinical phenomena as "narcissistic" of so little additional value? The answer lies in the fact that we cannot travel from the specific clinical phenomenon covered by the term "narcissistic need," etc., to the general theory of narcissism and return from this trip with a general principle of narcissism applicable to the specifics of "narcissistic needs." The opposite is true for any clinical drive phenomenon. We can turn to the theory of drives and then apply a general notion and body of information derived from the theory to enrich the understanding of the specific clinical drive phenomenon.

Let us for purposes of this discussion arbitrarily and incorrectly classify the productions of the analytic patient into two types: instinctually centered and narcissistically centered. The position of the analyst is quite different depending on whether he is faced by one or the other type of material. To understand the instinctually centered productions of the patient, the analyst has the necessary tools in the concepts of instinct, defense, superego, danger situation; but in the case of narcissistically centered material he has few if any guidelines. The clinical phenomena of narcissistic lesions run on one set of rails and the theory of narcissism runs on another, nonintersecting set.

Obviously, a closer connection between the *clinical data* covered by the terms "narcissistic supplies, needs, lesions" and the *theory* of narcissism needs to be established. I shall attempt to demonstrate that the connection between the "narcissistic lesions" and the theory of narcissism lies in the affect of pain of mental origin. My approach will be two-pronged. On the one hand, utilizing the clinical manifestations of narcissistic lesions, I shall attempt to demonstrate that feelings of humiliation, shame, and inferiority are genetically derived from pain. On the other hand, turning to the theory of narcissism, I shall attempt to demonstrate that pain of mental origin, like its counterpart, pain of physical origin, constitutes a lesion of the self. Therefore, an understanding of pain itself must be attempted.[2]

ELEMENTS RELEVANT TO PAIN OF MENTAL ORIGIN

I shall begin with some remarks on the affects of longing and sexual desire and discuss their relation to the two classes of objects, transient (need-satisfying) and constant. The concepts of narcissism and self and object presentations will be considered next and an operational definition of the self will be attempted. Then I shall briefly present Freud's views on pain of physical origin. Only after that will an attempt be made to formulate a dynamic, economic, and topographic scheme of pain of mental origin. With a formulation of

2 Such an attempt, beginning with clinical encounters in the analytic situation, may eventually lead to new perspectives on other affects as well (Lewin, 1961).

pain of mental origin available, I shall again turn to "narcissistic needs" and other clinical phenomena.

Longing

Freud (1926) elucidates the significance of longing in the following passage: "repeated situations of satisfaction have created an object out of the mother; and this object, whenever the infant feels a need, receives an intense cathexis which might be described as a *'longing'* one. It is to this new aspect of things that the reaction of pain is referable. Pain is thus the actual reaction to loss of object, while anxiety is the reaction to the danger which that loss entails and, by a further displacement, a reaction to the danger of the loss of object itself" (p. 170; my italics). Thus it is clear that Freud implied a relation between longing and pain. And the relation he implied is indeed in its subjective aspect quite simple; the longing for the longed-for object may at some time "turn into" pain or be replaced by pain.

In a more detailed discussion of object relations in early childhood Anna Freud (1952) implies the significance of longing, though she does not explicitly use the word: "In the earliest months of life it seems possible to exchange the object, provided the form of need satisfaction given to the infant remains unaltered. Later . . . the personal attachment to the object increases in importance; it becomes possible then to vary the satisfactions, provided the object remains the same. At that stage . . . separation from the object causes extreme distress. . . . As the ego matures and the pleasure principle yields to the reality principle, children gradually develop the ability to retain libidinal cathexis to absent love objects during separation of increasing lengths" (pp. 44-45).

How does "the ability to retain libidinal cathexis to absent love objects" show itself to the observer? Surely by signs of unsatisfied longing *despite* need satisfaction. We are all familiar with the longing of the lover for the absent beloved despite sexual satisfaction with someone else, or the longing of the exile for his native land despite need satisfaction in his present one.

It appears that longing has not been given sufficient explicit attention in our theoretical formulations. These observations and others point up the advisability of allocating a definitive place to the affect of longing in our discourse on object relations. (This attempt will be made below.)

Desire

The affect of desire is related, yet antithetical, to the affect of longing. Leaving on one side a qualitative differentiation between the two affects, they can be sufficiently separated for our present purposes by posing a simple question. What kind of object is needed to dissipate each affect? It is obvious that desire can be dissipated by the transient, need-satisfying object, i.e., by the external object whose presentation in the mind is inconstant. On the other hand it is obvious that longing will not be appeased by the need-satisfying object; it can be dissipated only by the constant object, the true love object, i.e., the object whose presentation in the mind is permanently cathected. This one-to-one relation between specific affect and type of object necessary for its dissipation is important for my later exposition of pain.

Narcissism and Presentation of Self and Object

A certain degree of obscurity prevails in the use of the terms self and narcissism (Hartmann, 1950; Jacobson, 1964; Lichtenstein, 1965; Sandler and Rosenblatt, 1962; Spiegel, 1959). The term self is often used as an equivalent of the total person, the "I" of ordinary speech. However, in the mental apparatus of any person, two large categories of presentations coexist, self and object.[3] The use of the term self to cover the totality of the person creates confusion because within that person *both* self and object presentations exist.

Second, narcissism is usually considered to be the cathexis of one's person (Hartmann, 1952).[4] As already noted, the mental apparatus of a person contains not only self presentations but object presentations as well. Surely, the idea of narcissism should not be blended with presentations of external objects.

A language relatively free of ambiguity and contradiction (in this area) can be achieved by using the terms *person* and *other one* to designate the totality of each individual in an object relation. The

---

3 For reasons of brevity, I shall not elaborate on my choice of "presentation" over "representation" except to note that Strachey uses "presentation" for *Vorstellung* (Freud, 1926, p. 171; Freud, 1917, p. 256), although that is not the only reason for my preference.

4 A modification of this view will be noted below.

person and the other one include the body and the mind of each individual. *Within the mental apparatus of the person and of the other one, both self and object presentations are contained.*

I believe that such a view results in a number of clarifications, the first being a modification of the definition of narcissism. Narcissism can now designate only the quantity of cathexis of the self presentation relative to the cathexis of the object presentation *within one individual*. It does not designate the cathexis of the total person in an object relation. Narcissism cannot be limited to the subject of the object relation alone. We can speak of the narcissism of both partners in the object relation.

If the preceding steps have been accepted, one is relentlessly driven to a redefinition of the meaning of the self that no longer allows the usual substitution of self for the "I" of casual speech. Since the self does not connote a totality (for which the term person is used in this paper) and since it therefore cannot imply the body, its place must be reallocated. The only place that can be found for it is as a *psychic entity within the mental apparatus.*

However, what then is the difference between self and self presentations, which are also within the mental apparatus? The self presentations are basically individual memory traces, with individual cathexes (and "facilitations") of the person's body and its functioning. The self, *in contrast* to the many cathexes of the individual self presentations, is the result of the ego's pooling and averaging of these cathexes to form a single overall constant cathexis. The self can be defined operationally (and usefully for daily analytic work) as the average constant cathexis of all the self presentations.[5] (See Spiegel [1959] for a more detailed presentation of the concept of pooling in relation to the self.) Similar views apply to the object and to the individual object presentations.

Pain of Physical Origin

Freud's formulation (1920) of pain of physical origin contains a number of elements: the penetration of the stimulus barrier in a

[5] The idea of a constant overall cathexis as distinct from a changing one can be found in "The Project" in the formulation of the ego: ". . . repeated reception will produce a group of neurones which retains a *constant* cathexis. . . . The ego may thus be defined as the totality of ψ-cathexes at any given time; and in these a permanent portion may be distinguished from a changing one" (1895, p. 384; my italics).

narrow sector by an external agent; the consequent disturbance within the psychic apparatus by the large quantum of unbound energies flowing from the periphery; the putting out of action of the pleasure principle until the more pressing task of binding these energies has been achieved. The pleasure principle reassumes its dominant role in the regulation of psychic events only when this task of painful binding has been completed.

A close reading of Freud's views on pain (1920, p. 30) shows that he implicitly assumed two conditions for its appearance, a necessary and a sufficient one. The necessary one is found in the penetration of the stimulus barrier and the resulting inflow of energies. But he also points out that the penetration of the barrier does not sufficiently account for the paralyzing character of pain and the impoverishment of all other systems. To explain the latter, a system must be assumed which reacts to and binds the inflowing masses of excitation. This is the sufficient condition, and I assume it is the ego which binds these masses of excitation.

Pain of Mental Origin

I believe it is possible to adapt Freud's model of pain of physical origin to pain of mental origin if certain emendations and amplifications are made. As the plan of the external world finds some kind of "representation" in the psychic apparatus, I shall assume a stimulus barrier within the psychic apparatus, in analogy to the barrier between the person and the external world, which tends to delimit the object presentations from the self presentations, i.e., to delimit object and self. Such a stimulus barrier would be the specific structural correlate to ego boundaries and the separation of self and object, whereas a weakening or a penetration of it would correlate to the phenomena of merging of self and object and dissolution of self.

Closely connected to the "density" of this stimulus barrier between self (presentation) and object (presentation) is Freud's formulation of the strengthening of the stimulus barrier through the hypercathexis of receptive systems (1920, p. 31). Such a strengthening of the stimulus barrier in my model would take place by an increased cathexis of the self (presentations). This means that impingements of cathexes of the object (presentations) on the self would have less chance of intruding into the systems of the self when the latter is in a state of increased cathexis. Cathectic currents flow in the direction of lesser resistance. If the stimulus barrier is especially strengthened, the cathectic current will be deflected away from it; and if the stimulus barrier is especially weakened, the cathectic current will tend to penetrate it.

I shall now describe what I assume to be the differences between the cathexis of the following four presentations: individual self presentations; the overall self (presentation); transient, need-satisfying object presentations; and permanent or constant object presentations. The possible role of the superego in these dynamics will not be considered here. All of these presentations are considered to be "open" to the id and to receive cathexis from it.

The cathectic flow from the id impinging on the individual self presentation and on the pooled self will be considered first. In order to account for both the openness of the self presentations to the continuing "upward" flow of cathexes from the id and the transient cathexis of these same presentations, it must be assumed that a continual transfer of cathexis from the individual presentations to the pooled self (presentation) takes place, leaving the former empty of cathexis. Only in times of instinctual surges is the volume of cathexis so increased that the individual self presentations themselves become cathected and are registered in consciousness as zonal sensations demanding discharge.

With the assumption of a continuing transfer of cathexis from individual to the pooled self (presentation), it becomes necessary to consider how this latter presentation can accomodate to the flow from the individual presentations. One can imagine that the pooling process involves a partial neutralization of these cathexes (Hartmann, 1952) and therefore makes them less demanding of discharge while permitting a rise in level. It will be noted that increased cathexis of the self presentations (whether individual or pooled) strengthens the stimulus barrier and renders the self systems less penetrable to the cathexes of the object presentations on the "other" side of the barrier.

The cathectic interchanges between individual self presentation, pooled self (presentations), id, and stimulus barrier apply equally to the need-satisfying object presentation and to the constant object (presentation) on the "other side" of the stimulus barrier.

A final assumption (the basis for which will not be discussed here) is: a mechanism resembling a "valve" is present in the id; this mechanism may at one time direct cathexis more toward the self systems, at other times more toward the object systems.

By manipulating the conceptual tools of self and object (presentations), it becomes possible to delineate a movement of cathexes between structures which can be meaningfully correlated not only to pain but also to desire, longing, anxiety, humiliation, and shame.

METAPSYCHOLOGICAL CORRELATES TO AFFECTS

Desire

The topographic, economic, and dynamic conditions which appear correlated to the affect of desire will be described first. Assume that the self (as specifically defined in this essay) is at its usual base cathectic level. The person is then in a sexually indifferent state. Then an inflow of cathexis from the id to individual self presentations (e.g., presentations of primary and secondary sexual zones) takes place. This dynamic-economic-topographic constellation (cathectic flow, change of cathectic level, and place of change) is reported to the ego and may appear in consciousness as sensations and feelings in the various sexual zones. If these erotic sensations are reported during the analytic session, they are usually referred to by the analysand as "I am having sensations, or feeling in. . . ." Or: "There are sensations in. . . ." But this feeling does not yet represent desire in the full sense of the word.

Desire in this sense occurs when the analysand says: "*I* am aroused" in contrast to "I have sensations in. . . ." This development can be ascribed to a shift from the increased cathexes of individual self presentations to a raising of the overall base cathectic level of the self as an organization. It is assumed that the pooling activtiy of the ego intervenes after a certain period of time to add the increased cathexes of the individual self presentations to the usual overall base cathectic level of the self. This *change* in base cathectic level of the self is transmitted to the ego and appears in the form of an affective change—"I am aroused" ("I desire").

At the same time cathexis is being continuously transferred along associative paths previously established to the appropriate transient (need-satisfying) object presentation. The ego, seeking to remove messages reaching it from the increased level of the self, uses this object presentation as a template to find a suitable external object. By "suitable" is meant one whose "possession" by (i.e., discharge via) the person abolishes the messages reaching the ego from the self. Once this discharge has taken place, the self returns to its resting base cathectic level and the person once again becomes sexually indifferent.

Longing

It is more difficult to establish similar metapsychological correlations for the affect of longing than it is for desire. It is not as obvious to which structures and cathectic events the conditions for longing should be assigned. As mentioned earlier, desire is dissipated by "possession" of a need-satisfying external object, while longing is dissipated only by "possession" of a constant or permanent external object. This means that as long as desire lasts, "possession" of the transient, need-satisfying object has obviously not taken place. It also means that a specific undischarged constellation exists in the mental apparatus during the state of desire, namely, cathexis of the self presentation. Similarly, if longing exists, the longed-for external, permanent (constant) object is not available to the person. Therefore, the presentation of this permanent object in the mental apparatus must still be cathected.

The question now arises whether the self (presentation) is also hypercathected in longing as it is in desire. The answer to this question must be no, for such a hypercathexis of the self would lead to sexual desire. In brief, desire is correlated to hypercathexis of the self (presentation) while longing is correlated to hypercathexis of the constant object (presentation) alone; in longing, the self remains at its usual base cathectic level. (As stated earlier, the cathected structures, whether they be self, transient object, permanent or constant object, are all within the mental apparatus of the person.)

Longing, which is generally considered to be more spiritual than desire, is in this schema seen as fed by the same libido as desire. The difference between the two affective experiences is here "explained" by correlating them, not to the drive alone, but to the differing structures through which the drive is refracted "on its way to consciousness." An attempt will be made to apply this style of structural conceptualization of affects to anxiety, pain, humiliation, and shame.

Automatic Anxiety, Pleasure, Unpleasure

When the external object is unavailable for "too long" a time, desire for the object disappears. We then also see the appearance of anxiety. Thus in the early stages of object relations a relatively simple connection obtains between desire and anxiety.

While we relate the *condition* for this early, economic anxiety to the absence of the need-satisfying object, we may not simply say that its absence is the *cause* for this primitive anxiety. Rather, the *conditions* for this anxiety can be more satisfactorily formulated as follows. The absence of the need-satisfying external brings about *conditions of unpleasure in the id* to which the ego responds with anxiety. These "conditions of unpleasure" arise in the id because the absence of the external object interferes with the smooth unfolding of id derivatives.

In the early stages of object relations, the appearance of pleasurably toned appetitive desire testifies to the "correct" unrolling of the drives, while the appearance of unpleasurable anxiety testifies to the contrary. The development of the defenses, the establishment of the superego, the expansion of the ego with its involvements in danger situations, the increasing complexity of object relations—all these may obscure but do not remove the early and fundamental relation of desire and anxiety to drive discharge and to the availability of the external object for this very purpose.

Since, given a sufficient number of assumptions, a schema (or model) can always be constructed to fit any set of events, the value and validity of a model (such as the one I have been using with regard to self and object) can be tested, when experimental verification is unavailable, by asking whether it throws some light on an additional phenomenon without increasing the number of assumptions. The phenomenon to which this model should obviously be applied is the change in sign from pleasurable desire to unpleasurable anxiety, i.e., from pleasure to unpleasure. (The terms are used in the ordinary sense of conscious experience.)

It is obvious that in confronting this aspect of problems of consciousness (Klein, 1959) only small advances in insight can be expected. The early interest in the so-called "transformation of affect" derives from an interest in the psychology of consciousness, but the ascendancy of the structural theory and the "new" theory of anxiety led to a deflection of interest from issues of consciousness.

In order to apply the model to the problem of change of affective sign (i.e., from pleasure to unpleasure), let us turn to the state symbolized by "I desire" in which the cathexes of the individual self presentations have been average and pooled into the overall self cathexis. In this state, the ego is anticipating (Hartmann, 1939) not only satisfaction but is also consciously anticipating pleasure as a result of previous pleasurable experiences. This ego is oriented toward the world of transient external objects as the source of anticipated pleasure.

The transient external object does not become available. After a suspenseful waiting period, the outward orientation of the ego switches inward. The cathexis of the transient (need-satisfying) object sinks back into the id. The cathexis, concentrated in the overall self presentation, is now redistributed to the individual self presentations and from there also sinks back into the id. This reversal of direction of the cathectic current from outward to inward appears to me to constitute the topographic correlate to the appearance of unpleasure in the shape of the affect of anxiety. The reversal creates a dammed-up state in the id through blocking the "natural upward" push of the drive into the self presentation.

Pain, Pleasure, and Unpleasure

Having described the primitive relation between desire and automatic anxiety, I shall now attempt a similar description of the relation between longing and pain. The thesis is essentially the same, namely, when the ego gives up its outward orientation toward the external object as a source of pleasure, longing disappears and pain appears. Obviously it now becomes necessary to specify those underlying processes which would explain the appearance of pain but *not of anxiety* as a response to the unavailability of the external object.

Before doing this, it may be worthwhile to note how very few people, with the exception of Freud, have expressed astonishment about the relation between pain and object loss. He said: "But why it is that this detachment of libido from its objects should be such a painful process is a mystery to us and we have not hitherto been able to frame any hypothesis to account for it" (1916, p. 306). Lifelong familiarity with the fact has obscured the need to explain its causes. While Freud (1926, p. 172) dealt with this relationship in some detail, his explanation of why at one time anxiety appears as a response to object loss (unavailability of the external object) but at other times pain remains somewhat obscure; regrettably he never returned to it.

The explanation I suggest is: anxiety is a response to the loss of the *transient* external need-satisfying object, while pain is a response to the loss of the *permanent* (constant) external object.[6]

I return to the connection between *longing and pain*. In longing the permanent object (presentation) has a permanent level of cathexis which is maintained partly by neutralization and partly by aim-inhibited discharge of cathexis onto the permanent external object. If the longed-for external object is unavailable for a long time, the urgency of the unneutralized components becomes greater. Finally, the ego gives up its suspenseful outward orientation and the cathexes are discharged inward.

Two directions appear open to the cathexes of the constant object presentation: one is to the id and the other is to the stimulus barrier between self and object. The question therefore is which one offers the lesser resistance to the flow of cathexes. Two factors blend to make the stimulus barrier less resistant: the upward push from the id and the weakening of the stimulus barrier due to lack of hypercathexis of the self in the state of longing (as contrasted to its hypercathexis in the state of desire). The cathexes of the constant object presentation are thus deflected to the stimulus barrier separating self and object and must finally break through in a narrow sector of this barrier.[7] Then *an identity with the first, necessary condition for pain of phys-*

---

[6] It may be noted that object loss usually refers to both types of objects condensed into one external object and that therefore a mixture of both affects can be discerned with careful observation. Anguish would be a more accurate word to denote this mixture, but it is unlikely that it will replace anxiety since the use of the latter has become so firmly established.

[7] The penetration of the stimulus barrier between self and object (presentation) by the object (presentation) constitutes the metapsychological explanation of introjection. This process, often erroneously described in terms of incorporative fantasies, is a *necessary and universal* condition for imitation, identification, ego ideal and superego formation; but it is not a *sufficient* condition. Other processes, among them neutralization, are needed to distinguish between them.

ical origin has been created. The continuing inflow of these foreign energies into the area of the self creates an excitation in it. This disturbance in the system of the self is responded to by the ego with attempts to bind the excess energies, *thus fulfilling the second and sufficient condition for pain of physical origin.*

In brief, loss of the transient (need-satisfying) external object leads to discharge of cathexis into the id, which in turn creates conditions leading to automatic anxiety, while the loss of the permanent (constant) external object leads on the other hand to discharge into the stimulus barrier between self and object creating conditions which lead to pain.

The Narcissistic Affects of Humiliation and Shame

The affects of desire, anxiety, longing, and pain appear to correspond to certain absolutes, at least in the view presented here, i.e., absolute possession of object (when desire or longing is satisfied) or absolute loss of object. But life usually presents us with less extreme situations; object possession is usually more or less partial and object loss is often likewise partial. In fact, partial object possession also means partial object loss.

In view of my previous discussions of absolute object (external) loss, it is apparent that some painful affects will also appear after partial object loss; and such affects, while painful, should be less painful than the anxiety and pain which result from absolute object loss. I propose that it is precisely the narcissistic affects of humiliation and shame which represent dilution of the more powerful unpleasurable affects of anxiety and pain. Such an attenuation of affect, corresponding to the taming of affects, leads to increasing complexity and maturation of the affective life.

In order to account for such a dampening of extreme affects, an additional assumption will be made; the intervention of a primitive ego ideal in the cathectic circuits previously described. I shall now attempt to delineate the structural conditions, including the ego ideal, which make the attenuation of these "narcissistic" affects from pain plausible.

I begin with Ferenczi's formulation in his remarkable paper on the sense of reality (1913). The scream of the child produces the mother. The scream of the child does not produce the mother. The scream of the child produces the mother and the affective state of pleasure and no pain. The scream of the child does not produce the mother, the love object is absent; misery and pain. *The efficacy of the child's ego in attaining the object becomes coupled with pleasure while its inefficacy becomes coupled with pain.* Later on in life ego efficacy becomes independent of object attainment and has a narcissistic premium attached to it for its own sake as seen in *Funktionslust.* But it is well to remember that this narcissistic premium has its origin in primitive object relations.[8]

Many such couplings occur early in life between efficacy and gratification, inefficacy and lack of gratification, bliss, misery and so on. Let us assume that the memory traces of these experiences become segregated, organized, and pooled, and their cathexes grouped into a special center. This center can then serve as a measure of the ego's efficacy in attaining the object and can be considered the beginning of an early ego ideal.

What is the effect of the introduction of such a center, of such a primordial ego ideal into the mental apparatus? To answer this question, I return to the schema representing the intrapsychic situation following loss of the *constant* external object, a loss that results in pain. With the introduction of an ego ideal, the cathectic circuit following object loss has become more complicated. The energies of the undischarged object presentation penetrate the stimulus barrier; however, the report of the disturbance created by this penetration into the self does not go directly to the ego (which would have responded by binding and by the consequent appearance of pain) but passes first to the ego ideal. Here the message is arrested for a greater or shorter period of time before it is permitted to proceed to the ego which only then can undertake binding measures.

A schematic example will show how the working and effects of such a center can be visualized under conditions of partial object loss. An infant lying in his crib screams a hundred times a day. Seventy times a day the mother appears in response to the screams, thirty times she does not. Gradually such experiences become organized into a center. The affective couplings (ego efficacy in object attainment—pleasure; ego inefficacy—pain) of this center have gradually

[8] A discussion of White's related work on competence (1960) is beyond the scope of this paper.

established a pleasure-pain level which corresponds to the habitual frequency of object attainment. This center, therefore, represents a kind of valve on which a certain pressure, a summation of stimuli, must be exerted before it yields and lets the message get through to the ego. When will the message get through to the ego? After the level established by pooling has been transcended; in short, when the mother does not appear thirty per cent of the times, but, let us say, fifty per cent of the times.

The effect of object loss when this more complicated cathectic circuit has been established differs in other respects from the effect of object loss when only the simpler cathectic circuit is available. In the latter constellation, object loss leads to pain for reasons which have already been given. In the former constellation, the effect of external object loss is held off from the ego by the ego ideal for a protracted time. Absolute object loss is thus converted into diluted object loss. I assume that the affect which results from this relative independence from the external object, from the "here and now" as Hartmann put it, is no longer pain but is humiliation.

I would then add that shame is humiliation experienced when someone else looks on (private humiliation, public shame). This formulation throws light on the early appearance of shame. The usual derivation of shame from the repression of exhibitionistic drives does not coincide with the observation that shame can appear before such repression has taken place, I belive it occurs in connection with previously described frustrations from the object.[9]

In the change from pain to the attentuated affects of humiliation and shame, we see that the introduction of an ego ideal into the cathectic circuit attenuates the impact of object loss. What happens if through some unknown process the ego ideal is lost? The simpler cathectic circuit would then be reinstated; as a consequence pain rather than the milder affect of humiliation would be experienced.[11] It is possible that a process of degradation of the ego ideal plays a role in the preliminary phases of melancholia so that a change from milder feelings such as humiliation to gross pain would be experienced with special intensity.

[9] This view differs from the position taken by Piers and Singer (1953) and is closer to that of Jacobson (1964).

[10] I owe the stimulus for this view to M. Masud R. Khan (London).

PAIN IN MOURNING AND MELANCHOLIA

If the model of pain and other affects which I have expounded should prove fruitful with regard to mourning and melancholia, it would increase the likelihood of its validity. The idea of applying the model elaborated as an explanation of pain resulting from object loss to mourning and to melancholia stems from the well-known clinical fact that pain is prominent in both of them. Of the many statements demonstrating that Freud considered pain of significance in these conditions, I cite only one from "Mourning and Melancholia": "We should regard it as an appropriate comparison, too, to call the mood of mourning a 'painful' one. We shall probably see the justification for this when we are in a position to give a characterization of the economics of pain" (p. 244).

The model explains the presence of pain in mourning since my formulations have been based on the absence of the constant object. The curative effect of the work of mourning, that is, the final disappearance of the *pain* of mourning, likewise becomes intelligible in terms of the model. For when the "total" cathexis of the object presentation has been withdrawn from it, penetrated the barrier, and entered the self, the work of mourning has come to an end and the necessary conditions for pain have finally disappeared.

The second benefit derived from this model is the easy explanation it permits of mourning in *economic terms,* so that it is no longer necessary to say with Freud (1917): "Why this compromise by which the command of reality is carried out piecemeal should be so extraordinarily painful is not at all easy to explain in terms of economics" (p. 245). The obvious explanation follows. The extraordinary degree of pain associated with the work of mourning can be understood economically by assuming that it is proportional to the intensity of cathexis of the object presentation which penetrates the stimulus barrier between self and object.

A third benefit of this model is that it offers a simple theoretical approach to the problem of infantile mourning in relation to reality testing. Freud said: "Reality-testing has shown that the loved object no longer exists, and it proceeds to demand that all libido should be withdrawn from its attachments to that object" (1917, p. 244).

This passage implies that mourning cannot occur before the dominance of the reality principle has been established.

My previous discussion of pain and longing showed that pain was brought about by internal discharge of object cathexis into the barrier separating self and object. What causes such an internal discharge? Only the absence of the longed-for external object, so that unsatisfied longing becomes replaced by pain. If we take pain to be the central feature of the state of mourning, then it appears that real loss alone can bring about mourning and that submission to reality is not a prerequisite. (Of course, the model requires the establishment of object constancy for pain to appear.)

But the growth of the reality principle does influence the affective response to object loss. This response becomes layered; for in addition to pain, *grief* is now experienced and this affect is linked to the ego's recognition of reality; *namely, the ego is completely incapable of changing the irreducible fact of object loss.*

In addition to the distinction between pain and grief, it is also useful to distinguish between the *state* of mourning as a clinical fact and the *work* of mourning as the cause of this state. We then realize that Freud's description of the state of mourning (1917, p. 244) refers to a mental condition which is characterized by the affect of mature grief, and not by primitive pain.

In childhood and adolescence the grieving state of mourning is usually not observed. However, this does not permit us to infer the absence of the *work of mourning.* In fact, according to the view presented here, the decathexis of the object presentation (the work of mourning) must inevitably take place *if a new external object is not found.* The difference in the clinical picture presented by children and adolescents following object loss (i.e., the frequent absence of grief) can be ascribed to the extraordinary mobility of their libido and to the availability of other external objects—a mobility and an availability no longer open to the adult to the same degree. Therefore in the case of children and adolescents, the work of mourning, the decathexis of the object, with its inevitable concomitants of pain or grief need not occur. The cathected object (presentation) can be adequately discharged onto a new external object (just as before object loss) and the work of mourning thus short-circuited. A comparable event is often seen in the young adult mother whose baby has died. The birth of another one usually solaces her; her libido has not been completely fixated to the first one and is displaced with relative facility onto the new one.[11]

Before applying the model to melancholia, it should be noted that there is general agreement in the psychoanalytic literature that some kind of object loss occurs early in this illness. Having accepted object loss as a factor in the genesis of melancholia, we need to inquire what special conditions exist to prevent the work of mourning from successfully decathecting the object (presentation) as occurs in normal mourning. Such a decathexis would leave energies free for finding a new love object and for sublimation and thus prevent the appearance of melancholia. I shall limit my discussion to a consideration of melancholia from the viewpoint of the cathectic circuit involved in pain.

The melancholic is as poor a mourner as the anxiety dreamer is a poor dreamer. The central feature which makes him an unsuccessful mourner is the cathectic fabric of the object. Jacobson (1957) has brought convincing clinical material which shows that mourning is "successful" when the object was more or less unambivalently loved. In contrast, in unsuccessful mourning, i.e., melancholia, we know that the feeling for the object was highly ambivalent.

The cathexis of the object in melancholia must have a large contingent of pregenital, destructive energies. It is assumed that such energies when they penetrate the stimulus barrier (introjection) between self and object make an incomparably greater demand on the ego than the more genitally toned energies which cathect the normal mourner's object. This demand depletes the ego of its store of neutralized energy. "The complex of melancholia behaves like an open wound, drawing to itself cathectic energies—which in the transference neuroses we have called 'anticathexes'—from all directions, and emptying the ego until it is totally impoverished" (Freud, 1917, p. 253). This impoverishment of the ego has several consequences. Those energies of the object which still remain unbound and unneutralized in its presentation now pass *unchanged* through the

---

[11] For different and at times related views on grief and mourning see Bowlby (1960), Fleming and Altschul (1963), A. Freud (1960), R. Furman (1964), Jacobson (1964), Neubauer (1960), Schur (1960), Siggins (1966), Spitz (1960), Wolfenstein (1966), Meltzer (1963), Wetmore (1963).

stimulus barrier into the self (introjection) by virtue of the depletion of anticathexis. The object (presentation), emptied of its cathexis, no longer sends further energies into the self and the ego no longer reacts. Thus the conditions for pain disappear.

This disappearance of pain also coincides with the stage when the self is occupied by an influx of aggressive energies. These pregenital aggressive energies, unlike the energies cathecting the self of the mourner, cannot be used to cathect an external object, or for sublimations and beneficial identifications with the lost object. They seek the only outlet available and that is the person—i.e., suicide. Thus the dangerous period of apparent clinical improvement in melancholia—i.e., loss of pain—and suicide become intelligible. As Freud put it, the object ultimately triumphs over the self.

SUMMARY

In this paper, the concept of self and object presentation has been used to construct a model for the derivation of a number of affects. A *variety* of affects could be "explained" by assuming the passage of the *same* psychic energy through a *variety* of structures. For example, desire is correlated to a hypercathexis of the self presentation, while longing is correlated to a hypercathexis of the object presentation.

The affects which have been discussed are desire, longing, anxiety, pain, grief, humiliation, and shame. The affect especially focused on in this paper is pain of mental origin. In analogy to pain of physical origin, it is treated as a narcissistic lesion, i.e., a lesion of the self (presentation). While pain of physical origin is generally ascribed to the influence of an external agent, pain of mental origin is ascribed, in this paper, to the absence of an external influence—to the *absence* of the influence of the constant external object.

Internalization explains this difference in causation; it creates an internal pain stimulus—the constant object presentation—in the interior of the mental apparatus.

Complete protection against pain of mental origin is achieved either by the attainment of the constant external object (which brings about dependence on the "other one" in order to avoid pain) or by relating to need-satisfying external objects only.

Since the establishment of lasting object relations brings with it a necessary potential for pain, the ego ideal appears to serve the function of attenuating the pain resulting from nonattainment of the constant external object. Humiliation and shame flow from this attenuation of pain.

The application of these views on pain to mourning and melancholia has two advantages: (1) an economic explanation of mourning becomes possible; and (2) the reality principle need not be invoked to explain the initiation of the work of mourning.

The concepts of self and narcissism are redefined; narcissism is here viewed as the positive balance of the overall cathexis of the self presentation, as compared to the cathexis of the object presentation *within one person*. Narcissistic needs, supplies, etc., are discussed in relation to pain.

BIBLIOGRAPHY

Bowlby, J. (1960), Grief and Mourning in Infancy and Early Childhood. *This Annual,* 15:9-52.

Fenichel, O. (1938), Ego Strength and Ego Weakness. *The Collected Papers of Otto Fenichel,* 2:70-80. New York: Norton.

Ferenczi, S. (1913), Stages in the Development of the Sense of Reality. *Sex in Psychoanalysis.* New York: Basic Books, 1950, pp. 213-239.

Fleming, J. & Altschul, S. (1963), Activation of Mourning and Growth by Psycho-Analysis. *Int. J. Psa.,* 44:419-431.

Freud, A. (1952), The Mutual Influences in the Development of Ego and Id. *This Annual,* 7:42-50.

—— (1960), Discussion of Dr. John Bowlby's Paper. *This Annual,* 15:53-62.

Freud, S. (1895), Project for a Scientific Psychology. *The Origins of Psychoanalysis.* New York: Basic Books, 1954, pp. 347-445.

—— (1916), On Transience. *Standard Edition,* 14:305-307. London: Hogarth Press, 1957.

—— (1917), Mourning and Melancholia. *Standard Edition,* 14:237-260. London: Hogarth Press, 1957.

—— (1920), Beyond the Pleasure Principle. *Standard Edition,* 18:3-64. London: Hogarth Press, 1955.

—— (1923), The Ego and the Id. *Standard Edition,* 19:3-66. London: Hogarth Press, 1961.

—— (1926), Inhibitions, Symptoms, and Anxiety. *Standard Edition,* 20:77-175. London: Hogarth Press, 1959.

—— (1931), Libidinal Types. *Standard Edition,* 21:215-220. London: Hogarth Press, 1961.

Furman, R. A. (1964), Death and the Young Child. *This Annual,* 19:321-333.

Glover, E. (1939), The Psycho-Analysis of Affects. *Int. J. Psa.,* 20:299-307.

Hartmann, H. (1939), *Ego Psychology and the Problem of Adaptation.* New York: International Universities Press, 1958.

—— (1950), Comments on the Psychoanalytic Theory of the Ego. *This Annual,* 5:74-96.

—— (1952), The Mutual Influences in the Development of Ego and Id. *This Annual,* 57:9-30.

Jacobson, E. (1957), On Normal and Pathological Moods. *This Annual*, 12:73-113.
—— (1964), *The Self and the Object World*. New York: International Universities Press.
Joffe, W. G. & Sandler, J. (1965), Notes on Pain, Depression, and Individuation. *This Annual*, 20:394-424.
Klein, G. S. (1959), Consciousness in Psychoanalytic Theory. *J. Amer. Psa. Assn.*, 7:5-34.
Lewin, B. D. (1961), Reflections on Depression. *This Annual*, 16:321-331.
Lichtenstein, H. (1965), Towards a Metapsychological Definition of the Concept of Self. *Int. J. Psa.*, 46:117-128.
Meltzer, D. (1963), A Contribution to the Metapsychology of Cyclothymic States. *Int. J. Psa.*, 44:83-96.
Neubauer, P. B. (1960), The One-Parent Child and his Oedipal Development. *This Annual*, 15:286-309.
Piers, G. & Singer, A. B. (1953), *Shame and Guilt*. Springfield, Ill.: Thomas.
Ramzy, I. & Wallerstein, R. S. (1958), Pain, Fear, and Anxiety. *This Annual*, 13:147-189.
Sandler, J. & Rosenblatt, B. (1962), The Concept of the Representational World. *This Annual*, 17:128-145.
Schafer, R. (1964), The Clinical Analysis of Affects. *J. Amer. Psa. Assn.*, 12:275-299.
Schur, M. (1960), Discussion of Dr. John Bowlby's Paper. *This Annual*, 15:63-84.
Siggins, L. D. (1966), Mourning: A Critical Survey of the Literature. *Int. J. Psa.*, 47:14-25.
Spiegel, L. A. (1954), Acting Out and Defensive Instinctual Gratification. *J. Amer. Psa. Assn.*, 2:107-119.
—— (1959), The Self, the Sense of Self, and Perception. *This Annual*, 14:81-109.
Spitz, R. A. (1960), Discussion of Dr. John Bowlby's Paper. *This Annual*, 15:85-94.
Szasz, T. (1957), *Pain and Pleasure*. New York: Basic Books.
Wetmore, R. J. (1963), The Role of Grief in Psycho-Analysis. *Int. J. Psa.*, 44:97-103.
White, R. W. (1960), Competence and the Psychosexual Stages of Development. In: *Nebraska Symposium on Motivation*, ed. M. R. Jones. Lincoln: University of Nebraska Press, pp. 97-140.
Wolfenstein, M. (1966), How Is Mourning Possible? *This Annual*, 21:93-123.

HOW IS MOURNING POSSIBLE?

MARTHA WOLFENSTEIN, PH.D.

I

The ability to form, and also, when necessary, to dissolve, object relations is essential to the development of every human being. At present we know more about the progress and vicissitudes of developing object relations than we do about reactions to their being broken off in different phases of life. In "Mourning and Melancholia" (1917), Freud described the phenomenon of mourning as it occurs in adults in reaction to the death of a loved person. There is a painful and protracted struggle to acknowledge the reality of the loss, which is opposed by a strong unwillingness to abandon the libidinal attachment to the lost object. "Normally, respect for reality gains the day. Nevertheless its orders cannot be obeyed at once. They are carried out bit by bit, at great expense of time and cathectic energy, and in the meantime the existence of the lost object is psychically prolonged. Each single one of the memories and expectations in which the libido is bound to the object is brought up and hypercathected, and detachment of the libido is accomplished in respect of it" (pp. 244-245). The lost object is thus gradually decathected, by a process of remembering and reality testing, separating memory from hope. The mourner convinces himself of the irrevocable pastness of what he remembers: this will not come again, and this will not come again. That the decathexis of the lost object is accomplished in a piecemeal way serves an important defensive function, protecting the mourner from the too sudden influx of traumatic quantities of freed libido. Painful as it is to endure, mourning serves an invaluable adaptive function, since by this process the mourner frees major amounts of

From the Department of Psychiatry, Albert Einstein College of Medicine, New York, New York.

libido which were bound to the lost object, which he can utilize for other relations and sublimated activities in the world of the living (Pollock, 1961).[1]

When in the sequence of development does an individual become capable of responding to a major object loss in this adaptive way? Bowlby, in a series of recent papers (1960, 1961a, 1961b, 1963), has been exploring reactions to separation and loss in young children. He has stressed the persistence of the demand, on a more or less conscious level, for the return of the lost object, the inability to renounce it, which he finds also characterizes nonadaptive reactions to loss in adults. Bowlby (1961a) raises the question: "At what stage of development and by means of what processes does the individual arrive at a state which enables him thereafter to respond to loss in a favourable manner?" And he adds his impression that "an early dating of this phase of development . . . is open to much doubt" (p. 323). Investigators who have reported on adult patients who lost a parent in childhood or adolescence have confirmed that expressions of grief, acceptance of the reality of the loss, and decathexis of the lost parent have not occurred. Helene Deutsch (1937) spoke of "absence of grief" in an adult patient whose mother had died when he was five, and whose inhibition of sad feelings had extended to all affects. Fleming and Altschul (1963) have reported cases in which the patients suffered the loss of parents in adolescence but had never mourned and continued covertly to deny the reality of the loss. Jacobson (1965), speaking of related cases, recounted persistent fantasies of finding the lost parents again.

In contrast to these observations, Robert Furman (1965a) has advanced the view that mourning can occur in quite early childhood.

[1] There has been some confusion in discussions of whether or not children mourn, because the discussants have attached different meanings to the term "mourning." I shall use the term "mourning" in the sense in which Freud used it in "Mourning and Melancholia," to mean that reaction to loss in which the lost object is gradually decathected by the painful and prolonged work of remembering and reality testing. Bowlby (1960, 1961a, 1961b, 1963) has extended the term "mourning" to include a wider range of reactions to loss. Those reactions in which the demand for the return of the lost object persists then become "pathological mourning." Bowlby feels that, in order to establish the relations between reactions to loss in early childhood and in later life, it is necessary to bring them under a common rubric. There is no logical necessity for this. All relations, whether of cause or similarity, can be established among distinct phenomena whether we call them by the same or different names. It seems to be in the interest of clarity to confine the meaning of a term to a distinct phenomenon rather than extend it to a range of differing phenomena.

He specifies as its preconditions the acquisition of a concept of death and the attainment of the stage of object constancy, both of which are possible by the age of four. I would suggest that these may well be necessary conditions, but they may be far from sufficient to enable the immature individual to tolerate the work of mourning. We need more empirical observations of how children in various phases of development actually do react to the loss of a major love object. Robert Furman (1965b) has reported the case of a six-year-old patient whose mother died while he was in analysis, and whose reactions Furman characterizes as "mourning." However, the main manifestation was that the boy painfully missed his mother in many circumstances where formerly she was with him. The expression of such feelings is no doubt useful in helping the patient to avoid the pathological affectlessness which developed in Helene Deutsch's patient. But the evidence remains inconclusive as to whether a mourning process, in the sense of decathecting the lost object, was under way. We can miss and long for someone we still hope to see again.

In the psychoanalytic literature there have been many contributions on adult reactions to loss, particularly those which take a pathological course, eventuating in one or another form of depressive illness. In recent years there have also appeared an increasing number of observations on reactions of very young children to separation from their mothers (notably A. Freud and Burlingham, 1943, 1944; Spitz and Wolf, 1947; Robertson, 1958; Bowlby, 1960, 1961a, 1961b, 1963). However, relatively little has been reported on reactions to loss of a major love object of children in the age range from the beginning of latency into adolescence.[2]

In this paper I shall draw on research data on children within this age range who have lost a parent by death.[3] Our subjects are chil-

[2] Some observations of beginning latency period children who had suffered the loss of a parent may be found in Scharl (1961) and Shambaugh (1961).

[3] The research project, some findings of which I am reporting here, has been conducted in the Division of Child Psychiatry at the Albert Einstein College of Medicine. Forty-two cases of children and adolescents who have lost a parent by death have been observed or are currently under observation. At the time of entering treatment the patients ranged in age from three and a half to nineteen years, the majority being in adolescence. We have had one child under six, eleven between the ages of six and eleven, eighteen between twelve and fifteen, and twelve between sixteen and nineteen. Sixteen of the patients came under observation within a year of the parent's death; eight within two or three years; eighteen from four to fourteen years later.

The following have participated in this project: Drs. Raymond Bernick, Peter

dren and adolescents in treatment in a child guidance clinic (and some cases from private practice). The clinical material has also been supplemented by observations of nonpatient subjects. The age at which our subjects suffered the death of a parent varied from earliest childhood to well into adolescence. The time of their coming under our observation also varied. In some instances our acquaintance with the child antedated the parent's death; in others, it began only years afterwards. However, as compared with efforts to reconstruct the effects of such a loss in adult analysis, we were in most instances much closer in time to the event. We were observing still immature individuals who had experienced a major object loss in the course of growing up, and we could see some of the more immediate reactions and the consequences for further development.

When we began our investigation we were aware that persons who have lost a parent in childhood more often succumb to mental illness in adulthood than those who have not suffered such a loss (Barry, 1949; Brown, 1961). From a therapeutic point of view we hoped that relatively early intervention might help to forestall such pathological effects. At the same time we did not know in what ways the vulnerability to later mental illness might manifest itself earlier in life. Also, since not everyone who has lost a parent in childhood shows later severe disturbances, we were alert to the possibilities of various adaptive reactions.

As our observations accumulated we were increasingly struck by the fact that mourning as described by Freud did not occur. Sad feelings were curtailed; there was little weeping. Immersion in the activities of everyday life continued. There was no withdrawal into preoccupation with thoughts of the lost parent. Gradually the fact emerged that overtly or covertly the child was denying the finality of the loss. The painful process of decathexis of the lost parent was put off, with the more or less conscious expectation of his return. Where depressed moods emerged, especially in adolescence, they were isolated from thoughts of the death of the parent, to which reality

Bokat, Betty Buchsbaum, Richard Evans, Daniel Feinberg, Karl Fossum, Lester Friedman, Paul Gabriel, Charles Goodstein, Phyllis Harrison, Leonard Hollander, Allan Jong, Saul Kapel, Dr. and Mrs. Gilbert Kliman, Drs. Sally Kove, William Lewit, Donald Marcuse, Manuel Martinez, Eli Messinger, James Pessin, Judy Roheim, Rita Reuben, Edward Sperling, Eva Sperling, Sherwood Waldron, Alex Weintrob.

testing was not yet applied. Thus we gained the definite impression that the representation of the lost object was not decathected, indeed that it became invested with an intensified cathexis.

It might be supposed that the nonoccurrence of mourning in our subjects indicates only some limitation in their selection. However, from our observations an increasingly strong impression emerged that there was a developmental unreadiness in these children and adolescents for the work of mourning. It is the purpose of this paper to explore this unreadiness and to offer a hypothesis concerning the developmental preconditions for being able to mourn. What I have said does not preclude an adaptive reaction to major object loss in childhood. Only, as I shall try to show, such a reaction follows a course different from mourning.

II

The following case of a young adolescent girl illustrates many of the reactions which we observed in our subjects following the death of a parent. The patient had been in treatment for half a year before the sudden death of her mother, so that it was possible to have some impression of the antecedent emotional situation. I shall focus on two mutually involved aspects of her reactions to the mother's death: the denial of the finality of the loss, and the defenses against the related affects.

Ruth was just fifteen when her mother died of a brain hemorrhage. In the months preceding the mother's death, Ruth had shown much ambivalence toward her. She shrank from her mother's demonstrations of affection and was intensely irritated by her little mannerisms. On the occasion of her mother's last birthday, she had left the present she had made for her at a friend's house and then had rushed to retrieve it at the last moment. At that time Ruth appeared to be in an incipient phase of adolescent detachment from and devaluation of her mother. Almost immediately following the mother's death, Ruth began to idealize her. She said repeatedly that she was just beginning to realize what a remarkable woman her mother was. While this in part echoed what was being said in the family circle, it also expressed an effort to purify her feelings and her image of her mother of the ambivalence which had been so noticeable previously.

In remembering her mother, Ruth reverted many times to an episode just before she had started treatment, when she had been greatly distressed and her mother had been very sympathetic and understanding. This incident became archetypal of her relation with the mother, who now appeared always to have been a comforter and protector. She tended to gloss over the many real difficulties and frustrations in her life with her mother. Periods of her childhood took on an aura of enveloping emotional warmth, though she knew that her diaries from those years told of much unhappiness.

What happened here was a reversal of the adolescent process of detachment from the mother. There was instead an intensified cathexis of the image of the mother, with a strong regressive pull toward a more childish and dependent relation, seen now in a highly idealized light. Freud (1926) said that there is a tendency toward hypercathexis of a lost object, just as toward a diseased body part. We can view this tendency as an effort to deny the possibility of loss of something so essential to the self.

Ruth had repeated fantasies of finding again mother substitutes from the past, a former therapist, a beloved teacher, neither of whom she had seen for many years. It was as if by a displacement from the dead to the absent she were saying: those I have lost can be found again. There was also an intensified attachment to a camp counselor, which was characterized by feelings of disappointment when they were together and desperate longing for the counselor when they were apart.

Expectations of the mother's return emerged gradually. In the second year following her mother's death, Ruth began a stringent course of dieting. She had had long-standing problems of overeating and being overweight, and her mother had repeatedly urged and encouraged her to diet. Now Ruth succeeded over a period of months in becoming surprisingly slim. She received many compliments on her improved appearance, to which she reacted paradoxically in a rather disappointed way. However, as it appeared later, these were not the compliments she was seeking, which would have had to come from her mother. On the eve of her birthday, Ruth went for a long ramble by herself through springtime fields and experienced a dreamy euphoria, a kind of oceanic feeling. When on her return home she tried to describe this experience to her father and felt he failed to understand it, her good mood began to dissolve into disappointment. The night of her birthday she started on an uncontrolled eating binge which continued for many weeks thereafter. Subsequent analysis disclosed that the sacrifice of delightful food represented a kind of bargain with fate, like a vow, in exchange for which she expected the return of her mother on her birthday. The oceanic feeling of oneness with nature may be taken as a symbolic realization of the wish to be reunited with mother, and was perhaps experienced as a portent of imminent reunion. Being confronted at home with her still grieving father precipitated the feeling that the wish was not coming true. The bargain with fate was vitiated and the self-imposed renunciation was abandoned.

Not quite three years after her mother's death, Ruth's father married again. Ruth was filled with emotional confusion, feeling as if her father had become discontented with her mother and thrown her out or as though he were committing adultery. While the father had gone through a period of concentrated mourning, following which he could turn to a new love object, the daughter was still unable to detach her feelings from the mother. She felt as though the mother's place should be kept open for her possible return. Thus father and daughter were out of phase with one another in their tempos of giving up the lost love object.[4] Ruth reported with grim satisfaction a dream in which her mother confronted her father and his new wife in their bedroom. It was as if she felt they deserved being called to account by the wronged wife. Before the father's remarriage she had had fantasies of her mother's return in which she imagined herself frustrated by her father's again asserting his greater claim to the mother. After her father's remarriage, she imagined her mother's returning and mother and herself going off together, leaving behind the strange new ménage.

Ruth repeatedly slipped into the present tense in speaking of her mother. Three years after her mother's death she admitted that she kept in her room a plant which had been dead for a considerable time but which she continued to water. At times when I had occasion to remind Ruth that her mother was dead, she had a pained, offended

---

4 The different tempos of reaction to loss in children and their widowed parents, which put them out of phase with one another, are generally a cause of much mutual misunderstanding.

feeling as if I should not say this to her.[5] At other times she forced herself to think of her mother's body decaying underground, but such thoughts remained isolated from the persisting fantasies of her mother's return. She said that there should be an arrangement for people to be dead for five years and then to come back again. She felt as though she was constantly waiting for something. Gradually she acknowledged thoughts of wishing the therapist could be her mother, but such thoughts occasioned feelings of painful compunction, as if they implied disloyalty to her mother.

Four years after her mother's death Ruth was facing a decisive separation from her therapist (she was about to start further analysis in the city where she was going to college). During the summer vacation Ruth wrote about a cantata in which she was participating, in which the chorus voiced the desperate feelings of drowning children. She quoted verses in which the children cry: "Mother, dear Mother, where are your arms to hold me? Where is your voice to scold the storm away . . . ? Is there no one here to help me? . . . Can you hear me, Mother?" And she said that the author of these lines had expressed for her what she felt.

I should like to elaborate further on the affective manifestations which accompanied this struggle to deny the finality of loss. Shortly after her mother's funeral Ruth found herself no longer able to cry. She felt an inner emptiness, and as if a glass wall separated her from what was going on around her. She was distressed by this affectlessness, and was subsequently relieved when, comparing notes with a friend whose father had died some time earlier, she learned that the other girl had had a similar reaction. The interference with affect was overdetermined by a fear of sharing her father's grief. Shortly after the mother's death, Ruth reported a dream in which her grandfather (standing for her father) leaned close to her and said: "Let us mingle our tears." This dream aroused feelings of intense horror in her: the sharing of such strong emotion was fraught with libidinal overtones and the incest taboo was invoked.

In the week following her mother's death Ruth said: "I guess it will be pretty bad this week." Thus she expressed her intolerance of the prospect of protracted suffering, her expectation of early relief.

---

5 Bowlby (1961a, 1963) has pointed out how much the bereaved person resents those who speak of his loss as a *fait accompli*. Hated are the comforters.

In the time that followed there were many alternations of mood, each good mood being hailed as the end of her distress. This illustrates what I have called the "short sadness span" in children, the desperate effort to recapture pleasurable feelings in whatever circumstances (Wolfenstein, 1965). Good moods are the affective counterpart of denial and help to reinforce it: if one does not feel bad, then nothing bad has happened.

Shortly after her mother's death Ruth appeared for her session in an exuberant mood. She had written a successful humorous composition, in which she congratulated herself on getting through her first year of high school with only minor mishaps. She explained this surprising statement by saying that she referred only to events at school, and proceeded to detail various embarrassing predicaments she had got into, which she turned to comic effect. Such denials, accompanied by euphoric moods, tended to be countered by catastrophic dreams, in which, for example, she and her father were taking flight from a disaster-stricken city, then turning back to try to rescue the dying and the dead. Conversely, sad moods were relieved by gratifying dreams.

Several months after her mother's death, upon returning to school in the fall, Ruth went through a phase of depression. She complained that nothing gave her pleasure any longer, not being with friends, not listening to music; everything she had formerly enjoyed had lost its savor. She felt she had nothing to look forward to, wished only to stay in bed, often felt like crying, and that any effort such as that involved in schoolwork was too much for her. Such feelings of sadness, loss of all zest for life, withdrawal and depletion are familiar components of mourning. What was striking in this instance was that these feelings were not consciously associated with the fact of the mother's death or with thoughts about the mother. Rather Ruth berated herself for the senselessness of her distress. At other times she blamed her unhappiness on her difficulty in ever feeling at ease with her schoolmates. This had been a long-standing complaint, but according to her now distorted view, she had felt much happier with her friends the year before, when in fact she had spoken constantly of the same malaise. Thus a strenuous effort was maintained to keep the feelings of sadness and despair isolated from thoughts of the mother's death. When the therapist repeatedly attempted to connect these feelings with the loss which the patient had suffered, the connection was accepted only on an intellectual level, and again the struggle to recapture pleasurable moods was resumed.

A major maneuver for achieving euphoric moods consisted in transitory identifications with her mother. Ruth would briefly engage in some activity which her mother had pursued and would feel extraordinarily well. Such incidents should be distinguished from the more stable perpetuation of characteristics of the lost love object which typically follows mourning. What Ruth was doing resembled more the play of a young child who, when mother is away, plays at being Mommy. This creates the illusion: Mother is not away, she is here, I am Mother. It operates in the interest of denial of a painful reality.

Other incidents exemplify the effort to keep painful longings and regrets isolated from thoughts of the mother. Sometimes in bed at night Ruth suffered confused feelings of desperate frustration, rage, and yearning. She tore the bedclothes off the bed, rolled them into the shape of a human body, and embraced them. She was quite uncertain and doubtful whether it was her mother she so longed to embrace. Walking through the different rooms of her house she reflected with regret how everything was changed from the time when she was a child. The furniture and drapes had all been changed through the years. She herself occupied a different room from that of her childhood. When she went back to the old room, it no longer was the way it had been. With all this there was no conscious thought that the great change which had occurred and which made home so different from what it had been was her mother's death. Ruth spoke of feeling at times when she was talking to me or other people that she was not really addressing the person before her. When asked to whom she was speaking, she replied that she might say it was to her mother. But this was a kind of detached speculation, carrying no conviction. When she became able to say that the song of drowning children crying for their mothers expressed her own feelings, the isolation between painful affects and awareness that mother was not there was beginning to break down.

At times of separation or impending separation from the therapist, Ruth was impelled toward trial reality testing of the loss of her mother. On one such occasion she said: "If my mother were really dead, I would be all alone"; and at another time: "If I would admit to myself that my mother is dead, I would be terribly scared." Thus we see incipient reality testing and alarmed retreat. The fears of what the finality of her loss would mean maintained the denial and persistent clinging to the love object, which continued to live in her imagination. We may consider that what is feared is the emergence of an unbearable panic state, in which inner and outer dangers are maximized. In the outer world there would no longer be any source of gratification or protection ("I would be all alone"). Within there would be a release of traumatic quantities of objectless libido.

It goes beyond the scope of this paper to consider the ways in which therapy may help an immature individual to give up a lost love object. However, there are a few points on which I should like to remark briefly. We have seen how the warding off of painful affects supports the denial that anything bad has happened. In therapy the child or adolescent can be helped to achieve a greater tolerance for painful feelings. One of the fears that children have of such feelings is that they may continue without letup and increase to intolerable intensity.[6] The therapist can help to insure that painful affects are released at a rate which the immature individual is unable to control independently.

In the case of Ruth, as in the case reported by Fleming and Altschul (1963), separations from the therapist repeatedly had the effect of initiating trial reality testing in regard to the loss of the parent. The current separation, for which the patient has been prepared, may serve as a practice exercise in parting. The fact that the patient can tolerate separating from the therapist may suggest to him that he may be able to bear the more final separation from the lost parent. In Ruth's case it was a decisive separation from the therapist which precipitated the desperate cry for the lost mother. In being able to bring together her feelings of desperate longing with the thought of her mother, in abandoning the defensive isolation

[6] A nine-year-old boy vividly evoked the awful prospect of unstoppable grief that would overwhelm children if they were not able to "forget" about a painful loss: "They would cry and cry. They would cry for a month and not forget it. They would cry every night and dream about it, and the tears would roll down their eyes and they wouldn't know it. And they would be thinking about it and tears just running down their eyes at night while they were dreaming" (from an interview by Dr. Gilbert Kliman on children's reactions to the death of President Kennedy).

previously maintained, she had taken one step toward acknowledging that her mother was really dead.

There were other instances in which Ruth underwent a trial giving up of lesser objects of attachment. I have spoken about her prolonged dieting. During that time she literally mourned the wonderful food which she had formerly enjoyed, remembering it with longing and sadness, which was quite different from her way of remembering her mother. This trial mourning did not at that time serve to advance her toward giving up her mother. There was an implicit *quid pro quo* in it, an expectation that through this ordeal of renunciation she would get her mother back. When this expectation was not fulfilled, the capacity for renunciation became for a time drastically reduced. A later trial giving up consisted in her decision not to return to the camp which she had attended for many years. After this decision was made, there was much regret and longing for beloved counselors and camp mates with whom she would not again enjoy the same close companionship as in the past. It would seem that the giving up of a major love object lost in childhood or adolescence requires many preparatory stages.

III

What we have seen in the case of Ruth was observed repeatedly in other children and adolescents whom we studied. Sad affects were warded off. When they broke through, they were isolated from thoughts of the lost parent. Denial of the finality of the loss was overtly or covertly maintained. Bowlby (1961a) has spoken of the importance of expressing what he calls "protest" in reaction to loss, that is, a vehement demand for the return of the lost object and strenuous efforts to regain it. He considers the full expression of such feelings and strivings essential to attaining the conviction that the object is in fact irretrievable.[7] "Protest" involves a painful aware-

---

7 According to Bowlby (1961a), a bereaved individual gives up a lost object when prolonged expressions of "protest" (clamorous demands and strivings for the return of the object) are seen to bring no result. These strivings then "gradually drop away or, in terms of learning theory, become extinguished" (p. 334). However, observation suggests that clamoring for the return of a lost object can continue indefinitely despite lack of response from the external world as long as the internal representation of the lost object is not decathected.

ness of the absence of the object, an awareness which may be for long postponed. The emergence of painful longings and crying for someone who does not come is a step toward reality testing and eventual tolerance for giving up the lost object.

Our subjects gave many indications that they denied that the dead parent was irretrievably lost to them. They frequently slipped into the present tense in speaking of the dead parent. They reported seeing someone on the street whom they fleetingly mistook for the lost parent. There was intolerance of any reminder that the parent was dead. Memories of the dead parent were not fraught with the painful feelings of the mourner who is in the process of realizing that these things will not come again. Where sad feelings emerged in relation to the lost parent, there was an effort to get away from them as quickly as possible. For example, a ten-year-old girl, whose father had died when she was seven, was moved to tears when her therapist said sympathetically that she must often miss her father. After being briefly downcast she proposed, "Let's change the subject," and was soon chatting in a cheerful and animated way about events at school. The intimate relation between tolerance for sad affects and reality testing appears throughout our material.

Fantasies of the dead parent's return often appeared in disguised form. Thus a ten-year-old boy, whose father had died when he was three, had a fantasy of a robot who would come out of the wall and teach him all he needed to know, so that he would not have to go to school. The robot (something both dead and alive) no doubt represented the omniscient father who could transmit his powers to his son. Perhaps the amount of distortion here is related to the age of the child at the time of the parent's death. We may recall Helen Deutsch's (1937) case of the patient who had lost his mother when he was five, and who remembered the childhood fantasy of a big mother dog coming into his room at night and showing him affection. Our material suggests that fantasies of the parent's return are either more clearly conscious or more readily admitted in adolescence than at earlier ages. It seems likely that the fantasy of the parent's return may be a more closely guarded secret in younger children. A readiness to admit the fantasy, thus risking confrontation with reality, may represent one of the many steps toward giving up the lost parent.

The denial of the parent's death coexists with a correct conscious acknowledgment of what has really happened. All our subjects could state that the parent was in fact dead, and could recall circumstances related to the death such as the funeral. Yet this superficial deference to facts remained isolated from the persistence on another level of expectations of the parent's return.[8] What we see here is a splitting of the ego in the defensive process. Freud (1927) observed the use of this mechanism in relation to the loss of a parent in childhood. He reported that two young men patients, one of whom had lost his father in his second year, the other in his tenth year, both had denied the reality of the father's death. They could feel and behave as if the father still existed. But this denial represented only one sector of their mental life. There was another sector in which the death of the father was acknowledged. In speaking of this defense against accepting an unbearable piece of reality, Freud remarked: "I also began to suspect that similar occurrences in childhood are by no means rare" (p. 156).

Following the death of a parent a child's image of him and feelings toward him undergo a change. It is not the parent as he last knew him in life, but the glorified parent of early childhood who is perpetuated in his fantasy. This, for a child in the age range we are considering, represents a regression. I may note parenthetically that a major loss suffered at any age precipitates some regression. The adult mourner becomes for a time "an infant crying in the night." The loss of a loved person evokes feelings of terrible helplessness, like those of a deprived infant who is powerless to relieve his distress. Children seem to respond to this predicament by conjuring up the fantasy of an ideally good and loving parent who can do everything for them. Their own feelings toward the lost parent also become, for a time, ideally loving. This is partly an attempt at posthumous undoing of bad feelings or wishes previously directed toward the lost parent.

Bowlby (1961b, 1963) has pointed out that young children express raging reproach against the mother who goes away and leaves them. In older children whose reactions to the death of a parent we have

---

[8] Furman (1964a) takes the verbal acknowledgment of a young child that his parent is dead and not coming back as indicating a readiness to mourn. What is overlooked is the defensive splitting of the ego as a result of which the death is at the same time denied and the attachment to the lost parent perpetuated.

observed, there seems to be a strenuous effort to divert such feelings from the image of the lost parent. Similarly, the negative sector of the ambivalence formerly felt toward the parent is split off. These hostile feelings are directed toward others in the child's environment, notably the surviving parent. Thus, far from being able to turn to substitute objects, the bereaved child often feels more at odds with those around him and alienates them by his angry behavior. His fantasied relation with the idealized dead parent is maintained at great cost. It seems to absorb most of his libidinal energies and involves a diversion of hostile feelings toward those who could help and befriend him.[9] With time, perhaps particularly in adolescence, reproachful feelings toward the abandoning parent emerge. Thus a twenty-year-old patient, whose father had died when she was fourteen, spoke of having idealized him following his death. Now, however, she was bitterly reproachful toward him, blaming his death, which had left her in such hard straits, on his reckless disregard of doctor's orders. The return of ambivalence toward the lost parent, like the ability to associate sad feelings with his loss, represents one step toward reality testing.

We have observed then that instead of decathecting a lost love object, which is what happens in mourning, children and adolescents tend to develop a hypercathexis of the lost object. Why do they cling in this way to a lost parent, unable to give him up? To understand this, we must consider what object relations mean in different phases of development. What happens when an object relation is externally severed gives us crucial clues as to what the relation meant to the individual who suffers this loss. Spitz and Wolf (1946) demonstrated dramatically that infants in the second half of the first year become radically retarded in all areas of development when they are separated from their mothers (and when no adequate mother substitute is provided). Recently Fleming and Altschul (1963) have presented strikingly similar observations about adult patients who experienced the loss of a parent as late as adolescence. They found that these patients had remained arrested in their development at the stage

---

[9] Lindemann (1944) called attention to the occurrence of rage in bereavement. Bowlby (1961a, 1961b, 1963) has stressed what he considers the omnipresence of rage in reaction to loss. He has also pointed out that, while its main object is the lost person, who is reproached for his abandonment, it is frequently displaced to others.

in which they were at the time of the parent's death. If the parent, or parents, had been lost when the patient was an adolescent, the patient was still, years later, living emotionally like an adolescent. These findings suggest that, despite the impressive development in so many areas which can be observed between infancy and adolescence, something in the child's relation to the parents persists throughout this time. The child needs the continuing relation with the parents in order to advance in his development.

I shall consider some of the indispensable prerequisites for the child's growth which the parents provide. While parents do not, in the normal course of development, remain exclusively need-gratifying objects, they do continue to provide for the child's needs until he is able to make his own way in the world. Apart from material needs, they are sources of narcissistic supplies. While with the infant and young child the mother provides support for his body narcissism, with the schoolchild the parents give essential support to his pride in his growing accomplishments. The parents also retain external ego and superego roles. With the infant and young child they mediate wholly between him and reality, for instance, guarding him from dangers of which he is not yet aware. They act as an external superego from the time they utter the first "No, no" when the toddler approaches some forbidden object. As the child develops internal ego and superego functions, these functions remain for a long time far from autonomous, dependent on external support from the parents.

To illustrate what happens when this manifold support is lost: we have observed repeatedly that some children and adolescents begin to decline in their school performance following the death of a parent. Other children begin to behave badly in school. In yet other instances, truancy and stealing begin after a parent has died. We may suppose that the child who in this way declines in his accomplishments or deviates from previous good behavior is suffering from the loss of narcissistic rewards and external ego and superego support. These disturbances are no doubt overdetermined. These children may be in part criminals out of a sense of guilt, seeking punishment for the guilt they feel for the parent's death (Bonnard, 1961). Another factor which may be operative is that the child's previous good behavior may have been predicated on a kind of bargain with fate. He was being good to insure that nothing bad would happen. When his parent died, the bargain with fate was abrogated. Such a sequence could be reconstructed in the case of the twenty-year-old girl, mentioned before, whose father died when she was fourteen. The father had had a heart attack when she was eight. Following this the girl had developed compulsive rituals and many scruples about bad thoughts and bad words, the unconscious purpose of which was presumably to prevent anything bad from happening to her father. When he died, of a second heart attack, it was as if fate had failed to keep the bargain and she was released from her part of it. Immediately following her father's death, her schoolwork, which had been excellent, declined. In adolescence she became promiscuous, and on starting treatment at nineteen she presented a picture of an impulse-ridden character.

I have tried to indicate in the case of Ruth that her clinging to her lost mother was motivated by incipient panic at the thought of letting go: "If I would admit to myself that my mother is dead, I would be terribly scared." I should now like to explore the factors which make for this overwhelming fear of acknowledging that the dead parent is irretrievably lost. One such factor has already been indicated in the discussion of the external ego and superego support that the child needs from the parents: without this the child fears the disintegration of the psychic structure he has achieved. On the most primitive level he fears annihilation: he could not survive if the parent were not still there. Ruth's saying, "If my mother were really dead, I would be all alone," expresses this. There would be no one to care for her, no one to gratify any of her needs, she would be abandoned in an alien world. This apprehension of annihilation in a child of Ruth's age is related to the evocation of a much more infantile image of the mother than that of the mother whom she recently knew. It corresponds to the sense of acute helplessness provoked by the loss of the parent.

A related fear is that of the breakthrough of massive amounts of objectless libido, of traumatic intensity. In mourning there is a gradual decathexis of the lost object, and this gradualness protects the mourner from a traumatic release of more unbound libido than he can cope with. I would like to suggest that children and young adolescents lack the capacity for this kind of dosage in emotional letting go. We know that in the sphere of action there is a gradual progression in being able to postpone action and to substitute the trial action of thought, in which smaller quantities of energy are involved. It would seem that there is a similar slow or late development of the capacity to release affective energies in any gradual way (Fenichel, 1945, p. 393). Children operate on an all-or-none basis. A tentative trial of what it would mean to let go of a lost parent thus evokes the threat of being overwhelmed and they revert to defensive denial.

Another factor contributing to the fear of acknowledging such a grievous loss is that the child still conceives of the parent as a part of himself. Jacobson (1965) has recently pointed this out, and has compared the desperate striving of a child to recover a lost parent with the little girl's longing to recover her lost penis.[10] That the parent is felt to be a part of the child, or an inalienable possession without which he is incomplete, helps to account for our repeated finding that children are deeply ashamed of having lost a parent. They often try to conceal this fact, or feel chagrined when it is revealed. The bereaved child feels a painful inferiority to children who have an intact family. Sometimes this feeling is displaced to material possessions.[11] For instance, the ten-year-old boy mentioned earlier, whose father had died when he was three, was particularly occupied with cars because his father had had such an impressive big car. He was keen on collecting toy model cars and became distressed when he saw another boy with a larger collection than his. He characterized the feeling evoked by the comparison of himself with such a more fortunate boy as "jealancholy," a term he coined as a condensation of "jealousy" and "melancholy." This boy was deeply ashamed of lacking a father and tried to conceal this fact from his schoolmates.

There is one further fear I would mention which reinforces the child's denial of the loss of a parent; that is the fear of regression. Repeatedly, children and adolescents have reported that they were unable to cry following the parent's death or that an inhibition of crying set in after a brief period of time. So, for instance, a thirteen-year-old boy said he felt nauseated on the trip back from his father's

10 In discussing the splitting of the ego as a defense against unbearable aspects of reality, Freud (1927, 1940) cited two main instances in which this defense was invoked: in relation to the castration complex, and in relation to the death of a parent.

11 Robertson (1958) has pointed out how young children, in prolonged separation from their parents, shift from longing for their presence to increasing demands for material gifts.

funeral and attributed this to the fact that he had swallowed his tears. Adolescents often feel distressed, uneasy, and self-accusing at this inhibition of crying, as we saw in the case of Ruth. We have to do here with an insufficiently explored topic: the relation of crying to different phases of development. Young children cry readily at any frustration, deprivation, disappointment or hurt. In latency there is normally a marked inhibition of crying and conscious repudiation of it as babyish. We are probably justified in suspecting that there is something amiss with a child in this phase who continues to cry easily. The inhibition of crying seems to extend well into adolescence. There is of course also a sex-typing in this regard in our culture: it is more shameful for boys to cry than it is for girls. However, in response to a major loss adults of both sexes cry more freely than children or adolescents.[12] The crying of adults in grief, if it is not indefinitely protracted, appears as a normal regression. Children and adolescents seem to hold back from such a regression, perhaps out of fear that once under way it would have no bounds and precipitate them to total infantility.

I should now like to consider a question which probably has already occurred to the reader: the child who has lost one parent still has a parent—why is the surviving parent not an adequate support for the child, an object to whom the child can transfer the feelings he had for the parent who has died? According to our observations, the child's relations with the surviving parent regularly become more difficult (Neubauer, 1960). There are many reasons for this, which I shall indicate here only in part. When a parent has died, the child is confronted with a widowed parent, afflicted, grief-stricken, withdrawn in mourning, sometimes otherwise disturbed. Whether the widowed parent is of the same or opposite sex, the child's incestuous strivings toward him are stimulated from seeing him now alone. But the parent seems to take little comfort from the child's presence; he is lost in grief. It is as if the child wished to say, "Don't you see me? I am here." And the parent replied, "You are no help." The child thus experiences anew the oedipal chagrin, the sense of his inadequacy in comparison with an adult marital partner. At the same time there is a futile but desperate urge on the part of both

[12] Studies of reactions to the death of President Kennedy showed that adults wept more than did children or adolescents (Sheatsley and Feldman, 1964; Sigel, 1965).

the child and the widowed parent to put the child in the place of
the missing parent. One of our most repeated findings is that, following the death of a parent, a child shares the bedroom and sometimes
the bed of the widowed parent. Many rationalizations are given for
this arrangement: the parent is lonely, the child is frightened at
night, the family has moved to smaller living quarters. One boy told
us that he had to go to his mother's bed because he was cold. When
the warm weather came he still had to go there because there was a
fan in her room. Evidently behind such trivial justifications there are
deep needs on both sides. Even when the child is not sharing the
parent's bedroom, incestuous impulses are intensified and arouse
alarm. In struggling to ward off these impulses, the child becomes
withdrawn or antagonistic toward the widowed parent.

There is also the child's tendency, as previously noted, to concen-
trate intensified positive feelings on the lost parent. The negative
sector of the ambivalence formerly felt toward the lost parent is split
off, and its most available target is the remaining parent. As the lost
parent is idealized, the surviving parent is devalued. Often there is
the conscious wish that he (or she) had died instead. Jacobson (1965)
has pointed out that on a deeper level the child blames the surviving
parent for the loss he has suffered. In the child's fantasy this parent
has destroyed the other or been deserted because of his unworthiness.
Thus for a child who has lost a parent, relations with both parents
become distorted. As to the narcissistic supplies and ego and superego
support which the child so needs, a parent withdrawn in grief is little
able to provide them. The child often feels and reacts as though he
has lost both parents.

IV

I have tried to show that there is a developmental unreadiness in
children for the work of mourning. I should now like to turn to the
question: what are the developmental preconditions which make
mourning possible? Adolescence has been repeatedly likened to
mourning (A. Freud, 1958; Lampl-de Groot, 1960; Jacobson, 1961,
1964). In adolescence there is normally a protracted and painful
decathexis of those who have until then been the major love objects,
the parents. The hypothesis which I wish to propose is this: not only

does adolescence resemble mourning, it constitutes the necessary precondition for being later able to mourn. The painful and gradual decathexis of the beloved parents which the adolescent is forced to perform serves as an initiation into how to mourn. The individual who has passed through this decisive experience has learned how to give up a major love object. In circumstances of later loss he is able to recapitulate the process.

It is not until adolescence that the individual is forced to give up a major love object. We have seen how little external loss enforces such a decathexis. The conflicts of the oedipal phase, as Anna Freud (1958) has pointed out, lead to a change in the quality of the child's love for the parents, making it love with an inhibited aim. But the parents remain the major love objects. It is only in adolescence that developmental exigencies require a radical decathexis of the parents. With sexual maturity, the adolescent is powerfully impelled to seek a sexual object. The images of the parents become relibidinized, but there the incest barrier stands in the way. The adolescent is confronted with the dilemma: to withdraw libidinal cathexis from the parents or to renounce sexual fulfillment. This may be likened to the dilemma of the mourner as Freud described it. The mourner is bound to the beloved object, no longer available; at the same time he is attached to life and all it may still have to offer. Eventually the decision is in favor of ongoing life and the renunciation of the past which this requires. The adolescent, impelled forward by his sexual urges, is similarly constrained to detach himself from his beloved parents and his childhood past.

We know that the struggle of the adolescent to achieve this detachment is a long and difficult one. Forward movement often alternates with regression. The adolescent has many possibilities, both in terms of opportunity and of his newly developing capacities for diverting freed libido into new love relations, friendships, and sublimated activities. But these newfound interests are often unstable; new relationships prove transient and disappointing. Libido reverts again to the old objects or becomes absorbed in the self and the work of inner reorganization. To the extent that freed libido remains objectless, depressed moods occur. Abraham (1911, 1924) has pointed out that depression is experienced not only when an object is lost externally, but when there is an inability to love someone formerly loved.

This is what happens with the adolescent as his capacity to love his parents declines. Jacobson (1961, 1964) has said that the adolescent experiences an intensity of grief unknown in previous phases of life.

Freud has stressed the crucial role of remembering in mourning and the reality testing by means of which memories are consigned to the irrevocable past. I should like to suggest that we find an analogue of this too in adolescence, that in adolescence a new feeling about the past emerges. There is a nostalgia for a lost past, a combined yearning and sense of irrevocability. The ways of remembering one's own past in different phases of development remain incompletely explored. We may consider, however, certain earlier phenomena in this area. The young child may yearn for the past, but he does not consider it irrevocable. He has not yet grasped the irreversibility of time. If he wishes to be a baby again, we will see him crawling on all fours and saying "da, da." He becomes a baby. In the latency period, with the repression which follows the oedipal phase, the attitude toward the past changes. It becomes one of repudiation. When his parents recall amusing and endearing things he used to do when he was little, the latency period child is inclined to disclaim these babyish things with some contempt. He puts his past behind him and prides himself on his new skills and accomplishments.

It is in adolescence that the sense of a longed-for past develops with the conviction that it can never come again. The past assumes a mythical aura. Fantasies of a golden age of the personal and the historic past probably have their inception in this time of life. Let me cite an early "memory" which a thirteen-year-old girl said had recently come to mind and which seemed to her very real. She recalled being wheeled in a baby carriage, in which she was cozily and contentedly ensconced, while her mother and father walked behind. She attributed to her infant self the thought, "Too bad this can't last." We would recognize this as a screen memory, in which memories and fantasies have been condensed. This girl had been the eldest child in her family and no doubt had envied the younger siblings whom she had seen replacing herself in the baby carriage, as they had in her parents' affections. In this memory she was again in sole possession of the parents. By ascribing to her past self the awareness that this could not last she was attempting to undo the traumatic surprise at the arrival of the next sibling. At the same time the sense of transience, of past pleasures having to be renounced, which pertained to her adolescent state, became part of the content of her childhood memory.

Probably nostalgic memories generally preserve something from very early childhood, antedating the oedipal troubles so painfully revived in adolescence. The theme of such memories, more or less disguised, is of the self as a greatly loved small child. As Wordsworth says, in his great nostalgic poem on recollections of early childhood: "Heaven lay about us in our infancy." The adolescent, in the enforced giving up of his parents, feels a sense of all he is losing. He conjures up regressively the most ideal aspects of being a child encompassed by parental love. We know that few real memories survive from the earliest years. Yet most individuals possess a history of themselves starting from birth, which is based on their parents' reminiscences. The parents themselves have felt nostalgic when they recalled to the older child the happenings of his first years. They have suffered some sense of loss as the confiding and affectionate small child seemed to grow away from them into greater independence. I would suggest that the adolescent, in his nostalgia for the past, identifies with his parents nostalgically recalling his early years.

The sense of the irrevocability of the past appears in many ways in adolescence. There may be an acute awareness of the transience of present pleasure, that every moment is slipping into the past, that life itself is ephemeral. Adolescents often find in their preferred poetry expression of these moods. A. E. Housman's poems, for instance, express an adolescent longing for a lost past, never wholly renounced. "That is the land of lost content,/I see it shining plain,/The happy highways where I went/And cannot come again." It has been said that Housman's poems are best appreciated by adolescents. Similarly, adolescent girls weep over songs of unhappy love, of partings and longing for an absent lover. Their conscious thoughts may be of a boy who has recently disappointed them. But the intensity of their grief is for the loss of a much greater love, the waning of their love for their parents, and the renunciation of their childhood.

In comparing adolescence with mourning we should also consider the ways in which they differ. The mourner is well aware that he is sad because of the loss of a beloved person and his mind is dominated by thoughts of the lost object. The adolescent does not know why he is sad or depressed and does not attribute these feelings to the loss of his capacity to feel love for his parents. Where the mourner has suffered an external loss, the adolescent undergoes an enforced renunciation because of internal conflicts. Whether the adolescent's renunciation is experienced as more active and voluntary than that of the mourner varies with the individual. This probably depends in large part on the relative strength of the forward impulsion and the regressive pull. The objects from which the adolescent is freeing himself are still there. Aggression can be directed toward them with some impunity since, in a reassuring way, they continue to survive. This is in contrast to the tendency to divert aggression from objects lost by death. While the mourner thinks of the object he has lost in a loving and idealizing way, the adolescent is devaluing the objects he is in the process of giving up. When the adolescent's struggle to withdraw from the parents becomes too difficult, he can still turn to them again, and, not without mixed feelings, derive gratification and support from their presence. In mourning a major amount of the libidinal attachment to the lost object is dissolved and the mourner is released from his painful, incessant preoccupation with the lost object. Yet he retains loving feelings for the one he has lost. Even more in adolescence, the decathexis of the parents is incomplete. Normally a positive attachment to them continues, though the feelings for them are no longer of such intensity or pre-eminence as those of earlier years.

The likeness of the adolescent process to mourning appears in the very considerable decathexis of major love objects, occurring over a period of time, accompanied by painful feelings, and with reality testing affirming the irrevocability of the past. The exigencies of adolescence which enforce this renunciation are without precedent in the child's antecedent life. Until he has undergone what we may call the trial mourning of adolescence, he is unable to mourn. Once he has lived through the painful, protracted decathecting of the first love objects, he can repeat the process when circumstances of external loss require a similar renunciation. When such loss occurs, we may picture the individual who has been initiated into mourning through adolescence confronting himself with the preconscious question: "Can I bear to give up someone I love so much?" The answer fol-

lows: "Yes, I can bear it—I have been through it once before." Before
the trial mourning of adolescence has been undergone, a child making the same tentative beginning of reality testing in regard to a
major object loss is threatened with the prospect of overwhelming
panic and retreats into defensive denial in the way we have observed.

We have seen that the younger child's panic at the prospect of
having to give up a lost parent is related to the characteristics of the
object relation. The parent is felt to be an indispensable source of
material and narcissistic supplies, an auxiliary ego and superego, a
part of the self. The renunciation of the parents in adolescence entails
a giving up to a considerable extent of the kind of relationship which
the child has had with them heretofore. Where the giving up of the
child-parent relationship is not accomplished, the individual may
merely turn away from his parents to seek others who will fulfill the
same functions. Where in this way the work of adolescence has remained uncompleted, the adult remains unable to accomplish the
work of mourning in response to loss.

V

We have considered the struggle of children and adolescents to
deny the finality of the loss of a parent and their unreadiness to
decathect the lost object through the work of mourning as we know
it in adults. The question arises whether there is an alternative way
for the immature individual to decathect a lost parent without undergoing the process of mourning. Such an adaptive alternative may
not be available to our child patients, handicapped as they usually
are by disturbances in development which antedate the parent's
death. To assess the range of possibilities it is important for us to
supplement our clinical data with observations of children whose
development has been relatively unimpeded up to the time of the
parent's death. I shall now turn to an instance of this sort, in which
we can see an adaptive reaction to the loss of a parent in childhood,
and at the same time contrast this reaction with that of mourning.

Walter, whose life course I have been able to follow from infancy
to young manhood, lost his mother at the age of ten. The mother died
of cancer after a period of progressive debilitation. During her last
illness both she and the boy were cared for by the young woman's

mother, who had great love and understanding for them both. Little by little, as the mother declined and became unable to satisfy the boy's needs, he transferred his affections to the grandmother. She was there, providing for his material wants, attentive to his accounts of his school days, appreciative of his accomplishments, involved with everything that concerned him. It was no doubt important that the grandmother was no newcomer in the boy's life. He had known her well before, and for a period of time she had cared for him in his mother's absence. Thus it was not a question of forming a new attachment, but of transferring a greater amount of feeling to someone already loved. What I believe happened here was that there was a piecemeal transfer of libido, detached from the mother, to an immediately available and acceptable mother substitute. This began while the mother was dying, and the boy turned gradually from her, withdrawn as she was in her illness, toward the grandmother. The process continued after the mother's death, when the grandmother devoted herself to Walter's care and upbringing.

Walter showed some of the same emotional inhibitions in reaction to his mother's death which appeared in the child patients we have discussed. He did not cry, and made strenuous efforts to deny and ward off feelings of distress. When his mother died he was sent to spend the day with friends of the family. In thanking these friends for their hospitality Walter laid exaggerated stress on what a happy day this had been for him. Unlike the adult mourner, he showed no diminution in his interest in usual activities. He was anxious to return to school at once and to carry on as if nothing had happened. In his spare time he began to immerse himself in incessant reading. We may suppose that partly this served to exclude painful thoughts and feelings. Partly his involvement with fictional heroes helped him to experience vicariously emotions which he could not acknowledge more directly. It was in relation to fictional characters that he experienced a belated breakthrough of his inhibited grief. Three years after his mother's death, when he came to the end of the series of books about The Three Musketeers, he wept profusely, saying, "My three favorite characters died today." I have characterized this phenomenon elsewhere as "mourning at a distance" (Wolfenstein, 1965).

The angry feelings in reaction to loss, which we have observed repeatedly, were not absent here. Following his mother's death,

Walter was diffusely irritable and quick to anger. In an altercation with his grandmother, intolerant of her rebuke, he said he was leaving home and stormed out into the night. When he returned, his grandmother said that they would have to talk about how bad they both were feeling because of his mother's death. She told him of the efforts that had been made to save his mother's life, that drugs had been flown in from other cities, and how sad it was that medical science was not yet sufficiently advanced to cure the terrible illness which she had had. Walter then was moved to confess that he blamed himself for his mother's death. Two years before she died she had had a breast operation and had returned from the hospital very weak. Nevertheless she had got up in the mornings to prepare Walter's breakfast before he went to school. He now felt that if she had not had to get up to get his breakfast, she would not have died. The grandmother assured him that this was not the cause of his mother's death, and that his mother's love for him and interest in him helped to keep her alive as long as possible. Their discussion went on far into the night, and at the end the boy, greatly relieved, and with the intolerance for prolonged distress characteristic of his age, exclaimed, "I feel great!"

While his mother was dying and for a considerable time after her death, Walter was insatiably hungry. He consumed great amounts of food and was particularly greedy for sweets. In this intensification of oral needs we may see a manifestation of the bereaved child's regressive longing for the all-fulfilling parent of earliest years. In this instance the regression remained circumscribed. The child's libido did not remain overly bound to the fantasy image of an idealized lost parent. The regressive greediness expressed only that part of the libido which was not yet transferred to the grandmother. But the greater part of the child's needs were being fulfilled in reality by the grandmother, who was able to supply material and narcissistic gratifications and to give ego and superego support.

In adolescence Walter showed strong feeling for and interest in friends, and developed an increasing capacity for sublimation in intellectual pursuits. At twenty-five he is married, with two beloved young children, and is progressing in his chosen career with pleasure and accomplishment.

Such an outcome requires a combination of favorable external and subjective conditions. The major external condition is the availability of an adequate parent substitute. Our culture generally makes little provision for such substitutes. The nuclear family, consisting of young parents and their growing children, entails an exclusiveness of attachment of children to their parents. Margaret Mead (1965) has pointed out that the nuclear family is especially well adapted to life in a rapidly changing culture. There is minimal boundness to old ways and customs. However, such a family is very little adapted to changes in its own personnel. In times and places where children have been raised in an extended family, there is a greater possibility of finding immediately available and acceptable substitutes if a parent dies (Volkart and Michael, 1957). In the context of our culture, the case of Walter is relatively exceptional in that a good mother substitute was immediately available to the bereaved child. The preexisting mutual attachment of grandmother and grandson and his previous experience of living with her in his mother's absence facilitated the transition. Moreover, the collaborative, noncompetitive way in which mother and grandmother had shared the boy's care probably lessened what feelings he may have had of being disloyal to his mother in turning to his grandmother.

The subjective factors favoring a major shift of object cathexis in childhood require further exploration. I can allude to them here only in a preliminary way.[13] We know that the fate of feeling toward a lost object is related to the ambivalence with which the object was regarded. Paradoxically the more ambivalent the relation has been, the harder it is to give it up. Where there has been strong ambivalence toward the object, its loss is likely to precipitate the protracted reproachful demands for its return which Bowlby has described. In the case of Walter, ambivalence toward his mother, whose only child he was, appears to have been of moderate intensity.

Freud stressed that no libidinal position is abandoned without great reluctance. More recent observations of children, however, have also made us aware of an opposite tendency, a developmental push which impels them toward more advanced levels of functioning.

13 We would expect a child's readiness to accept a substitute object to be related to the phase of development in which he was when he experienced the loss of a major object. Thus we would hypothesize that when a child is still almost wholly dependent on a need-gratifying object, he will be most ready to transfer his affections to someone who is able to provide for his needs (A. Freud and D. Burlingham, 1943, 1944).

There are probably great individual differences in the balance between the tendency to cling to early libidinal positions and the impulsion to move forward. In the readiness to welcome persons other than the mother, we can observe marked individual differences among children in the first years of life. Walter was one of those children who very early in life showed a great eagerness toward people. Thus a facility for forming object relations was probably another condition favoring his successful shift from mother to grandmother.

In the case of Walter, we have seen an adaptive reaction to the loss of a parent in childhood, in which apparently a major decathexis of the lost parent was accomplished. However, the process here differs markedly from that of adult mourning. There was no protracted sadness or withdrawal into painful preoccupation with memories of the lost object. In the gradual decathexis of the mother, while she was dying and after her death, Walter was able to transfer freed libido immediately to an already present mother substitute. If we imagined an analogue to this in an adult, we would have to picture a widower, let us say, having at his side a new wife, even one who had been an auxiliary wife before, to whom he could transfer at once the libido he was detaching from the wife he had lost. This is not adult mourning as we know it. The adult mourner can transfer his feelings to a new object, if one is found, only after a period of time in which he is emotionally occupied with detaching libido from the lost object. There is a hiatus here which the child is unable to tolerate.

VI

This paper has been concerned with determining the developmental preconditions for mourning. Observations of children in the age range from latency into adolescence, who have suffered the death of a parent, have shown that they are unable to mourn. In many instances, instead of a decathexis of the lost object, we find an intensified cathexis, with an overt or covert denial of the irrevocability of the loss. In the favorable instance of an adaptive reaction to such a loss, the process differed from that of mourning. There was an immediate transfer of freed libido to an available substitute parent. I have considered the factors making for the developmental unreadiness to mourn in children and young adolescents, in terms of the nature of the object relation to the parents. The hypothesis has been advanced that adolescence constitutes the necessary developmental condition for being able to mourn. Adolescence has been likened to a trial mourning, in which there is a gradual decathexis of the first love objects, accompanied by sad and painful feelings, with reality testing of memories confirming the irrevocability of the childhood past. It is only after this initiation into mourning has been undergone that the individual becomes able to perform the work of mourning in response to later losses.

BIBLIOGRAPHY

Abraham, K. (1911), Notes on the Psycho-Analytical Investigation and Treatment of Manic-Depressive Insanity and Allied Conditions. Selected Papers on Psycho-Analysis. London: Hogarth Press, 1942, pp. 137-156.
—— (1924), A Short Study of the Development of the Libido, Viewed in the Light of Mental Disorders. Selected Papers on Psycho-Analysis. London: Hogarth Press, 1942, pp. 418-501.
Barry, H. (1949), Significance of Maternal Bereavement before the Age of Eight in Psychiatric Patients. Arch. Neurol. & Psychiat., 62:630-637.
Bonnard, A. (1961), Truancy and Pilfering Associated with Bereavement. In: Adolescents: A Psychoanalytic Approach to Problems and Therapy, ed. S. Lorand & H. I. Schneer. New York: Hoeber, pp. 152-179.
Bowlby, J. (1960), Grief and Mourning in Infancy and Early Childhood. This Annual, 15:9-52.
—— (1961a), Processes of Mourning. Int. J. Psa., 42:317-340.
—— (1961b), Childhood Mourning and Its Implications for Psychiatry. Amer. J. Psychiat., 118:481-498.
—— (1963), Pathological Mourning and Childhood Mourning. J. Amer. Psa. Assn., 11:500-541.
Brown, F. (1961), Depression and Childhood Bereavement. J. Ment. Sci., 107:754-777.
Deutsch, H. (1937), Absence of Grief. Neuroses and Character Types. New York: International Universities Press, 1965, pp. 226-236.
Fenichel, O. (1945), The Psychoanalytic Theory of Neurosis. New York: Norton.
Fleming, J. & Altschul, S. (1963), Activation of Mourning and Growth by Psycho-Analysis. Int. J. Psa., 44:419-431.
Freud, A. (1958), Adolescence. This Annual, 13:255-278.
—— & Burlingham, D. (1943), War and Children. New York: International Universities Press.
—— —— (1944), Infants Without Families. New York: International Universities Press.
Freud, S. (1917), Mourning and Melancholia. Standard Edition, 14:237-260. London: Hogarth Press, 1957.
—— (1926), Inhibitions, Symptoms and Anxiety. Standard Edition, 20:77-175. London: Hogarth Press, 1959.
—— (1927), Fetishism. Standard Edition, 21:149-157. London: Hogarth Press, 1961.
—— (1940), Splitting of the Ego in the Process of Defence. Standard Edition, 23:271-278. London: Hogarth Press, 1964.
Furman, R. A. (1964a), Death and the Young Child. This Annual, 19:321-333.
—— (1964b), Death of a Six-year-old's Mother during His Analysis. This Annual, 19:377-397.

Jacobson, E. (1961), Adolescent Moods and the Remodeling of Psychic Structures in Adolescence. *This Annual*, 16:164-183.
—— (1964), *The Self and the Object World*. New York: International Universities Press.
—— (1965), The Return of the Lost Parent. In: *Drives, Affects, Behavior*, ed. M. Schur. New York: International Universities Press, 2:193-211.
Lampl-de Groot, J. (1960), On Adolescence. *This Annual*, 15:95-103.
Lindemann, E. (1944), Symptomatology and Management of Acute Grief. *Amer. J. Psychiat.*, 101:141-148.
Mead, M. (1965), Paper presented at Ciba Foundation Conference on Transcultural Psychiatry, London.
Neubauer, P. B. (1960), The One-Parent Child and His Oedipal Development. *This Annual*, 15:286-309.
Pollock, G. H. (1961), Mourning and Adaptation. *Int. J. Psa.*, 42:341-361.
Robertson, J. (1958), *Young Children in Hospitals*. New York: Basic Books.
Scharl, A. E. (1961), Regression and Restitution in Object Loss: Clinical Observations. *This Annual*, 16:471-480.
Shambaugh, B. (1961), A Study of Loss Reactions in a Seven-year-old. *This Annual*, 16:510-522.
Sheatsley, P. B. & Feldman, J. J. (1964), The Assassination of President Kennedy: A Preliminary Report on Public Reactions. *Pub. Opinion Quart.*, 28:189-215.
Sigel, R. S. (1965), An Exploration into Some Aspects of Political Socialization: School Children's Reactions to the Death of a President. In: *Children and the Death of a President*, ed. M. Wolfenstein & G. Kliman. New York: Doubleday, pp. 30-61.
Spitz, R. A. & Wolf, K. M. (1946), Anaclitic Depression. *This Annual*, 2:313-342.
Volkart, E. H. & Michael, S. T. (1957), Bereavement and Mental Health. In: *Death and Identity*, ed. R. Fulton. New York: Wiley, 1965, pp. 272-293.
Wolfenstein, M. (1965), Death of a Parent and Death of a President: Children's Reaction to Two Kinds of Loss. In: *Children and the Death of a President*, ed. M. Wolfenstein & G. Kliman. New York: Doubleday, pp. 62-79.

CLINICAL CONTRIBUTIONS

JULIE

The Treatment of a Case of Developmental Retardation

MARVIN ACK, PH.D.

In this paper I shall present the analytic treatment of a child who was, at age five and a half, severely developmentally retarded. The term "developmental retardation" is used in preference to mental retardation because when she was first referred to the Child Psychiatry Clinic of University Hospital, psychological testing revealed an I.Q. of 84. Therefore, according to current, accepted classificatory systems, she could not be considered intellectually retarded. Nonetheless, at this age, Julie could not speak in full sentences, had achieved no emotional independence, was irresponsible in body management, and was unable to play or get along with other children. All this will be amply demonstrated later.

A great deal has been written, by analytic and nonanalytic investigators alike, on the subject of the psychogenic factors involved in intellectual malfunctioning. However, as is the case in most areas of psychological functioning, Freud was among the first to call our attention to this problem. His first reference to this phenomenon was in 1901 in *The Psychopathology of Everyday Life,* where he described the dynamics involved in ordinary mistakes in reading, writing, speech, and forgetting. There are many more references to this problem in Freud's early contributions (in 1905, 1911, etc.), but the statements most relevant to the topic of this paper are to be found in *Inhibitions, Symptoms and Anxiety* (1926), where he characterized learning difficulties either as inhibitions of ego functions or as having the structure of a symptom.

Formerly at University Hospital, Cleveland, Ohio; now at The Menninger Foundation, Topeka, Kansas.

I would like to express my appreciation to Mrs. Alice Rolnick, who supervised the treatment, and to Dr. Anny Katan for her critical reading and many helpful suggestions.

According to Freud, there are three sources of such inhibitions. The first stems from the ego's attempt to avoid conflict with the id. "It has been discovered as a general fact that the ego-function of an organ is impaired if its erotogenicity—its sexual significance—is increased. . . . The ego renounces these functions, which are within its sphere, in order not to have to undertake fresh measures of repression" (pp. 89-90).

The second arises from the ego's attempt to pacify the superego. These inhibitions serve the purpose of self-punishment and can be seen in cases where success or gain is studiously avoided.

The third results from a depletion of energy. "The more *generalized* inhibitions of the ego obey a different mechanism. . . . When the ego is involved in a particularly difficult psychical task, as occurs in mourning, or when . . . a continual flood of sexual phantasies has to be kept down, it loses so much of the energy at its disposal that it has to cut down the expenditure of it at many points at once . . . [Therefore,] inhibitions are restrictions of the functions of the ego which have been either imposed as a measure of precaution or brought about as a result of an impoverishment of energy" (p. 90).

I shall try to demonstrate the applicability of these statements to the problem of pseudostupidity as exemplified by the patient and, more specifically, to show the effect of such massive inhibitions on the development of the ego functions of reality testing, aspects of cognition, and synthesis.

Authors since Freud have concerned themselves primarily with an elaboration of the content of the fantasies and the dynamics found to play a significant role in children with learning disorders. Following Freud's early remark regarding the impairment of a hypercathected ego function or organ, Abraham (1924) pointed out that both guilt over oral impulses and fear of erotization of oral impulses may result in an inhibition of learning. Thereafter, almost all authors have stressed the special significance of oral fixations in these cases. Sperry, Staver, and Mann (1952), in a study of a small group of children with learning difficulties, particularly emphasize the relationship of learning to destructive fantasies. Their opinion is that the symbolic expression of these fears (of learning) concern oral destructive impulses which during the course of development become related to phallic and genital impulses.

Other investigators of this problem have focused on the early relationship between mother and child and the role of identification in learning. Mahler (1942) suggests the two essential functions of pseudo-stupidity are that it "enables children as well as infantile adults to participate in the sexual life of the parents" (p. 149), and "to restore or maintain a secret libidinous rapport within the family" (p. 154). The child's stupidity is, therefore, linked to unconscious needs of both mother and child. Hellman (1954) also stresses the extreme and abnormally close bond between mother and child. Writing about a totally different group, David Rapaport (1951), in *Organization and Pathology of Thought,* suggests an inverse relationship between the importance of the original source of knowledge and the ability of the learner to make the knowledge his own. If we can extrapolate from this statement to the early mother-child relationship, it suggests that when the bond between the mother and child is pathologically strong the child may have difficulty integrating the knowledge derived from the mother. The information may exist as a foreign body or be so cathected with drive energies as to preclude the possibility of effective ego synthesis.

In presenting this case of extreme functional or developmental retardation I hope to elucidate those dynamic, genetic, and structural determinants which have general appositeness to the problem, as opposed to those dynamic factors which are idiosyncratic to a given child. The paper will also attempt to shed light on the diagnostic dilemma such cases present to clinicians by demonstrating, in this case, which ego functions proved prognostically valuable. Finally, I shall discuss some other factors that proved particularly important to the successful outcome.

CASE PRESENTATION

Personal History: Mrs. R. contacted a private psychologist when Julie was four and a half years old; the mother was apprehensive about the girl's development which Mrs. R. considered retarded. At that time, the mother stated that her greatest concerns were the child's lack of speech and her corresponding inability to understand her parents' verbal requests. Along with this, the parents also expressed concern about the child's severe and frequent temper outbursts and enuresis. The psychologist remarked on Julie's poor articulation, reported that the child showed no interest in him as a person and seemed unable to form a relationship. He recommended an evaluation at the Hearing and Speech Center. The speech therapist reported no hearing loss but also commented on Julie's inability to relate to the examiner. According to the Hearing and Speech Center's report, during the examination the child "talked constantly to herself although most often unintelligibly and resembling jargon." Some echolalia was also noted. The Hearing and Speech Center considered the problem to be an organic one, a sequela of anoxia related to prolonged labor.

Following this, Julie was referred to our Clinic where a complete psychiatric evaluation was undertaken. She achieved an I.Q. of 84, but both the psychologist and the psychiatrist emphasized her lack of involvement. Because it was impossible to distinguish between the various etiological possibilities, it was recommended that Mrs. R. be seen in weekly mother guidance and that Julie be enrolled in a nursery school. We hoped the special program created for Julie in the nursery school would enable us to determine the extent to which she could form a meaningful relationship.

The work with the mother was very rewarding. She was able to alter her methods of handling the child, and with support was able to establish firm and consistent limits. The nursery school experience however, was less clear-cut. There were occasions when Julie appeared to relate to the special teacher assigned to her, but most of the time she was off by herself or played like a dog with another child. She never participated in any group activity, and when frustrated would have a violent temper tantrum or cry inconsolably.

After about eight months, the child was again evaluated and psychoanalysis recommended for diagnostic purposes at least.

Family Background: Mrs. R. was the youngest of four children. Her mother first had a girl, and then a boy. The boy died when he was about ten or eleven, and the parents decided to try and have another son. After two more girls, they stopped. Mrs. R. described her mother as an extremely compulsive person, who was much more interested in her house than in her children. Mrs. R. was frequently told by her mother that she was not as pretty or as bright as her sisters. To the therapist, Mrs. R. spoke of her mother without any love or respect.

Mrs. R. was an attractive, young woman, who dressed precisely, applied cosmetics liberally, had bleached blonde hair and a "doll-like" appearance. She was born in Eastern Europe and at age thirteen was separated from her parents when they were forced to flee from the Russian invasion. She and her next-older sister came to America about five years later. Her sister married shortly thereafter, but Mrs. R. continued to live with her until her own marriage. Mrs. R. had always felt extremely inadequate and was extraordinarily vulnerable to criticism. Both her sister and her sister-in-law were very critical of her. Mrs. R.'s feelings of inadequacy were so great that for a long time she was almost unable to do anything for herself. She confided to the analyst that when she and her husband moved to Cleveland, she would buy a dress or coat from a local department store on approval and send it to her sister (who lived in a different state) for her comments before she would pay for the item. When Julie was an infant, Mrs. R. would often telephone her sister long distance to ask her how to do something pertaining to the baby, rather than call the doctor.

Before the child's analytic treatment started, Mrs. R. had been obsessively clean. She expected Julie to be perfect and would spend all her hours cleaning either the child or the house. Needless to say, this was a point of contention between the parents. Mrs. R. centered all her interests and energies on Julie. She had no interests outside of her home and was fearful of leaving her daughter with a babysitter. She maintained that because of Julie's violent temper outbursts no one would be able to handle her. When Julie first entered nursery school, the mother was so concerned about these tantrums that she was fatigued the entire first week of school and unable to do any of her usual housework.

Mr. R. was a tall, husky fellow who worked for a manufacturing company. He was an extremely passive man who seemed to do very little except work and watch television. During Julie's first year of life, Mr. R. was a very heavy drinker. He worked until 1:00 or 2:00 A.M., then went out drinking with fellow employees and did not come home until daybreak. This continued until his wife agreed to permit him to buy a new car if he would give up alcohol.

Until Mrs. R. entered guidance and put a stop to it, Mr. R. had been excessively stimulating to the girl. He often wrestled with her, tickled her, and played football with her. In this latter game, he would tackle her and lie on top of her, which both frightened and excited the child a great deal. The only thing that Mr. R. did not do was undress in front of the child or walk around the house in the nude. Mrs. R. had read that it was good to do these things and tried to get her husband to accompany her in such a program, but he refused. There were a few occasions, however, when Mr. R. bathed and Julie, who was supposed to have been asleep, wandered into the bathroom.

The marriage had always been a disappointing one. When Mrs. R. became pregnant—about six months after the marriage—Mr. R. abstained from any sexual contact. He became attentive and affectionate again after Julie's birth, but soon started drinking heavily. Mrs. R. visited a marriage counselor for four visits but discontinued when her husband refused to accompany her. They had no mutual friends, almost never entertained (except relatives), and were never invited elsewhere. About a half dozen times a year, the family went out to dinner and a movie, but this seemed to be the extent of their "social life."

Clinical Picture: At the start of treatment, Julie was five years, nine months of age. She was a tall, very attractive youngster with strawberry blonde hair. At first, she was almost always dressed in elaborate nylon "party" dresses. The most distinctive thing about the child was her speech. For a long time, it was very garbled and almost impossible to understand. She referred to herself as Julie rather than I or me. She confused pronouns, and transposed verbs and objects so that her speech had a "foreign" quality. She would often engage in clang associations; that is, she might say a few words correctly, but her next sentence would have no meaning except to rhyme with the previous one. She often omitted words such as, "That's an awfully . . . swimming pool," or transposed words such as, "Bring it tomorrow back." She misused tenses, "Mommy wented yesterday," or "Last week Mommy buy me shoes." Most frequently, however, she would make up and use nonsense words, for example, "Today Julie make a . . . dooby down." At the start of treatment most of her speech was of this personal and private type, with only occasional comprehensible words interspersed. All this, coupled with an imitation of the speech of a foreign-born parent, made it literally impossible to follow her.

Another striking aspect of Julie's total appearance was her physical coordination. Despite the fact she was actually well-coordinated when she tried to be, she appeared clumsy. She seemed always to be losing her balance, falling or bumping into things. Although she never seriously hurt herself, one was always able to find an abundance of minor cuts and scratches.

Course of Treatment

Initial Phase: Both child and mother accompanied me into the office. Julie remained silent and scared while I explained a bit about the purpose and method of treatment. She refused to permit her mother to leave the office for the first three days, during which she silently and compulsively played with dolls. Julie would line up toys in a row or the dollhouse furniture against the walls of the dollhouse. She said almost nothing, except on rare occasions when she would look at me and exclaim, "You're bald!"

After three sessions, and following a unilateral discussion on my part of how frightened some children were in my office, Julie permitted her mother to leave. Her behavior, however, remained the same. Her spontaneous verbalizations were nil. Yet, her activities gave many clues as to what could be expected to come. She played with the dolls and the dollhouse with mounting excitement, indicating fantasies of a great deal of oral aggression and thinly veiled heterosexual and homosexual activity. This would last for only five or ten minutes and was usually followed by the compulsive activities mentioned above.

She spent a good deal of time drawing, and despite the fact that the drawings were often bizarre, they clearly demonstrated her confusion of sexes and her strong wish for a penis. She drew pictures of boys and girls which were similar in almost every respect except that the girl carried a long "purse" in the genital area. In response to my questions, she would often call the boy a queen, or say the girl was either a princess or a king. Julie frequently drew bizarre animals. For example, she drew a horse with a long tail, then drew a face in the tail, and called it a "spider horse" or "duck horse" or other names that were unintelligible.

During this period, which lasted more than a month, Julie occasionally answered a question of mine, but most often she just ignored me. She mumbled a great deal to herself. I was not permitted to join in fantasy play by taking the part of any of the dolls and when I tried to suggest that a doll might feel a certain way, Julie would say, "Don't say that." When I suggested she might be feeling lonely or scared, she would violently scream, "Shut up." This reaction not only occurred every time I tried to mention a disturbing affect, but, confusingly, it also occurred very frequently when I tried to say something complimentary. Despite this, there was, on occasion, slight evidence that a meaningful relationship and transference were being established.

Near the end of the first month, she would greet me more excitedly, occasionally saying, "Hi! Doctor Ack," whereas prior to this, on the rare occasions she addressed me directly, she called me, "Talking Doctor." She sometimes brought a toy from home which I was permitted to hold or which we could discuss briefly. Every once in a while, she haltingly and laboriously told me something that had occurred at nursery school. Fairly often she started the sessions by asking whether I liked her dress or some other bit of clothing.

After about a month of treatment, I was obliged to miss two sessions because of a business trip. When I mentioned this to Julie, she immediately became visibly upset. In a confused manner, she conveyed to me that she would be unable to see me for a while because she had to go and visit "Proband." When I inquired into this, she became even more confused but managed to convey that it was a man who was bald like me. When her defense of turning passive into active was interpreted to her, Julie made one of her first completely intelligible and situationally appropriate remarks: she sadly said, "Don't forget my name." As it became clear that the child felt I was leaving because I did not like her, this of course was interpreted. Julie's reply to this was a plaintive, "I like you."

At this point, I knew nothing of any separations in the past, although mother had been seen weekly for almost a year. Nonetheless, it was clear that the girl's extreme reaction was a transference one. When I questioned Mrs. R., I learned that on two occasions—when Julie was approximately two years of age, and again at two and a half years—Julie had been left for two days with her maternal grandparents. On both occasions, the parents had made no attempt to prepare the child. Rather, they merely told her they were going to visit the grandparents, and while Julie was playing in the front room, they sneaked out the back door and did not return for two days. The maternal grandparents were very rigid, authoritarian, and totally insensitive to the emotional needs of children. Furthermore, neither grandparent was capable of speaking English, so they were unable to explain to Julie what was taking place.

When discussing Julie's development, Mrs. R. told me that the child's speech had been developing normally (albeit slowly) until around this age; however, she seemed never to connect these two events. From this point on, Julie stopped talking and would scream violently whenever her mother tried to talk with her. As a consequence, there was virtually *no verbal communication* between the two from age two to age four and a half, when Julie started nursery school. Such a disintegrating reaction to a separation at this age suggested a host of predisposing traumata; nonetheless, this was the event which appeared to precipitate her disorder. Because of the frustrations inherent in dealing with such a child and because of her feelings of inadequacy and hypersensitivity to criticism, Mrs. R. often followed anyone's suggestion regarding her handling of Julie. At times she was accused of spoiling the girl; she would then hit or yell to prove to relatives that this was not so. Just as often, she would give in to many of Julie's unrealistic demands, especially when others were present and a temper tantrum threatened.

When I returned from my trip, Julie was reluctant to join me in the office and whispered something in her mother's ear. Mrs. R. told me that Julie was angry at me for missing our sessions, and once inside Julie verified this. Following this experience, the child was able, for the first time, to display her anger toward me directly. There was also a slight but noticeable improvement in her ability to communicate coherently, and overwhelming evidence that she could relate, establish a transference, and effectively use the analytic opportunity. This experience ended the first or diagnostic (diagnosis in terms of her ability to be an analytic patient) phase of treatment.

Second Phase: During this phase of treatment, the bulk of our work was concerned with the working through of her defenses and the subsequent oral and phallic problems she displayed.

A great deal of work was done with her separation problem,

which had become inextricably intertwined with oral aggression and penis envy. Very suddenly after our first interruption, Julie became very exhibitionistic and excited in my presence. For example, one day I commented on a pretty bracelet she was wearing and she said, "It's a half one," then lifted her dress to show me her slip. In another session, she lifted her dress to scratch her stomach. She began to sit down with her legs wide apart or turned her back to bend over so that her underpants were clearly visible. This culminated in one session when she lifted her dress and wanted to pull down her panties.

She could not tolerate any attempt on my part to discuss the excitement engendered by being closeted alone with a male therapist. Since, at this point, I was not yet able to talk directly to Julie for more than a few sentences at a time, this presented a technical difficulty. However, knowing that Julie liked to have stories read to her, I asked for and she gave me permission to tell a story.

I told her of a fictitious girl patient, who used to lift her dress in front of me to show me something she didn't have. Julie immediately yelled, "A benis!" When it was ascertained that she in fact meant "penis," she demanded that I continue the story, so I repeated, "This little girl would lift her dress to show me that she didn't have a penis." At this point, Julie interrupted and made her second interpretation, "Yes, and she was angry." She again made me repeat the story and this time interjected that the patient was angry "at her mother." She then changed the subject, but following this surprising session she permitted me to talk much more and in turn conversed with me more often. Although she still screamed violently at me at times, I could usually circumvent this by offering my comments and interpretations in the form of a story.

As mentioned, the problem of separation became more prominent. She became increasingly more disturbed with each succeeding interruption. On one such occasion, when I suggested that my leaving made her feel as she had felt when she was a small child and her mother left her at the home of her grandparents, Julie immediately replied, "I was a small girl and I got out of bed and ate a loaf of bread." Then she amended this, saying she got out of bed and grandma put her into grandpa's bed, and she disliked that because it was smelly. She continued that "Father sleeps in pants and he has a big penis and it's smelly." This last statement immediately had to be undone, and Julie assured me that she had never seen her father's penis. This screen memory of eating the loaf of bread came to occupy a great deal of our time in the months and years to come.

Julie handled separations primarily by identification with the aggressor or by turning passive into active. She immediately would say she could not come the next day and wanted to quit early that day. The very first sign that Julie was learning to master anxiety constructively came at the time of the Christmas vacation. A few days prior to this interruption, Julie started playing with the toy telephone—a toy she had never previously used—making imaginary calls. When I remarked that it seemed as if she wanted me to call during the holiday, she could agree, and she added she really wanted me to visit her over the weekend. Our discussion of her wishes enabled her to manage the vacation with only minimal upset.

Despite this experience, separations continued to plague treatment, although for totally different reasons. In January, I became suddenly ill and had to cancel at the last moment. The next day, Julie fought with her mother, screamed violently in the waiting room, and refused to accompany me alone to my office. This all began when Julie asked her mother to call me and say that she was ill. I was forced to allow Mrs. R. to join us for the first time since the third day of treatment. Once in the office, Julie would not talk to me. Only by talking about Julie's feelings to her mother and pointing out that I knew how much she liked me and how hurt she had been to come all the way to the hospital and not find me there, was she able to allow her mother to leave.

On another occasion, following a two-day separation for which she was well prepared, I saw the most upset, disruptive behavior she had ever shown. She refused to talk with me and screamed violently whenever I tried to talk to her. This completely out-of-control behavior continued for two weeks until one day, at the start of a session, I predicted to her how she would act that day. When I finished, she calmly said, "You know what the trouble is—Treena [the name I had given my fictitious patient] wanted a penis and was mad at her mother," and she then added that she was mad at me. Following a discussion of her wish that I bring her a similar gift on my return, we were able to get at her affects about my trip.

This withdrawal from effective interpersonal contact whenever some event in the environment aroused anxiety was an often-used defense. Another similar and seductive defense this patient used a great deal was to flood the sessions with blatant sexual material whenever something was going on outside that she wanted to avoid. A vivid example of this occurred when Julie was about to enter kindergarten. The history of her kindergarten entrance was as follows. Early in the treatment, I suggested to the nursery school teacher that she make more demands upon Julie and insist that she do what the others do. Prior to this, because of her crying and temper tantrums, Julie had been permitted to participate or not participate as she wished. Plans were being made for the rest of the children to enter kindergarten in midsemester (February), and it was clear that Julie was upset about not going and also about being separated from the other children, who had accepted her. After the first six weeks of treatment, a frequent game in our interviews was "school." Julie would play the teacher and make me the pupil.

Although in these games she was very punitive (which was interpreted), it became evident that she could do many of the things expected of kindergarten children. This fact, along with the success of our nursery school program and her disappointment when she saw the others preparing to leave, made me decide that we ought to try her in the public school, despite the objections of her nursery school teacher and her mother's fears.

As the time for the change of schools drew near, Julie became more and more anxious. For a full week she refused to eat lunch at nursery school and also refused to go outside for recess—which had been her favorite activity. I heard none of this during our meetings; rather she filled the sessions with sexual material. Only when I could interpret that the id material was brought as a defense against her worry about going to public school did this material diminish and I was permitted to help her make the transition.

After some minor initial difficulties, her behavior and scholarship were excellent. At the end of the semester, she achieved the highest grades in her class. This achievement remained constant. Her report card has never shown any grade other than A (excellent) or B (very good)—and at one point, the principal and teacher asked Mrs. R.'s permission to skip or advance the child one grade. Not only did she do well at school, but Julie made many other ego gains during this semester at school. For the first time, she moved out toward other children. She became friendly with a boy classmate who lived across the street and for a while this was a very rewarding experience. However, she totally incorporated this child on a most primitive level. The boy, whose mother worked on weekends, was Catholic. Julie told everyone, in a most convincing manner, that she was Catholic and that her mother was going to find a weekend job. When I was able to review with her how desperately she wanted playmates, and explained that she could be friends with this youngster without being just like him, this behavior lessened and she began to interact more appropriately.

In our hours together during her first school experience, I spent a considerable amount of time working on her speech problem, both by interpretation and by educational techniques. Whenever she tried to converse with me, I helped her pronounce words, made her define odd words she used, and instructed her gently in speaking grammatically. This approach seemed necessary and proved very helpful, but nonetheless the greatest gains in speech came from the understanding and interpretation of the various causes of her problem.

The aspect of the symptom that had to be tackled first was the defensive use made of the difficulty. Once Julie made a conscious attempt to converse with me and participate in the treatment, it soon became apparent that she became confused, incoherent, and rambling when some event occurred which should have aroused sad or angry feelings. As mentioned, this was most noticeable when I had to cancel a session, following which she would become silent. We later learned that the purpose of this defense was to protect her and me against her oral aggressive wishes. One week, Julie's teacher was absent because of illness and in our meetings she was again totally impossible to understand. With the interpretation of her "crazy talk" as a way of avoiding any recognition of her feelings, more improvement was noticeable. She also used her inability to speak to protect herself against the demands made by others that she function adequately. I repeatedly pointed out how much she wanted others to think she was dumb whenever something was asked of her that she felt incapable of accomplishing.

Still another meaning of the symptom which became evident at this time was its association with her masturbation. One day, imme-

diately prior to her hour, Mrs. R. told me that Julie had been unable
to fall asleep the night before. During the session, I was told a very
confused story about a girl with brown shoes who could not stop
dancing. I recalled with her that she had some time ago told me she
had a secret which she, at that time, said she was too ashamed to tell
me and now it appeared she was trying to tell me what it was in this
story. At this point, she became even more incomprehensible than
before. I explained that this was her way of keeping anyone from
learning about her thoughts and actions in bed at night. She responded in her usual way, i.e., with violent screaming, but aided by
these interpretations and the educational techniques described, her
speech improved rapidly so that within a year she was able to make
herself completely understood when she wished to be.

There were innumerable times in the following years of her
analysis when she regressed to this stage and mode of functioning,
sometimes for the reasons mentioned and often for new reasons, but
always under the stress of some anxiety and never as totally as in the
past.

Penis envy, which displayed itself early in the treatment, arose
repeatedly and had to be worked through on many different levels.
At first, however, her fantasies were exclusively on an oral level. She
told a story of a girl and boy who, while walking down the street,
encountered a man selling candy. They bought some and when the
girl looked in her bag there was a penis. At another time, she drew
a picture of a cat called "Alley," with a big long tail, and then drew
another cat who she said was "Alley's sister," and who wanted a long
tail. She had Alley give his sister his tail, which she ate.

One day, Julie drew a series of pictures of a horse with wings.
His wife did not have wings. Then she redrew the wife and gave her
very small wings, and finally had the wife eat a long blade of grass and
her wings miraculously grew very large. At the same time, she spent
many hours playing games in which she would change things around.
Or she drew pictures with green grass, but before she was done she
changed it to orange; at times she drew pictures of boys who later
grew up to be girls.

Before the oral wishes and fantasies could be interpreted, however, we spent many hours on how dissatisfied she felt with herself
and how much she wished to be anyone or anything but Julie. She

also expressed the fantasy that she had at one time possessed a penis. On one occasion she said her mother took it away from her, while at another level, she believed it fell off because she touched it too much. Following this, her oral aggressive and libidinal wishes and fears began to disrupt her behavior and therefore became much more accessible to analysis. For example, for a number of weeks following the revelation that she felt her mother was responsible for her lack of a penis, most of the material she brought concerned her anger at her mother and, in the transference, at me. However, she denied feeling angry, saying, "I'm not angry, I don't like to be angry." The danger of recognizing her anger became understandable a short time later.

She told me a story of a fairy and a little boy with an axe who cut down trees. The fairy constantly frustrated the boy by hiding his axe. When I remarked that the fairy seemed angry, Julie had the fairy die. During this period, Julie became ill one morning and vomited, necessitating that she stay home from school. With me, she denied any worry and said this occurred because she had not eaten. When I asked why, she quickly blurted out, "Because I thought if I ate I would never see my mommy again—she would be in heaven."

The patient's oral libidinal wishes were displaced onto her grand-father and occasioned a great deal of anxiety whenever she had to come in contact with him. One time the grandparents were invited to dinner and Mrs. R. had prepared a turkey—one of Julie's favorite dishes. Nevertheless, she was unable to eat any of the meal. In sub-sequent interviews, it became abundantly clear that food (on that occasion) was equated with grandfather's penis and this fantasy was so intense that she had to inhibit her activity entirely when in his presence.

Despite the help Julie received from these interpretations and the subsequent insight, the strong oral fixation continued to color material from all levels. Whenever she was faced with great anxiety, she regressed to an oral aggressive level and became difficult to man-age. At such times, Julie sat down at the play table with her back to me and, using toys, puppets, animals, etc., would tell long, rambling, disjointed, and incomprehensible "stories." The "stories" seemed to have no beginning, middle, or end, and although individual words were understandable, I was never able to discern an intelligibly complete sentence. These "stories" would go on day after day, while at home she had eating and sleeping problems. Whenever I tried to make a comment, Julie screamed at me to shut up or threatened to break my furniture, throw something at me or leave the office. The "stories" were replete with incidents of animals eating other animals and humans, or humans doing the same to animals or other persons.

Whenever this regression occurred, a great deal of analytic work went into discovering the source of the anxiety which produced such a drastic reaction. In this fashion, all the problems usually found in a child analysis were encountered and analyzed. Yet each time this regressive behavior re-entered the treatment, an interpretation of the fantasy or wish or fear was only partially ameliorative. Only when the positive aspect of the regression was understood and explained, i.e., that this behavior was the patient's attempt, in fantasy, to re-establish the early mother-child relationship, was she able to give this up. This activity also seemed to represent the trauma and overwhelming excitement she had experienced as a preverbal child, as much with her father as with her grandfather.

The last new aspect of her speech difficulty was discovered in the latter part of her treatment. One day, Julie was telling me of some difficulty between her parents. During her account of these events, I was able to see and to point out her identification with her father. She responded to this by telling me that her father went to parties, played games, and drank whiskey. She then imitated his drunken walk and described how funny he talked when inebriated. I reminded her that when she was very small her father used to drink a great deal and that she seemed to have copied his speech. Her reaction was to close the discussion by feigning sleep—something she had never done, but exactly what her father did each time her mother began to argue with him. From this point on, there was further improvement in her speech patterns.

In the last year of her analysis, Julie never once resorted to this total, debilitating ego regression, which had been so prominent throughout the first three years of the treatment. However, this infantile tie with her mother was not yet dissolved although it never took this gross form again. Rather, what became evident was an excessive dependence upon her mother, not in the oral sense of the term but rather as an alter ego to interpret her capacities to her. Julie never seemed able to evaluate the adequacy of her reactions and responses. Once assured—by her mother or myself—that she was approaching a problem correctly, she could proceed with skill and agility. Nevertheless, her initial response to a novel task was always hesitant and abortive.

For example, about five months before terminating treatment, Julie was seen by a staff psychologist because the only recorded I.Q. was the pretreatment 84. In this test, she achieved an I.Q. of 111 (a 27-point increase), which the examiner felt was only a minimal estimate of her potential. The psychologist perceptively noted that her initial response to a task was consistently her worst effort, and that her evaluation of the correctness of her answers bore little relationship to reality except on the especially easy items.

It must be reiterated that throughout the analysis, even during its most turbulent periods, the patient's academic and social behavior in school was exemplary. As a matter of fact, each time she had a new teacher her mother was called in and told how well Julie was doing. Inevitably, the teacher closed by asking whether it was really necessary for this child to see a psychologist. However, the schoolwork in these early grades demanded mostly a rote kind of learning and provided little opportunity for abstract or problem-solving thinking. During the first and second grades, her marks in the academic subjects (reading and arithmetic) were A's. When she entered the third grade and the work became a bit more complex, her difficulty in problem solving and abstract thinking became more evident. Correspondingly, I learned from Mrs. R. that when Julie became a toddler she was not allowed the usual childish opportunities to explore and discover her world.[1] Mrs. R. restricted Julie not because of any fear of dirt (as I had expected), but because when Julie had started crawling she was discovered with some dirty inedible object in her mouth and her mother was desperately frightened she would eat something that would endanger her. When this period was reconstructed for her,

[1] Since this time, I have had my psychologist colleagues notify me whenever they test any child showing a similar inability to assess the adequacy of his responses. In four cases called to my attention, a careful study of the history reveals a similar restriction placed upon the child during the toddler stage—although these restrictions were imposed for entirely different reasons. If this interesting observation is a general one, it clearly demonstrates the continuity between early opportunities for ego expansion and the development of particular intellectual functions.

Julie began slowly to disentangle herself from the last remnants of the pathological aspect of her relationship with her mother.

Work with the Mother

A few words must be said about the work with Mrs. R. because this turned out to be a crucial factor in the outcome of Julie's analysis.

As is usually the case in the analysis of a young child, the mother was seen weekly for the first three years and bimonthly the last year. Not only did I depend upon her to keep me abreast of events at home and school, which Julie was unable to do, but I made considerable use of the closeness that existed between them by aiding Mrs. R. to make some interpretations similar to those given in mother guidance. This was done in an attempt to combat Mrs. R.'s proclivity to transfer all responsibilities to me, and to encourage and support self-reliance and self-esteem, which was the single most important problem in my work with the mother. Because Mrs. R. felt so unable to have a normal-acting child, the treatment of Julie hinged to a great extent upon her ability to alter this attitude.

As the treatment progressed, I was able to take up with her (on an experiential level) factors in her background that led to this self image. It was only with improvement in her picture of her own adequacy that Mrs. R. could truly permit Julie to become more adequate.

Another factor in the mother's handling of Julie that proved troublesome for a while was her inability to frustrate the girl. This resulted from the fantasy that her daughter would grow up hating her if she refused any demand. Mrs. R. was able to recognize the origin of this fantasy in her dislike of her own mother, who openly preferred her older girls and blamed Mrs. R. for not being a boy.

Discussion

Learning problems cannot be discussed as a single entity. Pearson (1952), Weisskopf (1951), and others have clearly demonstrated that a learning inhibition can be a symptom of a neurosis, a character disorder, or a more serious thought disturbance. And, if neurotic, it can result from a fixation on any psychosexual level of development and can involve any, and most likely all, of the psychic agencies of the mind. Nonetheless, we have every reason to expect some salient similarities in cases of extreme developmental difficulties.

The earlier literature implicates the oral phase as the most crucial one for learning. This case testifies to the accuracy of the analytic maxim that orality serves as the prototype of all later "taking in." As is the case with all symptoms, Julie's difficulty was overdetermined. A review of the data unearthed in this analysis suggests five major reasons for the patient's inability to master even the most common developmental task. From a familiarity with the literature in this area and from clinical experience with children with severe learning problems, I feel that the first three reasons presented below have general relevance to the problem and will, to some degree, be present in a majority of cases of pseudostupidity. The last two reasons seem peculiar to this patient and the special circumstances of her upbringing.

Despite the fact that each of the reasons contributed importantly to the ultimate clinical picture, her oral conflict and subsequent oral fixation seemed the most crucial factor. Her tremendous wish to devour and destroy, and the subsequent fear of retaliation that this wish aroused, decreed she avoid contact with others. The danger from this zone increased when her wishes and fears concerning oral destructive impulses became related to emerging phallic and genital drives.

The second reason arose from the unusual, intense, and pathological relationship between Julie and her mother. The child felt the need to "live down" to mother's opinion of her. Because Mrs. R. felt herself to be so inadequate, she was not at all surprised when her child was unable to function normally; rather, she unconsciously expected failure. Julie, on the other hand, felt it necessary to be stupid and inept in order to retain her mother's love. This abnormally close, almost symbiotic relationship allowed her to learn only what her mother could impart, and indeed not all of that. This would seem to substantiate Rapaport's (1951) statement referred to earlier.

Although this aspect of the problem of pseudostupidity has been commented upon by both Mahler (1942) and Hellman (1954), the dynamics outlined by these authors did not appear pertinent in this case. Julie's stupidity was not an attempt to gain more sexual knowledge, nor did she act castrated as a defense against castration anxiety. Also unlike the mothers of the children treated by Hellman, this mother had no guilty secret to divulge. In this connection, it appears to me that the probability of a "secret" producing a learning disorder is greatest when the "secret" relates to a current or recent activity of the parents. Whether or not this is so, the presence of a "secret" does not appear to be a necessary condition of gross learning inhibitions.

Another important cause of Julie's abnormal appearance was the excessive reliance upon regression as an indiscriminate defense against all anxiety. With the first experiencing of any signal anxiety, as a consequence of activities from within or without, she immediately regressed to a preverbal level. On these occasions, ego functions which had appeared and seemed functionally autonomous would become resexualized and reaggressivized. In the regressive process these functions became so contaminated with primitive drive-discharge characteristics that they seemed lost for varying periods of time in the analysis. The regression had to be analyzed from two sides, that is, from the pull exerted by the oral fixation and the child's wish to re-establish her early, primitive relationship with her mother (and in the transference with me), and from the side of the present danger that produced the anxiety.

The identification with her father during his "stupid" times was the fourth reason for her developmental anomalies. Despite Mrs. R.'s statement that her husband was never physically or verbally abusive during his drunken episodes, Julie clearly perceived him as a frightening figure. This early perception and her fear were further reinforced by later life experiences. Julie experienced her father's wild, exciting games, such as football and wrestling, as both exciting and scary, and her identification with her father was clearly an identification with the aggressor. This interpretation produced the last dramatic improvement in her speech disorder.

A final factor contributing to Julie's abnormal development was the limitation of reality-testing opportunities, a limitation imposed for two reasons. The first was an external one: as a toddler, Julie wore only dresses. Mrs. R. told me she handmade all the child's clothes, often using three to four yards of material for one dress. She then spent countless hours cleaning and ironing these dresses. Because of the mother's war against dirt and her fear that her child would ingest something poisonous, she did not permit Julie the usual exploration of the environment which so broadens the toddler's world and is so crucial to the development of reality testing.

The second important reason for Julie's poor reality testing was internal: her unwillingness and subsequent inability to use language. As Anny Katan (1961) points out, "Verbalization increases for the ego the possibility of distinguishing between wishes and fantasies on the one hand, and reality on the other. In short, verbalization leads to the integrating process, which in turn results in reality testing and thus helps to establish the secondary process" (p. 185). Julie's refusal to talk doomed her almost entirely to primary or drive-cathected modes of evaluation and tension discharge.

At this point, a brief comment regarding diagnosis in such cases seems called for, if for no other reason than to contest the current proclivity to diagnose all such bizarre behavior or atypical development as evidence of an underlying schizophrenic process. Discussing the treatment of atypical children, Anna Freud (1965) in her book, *Normality and Pathology in Childhood,* states:

> Where the libido defect is due to severe early deprivation in object relations, interpretation of the transferred repetition has no therapeutic results. Instead, the child may answer to the intimacy of the analyst-patient relationship, which is favorable for the proliferation of libidinal attachment because of the frequency and long duration of contact, the lack of interruptions, the exclusion of disturbing rivals, etc. On the basis of this new and different emotional experience, the child may move forward to more appropriate levels of libido development, a therapeutic change set in motion within the outward setting of child analysis but on the basis of "corrective emotional experience."
>
> [In a footnote to this point, Anna Freud explains:] Unlike the effect of analytic interpretation which is not restricted for the child by age or time of intervention, corrective emotional experience is limited by maturational considerations. It has to happen approximately within the same developmental phase in which the damage to the libidinal process has taken place. Once such limits have been overstepped, it is too late for correction [p. 231].

Anna Freud implies that traditional child psychoanalytic methods are not appropriate for such children. Therefore, cases such as the one reported here, treated successfully, are, in restrospect, cases of "pseudo" arrest. A careful diagnostic study intimated that the child had more potentialities available than she manifested. The social history suggested that the child had made tentative moves forward—

some behaviorally and some in fantasy—but enough to produce structural change despite the fact that the functions associated with these structures were not consistently available.

The psychological tests also hinted that there was more potential than met the eye. An I.Q. of 84 in a girl who behaved as bizarrely as she did is an unusually *high* score; however disturbed she was, Julie was able to understand verbal requests and respond to verbal instructions. She also scored a good deal higher on some nonverbal subtests which captured her attention and interest. This unevenness of performance spoke as much to the fact that in some respects she was developing "normally" as to the fact that she was also very disturbed.

Julie's ability to understand language was an important diagnostic and prognostic sign as well. In the absence of signs of organic impairment, this ability indicated that she was capable of using language although the expressive function of speech was inhibited. Inhibitions, we know, are subject to psychoanalytic understanding and possible amelioration.

Despite the importance of the understanding and interpretation of the dynamics enumerated above, I feel the analysis owes its successful outcome to another very simple fact which, in our sophistication, we may at times ignore. That is, the expression of confidence—to both mother and child—that they were capable of functioning more adequately. No one had ever acted as if the child could do anything independently, certainly not her mother but also not her nursery school teacher. By permitting Julie to act as she pleased at school, the teacher covertly conveyed to the child her belief that this was all she could do. As a consequence, it came as an enormous but pleasant surprise to Julie when I encouraged her to enter public school and conveyed to her my conviction that she could learn and behave like others. In this decision, I took advantage of the very positive transference, i.e., her wish to please me in the transference, and did not analyze this until she had enough corrective experiences of success at school to be able to continue her good work without the transference crutch.

Likewise, my expressions of confidence in the mother encouraged her to look at and change her perception of herself as well as of her daughter. I doubt that the outcome would have been as rewarding if this had not been done.

BIBLIOGRAPHY

Abraham, K. (1924), The Influence of Oral Erotism on Character-Formation. *Selected Papers on Psycho-Analysis.* London: Hogarth Press, 1927, pp. 393-406.

Freud, A. (1965), *Normality and Pathology in Childhood.* New York: International Universities Press.

Freud, S. (1901), The Psychopathology of Everyday Life. *Standard Edition,* 6. London: Hogarth Press, 1960.

—— (1905), Three Essays on the Theory of Sexuality. *Standard Edition,* 7:125-245. London: Hogarth Press, 1953.

—— (1911), Formulations on the Two Principles of Mental Functioning. *Standard Edition,* 12:213-226. London: Hogarth Press, 1958.

—— (1926), Inhibitions, Symptoms and Anxiety. *Standard Edition,* 20:77-175. London: Hogarth Press, 1959.

Hellman, I. (1954), Some Observations on Mothers of Children with Intellectual Inhibitions. *This Annual,* 9:259-273.

Katan, A. (1961), Some Thoughts about the Role of Verbalization in Early Childhood. *This Annual,* 16:184-188.

Mahler, M. S. (1942), Pseudo-imbecility: Magic Cap of Invisibility. *Psa. Quart.,* 11:149-164.

Pearson, H. J. (1952), A Survey of Learning Difficulties in Children. *This Annual,* 7:322-386.

Rapaport, D., ed. (1951), *Organization and Pathology of Thought.* New York: Columbia University Press.

Sperry, M., Staver, N., & Mann, N. E. (1952), Destructive Fantasies in Certain Learning Difficulties. *Amer. J. Orthopsychiat.,* 22:356-365.

Weisskopf, E. A. (1951), Intellectual Malfunctioning and Personality. *J. Abnorm. Soc. Psychol.,* 46:410-423.

DEPRESSION: THREE CLINICAL VARIATIONS

STUART S. ASCH, M.D.

The classical formulations of the dynamics of depression as worked out by Abraham (1911) and Freud (1917), have remained relatively intact until recently. With the advent of ego psychology, it has been possible to develop additional hypotheses which have led to an enriched understanding of depressive states. Substantial additions to our knowledge have come from studies of self-esteem regulation, of discrepancies between the ego ideal and a paralyzed or impoverished ego, and especially from Bibring's study of the helpless ego (1953). The present study, concerned specifically with the classical formulations of the depressive process, is an attempt to delineate the underlying mechanisms more discretely, and to postulate and illustrate several variations.

In "Mourning and Melancholia," Freud (1917) described this process essentially as follows: a lost object, of great narcissistic value, is incorporated into the ego in order to recover that object and preserve it. But now the ego becomes the object and experiences the ambivalence, which had been originally directed toward the object, with increased aggression. The source of this attack is located in the superego. Heightened libidinal impulses are evident in the tenacity with which the ego holds onto this object.

This classical concept of the depressive constellation, with its overly schematic outline of "aggression turned against the self," turned against the introject, has to be re-examined in the light of recently gained insights into the contents and structures of the ego.

The affects usually associated with this clinical picture of depres-

Presented at the New York Psychoanalytic Society on February 25, 1964.

Associate Attending Psychiatrist, Department of Psychiatry, Institute of Psychiatry, M. Ralph Kaufman, M.D., Director; The Mount Sinai Hospital, New York.

I am grateful to Dr. George Gero for his helpful suggestions after an early reading of this paper.

sion are feelings of a loss (emptiness and loneliness), guilt, self-criticism, and inferiority. Other symptoms and signs are more variable, but generally include anorexia or overeating, insomnia or increased fatigue with constant sleeping (even a kind of sleeping addiction appears at times), constipation, somatic complaints, inhibition of thinking, and psychomotor retardation.

However, we are becoming increasingly familiar with clinical conditions that differ from this classical picture and yet are dynamically related to it. We are becoming aware of the fact that the term "depression" includes various clinical states with similar, but not identical psychopathology.

Clinical variations appear along a continuum of feelings, self-evaluations, and functioning. I am postulating that these variations are a function of the vicissitudes of the "introject." The incorporation of this introject involves the modification of some structures or functions of the ego to resemble those significant attributes of the introject which have been cathected. Although the concept of "introject" refers only to the psychic representation of an object, the "introject" nevertheless is often experienced as if it had actual substance. This introject can be experienced (unconsciously, but sometimes also consciously to some extent) in different ways, apparently depending upon the structures and functions involved in the incorporation or identification and on the ego attitudes toward it.

Is it the self representation that has been endowed with the attributes of the introject? Is it mainly the body-image part of the self representation that is involved? Is it only a *part* of the body image? And if so, which part of the body image? (All of these are conceptualized as different structures within the ego itself.) Or perhaps the internalization is into the structures that subsequently evolve from ego functions, such as the superego.

These "spatial" relationships, as mentioned throughout this paper, are conceptualizations of psychic constructs of the object and self representations. However, they are more than just intellectual constructs, since they are also often experienced almost concretely in such spatial ways as, "I feel rotten inside," in contrast to a more tangential, "There is a weight on my shoulders."

Later accretions to the self representation tend to be experienced as more or less separate from and even superimposed on the earlier developed body image. To some extent these new elements never lose their stigma of "newcomer," even "parvenu," in contrast to the self perception of the "real me." They are, in fact, more labile than the fixed and more firmly bound primitive self images of the earlier identifications. Freud (1891) spoke of this principle in his monograph *On Aphasia:* "under all circumstances an arrangement of associations which, having been acquired later, belongs to a higher level of functioning, will be lost, while an earlier and simpler one will be preserved" (p. 87).

The "bad" or "toxic" stool that must be expelled, or the "depressing roll of fat that must be dieted off," are certainly parts of the self image of the ego, but they certainly also are perceived as more peripheral parts of the self representations than is expressed in the feeling "I am just no good, of no value at all." Between these two attitudes exists a continuum of feelings and evaluations, all dependent on the locus of the cathexis, on just *where* this "introject" is experienced.

The clinical picture finally presented seems to be influenced by which part of the ego has been identified with the "introject," its "distance from the ego core," to use Loewald's term (1962); or the introject may even be outside the ego, e.g., when it is part of the superego; or it may be entirely outside the self, displaced or projected onto some other object.

In this presentation I shall focus on three variations in the clinical picture of depression. I shall demonstrate that such variants reflect modifications in the ego corresponding to a hierarchy of object relations, a hierarchy evolved in response to developmental and maturational influences on the ego.

Hypochondriasis
DEPRESSION WITHOUT DEPRESSED AFFECT

The early body image is cathected and outlined through inner perception of the self, such as touch and proprioceptive impulses. "The nuclei of the early infantile self-images are our first body-images and sensations" (Jacobson, 1953, p. 56). As new body-image boundaries develop, this depletion of the self is normally compensated for partly by retaining some of the characteristics of the separated object through identifications, and partly by a continued relationship with the object.

A current real or anticipated loss of a narcissistically cathected object may lead to a recathexis of the earlier body image now threatened with loss of part of itself. This current loss may then be experienced as a threat to one of those early intrapsychic organ representations. If the object being lost is regressively experienced in this way, as part of the body ego, one attempt to avoid such a loss can be a hypercathexis of that body part.

Attention is then focused on its psychic representation, often resulting in this part of the body being experienced as *extra*ordinary. This heightened "self-esteem" (limited to the afflicted body part) is all the more in contrast to the complementary depletion of cathexis, from the mental images of real objects, from the rest of the self representation, and even from the rest of the body.

Such draining of energy due to the hypercathexis of a psychic organ representation is a major factor in the clinical picture of ego restriction, with limited abilities in thinking, functioning, and interests. Ego functions are further depleted by energy withdrawn for the superego's use in attacking the introject; they are drained still further by energy withdrawn to strengthen the countercathexis against the increased rage provoked by the loss of the object.

Clinically, the patient becomes preoccupied with this one part of his body in a tenacious, unyielding manner. At the same time, this body part provokes anxiety, since it is experienced as toxic and diseased, something that must be removed. This is the classical picture of hypochondriasis.

Since it is the sensory intake apparatus, i.e., pain, proprioception, etc., that stimulates development of the body image, the hypochondriacal complaint usually involves one of the more obvious organs, one whose psychic representation is a conscious one, the stomach, the heart, the bowels, etc. (It becomes a somatic delusion when there is an associated ego defect in reality testing.)

Hypochondriasis is not only an attack against part of the body image but is also a *libidinal* hypercathexis of the same part.[1] The

---

[1] It is especially in this symptom that one sees the double facet of depression of which Lewin (1961) speaks, the tenacious clinging to the breast, while at the same time attacking oneself for this activity.

affected organ, having come to represent the lost object, is now being treated like the ambivalently cathected introject in depression.

At this point, however, one is impressed with a major discrepancy between hypochondriasis and the classical phenomena of depression. When hypochondriasis is present, there may be *no* guilt and no depressed mood. The only affect consistently present is anxiety. In reviewing this group of patients clinically, it is quite striking to see the frequency with which hypochondriasis is seen without the classical depressed mood, without guilt or self-criticism; although the depressed affect may appear inconstantly. It is very tempting to consider such hypochondriasis (and perhaps psychosomatic illness as well, see below) as manifestations of "unconscious depression." This would be similar to our use of the term "unconscious guilt" to explain self-punitive acts, even while recognizing that affects are actually not a part of the unconscious.

However, the clinical significance of the finding that the affect of depression is sometimes not seen at all in hypochondriasis and is often not present consistently is that the hypochondriacal complaint may not be recognized as part of a depressive picture. Thus, even though a common phenomenon in medical practice, hypochondriasis is rarely recognized by physicians as a manifestation of depression. Of the 70 to 80 per cent of patients seen in general medical practice whose physical complaints are considered to have a psychiatric basis, the majority present hypochondriacal complaints (Kaufman et al., 1959; Mannucci et al., 1961). These figures become even higher if one considers the older age groups, in which depression is so much more frequent. An example would be the postpartum patient who is anxiously complaining about her episiotomy, way past the time appropriate for such concern. This patient may be a melancholic, regressively trying to undo the loss of part of her body.

I am suggesting that in the hypochondriacal condition, a loss is recaptured as part of the archaic body image, in an organ representation, rather than through incorporation into the self representation. I believe that it is just this involvement of the archaic body image, rather than the rest of the self representation, that explains the inconstancy of the depressive affect in hypochondriasis.

Support for the thesis that hypercathexis of the body image may "bind" the mood comes from a related clinical source. This is the lifting of the depressive mood so often seen during periods of actual organic illness, including psychosomatic illness. Recently an agitated depressed patient was admitted to the hospital. Prior to admission, her doctor had placed her on Thorazine. She developed hepatitis and the depression lifted. When the hepatitis cleared, the depression returned and she was hospitalized. When seen at this time, she bemoaned her state and insisted she preferred hepatitis to the depression.

A similar sequence often occurs with psychosomatic problems. Some years ago, I followed a hospitalized patient with status asthmaticus on a psychosomatic basis that kept her close to death. When the asthma cleared during psychotherapy, the patient found herself in a severe and profound depression and actually begged to have her asthma back.

Related psychosomatic studies by Heiman (1962) convincingly indicate that the recurrent or intractable uterine bleeding of certain women should also be recognized as reactions to a loss, even though the depressive affect is once again absent.

Here then, in hypochondriasis, we have a condition which permits us to postulate a more precise location of the introject. It is a specific portion of the archaic body-image part of the self representation of the ego that is being experienced as the introject, as the object of the superego's attacks. A more global identification exists when it is not just the primitive body-image part, but the self representation *as a whole,* which is closely allied or identified with the lost object.

Although the self representation includes the "body ego," it also encompasses the later accretions of attitudes, mannerisms, and characteristics of the self. It is these additional aspects of the self representation that are involved in the melancholic's identification with the lost object, not just the body image. The melancholic patient expresses a more direct self-criticism, *"I* am no good, *I* am inferior." *These* are the patients in whom the classical depressive affect is found.

For these reasons, it seems to me that the affect of depression is clinically apparent only to the degree that the self-representational part of the ego structure is the object of the criticisms of the superego attack. Anxiety rather than depression seems to be the main affect in hypochondriasis. Psychosomatic illness is probably related to hypochondriasis, but differs in its clinical manifestations. Psychosomatic illness can involve organs that are "unknown" so far as sensory impulses are concerned. These may be organs or parts of organs that have never been consciously cathected. Thus, psychosomatic illness, unlike hypochondriasis, can develop without the conscious awareness of the patient. In addition, it involves an actual organ, in contrast to involvement of the representation of the organ alone in the hypochondriac.

Conversion hysteria is to be differentiated from both psychosomatic illness and hypochondriasis. Again there is no actual organic change. Motor pathways are involved at least as often as sensory, in contrast to the exclusive sensory involvement in hypochondriasis. The hysteric's unconscious fantasy is concerned with the less primitive, more sophisticated body image, since hysteria involves a higher level of maturation and development. The conversion symptom is an attempted solution of a phallic conflict rather than an oral problem concerned with object loss.

DEPRESSION WITHOUT OBJECT LOSS
MASOCHISTIC SUBMISSION TO THE OBJECT

In certain clinical situations the patient presents a clearly depressed mood, including psychomotor retardation, low self-esteem, etc., but none of the accepted etiologies of depression can be found. There may be no powerlessness of the ego in Bibring's terms (1953), no obvious narcissistic injury, and no apparent loss of an object. On the contrary, there may even have been resolution of a threatened separation, so that the threat of a loss no longer exists.

As expected, such depressions are based on an intensely narcissistic relationship. However, the next step differs from the usual sequence of events in depression. In these cases, the origin of the danger of losing the object does not arise from a threat of abandonment by the object. It arises rather from the individual's *own* wish to give up the object. The patient experiences this wish to separate as an overt expression of his own hostile and destructive impulses toward the object. When he gives up the wish to separate and instead reunites with his object, his aggression is "turned against the self"; only at this point does clinical depression appear.

Case 1

Miss A. presented herself with a consistently depressed affect. As the analysis progressed, her depressed mood eventually appeared only with the analyst, as one of the main manifestations of the transference neurosis. She looked and felt "smothered" and depressed. Outside the analysis, however, her depressed mood lifted progressively; she developed new interests and functioned so much better that her friends were impressed by the striking change. This dichotomy of mood continued to grow until the depression became restricted to the analytic session (including a short period before and afterward).

Miss A., in her early twenties, sought treatment when she recognized an inability to leave her home and mother. She was in love with a young man, but an obsessional indecision prevented her from leaving her mother and marrying. She felt hopeless and depressed, and was ashamed of this inability to act effectively.

An apochryphal story of her birth appeared in her associations many times. Miss A. claimed that her mother had often told it. During the delivery the doctors found that Miss A.'s hair was strangling her mother. The baby had to be delivered (separated) quickly lest the mother die. In another version the baby was being strangled by the mother's hair and had to be removed quickly. In each story the hair was cut off and left behind (apparently a distorted version of a long umbilical cord).

In the first dream in analysis the patient was rescuing a little baby from the bottom of a washtub of water. She thought at first that she could revive the child herself with artificial respiration. This reassurance failed and mounting anxiety appeared as she began to feel that she was incapable of saving the baby by herself. She awoke from the dream in a panic.

All decisions were made by the mother, on the latter's initiative or with the help of her guidance. Mrs. A. was critical of the friendships sought by the patient and tended to belittle and ridicule other people. It became clear that Mrs. A. regarded her daughter as her own possession and resented any third party, including the father, who was derogated.

Miss A.'s depression in the transference neurosis was associated with a fear of losing the analyst (as she improved and became independent) and with her rage at the analyst for "requiring" this dependence. She felt that the analyst's reputation and career would be destroyed if she left the analysis. There were frequent impulsive attempts at separating from the analyst, but guilt and anxiety always brought her back, even more intensely submissive.

Miss A. made the first of these impulsive attempts to separate a year after treatment had begun. At the end of one session, on her way out the door, she casually mentioned for the first time that she would be away for several days of skiing with her boy friend. As soon as she reached the ski tow and grabbed the rope, she seized it incorrectly and promptly tripped and fell, breaking her leg quite severely. Thereafter, for almost six months, she came to the analysis on crutches, even during snow storms, when other, more able patients did not come.

Much of the analysis involved working through the tremendous rage Miss A. felt for her mother for requiring her to be helpless and the patient's belief in her mother's vital need for her. She also suffered from feelings of responsibility and great guilt whenever one of her objects was in *any* way injured.

Toward the end of the analysis, when Miss A. was making her marriage plans, there was a temporary repetition of her inappropriate helplessness, so that her mother had to take over and be closely involved with the floundering patient in order to get anything done. In the transference, Miss A. insisted that I was necessary to help her with her marriage plans, that she was unable to do it alone. She had to convince me she did not want the marriage and was really suffering; otherwise, she felt, I would be angry at her for marrying and leaving me. She then had a dream of her mother dying when she married. When her masochistic submission to her mother and the rage deflected back onto herself were once more analyzed and worked through in the transference, the patient was able to take over independently and marry without difficulty.

Case 2

Mrs. B., twenty-eight years old, had a sadomasochistic marital relationship. Whenever she attempted to leave her husband, she impulsively had to come back in panic. Mr. B. was a depressed man who insisted that his wife accept his verbal abuse and criticism of her. It seemed quite clear that all his *self*-criticisms were being displaced onto the patient whenever his depression became too severe. Certainly the epithets he used seemed more appropriate an appraisal of *his* behavior than of hers. Nevertheless she felt forced to submit masochistically and accept his abuse without contradiction. Continuing the marital relationship under these conditions, Mrs. B. would then become depressed and self-critical and function ineffectively.

In treatment, Mrs. B. gradually reached outside the marriage in attempting to build up some self-esteem independent of her husband. These attempts were always made very tentatively and were inevitably followed by overwhelming anxiety. She felt that her impulses (both libidinal and aggressive) would burst out uncontrollably and spill over into action unless her husband were there to keep them in check. Allied to this was the patient's conviction that if she left her husband, he would either become a hopelessly institutionalized patient or commit suicide. She could not leave and do this to him.

As she improved in treatment and became less afraid of her own wishes to separate and develop herself further, Mr. B. became increasingly and seriously depressed. He made frequent, drastic attempts to re-establish the sadistic relationship, and at times the patient would feel "forced" to submit. At *these* times the husband's depression would lift, while the patient in turn would become seriously depressed herself. In addition, at these times (not only as part of the inferiority feelings of her depression, but more as part of the masochistic submission) she would feel herself to be incomplete, unable to stand alone, and in need of being attached to her husband.

Genetically, this relationship with the husband could be traced back to a strikingly similar sadomasochistic tie to her mother. As a little girl the patient had been forced to submit physically to her mother (frequent painful enemata, beatings, etc.). In her conscious fantasies Mrs. B. pictured her mother in all kinds of overt sadistic acts. To a much greater degree than in Case 1 the mother attacked the child's spontaneous activities as disgracefully indecent or as destructive to the family reputation. Later, Mr. B.'s accusations about Mrs. B.'s gradual self-growth had an almost identical content.

This group of depressions is characterized by a specific clinical feature: the depression seems to be a function of the *continued* relationship with the object rather than of the *loss* of the object. In these patients, actual separation from the object may relieve the depression or at least change its character. However, the fact of separation arouses panic at the thought that *they* have destroyed the object, which now must be reconstituted by once again masochistically submitting to the object.

The special character of such attempts at resolution of the threatened loss of an object seems to stem from a specific problem in the development of these patients' early separation and individuation. They seem to feel that the act of separation from their partners —spouse, mother, child, analyst, etc.—is an aggressive act that will damage, mutilate, or destroy the partner. Miss A. was convinced that my career and reputation would be destroyed if she left; Mrs. B. was convinced that her husband would commit suicide and that her children would be physically damaged. Stein, in his paper "The Marriage Bond" (1956), describes a similar case, a husband who could not leave his wife because of "his belief that she couldn't survive without him because of her helplessness."

When the conflict is expressed on a primitive oral level, such patients feel that they must masochistically submit to and be engulfed and devoured by the object in order to fuse with it. On other levels the goal may be to remain a part of, an appendage to, the object, e.g., as mother's phallus. The aim, however, remains constant: a masochistic submission in order to preserve the object.

The rage at having to play this role and the shame and inferiority engendered by such a narcissistic devaluation are dealt with by the familiar mechanism of "aggression turned against the self." The rage is directed mainly against their *own* self representation, which does not include the object whose introject is more or less bypassed. The psychic representation of the object is preserved in this way and protected from their destructive rage, since to a large degree they have substituted themselves for the object. "We know that the helpless little child with a hostile, rejecting mother will rather accept and submit to this powerful though aggressive love-object than give it up altogether" (Jacobson, 1953, p. 58).

The need to remain a narcissistic part object of mother, inherently a regressive wish, is strengthened by the need to avoid the destruction of mother. The mechanism of "turning against the self" readily lends itself to this aim. Thus, the preservation of the object and the attachment to it are perpetuated, but at the price of incomplete self-individuation.

This pathology seems to be based on difficulties in the separation-individuation phase of development, described and documented by Mahler and Furer (1960). The child's ego fails to develop an adequate self image; i.e., it fails to delineate its boundaries from the more primitively assimilated body image that originally included the mother. (Perhaps in the depressive's ego structure a "proper" delineation of the body image is not achieved?)

Such a failure of development occurs when a mother is unable to tolerate her child's independence. Owing to her *own* developmental failures in separation and individuation, she tends to propagate such ego defects by continuing to perceive her child as part of her own image or even body ego. Even the separation at birth is experienced as an actual depletion or mutilation of her own body ego. The apocryphal story of her birth recounted by Miss A. is a symbolic representation of this concept of separation from the mother as a mutilating experience. We also see this clinically in the "smothering mother," who repeatedly impresses upon the child that he is part of her body, "my heart, my insides, etc.," and clutches him closely, literally and figuratively, to reassure both that they are still united. Such a mother seems to feel she must maintain an attachment to the child in order to maintain her own ego integrity. This attitude inevitably has a profound effect on the infant's nascent ego. The infant's body ego still includes the mother within its boundaries, and the child can readily experience separation from the mother as a loss of part of his own ego unless he is reassured by his mother and comforting experiences.

The child needs to learn how to deal with his mother, what kind of responses she expects. If the mother tries to prevent loss of "her body extensions" (of her narcissistic objects), then the child quickly learns that any separation from mother means both a loss of part of himself and an aggressive, destructive act against mother ("you are tearing out my heart"). The resulting self image of the developing child is defective and requires some continued connection with the image of mother (whose ego is also needed as an additional control over the child's dangerous instinctual drives). This leads to further regression to reunion with the mother (or, more correctly, to feeling part of the whole again) in order to protect the mother from destruction or mutilation.

To summarize, the depression of persons who relate to their objects in this special masochistic way is *not* an expression of ambivalence toward an incorporated lost object. Rather, a part of the self representation takes the place of the object representation in order to deflect the intensely ambivalent strivings away from the object and yet gratify them at the same time. "Better me than her" seems to express the intent of this process, which also gratifies the aggressive drives that could not be directed toward the object without destroying it, and thus represents a motivation for turning aggression against the self.

While protecting the object, such a mechanism also serves the additional ego aims of mastery and activity rather than dependency and passivity. Moreover, it is a ready-made mechanism for dealing with the later-appearing superego restrictions. By first being the victim, such a person can take what he wants without guilt. His aggression is already discounted. By submitting to the aggressive mother, he feels entitled to get her to give to him, to take from her, as he first let her take from him. Both drives and ego are gratified, and the later-appearing superego is placated.

Guilt, as a motivating agent in the substitution of the self for the object, seems to be involved inconstantly and secondarily. When guilt is present, it concerns some fantasied (or perhaps real) injury suffered by the object. (In Case 1, Miss A. later felt guilty about an early abortion of her mother; while Mrs. B. experienced guilt about her mother's castration.) These guilt feelings seem to become attached to this constellation of "depression without object loss" much later in life, in the postoedipal period, as expected, when the superego develops. The pattern of replacing the object, or part of the object, with the self begins much earlier—toward the end of the first year of life, during the phase of separation-individuation.

DEPRESSION WITH RAGE
PROJECTION AND DISPLACEMENT OF THE INTROJECT

When identifications with an ambivalent object are made at later developmental stages, they tend to form newer and less stable structures in the psychic apparatus (Freud, 1891). The relationship of these new identifications to the body ego is more tenuous than that of the earlier, more primitive, and more firmly fixed identifications. This is especially true of the identifications resulting from the resolution of the oedipus complex.

Some of these later identifications do enter into the ego and enrich it. Others are incorporated more "distally" to the ego core (Loewald, 1962) and may not be consistently experienced as an integral part of the self representation. They are more readily displaced outward, to clothing, hair, spouse, automobile, etc. They may be drawn either into the object representations or into the self representation. Finally, a large part of these later identifications forms the discrete group of attitudes and functions of the conscience, the superego, and is often experienced as if outside the self representation.

When these later, more "peripheral" (more labile) additions to the self representation are involved in a depressive process, their clinical manifestation may be a wish to get rid of the "bad part." Getting rid of an old article of clothing, or extra weight, or a bowel movement, or a husband, may lead to temporary relief.[2] This getting rid of the bad part must be distinguished from the use of sacrifices as a penance, as bribes to a guilt-provoking superego; the latter mechanism has quite a different significance.

The orthodox Jew in mourning would ritualistically tear his clothing at the grave of his beloved. This is penance, and is symbolic of his body being rent (in preparation for being eaten), and is punishment for his aggression toward the destroyed object; but it is

[2] This wish has always an implicit or even explicit sequel: "I must get rid of the bad part, *but* it must be immediately replaced by another good one."

also an identification with this eaten lost object. The clothing has come to serve as an outward displacement of the introject. In recent years, even this symbolic article has become more tangential. The mourner now pins a little black ribbon to his clothes, and it is this ribbon alone that is cut. The introject is treated as if it were detachable and outside the self, rather than a cathected integral part of the self representation.

As the introject begins to be displaced peripherally, and is experienced more as part of the object representation than the self representation, the affect of depression once again becomes less prominent and less consistent.

Pregnancy occupies a useful place in the study of the depressive process. It is one of the few situations in which an actual physical condition so closely resembles the concept of psychic introjection that the mental representation of the physical phenomenon is cathected with the mental representation of the introject.[3] Just as the "family romance" fantasy of the adopted child has some basis in reality, pregnancy lends reality and heightened significance to fantasies of incorporation and introjected objects. In the course of several years of consulting in a large prenatal clinic I have learned a good deal about the many conscious and unconscious fantasies that pregnant women have about the fetus inside themselves. I am convinced that many of these fantasies and the mechanisms operating in depressed patients are quite similar (Asch, 1960).

When the fetal movements appear in the twenty-first week, the pregnant woman is experiencing a live being inside herself that is nevertheless separate from herself. The sudden appearance of anxiety at this point is quite common, although it is usually mastered. Reversals of identity with the fetus, which are reversals of self and object representations, also appear frequently, and so does claustrophobia. Infantile fantasies of oral impregnation are recathected, although they usually remain unconscious. Almost every pregnant woman treats the "introject-fetus" to some degree as an ambivalently loved object, while her ego acts as the superego. She may feel that

[3] There are at least two other actual experiences of "introjects"; one is the fecal mass in the bowel, animistically experienced (usually unconsciously) as an incorporated object separate from the self (Van Ophuijsen, 1920); the other situation occurs when there is awareness of a tumor growing in the body.

the fetus is defective, inferior, deformed. She may feel it is "bad"; it just sleeps and eats; it is "evil," eating her up inside. She may wish to get rid of it, to kill it (and sometimes does).

I strongly suspect that these fantasies during pregnancy are universal, but of different strengths in different women. The experience of childbirth itself, with the actual physical separation of mother from the child, with the confusion of identities and roles, has been studied and found to result in some degree of depression within the first twenty-four to forty-eight hours in almost all women (Pleshette et al., 1956). This depression apparently lasts until the mother is able to recathect the new baby, by reinvesting it with the values of the lost object; that is, until she is able to appreciate the baby as having some connection with the lost "introject-fetus." Some women are unable to make such a transition. The birth separation is too traumatic. They continue to identify the baby with the lost "introject-fetus" and are unable to cathect the real baby in a meaningful way. The feeling of loss persists, and they remain depressed.[4]

Suicide occurring in the postpartum period can be understood as an attempted reunion, a libidinal expression of the wish to re-enter the womb of mother, to re-create the mother-fetus state (in addition to its direct discharge of rage at being abandoned). In these patients the birth separation experience revives earlier traumatic separation experiences with *their* maternal objects. In such women, however, the confusion of identities between mother and baby, the confusion of self and object, can also interfere with their distinction between suicide and homicide. Aggression toward the infant, even murder, may then occur as an acting out by the mother of the superego assaults on the introject. The infant embodies the introject that has been displaced outside the mother's ego. Attacks on the child may not induce feelings of guilt and may even be experienced as justified in much the same way that the melancholic justifies his self-criticisms and self-punishments, insisting he deserves them.

A logical conclusion would seem to be that the choice between suicide and infanticide, in postpartum depressions, depends on the

---

[4] Cerebrovascular accident victims show an attitude similar to that of such mothers to their babies. The recent stroke victim needs time to reintegrate the paralyzed part into his self representation and in the meanwhile experiences a partial depersonalization (and depression). He may not recognize his paralyzed arm and leg as part of his own body and may attack this "stranger" and even try to push it out of his bed.

"location" of the introject, on whether it is conceptualized *within* the self representation or outside it. Reasoning on this basis, I suggested (1960) that the actual incidence of infanticide was probably much greater than the figure being reported and at least as frequent as suicide in such women. It is possible that many of the deaths of infants listed as due to other or "unknown causes" (10,000 annually) are actually infanticides, either unrecognized or masked for "humanitarian reasons" by the family physician. In recent years an increasing awareness of this phenomenon has begun to appear with the reporting of the "battered child syndrome" (Kempe et al., 1962). These are infants and young children who are found severely and sometimes fatally injured, the first injuries almost always occurring during the postpartum period. These children are now being recognized as victims of sadistic parental attacks. The following clinical history illustrates several of these points.

Case 3

A twenty-seven-year-old woman, Mrs. C., sought treatment because of chronic depression. She had always been "nervous," shy, and ineffectual. Five years ago she married a childhood friend, a weak, ineffectual man. They had one child, a two-year-old daughter whom Mrs. C. did not want, although her husband did. The present severe depression appeared after this child was born.

Mrs. C.'s mother was a domineering woman, who constantly manipulated the patient and used her as an appendage of herself. The father was a severe alcoholic and a complete failure, for which Mrs. C.'s mother blamed the patient. Mrs. C. disliked her mother, although she never really let herself become aware of her great hatred. Instead she felt completely tied to her mother and was really unable to separate from her. Even at the time of treatment, Mrs. C. felt a great need to convince "people" that she was helpless and could do nothing without their help.

Mrs. C. gave her little daughter her own first name Catherine, "because I wanted her to have the nickname Kitty," even though this was not the patient's nickname. Later material disclosed the ambivalence more distinctly, in that Kitty was found to be the name of the beloved godmother. The patient had given Kitty her *mother's* name as a middle name but could never explain why. Mrs. C. had loved cats all her life, and still kept a stuffed cat that she had had as a baby. "I've always liked cats more than people." At the time she sought treatment she had two cats at home.

Mrs. C.'s relationship to her daughter was overtly sadistic. She felt Kitty was dirty, smelly, and loathsome (she was not toilet trained); for this reason she beat Kitty unmercifully, choked her until she was blue, and constantly attacked her verbally. Her cats also messed up the house occasionally, but Mrs. C. never punished or criticized them. The fury at Kitty was accompanied by conscious murderous thoughts for which she gave two rationalizations: the child was dirty and smelly; and she came between the patient and her husband. Mrs. C. painted a picture of this child as evil incarnate, malevolent and foul.

Soon after Mrs. C. began treatment, she became pregnant again. This was an unwanted "accidental" pregnancy, and very disturbing to the patient. (It was quickly apparent that conception occurred the night after she knew treatment with me would begin.) As the pregnancy progressed, the patient's rage toward her daughter increased. Mrs. C. hated her pregnancy, but would not consider abortion. The feelings about the pregnancy were suppressed and repressed, and for the most part came out only after direct questioning. In contrast, she was conscious only of her rage at Kitty. When the fetal movements appeared, Mrs. C. experienced a great increase in anxiety and insomnia. It was not possible to induce Mrs. C. to recognize her obvious rage at her own mother. Kitty, and, to a lesser extent, she herself, remained the main object of her rage. She was finally prevailed upon to send Kitty away to her mother (in a distant city). Only then did the self and the fetus become objects of conscious anger; simultaneously her depression also became more evident.

One month before her delivery date, after Kitty had been away for several weeks, Mrs. C. went to visit her mother, planning to take Kitty home with her. When she arrived, she had a furious fight with her mother, went to her old room in her mother's house, and swallowed a full bottle of sleeping pills which she had secretly obtained four months previously. She was never revived. The suicide note to the husband stated: "It is best for Kitty and you." This was the only time I had ever known her to consider what would be good for Kitty.

In this patient, there was an extreme confusion of the identities of herself, daughter, fetus, and mother. The mobility of cathexis was in part a measure of her regression, indicating the degree of primary-process ascendancy. This mobility also served the function of preserving the union with mother, even to the point of re-creating an intrauterine life, and facilitated the easy substitution of the objects of the drives. The libidinization was apparent in Mrs. C.'s difficulty in separating from her mother, Kitty, and the fetus. In her urgent need for this union, she refused to consider abortion. Her aggression was initially directed to Kitty and herself, with suicide or murder being a very real danger. When Kitty was finally removed for reasons of safety, Mrs. C.'s attacks on herself and the fetus increased. Her open outburst of anger at her own mother was followed by the fatal attack on herself. The suicide note suggested that the wish was to destroy the "bad" mother, in order to protect the weak child (and the husband who was *also* the weak child).

During the period of violent attacks on her child, Mrs. C. was relatively less depressed. Self-criticism for these attacks was unusual. While the patient was pregnant, the attacks on Kitty became even *more* violent. The depression became more prominent and severe, although it was still inconstant. When Kitty was *not* available, the depression deepened, the self-criticism mounted, and anxiety over the previously disregarded pregnancy increased; i.e., the introject, earlier displaced outward, was reincorporated. Mrs. C.'s sadistic mistreatment of the child was an expression of the sadistic superego attacking the introjected object. Since the child *replaces* the self representation, the affect of depression may be absent or diminished (although it is usually present in the interval between attacks on the child).

The person who needs a scapegoat to attack may be utilizing a similar mechanism. This seems to be true in those situations in which the person clearly holds onto the scapegoat and cannot abandon it; i.e., when there is also an obvious libidinal tie. In such situations, one finds that the unacceptable impulses of the attacker are being projected onto the victim; in addition, there also occurs a displacement of that part of the self representation which would otherwise be assaulted by the superego as the source of these disowned impulses. If the victim is lynched or burned, the attacker can for the moment feel purified and cleansed. But a *new* scapegoat must soon be found; otherwise the introject will reappear *inside* and cause an increase in guilt and self-criticism. The same phenomenon is seen in certain people who temporarily have a good feeling following catharsis of a so-called "toxic" stool.

This phenomenon can also be observed in certain types of sado-masochistic marital situations, some of which are curiously stable (Stein, 1956). "When we have an opportunity to observe both, the patient and his partner, we frequently find that they live in a peculiar symbiotic love relationship to each other; they feed on each other" (Jacobson, 1953, p. 67).

The depressive constellation of a sadistic superego and its willing partner of a masochistic ego is fragmented, projected, and displaced, and then acted out by the marital partners. One partner accepts the masochistic position with regard to the spouse's sadistic attitude. One partner plays the role of the sadistic superego, the other the role of the bad introject. The motivations of each partner are quite different. One is trying to ward off the feelings of depression, and does this by displacing onto the spouse that part of his self representation which represents the introject. The other partner is trying to avoid destruction of the object, and so substitutes himself for the object. Since his self representation continues to be the masochistic victim (albeit of a projected superego), he experiences depression. Mrs. B. (Case 2) lived in such a marital situation. When she accepted the attacks and criticisms of her husband, which were obviously more appropriate to himself than to her, his depression lifted. When she was able to disengage herself from this sadomasochistic relationship and refused to allow herself to be used as his "bad part," his depression increased.

SUMMARY

Three variations of depression have been presented. The attempt to explain these phenomena utilized the concepts of ego psychology and intrapsychic structure. The variants of the depressive process reflect a hierarchy of object relations which is determined by the particular developmental level of object and self representations involved in the conflict.

1. *Hypochondriasis—depression without depressed affect.* The experience of the affect of depression requires that the self representation be the object of self-criticism. Thus, in some clinical manifestations of depression, such as hypochondriasis, the affect of depression may be absent, because the body-ego part, rather than other elements, of the self representation is being attacked. In hypochondriasis, the main consistent affect is *anxiety* rather than depression.

2. *Depression Without Object Loss—masochistic submission to the object.* A special variation of depression that does not involve introjection of a lost object occurs in certain relationships. Here the depression is a function of the *continued* relationship with the object. A depressed mood does exist, but the intrapsychic attack is directed less toward an incorporated lost object and more toward a part of the self representation, which replaces and is quite distinct from the object representation. This syndrome seems to result from specific difficulties in the separation-individuation phase of development.

3. *Depression With Rage—projection and displacement of the introject.* Fragmentation of the depressive constellation with projection and displacement of its component parts from the self representation onto the object representations makes it possible to ward off the affect of depression. Some phenomena of pregnancy, postpartum suicide or infanticide, sadomasochistic marital situations, etc., may be clinical expressions of this mental mechanism.

BIBLIOGRAPHY

Abraham, K. (1911), Notes on the Psychoanalytical Investigation and Treatment of Manic-depressive Insanity and Allied Conditions. *Selected Papers on Psycho-Analysis.* London: Hogarth Press, 1927, pp. 137-156.

Asch, S. S. (1960), Mental and Emotional Problems in Pregnancy. *Medical, Surgical and Gynecological Complications of Pregnancy,* ed. A. F. Guttmacher and J. J. Rovinsky. Baltimore: Williams & Wilkins, pp. 375-385.

Bibring, E. (1953), The Mechanism of Depression. In: *Affective Disorders,* ed. P. Greenacre. New York: International Universities Press, pp. 13-48.

Freud, S. (1891), *On Aphasia.* New York: International Universities Press, 1953.

—— (1917), Mourning and Melancholia, *Standard Edition*, 14:243-258. London: Hogarth Press, 1957.

Heiman, M. (1962), Functional Uterine Bleeding as a Psychosomatic Disorder: Separation Bleeding, *Psychosomatic Obstetrics, Gynecology and Endocrinology*, ed. W. S. Kroger. Springfield, Ill.: Thomas, pp. 262-271.

Jacobson, E. (1953), Contribution to the Metapsychology of Cyclothymic Depression. In: *Affective Disorders*, ed. P. Greenacre. New York: International Universities Press, pp. 49-83.

Kaufman, M. R., Lehrman, S., Franzblau, A., Tabbat, S., Weinroth, L., & Friedman, S. (1959), Psychiatric Findings in Admissions to a Medical Service in a General Hospital. *J. Mount Sinai Hosp.*, 26:160-170.

Kempe, C. H. et al. (1962), The Battered-Child Syndrome. *J. Amer. Med. Assn.*, 181:17-24.

Lewin, B. D. (1961), Reflections on Depression. *This Annual*, 16:321-331.

Loewald, H. W. (1962), Internalization, Separation, Mourning, and the Superego. *Psa. Quart.*, 31:483-504.

Mahler, M. S. & Furer, M. (1960), Observations on Research Regarding the 'Symbiotic Syndrome' of Infantile Psychosis. *Psa. Quart.*, 29:317-327.

Mannucci, M., Friedman, S., & Kaufman, M. R. (1961), Survey of Patients Who Have Been Attending Non-psychiatric Out-patient Department Services for 10 years or Longer. *J. Mount Sinai Hosp.*, 18:32-52.

Pleshette, N., Asch, S. S., & Chase, J. (1956), A Study of Anxieties During Pregnancy, Labor, and the Early and Late Puerperium. *Bull. N.Y. Acad. Med.*, 32:436-455.

Stein, M. H. (1956), The Marriage Bond. *Psa. Quart.*, 25:238-259.

Van Ophuijsen, J. H. W. (1920), On the Origin of the Feeling of Persecution. *Int. J. Psa.*, 1:235-261.

PATTERNS OF ANGER

GUSTAV BYCHOWSKI, M.D.

Observations of the behavior of children and adults, so-called normal, neurotic or psychotic, lead us to believe that anger may be one of the principal emotions experienced by man. From observations of infants one may conclude that anger is also the first emotion felt by the child. Vague and diffuse at first, like the uncoordinated movements of a displeased infant, anger appears as an expression of unpleasure without focus or object. I would assume that at this early stage it is difficult, if not impossible, to distinguish between anger and distress.

Infants and young children manifesting symptoms of separation anxiety in its various forms and shadings show anger and rage mixed with anxiety. In many instances anger prevails when the initial display of distress fails to achieve the desired objective; the mother leaves the child either literally or symbolically, e.g., by not dedicating herself completely to him, continuing some activity of her own, paying attention to another person, etc.

In such instances anxiety becomes, as it were, overshadowed by anger. Motor manifestations of the latter become a prototype of reactions to distress at later stages of development. Kicking, biting, spitting, scratching, tearing, and, in some more regressive situations, resorting to urinary or intestinal elimination develop with a lightning speed when the wish of the child or, for that matter, of an older individual is not satisfied completely and immediately. Significantly enough, such a wish may simply aim at the mother's constant and fully absorbed presence or at her gratifying some other desire and thus proving her true love and devotion. Through various symbiotic and associative connections similar reactions may be provoked by

Clinical Professor of Psychiatry, Downstate Medical Center, State University of New York. Mount Sinai Hospital, Institute of Psychiatry.

other frustrations or deprivations which to the unconscious ego have the implication of separation, rejection, and lack of love. This construction holds true for a great many manifestations of individual and collective psychopathology.

Gradually, with the development of psychic structure and the beginning differentiation of the ego, the first vague perception of the somatic self allows the infant to focus the feeling of unpleasure around the perception of bodily sensations and bodily needs. In this way anger may become focused on certain somatic zones and organs which may alternately be the source of unpleasure or of delight. At that early stage general feelings of unpleasure and consequently of vague anger are probably still more frequent than such focused anger. The decisive step in the structural development of anger occurs when the perception of persons and objects becomes possible, thus laying the foundation for the development of object representations and object cathexis. This new step leads to the establishment of associative links between anger and objects, anger and the idea of an external cause—a formulation that closely resembles Spinoza's famous definition: "Hatred is the feeling of pain accompanied by the idea of an external cause."

Obviously, the persons closest to the infant are responsible for satisfying his essential needs. While they thus provide pleasure, they inevitably must also deny some gratifications. This, then, makes them the source of unpleasure and hence objects of anger. For this reason the early objects emerging in the dim and vague world of the infant can be truly called love-hate objects. They are hate objects because in the infant's awareness they cause his feelings of pain and unpleasure instead of relieving them without delay and with magic omnipotence.

In denying this service to the child they make him feel his helplessness. This experience lays the foundations for the essential association between the feeling of helplessness caused by a person in power and anger-rage directed at that person. As the behaviorist Watson put it, in a natural and almost classical limitation: "Rage is a reaction to the impairment of the freedom of movement."

An important corollary to the development outlined above is the early establishment of a dichotomy between the good and the bad objects. Obviously the former neither withholds nor delays gratification while the latter denies it more often than gratifies it, and thus has to be forced to provide gratification by coercing it into submission.

This definition implies not only anger but anger acted out as overpowering violence, since in this case the essentially weaker creature, the child, attempts to force the stronger, but bad object into gratifying his wishes as unconditionally as possible. We know that under certain conditions the dichotomy between bad and good object persists and leads to the preservation of the representation of the bad object in the unconscious, isolated from the rest of the conscious ego. This process interferes with the establishment of positive and integrated object representations and thus threatens the integration of the ego. It naturally occurs in individuals who have an inborn tendency to split, or who receive contradictory love- and hate-bearing messages in their early lives, or in whom endowment and environment interact in specific ways.

Since the bad object representations remain an important depository of the original primitive anger, its vicissitudes should be studied. These become even more complicated when new elements are introduced into the original dyadic situation between mother and child. There is the appearance of the other parent, who in the beginning usually remains more in the background and who becomes another object of ambivalent cathexis, a source of pleasure as well as unpleasure: in this way the foundation is laid for the complexities of the oedipal situation; and in most cases, there are other new arrivals, a new family member, who takes away a good part of the mother's attention and relegates his predecessor, at least for the time being, to a secondary role.

In these most general terms I have covered some basic situations responsible for the emergence of anger, envy, hatred, jealousy, and for the establishment of the representations of the bad objects as a focus of these emotions.

We learn from the analysis of severely disturbed persons, such as borderline or latent psychotics, narcissistic character disorders, generally speaking, persons with what I call a psychotic core or a primitive archaic ego nucleus, that in them the original object representations remained intact. In particular, the bad objects retain their original characteristics. In these cases I propose to speak of the archaic objects. We find that the latter are a preferred depository of primitive original anger, and thus a source of possible release in the form of violent acting out.

A few examples will serve to illustrate the concept of the archaic object, some of its implications, and some of the ego's ways of dealing with primitive, original anger.

Case 1

Mr. X, a college student, in his early twenties, developed a pattern of persistently showing up late for his 8 A.M. session. Repeated discussions revealed that when his alarm clock rang he turned it off and went to sleep. Upon awakening he felt remorse; an inner voice blamed him and he remembered that when he was admonished by his parents in his childhood he used to say: "Don't scream at me." He addressed the same warning to me although he realized that I did not even raise my voice. Yet, this was what he anticipated and "heard" because he obviously confused me with the original distorted representations of his parents. They, too, never really screamed at him. On a recent home visit he arranged with his father for a morning visit to an art museum, but when his mother woke him up he addressed her with the very same words which his parents remembered so well from his childhood: "Don't scream at me." On recalling and recounting this scene he experienced old anger and rage.

Mr. X had to admit that his parents never screamed, nor did they resort to violence of any kind. In fact, they were pleasant, highly civilized, and astonishingly tolerant and permissive. However, their images were blurred by the admixture of his own projected hostility. The distortion of the actual object representations by the confusion with the archaic objects colored Mr. X's perception of his parents and of persons in his actual experience.

Since his mother was a treacherous Amazon who "deserted him" for his two younger brothers, she and other women appeared as hostile and unloving, and he felt compelled to punish them by degrading them through sexual possession and abandonment. In his fantasy he expected of them that he would be reborn and returned to the lost paradise of maternal love. Yet, at the same time, since they were the representatives of the bad mother, he saw himself in fantasy entering the vagina as a mouse and leaving it through the anal orifice as a bat or some other demoniacal animal.

In analysis Mr. X vividly recalled a scene when he so annoyed his mother, who was nursing his little brother, that in exasperation she threw him out of the room and slammed the door. He then threw himself on the floor, kicked, screamed, and hit his head violently against the floor.

Rage at his mother and his younger brother remained one of the dominant elements of his personality. The oral coloring of this early rage appeared in the image of the woman as a vampire bent on destroying him. On the other hand, in reversing this situation the patient saw himself as a bat or some other animal who would degrade and destroy the woman and abandon her as soon as she began to show signs of attachment. The interchange of the oral-sadistic imagery between himself and the archaic mother shows an important characteristic of the archaic object. The archaic image of the self and the archaic images of the original love-hate objects undergo a process of interpenetration as a result of early projections and introjections. In the last analysis the coalescence of both archaic images is at the basis of a symbiotic relationship, which I shall discuss later.

To continue with the clinical illustration. In our further discussions of Mr. X's lateness I mentioned that I was disappointed in his obstinate clinging to this symptom. He was impressed by this, but in the next session described his afterthoughts: he felt that I wanted to trick him, like his parents, gain his confidence, in order to subdue him more effectively.

Additional material from the first stage of this analysis offered further illustrations of the image of the mother as a domineering, depriving, and emasculating monster, and of the father as a castrating killer—images which became completely modified in the course of further analysis and which, obviously, had nothing to do with reality. Anger was directed at both archaic images and the actual substitutes. Since they were the source and the representatives of the primitive superego, the commandments and the prohibitions, they themselves seemed to be objects of violent anger and opposition. This manifested itself in the patient's self-defeating and self-destructive acting out, in the course of his studies, and in the style of his love life.

Elements of oral aggression prevailed in the construction of the archaic objects, with subsequent additions from other stages of development. This predominance could be traced back to the frustration caused by the arrival at brief intervals, of his two younger brothers and, still further back, to pyloric stenosis from which he suffered in the first six weeks of his life and for which he was operated.

Narcissistic vulnerability manifested itself in various ways, among others in violent anger at whoever was supposedly depriving him of what he felt was coming to him or whoever was forcing him to accept something for which he was not ready at that particular moment. While these occasions for anger presented themselves in various situations, analysis showed they were experienced with particular poignancy on the oral level. A teacher was forcing him to listen, i.e., to absorb material; this was an "oppression" which he resisted with anger and violence. At other times he did not receive the praise and the mark he had expected, or a young coed refused to meet him or to yield without much ado to his entreaties. These were occasions for distress and anger.

During examinations Mr. X would spend too much time on the first question: he had to show his superior knowledge and could not admit to being limited by the exigencies of time imposed by the instructor. In this way the latter became fused with the general idea of a hostile parental object. As such he had to be resisted and fought against. To accept him would mean to renounce one's birthright, to be confused with the anonymous crowd of common people —his younger brothers. Not fighting and resisting might lead to renunciation of his peculiar grandiose image of the self.

In analysis resistance manifested itself frequently as anger at interpretations which seemed to attack this bastion of primitive narcissism and reduce his philosophical aspirations and speculations to the level of infantile fantasies. Could he really and truly acknowledge the infantile origin of his lofty ambitions and superman feelings?

Mr. X fought with vehemence against such surrender and such degredation. Anger at his parents and his brothers, accumulated in years of conflict, did not spare his own self, which became an object of remorse no less violent than his anger at all his adversaries. In his dreams and fantasies he saw himself as Prometheus punished by the gods for wresting from them their jealously guarded secret, or as

Icarus who deployed the wings fashioned by his father, but in disobeying his injunctions came too close to the blazing sun and was hurled down as it were, as a punishment for his hybris. The reference to the Icarus myth obviously reflected the growing insight into his oedipal conflict and the self-pity which was a close companion of his anger and frustration.

The aspect of anger directed at the same time against the original love-hate objects (or their substitute) and against the self will be discussed later. At present I wish to stress that this mechanism which led to fantasies of suicide was based, in the last analysis, on elements of early identification and persisting partial symbiosis with both parental objects. To deny this closeness Mr. X mobilized his anger against both parents and remained in emotional isolation from his peers of either sex. He could allow himself neither love nor friendship.

This mobilization of hostility in the struggle for emancipation from symbiotic attachments is strikingly illustrated by the following case.

Case 2

Mrs. Y, a professional married woman in her thirties, sought analytic help because of crippling phobic symptoms of long standing. In her analysis it appeared that she had built and preserved the image of her mother as a witch and a prospective killer. It could be shown that this nucleus had initiated the persecutory symptoms which she had experienced in her first summer on a college campus: she feared that some of her fellow students would poison her. An additional source of this paranoid nucleus was the image of her younger sister to whom she was bound by the ties of a deeply ambivalent symbiotic relationship. Similar ties bound her not only to her mother and her sister but to her husband and children as well. In a dream she saw her mother as a composite of Lady Macbeth and Juliet, that is of the romantic image of herself and the ambitious, lusting-for-power murderess who could never cleanse her hands from the stain of blood. This image was a clear result of the interpenetration of the archaic image of the mother and the image of her own self with its destructive impulses of manifold origin.

In her identification with her mother, Mrs. Y emanated, as it were, the same hostility which she felt was coming at her from her mother, as though by some dangerous rays of atomic radiation. It appeared in analysis that she was as afraid of her mother's anger as she was of the effects of her own hostility. The former led to serious hypochondriacal fears: cancer or other incurable diseases would in turn affect various organs and systems of her body. However, her own hostility would destroy in succession her children, her sister, her mother, and her husband.

As a defense against these murderous wishes, Mrs. Y developed fleeting, though extremely painful, bouts of anxiety concerning the health of her various family members. I repeatedly observed that whenever she became aware of her symbiotic ties and her own devouring feelings for her children and the necessity to free them and herself from this bondage, she mobilized violent anger at them which she then found hard to control. She would follow, glued to the telephone, with extreme anxiety the course of the plane carrying her daughter home from college and as soon as the daughter had safely arrived at home Mrs. Y wished that the girl would move out. It became obvious that the patient was reliving her hostility in her anxiety about her daughter's health.

Her children's social successes provoked violent envy, camouflaged by anxiety. This envy centered equally around the budding loveliness of her younger daughter and around the emerging manliness of her sons. Thus penis envy was as important as the envy of femininity and combined with the despair of not being loved as a woman. While in her dreams she would kill her sons, after having destroyed their virility, upon awakening she would be seized by "insane" anxiety about their health.

Orality emerged as an underlying core of some transient symptoms Mrs. Y developed during the analysis. As a reaction to any real or imaginary slight, deprivation, or frustration on the pseudo-masculine as well as the feminine front, she regressed rapidly to the stage of oral incorporation. She compulsively ate huge quantities of ice cream or other sweets or foods at inappropriate times. She then became somnolent, found it hard to wake up and get up in the morning, slumbered during her sessions, and despaired of the future. Once she described how on the previous day after a normal meal, she sneaked to the icebox and without any pleasure proceeded to devour a large container of ice cream. I asked her what she would do if I was there and would try to stop her and to take the ice cream from her. She replied, with great anger, "I would kill you." This led to a rich cluster of memories and associations which dealt with the breast and penis envy. The mother became the denying, punishing witch, while the father became the teasing, sneering, never-pleased ogre who never gave her any love or recognition. The symbolism of oral envy and hatred directed toward the mother emerged in a childhood memory in which she and her sister, with two visiting boys, had eaten up a box full of candy which her father had brought for her mother.

One source of rage at the mother was the envy of her successive pregnancies; Mrs. Y was the oldest child.

While this envy and anger were being worked through in analysis, the patient gratified the wish for a child in an autoplastic way by a pseudopregnancy with changes in her body, massive fluid retention, and nausea. In dreams she would experience delivery.

Here then we see that the primitive ego, as one of the ways of dealing with anger and rage, renounces object gratification, withdraws from the object or objects, and tries to resort to some form of primitive autarchy. During such brief periods, the patient would become depressed, apathetic, and withdrawn.

In this brief clinical vignette I wish to emphasize once more the role of symbiotic relationships which pervade and underlie all the affective bonds of the patient. In her attempt to liberate herself from this bondage she had displayed anger in various forms throughout her life. What in childhood led to temper tantrums and fights with her parents led in later years to conflicts with school authorities and finally to anger and indignation at all the elements of the Establishment. This included, of course, the authorities, the analyst, the medical profession, etc.

The parental imagos, incorporated as ambivalent introjects, remained both objects and sources of intense hostility. As the source of the superego they drove her on to early achievements, while denying her satisfaction in the area of female as well as masculine pursuits. Constant guilt feelings and dissatisfaction accompanied every achievement, so that she could as little enjoy her marriage and family life as her considerable professional success. Indeed, she was both the

"Angry Young Man" and the "Angry Young Woman" of our generation.

It should not surprise us that anger was for a long time the prevailing mood of her transference and the predominant mode of her resistance. In her attempt to deny this by way of projection, she attributed anger to the analyst, accused me of scolding her with my interpretations. Evidently in these projections she not only attributed to me her own hostile impulses but also the hostility which she felt her parents were hammering at her.

She remained so closely identified and allied with her hostile mother that on numerous occasions she echoed her mother's hostility in her dealings with her own family and in her painfully obsessive remorses. The effect of both parental introjects could be perceived clearly in the destructive and inhibiting impact of her superego and its interference with enjoyment on all levels of instinctual and sublimatory gratifications. She could not allow herself to be intimate with her husband when she was or had been angry at him. Nor could she enjoy reading when this "innocent" activity mobilized guilt feelings as a result of internalized criticism of her mother who was "working herself to death for her ungrateful children."

As I have previously mentioned, in the course of analysis episodes of transient bulimia were accompanied by bouts of depression with somnolence, feelings of despair, and thoughts of death. This was the only way in which she could atone for her attempts to emancipate herself from the parental introjects and for the release of anger which accompanied this painful process.

In this patient we see one of the better known vicissitudes of hostility—the turning of anger against the self. The parental imagos, incorporated as a punitive superego, release their aggressiveness which cannot be sufficiently discharged either on the original objects or on such substitutes as the husband and the analyst or, to be more exact, these discharges occur spasmodically while the punitive aspect of the superego still holds sway. Under the impact of this configuration the patient herself becomes the object of her own wrath. In destroying her parental introjects she depletes herself of what to her appears to be the most important content; and by the same token she forfeits any chance of reconciliation, that is, of being loved by her parents and thus being granted a lease on life.

Among the conflicts in which anger involves the vulnerable ego of the child, we have to count the conflict between activity and passivity. When he experiences intense anger at a parental figure, the child may feel intense signal anxiety. Does he not intend to hurt or to destroy the parent or at least, to defy and to turn away from him? Yet, it is this parent who is not only the sole purveyor of the gratification of the child's vital needs, this parent is also the only source of loving care. Thus, hurting him may deprive the child, if not of sustenance, then at least of love. Abandonment, desertion, and existence in an arctic loveless climate loom as the ultimate fate and supreme punishment. This anxiety may assume a different aspect and lead to a different solution depending on the sex and personality of the parent, and the stage of development of the child. For instance, a boy who has reached the phallic stage and begins to show growing signs of independence may encounter encouragement from his father but signs of rejection from his mother; because of her own narcissism she can "love" him only as long as he functions as a part of her and idolizes her. Or, to take another configuration, the boy's defiance of the father may provoke the latter's anger and cause castration anxiety. The boy then may find solace in the mother and lean on her heavily, a situation which, in its turn, may result in such widely divergent solution as feminine identification with renunciation of masculinity, or a preparation for the oedipal phase through curbing and sublimation of hostility and lifting of the anaclitic love for the mother to a building of a rich and complex object relationship.

In all these and many other solutions, the conflict between activity and passivity comes into focus. In addition to solutions resulting from the clear choice of passivity as a defense against anxiety, or of the taking up the challenge of activity, we see individuals who in these situations of crisis oscillate between both ends of the spectrum. It is my impression that this factor may become an important contribution to the origins of the symptom or the state of depersonalization.

Case 3

The following clinical vignette serves to illustrate the role of anger in the origins of depersonalization. No general conclusions can of course be drawn from this single observation.

Mr. N, a professional man in his forties, sought help for the distress he felt in the course of dissolving his second marriage. Anxiety, difficulty in concentration, and early signs of depersonalization developed more sharply after the termination of his marriage and the initiation of a love affair. Thereafter full-blown depersonalization and feelings of unreality dominated the clinical picture. These feelings extended to his ideas, emotions, and sexuality and culminated in doubts about his potency and in the termination of his liaison. Mr. N noticed that something peculiar happened to him when he said good-bye to me and I turned away. "This makes it unreal. There should be a constant fusion between the two of us."

However, where can one find such an absolute union in love and understanding? Surely not in professional friends and colleagues, most of them rigid members of the Establishment. Mr. N was angry at them during their discussions and meetings and felt inclined to protest and oppose them, yet was frightened by the possibility of scorn and rejection. However, this made him "feel hollow on the inside," a feeling which he re-experienced whenever he discussed his rage at his colleagues and friends with me or whenever he allowed himself to feel and to express anger at me. In the transference and in the analysis of dreams, we could see most clearly and poignantly the ego's reaction to the dangers of rage—an immediate shift to passivity, ultimately leading to the surrender of the ego feeling.

His anxiety in feeling his mounting anger and rage toward the analyst was such that he could alleviate it only by not taking seriously the entire analytic situation. Then "everything becomes a joke" and he must not take his own feelings seriously. Unfortunately, however, this also led to his derealizing my interpretations, our whole relationship, and the eventual outcome of analysis. Yet with his friends, like with me, Mr. N oscillated toward the other pole: he felt that he had to endear himself to them, to bribe them, as it were, through the surrender of his self. This shift to passivity led to the painful loss of his ego feeling. While leaving a particularly good analytic session, he felt the urge to throw his arm around me and recoiled, frightened by what he considered an onrush of homosexuality.

Genetic factors of Mr. N's history throw some light on the role of anger in his love life. As a child Mr. N felt that he could not allow himself to put his mother in the wrong, nor could he in any way consider himself superior. Yet at an early age he began to feel that he was smarter, but his mother would blow up and "act crazy" if one criticized or accused her. "She frightened me with her contorted face: she appeared as dangerous as my angry father; they became confused as a source of danger."

Mr. N's mother would change her feelings so rapidly that he could not count on her. To his anger or attempts at autonomy she reacted with anger and withdrawal. Mr. N found out that self-assertion was dangerous. "I had to suppress my anger at her as the price I had to pay for my safety." As a defense against his rage at and his devaluation of his mother, he built her up as an idealized object and dedicated himself to her service. With the help of this mechanism he could in the preoedipal period preserve her as an object of anaclitic love and worship, and could secure her constant enveloping love by allowing her domination and renouncing his autonomy. On the oedipal level he further developed this "mythology" to cover up his rage and scorn of her and, by derivation, of the female. In this development mother became an ideal of purity and wisdom, contrary to his "real" suppressed image of her as a silly, limited, narcissistic coquette. He remembered that his mother would sulk or pretend that she did not love him. "How shaky were the foundations of my existence!"

At the same time he not only had to deny his sexual impulses but give a further repressive push to his hostility. A nice, sweet boy— this was the image he had to create of himself, while his rage against his mother was mounting as was his anger about the game he felt compelled to play to appease her seductiveness. These processes led to the regressive moves, with orality and cutaneous erogeneity reasserting themselves, elements of which colored his later relationships with women.

These developments found support in the outcome of his oedipal conflicts. Mr. N described his father as an aggressive, tough person, who wanted to see his son grow up as a "little man" and who was disappointed to see that his son was sensitive and vulnerable. The boy feared his father's wrath and, under the impact of castration fear, increasingly tended to adopt maternal identifications. Thus, a circular reaction developed between the father's expressed anger and the son's suppressed anger and fear. The beneficiary from this was the mother who could perserve intact the image of her darling boy. Mr. N's father rejected the boy because he was not manly enough: not being able to gain love in this way, the child resorted to submission, that is, to a further curbing of his anger.

In the course of his sexual development Mr. N resorted to various devices in order to break away from "the no-man's land" in which he found himself caught: submission to and idealization of the mother, with underlying hostility on the one hand, and renunciation of his masculine self on the other. This "no-man's land" could also be defined as an ambiguous region between symbiosis and full individuation. He felt that he had to break away from the idealized maternal introject, since this bondage meant insanity. Thus, his first marriage was to an infantile woman who leaned on him parasitically.

In his second marriage he broke away from his mother only to build up a new version of a maternal introject. This woman was considerably older than he was. With her, he dreamed of establishing a paradisaical existence that would exclude the rest of the world (this meant, at least to his wife's mind, also Mr. N's children from his first marriage). Here, too, his anger broke through the camouflage of romantic idealization. He felt that he had to break away from this encirclement if he wanted to preserve, or rather to regain, his sanity.

In his love affair, whose vicissitudes could be followed in analysis, Mr. N attempted in vain to avoid former errors. In his beloved he re-created the idealized maternal imago: he wanted to serve her and thus earn her complete and total love and acceptance. Yet, here too, anger lurked beneath idealization and was easily provoked by anything resembling rejection. The distressing experience of depersonalization occurred at moments when he oscillated between anger and assertion of male autonomy on the one hand, and self-sacrificing submission on the other.

In his analysis Mr. N realized that he was always frightened of real, independent women, while his passivity served as a cover for his "viciousness," that is, murderous hostility. It was this violent rage that became camouflaged in his original submissiveness to his mother: he was unable to change his murderous wishes into the wish for mastery and domination. In suppressing the former he felt compelled to curb his actively masculine attitudes and resort to passivity as the best possible solution of the conflict. However, in his love affair, as well as in the analytic situation, he realized that if he wanted to snap out of depersonalization, he had to "make himself angry" and to express it. He could afford to risk it in analysis; yet the danger seemed too great in his love relationship, in which he suffered from increasing depersonalization, that is, from de-egotization of his feelings and of his self.

Mr. N felt that in order to re-establish, to regain his lost identity, he had "to squeeze the last drop of slave blood from himself" (quotation from Chekhov) that is, to give up his tendency to submission and passivity. It was a frightening experience for N to realize, in the course of his analysis, that whenever he perceived his mistress as a little girl, he wanted to kill her: he felt that she was encroaching on him and wished to merge with him, a wish which came dangerously close to his own.

Memories from the fourth and fifth year of life revealed his rage at his mother for playing with him in the parental bed after the father got up, and then letting him down by turning away. It was at that age that he began to feel uncomfortable with girls: he blushed and was tongue-tied. He remembered that he used to accompany his mother on her charity missions when she was distributing clothes to poor people. He was angry at her for expecting gratitude and thus "robbing them of their identity."

In the course of his analysis Mr. N relived his anger at his mother in various ways: in his love affairs, in the transference, and, finally, in direct confrontation after his mother returned from a long trip abroad. Mr. N re-experienced most of his early feelings and could work through his rage at her and his various reactions and defensive maneuvers. While these had been initiated in his infantile relationship with his mother, they set the model for his future interaction with his father at the peak of the early oedipal situation and in adolescence.

Mr. N's rage was his "central problem": "If a real me came out of me, I would be a sane killer. How come I do not fall off the bridge while I am driving?"

As a first line of defense the ego repressed hostility and with it the attempts at self-assertion and affirmation. In assuming the image of the self as a sweet little boy he avoided the dangers threatening

him from the abandonment by the mother and castration by the
angry father. Another aspect of this defensive maneuver was making
himself helpless and thus throwing himself at the mercy of the adults.
He felt that this led to "deviousness," because he could then insinu-
ate himself into their good graces and thus benefit from the "fleshpots
of Egypt." However, this process led to the second line of defense:
derealization and depersonalization. These reactions helped him to
deny his weakness: it was not *he* who allowed himself various maneuvers of compliance and surrender. This reaction became conspicuous
in his dealings with men and women in actuality, and in the analytic
situation. "My secret power was to allow the other person to possess
me. After that I can say no and detach myself like a woman withdrawing after an apparent surrender."

It was a momentous step for Mr. N when he could allow himself
to experience and to express anger at me. He felt that he did not
count with me unless he could have my complete approval. "I stand
convicted here if I am different from you." The same held true for
his relationship with a woman: "I have to be her, I cannot remain
myself. Otherwise she will kick my balls." The frightening experience
of loneliness seemed to be the price he had to pay for being a person.
In going back to his infantile struggle for individuation, Mr. N was
painfully regaining and constructing a feeling of the self that could
not be surrendered and denied. The experience of unreality and
depersonalization reappeared in the analysis whenever he allowed
himself to express rage at me and thus provided us with firsthand
evidence of the origins of his basic illness.

The deflection of anger from the original objects toward the self
is a well-known vicissitude of hostility and is hardly in need of further documentation. If I mention a few fragments from the following
observation, it is to demonstrate the destructive power of a drive
which has been invested in the binding shackles of a relentless and
punitive superego.

Case 4

Miss V, a thirty-year-old professional woman, sought analytic help
for a depression which developed following the loss of her mother.
After a period of initial improvement the depression deepened in
the course of her analysis. Unfortunate external circumstances and

the patient's stubborn refusal to be hospitalized (she lived alone) resulted in a suicidal attempt. She was saved after a coma of three days' duration and resumed her analysis, which was ultimately successful. The affect of anger was so prevalent that, even upon her awakening from coma and the realization that she was alive, Miss V was more angry at us for prolonging her hospitalization than she was appreciative of our efforts and merits in rescuing her. She disclosed that she tried to kill herself in anger. She was furious at her father, her friends and colleagues, and last but not least at her analyst. In a moment of final despair and helpless rage she decided to put an end to all her misery and to punish all those whom she considered responsible for it.

A brief outline of these various vectors of anger will offer an insight into the complex orchestration of hostility. Miss V was angry at all of us for trying to discipline her erratic behavior and for frustrating her in various ways. Unresolved oedipal problems were a source of anger at her father, her physician friend, and her analyst. Her father was in the process of separating from his second wife (his first wife, the patient's mother, died a few years earlier) and starting a new relationship. Her physician friend disappointed her in her fantasied erotic expectations. The same was, of course, true of her analyst; moreover, I aroused her wrath by my attempts to control her psychotic behavior and my insistence on hospitalizing her. I was also trying to interfere with her magic belief that she could increase her work load and reduce below the minimum her sleep and her food intake.

Yet, behind all these sources of anger, her burning wrath was directed primarily at the greatest love of her life, her mother, by now several years dead. Miss V was angry at her for having abandoned her, and this anger lay beneath the grief at her passing. However, even in the past, at times with full awareness, at times unconsciously, Miss V had been angry at her mother for exerting her strong authority and curbing her lively and temperamental daughter. It was the mother who played the dominant role in the family and who instilled in the little girl ambitions and aspirations exceeding by far the modest circumstances under which the family lived and struggled for existence. In brief, it was the mother who was mainly responsible for instilling in Miss V a strict punitive superego and a demanding ego ideal.

This process had started with premature toilet training and the imposition of anal repressions and taboos which, transformed and sublimated in later years, were rationalized and justified by the dire conditions of the family economy. Ambitions to learn and excel served to curb and to repress the libidinal impulses and, in conjunction with economic restrictions, to build up an ideal of ascetic self-restraint. The mother, who herself had little education, imparted her own frustrated ambitions to Miss V, who went through school with flying colors and became highly proficient in her profession. Finally, all these strict principles found their ultimate sanction and rationalization when Miss V's mother induced the child to join a religious sect known for its strict unrelenting orthodoxy. While this line of development required constant self-restraint and discipline, which remained permanent derivatives of maternal aggression, the mother endorsed them by a system of rewards and punishments. She forced her daughter to accept the maternal injunctions without protestations, since talking back and showing displeasure were frowned upon and led to increased punishment and discipline.

Eventually Miss V became the only member of her family who had a higher education and a substantial earning power. At the same time Miss V's aging mother went through bouts of depression and physical illness. Miss V was increasingly cast in the role of a parent toward her mother, the latter becoming, as it were, the daughter's ward and child. Ultimately Miss V renounced her feminine aspirations and saw herself as a missionary, a bearer of high moral, religious, and social ideals. All this was possible only at the cost of great effort, restraint, and repression of libidinal and aggressive impulses.

With the passing of her mother Miss V lost a good deal of gratification which she had received from the mother's adoring love. At the same time with the loss of this source and prototype of her superego and ego ideal, she found it more difficult to maintain the repression of the instinctual drives. As a reaction there set in an increase of compulsive symptomatology rationalized and defended by moralistic, sectarian religiosity.

While the process of mourning was laid bare by psychoanalysis, the maternal imago became open for inspection and the ego was increasingly flooded by quanta of love, both requited and disappointed, and, above all, by high charges of hostile aggression. Further analytic exploration of the ideal and prohibitive norms led to the exposition of the prototype of the superego and the release of her own repressed hostility and the introjected maternal aggression.

Processes of early identification between the mother and the child strengthened the underlying symbiotic tie. Consequently intense hostility was mobilized in the struggle for individuation. However, this hostility had to be repressed because it threatened the maternal love and incurred not only the mother's wrath but, above all, the displeasure of the superego.

In working through the ambivalent feelings about her mother, Miss V was confronted with her hostility, her intense and constantly repressed anger at her mother. This led to the intensification of guilt feelings and the deepening of the depression.

In her "abandonment" by all her substitute love objects, Miss V saw the ultimate punishment for her wickedness and the repetition of her bereavement. As Freud (1923) put it: "the ego gives itself up because it feels itself hated and persecuted by the super-ego, instead of loved. To the ego, therefore, living means the same as being loved —being loved by the super-ego, which here again appears as the representative of the id. . . . It [the ego] sees itself deserted by all protecting forces and lets itself die" (p. 58).

SUMMARY AND CONCLUSION

This survey of the vicissitudes of the hostile drive, though far from complete, suggests some general observations.

Anger appears as one of the earliest emotions. At first it is probably not differentiated from distress and anxiety. Hostility focuses on the first object representations whenever the object appears as a source of unpleasure and deprivations.

As long as the self and the world of objects are poorly differentiated the primitive hostility flows freely in both directions toward the self and the original objects. The infantile ego easily absorbs radiations of aggression emanating from the significant persons and sends them back distorted and potentiated.

This interpenetration of hostility contributes to the formation of archaic object representations, which become an important depository of primitive destructive hostility. In a predisposed psychic organization these distorted representations of the original love-hate objects remain split off and isolated from the rest of the ego, and therefore may at some future time become the source of serious psychopathology. In such formations hostility is externalized and projected onto the original love-hate objects or their derivatives, which then assume the status of an arch enemy and persecutor.

Since the curbing of primary narcissism is the source of frequent frustrations and anger, it is natural that individuals with strong narcissistic and aggressive endowment are more likely to develop violent hostility, which becomes stored, as it were, in the ego as a source of later pathology.

In view of the early somatic origins of the ego, hostility can become focused on specific somatic zones, which consequently acquire an important symbolic meaning. In this instance, too, later pathology may choose these zones as foci of aggressive tension and lead to psychosomatic disorders, conversion symptoms, hypochondriacal and delusional symptomatology.

Hostility is an important factor in the struggle for individuation. Thus, whenever an increase of the symbiotic links between the ego and significant love-hate objects occurs, hostility is mobilized, reaching violent and excessive proportions. At the same time increased hostility may intensify the fear of object loss and thus lead to the tightening of the symbiotic bond. In certain individuals these circular reactions result in closely enmeshed symbiotic ties, wrought, as it were, by violent hostility.

The role of aggression in the formation of the superego has been intensively studied in psychoanalysis. My own studies (1952, 1956, 1958) have demonstrated the release of this aggressive charge in psychosis and in the course of the psychoanalytic process. The violence of the aggressive charge invested in the formation of the superego is illustrated by cases in which the destructive hostility is deflected toward the self.

Finally, it seems that intense repression of anger may lead to a weakening of self-assertion and affirmation and to the impairment of the ego and reality feeling.

Repression and isolation of aggressive impulses interfere with the sublimatory potential of the ego and reflect on the level of object cathexis and creative spontaneity.

BIBLIOGRAPHY

Bychowski, G. (1952), *Psychotherapy of Psychosis*. New York: Grune & Stratton.
—— (1956), The Release of Internal Images. *Int. J. Psa.*, 37:331-338.
—— (1958), Struggle against the Introjects. *Int. J. Psa.*, 39:182-187.
Chekhov, A. From a letter in *The Portable Chekhov*, ed. A. Jarmolinsky. New York: Viking Portable Library, 1947, p. 1.
Freud, S. (1923), The Ego and the Id. *Standard Edition*, 19:3-66. London: Hogarth Press, 1961.
Spinoza, *The Ethics*, Part III, Proposition XIII, Corollary and Note.

PROBLEMS OF OVERIDEALIZATION OF THE ANALYST AND OF ANALYSIS

Their Manifestations in the Transference and Countertransference Relationship

PHYLLIS GREENACRE, M.D.

In this paper I shall limit myself to a relatively small but I believe important area in the vast field of transference and countertransference relationships. I shall deal only with overidealization of the analyst and of analysis. Before discussing this specific problem, however, I want to say a few words about the development of transference in general for it is a basic and most sensitive tool in the work of psychoanalysis, and its neglect or mishandling may interfere with the successful course of therapy by those who understand other aspects of psychoanalysis quite well.

The phenomenon of "transference" seems to be omnipresent in human relationships (Greenacre, 1954). It is based on two essential psychological ingredients: first, the difficulty of the individual to exist long in emotional isolation; and second, the capacity to shift or transfer patterns of emotional relationship from one person or situation to another, provided there is a connecting link of some similarity between them.

The imperative nature of the demand for human contact was brought home to us in a dramatic way some years ago by the pediatric observations of foundlings (Bakwin, 1942). The efforts to improve the lot of these infant waifs had been focused mostly on bettering their physical care in the early months of life, in order to give them as good a start as possible before placing them for adoption. It was obvious from this investigation, however, that babies

Presented at the Pan-American Psychoanalytic Congress, Buenos Aires, August 2, 1966.

abandoned at birth or in the first weeks of life did not thrive and rarely survived infancy under adequate or "good" physical conditions (warmth, care of nutrition and cleanliness) unless this included some mothering.[1] In other words, mechanical or impersonal substitutes for personal care simply do not work adequately. This demand for emotional contact, which is at first mediated through body contact, continues throughout life. Naturally in the first years after infancy, speech, memory, and imagination can offer substitutes for much of the physical contact which is so necessary in the early months. Still, solitary confinement in adult life is one of the severest punishments we know; an enforced abandonment by others, it rivals physical torture in the hierarchy of cruelty. Under conditions of confinement, too, those who enter imprisonment with some substantial emotional attachment to a person or a deeply felt cause have better chances for survival than the stranded ones (Jacobson, 1959).[2]

The second point, the ability to shift emotional patterns from one person to another on the basis of resemblances of varying importance, is so much taken for granted in ordinary life that it may seem an unnecessary belaboring even to mention it. Yet because of the universality of this transference ability we may overlook its importance, on the one hand, in stimulating and promoting the sound incorporation of new experiences into the process of growth if the transference is based on valid and significant similarities; or, on the

[1] The experimental work of Harlow and Zimmerman (1958, 1959) on the rearing of infant monkeys seemed to indicate that the body warmth of a mother, even an artificial one constructed from a wire body covered with terry cloth and heated by electric light bulbs, was the most important element in contributing to the developmental welfare of the babies. They showed further that the young monkeys needed to have a mother to whom they could literally cling at the same time that they experienced the body warmth. These findings are important contributions to the understanding of the needs of human infants. It may be risky, however, to extrapolate from them completely and apply them too literally. It is obvious that the arboreal life of monkeys demands the development and persistence of clinging far beyond the requirements of humans. It is my impression, however, that in early psychoanalytic theory, anchored too strongly in the libido theory, there was too exclusive an emphasis on orality, in the first phase of life, and that the importance of clinging (Hermann, 1936), touch, smell, vision, and kinesthetic stimulation was insufficiently appreciated.

[2] Also note the effect of imprisonment on fertile and active, but alienated minds: Adolf Hitler who wrote *Mein Kampf* while in prison; or the murderer Perry, whose waning warmth for humans turned to burning coldness touched with sentimentality as described by Truman Capote in *In Cold Blood* (1966); or the elaboration of a cult of hate during a period of confinement of Malcolm X—to be reversed later into a frank religious conversion to Moslemism (Malcolm X, *Autobiography*, 1965).

other hand, in contributing to the development of strongly preju-
diced attitudes based on highly charged personal emotional elements
which have a specious or at least not very significant similarity to
other personal or more general situations.

A corollary to all this is that when a few people are gathered
together, especially under conditions of relative isolation or secrecy,
the lines of emotional relationship become intensified. This is more
marked if the situation is protected against the influx of new stimulations bringing in new problems. There is then a tendency to a definite shift of emotional expectations into some kind of patterning
representing the combination of repetition with compromises, as
each individual seeks to adjust the attitudes generated by past experience to utilize the present situation for his own needs.

In the setting of analytic work, the group is reduced to two: the
analyst and the analysand. Every care is taken to avoid intrusion of
extraneous stimulations. The analyst then can give his attention
entirely to the analysand who attempts through the various channels
at his disposal to lay bare his innermost thoughts and feelings. The
analyst's aim is to gain an understanding of the nature of the patient's disturbance. This understanding is then communicated to the
latter at appropriate times and in appropriate terms. Naturally, such
an undertaking cannot be begun unless the analysand has some
basic confidence in the analyst or in the method of analysis or in
both. He is further propelled by his wish to be relieved. The emotional attitudes of the analysand may then develop and be strengthened since they are not met by conflicting reactions from the analyst
who ideally makes no effort to argue, to persuade or to direct the
analysand, but solely listens, clarifies and interprets. The relative
privacy usually serves as a protective isolation furthering feelings of
safety rather than of loneliness. This part of the situation with its
progressively developing confidence forms the primitive basis of the
working alliance (or therapeutic alliance), which is essential as the
medium of new understanding for the analysand. It is evident, I
think, that it has many characteristics of the early infant-mother relationship in which the mother is the protection against unwelcome
intrusions as well as against coldness and loneliness for the infant.
I believe, indeed, the transference has its roots in this early and
necessary relationship of infancy. However, in therapy, communica-

tion through bodily contact and direct gratification (other than that of privacy and watchful attentiveness) is replaced as much as possible by verbal communication. This situation makes possible the utilization of the adult's self-critical capacities, which probably could not operate well without anchorage to this primitive infantile trust.[3]

On this foundation the analysand finds himself developing attitudes, reactions, and illusions in regard to the analyst which are surprisingly inappropriate to and sometimes in marked contrast to his basic confidence. It becomes evident then that these are repetitions or revivals of earlier states arising from experiences with those with whom he has been in close relationship in years past. Although these attitudes may seem to carry hostility or suspicion, they have been able to develop because of the strength of the basic confidence reinforced by the absence of personal reactions from the analyst; and they may appear in remarkably clear outline in the analytic relationship. I am speaking here of course of the development of the transference neurosis or what I prefer to call transference neurotic attitudes.

It is probably obvious that the transference relationship in analysis contains by its very nature the seeds for idealization of the analyst in its rootedness in the early omnipotent stage of the mother-child relationship. It is my intention to examine certain other elements of early life which, if exaggerated, may favor an overidealization of analyst or analysis to a degree that is not helpful and may become rigidly binding and tenacious.

In years past, the basic importance of the mother-child relationship could be deduced from the very nature of its transference reproductions on the stage of the analytic relationship. But the growing concern with ego development pushed our interest back to the earliest months of life, and the utilization of direct observation of babies has enormously enriched our knowledge and made it more precise. It is noteworthy, however, that the role of the father in the first two years of the child's life has on the whole been rather neglected. This may be due in part to the fact that studies of well babies, and in some instances of severely disturbed ones, have necessarily been carried on mostly in clinics and day nurseries. Here the

---

[3] This was first described by Sterba (1934).

contact was largely with the mother through the use of techniques to gain information about the infant and to supply necessary aid and support to her. It is my belief, however, that the father is very important in these early months, not only as his influence is medi-ated through the mother but by his own contribution to special magic and omnipotent qualities of the child's life in ways which may be important in tendencies to overidealization, later appearing in the transference relationship to the analyst and to analysis itself.

Under most conditions, the mother is the infant's constant com-panion and very much the center of his universe, while the father is a more peripheral figure. This is especially marked during the first six to eight months. In caring for the baby's physical needs and alleviating his distresses, the mother's activity must contain a great variety of bodily contacts and handlings. There is a play of emotional responses—observable in her facial expression, her tone of voice, the briskness, smoothness or tension of her muscles, and in any number of details which may soon become significant to the infant. He prob-ably senses her at first almost wholly insofar as she gratifies his needs and literally comforts him, or fails in these functions. But there is gradually increasing awareness of her separateness as he gains recip-rocal awareness of his own body parts and sensory functions.

The father, on the other hand, is never as close and constant in bodily relationship with the young infant as the mother (or her representative) must be. Nature has seen to that. At first he is prob-ably most frequently sensed as a twilight figure, taking shape one way or another, actually associated with morning and evening; only appearing periodically in the full light of day as on weekends or holidays. Sometimes he is a nighttime marauder or ogre, but I shall say more of that later. How much he remains a distant figure or what part he plays in his own right or as an adjunct or an interference in the relationship to the mother depends on his own temperament, that of the mother, and especially on the nature of the relationship between them. The presence or absence of other siblings also plays a role.

If the father is a physically active person who really enjoys his children's infancy, he will play with the baby in a romping way, generally after the child has learned to sit up or shown an inclina-tion to walk or stand. Playing with the child with wide tossing or sweeping movements or carrying the little one on his shoulders astride his head seem to be favorite paternal games. They are most exciting, especially in that period toward the end of the first year and during the second year when the child is beginning or has recently learned to walk. It seems then that the baby may feel a strong push for muscular activity and become demanding in seeking it. In this, there is not only a diffuse body erotism but, on the ego side, an increase in the sense of body self and a degree of exploring of space. Some identification of his own movement with that of his father may occur with great exhilaration. The child may temporarily take on the illusion of being very big and active and the ensuing excitement may be enhanced by his for-real experience of being smaller, but on the way up.

Watching this as an onlooker I have thought that this illusion was a beneficial one, giving the child a sense of vigor and power through participation with the father, in contrast to some other father-child games in which the child continuously feels his own smallness and helplessness. Here again the effect may depend as much on the father's use of the game as on the child's. When the game results in overwhelming excitement, it may produce a premature genital stimulation associated with submission and leave some distorting influence on the later sexuality.

In either event I have been struck with the fact that children of both sexes seem to enjoy this sort of romping play much more with the father than with the mother, who may, it is true, be less well equipped muscularly to undertake it and consequently less smooth and assured in her movements. The child is more likely to initiate hide-and-seek games with the mother, dosing himself and her with his needs for separateness.

Thus, after the first weeks of life, the movement in the child is toward a gradual separation from the mother, which may ultimately allow the growth of a relationship on a different level. The father, however, must emerge from a murky figure "off there" to one with whom the child is familiar, after which at least an incipient object relationship is possible. This difference in relationship to the parents progressively diminishes but is not lost as long as the child remains at home. For usually the mother is concerned with the details of the immediate care of the children, the management of the household, food, clothing, and cleanliness, even though her care no longer requires much direct bodily handling. The father, on the other hand, is off at work during the day, because his provision and care for his children consist in his being the breadwinner. To the preschool and young school child the father's activity is generally more mysterious, powerful, and glamorous than the everyday familiar concerns of the mother. These earliest of all parental figures, the all-giving mother and the more than life-sized heroic father (dating actually from the first two years of life and representing the positive form of the murky figure at first sensed) tend to persist more or less until the oedipal period and the entrance into the school world, which usually occurs about the same time. But they are the parental figures which reappear later in a new embellished form in the family romance[4] if there has been an especially strong disillusionment regarding the parents in the oedipal and again in the pubertal periods.

What I have presented thus far deals only with the perception of the *good* parents. It is obvious that there are other aspects which the young child reacts to—the angry parent, the distant unresponsive parent, the punishing parent, etc. In general these different parents tend to line up into the two categories: good and bad. These parental images with their roots in the first year or two of life are formed not only from the perceptions of the actual parents (or substitute parental figures) but also from the good (comfortable) or bad (uncomfortable) feelings in the child himself; for they originate in a period when the differentiation of the self from the other is in process.

We can deduce then that the more troubled and painful the early preoedipal years are, whether through endogenous physical distress within the child or injurious influences from without (i.e., any situations in which distress is of such proportions that it cannot or at least is not alleviated readily by comforting ministrations), the greater will be the increase in the natural ambivalence of the child. While this develops most often in relation to the mother with whom early contact is the greater, it may spread readily to include others in the environment. Commonly the hostile distrust becomes covered

---

[4] Frosch (1959) has described extensively the appearance of derivatives of the family romance in the transference.

with an anxious overattachment and overvaluation of the parent(s), which is, however, extremely susceptible to being upset.[5]

Some years ago as a consultant to a group of institutions caring for children from broken homes, I was much impressed with this state of affairs. In some instances these children had parents who really were *bad* parents in that they were neglectful, cruel, and not to be depended upon. However, rarely is any parent completely bad and the child generally had some kernel of pleasant memory to use as the basis of an expectation. The tendency of these children was to idealize, even glamorize, the absent parents. But if they went "home" to visit, there was likely to be trouble, as reality forced itself upon the child and outbursts of anger or other forms of aggression were frequent and severe. The social stratification of the children among themselves within the institution depended not so much on skill in competition of one sort or another but on how much the child was in contact with his parents: how often they visited, wrote, or sent him presents.

This is a rather long prelude to the consideration of the over-idealization of the analyst and sometimes of analysis, a development which may present a subtly based transference problem with severe sequelae after the analysis is over, especially if it is not understood during treatment.

It is evident that the analytic situation, characterized by the analyst giving his total attention to the analysand in an atmosphere of privacy and protection with the aim of ultimately relieving the analysand, is one which meets many of the requirements of the good parent. And this is helpful for the formation of the basic transference, the site of the working or therapeutic alliance. But it also has some hazards in permitting a degree of idealization of the analyst or of analysis which is not beneficial.

The general transference situation develops according to several different combinations of factors which impinge upon and may influence the intensity and configuration of the developing oedipal attachment. (1) If there has been a preponderance of discomfort in the earliest months but the care of a good parent has been available,

---

[5] I discussed this somewhat in my papers on the predisposition to anxiety (1941). The emphasis there was on the earliest distresses of all, those occurring at birth and the very first months of life.

then there is generally enough margin of positive response for the development of a sound basic transference and a workable transference neurosis. There may be a special tendency to idealization of the analyst which does not get out of bounds, however, unless it is augmented by a strongly seductive or protective analyst. When the idealization of the analyst is extreme, the patient may "analyze" to please the analyst and be fearful of admitting any hostile feelings. Characteristically, then, the analyst is nearly perfect, but the world remains insidiously hostile, and the analysand does not realize fully enough his own ability to deal directly with disturbing situations. Instead he is likely to resort to analyzing others before or in place of taking appropriate action himself. (2) There are some patients who have suffered *severe* physical distress in the preoedipal years (but not in the first months of life) and have been well cared for through the illness, who show in analysis an expectation of magic relief through simply coming to the analysis itself. They express few emotional reactions to the analyst, and in fact have generally a limited vocabulary for emotions, sometimes reacting as though an expression of any feeling is an indication of weakness. Their dreams may be vivid and show marked transference allusions of which they remain insistently unaware. One cannot say that the patient specifically idealizes the analyst or analysis, but rather that on a very primitive emotional level he expects magic relief from a procedure. (3) In a third group of patients, in whom there has been a prolonged severe degree of sensory and emotional deprivation soon after birth, no adequate clinging seems ever to have developed. In these cases, I believe, hostile attitudes will appear and persist from the beginning of the analysis. I am thinking here of a few patients who were institutionalized soon after birth or cared for under practically institutional conditions because of severe illness of the mother combined usually with unfavorable socioeconomic conditions. The care was not as sterile as in the case of the babies reported by Bakwin, but was grossly lacking in warmth and responsiveness. Subsequent to these early conditions the patient finds the privacy of the analytic relationship disturbing as it demands more than he is ready to give. His fear of passivity is so great that it is met by a need to feel omnipotent. In rare instances when a positive transference to the analyst does develop, it may tend to become persistently clinging and to

exclude the hostile elements, which are deflected onto accessory transference figures and subject to some analytic work. It is not a very
satisfactory or complete therapeutic procedure.

In type 3, however, if the patient shows a prolonged open hostile
attitude toward the analyst or analysis, and his history indicates that
he has not been able to sustain any good relationships in his life,
then I think it is generally useless to attempt to analyze. I would
emphasize the significance of the history of interference with sustained personal relationships rather than with achievements. For
there are many bright and even perceptive people who have stacked
up an impressive number of achievements which are nonetheless
built with a pervasive hostile attitude and a drive to be on top at all
costs. I have not been successful with such patients myself, but have
heard other analysts report some favorable results when the analysis
was undertaken after a prolonged period of psychotherapy. Such
patients sometimes seem to idealize themselves as part of the narcissistic inflation necessary to counteract their fear of passivity. They
occasionally seek analysis because of loneliness.

The group of patients who are chiefly to be considered here are
patients of the first type described. They do not show *open* marked
ambivalence. Hostility has early been controlled by reaction formation and superego development, but there are also pockets of denial.
They may be gentle and quiet people, or the latent aggression may
appear in a pressure of fervor and too consistent goodwill, associated
with a general tendency to idealize. Their compensation in life is
fairly good, and they may seek treatment with fairly typical and not
very severe neurotic symptoms. As has already been implied, some
idealization of the analyst is to be expected from the very nature of
the analytic situation. In these patients there is at first very little
to mark any problems as more severe than in most neurotic patients,
unless it is that they seem to be unusually "good" patients. They
accept intrepretations overreadily, complying with free associations
which will support or elaborate what the analyst has said. They tend
to keep overt hostile reactions outside of the transference responses,
and often deal with hostility by converting it into too great be-
nevolence.

These patients do not want ever to relinquish the analyst. This
wish to hold on expresses itself further in the wish to be an analyst

or to do something at least related to analysis. It is easy to consider this idealization as part of a postoedipal identification and to accept it as the development of postoedipal values established as part of the resolution of the oedipus complex. But the fact that some of these patients never free themselves from the analyst or from the defensive use of analysis becomes apparent in later years and is rationalized as part of the analysis terminable-or-interminable question. As a matter of fact, this is not the case. It seems rather that the analyst and then analysis have been accepted as part of a special and magic world of omnipotence, which really belongs to early childhood. There is not as full an assimilation of the content of interpretations as one would have expected in the course of analytic work. Analytic concepts are understood in a quasi-intellectual way and, being used too much in the service of defense, they do not enrich life so much as replace it. The phase of analyzing others, which practically every analysand goes through in the course of his own analysis, persists, is indefinitely prolonged, and gratifies a narcissistic sense of in-ness and power. There are other patients who cannot sustain this clinging attitude toward the analyst or analysis; they again repeat the disappointments that they have experienced with their own parents, often in a peculiarly bitter way and become aggressively hostile. In either case, whether the postanalytic attitude is one of persistent clinging or of hostility to the analyst or to analysis, it is likely to be one of fervor approaching fanaticism.

A complicating set of circumstances in a number of patients belonging generally to this group is found in the consistent and repetitive exposure to the primal scene beginning in the first weeks after birth and continuing without great interruption until puberty or even later. It has seemed to me that such a state of affairs, while usually occurring together with other untoward experiences, did nevertheless produce rather characteristic disturbances. It would take a more detailed careful study of a larger number of cases than I have yet had time to make to give a report on the variety of ways in which these experiences impress the child and combine with the fantasies endogenously generated in him, resulting then in rather severe distortion of later sexual interests and of passive and aggressive attitudes (Zetzel, 1965). The instances of prolonged sharing of the parental bedroom involving repeated primal-scene exposures occurred in my patients almost exclusively in only children or in the youngest of several children. This situation may be contrasted with that in which there are sporadic chance participations in the primal scene, but then the experience is regarded as exceptional. In the latter instances, there is more likely to be a shock reaction and the impact on the child depends very much on the age of the child, the actual nature of the primal-scene exposure itself, the circumstances surrounding it, and the reactions of the parents to the child's intrusion. In any event, the experience is likely to color the child's developing sexual theories and expectations. In the cases of repeated exposure over a number of years, it was necessary for the child to develop strong defensive reactions which shaped not only his sexual attitudes and expectations but invaded other parts of the character as well.[6]

In two cases (one an only child and the other the younger of two) the child shared the bedroom with the parents for several months of the year until well after puberty. The situation in both instances was furthered by the fact that the family lived in a Southern community in which the house, though sufficiently ample in size, was not heated throughout and during the winter months the family all slept in the one warmest room of the house. In other instances of only children of moderately poor but not really impoverished families, the child had been kept in the parents' room, while another room was rented out to a roomer. The arrangement was due to frugality rather than to real need. In still other families, well-to-do and with no special economic pressure, a variety of factors seemed to promote this sleeping arrangement: the parents might enjoy having the little one at hand and treat him more or less a plaything; or a sexually inhibited mother might keep the child at hand as a barrier to frequent sex relations. A neurotic anxious parent might need to reassure himself of the child's safety during the night. It is my impression, in fact, that the situation of such prolonged sleeping-together arrangements is rarely due as much to drastic impoverishment as to a kind of clinging, a continuation in one or both parents of old infantile wishes for closeness due to many different neurotic reasons. I shall describe some of the typical developments and then

[6] Some variations of the primal-scene experience are indicated but not elaborated in my paper on "Screen Memories" (1949).

whatever visual memory associated with the sounds is aroused. This may be felt as though in the body or projected outward, with a reconstruction of the sense of being at the breast or close to the mother's body.[7] In some instances there is also a marked and circumscribed disturbance in the infant's motor and kinesthetic sense, due to special awareness of the rhythmic motions of intercourse and the shaking of the bed.

In one patient who showed this disturbance in a marked degree during the analysis, I finally made a tentative interpretation that it seemed she actually might have shared the bed with the parents for some time and participated unusually intimately in the movements of their sexual relationship. After a pause she confirmed this probability, saying it was true that during her second year the parents had taken her with them on a belated honeymoon in which she had shared their bed in the various hotels in which they stayed.

The specific direct stimulation of visual curiosity in this situation ordinarily comes, I think, at a later date—perhaps beginning in the latter half of the first year and continuing especially in the second and third year. There is then a clearer differentiation of self from the other, and the child is able to stand up in his crib and take in the situation more fully if there is even a dim light on. This situation is stressed by Zetzel (1965) who indicates that a later desire for visual mastery may be stimulated, although free fantasy is interfered with. I had come to the same conclusion in my cases, but would emphasize that the mastery is highly narcissistic with strong competitive and exhibitionistic content, while the inhibition of imagination robs it of richness. In some cases the process of learning is even more drastically involved. The intensity and elaboration of curiosity also depend upon the specific nature of what the child sees and on the parents' reaction to his activity. In this later period, too, he is more likely to feel some beginning genital stimulation accompanying the pressure for excretory discharge. Furthermore, jealousy may now begin to be a strong ingredient in the feeling of exclusion and intensified loneliness.

[7] Here then may be one source of the later experience described by Isakower (1938) and known rather generally as the "Isakower phenomenon," which was elaborated in Lewin's studies (1946, 1953) of the "dream screen."

My experience with patients in whom the sharing of the parental bedroom has extended practically uninterruptedly well into latency has impressed me with the degree to which selective denial and an amnesia of varying dimensions have developed. As a result, what the analyst hears about may be a few or many screen memories which are more than ordinarily inaccessible to elaboration, reconstruction, and interpretation. There may be an extremely strong resistance even on the part of very intelligent reasoning people to the idea that the parents indulged in sexual activity at this period and sometimes very improbable rationalizations are offered to account for such an asexual life.

It is very difficult to generalize about these cases. The clinical symptomatology varies according to the form of early stimulations and the ways in which they combine with later specific traumas and disillusionments affecting the oedipal struggle and its solution. There are many patients who overtly cling not to the analyst, but to the analysis in a paradoxical way. In spite of a continued rigid resistance and apparent discouragement they are quite unwilling to give up analysis. If induced by the analyst to discontinue treatment, they return later hoping this time it will be better. It is noteworthy that the maintenance of an extraordinarily enduring attachment to analysis may be their means of keeping an idealized version of the parents.

In general whether there was direct clinging to the analyst or to analysis, what the patient absorbed from interpretation was accepted pretty much on an intellectualized basis. Often this was hazy too. In some of the overt clingers there might be an attempt at cliché learning of analysis and a repetition of bits of analytic theory which the patient accepted as belonging to himself. Or there might be expressions of devotion to the analyst and of aggrandizement of him, but without the development of any clear transference neurosis. In some, such an attitude was punctuated by episodes of acting out which really expressed deep hostilities to the analyst and which were difficult to analyze (Greenacre, 1963). Then again there might be a kind of Chinese wall shutting out of the analysis any frankly sexual thoughts, memories or feelings, even when their presence was startlingly clear in dreams or definitely implied in reactions to current situations.

One patient of this type had sought treatment because of impotence, beginning relatively soon after marriage and apparently in connection with his wife's desire to have a child. He could not accept the fact that the time relationship pointed the way to a possible connection worthy of exploration, but strongly insisted that it was a pure coincidence. He was more than reticent about the details of his sexual life, and did not mention spontaneously sexual successes or failures.

A prolific dreamer, this man brought clear, informative dreams, which appeared to tell the story of his difficulties in an almost forthright way. But he was singularly incurious about them. He would give a few associations and then tend to paraphrase the dreams. When there were "wet dreams" or specific sexual references, he would then admit that the dreams *might* have something to do with his sexual symptom, but he would not venture much beyond that. When I gave a tentative interpretation, I would get a cautious admission that what I said *might* have some significance, usually followed by a firm assertion, "But of course I don't remember anything about it!" With that he firmly shut the door which had momentarily been slightly ajar.

The patient was one who had shared the parental bedroom in winter into his adolescence because it was the warmest room in the house. (The details of childhood, though important, are not here enumerated.) He had graduated from the foremost professional school in his field with a magna cum laude. Now in his mid-thirties he was very inhibited in his social relationships, but in his work seemed efficient and self-assured (as I happened to hear from outside sources). It is true that he had somehow found a specialty within a specialty in which his sharp intellect could stake out problems with great skill and clarity. But he lacked encompassing vision and was restricted in professional areas requiring appreciation of human emotions.

He clearly used his concern with professional worries as a defense against his sexual problems. When he could not go to sleep readily or was awakened by an anxious dream, he shifted immediately to thoughts about unfinished work in his office and planned the work of the next day in detail.

He could not admit even the possibility that his parents had had intercourse or any other sexual activity at any time after his birth. Neither did he seem to feel that the absence of any sexual relationship between them would have indicated some severe personal problem. What did emerge fairly clearly and repetitively—to an extent that seemed convincing to me—was that the father had been involved with a young girl in some way which caused gossip. This would come up with associations to older men who had impregnated young girls. Just what the facts in regard to his father were, I could not tell, but his unadmitted fantasies were clear enough. The father was certainly a well-respected man in the community, and the patient emphasized this with such strength that one suspected a certain defensiveness in it. He seemed to have a need to keep an early idealized vision of the powerful all-good father. This he did in his symptoms, his character defenses, and his transference attitudes.

It has been the aim of this presentation thus far to indicate some of the general and specific situations in the early years of the later analysand which contribute to the development of overidealization of the analyst or to passive magic expectations from the ritual analysis, and further to describe the relation of these to the origins of transference itself. I believe this is rooted most deeply in the physical dependence of the infant on the mother (partaking of the oceanic feeling described by some as religious); however, it also contains elements of the second year of life when the infant is accomplishing his own separateness but would still react to the parents, especially the father, as being all-powerful and godlike. The regression that occurs in the analytic transference relationship contains elements of both, but one or the other may be so accentuated as to focus the overly strong transference dependence on the analyst in a personal way or on the method of analysis, which then cannot really be utilized because it serves such a strong defensive need.

In the patient whose case has been scantily sketched, it appears that his normal postoedipal idealization of his father was interfered with both by the fantasies of violence repeatedly and annually reinforced by subjection to primal scenes, and further by hints and gossip concerning his father's behavior in the latter's young manhood. Both sets of experiences had obviously made indelible impressions on the boy, but had to be obliterated from consciousness by one of the strongest walls of denial I have ever encountered. It should be added, however, that in prepuberty the patient had a physical illness which focused attention on his genitals intensifying and fixating castration fears.

What interests me specially, however, is the way in which he built a strong reaction formation of almost religiously ritualized aims of perfection in his work. Although engaged in a profession dealing essentially with human relations, he had succeeded in finding a place for himself in which he could do a very specialized piece of work which did not demand that he look deeply into human motivations. In his own way he was courageous and efficient to an extreme degree. It was not that he sublimated conflicts but rather that he transferred them, in life as well as in analysis, to rather institutionalized social goals in which concepts of right and wrong played a considerable part. In this way he reinstated the glorious powerful father of his early childhood—the figure which might under some circumstances be the basis of a family romance fantasy. In the analysis itself, he clung to the feeling that if he followed the rules of analytic procedure conscientiously he *must succeed*—thus giving the analysis too a rather firm disciplinary ritualistic quality resembling some religious practices.

But what are the countertransference attitudes of the analyst which permit or even promote his overidealization by the analysand? They appear as precisely those counterparts of the transference problems which occur in the analysand. Mainly they consist of the persistence in the analyst of strong narcissistic competitive drives with high demands for success. This appears under the guise of therapeutic enthusiasm. This may have been dislodged from its original appearance as personal ambition and give rise to an overvaluation of the power of analysis itself. Such analysts will see "more analysis" too readily as the answer to recurrent neurotic difficulties, without giving sufficient attention to why the previous analysis failed. They may be too ready to attribute a failure to the inadequate work of the first analyst, without assessing the real complexity of the neurosis. If they concur with the patient in blaming the previous analyst and sympathize with him, they are likely to find themselves enmeshed in too strong a positive transference in which it is difficult to decipher the negative elements. This is particularly likely to be true when the analyst has himself a need for emotional gratification—to be loved and admired by his analysands. In such instances the analyst often appears disarmingly modest, but has a faith in the almost divine power of analysis.

The expectation of therapeutic omnipotence in the process of analysis was more frequent in years past. Freud's early discoveries were so profound and far-reaching and the realization of the power of unconscious forces to modify the course of life was so startling that the process of uncovering these forces and diminishing their effects was awe-inspiring. At the same time the analyst's position in the community set him apart in a way which tended to enhance or to wound his narcissistic image of himself. With the increase of the general public's knowledge about analysis, the analyst no longer occupies this special role, and this particular social increment to his narcissism is largely relieved. But the total problem is by no means eradicated.

It is not only the narcissistic needs of the analyst but his failure to recognize his own hostile aggressive drives which seem to make trouble by dovetailing with the problems of these analysands. He may then too readily identify with his patient and accept the latter's splitting of transference with projection of negative transference onto others, especially accessory members of the patient's family or of the analytic community. The therapeutic enthusiasm of the analyst is sometimes part of a latent rescue fantasy (Sterba, 1940), which is aroused by the analysand's suffering and pleas for help. An intense transference situation approaching a family romance may then develop. The patient's wish to find an ideal and all-powerful parent is met by the analyst's gratification in being the sympathetic parent through whom the patient will find a complete cure, approximating even a rebirth.

In such rescue operations the analyst's aggression may be allocated to those relatives or therapists who have previously been in contact with the patient and are, in fact or in fantasy, contributors to his disturbances. The analyst then becomes the savior through whom the analysand is to be launched. If this situation is further complicated by the analyst's succumbing to the patient's clinging seduction to the point of modifying the analytic treatment by interventions and active procedures, this naturally increases the attachment of the patient and tends to augment the secondary narcissism in giving him a sense of being specially favored. However, it further acts to keep him in a state of continued dependence or even transference bondage. This is sometimes gradually altered by time, but it is also prone to feed upon itself to the point of becoming irksome to either analyst or analysand, after which the latent negative transference may emerge in a troublesome or destructive way.

There is one situation which may interfere considerably and insidiously even in the treatment of patients whose problems are similar but less severe than those of the group described in this paper. This situation arises when the analyst is very well known and carries considerable prestige in the community from which the analysand comes. These circumstances, outside the control of the analyst and analysand, tend to enhance the image of the analyst and give the treatment a kind of magic power, with improvement deriving from association with the analyst rather than from the analysand's own development. It is impressive how many analysts, wrapped in the cloak of supposed anonymity in the consulting room, do not genuinely realize the complication of being well known and even in contact with the analysand in the outer world. In such situations transference cures may result without fundamental change or growth in the patient. This constitutes a special complication in the training of analytic students, but it is also met in other patients. It approximates a reality gratification to the patient by the analyst, and tends to fixate special problems in the analysand. It is a situation which cannot be entirely eliminated; but awareness of its significance may modify therapeutic results considerably.

BIBLIOGRAPHY

Bakwin, H. (1942), Loneliness in Infants. *Amer. J. Dis. Child.,* 63:30-40.

Frosch, J. (1959), Transference Derivatives of the Family Romance. *J. Amer. Psa. Assn.,* 7:503-522.

Greenacre, P. (1941), The Predisposition to Anxiety. In: *Trauma, Growth, and Personality.* New York: Norton, 1952, pp. 27-82.

—— (1949), Screen Memories. *This Annual,* 3/4:73-84.

—— (1954), The Role of Transference: Practical Considerations in Relation to Psychoanalytic Therapy. *J. Amer. Psa. Assn.,* 2:671-684.

—— (1959), Certain Technical Problems in the Transference Relationship. *J. Amer. Psa. Assn.,* 7:484-502.

—— (1963), Problems of Acting Out in the Transference Relationship. *J. Amer. Acad. Child Psychiat.,* 2:144-175.

Harlow, H. (1958), The Nature of Love. *Amer. Psychologist,* 13:673-685.

—— & Zimmerman, R. R. (1959), Development of Affectional Responses in Infant Monkeys. *Science,* 146:421-432.

Hermann, I. (1936), Sich-Anklammern, Auf-Suche-Gehen. *Int. Z. Psa.,* 22:349-370.

Isakower, O. (1938), A Contribution to the Pathopsychology of Phenomena Associated with Falling Asleep. *Int. J. Psa.,* 19:331-345.

Jacobson, E. (1959), Depersonalization. *J. Amer. Psa. Assn.*, 7:581-610.

Lewin, B. D. (1946), Sleep, the Mouth and the Dream Screen. *Psa. Quart.*, 15:419-443.

—— (1953), Reconsideration of the Dream Screen. *Psa. Quart.*, 22:174-199.

Sterba, R. F. (1934), The Fate of the Ego in Analytic Therapy. *Int. J. Psa.*, 15:117-126.

—— (1940), Aggression in the Rescue Fantasy. *Psa. Quart.*, 9:505-508.

Zetzel, E. R. (1965), Repression of Traumatic Experience and the Learning Process. (To be published.)

FURTHER CONSIDERATIONS OF THE ROLE OF TRANSFERENCE IN LATENCY

SELMA FRAIBERG

I

Some years ago one of the first of my child analysands returned to me at the age of sixteen and told me that she felt she needed help once again. Dorothy had been in analysis between the ages of seven and ten. She was, in fact, one of the children whose case material was used to illustrate my earlier paper on transference in child analysis (1951). The treatment of Dorothy in adolescence gave me an extraordinary opportunity to re-examine the role of transference in child analysis and to reconsider my earlier views.

Dorothy had been an aggressive, insatiable, and uncontrollable child when she entered analysis. Learning was impaired. She chose for her friends the neglected, quasi-delinquent children in her neighborhood, and, at the age of seven, seemed ready to form her own identity on the basis of "no good," "worthless," "cast off."

For the purposes of this essay there is no need to elaborate on the case history or on those details of the analysis which are summarized in the earlier paper. The analysis brought about radical changes in the child's personality, the oedipal conflicts were brought to a favorable resolution, anxieties over sex play and masturbation were extensively dealt with, and at the time of termination Dorothy showed all the signs of a favorable development in her femininity, her pleasure in learning, her relationships to parents and friends, and her self-valuation.

In this sketch I should call attention to one symptom that had

Associate Professor of Child Psychoanalysis at the University of Michigan Medical School, Ann Arbor, Michigan.

Presented at the Panel on Latency at the Fall Meeting of the American Psychoanalytic Association, December 4, 1964.

been prominent in the early phases of the analysis. There was a dog phobia that had once been so pervasive that Dorothy could hardly bring herself to go outdoors at certain times, and during one period of the analysis the dog phobia had manifested itself in relation to me and to my house. (Later, I shall return to this detail.) It is also important to note that Dorothy had been enuretic until the age of four and that an ill-advised cystoscopy had been performed at four. Following the cystoscopy the enuresis ceased.

Between the ages of eleven and sixteen Dorothy sustained all of her gains, and early adolescence brought forth no extraordinary conflicts. I had followed her development through occasional visits with the parents, and Dorothy herself somehow kept in touch with me. Occasionally she sent a greeting card or called me to tell me about something nice that had happened to her. Twice, when she was thirteen, she asked to see me and on one of these visits told me that she sometimes still worried about the cystoscopy. She was afraid that it might happen again. Since Dorothy's overall functioning was unimpaired, I was not too concerned about this problem and felt that the old memories had been revived under the pressure of pubertal conflicts.

At sixteen Dorothy was an attractive, poised, very articulate girl, riding a tide of popularity at school and sustaining good grades along with an active social life. In general, she presented a picture of such wholesome good health that later, when we requested that she be excused from school for regular appointments with me, the school refused the request on the basis that there could not be anything wrong with this girl that would require her to be excused from school for psychiatric treatment. The hint was strong that either Dorothy was malingering or the therapist was making a mountain out of a molehill.

When Dorothy came to see me at sixteen, she stated directly that she needed further treatment. In a forthright and adult way she told me that in the past months she had come to recognize that she had a problem in relation to boys. She knew many "nice boys" with whom she went to parties and dances, but she felt very little sexual attraction for the nice boys. On the other hand, she formed an attachment to a boy who was coarse and really repulsive to her and yet she found kissing and sex play with him very exciting. She felt there were some problems that had not been worked out in her childhood analysis; in fact, she remembered deliberately concealing certain things from me. As I talked further with Dorothy, I reached complete agreement with her that further treatment was indicated at this time.

I saw Dorothy twice a week for a thirteen-month period. The story of the adolescent treatment may one day be reported in greater detail, for it illuminated the child analysis in an extraordinary way. From the material in the adolescent therapy I shall excerpt only a few details that throw light on the problem of transference in a child analysis.

In the early weeks of treatment Dorothy described her sexual relationship to Joe, the boy she described as repulsive and attractive to her. There was no genital sex play; the erotic high point of her relationship was achieved by having him lie upon her (both fully clothed) while she, imprisoned beneath him, moved her thighs and reached orgasm. Her shame as she described this act was overwhelming to her.

Dorothy's associations led back to the childhood cystoscopy at age four. She remembered being held down, screaming, while "that thing" was put into her. The memory was vivid and she could re-experience the terror as she told me. She had no difficulty in seeing the connection between her sex play with Joe and the cystoscopy. Then followed a period of resistance in the treatment, candid acknowledgment that she was withholding something from treatment, and even an admission that this was the same "something" that she had withheld in her childhood analysis. She was finally able to tell me that for years she had practiced a form of masturbation which involved thigh friction alone. The exciting fantasy for the masturbation was the memory of the cystoscopy. She was certain that she had never told me about masturbation in her childhood analysis. She was mistaken, but I shall return to this point later.

I was now able to show Dorothy how the sex play with Joe was the acting out of the masturbation fantasy. As we dealt with the masturbation fantasy in subsequent sessions, the relationship with Joe began to dissolve and within a few weeks Dorothy discovered that she no longer needed him. From this point on there was no longer a need for a degraded lover.

A new boyfriend now appeared. His name was Arthur. He was homely, tender, good-humored, and an amateur psychologist. The erotic high point of this relationship seemed to be an interminable psychologizing during the late hours, a sharing of adolescent woes, a continuous diagnosis of each other's weaknesses and failings, and clinical interpretations which sometimes led to quarrels. It was a long time before Dorothy was able to see some of the transference implications of this new friendship.

Soon this relationship, too, was caught up in conflict. One evening Arthur had his arms around Dorothy and Dorothy found it exciting. Then Arthur began to nibble gently at the back of Dorothy's neck. At this point she had a feeling of panic. The thought occurred to her that Arthur was going to bite her. The sensations in her own genitalia stopped abruptly. The feeling of terror would not leave her and when she left Arthur that evening she was in tears.

In her session with me Dorothy immediately associated to this incident her old fear of dogs. She remembered, she told me, that her fear of dogs was one of the problems that had brought her into analysis in childhood. In the hours that followed we were able to trace the connections between genital sensations, the fear of attack by a dog, the masturbation fantasies, and the cystoscopy. For many weeks Dorothy remained completely anesthetic when Arthur held her or kissed her, and even later, when she recovered genital sensations, there were transitory occurrences of complete frigidity which required analytic work for months. The fear that she would not be able to control her excitement, that she would abandon herself and degrade herself, entered the treatment later. Unresolved residues of the oedipal ties to the father appeared as further obstructions to the experience of pleasure and were dealt with in treatment. And, finally, the very core of self-degradation, the early childhood experience of outright rejection by her mother, the feeling of lovelessness and worthlessness came into the adolescent treatment through the analysis of the transference.

This concise summary clearly implies that the childhood analysis had not effected a genuine resolution of the central conflicts in the neurosis. In the case of Dorothy I believe that resolution might have been achieved through a deeper analysis of the phobia in the transference.

When I reread my notes of the child analysis, I was struck by the fact that the method of that analysis was entirely alien to me only a few years later. Repeatedly I found instances in which my technical handling would now be very different. Even the criteria I had employed for termination of the analysis seemed questionable to me. It was in the area of transference that I found myself most critical of the early work. And it was in the handling of transference that I felt I had cut off access to precisely those conflicts that had re-emerged in the adolescent neurosis.

In reviewing the case notes of the child analysis, I found these differences in method and technique between the child analysis I practiced in those days and that which I consider my present-day practice. To a large extent these differences also reflect the changes in the field of child analysis.

First, my attention was drawn to the ways in which I dealt with the earliest transference reactions in the childhood analysis. When the aggressive behavior first manifested itself in the analytic sessions, I employed techniques to arouse the child's anxiety in relation to her behavior. I showed great concern about the possible consequences of her uncontrolled behavior and brought about a situation in which the child made conscious efforts to control herself. The benefits in improved family relations were apparent very soon. The effort at self-control produced a mouth tic which appeared from time to time during the early months of analysis. In the child analysis of that period we regarded this as a favorable sign. This meant that we had converted the behavior disorder into a neurosis and had created a favorable situation for analysis.

Today, confronted with the same behavior manifestation in transference reactions I would view the aggressive behavior as defensive and begin to show the child how the aggressive behavior appeared whenever she was afraid of something. I would explore the anxiety in relation to me, trace it in its other connections, and help the child see her behavior as an identification with the aggressor. This would lead us into the analysis of the mother-child relationship and the same path would lead into the analysis of the cystoscopy. The analysis of the sadistic behavior as defense would bring me into direct contact with the phobic substructure of the behavior disorder and, by addressing myself to fear and helplessness, I would hope to bring about the kind of transference which we obtain with hysterical patients; i.e., the analyst becomes the ally against danger and the analysis has the purpose of freeing the child from anxiety. I would avoid, as far as possible, any measures that deliberately create anxiety in the child. The anxiety is there, it only needs to be uncovered through analysis of defense; and by following this analytic approach I would be in a favorable position to deal with transference reactions. I cannot easily show a child that her fear of me is unrealistic, and introduced by her neurosis, if I have, in fact, induced anxiety in her through the therapeutic approach I followed in Dorothy's case. Further, I would expect that through analyzing the relationship between anxiety and the aggressive behavior, the aggressive behavior would diminish without a heroic effort at self-control on the part of the child, an effort which in this case produced a new symptom. Experience tells us that the analytic approach which I would prefer in such an instance should bring about a more durable form of self-control than that obtained through turning the sadistic impulses back upon the self.

The dog phobia in the child analysis is of special interest. In my earlier essay on transference in child analysis, I described the way in which the dog phobia was manifest in the transference during one period of the analysis. As the analysis began to center upon Dorothy's relationship with her mother, and at a time when internalization of aggression had been achieved to a large extent, the dog phobia appeared in relation to me and to my house. Resistance was manifest in the analytic hours through a kind of frozen silence; then the child became afraid to come to her hours because of a little dog who lived on my street. During the same period the mother's own destructive feelings toward the child came to the foreground. Dorothy's mother was afraid that she might strangle her child. As I saw it, then, the phobia which represented in part the child's fear of her aggressive wishes and projection onto an external object had received massive reinforcement through the real danger of the mother's hostile feelings toward the child. When analysis centered upon the conflict between the child and her mother, danger was experienced as coming from the analyst and the dog phobia was transferred to the analyst. Thus far, I think, I would have no objections to the formulation I had worked out. In the earlier essay I also showed that there was no correspondence between the transference of the dog phobia and a transference neurosis because the conflict still centered in the relationship with the original objects, the still present objects for a child. In the illustration from Dorothy's case, we saw that the phobia was not withdrawn from the home ground as it were, but extended into the analytic situation. From the evidence available to me at *that* time, I would not alter my views on this point either.

But my handling of the dog phobia in the transference struck me as quite alien to my present-day technique. In the child analysis I dealt with the transference of the dog phobia by showing the child verbally and through play devices that she behaved toward me as if I were a dangerous dog who might hurt her, and then in play and games with her I represented myself as a harmless old dog who would never hurt a little girl. On the basis of this reassurance to the child the dog phobia was withdrawn from the transference, the positive transference was restored, and the analysis went on to explore the conflicts of ambivalence in relation to the mother. With analysis of the oedipal conflicts the dog phobia disappeared. But it was the unlaid ghost of this dog that returned in adolescence.

Today, I reflected, I would have worked with the transference of the dog phobia in quite a different way. First, I would have educated the child patient to the meaning of transference reactions and through many demonstrations during the early period of the analysis would have shown the child how feelings and ideas can attach themselves to me and seem real yet belong someplace else. I would teach the child to trace these reactions and to find their origins. I would deal with the earliest negative transference reactions in a way that would make it possible for a child to express them and to see how we make use of them analytically. And through dealing with the dangerous affects in small quantities during this early period of analysis I would expect that the child will be less likely to feel overwhelmed by her feelings when certain conflicts appear full strength in the analysis. With this groundwork, if a dog phobia should make its appearance in the transference, I would have a patient who understood the meaning of transference, who would feel that the danger now emanating from the analytic situation was somehow alien and would work with me in unmasking the dog and her own resistance.

If I had analyzed the dog phobia as it was manifest in the transference, where might the dog phobia have led us? From the material in the adolescent therapy we know that there were links between the dog phobia and the cystoscopy in the fear of a genital attack. If I had analyzed the dog phobia in the transference, would the paths have led us back to the cystoscopy and the masturbation fantasies? Was the dog phobia another manifestation of a doctor transference, a "fear of the examination" that was analysis? Perhaps it is unprofitable to speculate, but it is very clear that by managing the transference instead of analyzing it I could not know exactly what was transferred.

As it happened both the cystoscopy and masturbation later appeared prominently in the childhood analysis and were analyzed on the basis of stories, daydreams, and play. But it struck me, as I reread the notes of that period, that the affective quality of these communications was thin, and diluted, I felt, in the context of play, storytelling, and "make-believe." The memory of the cystoscopy was a pale ghost of the memory that was reported to me in adolescence; there had been no reliving and re-experiencing of the event in the child analysis. Again, I do not attribute this to endogenous factors in the child analytic situation; the limitation lies in the method I employed. If transference analysis had been employed in the childhood treatment, the memory of the cystoscopy would have emerged in transference, made real and present to the child through the transference. Following closely the model in adult analytic technique, we would expect to revive this memory with a good measure of its original affective charge and the analysis of the event would have given meaning to dread of genital attack and castration anxiety.

In the child analytic notes the sadomasochistic fantasies appeared and links were established with the earlier cystoscopy, but I cannot find in my notes any connections that were established between the sadomasochistic fantasies and the masturbation itself! There were a group of masturbation fantasies, specifically oedipal in character, that occupied many months of analysis, but the sadomasochistic fantasies that Dorothy revealed in the adolescent treatment (the cystoscopy fantasies) were maintained in isolation from the masturbation itself. Only a young and inexperienced analyst could have overlooked this. We then have another explanation for the isolation of the memory from its attendant affects in the analysis. As long as the sadomasochistic fantasies could be maintained in isolation from the masturbatory context, the affects could be maintained in isolation.

Now, I think we can understand why Dorothy felt that she had concealed her childhood masturbation from me. Since she had never told me the cystoscopy fantasies as masturbation fantasies, she felt, in fact, that she had not told me. I also feel that so much of this analysis was carried on within the context of play and make-believe that even when masturbation was handled in the analysis it was somehow "not real" to the child.

This re-examination of a child analysis cannot stand by itself as an illustration of the role of transference in child analysis. At best we have only a kind of negative evidence that if the transference had been analyzed, the outcome might have been different. It might be more profitable to turn to another case illustration from latency in order to examine the role of transference.

II

Nancy was eight when she began her analysis. Six months prior to referral seizures were observed and an EEG confirmed petit mal with grand mal components. A number of anticonvulsants were tried without success in controlling the seizures. With the onset of seizures there was marked deterioration in all areas of ego functioning and an impoverishment of affect that alarmed the parents. Analysis was begun with the hope of restoring ego functioning, but only after treatment was underway did we have hope that analysis might have some success in controlling the seizures. When analysis was terminated at the end of four years, Nancy was symptom free and there were significant characterological changes.

I shall not attempt a detailed history of the analysis. I have excerpted material from the third and fourth years of treatment in which analysis of the transference led to the uncovering of memories from the age of three. This was a critical year in the etiology of the neurosis, but it should be clear that the events that we later learned about cannot be construed as an etiology for the convulsive disorder itself.

During the first two years of analysis we dealt with the defenses against affect, masturbatory conflicts, a ball fetish, erotic looking

games with an older brother, Fenton, and some aspects of the positive and negative oedipus complex. Nancy brought in dreams for
analysis, learned to associate on the basis of a "What Pops into your
Mind Game," and learned to candidly report reactions and feelings
toward the analyst. At the beginning of the third year of analysis
manifest seizures were rare, ego functioning was restored in all areas,
and the affective picture was favorably altered. From a number of
details in dreams and fantasies I was certain that there had once
been a sexual observation of a couple, but the threads of this material
seemed to lead nowhere.

In the middle of the third year of analysis a compulsive finger
game appeared in analytic sessions and soon Nancy reported that she
found herself playing the finger game at home and at school. In the
finger game one hand was opened partially in a clawlike formation;
the other hand with fingers partially closed entered the open hand
in a rhythmic motion. Her associations led her into "what grownups
do to get babies," then into "penis and mouth," and suddenly an
interruption of associations and the experience of violent nausea in
the hour. In later sessions the threads led back to sex games with
her little friend Arthur which she herself blamed for bringing on
her seizures, and the recovery of a memory from this period in which
Arthur's mother, coming upon the children, had made a threat
against Arthur's penis. Other threads seemed to lead back once again
to a sexual observation of a couple (but I did not suggest this). The
finger game ceased and there followed a period of strong resistance
in the analysis.

One day Nancy arrived for her hour and immediately reported
a thought that had been running through her head all during her
trip from her house to my house. The thought was "Selma is a blackmailer, Selma is a blackmailer." I said, "Do you really think Selma
is a blackmailer?" "Of course not!" she said, "I'm just telling you
my thoughts!" She went on. Along with the thought was a fantasy
that I would tell her parents that if they did not pay me more money
I would discontinue treatment. There was no one else to go to, so
her parents had to pay me more money.

Now I should mention that nothing in the objective picture
could account for this fantasy. At no time in the analysis had the
analytic fee been a problem for her parents or for me. Nancy herself

was baffled and could provide no associations. I reminded her of criminal games in analysis the previous spring and the blackmailer who threatened to get the criminal if he did not pay off. "Yes," she said doubtfully, "but I'm not really afraid that you would tell any-one about anything I've told you, or that you would really blackmail anyone." I tried other leads. I reminded her of a maid who left Nancy's family because she thought she could get more money else-where. Yes, Nancy remembered. Then was I like a maid in this fantasy? "Yes." And the trail broke off again. Then, abruptly Nancy said, "Now I think of another blackmail. A black *male*. [This had turned up too in the blackmail fantasy the previous spring.] And that reminds me of a game Sally [her best friend] and I play. She's an all black horse and I'm an all white horse and we love each other." "What do you do?" "Oh, we just run alongside of each other. Play together. See, that's where the black *male* comes in." We pursued this further. "Were there any other associations to a black male?" "No."

I asked her if another possibility of a black male was in connection with night. A white male would look like a black male at night. "No," Nancy said flatly. "You just lost the $64,000 question. I thought we were getting some place before, but that doesn't sound right to me. I keep thinking it was a *black* male." And we could not pursue this further that hour.

Soon afterwards, baffled by the detail of a black male and the child's own conviction, I found an opportunity to ask Nancy's mother some questions. I could not believe in the possibility that a pro-tected middle-class child would have had an opportunity to see "a black male." Nancy's mother then told me that when Nancy was three and a half she and her husband had taken a two-week holiday in another city. The children were in the care of a Negro maid. When the parents returned they learned from neighbors and from the children themselves that Cassie's boyfriend had visited her at night. Cassie was dismissed shortly afterwards. The parents had no evidence that the children had observed the couple in bed; Cassie's room was on another floor. The parents had never considered the possibility that Nancy could have observed a sexual act and had never told me about this incident.

I never told Nancy what I learned from her mother. The material that I now bring together emerged entirely through the analysis of the child's own dreams, fantasies, and transference behavior.

Soon after the appearance of the "blackmail-black male" material Nancy developed an upper respiratory infection and was in bed for a week. I did not understand until a year later that the upper respiratory infection belonged to the memory of the sexual observation. Only later, when still another sequence linked the observation and an illness and a separation from the parents, was I able to see this and use it analytically. (In the reconstruction, the three-year-old Nancy had wakened at night with cold symptoms and perhaps a sore throat. She had gone in search of Cassie. At the door of Cassie's room she heard voices. She opened the door and went in.)

When Nancy returned to analysis after her illness she reported that the fantasy "Selma is a blackmailer" had returned. Her associations were: "Selma is a robber. . . . You took my good feelings away." She was very careful to assure me, "These are just my thoughts you know. I don't really think this." She had lost all genital sensation that week and somehow felt I was to blame. There was a fantasy that I would cut off her hands at her wrists so that she could not touch herself. Then, still associating, she told me for the first time about "a picture" that kept coming into her mind during the time she was ill in bed, a "picture" that she had had before, when she was ill, and sometimes when she was not ill and was alone. The "picture," as she described it to me, had the quality of a hysterical hallucination in vividness and intensity. It was the picture of a chessboard with black and white squares and on the chessboard were "little creamy, skinny blocks" arranged on the board for a game. When she sketched it for me she showed a mass of little blocks placed in one corner of the board and two blocks isolated in the opposite corner. Along with the hallucination was a noise, "a noise," said Nancy, "that sounds like a big wh-i-ish."

In this hour and the next Nancy's associations again led in the direction of mutilation fears ("Someone will cut off my hand") and her associations to the chessboard blocks went on in this way: "They're people. It's as if the ones in the corner are mother and father with lots of children and a couple in the other corner without children." Then the phrase, "Evening Star" came into her mind. And then there flashed through her mind a picture. "A couple in the moonlight kissing. And there's the wh-i-ish sound again. . . . Another picture. A couple riding a horse in the moonlight." And then the associations stopped. There was a trancelike quality in Nancy as she gave these associations. Finally, I asked her if she could ever have seen a couple in the moonlight. She said, immediately, "Oh, yes!" I am not sure whether or not she had a brief seizure at this point. When I asked her about her last words, "Oh, yes!" she was surprised, and had not known she said this. She assured me she could not remember anything about seeing a couple and could not imagine what made her say that.

For over a month following this session, the analysis was at a standstill. Nancy had no problems to report, no conflicts, no fears. The seizures had practically disappeared from the picture, but something new had taken their place. Nancy told me that she was "forgetting" all kinds of things and she wanted to make it very clear that these episodes of forgetting were not at all like seizures. She carefully explained the difference. "In my forgetting spells I would blank out. Like the telephone gets disconnected. But this way I don't get disconnected. It's like I hear a person talking, but I can't remember what they said." Through careful questions I ascertained that Nancy was making clear that she never lost consciousness at such moments and that she was actually describing a hysterical absence.

This brought us close to the summer holidays. Nancy was obviously marking time in analysis until summer camp and when the time for departure came, she was relieved. It was an excellent summer, according to all reports. There were no symptoms, no conflicts that interfered with her pleasure at camp. It was as if banishing the analyst erased the memories.

Before proceeding to a new phase in the analysis of the primal scene material I shall briefly summarize the first appearance of primal scene material in the transference. We recall that much earlier in the analysis I had seen evidence of primal scene material in dreams and fantasies. None of this was available to analysis until it entered the transference. When the memory made its first breakthrough it appeared in the form of a transference symptom, the compulsive finger game, which manifested itself first in the analysis, then at home and school. In the finger games the memory of a sexual observation was still screened by later memories of sex play and masturbatory experiences. *However, when components of the memory of the original sexual observation became preconscious in the next phase of the analysis they no longer sought representation through compatible screen memories but found a new and independent route to preconscious representation in a transference fantasy: "Selma is a blackmailer."* Through the analysis of this fantasy we obtained almost immediately the associations that led back to "a maid" (the analyst in the fantasy, threatens to quit for more money) and "a black male" (from blackmail). In a rapid development in the next few weeks there appeared an upper respiratory infection, which, as I later learned, was a factor in the original observation, and the chessboard hallucination, a highly abstract representation of the act. I think we are justified in speaking here of transference neurosis.

The beginning analysis of the chessboard hallucination very shortly led to an impenetrable resistance. In the fall, when Nancy returned from camp, the resistance was still manifest. She had stopped working in analysis and the characteristics of the resistance eluded me as I tried to find a route back into the analysis. One evening, as I was reviewing my notes, I was struck by the fact that my interpretations seemed scattered and without focus and that many of them had a "pushing" quality that I did not like. I seemed to be trying to get her back to work by pressing and I was not sure why I was doing this. In the next hours I made no interpretations and resisted the temptation to get Nancy back to work and then, from various reactions, I had the impression that Nancy was inviting me to push her, to make her go back to work. Then a fantasy emerged. What would happen, Nancy wondered, if she should quit analysis? Her fantasy was that she would be forced to return. I would force her to return, she thought. Would I, though? Well, probably not, she considered. Well, then, her parents would force her to return, she decided. It was clear that this idea was somehow exciting to her and she saw it as real. When I pointed out to her that nobody had ever forced her to come to her analytic hours and that there was no reason to expect that anyone would, that I myself would not want this, Nancy still clung to the idea. When the fantasy persisted in the next hours I began to bring her attention to the detail of "forcing" as an analytic communication. I suggested that there was something in the idea of "being forced" to do something that could not be put into words, and was coming out in the form of a fantasy in which she would be forced to come to analysis. The meaning of the resistance was revealed very shortly afterwards.

One day Nancy arrived for her hour with a "back to work" manner that I could recognize. She began her hour. "Isn't it funny," she said, "how many of my daydreams are torture daydreams?" (It was indeed "funny," since she had never told me any torture daydreams during the three years I had known her.)

The torture daydreams I now learned were also incorporated in games which Nancy played with her friend Sally. In the games the two girls played horses together. One of the games we already know from Nancy's story of last spring. Nancy was a white horse and Sally was a black horse. Today, as Nancy began to give details of the current game with Sally, she made it clear that the game originated in her own daydreams and that she and Sally acted it out.

In Nancy's daydream there were two children who were captured by animals and enslaved by them. They were forced to do the work of dray horses. When they were too slow at work they were tortured. In one of the tortures a bit was placed in the mouth so that each effort at pulling would cause the bit to cut into the mouth. In another torture the girl was put in stocks, with head, arms, and legs through holes, while a man behind her threatened her with a whip (but did not actually beat her). The boy, however, was beaten on his arm by the whip. In still another torture the boy and girl were driven like horses while carrying heavy weights suspended from their backs.

In the following hour Nancy was nearly inarticulate with shame for having told me the torture daydreams. They belonged to masturbation, she needed them to get "a very strong feeling." Now each of the details of the sadistic fantasies came into the analysis. She associated to the bit in the mouth of the horse-humans her own hands in masturbation. "When I tighten up there with my hands." It was an exact displacement from vulva to mouth. The weights on the horses reminded her, she said, of "the balls . . . they hang down." The whipping did not yet yield any associations.

Gradually we established the links between the sadomasochistic masturbation fantasies and earlier sex games. Then the chessboard hallucination returned, and this time something new had been added. There were associated noises. "It sounds like people mumbling or jabbering and I can't make out what they're saying." Here the threads broke off once again and it was several weeks before Nancy provided another clue through a game with Sally. Again the game was confided with deep shame. The two girls pretended that they were two dogs, a male dog and a female dog. The male was wrongly thought to be savage and was chained up. Nancy, the female dog, tried to free him. She was to be punished by The People. In a climactic scene the Nancy dog is on her back (tied down) and the Sally dog is crouched over her legs with his paws under her while The People lower a heavy metal cast over Nancy's body. At first she can barely feel it. Then it hurts a little, then it hurts a lot and Nancy, in the game, can hardly breathe.

Nancy began to ramble. She confessed she did not want to associate to this material. "It makes me ashamed." Then she said, "There's a word that keeps coming into my mind and I keep forgetting it." And at this moment she had a seizure. The word was "intercourse" and when she remembered it shortly afterwards she said, "I feel like getting out of here, right now!" As we talked about her feelings she suddenly interrupted to ask urgently, "What would happen if something went wrong and instead of the seed coming out of the man, urine came out?" She looked ill again and I asked her about her feelings. "Like throwing up," she said.

As we worked over this material in this hour and the next I drew Nancy's attention to the themes of torture and intercourse and fascinated looking and now I suggested for the first time that she might, in fact, once have seen a sexual act between a couple and that it might have seemed to her like a torture. She regarded me wide-eyed and then let out a little cry of disgust and horror. Yet she did not deny it. "Maybe when I was little." She was silent for some time. Then I heard her say "Wa-wa-wa" in a musing voice, meanwhile blowing her bubble gum into a large, full bubble. Then she said, "Look at what I am doing with this!" She had blown it to the fullest extent, then inhaled and caused it to collapse. She stopped short in amazement and said, "I think that's what I saw! A penis, I mean. . . . Now I want to go home. I feel like getting out of here in a hurry!" I told her that if she had, indeed, once seen such a thing, she might have felt like getting out in a hurry.

There followed two hours during which Nancy found herself quite unable to talk and empty of feeling. When I asked what had happened to all the strong feelings she said, "All gone, I guess. Or maybe I should say they are in forgetting spells now." I then suggested that the inability to talk might be part of the memory, too. If I were right that she had once seen something between a couple, she might not have been able to talk about it afterward. She listened to this with some interest and then said, "You know what pops into my mind? That maybe someone told me I *mustn't* tell."

It was nearly two weeks later that Nancy brought a report of nausea and stomach pains and a new fear. In the darkness of her room at night she saw a picture. "A man with horns growing out of his head. A horrible monster. And I kept thinking about it [last night] and I couldn't fall asleep. . . . But today in class I thought of something. I think it's connected with what I must have seen when I was little, seeing intercourse, I mean. I don't know why, but when I made that connection I was *really sure* for the first time since we've been talking about it that I saw it. . . . He had a black face. Very ugly horns."

I have reported this segment of the analysis in some detail in order to permit close examination of the transference and a comparison with the adult model. The material shows that following the initial breakthrough of the primal scene memory in the transference fantasy "Selma is a blackmailer" a resistance appeared. The analysis of the resistance and the fantasy "to be forced" (in analysis) led us into the sadomasochistic masturbation fantasies and the torture games with Sally. The analysis of the sadomasochistic games led back to the original observation of a couple, the recovery of partial memories in the transference, and the associated affective reactions—anxiety, guilt, nausea, an urge to take flight. There followed a period of resistance, conversion symptoms of nausea and stomach pains, anxiety at night, and the hallucination of the black man with horns. It was this that led to the patient's conviction that she had really seen intercourse.

In all the significant ways I think we can demonstrate a correspondence to the adult model of a transference neurosis. We note, too, that the technical handling of the transference followed closely the model of the adult analysis.

It may be useful to pursue the threads of the primal scene material in the next period of analysis. I should mention that the conviction that she had in fact witnessed a sexual scene remained with Nancy, but further analysis of the primal scene material encountered a new resistance. The defenses which now appeared led us into the analysis of bisexual fantasies, her masculine identification, and only many months later to the further analysis of the primal scene material.

Once again it was the analysis of the transference that led us back to the primal scene material. There was strong resistance, a fear of me that became explicit in a fantasy that analysis would take away her "boy part" (i.e., masculinity), and occasionally a feeling that analysis itself was a kind of torture. At the same time there was acting out in two directions. The torture games with Sally were back in the picture, and Nancy would give me only vague hints that the new games had something to do with a master and a slave and the command to the slave that she must exhibit herself to strange men. During the same period Nancy became provocative with her brother and, to a lesser extent, with other boys, teasing and goading until Fenton threatened to beat her up, then exciting herself through fantasies of being beaten.

In daydreams and one nocturnal dream of this period I could clearly see that I was represented as a sadist who exerted hypnotic effects upon a girl or a boy who was obliged to obey commands, and Nancy herself could acknowledge the transference implications. But it was much more difficult for Nancy to see the games with Sally or the provocation of Fenton as "acting."

During this period of acting I chose to deal mainly with the defensive aspects of the acting. I was able to show Nancy how she was afraid that her analysis would take away what she called her "boy part," how being a girl made her feel helpless at times, and how with me, with Fenton, and with Sally, she seemed to be telling a story over and over again of a helpless girl and a dangerous and terrible man who would command the girl to do all kinds of shameful and humiliating acts for his pleasure. The resistance dissolved and then, one day, Nancy arrived for her hour visibly distraught and told me a terror dream which she had the night before.

"My cat had kittens, but she had four kittens and two snakes. I watched them come out of her. The snakes escape and the whole family tries to get them out of the house. There are three little panels like doors in the house and if you could get the snakes through the little doors you could get them out of the house. . . . Then the snakes got into a fight. One was 'a rattler' and one was 'a gardener snake' [her words] and it was like they were wrestling together. Then the rattler stuck his head right into the mouth of the gardener snake and killed him."

It was this dream that led us into another dimension of the primal scene material. The anxiety centered in the snake fight; as Nancy described the killing of the "gardener snake," she cupped one hand and pushed a finger through the hole, a gesture that she had employed earlier in analysis during a period when she was trying to figure out with my help how the penis could enter the woman. As other details of the dream emerged in this and subsequent hours Nancy herself could make the connections between the terror dream and a sexual observation. "The whole thing must have looked like a fight to me and I thought someone was going to get hurt. The woman." Other details brought associations to mouth, teeth, biting, and the thought, "He had stolen the penis from the woman."

During the analysis of this material Nancy's parents took a two-week holiday. Typically, during parental holidays Nancy reacted with no conscious feelings of loss, but almost invariably she developed a cold, a sore throat, or an earache. Within a few days Nancy called, asking to cancel her appointment because she had a sore throat and sniffles. She had no temperature. I encouraged her to keep her appointment. When she arrived she looked quite miserable. She complained of a stuffy nose. Her eyes were tearing. "But I don't feel really sick. And the worst thing isn't the cold. I feel *hungry*, terribly hungry, just starving. But not *really* hungry. It isn't like I could eat something and feel better."

I was able to show Nancy how the hunger was connected with longing for her mother and how the tearing eyes and congested nose represented the suppressed tears. And then I could encourage the expression of grief and longing more directly. During the next three hours Nancy was overwhelmed by feelings of love for her mother and longing for her return. As the tears began to come freely in analytic hours the cold symptoms diminished—an exchange that greatly impressed Nancy. Then through a piece of acting and a new set of symptoms we were able to establish connections between this separation from the parents and an earlier, traumatic separation.

There was a fight with Fenton, not so different from a number of other fights with Fenton, and again there were the fears of Fenton and what he might do to her. But this time Nancy's own destructive rage toward Fenton broke through. "I'm afraid I could kill him! I hate him! There will never be enough years to get rid of my hate by talking about it."

Then, in a rapid development during the second week of the parents' absence, a group of facial tics made their appearance. These consisted of a widening of the eyes, a wrinkling of the nose, a distorted grimacing and stretching of the mouth. When I now saw this group of tics in a constellation, I realized that each of these tics had appeared fleetingly at one time or another during the past months, but until this week we had never seen anything like this. I drew Nancy's attention to this new group of symptoms and began to suggest a meaning in terms of body language. When Nancy could finally acknowledge the tics as symptoms, she also told me with some surprise that they appeared *only* in her analytic hours. I was later able to confirm this.

Nancy could provide no associations to the tics and I had to suggest the meaning to her, i.e., "To see something frightening," "disgust," "horror." I suggested to her that the tics represented memories in the same way that the cold symptoms and the hunger were ways of remembering an earlier time when mother and father were away. And if we added to this group of symptoms the fight with Fenton, and the dream of the snake fight that we had left incompletely analyzed, we now had a picture, I proposed, of that time that was not remembered, when Nancy had observed the couple. The tics and the cold symptoms disappeared shortly afterwards.

The analysis of the snake dream, the repetitious features of the illness during separation from the parents, the acting with Fenton, and the tics were employed for reconstruction in this child analysis in a manner that closely follows the adult model. As memories and their associated affects were revived and re-experienced by the child, I helped Nancy see how the memory had been broken up into several components and how the fragments could be reassembled to tell a story. In my own reconstruction I proposed that during the period of the parents' absence at three, Nancy had experienced the same sadness and longing for her parents that we had seen in the more recent separation. I suggested that the three-year-old Nancy might have developed a cold or a sore throat in the same way as she repeatedly did when her parents were absent during the time I had known her. She may have awakened at night in discomfort or pain and gone in search of Cassie. At the door of Cassie's room she heard voices which later appeared in the chessboard fantasy as mumbling or jabbering. She entered the room and saw the couple in intercourse. What she saw she interpreted as "fighting," "attack," and the castration of a woman by a man, as we saw in the analysis of the snake dream. She was frightened and "left in a hurry," as we saw in the transference during the analysis. She was either afraid to tell about what she had seen or had been told not to tell, something we inferred through transference behavior at one point in the analysis. During the first period following the observation and before the memory was completely repressed, a group of tics may have appeared; in these the experience which could not be told was represented in symptoms, possibly identical with those she had recently experienced in the analysis. (I should mention, however, that the parents were unable to confirm my hypothesis regarding the tics. They had never seen these tics and had no memory of ticlike symptoms at an earlier age.)

This phase of the analysis of the primal scene observation produced demonstrable effects in Nancy's personality. In the months that followed we began to see the emergence of a new integrity of the ego replacing the unstable bisexual integrity that had disposed the ego to neurosis. There was a new energy and self-confidence, satisfaction in femininity, and heightened pleasure in learning, friendship and new endeavors. No new symptoms appeared and the old symptoms which had dropped out or receded in the earlier phases of analysis now seemed definitely out of the picture.

DISCUSSION

The excerpts from the case of Nancy were arbitrarily chosen in order to follow a single theme, a primal scene memory, as it emerged in the transference. The material demonstrates that a transference

neurosis appeared in the analysis of this child in latency, that it manifested itself in ways analogous to those of the adult model, and that
the analysis permitted technical handling which closely followed that
of adult analysis. My own experience and that of other child analysts
can provide a number of such examples in practice.

Both Sara Kut (1953) and Sylvia Brody (1961) have written about
transference in prepuberty and puberty and have provided illustrations which show a close correspondence in certain features to the
transference neurosis obtained in adult analysis. Both writers attribute
the readiness to form a transference neurosis in prepuberty and
puberty to the growing independence of the child from the original
objects. Sylvia Brody asks the question "whether we have not discounted too readily the significance of transference neurosis in children, or relied too little on its appearance" (p. 252). Anna Freud
(1945) wrote of "the open and controversial question as to whether
the relationship of the child to the analyst is really wholly governed
by a transference situation." She said, "Even if one part of the child's
neurosis is transformed into a transference neurosis as it happens in
adult analysis, another part of the child's neurotic behavior remains
grouped around the parents who are the original objects of his pathogenic past" (p. 130).

The illustrations from Nancy's case show us that latency may also
provide conditions favorable to the establishment of a transference
neurosis, that the factor of independence from the original objects
is not the only criterion. But "the open question" which Anna Freud
raises must be raised in this case, too. For while the primal scene
material appeared in the form of a transference neurosis and its
correspondence to the adult model is demonstrable, the full report
of this case would demonstrate that the whole of this child's analysis
did not come under the influence of a transference neurosis.

During the first two years of Nancy's analysis transference manifestations were employed extensively in the analytic work and with
great profit in reviving memories and affects of certain events that
had preceded the outbreak of the neurosis. As these memories were
revived they were transferred, but they were also relived or re-experienced with the original objects, and this does not correspond to "acting in the transference" but to the mode of childhood, the translation

of memories into actions and the availability of the original cast of characters for repetition and undoing.

Examples: When the analysis revived a memory of a traumatic episode of sex play between Nancy and her little friend, Mike, and Nancy experienced in her analytic hour the feelings of longing and humiliation, she did not re-experience this in the form of a love conflict or a feeling of rejection in the transference. She left the hour full of fury toward her faithless friend of four years ago and went in search of him. She found him dawdling in the front yard of his house, picked up a handful of mud and pelted him. She pursued him down the street flinging mud and insults at him.

Similarly, when Nancy in the second year of analysis re-experienced the love and longing for her mother that had undergone a transformation with the onset of the neurosis, it came about in this way: she produced fantasies in her analytic hours in which the queen was stolen from the king by a robber. However, when the affects themselves were revived during this period, they were not transferred to me, but re-experienced as love and yearning for the mother. In these examples we only confirm that which we already know about the child patient in analysis, namely, that the child who still possesses the original objects can relive on the home grounds certain conflicts which, in the adult patient, can be reproduced only in transference.

But now we are obliged to take into account that the primal scene material in Nancy's case was reproduced in the form of a transference neurosis and that the recovery of memories from the third year was achieved almost exclusively from the analysis of the transference neurosis. The analytic material provides its own answer. *For this memory was, properly speaking, "repressed."* It could be revived only in transference, in analogy with the conditions that facilitate the formation of a transference neurosis in adults. In the earlier period of analysis, when the analytic work centered mainly on the defenses against affects and the recovery of experiences that had led to the onset of the neurosis, the case material would show that these memories had undergone only partial repression. Once the affective links were restored each of the memories came through clearly and without distortion. To a very large extent these memories were re-experienced with the original cast of characters.

I believe that the question of "availability of the original objects" can also be qualified by a study of "kind and degree of repression." A brief example from Nancy's case illustrates the problem. I have already mentioned that the tender tie to the mother was revived in the analysis and experienced directly in relation to the mother, without transference manifestations as far as I could judge; but the erotic tie to mother emerged in the later analysis in the form of a transference fantasy. In one of Nancy's fantasies I was represented as a seducer of girls. When the fantasy was analyzed in the transference, memories of a very primitive kind emerged, a tactile memory of a hand, the rough texture of cloth, sensations of smoothness and roughness, and then a picture swam into consciousness of a mother bathing a little girl and washing her genitals. This memory, from a period under three years of age, could find its way into consciousness only by means of the transference. And unlike the earlier example of the tender feelings toward mother, the erotic tie to mother did not seek repetition with the mother herself, but found representation in a transference fantasy. Here, we have another demonstration of a memory that is, properly speaking, repressed and a libidinal aim that has undergone repression, both of which unite in a transference fantasy and in a manner entirely analogous to that of the adult transference neurosis. And while the original object, the mother, was still available, repression of the libidinal aim had prevented the repetition with the original object.

Where even a part of the child's neurosis is transformed into a transference neurosis the advantages for the child analysis will be as great as for the adult analysis. For it may be that only in this way can the analyst have access to the deepest layers of the neurosis. In the case of Dorothy, which I cited at the beginning of this paper, it was my failure to explore the dimensions of the transference that left untouched a pathogenic core that lay dormant and in a state of readiness to produce new symptoms in adolescence.

BIBLIOGRAPHY

Brody, S. (1961), Some Aspects of Transference Resistance in Prepuberty. *This Annual,* 16:251-274.
Fraiberg, S. (1951), Clinical Notes on the Nature of Transference in Child Analysis. *This Annual,* 6:286-306.
Freud, A. (1945), Indications for Child Analysis. *This Annual,* 1:127-149.
Kut, S. (1953), The Changing Pattern of Transference in the Analysis of an Eleven-year-old Girl. *This Annual,* 8:355-378.

SOME COMMENTS ON THE SIMULTANEOUS ANALYSIS OF A FATHER AND HIS ADOLESCENT SON

HAROLD KOLANSKY, M.D. and WILLIAM T. MOORE, M.D.

In the history of child analysis, the technique of dealing with parents and their involvement in the analytic process have been important problems. From the first case of child analysis the part played by parents has been a primary consideration. Freud (1909) set this pattern in "The Analysis of a Phobia in a Five-year-old Boy" by utilizing the important relationship of the boy's father and conducting the entire analysis through this parent. To our knowledge there have been no other reported cases of a child analyzed by his parent, and in general the difficulty in establishing transference and maintaining objectivity would appear to militate against such a procedure.

As early as 1945 Anna Freud stated that during the evaluation of a child for analysis, one must assess the ego of the parents and borrow from the parent's ego during the analysis of the child. In the psychoanalytic treatment of children, the analyst must depend upon the parents' cooperation, and he must be mindful of the part parents play in the resistance to the resolution of the neurotic process in the child. The child analyst must therefore deal not only with the child but also with one or both parents so that the child can become free of his regressive fixations and move forward developmentally. These efforts are frequently diverted by the intensity of a parent's neurosis and its effect upon the child. In such instances the analysis of the child does not succeed unless the involved parent is also analyzed. Anna Freud indicated that most of the cases seen in the earlier period

The authors are members of the Child Analysis Study Group and the faculty of the Institute of the Philadelphia Association for Psychoanalysis.

The paper was read before the Baltimore, Cleveland, Philadelphia Psychoanalytic Congress, in Washington, D.C., June 11, 1966.

of child analysis were children of parents who had already been analyzed or who were at least sympathetic to the needs of the child.

We would like to present a brief summary of previous work with parents as described in the analytic literature. It has been known for a very long time that the parent's conscious and unconscious attitudes and fantasies play a distinct part in the child's development (Johnson and Szurek, 1952), and if these are not taken into account, one can neither fully understand the child's productions nor can one gain the parent's sympathetic support of the treatment. Burlingham (1932) indicated the need to maintain the cooperation and the sympathy of the parents throughout the entire analysis of the child, and stressed that "if one does not succeed in this the analysis moves inevitably to an abrupt and premature interruption" (p 69). For this reason the analyst has to "keep the child's parents in a favorable attitude toward the analysis" (p. 69). She further indicated that the analyst must keep contact with the mother and emphasized that "The power of unconscious forces is especially marked in its interplay between parent and child. It is so subtle and uncanny that it seems at times to approach the supernatural" (p. 71). Although Burlingham did not explicitly refer to the simultaneous analysis of parent and child, she laid the groundwork for it by stating "When an adult has successfully completed an analysis, he knows what to do with his released potentialities; but a child, just because he is a child, still has to be guided and helped and given opportunities to use these related powers. In the development of a child, this is a part of his normal education" (p. 73). Often enough the parent is not capable of guiding and helping the child unless he himself has had an analysis.

Almost all workers in child analysis, as those in child psychiatry, have felt the need to work with the parent in one way or another. Burlingham (1951), reviewing the various methods, spoke of preventive work with the mother, involvement of the entire family, and group therapy, all having limited value in their effect on the treatment of the child. She further indicated that there still remained a large group of children who could be helped only by psychoanalysis. She described less serious situations in which a person other than the child's analyst worked wtih the mother in an effort to resolve the more superficial childhood problems and to decrease her jealousy of the child's analyst. Burlingham then described a case in which analytic advice was given to the mother of a two-and-a-half-year-old who had eating, soiling, and speech problems. In this instance there was some beneficial result because the mother cooperated. However, when the child was three and a half it was found that he needed analysis because he had developed an obsessional neurosis. At this point the mother reacted as if she had never heard the advice given her previously. Her unconscious fantasies had not been touched. While the child was in analysis the analyst also worked with the mother and the child made some progress. Burlingham discussed this case again in 1955.

Erna Furman (1957) reviewed the ways in which parents had been seen therapeutically or prophylactically in work with children. She stated there were three main approaches: (1) advice on upbringing; (2) treatment of the mother by psychoanalysis or other techniques; (3) a method aimed at keeping the focus of work centered on the child within a nursery school setting while having discussions with the mother.

Other modifications of work with mothers have been successfully used while directly treating the young child. These have to do largely with inclusion of the mother during certain therapeutic sessions with the child. For instance, Berta Bornstein (1935) occasionally included the child's mother in the treatment of Lisa, as did Steff Bornstein (1935) in treating a three-year-old. Schwarz (1950) and Kolansky (1960) also stressed that the mother's presence during certain sessions has a beneficial effect and increases her ability to understand the young child.

Simultaneous analysis of husband and wife has been practiced since the early years of analysis. It has often been observed that as one partner begins to free himself through psychoanalytic treatment from a severely neurotic relationship with his spouse, the other partner will seek analysis as a result of the loss of neurotic interaction. The neurotic economy of the marriage has been severely disturbed. It is therefore not surprising that such simultaneous analysis is occasionally necessary when a mother and child are locked in a severely neurotic adaptation to life.

Simultaneous analysis of child and parent conducted by two analysts, was first described by Burlingham, Goldsberger, and Lussier

1955). Burlingham elaborated on the case of Bobby first mentioned in her 1951 paper. Bobby was one of many children in whom much effort resulted in disappointment. Unconscious forces in the mother could not be dealt with short of the mother's own analysis.

Most cases of simultaneous analysis have originated in the Hampstead Clinic in England. Such a clinical setting seems to lend itself well to careful and systematic investigation of this treatment.

Anna Freud, in her introduction to Kata Levy's report (1960) on "The Simultaneous Analysis of a Mother and Her Adolescent Daughter," stated that the material gained from the nine mother-child analyses in the Hampstead Child-Therapy Clinic has served a number of useful purposes: "It is invaluable for highlighting the points of interaction between the abnormalities of mother and child. . . . The detailed clinical demonstrations . . . represent a welcome step forward from child-guidance work to the effect that precise information backed by analytic . . . findings takes the place . . . of the former rather vague generalizations" (pp. 378-379). She made three additional points:

1. The Hampstead material suggests that not all children react directly to their mother's symptoms; some children are affected only indirectly, e.g., by the interference of the mother's illness with her capacity for mothering. The resultant disturbances in the child are often completely different from those in the mothers. They show none of the characteristic consequences of overlapping fantasies and *folie-à-deux* phenomena.

2. The studies demonstrated that when neurotic symptoms, conflicts, and repression in the child were reinforced by powerful emotional forces in the parent, the therapeutic action of child analysis was slowed up or rendered inadequate.

3. The tool of simultaneous analysis can be used profitably in understanding other developmental problems. The interaction between parents and child is fundamental to elucidating the *foundations of personality* or the *roots of mental illness*. Moreover, "as a child moves forward on the developmental scale, each step demands the giving up of former positions and gains, not only from the child himself but also from the parent" (p. 379). Often the child wants to make the progressive move and is held back by the parent. In the most difficult cases "mother and child may join forces in a regressive

move. Such interlocking then becomes particularly fateful with the onset of puberty. . . . [In these cases] simultaneous analysis enables us to trace the contributions made by both sides to the success or failure of this particular developmental task" (p. 380).

Anna Freud's comments, particularly those referring to the adolescent, were of special interest to us because we were analyzing an adolescent boy and his father. This is unusual because all of our other cases of simultaneous analysis involved mother and child, as did the cases reported by the Hampstead Clinic. In our other cases the mothers began their analyses a year or two after the children upon the recommendation of the child's analyst. In the case described in this paper, the father was in analysis for two years before his son entered analysis; however, four years previously, the boy had been seen once weekly in psychotherapy by a nonanalyst for a ten-month period. This treatment was terminated by the father.

In the cases reported by Dorothy Burlingham et al. (1955) and Ilse Hellman et al. (1960) mother and child were seen by different analysts in training who reported the material to a senior analyst. In this way they avoided the pitfalls of double transference, which Melitta Sperling (1950, 1951, 1954) encountered when she analyzed both mother and child. We have adopted a different procedure and have in the past eight years discussed our cases of simultaneous analyses. At first we did this somewhat infrequently. When we observed no transference and countertransference difficulties, we became more active in the exchange of material.

We were impressed with the degree to which our experiences confirmed the findings stated in the literature, especially those coming from the Hampstead Clinic. We were repeatedly able to corroborate specific unconscious influences exerted by the parents on the children, influences which might otherwise have remained for the most part speculative. We have also had opportunities to observe direct cause-and-effect relationships as the simultaneous analyses of both patients progressed.

Simultaneous analyses had other advantages: (a) We obtained a clearer picture of the child's developmental lines—his inhibitions, regressions, and progressions. (b) We gained much better insight into the mutual psychopathology and its effects. (c) In some cases more severe psychopathology in the child could be prevented. (d) The exchange of material between the two analysts often highlighted specific trends before they would have become apparent if the individual analyst had known only the material of his own case. (e) When the parent's pathology interfered with the progress of the child's analysis, the child analyst could refer the parent to his own analyst.

In general we have referred a parent for analysis when his psychopathology was so severe that it interfered with the child's development and progress in analysis. In these instances, although the child's conflicts were of course intrapsychic, the parent's neurosis enforced a continuation of the child's neurosis. Changes in the child would induce too intense anxiety in the parent. In some instances the parent's psychopathology, regardless of its effect on the child, was severe enough and sufficiently incapacitating to warrant treatment.

In Philadelphia, it is not infrequent for two analysts to be conducting such simultaneous analyses. Over the past eight years the authors have worked together on four cases of simultaneous analysis of a parent and child. In the first case, we found that a latency girl could not sufficiently work through her feelings of murderous rage toward her mother and the projection of that rage onto the mother until the mother entered her own analysis and worked through unconscious feelings which led her to react to her daughter as she had to her own older sister whom she hated and feared. This woman treated her daughter in a cruel and sadistic fashion, which played an important part in the development of an obsessional neurosis in the child. The daughter was able to deal with her ambivalence toward the mother only after the mother had gained some insight into her own childhood conflicts. Then the analysis of the child also began to move forward.

The second case was that of an early latency boy who was in analysis because of marked effeminate tendencies. His progress was quite limited until his mother, a pregenitally fixated character with intense penis envy, entered analysis and began to work through her own dissatisfaction with him. From his birth on she regarded him as a defective child and unconsciously attempted to castrate him; but she also had projected an image of herself as an unwanted child onto him and rejected him at every turn.

In the third case, an adolescent girl had been in analysis for a year prior to her mother being referred for analysis when it became obvious that the girl's intensely sadomasochistic relationship with her father was unconsciously sanctioned by the mother. The mother's analysis disclosed that she was using the girl as a foil to ward off sexual relations with her husband. Herself being frigid and castrating, she again and again threw the girl at her husband. The result was a mutual acting out of sadomasochism, which created the greatest of difficulties in the analysis of the girl.

The fourth case, which we are presenting here, involved the simultaneous analysis of a father and his adolescent son. This father projected his unconscious impulses onto his son and then warded off these projected wishes by certain reaction formations against them. Further, the father used identification with the aggressor (his own father) as a means of protecting himself from anxiety about his own passivity, while at the same time he unconsciously perpetuated the family pattern of male passivity. The son identified with the model of behavior set by the father and developed a compliant personality virtually identical with the father's. The son could be analyzed only after the father had worked through part of his need to insure the son's passive allegiance to him. Repeatedly, the son's analysis progressed only after the father had analyzed aspects of his fate neurosis, passivity, and anxieties about possessing a small penis.

In the case material which follows we have concentrated on demonstrating the advantage of simultaneous analysis to obtain a clearer picture of some aspects of the child's development, the mutual psychopathology and neurotic interaction of parent and child, and the ability of the child to make progress in his own analysis at times when his father's analysis became effective. The technical procedure of an exchange of information between the analysts and the utilization of such information to highlight events in the analyses of parent and child will be discussed in a future paper.

Treatment of the Child

Dick B. appeared in my office a passive, reluctant, affectless mass. He seemed quite preoccupied and somewhat detached and was very disinterested in treatment. With an occasional question I managed to keep the conversation going during the first hour. In the second interview he blandly suggested that the treatment was a waste of time and money. "It won't do no good. I don't see wasa use." He ran his words together, a characteristic of his form of speech at the time. He later informed me that he had had speech therapy at the age of seven, but "it dint do no goot." He seemed to begrudge the energy necessary to carry on a conversation. He said he had tried psychiatrists before, but it always ended up the same way: "Nuffin is complished. Ya coont get nowhere. Ya coont change nuffin." Following this he became sullen and silent.

At the beginning of his analysis Dick was thirteen years old and had recently been Bar Mitzvahed. He was referred for analysis because of his very poor academic performance (I.Q. 105) and lack of any initiative or responsibility. Both parents expressed concern about the effect of the father's frequent beatings of Dick. The boy told me that they began when he was six or seven years of age.

He had been in once-a-week psychotherapy at the age of eleven for approximately nine months. At the age of twelve there had been an abortive attempt at analysis with another child analyst. Dick said, "It dint last cuz I dint like him and he coont help anyway." Mrs. B. was opposed to treatment because the analyst's office was too far away (a realistic consideration). It was quite apparent to both parents that they did not want Dick to be analyzed as they quickly terminated the treatment. Mrs. B. stated that "Dickie" was her oldest and favorite son (the younger ones were Alfred, ten, and Edward, seven). At the time I saw Dick, Mr. B. had been in analysis for two years. While he thought he was in favor of Dick's analysis, he admitted that he had been active in terminating his son's previous attempts at treatment. Both parents still felt that Dick would be fine were it not for his poor schoolwork. Except for that they doubted that they would even consider analysis for him. They recognized, however, that Dick had no friends and strenuously avoided any competitive situation. When Mr. B. tried to interest Dick in golf and skiing, "he would stop before he got started." Dick had failed physical education and did poorly in all school subjects. He seemed to have no interests at all. He rarely talked to his parents and communicated with them only in a perfunctory manner. His only activity seemed to be beating up his two younger brothers. In turn he was chased and beaten by his father. As the father would strike, Dick fell to the floor and Mr. B. would either jump on him and punch the boy about the head, or he would kick him in the torso as Dick tried to roll out of the way.

Dick had a long history of periodic abdominal pain, nausea, and diarrhea. On several occasions a diagnosis of peptic ulcer and spastic colitis was made, but the former was not demonstrated by X-ray. The final conclusion was that the symptoms were of emotional origin.

As the analysis began Dick told his mother it would be of no use because he would not tell his analyst anything, nor would he tell her regardless of how much he was beaten. Both parents were afraid that Dick would get out of control if they could not find a punishment to substitute for the beatings. They feared they could not *make* him do what they wanted, i.e., to improve in school and not fight with his brothers. He might not show them a *proper* respect or do their bidding. They immediately invited me to find an effective punishment since they knew the beatings must stop. I of course refused to "offer" one.

Shortly thereafter Dick told me that his parents seemed to beat him less often. He thought it was because they feared what I would think of them. He smiled and added that it would be of no use; before long his father would revert. "He always went back before. That's why I stopped seein Dr. W. [first psychiatrist] cuz he coont change my father and you coont neither. Nuffin works wif him. It coont do no good to see me." I asked Dick if he had any hope that his father might stop beating him once his father had gained some understanding of his own problems through analysis. Dick thought for a moment, then replied, "It dint do no good so far." Once Dick had agreed to give his own analysis a try, "even if it didn't do any good," he came to his own sessions regularly without complaint. He stipulated, however, "Ya mustn't spect me to do alla talkin. I don like it when someone spects me to do somethin."

He started out by telling me he thought his father was right in punishing him; otherwise he, like any boy, would never behave. His discussion became quite heated when I wondered why it must be by beating. He said all fathers have to beat their kids, "it's the only punishment and if you don't punish children they are bad." He stated further that he knew that was what I did to my children, as did all the other fathers in the world; it was stupid not to punish children. In this way he frantically protected his parents from *his own* criticism and hatred. On one occasion his eyes filled with tears as he told me it was really only his father who beat him (not completely true), and his mother tried to protect and save him from his father (a frequent occurrence). He added, "I love my mother, she is so nice."

After six months he told me of his earlier interest in stamp collecting. When he was eight years old his father gave him his own boyhood stamp collection. Although Dick had not bothered with it for several years, he thought he should renew his interest. He began collecting commemorative sheets after seeing some on my desk. Since I knew a little about stamp collecting, we talked about it at great length. Frequently he was quite discouraged about collecting stamps because his father did not permit him to use some of his own savings (from Bar Mitzvah gifts).

Dick began to express some concern that his father would not change and the beatings would continue. He thought I should see his father again even though he felt it would do no good. One day Mr. B. called me in an excited state. He overheard Dick gambling (matching quarters) with some other boys in his bedroom. Mr. B. insisted that his son be punished for this "inexcusable practice." He knew he should not beat him, but what punishment should he use. I asked him why he was so upset about it and indicated that his reaction seemed to be out of proportion to the situation. So he went directly to his own analyst with the problem. When Dick noted what had happened, he became more courageous in his criticism of his father, "You know he shoont hit me so much. Other fathers don't. I asked some of my friends and my father is the worst. Some boys have only been hit one time in their whole life."

Dick began to discuss the fights at home in more detail. Usually arguments or teasing with one of his younger brothers would lead to the father attacking Dick. "I try to get away. I run and go limp cause he can't hit me so well when I fall down." He gradually realized that Alfred would provoke him to hit when his father was around. As Dick expressed it, "He *framed me* so I cood git hit by Dad." He also told me that he could neither refuse nor criticize his mother's cooking without being sent to his room or hit by his father. He felt this was hard to understand because his father always complained or refused to eat many foods himself. Dick noticed that his mother would tell his father about things he had done earlier in the day. "Then he starts wif me. Sometimes it's her fault too. Wize she doot?" Dick by now had become adamant about his father. "He can't make me do nuffin. He can beat me all he wants. I won't eat. I won't let my brothers alone. I won't study. I won't do nuffin he wants." When Dick now argued with his father and anticipated anger and attack, he would say, "Go ahead and hit me, thas what you want to do anyway." He was quite pleased with himself when this action seemed to abort the attack.

I recalled a comment Dr. Kolansky had made to me in the course of our discussion. He stated that Mr. B. equated his own masturbation with beating his son "Dickie." Mr. B felt he must control his son as he controlled his penis with masturbation (beating). At a later time Mr. B. himself told me of his fears that if he did not keep Dick and the other boys "under his thumb," they would "get out of hand." He commented that this was a problem he had been working on in his own analysis.

Dick also became more critical of his mother. Her informing the father of Dick's misbehavior resulted in Dick being beaten by his father, whereupon she would criticize the father for beating Dick. "If she dint want him to hit me, why'd she start to begin wif. She's no better than he is."

Dick's massive repressions were a severe handicap to him in every sphere of his life. We concentrated considerable attention on his inability to remember things from one day to the next. I indicated how he could not remember even the simplest details. He would begin each session by announcing, "Nuffin happened since last time." He was quite impressed when he began to realize how many things had happened that he had forgotten. Even though he at first resented my calling his attention to the matter, he changed his greeting to, "I don't think anything happened, but I'll probably find out plenty did." (I noted that his slurred speech began to disappear.) I told Dick that his fights were so unpleasant to him that he had to protect himself by forgetting anything that might act as a reminder.

As Dick became aware of how little he could remember, he developed some enthusiasm for the analysis. Once he was most impressed to find he could not even remember the full names of five friends. He commented himself that in addition to not remembering, he did not even seem to notice what went on around him. He became acutely aware of his lack of attention and the amount of daydreaming in school. The latter, he said, he could never tell me about. These were *too personal* and he wanted to keep them to himself even if he *ever* could remember any of them. He realized he could not remember what he read even though he was a voluminous reader. Nor could he memorize any material for tests. This realization alarmed him. He would frequently test his memory. One day he commented, "No wonder I never do any good. I study and forget everything. It's discouraging." He said his mind was like a "steel door" because it would not let anything in or out. I welcomed his steel door comment and used it frequently in our discussions.

Dick now began to compare himself with his father and paternal grandfather. The grandfather was a wealthy businessman who was in a successful partnership with a "real tycoon." The grandfather lived in awe of his partner and often spoke of his gratitude for being associated with this man. He felt he owed his financial success to this partner. Dick wondered why his own father, at almost forty, was just starting his own business after working many years for the grandfather. The boy spoke of the grandfather's frugal living and his meager furnishings. "Why does he when he is a millionaire?" Dick noted that his grandfather was not as rich as the partner. He understood it though. "Mr. A. gets all the business and gets things to work for him, so it's only right he grabs most of the money." Dick wondered whether his grandfather gave up too easily. "Maybe it's because he has all those heart attacks. Before that, though, he got up early and worked hard." He was puzzled about why his father still had to tell grandpa everything and seemed afraid of him. He wondered whether his grandfather had beaten his father when he was a boy. (Later Dick confirmed this by asking his grandfather during a visit.) He wondered whether the *men in his family* passed on the feeling that *it's no use* because everything works against them. He hastily added that usually it was just *bad luck*. As proof he cited his father's bad luck on two recent business ventures. Dick pointed out that he always had the bad luck to hit his brother every time his father was around. I reminded him that he thought Alfred "framed" him; yet he seemed willing to go along with it over and over again. Perhaps *some* of the "bad luck" was his own doing.

Dick started to bring problems about homework to the analytic sessions. He asked me whether I could help him with definitions and spelling, about which he was most concerned. It became apparent that he usually miscopied assignments and then learned misspelled words as well as wrong definitions. When I called this to Dick's attention he was impressed with the idea that he surely would fail even if he learned everything he had prepared. As a result of our talks he learned words correctly and passed his tests. To his dismay, however, he began to lose the word lists or forgot to bring them to the sessions. Two days before a history test he mentioned that he would have to flunk because of *bad luck*. He had lost his notebook with all the questions and answers. When I suggested that he could get them from another student or consult his teacher, he replied, "No! I can't bother him. It woont do no good. Nuffin ever does." I commented that it seemed to me he was giving "bad luck" a helping hand and thereby insuring his failure. He smiled, "Just like pop and grandpop, huh?" Later he brought his report card and surreptitiously placed it on my desk, without my noticing it. Several times during the hour I commented on his mysterious smile. He laughed and replied, "You will find out why." When I discovered the report card, it was his worst ever and had followed a report card which indicated that he had improved. "I fooled you," he laughed, "see nuffin does no good. Nuffin ever can." I commented that he seemed pleased with the idea that he had disappointed me and that analysis could do him no good. But I believed he was really worried and still felt he had to prove that no one could make him do anything, including me. He replied that his father was angry, but that could not make him improve. "He used to yell and beat me, but it did no good." He added that it had always been important to his father that he did well in school. This was followed by a long discussion of his father always calling him "stupid." "So I showed him he is right. I *hate* him [first time]! I will never like him til he dies no matter how he treats me now. It's too late. The hate is too much."

Dick began to realize that one way he could get back at his father was to see his father helpless with rage and frustration at not being able to control his school performance. He said he could prove his father was not powerful enough to *make him do good*. "I guess I like to see him mad because he looks so foolish. It used to be the madder he got, the more he would beat me even for little things. Any little thing would set him off. But I could never give in. He ought to know by now he does no good. He says I have no interests and I don't care. I hate him so much I don't think I could ever get over it." Thus it seemed Dick was able to stimulate his father's anxiety by becoming his father's uncontrollable penis no matter how much he was beaten. Father and son were locked in a neurotic conflict that would indeed be difficult to break.

Shortly thereafter Dick, stimulated by a younger friend, developed an interest in ham radio. He enrolled in a course at the Franklin Institute, then decided he would save his money to buy amateur radio equipment. He also became very interested in making money and obtained a morning paper route for which he got up early (as he knew his grandfather had). The announcement of the job brought negative and discouraging comments from the father. Dick developed a small baby-sitting business with limited success. He frequently stated he did not want his father's money because he was too petty and "cheap" about all money matters.

After Dick had been in analysis for a year and a half, Mrs. B. gave birth to a fourth son, and while she was hospitalized Dick went to live with an aunt and was most impressed with the easy atmosphere in her home. He openly did not want to return to his own home, having now a fuller realization of the neurotic behavior prevailing there: "They always have something going. Mom and Dad or my two brothers. I wish I never had to live there again because there's always something in the air." After making his wishes quite known to his parents, they finally insisted that he return.

When Dick again had a poor report card, his reaction was: "Boy, those D's got to me this time, like never before. I decided I better do something." He wondered how he had recently done on Iowa Achievement Tests. He wanted to know whether he was "really stupid like Dad says." He asked me to get the test results from his school so that he could find out in which areas he was doing poorly. "Maybe I can get a tutor and do better." He gradually improved his study habits and worked harder at the amateur radio course as well. He said, "I hate that steel door. I hope we can get rid of it. It's so hard to remember things when I study."

I have presented only those aspects of the case which I feel have a direct bearing on our discussion of simultaneous analysis of parent and child.

If Mr. B. had not been in analysis himself, Dick certainly would never have received analytic treatment. Even if he had, it is extremely doubtful whether it would have been possible to analyze him. The beatings would not have stopped; hence the mutual neurotic involvement with his father would have presented an unsurmountable hurdle. Moreover, assuming that Dick had developed some insight into his behavior, his father, without his own analysis, would not have stood by and allowed the disruption of his own neurotic need satisfactions. With a continuation of his father's brutality, I believe it would have been impossible in Dick's analysis to reach a point at which Dick could understand his fear of his father as a projection of his own aggressive and hostile impulse. Therefore it seems to us, as we have indicated in the introduction, that a child who is an integral part of the neurotic economy of a parent cannot successfully start or complete an analysis unless the parent has previously had an analysis or is simultaneously undergoing an analysis. Otherwise the parent will not allow the child to be analyzed, nor will the child be willing.

ANALYSIS OF THE FATHER

Mr. B. was an extremely tight and rigid man of thirty-five, who showed evidence of a lifelong struggle with his impotent efforts to assert his masculinity. He came for analysis when he recognized his considerable anxiety and difficulty in his father's business. His father had a secondary role in the business, which was originally jointly owned by Mr. B.'s father and another man. Due to the passivity of Mr. B.'s father, his partner had at an early time taken advantage of him and as a consequence Mr. B's father had lost approximately one third of the multimillion-dollar business.

When Mr. B. arrived for his first appointment he appeared to be timid, frightened, overly respectful, and cautious, although he obviously wanted to talk about his worries. He was thin, in fact somewhat asthenic looking, balding, wore metal-framed glasses, was somewhat hunched over, spoke in a quiet way with obvious discomfort in speaking, and his manner of speaking did not convey the fact that he had

had a college education; he used words incorrectly, and his sentence structure was often faulty, due to tension. There were elements of some depression, and the overall impression was of a man completely lacking self-confidence.

Mr. B. early complained about the fact that he assumed great responsibility in the business without having the authority to back it up, especially on the two occasions when his father suffered a coronary occlusion. Mr. B. often thought that he should leave the business, but never felt free to do so because of the fear that his father would be upset, have another coronary and die. His younger sister recently also had had a coronary.

Because of his fears of a heart attack, Mr. B. placed himself on a stringent diet, so completely lacking in cholesterol content of any kind that it was tasteless. Mr. B. also felt extremely anxious when his father ate food containing cholesterol. All day long he worried about his father's health, and went through countless obsessional rituals and routines to protect himself from an awareness of his death wishes toward his father, especially when the father traveled by air.

Mr. B. showed the anal character traits of parsimoniousness, obstinacy, and orderliness, described by Freud (1908). He was meticulous in his appearance, conscientious, trustworthy, and had intense reaction formations against disorder, dirt, and food remaining on dishes after a meal. He was plagued by the fact that his wife was, in his own description, "a slob who never cleans dishes, the house or the children." On the other hand there were breakthroughs of his sadism in the form of rage and revengefulness, coldness and ambivalence toward his wife and his eldest son, Dick. He also had premature ejaculations, and as a consequence of his impotence frequently avoided his wife sexually. He was consumed with the feeling that his penis was too small and from adolescence on had avoided shower rooms for this reason. He complained that his wife did not control her eating habits, was overweight, and took little care of the children. He talked a lot about food and his food anxieties, which had many roots. The wrong foods could lead to coronary occlusion; this anxiety appeared to be the result of castration anxiety, in relation to his murderous feelings toward his father. He was angry at his wife for not feeding the children before they went to school; this appeared to be a displaced resentment because his own passive longings were not fulfilled. He reacted with disgust to food partially eaten and left on plates following a meal; this disgust was a reaction formation against anal impulses. His wife's overeating made her sexually unattractive to him, which he used as a rationalization for his impotence.

He told me that he was never able to confide in his father; a void existed in Mr. B.'s relationship to his father, as it did between himself and Dick. As previously described, Dick had marked learning difficulties in school and suffered from a spastic colon. He too was obstinate, stubborn, defiant, opinionated, and quarrelsome. In brief, he showed evidence of an anal character structure similar to that of his father. Mr. B. reacted with intense rage to these characteristics in his son, which were caricatures of his own personality. He could not tolerate Dick's "freshness and disobedience which no boy should show toward a father." He could not stand his children's bickering and rarely took them out to dinner because of it.

Several months after the analysis began Mr. B. reported his first dream: His father was lying down and began to drowse and mumble while playing cards with his partner. Mr. B. anxiously shook his father to see whether he was alright. This made his father angry and confused about where he was. In his associations Mr. B. revealed his apprehension about a feeling that his father was losing his memory, as his grandfather had, and that his father would not wear glasses although he was losing his vision. His father did not protect his health, often stayed up too late playing cards. His father often withdrew from important decisions, as if lying down on the job, leaving the decisions to his partner. This had in fact happened on the day of the dream, and Mr. B., acting like a watchdog, had asked his father why this happened, only to get a gruff retort. The partner told Mr. B. that his father was no longer very capable and that more would be expected of Mr. B. Mr. B. said that he knew he was overly concerned about his father's health; however, he had also noticed some cloudiness in his father's eyes![1]

The dream showed both Mr. B.'s reaction formation against his death wishes toward the father and the elimination of the father

[1] The following day, Mr. B. had another dream in which he saw his sister lying dead, while he asked: "Why did it have to happen to you?" In his associations, he mentioned the fact that the only person he ever saw dead was his grandmother, who died after a cataract operation. This was significant, because on the previous day his associations had been concerned with his father's probable need for cataract surgery.

from the card game. He was being "dealt out" by his son and felt insulted. In brief, Mr. B.'s father perceived this as a castration threat. Mr. B. mentioned that he also acted as a watchdog toward Dick, but Dick rebelled primarily because his father acted as if he were castrating him by emphasizing his faults and by preventing him from becoming independent.

Mr. B. often mentioned Dick after mentioning a struggle with his father. On one occasion, he told me about being rebuffed by his father when he really wanted to be praised. Abruptly he talked about Dick wanting praise for a good mark the previous night, and that his wife had to nudge him to say something supportive. He mentioned his father's unconstructive criticisms, and then, without being aware of the connection, talked about criticizing his wife for her weight and an argument with his son about a poor grade in school. Thus, whenever Mr. B. felt criticized in his business, he would be highly critical of his wife or Dick, as if to restore his narcissism, through the mechanism of identification with the aggressor.

Mr. B. indicated that Dick never gave him any sense of gratification. Later he mentioned that his father continuously told him, " want some *naches* [pride and pleasure] from you before I die." Mr. B began to consider starting a business of his own. During this period his resistance in the treatment mounted and was characterized by many silences. At the same time, in response to his father's anger about his leaving, Mr. B. began to beat Dick severely.

His worry about having a small penis emerged again. He had been unable to change his clothes in the locker room of his club and remembered that in junior high he used to go to the gym with some of his friends, who would say, "You have a small prick." When asked how real this concern was, he said his penis was smaller than most he had ever seen, but when erect he guessed it was of average size. Although he said his other sons were normally endowed, he felt Dick's penis was as small as his, and Dick seemed to suffer from similar embarrassment. Mr. B. remembered that as a child he had secretly resented his father because he felt he had inherited a small penis from him.

At times when Mr. B. was struggling with his competitive feelings toward his father and his wish to break away from him, as if to demonstrate the size of his own penis, he would have dreams that reflected his attempts to solve his phallic conflicts on an anal level. Thus, he was defecating a huge, long, and narrow piece of feces. Castration anxiety was of course prominent throughout. He mentioned one day that his son Edward, then almost five years old, was handling his genitals and that his wife had removed the boy's hands from his genitals. Mr. B. remembered masturbating at the same age and being told to stop. Edward quite obviously had erections and began to develop reaction formations by saying that his penis was hard and hurt. Mr. B. recalled, "When I was eight or nine I liked to fondle myself, but I was guilty all the time, and I would wash my hands for five minutes as if to wash the guilt away. When I was twelve I thought of a Tarzan comic strip, in which a white princess was anointed with oil in a ritual. This excited me and called my attention to her breasts." In connection with masturbation, he mentioned that his younger sister had been his father's favorite. It was clear, although not to the patient, that his masturbatory fantasies had to be warded off because of their oedipal content. He regressed to the anal phase, and subsequently developed obsessional rituals as a defense.

During this period the patient's analysis dealt with three themes: the masturbation memories that had been stirred up by his son, his sexual impotence, and the anxiety about failing in business (which in actuality also represented a wish to fail, so that he would not be in competition with his father). He lacked enthusiasm, lacked confidence, and wondered whether he had the ability to succeed, but he could not stay in the business with his father because he hated taking orders like a schoolboy. An interpretation was made that his fear of leaving the business and being on his own was related to his feelings of opposition to his father whom he desired to hurt. Thoughts about leaving the business certainly brought his passivity, and homosexuality, his concern about the small penis, his fate neurosis, his sadistic attitude toward Dick, and his castration anxiety into focus, as will be seen in what follows.

After expressing some mild resentment about his father, Mr. B. had several overt castration dreams. These further elucidated his hand-washing compulsion. Each time after masturbating he had to wash seven times—a practice that had stopped only two years prior to the analysis. The feelings of inadequacy continued to be expressed in dreams about playing baseball and not being able to get the ball up in the air. This led to associations about his small penis, his inability to satisfy his wife sexually, and about Dick not being able to measure up.

As his anxiety about leaving the business mounted, he became increasingly restrictive with his children. I interpreted the symptomatic nature of this behavior which interfered with his children's lives and bound him down as well. He became very disturbed, saying that what he had considered to be an asset now turned out to be a liability. On further reflection, however, he conceded that his restrictiveness needed consideration. He knew he was inhibited and could use his energies better and wondered whether his troubles had all started with his masturbation at eight or nine. He remembered that at that time he stole stamps from a store, felt ashamed and guilty, lay awake nights waiting to be caught, feeling he was a little crook. His orderliness and collecting of all kinds of things had begun shortly thereafter at the age of ten. At this time, too, as he put it, "I displaced the cleaning of my soul to my body with the hand washing." I said that this was like the orthodox Jewish custom of thoroughly cleaning before the High Holidays partially to relieve guilt over sins, and this brought to his mind his father's actual orthodoxy and the beatings father gave him as a child when he broke the Sabbath rules. The stamp stealing, a displacement from the masturbation, represented an unconscious effort to be caught and punished.

His death wishes and his obsessional preoccupations and their relationship to masturbation were clearly evident when his wife and children went to Florida by air. He had to put a coin in a certain drawer so that Alfred would come back alive, and again his thought led to masturbation and washing his hands seven times. In other words, death wishes toward his family were really part of the masturbatory fantasy, and the obsessional preoccupations were efforts to undo the aggression, just as the washing was. Seven days a week you should be clean. Therefore seven days a week you should have it on your mind not to masturbate. Cleanliness was next to Godliness, and it wiped out sin. He said, "I wonder if my compulsions aren't related to my guilt about my wife, father, and children, since I never atoned for the masturbation. God will overlook my sins." I commented on his effort to dupe his conscience for the guilt he felt about his anger and masturbation.

In essence, following his prepubertal masturbation, he had regressed from the phallic phase to an anal-sadistic level, but there were constant breakthroughs of the sadistic impulses toward his wife and children. In Mr. B.'s analysis, Dick's reactions to poor schoolwork were discussed and I told Mr. B. that Dick appeared to react to his inadequacies in school by bullyish and impulsive anger or by withdrawal. Mr. B. responded by saying it sounded like himself.

After six months of analysis, I pointed out the pleasure that Dick and Mr. B. obtained in tangling with each other, and that the patient operated by a double standard: Dick was to follow the father's verbal prescriptions but not the example set by the father's behavior. Mr. B. expressed concern about a breakdown of discipline. He could not stand his wife and children talking back to him, but he had not recognized how he encouraged precisely that. In complaining about Dick going to his mother instead of to him, he mentioned that the boy would say "Dad," and he would respond, "Yea doll"; thereupon Dick would angrily mutter, "Oh never mind," and go to his mother. Further discussion brought out the fact that his own father called Mr. B. "Sonny boy" or "Sonny dear" to this day, and he himself for the longest time felt angry at his father for this derogation. Again one could see the identification with the aggressor, and also how Mr. B. paved the way for his son's passivity and abortive rebellion.

Latent homosexuality as a defense against heterosexuality and aggression was clearly evident. He avoided intercourse for weeks at a time, and had many rationalizations to explain the avoidance, including an anal regressive complaint that his wife did not douche. When he had intercourse, he had dreams of homosexuals.

The essence of this man's neurosis could be understood from the material of the late latency and pubertal period during which he actively masturbated with much guilt and developed reaction formations against the regressive anal impulses. At that time, he fought with his sister, was beaten by his father, and began to feel quite inadequate because of his small penis. The anxiety thus engendered was displaced onto his schoolwork and eventually onto his business activities. The oedipal nature of his masturbatory fantasies was thinly disguised, and regressively acted out in relation to his sister.

When he finally established a business of his own, he had thoughts of killing his father and feared that the competition would be too much for him.

While Dick was in the hospital for a spastic colon and Mr. B. was preoccupied with his own sexual inadequacies, he was very critical of a model Dick had made, thus interfering with Dick's constructive efforts. I pointed out to him that he did to Dick what his father had done to him, and that his actions seemed to be motivated by a need to master his own anxiety. His fear of his own aggression became evident while Dick was hospitalized; Mr. B. had a dream of volunteering for tests with live cancer virus; he died, and the newspaper carried an account. He remembered reading about several male Hollywood actors who were at that time dying of cancer. He spoke of their fame and his wish for newspaper fame. In essence, this was a punishment dream for the wish for notoriety and aggression.

That night he had intercourse following which he had another dream: he heard noises, investigated, and found that the basement lights were on. He opened the door, and at the bottom of the steps was a colored fellow and a girl having intercourse. He closed the door and yelled.

The primal scene elements were evident and were reconstructed. He then mentioned that at the age of seven to nine he had nightmares of robbers coming halfway up the steps in the dark, pointing a gun at him, and frightening him, after which he screamed. Further associations led to a movie he had seen that night. Jack Carson, whose death of cancer he had mentioned the previous day, was in the movie that dealt with a husband, wife, and lover triangle. Thus the movie reinforced his unconscious feeling that he was a sexual robber who should die. His old ideas were that colored men had loose morals, were violent, and could be sex maniacs. He remembered his violence to his younger sister. The fear of robbers followed a beating by his father for the violence to his sister. The wish for notoriety and the big penis appeared to belong with his oedipal wishes, the punishment for which was identification with a cancer victim and with a robber who would be killed or die.

As on many previous occasions, that night he beat his son Dick for interfering with the family. When his acting out was interpreted, he could see the projection of his own impulses onto Dick and the identification with Dick, following which he had to punish Dick as he himself felt the need to be punished. In response to this interpretation Mr. B. had a dream in which he beat Dick for smoking and driving his car at age twelve. Dick drove past a house in which Mr. B. lived when he was twelve, thus confirming the identification and projection. In his associations, Mr. B. said that Dick was also doing forbidden things in the dream. Mr. B. told me that when he himself was between the ages of ten and twelve he used to take his mother's cigarette butts, though he feared his growth would be stunted. This was the period of active masturbation and guilt. On the following day Mr. B. again discussed his anxieties about starting a business of his own. He especially feared the competition of others in his field, and this again was portrayed in a dream with associations about Dick being a competitor. It thus appeared that Mr. B.'s clinging to the idea of his small penis was in part a defense against the wish for a large penis which would enable him to compete successfully with his father. He projected this conflict onto his first-born son, making Dick the representative of himself (Dick stole comic books, gambled, and beat his siblings). He attacked Dick mercilessly for having so many of his own characteristics. Mr. B.'s emphasis on precisely what he was warding off induced Dick to act out his father's unconscious wishes, whereupon the father would react to the projected wishes by beating Dick as though, via identification, to receive punishment himself. However, Mr. B. also punished himself in reality. His passive defenses as well as many other circumstances in which he had maneuvered himself into the position of the victor had resulted in a genuine fate neurosis. As a consequence, leaving his father's business had the significance of doing his father in; hence Mr. B. needed Dick as a scapegoat.

In the course of discussing his sexuality, it became apparent that his wife never reached a climax during intercourse because he usually proceeded without any preparatory foreplay and ejaculated almost immediately upon penetration. At the time when Mr. B. was preoccupied with this material, an incident at home betrayed the unconscious interaction of father and son and Dick's compliance with the father's wishes. Dick was sitting up in bed with his mother watching television, quite obviously an oedipal situation; as could be expected Mr. B. immediately had to find some things to fight with Dick about and punished him severely. Following this, he had a castration dream in which someone was to have a prostate cut out while he slept. Mr. B. tried to defend himself against this: he was to be cut on his arm. His associations led to his father's prostate operation two years previously, and to Dick having playfully teased Edward with a knife. He had fantasies of his penis withering from nonuse, as an obvious punishment for the oedipal wishes active at that time.

He began to restrict Dick's TV watching by pulling out the plug when he went out. When he found that Dick had put the TV plug back in, Mr. B. screamed and cursed Dick, calling him a robber and a thief and a criminal. In this way he conveyed his wish for Dick to do what he had done in childhood. He had his scapegoat, but his conscience was not fooled: the castration dreams continued.

Fifteen months after Mr. B. started his own analysis, he consulted another analyst about Dick, took Dick to Dr. T. for analysis, and in his usual passive way misheard what the first doctor said, did not know what the analysis would consist of, and began to oppose it once he got to Dr. T. Mr. B. showed his opposition to Dick's analysis by wanting Dick to tell him his dreams, by refusing to go to the center of the city and especially to a woman analyst, by complaining that analysis took up too many hours, by insisting that Dick's appointments be scheduled only after school.

Technically the working-through process was long and arduous. Month after month the same issues were repeated in the same way. Mr. B. was timid, respectful, quiet, dutiful, obedient, and punctual. These elements entered the transference as did his rebellion, though in more subtle ways; he attempted to keep his emotional distance from me and made as little progress in the analysis as he did in the business. Although he talked and talked, the material was not connected, and there was always tension and silence, as with his father. This behavior was slowly interpreted and gradually changed.

Toward the end of his first year of analysis, Mr. B. mentioned, with anxiety, his efforts to control his masturbation and his "wet dreams" at thirteen or fourteen. In the same session he reported a dream about Dick doing well on an examination and receiving a mark of eighty. Eighty brought to mind the death of a former business partner who was eighty. Mr. B. also feared his father's death when he established a business of his own. The associations had to do with his ambivalent attitude to his father, and he believed if he controlled his masturbation he could keep his father alive.

During the second year of his treatment a change occurred. He began to be somewhat more tactful with people, having recognized that he displaced the antagonism to his father to other men in authority. Being diplomatic made him feel degraded, however. This was a frequently recurring pattern: he rationalized that what seemed to be mature behavior was degrading and small-boyish, an attitude which often led to further fights with Dick.

He slowly became aware of the fact that his involvement with Dick had a sexual determinant: by means of the beatings he obtained satisfactions that he could not obtain in intercourse with his wife. Moreover, his fear of intercourse also frequently led to fights with his wife. His passivity manifested itself in his wish to be seduced by his wife and to have intercourse with her on top of him. His fear of not having an ejaculation led to premature ejaculations. He often worked until 2:00 or 3:00 A.M. to avoid intercourse. He complained bitterly about his wife, felt that all problems were caused by her, and talked of divorce. His passivity and homosexual conflicts showed up in a dream in which he caught his wife having intercourse with another man, the world found out how she cheated on him, and she should be punished.

Only slowly could Mr. B. reveal other aspects of his fear of sexual contact with his wife. These were frequently cloaked in such terms as, "I just don't like physical contact with her in bed because I get so warm and have to throw the covers off." In actuality, he could not look at his wife nude, could not sleep in a double bed with her since the first year of marriage, could not sleep after having intercourse, and when she spoke of her strong wish to sleep in a double bed, he replied: "You will drive me to setting up separate rooms for both of us." His castration anxiety in relation to direct contact with his wife was often cloaked in anal regressive terms, e.g., "I can't stand being in bed with her. She piles such a mess up around me with her readings and so on. The books are all piled around me." It was apparent that in a regressive sense, he often viewed his wife as being part of the dirt and mess that surrounded him.

Finally, in the second year of analysis, he established his own business. On the first day he felt content and had a dream in which

Edward and he showed each other their big penises. This ushered in a period of almost total withdrawal from intercourse. After several months he himself broached the topic of his virtual lack of contact with women while he was so completely immersed in work with thoughts about men, that it frightened him to think of the homosexual implications. I interpreted that his going into business also made him fearful of his sexual competitiveness, and he defended himself by thinking only of men. Then he pushed himself to have intercourse, and had frequent premature ejaculations. At this time, in the transference, Mr. B. blamed me for his own increasing difficulties in making decisions, which he attributed to the need to analyze. He was saying in effect that I was making his penis smaller. He feared the analysis would take his magical obsessional rituals away, and that his father might die in a plane crash. Fortuitously and tragically a plane crash occurred at this time killing many of his friends who had gone on a golf trip. This increased his anger and apprehension. He had to perform special rituals to protect his family on their next plane trip. However, in analyzing his fear of having a car accident in which he would be killed, he began to have some insight into the projection of his own impulses onto the analyst and his own unconscious need for punishment.

Meanwhile, there was an increase in what Mr. B. called "depantsing." The boys would wrestle with each other and sometimes he would join in, and then one boy would pull the other boy's pants down, and say "Woo woo." He beat Dick for punching Alfred in the groin when Alfred tried to depants Dick after Dick had done this to Alfred. In the same period he began to burst into Dick's room as if to discover Dick masturbating, although Mr. B. was not conscious of this intention.

A school counselor told Dick that he needed intensive treatment if he wanted to get well and to do well in school. Finally the parents made arrangements for Dick to be analyzed by Dr. Moore in a few months.

After some analytic work on Mr. B.'s homosexual fantasies and feelings, his anxieties concerning the business, and his sexual inhibitions, he began to function better, had more control of his erections, and found intercourse with his wife more enjoyable.

He began to discuss his desire to learn from capable men in

authority. He mentioned that Edward at age six had a larger penis than Dick at twelve, which Dick resented. The wish to learn from the big man thus expressed the wish to have the big man's penis. Learning, however, really meant having a small penis; therefore he had learning inhibitions. Every day brought new complaints about fate dealing him cruel blows, and it took many months before he could see that he himself brought about these situations.

The following incidents are typical of the way in which Mr. B. made his fate complaints. His wife needed a new car, and he planned to spend a certain amount of money. He went to the auto showroom with his wife, without having told her how much he would spend. She fell in love with a model costing $1,000 more, and he protested only meekly. She bought the car, whereupon he violently cursed her and found an excuse to beat Dick. On the next day he complained to me: "You see what fate does to me?" He formed business associations with men of questionable honesty who disposed of large sums of money and were much envied by the patient. Invariably he would agree to their propositions, which could only hurt him, but as if to prevent recognition of what he was doing, he told me about these deals only after he had been hurt by them, again with the same fate complaints. Invariably, when these deals were examined, it turned out that the disadvantageous outcome could easily have been prevented. By setting up these situations, he was in effect saying, "You see I'm not aggressive or competitive, but am simply reacting to what others do to me." Then he could restore his narcissism by beating Dick. The beatings were followed by dreams of his boys being piranhas destroying him and the dreams in turn would leave him feeling lonely, empty, and depressed.

Mr. B. was a man of average intelligence who had received a college education. Yet there were clear indications that he, like Dick, had had severe learning difficulties while growing up. The interference of anxiety with the learning process was reflected in his use of language. For instance, he used "remembrance" for memory, "arousement" for arousal, "tumult" for turmoil, "revolvement" for revolving, "analyzation" for analysis, "jungle" for jumble, "presentment" for presentation, and "lackadaisial" for lackadaisical.

As Dick prepared for his Bar Mitzvah, Mr. B. became hypercritical of him; Dick had no singing voice and would disgrace Mr. B.

in front of his own father. Dick was his product and Dick's performance would reflect on Mr. B. In this attitude the patient resembled his own father. When Mr. B. told his father about a successful business venture, his father was pleased, but had to add, "Show me some real *naches* before I die."

As the time for Dick to see Dr. Moore drew near, Mr. B. thought again and again of Dick's treatment as being doomed to failure; only by making conscious the sabotaging wishes behind this could I help him to allow Dick to get started. Mr. B. dreamed, "I am a doctor, washing my hands more than once as if I was going to operate." It was clear that Dick's analysis represented the wish for and fear of castration of Dick and himself. There were also hints that Dick's problems had something to do with his own masturbation, although what this was was not yet fully evident. Mr. B. felt very inadequate having a son in analysis. I said that Mr. B.'s father felt so inadequate that he had to live through Mr. B., as Mr. B. had to do with Dick. On the eve of Dick's treatment, Mr. B. dreamed of losing his wallet which had been in the left side pocket of his pants near the groin. His associations dealt with Dick having the same conflicts about a small penis and Mr. B.'s fear of losing the penis and Dick. Putting Dick into analysis meant revealing his secrets. No one but Mr. B. had ever seen the contents of his wallet, which, he said, "is my most private possession." One could clearly see why Dick's previous treatments had to fail.

Gradually Mr. B. stopped interfering with Dick's treatment. However, he still felt he was losing authority if he could not punish his children. I interpreted that he felt emasculated by not punishing them. He then revealed an important fantasy: "I use my hands to mete out punishment. I use my hands to masturbate after a period of depression or frustration. I daydream of the luxury of getting rid of all irritants. Father hit me and became a symbol of masculine authority." I interpreted that the pleasure of hitting relieved his tension, as did masturbation. He agreed and said he could go further: "Dick constantly stands up to me and won't take my control or authority. Dick is erect like a penis, I think I will knock that kid off and reduce him to a limp form."

He came to understand that his business failure was not only a passive way of saying to his father, "I'm not a competitor," but it was also a rebellious way of saying to his father, "I will not do your bidding. I will give you no *naches*." In turn Mr. B. felt that the frustration he thus caused his father would increase the danger of a heart attack.

After three years of analysis his fate neurosis began to change. He no longer set up problems in his work or with his wife. As a consequence he enjoyed intercourse somewhat more and his business improved. But then he announced his wife's pregnancy and in exploring the events, he became aware of having calculated ovulation as fourteen days following the *end* of period! This led to a rediscussion of his fate neurosis. Shortly thereafter he again had more physical contact with his boys; Mr. B. also stated that he wanted to be loved by the children as if he were their mother. Once again one could see his use of homosexuality as a defense against his intense guilt feelings over heterosexuality and, in this instance, impregnation. To know about the menstrual cycle meant to be clear-minded, decisive, and definite, but that meant to oppose his father. This defensive stance, however, also contained an indecisiveness that could and did result in impregnation, which was a declaration of manhood. It was the latter which made for his unconscious need to turn to latent homosexuality.

In the fourth year of analysis, he mentioned for the first time childhood memories of his relationship with his mother, which showed his identifications with her in his passivity, his health concerns, and his stubbornness. He felt like a woman who let herself be taken advantage of, following which she complained. He then became aware of his attempts to make Dick passive in an effort to externalize this part of his personality. This insight stimulated a continuing improvement. He no longer beat Dick. He was more supportive and affectionate with his wife, although he continued to be somewhat anxious about sexual relations.

CONCLUSION

On the basis of our experience with simultaneous analysis of four sets of parent and child, we are inclined to state that active interchange of information between the analysts appears to broaden the understanding of each case as well as of the parent-child interaction, as long as the extraneously gained knowledge is not misused by the individual analysts.

Our findings in this case of simultaneous analysis of a father and son repeatedly confirmed what Anna Freud had suggested: again and again precise information took the place of generalized statements concerning the meaning of specific phenomena. For example, this could be seen in the unconscious masturbatory aspects of the father's beating of the son, which the father once characterized, in a most naïve way, as "beating my Dick."

The analyses of this father and son also bore out Anna Freud's statement that child analysis alone is inadequate when the unconscious forces in the parent work in the direction of enhancing the child's psychopathology. For example, the child's analysis could not even get underway until the father had sufficiently worked through his fear of loss of so important an object as his son (Dick-penis), and until he felt less threatened by exposing his defects to another man (the boy's analyst). Another example was the erotization of the beatings by both father and son. As long as the father continued to act out this form of his masturbatory complex the boy would have been able to produce a beating response without gaining insight into his own provocation. Moreover, the child's analysis would have had little effect as long as the father continued to reinforce the boy's tendencies toward and pleasure in passivity, by acting out his unrecognized need to keep his son in an inadequate position as a means of warding off his own inadequacy. Furthermore, Mr. B. could incite certain latent impulses in the boy by referring to him as "robber, thief, and criminal."

Anna Freud indicated that simultaneous analysis could provide more definitive information about the foundations of personality and the roots of mental illness. The cases described illustrate this in a variety of ways:

1. When the father felt overwhelmed by passive experiences, he acted in a brutal way to his son; by identification with the aggressor, the boy did the same thing under the same circumstances with his younger brothers.

2. Reaction formations against stealing, gambling, and lying were so frequently and grossly exhibited by the father that the boy

acted out precisely these warded-off impulses to gratify the father's repressed wishes.

3. The father unconsciously conveyed a pattern of expected character development at precisely those points in the child's development at which the father himself acquired the same characteristics. For example: (a) When Dick was six or seven years old, the father began to beat Dick, encouraging erotization of beatings, an unlucky fate, and passivity. He had been beaten by his father at just that age. (b) When Dick was eight, the father gave Dick his stamp collection, which he had begun at the age of eight to reinforce his reaction formations against the "dirt" of masturbation. (c) When Dick was fourteen, the father repeatedly burst into Dick's room to discover him masturbating. In the father's analysis, we learned that his own greatest struggle against masturbation and ejaculations had occurred at fourteen.

It was also of interest to note that the unconscious wishes of father and son coincided. What Dick wished would happen to his father was precisely what the father wished for Dick. Dick liked to see the father helpless with rage at not being able to control his scholastic performance; in essence, Dick was making his father's penis limp and impotent, as the father so often wished to knock Dick limp.

BIBLIOGRAPHY

Bornstein, B. (1931), Phobia in a Two-and-a-half-year-old Child. *Psa. Quart.*, 4:93-119, 1935.

Bornstein, S. (1933), A Child Analysis. *Psa. Quart.*, 4:190-225, 1935.

Burlingham, D. T. (1932), Child Analysis and the Mother. *Psa. Quart.*, 4:69-92, 1935.

—— (1951), Present Trends in Handling the Mother-Child Relationship during the Therapeutic Process. *This Annual*, 6:31-37.

—— Goldberger, A., & Lussier, A. (1955), Simultaneous Analysis of Mother and Child. *This Annual*, 10:165-186.

Freud, A. (1945), Indications for Child Analysis. *This Annual*, 1:127-149.

Freud, S. (1908), Character and Anal Erotism. *Standard Edition*, 9:167-175. London: Hogarth Press, 1959.

—— (1909), Analysis of a Phobia in a Five-year-old-Boy. *Standard Edition*, 10:3-149. London: Hogarth Press, 1955.

Furman, E. (1957), Treatment of Under-fives by Way of Their Parents. *This Annual*, 12:250-262.

Hellman, I., Friedmann, A., & Shepheard, E. (1960), Simultaneous Analysis of Mother and Child. *This Annual*, 15:359-377.

Johnson, A. M. & Szurek, S. (1952), The Genesis of Antisocial Acting Out in Children and Adults. *Psa. Quart.*, 21:323-343.

Kolansky, H. (1960), Treatment of a Three-year-old Girl's Severe Infantile Neurosis. *This Annual,* 15:261-285.

Levy, K. (1960), Simultaneous Analysis of a Mother and Her Adolescent Daughter. *This Annual,* 15:378-391.

Schwarz, H. (1950), The Mother in the Consulting Room. *This Annual,* 5:343-357.

Sperling, M. (1950), Children's Interpretation and Reaction to the Unconscious of Their Mothers. *Int. J. Psa.,* 31:36-41.

—— (1951), The Neurotic Child and his Mother. *Amer. J. Orthopsychiat.,* 31:351-364.

—— (1954), Reactive Schizophrenia in Children. *Amer. J. Orthopsychiat.,* 24:506-512.

OBJECT LOSS AND MOURNING DURING ADOLESCENCE

MOSES LAUFER, M.Sc.

The psychoanalytic study of childhood has given us a clear picture of the changes in the mental apparatus which are expected to occur at various stages of development (A. Freud, 1965). If these changes do occur, we assume that progressive development is continuing and that the child does not have to seek solutions which will result in a distortion of his relation to himself and to external reality. A similar statement can be made about adolescence as a developmental stage. Unless a person succeeds in accomplishing certain defined tasks during adolescence (Laufer, 1965) his ego functioning as an adult will contain areas that are impaired. How the adolescent experiences these tasks is determined by a number of factors—the level of object relationship reached at the time of superego internalization, the defenses available to deal with anxiety, the strength of the fixations, the quality of the fantasies, the uses made of identifications. In the adult, however, we see the result of the various compromises. When we meet adult patients, we always find that, whatever their manifest complaint, its internal equivalent is similar: they are aware of failure in one or more of those areas which should have actively been dealt with in adolescence. On the other hand, the clinical pictures presented by adults also show much greater deadlock and much more distortion than those of adolescents.

The author is a member of the Hampstead Child-Therapy Clinic, which is maintained at present by The Field Foundation, Inc., New York; The Anna Freud Foundation, New York; The Grant Foundation, Inc., New York; The Estate of Flora Haas, New York; The Walter E. Meyer Research Institute of Law, New York; The National Institute of Mental Health, Bethesda, Maryland; The Old Dominion Foundation, New York; The Psychoanalytic Research and Development Fund, Inc., New York; The Taconic Foundation, Inc., New York.

Part of this paper was presented to the Chicago Institute for Psychoanalysis, April, 1966; and to the Canadian Psychoanalytic Society, Montreal, April, 1966.

This paper examines how the death of a parent during adolescence can interfere with normal development by preventing the necessary internal changes from taking place. The first part briefly discusses the literature related to adolescence and mourning. The second part contains the relevant analytic material from the treatment of an adolescent boy. The last part is a discussion of some of the case material, followed by comments on the possible consequences of object loss during adolescence.

REVIEW OF LITERATURE

Adolescence

In recent years a number of psychoanalytic papers have examined the structural and adaptive changes occurring during adolescence. One of these changes is related to the adolescent's need to detach himself libidinally from the parental figures—a process which has been described as comparable to that of mourning (Frankl and Hellman, 1962; A. Freud, 1958; Lampl-de Groot, 1960). There seems to be general agreement that this process is crucial and must be successfully completed to enable a person to proceed emotionally to adulthood (Blos, 1962; Frankl and Hellman, 1963; Root, 1957; Rosenblatt, 1963; Sprince, 1962).

Adolescence as a recapitulation of one's earlier life was described by Freud (1905) and Jones (1922). That this recapitulation takes place in the context of physical genital dominance means that the ego is faced with stresses which are qualitatively and quantitatively different from earlier ones. In the course of coping with these stresses the adolescent may manifest temporary id and ego regressions, changes in the uses made of identifications, and alterations in the types of object relationships (Blos, 1962; Eissler, 1958; Fraiberg, 1961; Geleerd, 1961; Harley, 1961; Jacobson, 1961; Laufer, 1964).

Despite these many contributions to the literature on adolescence, we still need to know a great deal more about normal adolescence before we can assess the precise meaning of the variations of behavior which are observed during this period (A. Freud, 1965). On the other hand, there is at present much greater recognition than existed earlier that this phase plays a crucial part in the development of the person (A. Freud, 1958; Lampl-de Groot, 1960).

Mourning

Freud's study of mourning is the psychoanalytic source of the dynamic understanding of this process. He wrote: "Mourning is regularly the reaction to the loss of a loved person, or to the loss of some abstraction which has taken the place of one, such as one's country, liberty, an ideal, and so on. . . . We rely on its being overcome after a certain lapse of time, and we look upon any interference with it as useless or even harmful" (pp. 243-244). In explaining what the work of mourning consists of, he states, "Reality-testing has shown that the loved object no longer exists, and it proceeds to demand that all libido shall be withdrawn from its attachment to that object. This demand arouses understandable opposition—it is a matter of general observation that people never willingly abandon a libidinal position, not even, indeed, when a substitute is already beckoning them" (p. 244).

There is disagreement in the literature on the age—or developmental stage—at which a person is capable of mourning (Bowlby, 1960, 1961, 1963; A. Freud, 1960; Furman, 1964a; Klein, 1940). The different views held by these authors reflect differences in theoretical assumptions and are not related to the process of mourning itself. Anna Freud (1960) described the process of mourning as follows, "The process of mourning (*Trauerarbeit*) taken in its analytic sense means to us the individual's effort to accept a fact in the external world (the loss of the cathected object) and to effect corresponding changes in the inner world (withdrawal of libido from the lost object, identification with the lost object)" (p. 58).

Much less has been written about the possible consequences of any interference with the work of mourning following actual object loss, and only a few clinical papers deal with mourning during adolescence (Bonnard, 1961; Fleming and Altschul, 1963; Root, 1957). Several authors imply that mourning following object loss fulfills an important function and follows a predictable course. Helene Deutsch (1937) states that "The process of mourning as reaction to the real loss of a loved person *must be carried to completion*. As long as the early libidinal or aggressive attachments persist, the painful affect continues to flourish, and *vice versa*, the attachments are unresolved as long as the affective process of mourning has not been accomplished" (p. 21). In a number of clinical examples of adult patients in analysis she shows the possible consequences of this failure—affectlessness, depression, compulsive weeping, shallowness of object relationship. Deutsch's paper contains important observations on the damage to progressive development if mourning is, for whatever reason, interfered with (see also Fleming and Altschul, 1963; Furman, 1964b; Pollock, 1961; Root, 1957).

The observations made by these authors stimulate many questions concerning adolescent development. What happens if the adolescent loses, in reality, the object from whom he is trying to free himself? What internal factors play the most important part in determining the outcome? How does the failure of mourning in adolescence manifest itself in adulthood? These are the questions which will be discussed.

CASE ILLUSTRATION

Michael's mother initiated the referral for treatment.[1] She had been worried about him for years. He was now doing very poorly at school, he was extremely shy, and although he had some friends he was lonely and felt isolated. At the beginning of his treatment, when he was fourteen years and eight months, he impressed me as a very disturbed and frightened boy. His mother had said of him: "There is something in him that can't come out"—a rather apt description of his inability to express any feelings which represented aggression against the object. Eight months after treatment began, his mother suddenly died of a coronary thrombosis. She was then in her mid-forties.

Although the event of death had tragically affected other members of his family in the past, Michael himself had never experienced the loss of a loved one by death. He never knew his real father who had died in a concentration camp, but kept a photograph of him which had been given Michael by his mother. When Michael was four and a half years old, Mrs. M. married a man much older than herself. After spending three years in Sweden, the family arrived in London when Michael was seven. At school he felt like "the local freak," being shy and unable to speak the language. Mrs. M. worked at home

---

[1] I wish to acknowledge the help of Miss Hedwig Schwarz who supervised the first part of the treatment.

as a dressmaker. Her mother, aged seventy, lived nearby and visited daily.

Five months after treatment began, Mrs. M. had a coronary thrombosis and was hospitalized for some weeks. Michael attempted to deny the seriousness of the illness by referring to it as "indigestion." He kept on insisting that she was perfectly alright, and that a fuss had been made unnecessarily. However, his stepfather informed me that she could not be moved for at least two weeks because of the seriousness of her condition.

At the time of her death, Michael's analysis had reached a point at which he began to recognize the existence of a feeling of hopelessness which alternated with a feeling that one day things might change in his life. He had previously referred to the belief that people did not have to do things which they did not want to do. Nobody could force another person to do anything—one always had the final choice of killing oneself. Although his thoughts of suicide had come into the analysis from time to time, I had used these references only as a means of showing him the relationship between suicide and aggression directed at another object.

Michael telephoned the day after his mother's death and said, "I won't be coming tomorrow because, you see, my mother died yesterday." It seemed that he started to cry. (I mention this because his inability to cry about her death was important later in the treatment.) When he returned to treatment a week later he described in detail how his mother had become ill. She was admitted to the hospital, "but I didn't think there was much wrong with her." His stepfather was called to the hospital during the night, "and I thought I heard the phone in the middle of the night, but I didn't take any notice of it." When Michael awoke the next morning, his stepfather told him: "You don't have a mother." Michael said he had never seen his stepfather in such a state. "He's completely broken up." His only reference to his own reaction was the statement that when he heard the news he walked back to his room and lay on the bed.

Both stepfather and grandmother found it impossible to carry on with their work or household duties. Michael described the unbelievable reality of his mother's death and the extent of the adults' misery. He himself was bewildered by the death and by the reactions of his stepfather and grandmother.

Michael assumed some of the responsibility of running the home, e.g., shopping for food, preparing it, seeing that the house was properly heated. This behavior seemed to reflect an identification with the feeding mother and a wish to keep her alive by doing the things she ordinarily did. (His interest in catering, his need to avoid being hungry, and his interest in preparing foods were linked with the fantasy, obtained much later in treatment, that the idealized real father may have died of starvation in the concentration camp.)

For weeks, Michael talked of the mood changes in his stepfather, the visits to the cemetery, his grandmother's crying spells, or the future plans of the family. Michael had adopted the role of looking after his stepfather and grandmother—a step that was crucial in enabling him to begin to integrate the meaning of the reality of his mother's death. The manner in which the adults showed their reactions to the loss made it possible for Michael to experience sadness mainly via these people. His way of mourning appeared only in his identification with the dead mother. By this means he could perpetuate his relationship with her, and at the same time keep the oedipal aggression under repression, thus avoiding the need to feel responsible for her death. There emerged a pattern of reaction which was representative of his pathology and which might prove to be very dangerous for his future development (Deutsch, 1937; Root, 1957). It was as if he could not allow himself to feel as sad as he knew he was. This manner of dealing with the affects related to the mourning influenced the whole process of withdrawing cathexis from the internalized object.

His treatment sessions were now taken up by a number of concerns in his daily life. The first was his feeling of urgency in deciding on his future work. A plan had to be made quickly and must be acted upon at once. Secondly, his current masturbation conflict, the changing content of his masturbation fantasies, and his manner of dealing with this conflict gave me the most important insight into the dynamic meaning of his behavior (Arlow, 1953; A. Freud, 1958; Reich, 1951). Thirdly, he developed a compulsive need to gamble. And finally, the manifestations in the transference and his changing attitude to treatment enabled me to examine his reactions to certain types of object relationships and to fear of genitality (Eissler, 1958; Harley, 1961). Each of these concerns contained his mourning reaction as well as his reaction to his adolescent development. Although it was often very difficult to distinguish between them, the attempt in treatment to separate these reactions was crucial in understanding the meaning of his behavior.

Although Michael had previously speculated about his future work, he suddenly decided definitely to study catering. This plan was encouraged by a family friend, who had a number of restaurants and who had been very successful financially. Michael idealized this man and constantly held him up as an example of success. This man was used as an ally in resisting any understanding of the meaning of the feeling of urgency to secure his future. He saw himself as very soon being able to take care of his stepfather and grandmother rather than as dependent on these two old people. He felt he now had to rely on himself because his stepfather and grandmother were not really related to him in the same way as his mother. He showed the same attitude in relation to me as well. He made plans without mentioning them or he told me only of what he had already done.

The anxiety which Michael expressed about his future was also determined by other factors. His actual life was filled with dreariness, sad people, old and ill relatives. He felt that his stepfather and grandmother were vulnerable because of their ages, and therefore he must plan his life so that he could predict what would happen to him in the future.

Michael felt he could not "do anything" because his mother's death was still so close. He could not tell his teacher about her death; he wore the same clothes for many weeks; he spent much time by himself. He did not want pity, he repeated. He sympathetically and critically described his stepfather's visits to the cemetery and how his stepfather talked to mother "as if she can hear him." When I suggested that at such times he might have an odd feeling of being angry with the dead person for having died, he reacted with great relief. He could then tell me that during the previous month, he sometimes felt as if mother had no right suddenly to land him in this situation. He knew such a feeling was silly, but it made him feel awful. He felt peculiarly ashamed of his stepfather's behavior. With much anxiety, Michael described having noticed that he often did things like his stepfather, that he had similar mannerisms and sometimes talked in the same way. Angrily, he described his stepfather as an ineffectual, sad, failed man, who might have extended his mother's life if he had earned more. Michael often returned to the idea that he was becoming a helpless, ignorant, depressed person, and if this was so then why bother to make the effort to grow up. Michael's need to organize his future life quickly in order to be different from his stepfather reflected his struggle against identification with the stepfather (Greenson, 1954) and now colored much of his behavior.

His masturbation conflict is relevant in this context. Before his mother's death, Michael had been surprised when friends at school told him that masturbation was not as unusual as he seemed to think. His masturbatory activity had consisted of touching his penis, but he would not ejaculate. Following the death, he found it impossible to touch his penis. He felt that he must not get pleasure from his body. To do so would be to show disrespect to his mother and to risk forgetting her too quickly. The guilt he expressed in this way was a complex phenomenon because it also contained his earlier reaction to masturbation, his present ambivalence to mother, as well as the defense against an ego-dystonic masturbation fantasy.

Michael feared now that if he enjoyed something too much, it would prove that his mother did not mean much to him in the first place. He did not listen to the radio or go to the cinema. At the same time, however, this was his way of conveying to me that without mother it felt as if there was no purpose in being alive. He began actively to question his whole past life and who he really was. The central theme was related to the "awful thought" that he might be illegitimate. But to raise this question now meant that he would be implying that mother was a whore. How could he think such a thing? He tried to stop himself from having such "terrible thoughts." Clearly, such talk about mother meant that the character and behavior of the idealized real father would also begin to be questioned. One day he produced a photograph of his father in the company of other men, with the remark, "Guess which one is my father?" When he did speculate about his history, he became very tense, and he tried constantly to switch to a more neutral topic. He feared that he might say things which he would then not be able to live with. It was as if he might talk about mother without her being able to defend herself.

His effort to overthrow the earlier identification by hinting that he had little to do with the oedipal objects (Laufer, 1964) brought with it the fear that he would find himself completely alone. Although such behavior may be part of normal adolescence, for Michael it meant that he would be nobody and he would mean nothing to anybody. Again, the fear of being abandoned by the love object manifested itself in his effort to keep himself from having thoughts about the details of his birth. I became the powerful person who was trying to reform him, and in this way I would have so much power over him that he would not be able to criticize me. Perhaps I was not satisfied with him? Did I think of him as a stupid and ugly child? Was I like his mother who pushed him to become somebody special? His active effort to do nothing, which appeared to the observer as passivity, created the feeling in him that he could manage alone— nobody had power over him; he was free to do as he pleased; his mother was dead and he had to look after himself. His long-standing means of denying his fear of mother, and his oedipal aggressive wishes toward her were now being used in his endeavor to deal with her actual death. The danger contained in this behavior was that the aggression would prove to be unanalyzable, lead to further depression, and increase the possibility of suicide.

It was at this point that the understanding of the ego-dystonic masturbation fantasy became crucial to any treatment progress. He could not masturbate for two months after his mother's death. Then he would touch his penis without allowing himself to ejaculate. In the accompanying fantasy he was having intercourse with a middle-aged woman. Sometimes he thought of his friend's mother, sometimes it was a woman whom he had noticed on the street. He expressed the feeling that it was like having intercourse with his own mother. He felt shame, disgust with himself, and the wish not to masturbate at all.

Although masturbation fantasies are the most important clue to the understanding of a person's sexual life, fixation points, and the dynamic meaning of conflicts, masturbation fantasies in adolescence are so overdetermined that it would be correct to speak of various meanings of these fantasies (Laufer, 1964). This was true of Michael's fantasies. They contained his effort to perpetuate his mother's life, the attempt to prove that his own oedipal aggressive wishes had not

really harmed her, and the wish to obtain his mother's permission
to use his penis for his own sexual pleasure.

In his associations to this fantasy, he pictured mother's body and
wanted to know what had gone wrong. He would imagine looking
into her body to discover why she had died. If he had a million
pounds, he said, he would give it to medical research to try to make
sure that people did not die so young. But, when thinking of intercourse, he could not imagine mother, and he had to substitute another
woman. He then thought that something might have happened to her
when she gave birth to him. Who was to blame—was it Michael, or
the real father, or was it the stepfather? "It could be anybody's fault,
couldn't it? If I'm illegitimate, which I know I'm not, then it could
be anybody."

I decided not to encourage any examination of the fantasy content beyond its link to the dead mother. I feared that an interpretation relating this fantasy to the oedipal parent would lead to further
repression of affect. At the same time, I was confronted with a serious
technical problem because it was obvious that the mourning of
mother could not proceed until the oedipal relationship to her had
been analyzed. At this point I interpreted only Michael's wish to
keep his relationship with the mother whom he loved, though he
always found it difficult to show appropriate feelings for her. I said
that he was also trying to understand his worry that he might have
been responsible for her death, and that the extent of his sorrow
following her death could be seen in his effort to keep her alive.

His ability to talk of the masturbation fantasy and the understanding of one part of it brought about important changes in his
behavior. He was greatly relieved when he recognized his love for
mother and the feeling that he was not "taking advantage" of her
death. Masturbation was experienced as less of an awful thing, and
he began to make more of an active effort to organize his life around
the reality of her death. He began to wear the new clothes which
had been bought before her death, he risked listening to the radio,
and he listened to pop records at friends' homes.

This was the extent of his progress about a year after his mother's
death. By that time he had been at the catering school for some
months. At first he talked very little about the school. He was pleased
to meet new people who did not know much about his history. When

he began to learn about food preparation, he cut himself severely a number of times. He attributed it to preoccupation with home worries and the difficulty in getting used to the new setup.

A short time later he began to gamble at school and to bet on the horses. At first he described it as a nice way of spending his free time and getting to know people, but it quickly developed into something he was compelled to do. He would organize five or six boys each day. Most often he played against all the others. He also began to cheat. At first the bets were three- or six-pence, but then they became ten shillings, a pound, or more. He used the money which he had saved from his weekend work, or he risked the money which his stepfather had given him as a clothing allowance. In some games, the boys would win or lose as much as twenty pounds.

The gambling was undoubtedly motivated by some homosexual elements—the fantasied power over all the other boys; the accumulation of money belonging to the other boys; the ability to take away their power; showing the onlookers that he could match any of the players in taking risks. However, the homosexual implications were incidental to the much more important meaning related to the mourning process and to the serious masturbation conflict which still existed. In gambling, he could temporarily create the feeling of omnipotence and deny the reality that he might lose rather than win. Gambling thus served the purpose of making him feel completely in control of what he described as "fate" (Freud, 1928; Greenson, 1947). However, it did not enable him to overcome the preoedipal attachment to the powerful and frightening mother.

At school he became known as the most daring gambler; ready to take unusual risks; giving fantastic odds; predicting the outcome of the game; betting against five or six boys at one time. When he won, he would say that this was expected. When he lost, which happened often, he explained it as an accident, as something reversible, or something due to a lapse of attention. He described the excitement and the physical reactions during the gambling—perspiring, quickening heartbeat, sometimes the need to urinate, and often much pleasurable tension around the anal opening. After the game, the excitement changed to a temporary feeling of fatigue, usually followed by a short period of sadness, but then plans for the next game. When he was alone at home, he practiced throwing dice or dealing cards. (During

the first weeks of treatment when Michael was still very frightened
of me and came to treatment under protest, his way of communi-
cating was showing me tricks—the penny that would disappear up
his sleeve, etc.)

During this period occurred a number of external events which
significantly increased the anxiety he was experiencing. At home
there were awful scenes between his stepfather and grandmother,
each accusing the other of being useless. The grandmother told
Michael that his stepfather was meeting other women for coffee and
that he no longer visited the cemetery regularly. Michael also learned
that the man who was his "hero," who owned restaurants and had
promised him work, was thinking of leaving his business. He felt
extremely vulnerable, "Anything can happen, you can never be
sure."

Michael was now regularly invited to parties and he began to stay
out much later than either stepfather or grandmother approved. He
stated that he would stay out as late as he pleased, that neither of
these two "old people" were really related to him, and they had no
business ordering him around. But he also reasoned that they had
suffered a great deal, and there was no need to make them worried
or sad. In fact, he obviously was aware of the fact that both these
people meant a great deal to him. It was precisely this inability to
give them up—especially following his mother's death—which added
to his efforts to ignore them. He felt very much alone and made many
attempts to induce me temporarily to assume the role of his guide
or adviser or authority. In this way, he tried to re-create with me the
same dependent relationship which he had had with his mother and
hated. To some extent, he also tried to establish such relationships
with his friends and with adults whom he considered to be successful.

Gradually Michael developed a greater ability to deal more actively
with some of the affects which he had been avoiding. He talked less
of his stepfather and grandmother; he began to risk masturbation
more often; he began to refer to his sadness; he could criticize me
and talk of his envy of me. He began to realize the meaning of the
loss of the oedipal as well as the real mother, and to face his inability
to cope with feelings of aggression toward her except by compliance
and withdrawal. He also could begin to question his idealization of
his real father and of me.

He still masturbated with the fantasy of having intercourse with an older woman. Although he now masturbated to the point of ejaculation, he often stopped before ejaculating, explaining, "I feel I shouldn't go on enjoying myself like that." He felt he was no good and dirty, that he was letting mother down, and he wondered whether suicide would be the answer. At school he continued to cut himself.

He often ate before or after gambling. It made him "feel good" and less worried about whether he would win or lose. He went to a café to have a snack before coming to each session. If he did not eat before his session, he felt he would be unable to associate and want to leave early. One day he stated upon his arrival that he felt like vomiting because he had eaten too much at school. He recalled his earlier proneness to vomiting. At the age of seven or eight his mother and stepfather often left him in the care of a neighbor. They would go out regardless of whether he cried or not. He then used to vomit, but even this did not stop them from going out. He then recalled his relationships to other children at that time. Next door lived a girl whom he masturbated anally. He would promise her sweets if she agreed to let him touch her anus. This was a secret which they shared.

This anal masturbation had a number of meanings. It was used defensively to ward off the fear that his mother could take away his penis. Michael saw her as a phallic woman who could frighten him into doing what she wished and who inhibited any instinctual pleasure he sought. His behavior with the little girl also embodied his belief in the great power one has when one is able to supply quantities of food. Similar reactions could be observed in his current behavior when he prepared food. Bribing a person, avoiding his anger, and temporarily feeling omnipotent were important factors in his pleasure in catering.

He remembered that his mother had often accused his stepfather of being a failure. During these scenes Michael crawled into bed and pretended to be asleep. He constantly feared that one day his mother might leave him. He could describe this fear only as a feeling that mother was very tense and argumentative. From this description, it seemed that she had always been a dominating woman who had not understood Michael's abilities and limitations. This was certainly obvious during her last year of life when Michael was already in treatment. On the other hand, she was very devoted to him. She very much wanted him to grow up to be a "happy person," to go to university, and become a professional. As the treatment progressed, it was possible to see that his description of mother's expectations of him contained his own thoughts about the life and character of the idealized real father.

Michael could not recall the time when his stepfather was suddenly presented to him (he must have been four years old), but he remembered the lovely time in Sweden, where the teachers at his school were very kind to him. He compared this lovely time to the awful period which soon followed after he arrived in London, when he was alone, felt like "a freak," had no friends, could not speak the language, and was too shy and frightened to make friends.

These recollections led to material that helped to elucidate his relationship to the idealized real father (Kris, 1956a). This relationship was built around the fragmentary information which Michael's mother had given him about his father and the one treasured photograph of his father. Although the details of the father's death were never confirmed, the family believed he died in a concentration camp. Michael secretly believed his father had starved to death. This central fantasy was completely repressed, but played a crucial part in determining his long-standing interest in food. For a long time in treatment, Michael was unable to think about his father because this would have brought forth his speculations about being illegitimate. One of the main determinants of his choice of catering— preparing and offering continuous quantities of food—was to keep active the relationship to the real father, and to do (provide food) that which would have prevented the death of his father. (Although I believed that the idea of food might also have been associated with the guilt he may have experienced about his father's death, there was never any clear analytic material to substantiate this meaning.)

Thereafter it became possible to reconstruct his oedipal relationships and to gain insight into his inability to mourn his mother actively. Although as a small child he had apparently heard his real father mentioned, in reality he had this sad, anxious, and bewildered mother all to himself during the preoedipal period. From his recollections of the nice time in Sweden, followed by the awful time in London, it seemed that this was exactly his reaction to being presented in the oedipal period with a new father who suddenly took over Michael's position. The catering also contained the identification with the feeding and giving mother, but this identification was used primarily for defensive purposes to avoid the ambivalence he felt toward her. A similar reaction could be observed in his way of dealing with his mother's actual death; he was unable to experience the loss as something real and tragic. Although Michael recognized some of his anger to the oedipal mother, he found it extremely difficult to allow himself to see the link between his own frightening feelings, his fear of mother, and his compliant behavior. This reaction was examined in treatment, but it was not adequately worked through and remained an important area of potential future danger to Michael's development.

As Michael gained a somewhat better understanding of his oedipal ambivalence to mother, it became possible for him to react to her loss much more appropriately. He said he knew that "hope" or the thought of great medical research would never bring her back. He sometimes would wake from a dream being sure she was alive, and then the horrible truth would hit him. Therafter he could talk of the very few tears he had shed at her death. For the first time, he cried in his session.

The content of Michael's masturbation fantasy changed. He would think of petting or having intercourse with one of his schoolmates, a girl whom he liked. He could ejaculate. Although there was some guilt when he masturbated, interpretation of the oedipal aggression and of his fantasies connected with mother's death enabled him to feel that his body and his sexual feelings were his own and separate from mother. His gambling activities diminished a great deal.

In contrast, his social relationships remained an area of difficulty. He felt uneasy about his blushing and shyness. Although he had close friends, attended parties, and started to go out with girls, he still found it most comfortable to do things for people, e.g., helping at a party; making arrangements; listening to other people telling stories. Whenever he was invited to a party, he spent much time in his sessions on finding reasons to stay away, but he usually would go. It was much easier for him to deal with the difficulties at home, even though he still felt that he should perhaps not be enjoying himself with his friends as much as he was. He could invite friends to his home, and he was finally able to tell them about his mother's death and about the many difficulties which existed in his home and in his own life.

At this point Michael demanded that treatment come to an end. He had finished his training at school, where he had done extremely well. He was planning to work in one of the large restaurants to gain experience. Although his wish to end was certainly a normal move on his part, we had not yet succeeded in understanding his attitude to his body, his castration anxiety, and the various meanings of his feminine identification (Freud, 1914a; Stewart, 1963). These areas had been discussed, but a good deal of work remained to be done. Nevertheless, treatment was terminated.

Follow-up

I arranged to see Michael one and a half years after the end of treatment. He was then almost twenty. He looked very much a young man, was very pleased with his progress at work where he had just been given a better position. Until recently he had had a girlfriend, who had given him up for another boy. He had felt very sad at the time, but "I'm back to normal." He said that his stepfather and grandmother were still bickering, but he now spent much more time away from home with his friends. Occasionally he still became very sad, thought of his mother, and felt that he had had a hard time in the past. My own feeling in this interview was that he would need further help as an adult.

DISCUSSION

In the presentation of the case of Michael, I have tried to show the direction of the mourning process following the death of his mother, and the danger which existed that he would confuse his reaction to her death with the normal conflicts of adolescence. The material also demonstrates how the conflicts of the oedipal period and the severe inhibition of oedipal aggression interfere with the dynamic and structural changes which must take place if mourning is to be "carried to completion" (Deutsch, 1937).

From the details available of Michael's history, it is obvious that he was already vulnerable to depression (Abraham, 1924; Bibring,

1953) and to a severe interference with ego achievement long before his mother's death. Nothing is known of his infancy, but as a toddler he was described by his mother as a frightened and clinging child who followed her around a great deal. He did as he was told, seldom smiled, and never complained. In early latency, he was friendless and felt like "a freak." His mother described his uncommunicative manner by stating, "There is something in him that can't come out."

In the preoedipal period Michael lived alone with a sad but powerful mother, and at the same time carried on a fantasy relationship to a nonexistent but idealized father (as the mother herself probably did). Therefore his relationship to the outside world was also distorted. Michael seemed to believe that the expression of aggression would lead to the loss of the all-important and all-powerful mother. The result was an inhibition of experiencing any feelings which might represent anger or disappointment in the object. His way of dealing with such feelings could be seen in the phrase, "You don't have to do anything you don't want to." This seemingly passive attitude represented Michael's reaction to his long-standing inability to deal with his ambivalence to his mother. The dangerous element was that aggression might be turned against the self in suicide. His mother's death greatly increased this danger because suicide might also have represented both a means of bringing about a fantasy reunion with his dead mother and a punishment of himself for his death wishes directed at her.

What kind of child was Michael during the oedipal period, and how did he solve his oedipal conflict? Or, asked another way, what was the quality of the superego following the resolution of the oedipal conflict, how did it influence his development in adolescence, and what was its impact on the mourning process following object loss?

To believe in the omnipotence of the oedipal objects is a normal attitude of the child. Such a relationship normally enables the child to identify with the parent of the same sex. At the same time his day-to-day experiences with his parents introduce the child to a variety of affects such as love, disappointment, anger. The ability to express such affects, however, requires a safe environment, which makes it unnecessary for the oedipal child to fear that his fantasied loss of the object might be turned into a reality event. Michael had a fantasy relationship to a dead but idealized father.[2] This relationship, therefore, did not make it possible for Michael to experience the consequences of his ambivalence to the oedipal object. Michael repeated this type of idealization in adolescence in his relationship to the man who assumed temporary responsibility for arranging for Michael's future and in the transference.

Michael's defensive organization was only partially effective in dealing with anxiety. This statement applies to him as a child and as an adolescent. As an oedipal child, he used such primitive defenses as regression and projection to avoid anxiety. My impression is that withdrawal into fantasy also played an important part, but I do not have very much clinical material to substantiate this. In adolescence, the use of primitive defenses need not in itself be a hindrance to progressive development if the person also has available other defenses that help him maintain a higher level of ego functioning in situations of anxiety. This was, however, not the case with Michael. In early adolescence he still grappled with internalized conflicts and with the demands of the outside world by withdrawal, denial of affect, and regression.

Michael could not at all use aggression, of which the normal child avails himself, in his effort to change the relationship with the parental figures. It was clear, from his behavior, that this inhibition of the expression of aggression seriously affected his adolescent development (Laufer, 1965). If Michael's mother had not died, his inability to deal with his aggression to the oedipal mother would have been a central task of treatment. With her actual death, this became even more important because the inhibition now seriously interfered with the mourning process. The guilt he felt because of mother's death would inexorably tie him to the very relationship from which he had to free himself. The idealization of his mother (although a normal reaction to the death of a loved object) made it impossible for him to do anything except deny the hostility which existed, and to continue to allow the adults at home to act as auxiliaries for his own positive feelings. The resulting dilemma seemed insoluble because

[2] In a discussion of this paper, Dr. Jerome Kavka made the point that when Michael lost his mother, he also lost the figure that nurtured the relationship to this idealized father.

he wanted to get away from them but at the same time felt that they were really still a link with his mother.

When Michael's mother became seriously ill and had to be hospitalized, it was impossible for him to recognize the severity of her illness. His earlier assumption that mother was all-powerful and indestructible had never really been questioned; therefore, when Michael was suddenly confronted with her vulnerability, he reacted with outward casualness, but an underlying panic. Even at this stage it was possible to see how Michael used his stepfather and grandmother to express his own feelings. When his mother's death occurred, it was as if Michael could deal with this unbelievable reality only by proxy—by acknowledging their sadness and grief. He himself did not experience these affects, but instead he tried to extend her life by idealization.

Michael used identification for a number of purposes, but his assuming the characteristics of other persons did not resemble the process usually seen in adolescence. It was more a regressive means of dealing with the serious internal and external problems existing in his life. For example, his mother's death strengthened his identification with her; he temporarily behaved toward his stepfather and grandmother in a way which resembled his mother's attitude. The danger in this was a double one—it hindered his ability to mourn her loss more actively, and it completely handicapped him in his beginning effort to accept his masculinity. Such behavior was an expression of his pathology rather than an age-adequate use of certain mechanisms, and I felt that the internal changes which should be taking place during this developmental period were not occurring. As treatment progressed, there were important changes in this area (in his manner of wearing clothes and his hair style; his attitudes; his use of friends to fight the standards of his stepfather and grandmother; his ability to risk making adults angry with him). These new ways of using identification showed that once he had dealt with the mourning more actively, the normal changes occurring in adolescence could also get under way.

Michael's wish to become a caterer had certainly existed long before his mother's death, but the urgency to make definite plans immediately followed her death. Although the choice of catering and the sudden decision contained neurotic factors, they also provided a link with the future as well as with the past. It seemed to hold the promise that he could get on without mother, and at another level did not force him to give her up. At first he used catering as a means of doing what mother had done, i.e., supplying food to others. In this way he could temporarily postpone the mourning. When he understood that this activity served to ward off people's anger and was linked to his fear of his own aggression, he began to mourn more actively. Temporarily, it seemed that the identification with mother also contained the effort to re-establish a feeling of union with her. I was concerned that he might act on this fantasy of union with the idealized dead mother and commit suicide, but the safeguard against this danger lay in the fact that catering partially fulfilled this fantasy and also the fantasy surrounding his father's death. In this sense, the choice of catering was certainly a "neurotic" one and contained dangers for his future development.

Some of the factors mentioned can also be applied to elucidate the role of gambling and of the ego-dystonic masturbation fantasy of having intercourse with an older woman. Michael's paniclike efforts to avoid the affect connected with his mother's death manifested themselves in the form of tempting fate, behaving in an omnipotent way by betting against ridiculous odds (Ferenczi, 1913), and creating the fantasy of having mother's live body to himself. Although the oedipal aspect of this fantasy had to be understood before it was possible for him to mourn his mother, it was necessary to postpone its understanding until he could cope with the initial shock of the reality of her death. Without an understanding of the oedipal connection, however, there was the danger that his mother's death would act as a confirmation of his fears concerning the existence of some link between aggressive thoughts, body pleasure, sexual intercourse, and actual death. The persistence of such a link would have grossly interfered with his present and future sexual life. At the same time, this masturbation fantasy expresses Michael's inability to change his relationship to his own body which he felt as belonging to his mother rather than being his own.[3]

Michael's gambling was linked with his masturbation conflict and his wish to reverse the irreversible. It was as if he needed to face

[3] A point made by Dr. Heinz Kohut during a discussion of the paper.

repeatedly the reality of loss of money to be able to integrate the reality of mother's death. But the gambling (and cutting himself) also contained the guilt about his masturbation, and therefore perpetuated the need to go on losing. When he won, it was as if the superego approved, and this acted as a temporary alleviation of his guilt. Losing, on the other hand, represented punishment for his thoughts and at the same time served as a reminder that he must not attempt to get pleasure from his body.

The gambling also contained his homosexual wishes—as could be seen in the pleasure he derived from overpowering the other boys, making up after arguments, cheating, and the excitement in the play. But this statement should be clarified, because his object relationships did not at all have a homosexual quality (Fraiberg, 1961). In early adolescence his object relationships were characterized mainly by a desire to do things for people and the wish to be included by them. I do not think that homosexuality itself was a danger. The real danger lay in the detrimental effect which idealization of the all-powerful perfect man might have on his further ego development. This could be seen in the transference, as well as in his readiness to form pseudoidentifications with men who were prepared to take over and decide things for him (Laufer, 1964). These inclinations might, in adulthood, make him a very ineffectual husband and father. While these factors were to some extent dealt with in treatment, they were not completely worked through, and therefore still exist as potential dangers.

Further Comments on Mourning During Adolescence Following Object Loss

When we describe the work of mourning following object loss, we refer to the libidinal detachment from the object and expect that this process will finally result in renewed interest in the outside world and an ability to cathect other objects. This implies that the mental apparatus is capable of *actively* dealing with the affects experienced during this period. The argument I have used in this paper is that if normal mourning does not take place, i.e., if the work of mourning is not "carried to completion" (Deutsch, 1937), the affects originally attached to the introjected parental figure remain unchanged and additional defenses must be employed to avoid the experience of these affects. As a result the person's ego functioning is impaired and his relation to himself and the outside world becomes distorted. This danger is even greater in adolescence when the ego is normally exposed to many stressful demands.

However, the loss of a parent—whether through death, separation, illness—does not automatically lead to pathology. The impact of such an event on a person's psychological development will be determined by the level of drive development, the quality of his object relationship, and the degree of ego maturity attained before the event (A. Freud, 1960; Furman, 1964b). While itself not pathogenic, object loss can become the nucleus around which earlier conflicts and the latent pathogenic elements are organized. A great deal can be learned about the state of the ego and the developmental level of the various ego functions by observing the way in which a person attempts to cope with the actual loss of a parent.

The detachment from the oedipal object is a normal developmental task in adolescence, which may be greatly complicated by the actual loss of the object. The oedipal ambivalence to the object which is normally re-experienced in adolescence may then be kept under repression by the idealization of the lost object. This idealization becomes an insurmountable obstacle to the relinquishment of the object, resulting in further compromise formation and further defensive measures and ego (character) deviations which otherwise might not have occurred.

In this context, I refer to Furman's recent statement:

> The mourning task is initially dependent on the ability to have a concept of death. But further maturations of the mental apparatus must have transpired, foremost among them being the achievement of a phallic level of object relationships. This would mean the child would essentially have mastered the high degree of ambivalence of the anal-sadistic phase of relationships, referring here to the phases of object relationships described by Anna Freud in 1963. Unless the phallic level of relationship had been reached, the anxiety engendered by the fear of the destructive component of the ambivalence could force the denial of the external perception of the object's loss. Or the unmodified aggressive component could obliterate the internal representation of

the lost object. If the representation of the object cannot be maintained in the object's absence, the decathexis cannot occur [1964a, p. 325].

While these remarks were made about childhood, they are relevant to a discussion of the possible repercussions of object loss in adolescence. Normally, during adolescence, there occurs a change in a person's way of dealing with the reactivated ambivalence to the original object. If intrasystemic changes are to take place during adolescence, a person must have the freedom to regress temporarily, to use identifications in various ways, to experience oedipal aggression in a new and less frightening context, and to engage in masturbation and diverse trial actions. The loss of the oedipal object in adolescence may constitute a developmental interference in the sense described by Nagera (1966). The normally expected changes will not take place because of the idealization of the dead object and the total repression of ambivalence and feelings which represent anger or disappointment with the object. The extent to which the work of mourning will interfere with the normal adolescent tasks is determined by the kinds of defenses available to deal with the oedipal ambivalence and by the quality of the relationship to the object. Conversely, the developmental task of adolescence as well as previously existing conflicts may interfere with the work of mourning the lost object and result in such well-known pathological solutions as depression; flattening of affect; repetitive acting out as a way of dealing with the affect related to the loss; disturbances of sexuality due to the guilt feelings attached to the death of the object; or a glorification of the past resulting in a distortion of present reality.

SUMMARY

This paper focuses on the impact of object loss during adolescence on normal development. Case material from the treatment of an adolescent boy whose mother died suddenly is presented. The discussion points to the various ways in which the reaction to the loss may interfere with the normal developmental tasks that every adolescent must deal with.

BIBLIOGRAPHY

Abraham, K. (1924), A Short Study of the Development of the Libido. *Selected Papers on Psycho-Analysis.* London: Hogarth Press, 1949, pp. 418-501.

Arlow, J. A. (1953), Masturbation and Symptom Formation. *J. Amer. Psa. Assn.,* 1:45-58.

Bibring, E. (1953), The Mechanism of Depression. In: *Affective Disorders,* ed. P. Greenacre. New York: International Universities Press, pp. 13-48.

Bird, B. et al. (1966), Panel on Working Through, rep. H. T. Schmale. *J. Amer. Psa. Assn.,* 14:172-182.

Blos, P. (1954), Prolonged Adolescence. *Amer. J. Orthopsychiat.,* 24:733-742.

—— (1962), *On Adolescence.* New York: Free Press of Glencoe.

Bonnard, A. (1961), Truancy and Pilfering Associated with Bereavement. In: *Adolescents,* ed. S. Lorand & H. I. Schneer. New York: Hoeber, pp. 152-179.

Bowlby, J. (1960), Grief and Mourning in Infancy and Early Childhood. *This Annual,* 15:9-52.

—— (1961), Processes of Mourning. *Int. J. Psa.,* 42:317-340.

—— (1963), Pathological Mourning and Childhood Mourning. *J. Amer. Psa. Assn.,* 11:500-541.

Buxbaum, E. (1958), Panel Report: The Psychology of Adolescence. *J. Amer. Psa. Assn.,* 6:111-120.

Deutsch, H. (1937), Absence of Grief. *Psa. Quart.,* 6:12-22.

Eissler, K. R. (1958), Notes on Problems of Technique in the Psychoanalytic Treatment of Adolescents. *This Annual,* 13:223-254.

Ferenczi, S. (1913), Stages in the Development of the Sense of Reality. *Sex in Psychoanalysis.* New York: Basic Books, 1950, pp. 213-239.

Fleming, J. & Altschul, S. (1963), Activation of Mourning and Growth by Psycho-Analysis. *Int. J. Psa.,* 44:419-431.

Fraiberg, S. (1961), Homosexual Conflicts. In: *Adolescents,* ed. S. Lorand & H. I. Schneer. New York: Hoeber, pp. 78-112.

Frankl L. & Hellman, I. (1962), The Ego's Participation in the Therapeutic Alliance. *Int. J. Psa.,* 43:333-337.

—— —— (1963), A Specific Problem in Adolescent Boys: Difficulties in Loosening the Infantile Tie to the Mother. *Bull. Phila. Assn. Psa.,* 13:120-129.

Freud, A. (1958), Adolescence. *This Annual,* 13:255-278.

—— (1960), Discussion of Dr. Bowlby's Paper. *This Annual,* 15:53-62.

—— (1965), *Normality and Pathology in Childhood.* New York: International Universities Press.

Freud, S. (1905), Three Essays on the Theory of Sexuality. *Standard Edition,* 7:125-145. London: Hogarth Press, 1953.

—— (1914a), Remembering, Repeating and Working-Through. *Standard Edition,* 12:145-156. London: Hogarth Press, 1958.

—— (1914b), On Narcissism. *Standard Edition,* 14:67-102. London: Hogarth Press, 1957.

—— (1917), Mourning and Melancholia. *Standard Edition,* 14:237-260. London: Hogarth Press, 1957.

—— (1928), Dostoevsky and Parricide. *Standard Edition,* 21:175-196. London: Hogarth Press, 1961.

Furman, R. A. (1964a), Death and the Young Child. *This Annual,* 19:321-333.

—— (1964b), Death of a Six-year-old's Mother during His Analysis. *This Annual,* 19:377-397.

Geleerd, E. R. (1961), Some Aspects of Ego Vicissitudes in Adolescence. *J. Amer. Psa. Assn.,* 9:394-405.

Greenson, R. R. (1947), On Gambling. *The Yearbook of Psychoanalysis,* 4:110-123. New York: International Universities Press, 1948.

—— (1954), The Struggle Against Identification. *J. Amer. Psa. Assn.,* 2:200-217.

Harley, M. (1961), Some Observations on the Relationship between Genitality and Structural Development at Adolescence. *J. Amer. Psa. Assn.,* 9:434-460.

Jacobson, E. (1961), Adolescent Moods and the Remodeling of Psychic Structures in Adolescence. *This Annual,* 16:164-183.

Jones, E. (1922), Some Problems of Adolescence. *Papers on Psycho-Analysis.* London: Baillière, Tindall & Cox, 5th ed. 1950, pp. 389-406.

Klein, M. (1940), Mourning and Its Relation to Manic-Depressive States. *Contributions to Psycho-Analysis.* London: Hogarth Press, 1948, pp. 311-338.

Kris, E. (1956a), The Recovery of Childhood Memories in Psychoanalysis. *This Annual,* 11:54-88.

—— (1956b), The Personal Myth. *J. Amer. Psa. Assn.,* 4:653-681.

Lampl-de Groot, J. (1960), On Adolescence. *This Annual,* 15:95-103.

Laufer, M. (1964), Ego Ideal and Pseudo Ego Ideal in Adolescence. *This Annual,* 19: 196-221.

—— (1965), Assessment of Adolescent Disturbances. *This Annual,* 20:99-123.

Levin, S. (1966), Panel report: Depression and Object Loss. *J. Amer. Psa. Assn.,* 14: 142-153.

Nagera, H. (1966), *Early Childhood Disturbances, the Infantile Neurosis, and the Adulthood Disturbances.* New York: International Universities Press.

Pollock, G. H. (1961), Mourning and Adaptation. *Int. J. Psa.,* 42:341-361.

Reich, A. (1951), The Discussion of 1912 on Masturbation and Our Present-day Views. *This Annual,* 6:80-94.

Rochlin, G. (1959), The Loss Complex. *J. Amer. Psa. Assn.,* 7:229-316.

Root, N. N. (1957), A Neurosis in Adolescence. *This Annual,* 12:320-334.

Rosenblatt, B. (1963), A Severe Neurosis in an Adolescent Boy. *This Annual,* 18:561-602.

Spiegel, L. A. (1958), Comments on the Psychoanalytic Psychology of Adolescence. *This Annual,* 13:296-308.

Sprince, M. (1962), The Development of a Preoedipal Partnership between an Adolescent Girl and Her Mother. *This Annual,* 17:418-450.

Stewart, W. A. (1963), An Inquiry into the Concept of Working Through. *J. Amer. Psa. Assn.,* 11:474-499.

INTELLECTUALITY

Aspects of Its Development from the Analysis of a Precocious Four-and-a-half-year-old Boy

HERBERT WIEDER, M.D.

An early, out-of-phase organization of intellectual functions used as a preferential mode of defense and adaptation represents a specific expression of premature or precocious ego development. The psychoanalytic literature contains extensive discussions of the predisposing potentiality of such prematurity to obsessional neurosis (Freud, 1913; Wulff, 1951; A. Freud, 1965; Sandler and Joffe, 1965) and to disharmonious developmental patterning that may contribute to psychopathology (Escalona, 1963; Lampl-de Groot, 1964; A. Freud, 1965), as well as to giftedness (Greenacre, 1952, 1957). The factors nurturing the genesis of precocity itself, though less extensively documented, have been sought through direct observation of young children and infants (Fries and Woolf, 1953; Greenacre, 1941; Bergman and Escalona, 1949; Leitch and Escalona, 1949; Greenacre, 1952, Alpert, Neubauer, Weil, 1956; Bowlby, 1958; Rank and Macnaughton, 1950) and through reconstruction from adult analyses (Boyer, 1956) as well as from biography (Greenacre, 1955; Eissler, 1959).

It is well known that gratification, frustration, conflict, and anxiety, in optimal degree, are necessary for stimulating ego differentiation, integration, and development (Hartmann, Kris, Loewenstein, 1946; Kris, 1949; Hartmann, 1939, 1950). Detailed studies have documented the fact that these experiences beyond the optimum range on either end of the spectrum have a deleterious inhibiting effect on the intellectual development and functioning of children (Mahler, 1942; Spitz, 1945; Beres and Obers, 1950; Pearson, 1954). The experiences that have an excessive stimulatory effect on intellectuality, however, have not been emphasized.

The literature contains several case reports of adults with hypertrophied intellectuality occurring in the presence of obsessional neurosis and disturbed object relations (Rosen, 1958), distortions of the body image (Keiser, 1958), and in conjunction with an inhibition of other specific intellectual functions (Boyer, 1956; Vereecken, 1965). An analytic report of a precociously intellectual preschool child is not available. Excessive intellectualization, obsessive rumination, and isolation, though not uncommon in latency, are usually not the principal symptoms or defenses in preschool children, if the dearth of reported cases is used as an index of incidence. There seems to be a connection between these defenses, precocity, and obsessional neurosis (Hartmann, 1950; Sandler and Joffe, 1965).

No doubt, intellectuality serves adaptive functions and is highly valued. For this reason, parents will not regard its precocious development as a symptom or problem during the preschool years, and will not bring such children for treatment until some other, bothersome problem emerges. In this paper I shall present material from the analysis of Abel, a four-and-a-half-year-old boy, whose intellectuality developed precociously. Although Abel's precocity was the result of excessive trauma and conflict in a highly endowed child, some aspects of his development are pertinent to an understanding of the intellectual growth of academically brilliant children with less overtly disturbed backgrounds.

Intellectuality as used in this paper refers to a mode of ego functioning which becomes organized from an extremely complex substrate of innate capacities, tendencies, or endowments. The capacities to perceive, recall, learn, and intellectualize are some of the elements constituting this substrate (Hartmann, 1939). As intellectuality evolves from the coalescence of ego functions into a hierarchically superordinate function, it may under certain circumstances become a preferential and exaggerated mode or style of defense and adaptation, adding distinctive features to a person's character (Kupper, 1950).[1] As a mode, intellectuality matures through different phases of development whose pathway may be traced.

Intellectualization is familiar as the term describing the defense or resistance in which drive energy is bound by an idea or word. In

[1] The antonym of intellectuality in this context is motility (Mittelmann, 1954); an approximate synonym, mentation.

her discussion of intellectualization, Anna Freud (1936) emphasizes that "the association of affect and instinctual processes with ideas of words is . . . the first and most important step in the direction of the mastery of instinct. . . . This intellectualization of the instinctual life, the attempt to lay hold on the instinctual processes by connecting them with ideas which can be dealt with in consciousness, is one of the most general, earliest and most necessary acquirements of the human ego" (p. 178). Intellectualization as a defense in puberty is conceived as representing the exaggeration of a general ego attitude, under the conditions of a sudden increment of libido, to master instinct by means of thought. Infancy and puberty represent phases of instinctual danger which can function as objective danger, and "make humans intelligent."

Hartmann (1939) points to the reality-oriented and adaptational aspect of this defense: "When a defense against instinctual drive results in heightened intellectual achievements, this shows that certain forms of conflict solution may involve biological guarantees of an adaptation process to external reality. This does not hold for all defense processes, of course, but it does hold for intellectualization even outside of pubertal development. . . . Thus, the description of this phenomenon as a defense does not fully define it. The definition must also include its reality-oriented and adaptation-facilitating characteristics and regulations" (pp. 14-15).

In this report, intellectualization will be considered as the expression of an innate capacity of the ego to bind drive energy to ideas. Intellectualization may develop as a distinct and preferred mode of psychic functioning that is simultaneously oriented in two directions. As a defense it reduces anxiety and tension; as an adaptation it enriches a person's familiarity with external and internal reality.

Learning, a widely used term, cannot be adequately defined. However, we can conceive of a learning function emerging from a hypothecated innate capacity to learn. The learning function, itself the result of a highly complex coalescence of ego functions, organizes drive cathexes, introjection and identification mechanisms, along with perception, retention, recall, and other autonomous functions into a superordinate function. In the search for accumulation, synthesis, and organization of data, it serves the ends of mastery, survival, and gratification. As is the case with the more inclusive function of

intellectuality, to which it contributes, the development of the learning function can be traced from its early emergence in the mother-
child relationship to its highly specialized activity of independent
academic pursuits.

CASE HISTORY

Abel's parents sought consultation after his nursery school director complained about Abel's disturbed peer relationships, his unpredictable and impulsive running from class to the bathroom, and his
preoccupation with drawing snakes. The parents expressed their own
worries over Abel's eating and sleeping habits, his brooding concern
over "making a stain," and his frequent scratching of his anus. They
felt that he was immature and not progressing physically, and were
perplexed "that such a brilliant child, who knew so much, couldn't
learn to get along."

The initial interviews, apart from yielding Abel's history, illuminated many of the parents' characteristics which had a direct bearing
on Abel's development (Sandler, Daunton, Schnurmann, 1957; Kris,
1962). Strikingly opposite beliefs coexisted with mutually shared con-
victions, producing conflictual tensions or exaggerated dogma. Vague
and unreliable, the mother spoke with much wordage and unclear
content. Precise and detailed, the father related genetic and anecdotal
data in a well-defined pattern. The marked contrast in their use of
speech was a particularly important influence on Abel's development.
In their emphatic attitude to educational achievement, "brains"
never went with "brawn," athletics were derogated, and the dichotomy of mental and physical was literally equated with "good" and
"bad."

As a marital couple they appeared to be libidinally inhibited.
One of the father's interviews was filled with complaints about
his wife's mothering abilities; yet in the same interview he remarked
that her frigidity imposed only a mild degree of conscious frustration on him. He had often wondered, however, whether something was amiss in their sexual life because neither he nor she felt
passion strongly. When the mother discussed Abel's sexual behavior,
she revealed a preoccupation with looking but also a marked naivete
in recognizing what she observed. She flustered and defensively ex-

cused Abel's erotic behavior as caused by his sleepiness, hunger, or need to urinate. Neither parent demonstrated empathic understanding of each other or of the child; instead they unquestioningly relied on proscribed patterns of socially correct behavior in human relations. Their inflexibility and inappropriate application of principles had many adverse consequences. For example, since older children "*should* resent a new sibling," Abel's jealousy was encouraged. However, "one should *not* hit babies"; therefore Abel would be punished for expressing his anger. That Abel then developed an intense hatred for his little brother was completely incomprehensible to them.

When Abel was irritable or difficult, the father tried to find a medical disturbance to alleviate. When Abel was tractable and easier, the father thought more constructively, though academically, about child rearing. The mother, however, would cry, cajole, argue, or hit when he misbehaved; and talked, praised, and explained what a "good boy" was when he was "behaving." Unfortunately for Abel, both parents indiscriminately equated good, tractable, and "behaving" with control, submission, and passivity; and bad, misbehaving, or difficult with activity of all types.

The parents' sharply contrasting personal thought patterns, their overtly contradictory behavior, the marked dichotomized attitudes, the lack of empathy, and their emphasis on intellect and brains were environmental influences which had a severely traumatizing and conflict-producing effect on the child.

The first consultation with the mother revealed a clinically important area which later led to therapeutic difficulties. While attempting to relate Abel's history, she alternated between giving vignettes of his and then of her life, and frequently interchanged "me" and "he." At times I found it difficult to decide whom she was discussing. For example, "As an only child I felt overwhelmed when I had Abel, and didn't know what to expect from him, and when Abel had his little brother he got very upset and angry. I was very overprotective and didn't let anyone near him, so we had no one to play with until he was three. We got along fine except that he had a vile temper and would upset me when he wouldn't eat. All his problems were triggered off by going to school because at home we were fine." These remarks of the mother suggested the indistinctness of the boundary between herself and the child. Her inability to establish separateness perpetuated a symbioticlike relationship with Abel, in which she viewed any intervention, e.g., his school, friends, analysis, or any independent strivings on Abel's part, as threats to her own stability. As she continued to talk about Abel and herself interchangeably, she reported how irritable she became during her menses and how ultra-sensitive Abel was about physical injury; they cried easily; she didn't let Abel touch things and he didn't let the baby touch things; she had wished for a girl because boys upset her with their aggression.

Most of the following data were revealed by the father who had a clinical and obsessive preoccupation with detail. Abel was a normal, healthy neonate. His tendency to hyperactivity and restlessness upset the mother. She tried to comfort and hold him, but tensed and cried along with Abel when her efforts failed. When Abel relaxed, she relaxed. The feedings, which had been "on demand" in accordance with the father's request, were ordeals of urging Abel to finish each bottle. Since every cry meant "feed" to the mother, her attempts to satisfy hunger were often refused, and a turbulent interaction developed. "She couldn't let Abel take what he wanted and be satisfied. He would eat, and then trouble would start when he refused more. When he ate, she felt better."

The father had worried about Abel, who was often tense and restless, cried, slept poorly, ate erratically, and only rarely seemed peaceful. An interesting observation of the father, confirmed by the mother, was that "she didn't animate" toward Abel for six months. She believed that babies were like vegetables, and Abel's cries stimulated in her no responses other than confusion and the urge to "shut him up." She never established a consistent, predictable soothing reaction to Abel's distress, nor could she discriminate between his crying signals. As a consequence, Abel often experienced states of increased tension and only partial tension reduction.

The father was impressed by the intensity with which Abel, at about four months of age, would peer at or study objects or people, "as if he were gluing his eyes on you." By six months, fascinated by his many stuffed toys, Abel cried when not all of them were in his crib or playpen. Replacing the missing doll usually satisfied him. His intent awareness of his external environment persisted; and as he matured, "looking and listening" became his characteristic state of alertness.

The mother was initially enthusiastic about his achievement of crawling. However, when he energetically maneuvered about the house, she was concerned that he would hurt himself and confined him to his playpen for considerable periods of time. Abel reacted by crying until set free for short intervals. Similarly, when he started to walk at fourteen months, the mother would suddenly become angry and scold or slap him if he "got away from her."

Babbling, a new development pleasing to the mother, was intimately associated with the feeding situation. The mother consistently read Abel a story while he looked at a picture book during mealtimes. She fed him in this manner until he was three and a half years old. From ten months of age onward his rapid acquisition of new words and sounds gratified her. For a while peace reigned during mealtimes. Then Abel dawdled or refused food, exciting the mother to scold and to remove food, story, and the book. The father dated a pattern of behavior which developed at about eleven months: "Whenever his mother was angry, Abel babbled a string of words which always made my wife laugh and she couldn't stay angry any more." When speech replaced babbling Abel screamed at, argued with, or reassured the mother during their frequent verbal exchanges. As he matured, he achieved greater sophistication and refinement of his technique to calm, excite, or control his mother's moods; he became a "charmer."

Bowel training, another set of turbulent experiences, was initiated at eighteen months. While Abel sat on the toilet, his mother read to him as was her custom while feeding him. But Abel preferred to defecate into his diapers, thus precipitating angry outbursts in his mother. In desperation she often inserted suppositories when he dawdled to encourage defecation in the toilet. Apparently this procedure continued until Abel was twenty-eight months, at which time the father forced its discontinuation. Subsequently Abel occasionally developed fecal impactions which the father removed digitally, on at least three occasions that he recalled, or by enema. Around three years of age Abel started a habit of inserting his finger in his rectum and became enraged if stopped. Continuing to defecate at will, he provocatively announced his encopresis with the words, "I just made boom," his word for stool. In a mood of angry frustration the father beat him at age four for having "dirty pants" and Abel abruptly became clean and constipated. A persistent fear that he would "make a stain" developed and he manifested fright during thunderstorms. He became meticulous about himself and his possessions, keeping them and his room in an exact order.

Bladder-control training was initially reported as successful and uncomplicated. However, in response to questions about Abel's masturbation, the father stated that Abel never touched his penis and that the mother always held it for him when he urinated. Although Abel was not a flooding bedwetter, he dampened his pajamas at night, called his mother, and then was toileted. The mother constantly reminded him to urinate, and the father accurately observed that "Abel never had to get the urge, she got it for him." She communicated the purpose of the bathroom via an invitation to imitate. As the principal object of imitation the mother reported that she stood up to urinate as he watched, clearly perceived her genital, and often commented on her absent penis. Both parents reported that Abel seemed to enjoy being wet, at times with urine, or a leaky nose, or dribbling spit, and insisted on mother wiping him dry. She also frequently examined his buttocks for fecal stains for which she thoroughly washed him.

Abel's remarkable ability to acquire information was apparent to those in contact with him and his brilliance charmed them. His encyclopedic knowledge was acquired effortlessly by looking and listening. Retention and recall kept pace with his perception. As his father said, "We always had to be careful in our conversations because he could reproduce them almost verbatim."

During the mother's second pregnancy, when Abel was three years old, he became extremely anxious. While he clung to her she verbally reassured him. He nightly demanded a protracted bedtime story before allowing her to leave. Sleep was interrupted by marked restlessness and crying out at night. He clearly perceived and was aware of the changes in his mother's body, and persistently questioned her about it. At age three and repeatedly thereafter, his father gave him a completely factual clinical account of insemination, gestation, and parturition. Anatomical differences between the sexes were already well known to him.

During this pregnancy the mother required bedrest for "stain-ing," a process Abel observed in different contexts and a word he heard on many occasions. Confined to bed for bloody symptoms of a threatened abortion, the mother became an object of Abel's intense curiosity. Under the pretext of wanting to talk with her Abel frequently climbed into bed with her and, according to the parents, he saw the signs of bleeding. After the baby's birth the ritual cir-cumcision was performed at home, and Abel, then aged three years eight months, present at this rite, saw the bloody penis.

Abel developed a hostile, sadistic attitude toward the baby brother, pinched or provoked him to cry, and generally emphasized his in-feriority. By this time Abel also tyrannized the parents. With daw-dling, drooling, encopresis, or tantrums, he could provoke a rage reaction from them and devastate their meal hours or nighttime sleep.

Entering nursery school shortly after his brother's birth, Abel attempted to charm his teacher with his bright conversationalism, his remarkable fund of information, and his intense desire to know everything. However, being antagonistic to peers, mocking "stupid kids," much to his chagrin he was counterattacked. Unable to par-ticipate in activities with other children, or to sit quietly to hear stories or learn songs, seemingly disinterestedly he left the group to make clay snakes, which fascinated him, or to draw numbers or letters or words, at which he was quite adept. However, when a story was repeated, he corrected the slightest change or omission. He fre-quently dashed off to the bathroom and upset the teacher with his preoccupation with "making a stain." The teacher cautioned him that he could not remain in class if he did not behave. Managing to control himself, he remained in the group, appeared "distant, squirm-ing, and distracted," but easily maintained the class levels of achieve-ment. He frequently did not finish his work, dawled over tasks, and after periods of silence and refusal to answer questions, blurted out answers to questions directed to other children. Abel complained to his father that the other children did not like him. A forlorn expres-sion accompanied his verbalized wish to "go to some kid's house and play." After his behavior became intolerable to the teacher, the par-ents were informed. Arrangements were made to see Abel four times weekly, and his analysis continued for three years on that basis.

Excerpts from the Analysis

Abel, a thin, owl-eyed, four-and-a-half-year-old, appeared for his first session dressed in long pants, Buster Brown collar and bow tie, with a scrubbed, combed look marred by a drool-covered chin and mucus-leaking nose. After an exchange of greetings, I invited Abel into the office and said: "I guess you know Mommy and Daddy have been to see me and I wonder if you know why you are coming to see me?" "Yes, you are going to teach me how to behave!" Characteristically, Abel conceived or spoke of relationships in terms of teaching or being taught.

In the early sessions Abel verbalized fantasies of going to school, where imagining himself to be the bus driver he gruffly and peremptorily told people to "get on," "get off," "shut up," "sit down." Talking all the while and orienting himself in the new, strange surroundings, he told me about all the "interesting things" in the office. Instead of asking questions he made declarative statements, "You wear glasses; I see you smoke; this is drawing paper"; and in an educative manner described many other self-apparent details.

From the start, the acuity of his perception, retention, recall and his attention to detail were evident. Not interested in using the material in the playroom, he preferred to talk about school, mother, or brother in a chatty, almost gossipy manner, or he would talk to himself. One day while chatting he suddenly remarked that eight jars of different colored paints were not in the same order in which he had last seen them. The accuracy of such observations could be checked at other times. He talked to himself while moving about examining the play materials, seemingly intently, while muttering, "I don't see medicines; Daddy's office is different; when I was sick the doctor took blood from my finger." In this manner he also revealed clearly his ability to split his attention, so that while he seemingly was involved in one activity or set of thoughts, oriented toward external reality, he was simultaneously involved with subjective experiences.

Abel insisted that I occupy myself with activities other than listening, such as looking at books or drawing, while Abel moved about giving reading assignments, reproaching me for not sitting up straight, for talking back, or for touching the play material. That

Abel was acting as the mother, teacher, or bus driver actively bossing me and thereby mastering some uneasiness was quite evident. At times silently absorbed in writing alphabet symbols and numbers, he attempted to construct words associating sounds with symbols. Apart from serving the function of learning and being an unverbalized communication (that did show his problems), this activity was predominantly an attempt to distract himself with images or ideation.

Talking and isolating himself in schoolwork were the means by which he maintained a seeming tranquillity in the new situation. This behavior was reminiscent of the nursery school experience in which separation from the mother and the loss of the gratifications involved in their relationship filled him with a restless uneasiness and led to some attempts at mastery. This behavior also expressed some elements of the relationship to the mother in which the process of split attention had received much encouragement, and of the feeding and bowel routines where looking and listening were important and simultaneous experiences.

I remarked that although Abel had wanted me to teach *him,* he seemed to want to teach *me.* He blurted out, "If you know lots of things you don't have to be scared." With this and other related remarks, I recognized the extent to which Abel used the mechanisms of projection, reversal of active and passive roles, identification, and identification with the aggressor in his attempt to structure the relationship to me along teacher-pupil lines. By encouraging Abel to direct me, to let me know how I should behave or feel, I gained access to his world. "He and me" became as interchangeable as "mother and he," and we communicated by means of transitory identity exchanges motivated in him by his need to master anxiety. Abel quickly recognized that my readiness "to be Abel" took cognizance of a make-believe which we both understood and which was consistently interpreted and clarified.

In the vacillating roles, Abel at times ordered me to read, clean up, or suffer punishment, depicting himself as a teacher modeled on the pattern of mother. Sometimes I was the teacher who was bossed, argued with, screamed at, and threatened. At other times I was quiet and ignored, while he drew numbers, snakes, or words, frequently muttering to himself and isolating himself from the stimulations of the analytic sessions. He offered, as teacher modeled after the father, informative, reassuring data; as pupil to the father teacher, he requested scientific information.

The absence of playfulness and play and the rather humorless quality of the educational theme were quite conspicuous. Talking as though I were Abel, I complained of not being allowed to touch or play with any of the toys which Abel kept describing; they were there to be used, but Abel wouldn't let me. "You can't touch what doesn't belong to you!" Abel retorted. I suggested that perhaps Abel really wanted to play with and touch them, and that was why he kept talking about them. "I'd rather talk, I don't want to get dirty," he responded. "Maybe you're trying not to get dirty and also not to feel scared by showing me instead how smart you are," I answered. Abel then remarked how angry his mother became when he made things messy, whereupon I interpreted that Abel thought I would be angered, too, and that he was trying to please me so as not to upset me. This prompted him to verbalize his concerns over whether I would be angry with "his nosiness"; thereby he revealed his fear of the new situation. His behavior in the sessions changed: an overture of talking associated with mounting uneasiness was followed by a dash to the toilet. Apparently talking, teaching, demonstrating knowledge had protected him from uneasy feelings engendered in part by stimulants in the session and fears associated with satisfactions or urges. The inhibition of physical playfulness represented both an undeveloped capacity and its employment as a defense against impulse discharge. As an undeveloped capacity it eventuated from the lack of playful, nurturing, relatively neutral body care by both parents—a lack for which they substituted intrusive, assaultive stimulation of erogenous zones—and from the inhibition of playful physical motility. As a defense, as expressed by the educational preoccupation, the direct discharge of danger-laden impulses was prevented. Nursery school and children, therefore, represented threats by stimulating warded-off urges, as the analytic setting and the analyst also did.

Questioning gradually replaced informing as his mounting anxiety stimulated his curiosity about the analyst. Seeking reassuring data, Abel, as pupil to the father teacher in the transference, wanted to know about my age, marital status, religion, and so on. Armed with some knowledge, Abel became less apprehensive and ventured to use the playroom facilities. Though reflections of the father-child relationship were present, the vacillating identifications and feelings of the mother-child interaction dominated the transference.

As he drew with paint and crayon, smelling each color and becoming distressed when he dirtied his hands or clothes, Abel verbalized his fear of "dirtying the place" and occasionally ran to the bathroom. While expressing his fear of dirtying himself and me, he attempted to wipe his paint-covered hands on both of us. I pointed out that although he claimed he did not want to be dirty, he seemed to want both of us to have dirty pants. Thereupon Abel anxiously looked into his pants and went to the bathroom to defecate. Two themes developed: the first concerned the beating he had received for his dirty pants; the second related to "stains" he knew the mother made in her pants. He was fusing and confusing the image of fecal stains with the bloody menstrual stains and the bloody penis of the circumcision of the brother. His conscious, brooding preoccupation with "making a stain" stimulated him to educate me about blood composition, function, production, and illnesses much as "anemia," with data obtained from his father: "Daddy taught me all about blood so there's nothing for you to be afraid of." "But sometimes blood scares me," I said. "Well," Abel reassured me, "stop worrying. If you lose some blood, you can always make more." When a tonsillectomy was imminent, he insistently reassured me by describing the procedure and the need for it since "almost everybody has it done." This information was given in a matter-of-fact way and with little trace of his emotional state. The analyst, however, as the passive victim, had to be frightened. Characteristically, these active pedagogic periods recurred frequently and repetitively when frightening material was on Abel's mind. At first, as teacher or doctor, he would project the anxiety onto me and then try to calm me with information. In these moments of teaching he communicated facts for the purpose of informing and reassuring me, expressing part of his identification with the educating father. "Teaching" and "being taught" could be viewed as expressing bisexual implications by virtue of the identifications with both parents and the vacillation of active and passive aims.

Abel's statement, "If you lose blood, you can make more," expressed his rumination about losses stimulated by various sources. He desired an abundance of "cars, trains, and snakes, so that if I lose one I can still have more." Frustrated in his wish to acquire the toys, crayons, and dolls in the playroom, he accusingly cried, "Everything I want to play with you take away! You are a bad man; you even take away food!" These remarks were references to experiences with the mother and suggestions, later confirmed, of deprivation suffered or anticipated at the hands of the father. The preoccupation and ruminative concern with snakes and trains were displacements from an anxious preoccupation with his body and its functions. In comparing his possessions to those of other people, he mainly resorted to disparaging criticisms. My toy plastic train could not compete with his "big, real electric Diesel and steam locomotive." He generally commented unfavorably on the things to play with or on my ability to draw snakes. The disparagements, although related to his attitude toward the little brother as well as to his feelings about himself engendered by parental attitudes to him, quite clearly indicated his envious and frightened awareness of big penises, little penises, bleeding penises, and the enigmatic vagina.

I remarked that "Abel didn't like and also seemed afraid to play with something he had only one of." Abel responded with his "I don't like to lose things," and initiated a game. When he and I were in the playroom he commanded me to leave and re-enter the room repeatedly. I complied and the game, which at first seemed a variant of hide-and-seek or peek-a-boo, continued for a few sessions. I did not understand the game and told Abel so. He angrily remarked, "You can't talk, just do!" "But what should I do now?" I asked. "You must do as I say, I'm the boss!" Thinking this was another reversed mother-child scene enactment, I acting as Abel said, "I won't be bossed!" Abel immediately became frightened, looked into his pants, and ran to the toilet to defecate. A well-hidden secret now emerged: that he "made his boom stick go in and out and sometimes it slipped out."

The encopresis, an irritant to both parents, culminated in the spanking that had abruptly inhibited it. The mother's reaction to his soiling had been to use it as a stimulant for sadomasochistic scenes of scolding, slapping, screaming, and arguing. The physiological control of the fecal column had important ramifications in this relationship to the mother: on the one hand, he secretly insured his anal, libidinal pleasures, and on the other, he apparently acquiesced in the training.

He also flirted with the danger of provoking his mother or father too far by inciting them to rage. He had hoped by this control of me to give himself a sense of mastery of these dangers. The mastery, or control, of the fecal column was associatively linked to father, mother, analyst, and other objects. When I appeared to be not in his control, Abel's fear of losing control focused on his anal masturbatory object. Thoughts pertaining to "going boom" were accompanied episodically by a fear of a bloody loss of the penis, a fear which derived from his identification with his mother and brother and the confusion of the images of bleeding and staining. The partial control of both anal and phallic physiological functioning served the end of stimulating the mother's anxious attention, thereby insuring the gratification of passive aims at both zones as well as the precipitation of sadomasochistic scenes.

I offered the interpretation: "Perhaps you like to play with your boom stick because when you lose it you can make more" and related this to fears and concerns about the penis. Abel rejoined, "Why do you want girls to have penises?" I replied, "Because I get frightened when I see it isn't there." Abel reassured me, "Boys and girls are born that way." Another period of repetitive pedagogic reassuring around the topics of reproduction, penises, and vaginas ensued. After another interpretation of his defense of reassuring and teaching me, he exclaimed, "Girls are born with vaginas, they are born that way! It's an awful-looking peepee hole, sometimes it bleeds, ugh, it's awful. I'd be afraid to have one. Sometimes I'm afraid my brother will bite mine off and then I'll be a girl. I don't like to talk about them, or penises. I don't like to even think about them. It makes me want to go boom and I get spanked. Let's talk about trains and snakes."

His seeking or giving educational information, his being pupil or teacher, indirectly expressed feelings and wishes of an affectionate quality, which also stimulated anxiety. He frequently inquired about the socially differentiated behavior of boys and girls, and then attempted to act as boys do. "Isn't it silly," he would say, "that people kiss or even shake hands?" "But you and I are friends," he asserted, and would become polite and socially correct. While verbalizing his friendship Abel expressed the wish to be taken to the bathroom to play water games, "so we can get wet." Wishes to get wet, to play with water, and to urinate accompanied wishes to make a fire that he could put out. After building a make-believe fire, he extinguished it with water and either spit in an undirected spray or aimed in a well-directed stream. The well-directed forceful stream and the undirected spray, though genetically related to his perception of the father's and mother's urinary performances, also represented the parental patterns of speech. Phallic exhibitionism had been displaced onto speaking and demonstrating knowledge, and voyeurism onto being taught through "looking and listening." Scoptophilic and exhibitionistic tendencies serving libidinal and aggressive ends were then discharged through intellectual channels. Interestingly, when Abel was more actively oriented, forceful spitting replaced passive drooling. A clear body-phallus fantasy was present, expressed, for example, when he would become a snake and wiggle across the floor secretly exciting his penis in the process. He thought of his head as dangerous to people he did not like because he could bite and poison, or spit at and blind them. Along with the heightened cathexis of its intellectual content, the image of the "head" and "brain" were hyper-cathected with libidinal and aggressive energy.

In the bathroom Abel told me that "Mother always gets excited when I won't do and she used to stick things in me to make me." He described how she read to him while he sat on the toilet and added, "I liked that. I like to make you read to me, too. Then we really are like friends." Feelings of affection and wishing to do "friendly things" stimulated penile, rectal, and urinary urges whose active-aim gratification threatened him with harm. When his wish that we both get wet was momentarily frustrated, Abel responded with rage and threateningly screamed, "I'll go boom!" We could now approach his use of "making a stain" or "making pee" which expressed his wish to hurt or get rid of "bad Mommy or Daddy" as well as to anger the parents for angering him. He experienced the active aim of his aggressive urges as equally threatening and dangerous as the libidinal ones.

The object of his urges, in the transference as at home, was the mother, an ever-ready gratifier of his passive aims, which he readily substituted for the more frightening and frustrated active ones. His passive aims unceasingly shunted back and forth from father to mother. Recognizing Abel's mounting libidinal and aggressive urges, actively oriented in the transference, and their confrontation by an overpowering fear realistically augmented by the memory of being beaten by the father, I became concerned that a persistent regression would be Abel's only source of relief from undischarged tensions. I therefore suggested to the father that he retract the threat of a beating by telling Abel he was sorry to have lost his temper; that he realized that Abel could not help himself and therefore should not have been punished. With this reassurance Abel's reaction formation diminished and a transient period of soiling and wetting set in.

Although the diminution of the objective fear did not relieve the anxiety stemming from the internalized aspect of his conflict, it did allow for actively aimed libidinal and aggressive urges to be present more persistently albeit conflictually. His active phallic urges then brought him into more direct conflict with his father. On the one hand, his wish to be a doctor, "to be like his Daddy," reflected his urge for the masculine identity; on the other hand, his penile urges, still associated with anal and urinary urges, threatened to bring him punishment. Abel solved the conflict by regressing to a passively oriented relationship to the father. Wishes for closeness and lovingness with the father led to the desire to know all about doctors and how to become one. His wish for knowledge brought him closer to his father; the uneasy closeness stimulated his wish to learn. The same theme with different content continued from the relationship to the mother. More conscious material pertaining to penile sensations and concerns about them appeared in the analysis. At first there was the usual quest for data, followed by his educating me in great detail about spaceships and rockets and the fuel which they utilized. He obtained factual data from his father, who enjoyed teaching him about scientific matters. This interest led into his concern about bodily functions, "gas," and passing flatulence, which was an exciting pastime but might produce "stains." He compared his "gas" with his parents' gas; though feeling less well equipped, he pretended he had more than they. He educated me about the symptoms and treatment of appendicitis, ulcers, and other illnesses with material supplied by his father.

That cars, trains, trucks, and rockets all carried gas eventually meant that penile sensations, erections, and detumescences were linked with other bodily functions, thus filling him with a need to know everything about them. However, just to think about these bodily phenomena as well as to feel his "itchy" urges to play with and touch his penis filled him with urges to "stain" and "get wet" and thereby with the threat of incurring punishment. He displaced these thoughts onto other less threatening thoughts and developed a lively interest in cars, rockets, and snakes, and later in hand puppets, which obviously represented a part of himself. He said about them, "I play make-believe that my hands don't make the puppets go, they go by themselves." "Yes," I replied, "you play make-believe about your penis, too; you believe it goes by itself when really you're making it go. You like to feel it's only Mommy who makes it go for you."

Other determinants of his castration fears and his wishes to perpetuate his gratifications could be elicited. His fear of "making a stain" was related to a fear of making "pee." His wish to be wet manifested in drooling, wet nose, and dampened pajamas represented his attempts to obtain satisfaction of his penile urges. Touching his penis carried the dual threat of releasing urges for which he would be punished and of being separated from the mother as a source of gratification.

The material about the rockets was presented in confused excitement: rocket heads broke up in violent explosions and went "boom." Then the rockets became snakes, which moved or could be killed. Rockets and snakes produced more rockets and more snakes. The excitement engendered by these images and activities led to urges to defecate and a desire to "make big ones." We learned that he was afraid to play with his penis because "it makes me go boom" and "Daddy will spank me." His increasing preference to make the puppets do tricks was accompanied by more frequent play with his penis at home. In the analytic sessions he would "push and pull" trains and trucks, make them bump into each other, and then substitute the puppets.

He reported a dream "about tracks" to his mother and added the remarks: "No one can say I want to push tracks, can they?" He was referring to an interpretation that pushing trains and snakes and puppets was his way of playing with his penis. During an exciting play session with puppets, Abel kept knocking my puppet down, picking it up, hitting it, and generally overwhelming it; with his other hand he held on to his penis and at times looked to see whether he had made a stain. The "fighting" of the puppets was interchanged with their making love, kissing, and embracing. Again he had to reassure himself that he "didn't make a stain." The fears engendered by his urges abruptly stopped his play with puppets, trucks, snakes, and penis. In its place appeared a period of rumination in which he insisted that "no one touches penises anyway."

His curiosity and anxiety about his urge to "touch" stimulated questioning and a search for data about atom bombs. His thoughts demonstrated that the urge to "pee" led him to want to touch his penis and to have it touched; and conversely, his urge to play with an "itchy" penis stimulated his desire to "go pee" and "make boom." Anxiety about his phallic strivings directed at the mother analyst initiated a regression to the wished-for anal-oral mode of affectionate relating and the wish to be read to while defecating, a situation in which Abel could "really feel friendly." This transference material disclosed that the wished-for feelings of closeness, achieved by being read to, underlay the development of his acquiring knowledge. Since passive aims characterized his libidinal orientation of the anal and phallic organization, a desire for closeness leading to the experience of positive affectionate suffusion may be represented by the wish "to be touched." The themes of touching or being touched were present in manifest and diffuse ways. The conflicts over them were expressed in his own anxious attitudes to touching things that did not belong to him and his insistent desire that he be wiped, dried, touched, or as the puppet manipulated. The conscious expression of this wish "to be touched" in the intellectual sphere was "talk to me" or "teach me."

The active urge to touch his penis filled him with the dread of consequences. "To be able to do what Daddy did" stimulated anxiety, as did the implied threat of the loss of mother's gratifications, and both were the sources of his wish for knowledge about what people do with and to penises. Abel asked me, "Do you think Daddy touches his penis?" "You think he does," I replied. "Well, maybe only to make pee. Maybe he doesn't always. Maybe Mommy helps him make, too!" He repeatedly asked his father for more data concerning reproduction and expressed his wishes for sufficient knowledge to be able to read his father's or my medical books. This period was also characterized by marked sexual identity confusion insofar as passive and active aims vacillated between male and female objects. Unquestionably, Abel's awareness of the angrily close and libidinally cold relationship between father and mother contributed to his confusion about who was to be feared the more. The father's passivity and apparent fear of his wife's outbursts enhanced Abel's image of the dangerous woman. The father's beating, the removal of fecal impactions, his big penis and physical strength linked to the image of the bleeding woman augmented the image of the father as the dangerous man. The parents' frequent verbal battles carried both libidinal and aggressive implications; first one and then the other parent would appear stronger to Abel.

Gradually, with the partial tolerance of the actively aimed wishes, his wish to become a doctor, to learn everything his father or analyst knew stabilized and consolidated the identification with the loving father. Another source of this wish was the desire to gain magic protection from illness, to be active master rather than passive victim. His active orientation had an important link with his motivation to learn. "I want to learn so I can be a doctor. Daddy told me all about the schools I would have to go to. I want to be a doctor children like." In this context, the anticipation of the future reality was a new acquisition and added a new dimension to his thinking. On the intellectual side the acquisition of knowledge was to serve a distant aim instead of some immediate gratification only. He was now consciously motivated to learn in order to master his environment. The safety of learning was enhanced by the father's pleasure in Abel's intellectuality. To have father's knowledge also meant to have father's strength, a weapon of attack and protection. This desire therefore also reflected Abel's covert aggression against the father, but it was experienced overtly in a manner mutually acceptable as a seemingly loving bond. If Abel had not possessed such a high intellectual endowment, a mutually less satisfying situation undoubtedly would have been the outcome.

During the first year and a half of Abel's analysis, he completed kindergarten. His behavior there was similar to that in nursery school, but was accompanied by less overt rectal play. His performance in first grade was characterized by an astonishing acquisition of knowledge and skills, but also by an unwillingness to finish his work. According to his teacher, Abel was "brilliant but uneven." If she allowed him to do as he wished, he showed his ability; if pressed to perform, however, he would refuse. The anal and oral libidinal history of this behavior is evident. Although his intelligence was objectively rated as superior, a sharp contrast existed between his fund of factual scientific knowledge and the presence of omnipotent wish-fulfilling fantasies. While he discussed reproduction and how boys are born with penises, he also verbalized his fears about undressing in the presence of his little brother, "who might bite off my penis and make me a girl." In this regard, however, he was not too dissimilar from other children his age. As Bornstein (1951) states, "For the sake of adults, the child behaves as though he were living by the rules of the secondary process. However, listening to children five to eight years old, when they are engaged in conversations with each other, convinces us that . . . their conscious thought processes . . . can during the latency period still easily dip into the primary process" (p. 279).

As chaotic as the analytic material seemed to be, his behavior at home and in school was more coordinated and adaptive. Toward the end of first grade and the beginning of second progressive changes were noted in his behavior. He established and maintained friendships, but required the acknowledgment of his superior intellectual ability. For example, he established himself as the arbitrator of disputes or as the class authority. Meticulous, precise, retentive, he was an ideal student performing eagerly for the teacher. Less afraid of "making a stain," although he still at times engaged in "boom stick" masturbation, he was more concerned with academic failure. As time went on his mother's inability to encourage and enjoy Abel's active strivings perpetuated his conflict; and his father's passivity offered him no support. With Abel's improvement, she recognized her anxiety and accepted referral to a colleague, but after a short period she stopped her own and then Abel's treatment.

DISCUSSION

Prolonged states of chronically unrelieved tension characterized Abel's neonatal period. The vacillations of the mother's moods, her helplessness to comfort, and her ineptness in discriminating or establishing signals produced, or occasioned, a particular danger for Abel in the loss of her need-satisfying function. His early perceptual image, we might postulate, was invested with sensations or feelings of only partial satisfaction (Spitz, 1955). Abel's realistic needs augmented by unrelieved tension increased the attention cathexis of this image and prolonged his orientation toward reality representations. "Gluing" his eyes on people and objects represented a prolonged scanning of external reality. He also reacted quite early to the absence of objects. At six months, for example, he perceived the absence of a doll and was quite disturbed by it.

The perpetuation of this awareness of, or search for, missing or misplaced objects was apparent in the analysis, for example, when he noted the misplaced jars. Undoubtedly, the later edition of concern about the missing object, the penis missing from the mother, received added stimulation from phallic and anal urges superimposed on the earlier oral experience of the missing "good mother." His tension quickened by the uncertainty of finding this satisfying or "good" object increased his need to search for it and for the means of re-establishing its presence. Satisfaction and tension reduction required oral possession and physical closeness which, when achieved, enriched his ideational representation of the object. The persistent inability to share possessions accompanied by his wish to acquire them in profusion represents greed, or his need to incorporate all objects.

The need for the object may be expressed in terms of intellectuality as a "need for representations" or as a precursor of a need to know. "Not knowing" thus symbolizes absence of the object, separateness and aloneness which threaten the subject with overwhelming tension. Incorporation and introjection of the object's qualities through sight and sound and food supplement each other in the acquisition of knowledge or in "knowing," decreasing absence and thereby tension. One might consider a "hunger for knowledge" to be derived from tension in which those ego functions capable of yielding satisfaction are cathected. In this regard, "knowledge" or representations contribute to the development of object constancy, promote the loosening of the symbiotic tie, and permit the physical distance of the object (Mahler, 1963). In Abel's experience, however, learning did not aid this maturation. Rather, his need for the object perpetuated his need for knowledge in a circular fashion. The learning function thus had a defensive aspect, but nevertheless also enriched the contents of the intellectual sphere.

The mother, by virtue of her reactions to actively aimed drives, persistently discouraged motility discharge patterns and exaggerated the satisfactions of passively aimed wishes and intellectual functions. Thereby she initiated the transmission of her own dichotomized attitudes of mental and physical. As motility developed the effective frustration of these emerging skills as well as the activity implied by them endowed this mode of functioning with a feeling of displeasure or sense of danger. Abel's restless, helter-skelter activity at age four and a half represented a tense expression of the wish to move around and explore, a wish counteracted by the fear of thereby inciting the mother's angry mood. These experiences resembled the frustrations of crawling and toddling during the first fourteen months. Babbling, on the other hand, was enthusiastically received and encouraged; and, in time, the speech function and apparatus received a heightened cathexis derived from the frustrated motility patterns.

The clinical data demonstrated that Abel's perceptual functions were simultaneously oriented to his outer and inner world, a process that led to the splitting of attention. The tendency to prolong this state of simultaneously scanning the external world and attending to inner sensations may have eventuated from the early excessive unrelieved tension. In these experiences the inner tension was prolonged, the cathexis of the object representation persisted, and the search for the object in external reality was maintained. The double orientation of his perceptive processes toward inner tension or danger and toward external sources of satisfaction or dangerous parental mood kept Abel alert to threats or sources of relief. This state was further exaggerated by the parents' reaction and constant vigilance to the anal and phallic impulses. The analytic material also demonstrated that Abel's concern about bodily functions stimulated him to seek knowledge about them, just as his search for knowledge of the world was stimulated by frightening events. This aspect of learning in the service of reducing anxiety supplements that aspect of learning which satisfies the wish for closeness and adaptively adds to knowledge.

Split attention, an avid incorporating of facts through looking and listening, the dominance of passive aims, subdued and restricted motility, and the strong need for closeness—all these appear to be traits that developed during the oral phase either as consequences of the unrelieved tension or as means to reduce it. They remained characteristic of Abel's later functioning.

Babbling is a developmental landmark in which the motoric and intellectual aspects of speech are fused. Abel's babbling expressed his imitative identification with, perhaps incorporation of, "the noisy, wordy mother." He used the sound elements of this identification in the active, or magic, mastery of mother's threatening moods and in the reduction of his own tensions occasioned by them. Sounds or words elicited or reduced tension as effectively as being slapped or held. "Making sounds" became, through learning, an important means of reducing his own anxiety or calming the over-wrought mother. Simultaneously "babbling at" and "listening to" mother established further contact and enhanced the feeling of closeness; this in turn led to the incorporation of more sounds and words and more detailed discrimination of the object. The active acquisition of new words represented a new edition of the earlier used technique of tension reduction either by achieving physical closeness to the object or by cathecting its psychic representations.

In the light of this material, Abel's neonatal tensions seemed to have availed themselves of his specific endowment to reduce this tension. The components of his emerging intellectuality are discernible in the operation of the mechanism of intellectualization and the learning functions. By the time Abel was a babbler, his ego had organized these components into a mode of defense which was further nurtured and perpetuated and eventually preferred to other modes.

As speaking developed the content of Abel's speech acquired a style referable to the mother's and a distinctly different style referable to the father's. In this way each speech style and content acquired a different sexual implication and expressed his identification with each parent. In the analysis this was clearly evident in Abel's vacillation between the roles of teacher and pupil, a vacillation which utilized the speech aspect for its expression. At times he was the wordy, threatening, arguing mother; or the logical, academic, reassuring father. As the pupil child he could enact an argumentative scene with the mother analyst or a teaching experience with the father analyst (see Helen Ross, 1965).

In his projection and role reversal Abel also utilized his fund of knowledge. Insofar as talking and demonstrating knowledge bound Abel's tension and controlled the threatening analyst, this behavior is genetically related to the babbling period and simultaneously expressed the defensive and adaptive aspects of intellectuality. Interpretations of the defensive aspect evoked anxiety, which impelled Abel to renewed questioning and further acquisition of information to relieve his anxious curiosity (Nunberg, 1961). The defensive aspect of learning was evident insofar as Abel felt reassured by being taught and masterful by teaching. He demonstrated his awareness of his ability to control his mother's anxious, angry moods by exhibiting his knowledge. This adaptive aspect of learning also had its roots in the earlier babbling phase.

The child's history and analytic data clearly depict the babbling period as an important early phase in the evolution of intellectuality. The functions of learning and intellectualization were principally used as means of reducing tension and anxiety and of achieving adaptive ends. Although in Abel's case the importance of babbling assumed exaggerated proportions, his developmental history nevertheless suggests what occurs in all children more or less overtly. The transition from babbling to speech represented, in the intimate though troubled interaction of this mother and child, the evolution of maturational and developmental trends toward intellectual functioning.[2]

By the time Abel was four and a half years old, his intellectuality was dramatically overworked. Talking, ruminating, learning, teaching constituted his preferred mode of discharging or coping with aggressive and libidinal drives, mastering anxiety, establishing relationships, and acquiring new knowledge. This level of intellectuality emerged from the more primitive phase of babbling, which in turn evolved from an even more primordial structure. The refinement of observational methods may yield insights into the crying of neonates, its maturation, and the mutual learning process by which the

---

[2] Echolalia may then be understood as a regressive, restitutive phenomenon or a fixation of development referable to the babbling relationship.

diffuse all-or-none cry signal is transformed into a communication between neonate and object (Karelitz, Karelitz, Rosenfeld, 1960).

In the analysis two processes were discernible. Under the impact of instinctual anxiety or drive tension occasioned by the fusion of phallic and anal drives, Abel attempted to bind energy to ideas, thereby diminishing the danger of retaliation for discharge. Simultaneously, he educated and wished to be educated, both of which led to closeness to the object, the incorporation of qualities and data representing the object, and increased knowledge *of* the object. These factors in turn aided the mastery of anxiety and the acquisition of knowledge for the mastery of reality.

The teacher-pupil relationship recapitulated both the mother-child and the father-child relationships. In the role of pupil Abel sought gratification of his passive yearnings from mother and father. As naughty pupil, he attempted to stimulate sadomasochistic scenes. As the teacher, he calmed or excited the analyst child and on other occasions identified himself with the analyst teacher to master fear of the object. In either role, teacher or pupil, knowledge and factual information were necessary requirements for the success of the identification and the transactions in the relationship. In this respect intellectuality contributed to his functioning in various roles. Certainly, intellectuality aided his attempts to construct an artificial masculinity in accordance with the learned model. His feminine identification and passive orientation protected him from his active phallic drives, which were overstimulated daily by his mother's seductive behavior. Active aims at all libidinal levels were associated with danger, both mother and father representing punitive agents. The encouragement and satisfaction of his passivity resulted in an exaggerated defense against and an estrangement from active phallic urges and facilitated too ready a flight from masculine attitudes. He then sought an external model around which to construct an artificial, but wished-for masculinity.

When anxiety or external threats mounted, Abel increased his split-attention vigilance and tended to use his intellectuality defensively. When anxiety diminished, intellectuality was used more adaptively. The material about snakes and atom bombs clearly depicted the consequence of alterations in the level of tension. During periods of increased drive tension these ideas linked up with his fear of "making a stain" and represented his defensive attitude against drive discharge. When tension diminished, the ruminating intellectualization was replaced by a search for knowledge and a pursuit of what were now genuine academic interests. The same ideation alternately served different ends depending on the tension level. Anxiety readily transformed problem solving, thinking things over, attempts at mastery into rumination, preoccupation with fantasy, and tension binding.

Vacillations in the active and passive aims and in the flux of anxiety tended to enhance defensive functioning and powerfully influenced the expression of the wish or fantasy of being teacher or pupil, of teaching or being taught. For Abel, to be actively oriented and teacher at times represented an adaptive expression of his identification with the father and an adaptive functioning of his intellectuality; at other times he "taught to be safe" as a defense against anxieties and fears. As the pupil, passively oriented and incorporative, wishing to be taught, he acquired knowledge and learned; or defensively achieved satisfactions and inhibited impulse discharge.

His material confirms impressions that a fluid, vacillating equilibrium of passive and active aims is necessary in the personality of the well-functioning student and teacher. A too one-sided favoring of either aim may interfere with the learning experience in particular, while anxiety may quicken the defensive aspects of intellectuality in general. The implications of these remarks for learning disturbances go beyond the intent of this report.[3]

As we have seen in Abel, conflict led to regression and the search for gratification of passive aims. In terms of his intellectuality, this represented a shift from "wanting to learn" to "wanting to be taught"; or, on another level, a regression from the "wish to know" to a "need to know." At a time of life when it is more phase adequate and appropriate for a four-year-old to move around and be intrusive, to use inanimate toys and children as objects on which to discharge impulses in play, Abel preferred either to talk or to isolate himself in intellectual activities. Thereby he bound the disturbing impulses, restricted his motility, and imposed an inappropriate task on his intellectuality.

[3] See Lewin (1939, 1958) for an interesting discussion of various factors bearing on education and educability.

The elements of this behavior are frequently, though less glaringly, seen in preschool children who may be as well endowed but not as intellectually fixated as Abel. Little children often wish to have stories read to them or to play school or teacher (Helen Ross, 1965), to withdraw into looking at books, or to draw and count when anxious moments or troublesome feelings appear. Anxiety frequently provokes urgent questioning and a wish to learn when curiosity eventuates from conflict.

In the analysis Abel experienced play with an adult who could hold him gently or allow him to sit on his lap, who did not stimulate or gratify erogenous zone excitations. The analysis thus realistically "taught" Abel the pleasure and safety of motility and play. Interpretation and experience were in accord and relieved his intellectuality of an inappropriate burden during periods of reduced tension.

On the other hand, anxiety repeatedly initiated the intellectual defense and limited play and playfulness with children. Abel's intellectuality has remained particularly sensitive to changes in drive-tension level, perhaps as a stigma of its genesis, and is not fully autonomous. His development suggests that unneutralized energy may of necessity be involved not only in the initiation but also the maintenance of special modes and abilities. "Fully autonomous" is a theoretical ideal; and perhaps we should view preferential modes of functioning and sublimations (as well as their disturbances) in terms of too much or too little unneutralized energy involvement. Abel's intellectual functioning in later years may well be characterized by periods of ruminative, encyclopedic data-gathering rather than by thoughtful, goal-directed, synthesizing search for knowledge whenever the level of unneutralized energy vacillates between "more and less." If he should develop academic disturbances, they would reflect characterological problems rather than damage to the intellectual functions themselves. His history will influence his performance in such matters as finishing papers or assignments, flirting with danger or provoking a teacher's patience, refusing to show what he knows. But he might also develop some hypertrophied function of intellectuality, helpful and adaptive on the one hand but utilizing energy more appropriately experienced in a love relationship on the other.

Summary

I have presented material pertaining to precocious intellectuality in a four-and-a-half-year-old boy as reconstructed from his analysis. The child, highly endowed intellectually, was exposed to prolonged states of tension by inept mothering and fathering. Conscious and unconscious parental attitudes favored the channeling of drive expression toward certain modalities, and away from others, thereby reinforcing and encouraging a preferred mode of intellectual functioning. Thus equipment and environment interacted to give intellectuality a heightened cathexis. A "need to learn" was gradually organized into a learning pattern that served tension reduction, the achievement of physical and emotional closeness, the mastery of drives and external reality. The babbling period is emphasized as representing an important phase in the development of intellectuality. Intellectuality is viewed as a mode of functioning adaptively or defensively, depending on the changing level of drive tension.

BIBLIOGRAPHY

Alpert, A., Neubauer, P. B., & Weil, A. P. (1956), Unusual Variations in Drive Endowment. *This Annual*, 11:125-163.

Beres, D. & Obers, S. J. (1950), The Effects of Extreme Deprivation in Infancy on Psychic Structure in Adolescence. *This Annual*, 5:212-235.

Bergman, P. & Escalona, S. K. (1949), Unusual Sensitivities in Very Young Children. *This Annual*, 3/4:333-352.

Bornstein, B. (1951), On Latency. *This Annual*, 6:279-285.

Bowlby, J. (1958), The Nature of the Child's Tie to His Mother. *Int. J. Psa.*, 39:350-373.

Boyer, L. B. (1956), On Maternal Overstimulation and Ego Defects. *This Annual*, 11: 236-256.

Eissler, K. R. (1959), Notes on the Environment of a Genius. *This Annual*, 14:267-313.

Escalona, S. K. (1963), Patterns of Infantile Experience and the Developmental Process. *This Annual*, 18:197-244.

Freud, A. (1936), *The Ego and the Mechanisms of Defense*. New York: International Universities Press, 1946.

—— (1965), *Normality and Pathology in Childhood*. New York: International Universities Press.

Freud, S. (1913), The Disposition to Obsessional Neurosis: A Contribution to the Problem of Choice of Neurosis. *Standard Edition*, 12:313-326. London: Hogarth Press, 1958.

Fries, M. E. & Woolf, P. J. (1953), Some Hypotheses on the Role of the Congenital Activity Type in Personality Development. *This Annual*, 8:48-62.

Greenacre, P. (1941), The Predisposition to Anxiety: Parts I & II. *Psa. Quart.*, 10:66-94; 610-638.

—— (1952), Some Factors Producing Different Types of Genital and Pregenital Organization. In *Trauma, Growth, and Personality*. New York: Norton, pp. 293-301.

—— (1955), *Swift and Carroll*. New York: International Universities Press.

—— (1957), The Childhood of the Artist. *This Annual*, 12:47-72.

Hartmann, H. (1939), *Ego Psychology and the Problem of Adaptation*. New York: International Universities Press, 1958.

—— (1950), Psychoanalysis and Developmental Psychology. *This Annual*, 5:7-17.

—— Kris, E., & Loewenstein, R. M. (1946), Comments on the Formation of Psychic Structure. *This Annual*, 2:11-38.

Karelitz, S., Karelitz, R. F., & Rosenfeld, L. S. (1960), Infants' Vocalizations and Their Significance. *Mental Retardation* [Proceedings of the First International Conference on Mental Retardation]. New York: Grune & Stratton, pp. 439-446.

Keiser, S. (1958), Disturbances in Abstract Thinking and Body-Image Formation. *J. Amer. Psa. Assn.*, 6:628-652.

Kris, E. (1949), Notes on the Development and on Some Current Problems of Psychoanalytic Child Psychology. *This Annual*, 5:24-46.

—— (1962), Decline and Recovery in the Life of a Three-year-old. Or: Data in Psychoanalytic Perspective on the Mother-Child Relationship. *This Annual*, 17:175-215.

Kupper, H. I. (1950), Psychodynamics of the 'Intellectual,' *Int. J. Psa.*, 31:85-94.

Lampl-de Groot, J. (1964), Remarks on Genesis, Structuralization and Functioning of the Mind. *This Annual*, 19:48-57.

Leitch, M. & Escalona, S. K. (1949), The Reaction of Infants to Stress: A Report of Clinical Findings. *This Annual*, 3/4:121-140.

Lewin, B. D. (1939), Some Observations of Knowledge, Belief, and the Impulse to Know. *Int. J. Psa.*, 20:426-431.

—— (1958), Education or the Quest for Omniscience. *J. Amer. Psa. Assn.*, 3:389-412.

Mahler, M. S. (1942), Pseudo-Imbecility: Magic Cap of Invincibility. *Psa. Quart.*, 11:149-164.

—— (1963), Thoughts about Development and Individuation. *This Annual*, 18:307-324.

Mittelmann, B. (1954), Motility in Infants, Children, and Adults: Patterning and Psychodynamics. *This Annual*, 9:142-177.

Nunberg, H. (1961), *Curiosity*. New York: International Universities Press.

Pearson, G. H. J. (1954), *Psychoanalysis and the Education of the Child*. New York: Norton.

Rank, B. & Macnaughton, D. (1950), A Clinical Contribution to Early Ego Development. *This Annual*, 5:53-65.

Rapaport, D., ed. & tr. (1951), *Organization and Pathology of Thought*. New York: Columbia University Press.

Rosen, V. H. (1958), Abstract Thinking and Object Relations. *J. Amer. Psa. Assn.*, 6:653-671.

Ross, H. (1965), The Teacher Game. *This Annual*, 20:288-297.

Sandler, A.-M., Daunton, E., & Schnurmann, A. (1957), Inconsistency in the Mother as a Factor in Character Development: A Comparative Study of Three Cases. *This Annual*, 12:209-225.

Sandler, J. & Joffe, W. G. (1965), Notes on Obsessional Manifestations in Children. *This Annual*, 20:425-438.

Spitz, R. A. (1945), Hospitalism. *This Annual*, 1:53-74.

—— (1955), The Primal Cavity. *This Annual*, 10:215-240.

Vereecken, P. (1965), Inhibition of Ego Functions and the Psychoanalytic Theory of Acalculia. *This Annual*, 20:535-566.

Wulff, M. (1951), The Problem of Neurotic Manifestations in Children of Preoedipal Age. *This Annual*, 6:169-179.

NORMAL AND PATHOLOGICAL DEVELOPMENT

THE ROLE OF SOUND IN THE
SEARCH BEHAVIOR
OF A BLIND INFANT

SELMA FRAIBERG, BARRY L. SIEGEL, M.D., and
RALPH GIBSON, PH.D.

In an earlier paper (Fraiberg and Freedman, 1964) the development of a blind infant, Toni, was reported. The study of Toni
opened up a number of problems which we are pursuing in our
current research with blind infants in Ann Arbor. The subject of this
essay, the role of sound in the search behavior of the blind infant,
grew out of some puzzling and inexplicable findings in the study of
Toni which required further investigation.

We shall briefly summarize some data of Toni's history which are
pertinent to the problems examined in this study. Toni demonstrated
a selective smiling response to the sound of her mother's voice and to
tactile stimulation by her mother in the period under three months.
At eight months she showed marked anxiety at being held by a
stranger and clearly discriminated the strange voice in other observations.

Her gross motor development followed the norms for sighted
children until the last quarter of the first year. At nine months,

This investigation was supported in part by Public Health Service Grant #MH
12281-01 from the National Institute of Mental Health, by funds from the General
Research Support Grant to the University of Michigan Medical School for 1965 from
the National Institutes of Health, and funds from the Department of Psychiatry, University of Michigan Medical School.

Mrs. Fraiberg is Associate Professor of Child Psychoanalysis, Department of Psychi-
atry; Dr. Siegel is Instructor in Psychiatry, Department of Psychiatry; Dr. Gibson is
Associate Professor of Psychology, Department of Pediatrics; University of Michigan
Medical School, Ann Arbor.

We are indebted to Dr. Peter H. Wolff for his comments and criticisms of an early
draft of this paper; these have been of inestimable value to us in studying areas of
correspondence between Piaget's developmental psychology and the psychoanalytic
theory of ego formation.

although Toni had demonstrated postural readiness for creeping, she could navigate only in a circle; and direct, linear creeping did not occur until fifteen months, at a time when she could already walk with support. From this we inferred that in the absence of a stimulus for reaching, there was no external incentive for the initiation of the creeping pattern. We were unable to explain, at that time, why a sound-making object should not have provided a motive for reaching.

In the absence of vision, adaptive hand behavior was markedly impeded. The mouth remained the primary organ of perception until well into the second year. The hand was employed minimally for fine discriminations. (When we consider the role of vision in facilitating adaptive hand behavior, the problem for the blind child assumes central importance. The adaptive substitution of the hand for the eyes, as a primary organ of perception, takes place via a detour, which we described in the earlier paper. It may not take place at all—which we demonstrated in the case of nine-year-old Peter and other blind children with arrested ego development [Fraiberg and Freedman, 1964]. These were children whose personalities remained frozen on the level of mouth-centeredness and nondifferentiation.)

Blindness for Toni was not a serious impediment in language development. The range and quality of vocalizations were good; imitative sounds followed the norms for sighted children. Naming of objects was slightly retarded by these norms, but as locomotion expanded her experience with objects, her vocabulary moved ahead rapidly, and in the period from twenty to thirty months her speech was well within the range for sighted children.

At the conclusion of the study of Toni, the investigators reported a finding that remained inexplicable: Toni demonstrated at ten months her first success in reaching for and recovering objects that were removed from her grasp. With this demonstration the investigators realized for the first time that they had *no observations that indicated that Toni was able to reach for and recover a sound-making object earlier than a soundless object.* A review of thousands of feet of film provided no further clues. Differential cues in search behavior had not been studied experimentally during the early months of this study.

Description of This Investigation

Purpose and Problems

In our current study of infants totally blind from birth, we have designed simple tests in which problems of search and recovery are presented to the blind infant at twice-monthly intervals. The tests, to be described later, have given us new information regarding the tactile and auditory experiences that lead a blind infant to search for and recover an object. Our evidence, derived from the study of three additional babies in the Ann Arbor series, suggests that search for and recovery of an object on sound cue alone are late achievements of blind infants, occurring in the last quarter of the first year. For three of the four babies whose overall development was rated by us as "good" to "very superior," the age for attainment of an object on sound cue alone was nine months six days, ten months nine days, and eleven months.

In this paper, based upon our study of Robbie, we can demonstrate that the problem of search and recovery is a conceptual problem for the blind infant. Sound alone does not confer substantiality to the object—as Robbie demonstrated through the absence of orientation, reaching or search on sound cue alone during the period under eleven months. In the absence of vision there is no information that can unite the tactile experience of a bell or a musical toy and the sound of the object, independent of tactile experience. The coordination of prehension and hearing is achieved by the blind infant late in the first year and correlates with a stage in the development of the "object concept," the beginning attribution of "permanence" to objects.[1]

The sighted child reaches for and attains an object "on sight" at the age of twenty-four to twenty-eight weeks. There is no equivalent of this achievement in a blind infant until the end of the first

[1] The term "object concept" as employed in this essay follows Piaget's usage; i.e., the concept of an object as permanent, substantial, external to the self, maintaining its identity whatever the changes of position—a thing that "exists" independent of the subject's perception of it. Piaget describes the stages leading to the achievement of an object concept in *The Child's Construction of Reality* (1937). It is in this sense only that we employ the term "object concept." We are not speaking of libidinal object in psychoanalytic terms, although there is reason to believe that the construction of a human object concept follows a parallel development.

year. In all those ways, then, in which the hand unites the infant with a world "out there," in those ways in which the purposeful reach gives intentionality to action and a sense of voluntariness in the formative period of the ego, the blind child is deprived for much of the first year. When Robbie at eleven months is able to make an accurate reach for and recovery of an object on sound cue alone, we can look upon this achievement as an adaptive feat.

The adaptive failure in many blind children may be read through the hands of the deviant blind child. For these children the hand remains in a morbid alliance with the mouth. The hand behaves as if there were nothing "out there." There is typically no search for an object if it is lost or removed. After loss it is "not there," "no place." Typically, the hands of these children at the late age of twelve, thirteen years, or later, are held at shoulder height in a neonatal posture. (This informs us of the role of vision as an organizer of midline behavior in the intact infant.) Along with this stereotyped hand posture occur stereotyped finger and hand movements which belong to the group of so-called "blindisms." The hands held at shoulder height go through stereotyped grasping or fluttering motions—simple reflex actions which testify to the failure of grasping to attain, to find purpose, and to give meaning to experience.

At the start of our investigation of the search behavior of blind infants we were unable to construct any useful hypotheses about the role of sound in search behavior. It is demonstrable that the blind infant who finds the adaptive solutions is able from the second year on to localize sound and employ sound for tracing objects. At fourteen months, for example, Robbie followed the displacements of a cardboard box on a thick pile rug, manipulated with great care by an examiner, and, by using cues that were nearly inaudible to us, he tracked and located the object each time. Dorothy Burlingham (1964) and Doris Wills (1964) describe the preschool blind child's tracing and placing of persons and objects through sound cues. Dorothy Burlingham draws attention to the blind infant's selective listening and "motionless attention" to sound in the first year of life. Before five months of age all of our babies demonstrated attention, smiling, and motor excitement in response to the mother's voice and other familiar voices. (We have reason to believe that selective response to the mother's voice comes in much earlier, but only one of our babies, Keith, was referred for study under four and a half months, and we have only the parents' retrospective histories to go on in these cases. Keith, however, showed a selective smiling response to the sound of his mother's voice at ten weeks of age, the time of our first observation.) Interest in sound-making objects and toys was demonstrable in all of our babies under five months, although handling and manipulation of these objects were rarely observed at this age as spontaneous or motivated activities giving pleasure.

In view of the fact that the blind child demonstrates a capacity both to respond to sound selectively and to trace objects through sound cues from the second year on, it was tempting to construct the intervening stages on the basis of the sighted child's model. In this way it *appeared* as if an adaptive substitution had taken place in which audition provided incentives and information for search behavior in analogy with vision. But here, as in other instances where our hypotheses were derived from the developmental patterns of the sighted child, the analogy proved treacherous. Our experience in the New Orleans study, which provided much valuable information on the characteristics of the blind child's development, disputed some of these assumptions regarding the role of hearing in the blind infant's first year and suggested an investigatory method which should be constructed naïvely, open to novelty and surprise.

Still another hazard appears in the form of inferences drawn from the mixed population that is designated as "blind." Those developmental data that are recorded and analyzed for blind infants and young children are based upon a population that includes all degrees of blindness and blindness acquired after birth. We have evidence that infants with even a small amount of useful vision follow closely the developmental patterns of sighted children. Light perception alone affords an advantage to the blind infant. Both Toni and Keith were found to have light perception in one eye. Each of these children played a game in which he moved a hand in front of the eye, cutting off light in one moment, experiencing light in the next. The game of "light" and "no light" was an absorbing occupation for the baby; light itself had become an entrancing spectacle! And, later, in the last quarter of the first year, both babies were aided in searching for objects by the object being moved across the field of the one eye and blocking light in transit. When Keith wakened in the morning he turned immediately to the window of his room, responding to the light.

For this investigation we have tried to select only babies who have been totally blind from birth and, within the range of certainty possible during the early weeks of life, babies who have no other sensory defects and who demonstrate adequate neuromuscular functioning. In the exceptional case in which light perception appears some time after selection of the baby for study, we have included the baby in the study, but we must take into account the slight advantage that light perception offers the baby in certain areas of development. In this report and in others, when we describe developmental patterns and problems of adaptation, our findings apply only to the infant totally blind from birth and the infant with light perception.

Method

Our findings with regard to the role of hearing in the search behavior of a blind infant are derived from direct observations and the subsequent study of films of Robbie between five and a half and twelve months of age. The observations by the team were made twice monthly, alternating a home visit and an office visit. Our observations covered the broad range of infant development in the areas of object relations, gross and fine motor development, behavior toward toys and inanimate objects, language, and development of the sense of self. Generous samples of all behaviors under study were recorded on 16 mm. film.

The study of search behavior was recorded entirely on film. Problems of search were presented to the baby during each of the observational sessions, and the cinema record was analyzed in staff meetings. We use a variable speed projector which permits us to slow down the film for a frame-by-frame analysis, if necessary. Our practice is to view the film at one-third speed, while one of the investigators using a Dictaphone records a narrative covering the action in fine detail. The entire staff reviews the film and listens to its description. When there is disagreement about a behavior observed, we can of course go back over the disputed sequence in the film until agreement is reached. In this way we obtain a written protocol for each film sequence, which can also serve as an index to the film itself. The written protocol is a reliable transcript of the events recorded on film and can be used flexibly as a document for analysis.

The data which we present from the study of Robbie are derived entirely from film study and the written protocols. Through the slow-motion film study we were able to trace in fine detail the subtleties in hand behavior, the fleeting first intimations of search, and the development of intentional reaching. The transcript of these developments in a written report cannot, of course, reproduce the effects of viewing the film and our descriptive language for the subtleties of hand behavior cannot do justice to the story told by the hand alone during the first year of Robbie's life.

The study of search behavior in the blind infant is only one facet of the larger study, of course. In each of the twice-monthly observational sessions we present the blind baby with problems of search and recovery. The test objects include a rattle, a ring, cubes, a bell, a cup, a cookie, and a small ball of yarn. The baby's own toys are used in parallel tests. The baby is presented with each of these objects and permitted to hold them and explore them by means of the mouth or the hand. The object is then withdrawn by the examiner and the child's behavior is recorded. We test the differential response to tactile and auditory stimuli by means of the test objects and the mode of presentation. Thus, the ball of yarn will give no sound cue when it makes contact with the surface of the testing table; if the child reaches for the ball of yarn after it is withdrawn, we can assume that tactile experience alone has provided the incentive for reaching. The bell is presented in two sequences. In the first sequence the bell is rung without presenting it to the child's hand. In the second sequence the bell is rung, presented to the child's hand, then withdrawn and placed on the test table. Each test is repeated several times in the course of each session, so that the child is given ample opportunity to familiarize himself with the object and demonstrate a behavior toward the object following withdrawal.

Robbie, Pertinent Background Details

Robbie Perrin was first seen by us at twenty-three weeks of age following the diagnosis of bilateral agenesis of the optic nerves made by our Department of Ophthalmology. Pediatric and neurological examinations did not reveal any other congenital defects. The parents had suspected blindness earlier and told the social worker who spoke with them after the examination that the diagnosis was only a confirmation of what they already knew. They warded off the social worker's tactful allusions to feelings and only gradually, in the months that followed, were they able to speak of their fears for the child's future and of their guilt: "Could we have done something. . . ? Is it bad blood in the family?"

The parents were both young and Robbie was their first child. The father was a factory worker and both parents had limited educations. In spite of their pain and self-reproaches, they demonstrated a considerable capacity to come to grips with the child's blindness; their tenderness for the baby and their pleasure in him were evident from the time we first knew the family.

Robbie, at twenty-three weeks was an extraordinary blind baby. He was alert, responsive, attentive to voices and domestic sounds, smiled joyfully in play with his parents, and displayed a good range of vocalizations. He was able to sit for long periods in a propped position and enjoyed the sociability of the living room. He had two brief naps, morning and afternoon, and the long and sustained waking periods spoke well for the amount of stimulation he was receiving. His adaptive hand behavior was very superior for a blind baby. He explored objects with his hands and used his mouth minimally for getting information about objects. (Typically, the blind infant employs his mouth as the primary organ of perception during most of the first year.)

Robbie's development throughout the first eleven months (the period covered in this paper) was consistently superior as judged by existing scales for blind infants. While we should note that none of the available instruments for testing blind preschool children is satisfactory to us, and we have no confidence in a developmental quotient based upon these tests, an analysis of each sector of development over the period five to eleven months showed consistent and stable gains for Robbie and a harmonious profile. Robbie's overall achievement placed him in the superior range for blind children on scales that were standardized for children with varying degress of visual loss. In general, the examiner can have more confidence in the assessments of blind children who maintain their leads in the superior or very superior range than in the assessments of those blind children who show unevenness and even great disparities in their developmental achievements at any given test period.

Robbie's superior development testified to adequacy in mothering —that he was being stimulated by his human environment. Yet it is important to note that Robbie's mother had depressive features in her personality which concerned us as clinicians, and we had reason to believe that they antedated the birth of the blind infant. She tried to ward off depression by eating and by defenses against painful feelings. We were impressed to see that as long as Mrs. Perrin succeeded in warding off depression, there were no apparent impediments to Robbie's development. This means that for the age period four to eleven months covered in this essay, the quality of mothering was at least adequate, and the language and social sectors of development, which are clinically relevant in the evaluation of the mother-child relationship, showed no impairment. (In the second year, by contrast, there was a four-month period during which the mother's withdrawal and loss of rapport with Robbie showed immediate effects in the language sector and a slowing down of the rate of development in all areas. With guidance and support the mother was able to re-establish her relationship with the child and Robbie's language and overall development leaped forward again.)

Our study of the parent-child relationships in the development of Robbie will be reported in a separate essay. At the time of this writing Robbie is two years three months of age. His mobility (running, climbing, walking up and down stairs, playing ball), his skill in the use of his hands for fine perceptions, his speech development (good simple sentences), his lively interest in people and objects, are within the top range for blind children. He is not easily identified as a blind child on the playground or in our office waiting room.

When we now describe the slow and laborious route that brought Robbie at eleven months of age to reach for objects on sound cue alone, we need to place this achievement in the context of his overall development which in this blind child was superior.

The question can be fairly raised: "Is it possible that the achievement of reaching and recovery on sound cue alone was delayed by some factor in the mother-child relationship that was not evaluated in this study?" We ourselves wondered if cathexis of the human voice might be such a factor. For although Robbie showed selective response to his mother's and father's voices from the time we first knew him, it seemed to us that his mother used a tactile mode of communication with Robbie more spontaneously than speech. Yet, since his language development was excellent during the period four through eleven months, there was evidence of adequacy in attending and responding to the human voice and vocalizing need and signals, from which we have to infer a cathexis of the mother and her voice.

As other babies came into the project the whole question of cathexis of the human voice and generalization to sound-making objects became even more complex. Jonny, for example, provides a good contrast study. His "dialogue" with his mother was very largely a vocal one; he came "alive and joyful" when he heard her voice and carried on "conversations" with her. At thirteen months Jonny has not yet demonstrated reaching for and recovery of the sound-making object, and judging by his present performance, he is several months away from this achievement. Toni, in the New Orleans study, showed such marked cathexis and discrimination of the mother's voice that the stranger's voice could evoke anxiety at nine months. She had an excellent vocal "dialogue" with her mother. She did not demonstrate reaching for and recovery of the sound-making object until ten months nine days. Keith, whom we rate as the most superior of our blind infants, had a rich repertory of signals with his mother, tactile and vocal, and was advanced in all sectors of development. Keith demonstrated search and recovery on sound cue alone at nine months and six days (one month earlier than Toni). It appears, then, that the information obtained from these four babies does not establish certain links between the cathexis of the human voice and the *age* at which the child recovers an object on sound cue alone. Moreover, the two babies who gave their first demonstrations of this achievement at nine months six days and ten months nine days (Keith and Toni) both had light perception in one eye and, as we have already mentioned, were probably able to construct an object's trajectory within a restricted range if the object passed before the one eye and momentarily cut off light perception.

We can employ the same data on "age of attainment" to construct a brief summary. Three of the four babies who demonstrated good to very superior overall development (Keith, Toni, Robbie) achieved the recovery of an object on sound cue alone between the ages of nine months six days and eleven months. One baby, Jonny, who is retarded in all sectors of development except language, has not yet demonstrated this behavior at thirteen months. We cannot generalize from this small number and we cannot select the factors at work until we have studied more babies, but there may be some significance in the fact that this "late achievement" in three of the cases appeared within the context of good to superior overall development.

With this background we now propose to describe the patterns of search behavior over a period of five months to eleven months which brought Robbie to recover an object on sound cue alone.

SEQUENTIAL STAGES LEADING TO SEARCH FOR AND RECOVERY OF AN OBJECT ON SOUND CUE

TWENTY-THREE WEEKS TO TWENTY-EIGHT WEEKS

If a sound-making object or a soundless object is removed from Robbie's hand, there is, typically, no vocal protest, no expression of displeasure on the face, no attempt to reach out and recover the object.[2]

Hand behavior: Typically, the hands remain motionless after removal of the object, but we begin to get isolated examples of a new behavior. In the slowed-down film we can see that after the object is withdrawn from the hand, the hand sometimes executes a brief pantomime of the action previously employed in holding the object.

[2] The examples cited in the text were selected from hundreds of items analyzed by us to trace the characteristics of each phase. Observations of search behavior covered spontaneous demonstrations of the child in play as well as the structured test situation. To encourage the child's best performance and to test the full range of his performance we varied the conditions in these ways: the mother herself was invited to present a favorite toy to the child in parallel search problems. When the examiner tested, he employed the child's own toys as well as test objects to obtain the most favorable conditions for search. The child was offered as many trials as he could tolerate within the range of his attention span. (Typically, there were five to ten trials for each sound object each session.) Such factors as duration of the sound stimulus and continuity or interruption of sound were experimentally varied. Not one of the variables introduced elicited search and recovery on sound cue alone until eleven months.

One example may be cited here which covers all the variables mentioned: Robbie's musical dog, one of his oldest and most treasured toys, was offered to him in nearly every session; the toy playing its music was within easy reach of his hands. Whether mother or father presented it, or the examiner, whether the music played for a few seconds or a few minutes, there was no reaching, no gesture of search, no attempt at recovery under eleven months.

The pantomime will occur only when there has been tactile contact with an object the moment before and will occur with the same frequency for a sound-making object or a soundless object. *On sound cue alone:* In repeated experiments we demonstrate that if the bell or the squeaky toy or one of his own noise-making toys is manipulated by the examiner to make sound, and if there is no antecedent tactile contact with the object, the hands remain motionless. The sound of neither bell nor rattle activates the hands in any way, although the child shows alertness and concentrated attention when he hears the sound. There is no orientation of the head toward the source of sound.

Pertinent developmental data: Robbie is sitting well, with slight support; in the prone position he elevates himself on hands, elevates the trunk. There is good coordinate use of hands in holding objects. He smiles in response to mother's and father's voices and tactile stimulation. He is generally attentive and alert to voices and domestic sounds. His language development is good; he coos, vocalizes vowel sounds. His favorite toy is a musical dog, which he embraces, brings to his mouth, and explores with his hands. Rocking is noted during periods of nonstimulation.

Examples of Test Behavior on Removal or Loss of Object

1. A soundless object

Age: 0;5.28

Robbie is given a small ball of yarn and is allowed to play with it on the tray of his low chair. With yarn in hand he moves his hand along the surface of the tray in a bouncing motion. He drops the yarn on the tray and makes no attempt to recover it. The hand, still formed as if grasping the lost object, begins to move along the surface of the tray in a bouncing motion, continuing the action employed during the interval that he had held the ball of yarn in his hand.

2. A sound-making object

No tactile cue

(a) The examiner rings the bell and places it on Robbie's platform. Robbie has not been given prior tactile contact with the bell in this trial. At the sound of the bell Robbie is attentive and motionless. There is no movement of the hands or articulation of the fingers.

With tactile cue

(b) The examiner touches the bell against the back of Robbie's fingers. The tactile contact now activates the hand. The hand makes an exploratory gesture, makes contact with the bell handle, and grasps it firmly. Robbie moves his hand back and forth ringing the bell.

(c) Immediately following sequence (b) in which Robbie held the bell in his hand and rang it, the examiner removes the bell from Robbie's hand and rings it within easy reach of Robbie's fingers. The hands remain still. There is no gesture, not even a flexing of the fingers in response to the bell sound, although Robbie held the bell in his hands and rang it only a few seconds before.

These experiments are repeated using a variety of test objects and the child's own toys. On sound cue alone there is no behavior of the hand that shows recognition or search; the hand remains motionless. Following tactile contact, the removal of an object will sometimes elicit a hand behavior that suggests continuation of the interrupted action.

From these observations we can see that sound alone does not confer substantiality to the object. Even after Robbie has held the bell in his hand and rung it, his behavior toward the bell sound in sequence (c) tells us that holding the bell and hearing the bell are discrete experiences for him. The sound of the bell does not evoke the schema of grasping, as evidenced by the stillness of the hand and the absence of an exploratory gesture.

In these and repeated observations during this period, however, we see that tactile contact with the object, whether it is a sound-making or soundless object, will activate the hand. In the yarn sequence, e.g., when he loses the object, he does not yet search for it in the place where he lost it, but reproduces the previous action when the ball of yarn was held in his hand (bouncing the hand along the surface of the tray).

By reproducing the previous action in holding the yarn we can see that for Robbie the substantiality of the object is still dependent upon his own actions; it is "there" when he holds it in his hand; when he loses tactile contact with the object, it ceases to "exist"; hence, no search behavior. (At this age the sighted child will make a sure reach for the object on sight. When the object is removed before his eyes and concealed, he will not search for the object—it ceases to "exist," but his visual tracing of the object in this stage will lead him in the next stage, at about eight months, to search for the object behind the screen.)

TWENTY-SEVEN WEEKS TO THIRTY-SIX WEEKS

The beginning of search for the tactile object occurs. Following tactile contact with either a sound-making object or a soundless object Robbie begins to make exploratory motions with his hands and actually conducts a random search on the tray top or the table top.

Hand behavior: Following removal of the object from his hands Robbie will now give occasional demonstrations of the beginnings of search. The hand moves radially across the tray from the periphery, a global search which does not take into account the position of the object when he lost contact with it and does not take into account sound cues created when the object makes contact with the surface. Since the tray is his play table, his search at this time tells us only that now there is an expectation that the object lost may be discovered again within the circumscribed space of the tray. Moreover, since we ourselves usually return the object to the tray top, we reinforce his expectation that this is the place where the object can be found. On the other hand, the boundaries of this small space are not organized or mapped by him; his search is therefore unsystematic and he can easily bypass an object that is on the tray. When his random search does not rediscover the object in a brief trial, he makes no attempt to extend the search. If he makes accidental contact with the object on the tray, he grasps it surely. If the bell is rung by the examiner immediately after Robbie has held it in his hands, we now see the hand activated in a grasping motion. There is no search, but the hand executes a pantomime of opening and closing, grasping and ungrasping—or sometimes only a brief fluttering. *On sound cue alone:* If the bell is rung without giving Robbie prior tactile contact with it, there is no gesture of reaching, no searching, no hand pantomime. One new behavior is promising. We begin to get isolated incidents in which Robbie orients his head to the sound, turning toward the source of sound.

Pertinent developmental data: At 0;6.9 Robbie sits well unsupported; he can pull himself to standing position with assistance. He now transfers. He imitates banging the cup with spoon, after examiner demontrates using child's own hands in his. At 7.4 he patty-cakes in response to verbal request. He shows recognition of tin cup (test object) when his hand makes contact with the handle, by grasping the cup and bringing it to mouth.

Examples of Test Behavior on Removal or Loss of Object

1. On sound cue alone

Age: 0;6.28

Robbie is seated before a small table on his mother's lap. The bell is rung by the examiner and placed on the platform within easy reach for Robbie. There is no gesture of reaching, no special behavior of hands; the hands remain at rest.

Age: 0;7.11

A squeaky toy fish (a test object) is squeaked by the examiner, a few inches away from Robbie's hand. The hand remains still. There is no gesture of reach or recovery.

Age: 0;8.23

(a) Robbie's own squeaky hammer is made to squeak by the examiner in a range within easy grasp for the child if he could reach. Robbie is attentive, blinks his eyes each time he hears the sound, makes no gesture of search or recovery.

(b) Robbie's own beloved musical dog is made to play its tune within close range of Robbie's hand, but without touching the hand. Robbie appears to recognize the sound, stops what he is doing and attends. He does not reach for the toy; shows no attempt to search.

Repeated tests during this period demonstrate that *sound alone* will not elicit any behavior of reach or recovery. The hands themselves remain still; there is no motion of the hand or activation of the fingers that can tell us that the sound is meaningful to the child. There is no difference in his behavior toward the sound of his own toys or the sound of test objects. The squeaky hammer and the musical dog are two of Robbie's favorite toys, frequently handled, tasted, manipulated, and experienced as a sound-touch object. He himself can squeak the hammer to make its noise. But when the toy is caused to make sound independent of his own immediate tactile experience of it, he behaves as if it had no identity for him. Nothing in his hand behavior yet tells us that the sound elicits a tactile-motor memory of the object.

2. Sound cue following tactile cue

Age: 0;6.28

(a) The bell is placed in Robbie's hand, then removed and rung in front of him at midline. The face shows alertness and attention. There is no gesture of reaching, but the hands open and close, in a gesture of grasping. (The experiment is repeated several times with the same reaction.)

Here, we see a behavior that is, properly speaking, only an extension of hand behavior in the twenty-three- to twenty-eight-week period, when following loss of the object, the hand reproduced the action previously employed in holding the object. Now, however, something new is emerging. The bell sound now elicits the motion of grasping when there has been an antecedent tactile experience with the bell and when there is temporal contiguity of the two experiences. (On sound cue alone, without prior tactile contact, there is no specific hand behavior as we have shown in 1.) But there is not yet any behavior (reaching or search) that tells us that bell sound is interpreted as a manifestation of the object bell in space.

Age: 0;7.11

(b) A cube is placed in Robbie's hand, then removed and tapped on the table. Robbie makes a tentative search on the table, makes accidental contact with it and recovers it. The experiment is repeated several times, but after this first success Robbie does not attempt a search.

Typically, during this period Robbie cannot employ sound to trace an object's trajectory or find an object's place through its sound as in (b). This means, of course, that if search is initiated at all following the removal of the object, it is tentative and exploratory, and recovery of the object is almost accidental. Even when we increase his chances of recovery (as we always do) by narrowing the field of search and bringing the object either to the tray or table or within a range of a few inches from his hand, the encounter with the object is a matter of chance, as we see in (b).

When we consider that in the sighted child of twenty-four to twenty-eight weeks, hand and eye coordination bring about a sure reach and recovery of objects, the problem for the blind child seems formidable. Before the blind child can "place" an object on sound cues, recovery is accidental, search will bring only rare rewards, and reaching is virtually purposeless.

THIRTY-SEVEN WEEKS TO FORTY-EIGHT WEEKS

Search patterns for the tactile object become organized. The tactile and auditory schemas begin to unite toward the end of this period. As late as forty-eight weeks he will not yet search for an object on sound cue alone, but we can predict from his hand behavior that he is nearly ready to take the step.

Hand behavior: The radial, global exploration of the table surface or space gives way to intentional reaching when there are cues for locating the object or following its trajectory. When the examiner removes an object, we begin to get more frequent demonstrations of reaching or searching in the place where he last had contact with it. Following tactile contact with a sound-making object, he occasionally is able to trace it through sound cues and to recover it. *On sound cue alone:* There is still no gesture of reach or search for either a test object or familiar toy on sound cue alone; but on sound cue alone we now see the fingers activated in a pantomime of grasping.

Pertinent developmental data: At 0;8.8 he fingers the holes of the pegboard. He protests the removal of objects. At 0;9.8 he is supporting himself well on hands and knees, rocking back and forth; at 9;10.10 he is bridging, balancing well on hands and one leg. He is standing with slight support, takes steps while supported; pincer grasping is demonstrated. He hits two spoons together. Robbie examines the interior of the bell and clapper with interest, reorients the bell in order to hold it by hand, rings it. He holds his own cup and drinks from it. He discriminates and shows preference among toys and test objects. He imitates sounds, "mama," "dada," "no." He reacts to strangers' voices by motionless attention; there is no manifest anxiety.

1. Examples of search following tactile cue alone

Age: 0;8.8

(a) Robbie is seated before a small table. The examiner touches a cube to Robbie's fingers. Robbie grasps it. The examiner attempts to withdraw the cube and the hand grasping the cube is pulled forward in resistance. The examiner removes the cube from Robbie's hand and holds it in midair within reach of the child's hands. Robbie withdraws his hand, then makes a sure reach in the direction and the area where he last had contact with the cube and recovers it. The reach itself reproduces the motor pattern in which the hand was pulled in resistance to the examiner's attempt to remove the cube from his grasp.

(b) A pegboard is placed before Robbie on the table. Robbie is helped to find one peg that is placed in a hole. He grasps the peg and removes it. The examiner removes the peg from Robbie's hand and places it in the same hole. Robbie makes a direct reach to the place where he last found the peg and grasps it. (There is no guidance from the examiner at this point.)

(c) Immediately following (b): Robbie is holding peg A with both hands at mouth level. The examiner places another peg, B, in the pegboard and removes peg A from Robbie's grasp. Robbie makes a sure reach for the place on the pegboard where he last encountered peg A and retrieves it. (Note: this was not, of course, the place where he had lost contact with peg A, which was at mouth level.)

These are examples of purposive reaching following tactile experience with the object. Before reaching became purposive, however, we caught glimpses in our early films of its origins. At an earlier stage, when the examiner attempted to remove a toy that Robbie held fast, the hand was pulled gently forward in the act of resistance. Here the motor pattern for reaching was established before reaching became intentional. (There is a parallel in the development of reaching in the sighted child in the period that precedes intentional reach.) Before intentional reaching appeared in Robbie's case there was a transitional behavior. We would sometimes see Robbie's hand reach out in space after an object was removed, reproducing the action in which the hand and arm were extended in resistance to the examiner's attempts to remove the toy —a continuation of the interrupted action. This act of reaching, not yet intentional, sometimes led to contact with the object and recovery.

In order for intentional reaching to take place Robbie needed to have some notion that the object lost was still to be found "someplace." This step in the development of intentional reaching has no parallel in the sighted child. When vision and prehension are coordinated, the child reaches on sight; the object is "there" because the child can see it. In this way vision confers an elementary form of "permanence" to the object months before the child searches for the hidden object (the demonstration of the emergence of an object concept). But when Robbie makes a purposive reach for an object he is not informed by vision or hearing. How does he do it?

In the examples (a), (b), and (c) and in a number of other examples in this section, it is clear that Robbie will conduct some kind of search following manual tactile experience with the object removed and that he is employing directional cues for the purposive reach. Earlier, in the twenty-seven- to thirty-six-week period, search behavior was demonstrated only after the lost object had been previously grasped. Now at eight months, search patterns are organized around the object that has been tactually experienced. This means that tactile experience with the object confers the beginnings of "permanence" to the object. In this respect, there is a striking parallel with the sighted child.

Piaget (1936) records a number of examples in which the sighted child at eight months will search with the hand, following a tactile experience, for an object lost or removed without employing vision in the search. This search is demonstrated only when the child has had an antecedent tactile contact with the object. Through these examples Piaget demonstrates how the child attributes the beginning of permanence to tactile objects. At a slightly later stage, eight to ten months, the concept of permanence emerges with regard to visual objects; the child will conduct a search for the hidden object when he has seen it disappear before his eyes.

In examples (a), (b), and (c) we can see typical search patterns for this period. In (a) Robbie makes a sure reach in the direction and the area where he last had contact with the cube (a point in midair between him and the examiner). While the action places this behavior in part as belonging to the pattern of "interrupted prehension," this is a big advance from the behavior of the earlier period, six to eight months, when the search did not take into account the point at which he lost contact with the object. The sure reach of this period contrasts with the random search of the earlier period and tells us that there is some belief that the lost object can be recovered, that it is "someplace." In (b) and in (c) he searches for the peg on the pegboard, accurately locating the hole where he first encountered a peg and removed it. There is not yet a deduction involved in this search behavior; there is only the expectation that the object can be recovered in a certain place, the place where he first found it. (Here there is some correspondence with the behavior of the sighted child of the same age who searches for the lost object in the place where he first encountered it. As Piaget points out, the child conceives of the object only in a special position, the first place in which it was hidden and found.)

2. Sound cue following tactile cue

Age: 0;8.8

(a) Robbie is given a squeaky rubber toy (test object) and is given time to explore it manually and by mouth. He squeezes it to make it squeak. The examiner removes the toy. Robbie reaches directly to the place on the tray where he first encountered it. He does not recover it. He does not conduct a further search.

(b) Immediately following (a) the examiner squeaks the toy to give Robbie a cue if he can use it. He begins to kick his feet. Hands are held together. No gesture of reach or search.

In this sequence we see that Robbie cannot yet use sound to guide his search. In (a) he disregards the sound cue given by the examiner and conducts his search along the lines of search for the tactile object which we described in Section A. He confers a position on the object, the place where he first made his tactile encounter with it. In (b) when the examiner gives him another sound cue, he makes no attempt to reach or search for the object following failure in (a) to recover it in the first position.

Age: 0;9.8

(a) Robbie is lying supine in his crib, fingering his cradle gym. (The trapeze is composed of rings and a bell toy, a clown.) Robbie reaches up surely to grasp the rings and sets the trapeze in motion, smiling joyfully as he engages the trapeze again and again.

(b) Immediately after (a) he is lying quietly, *not* in touch with the trapeze. The examiner rings the bell toy on the trapeze which Robbie engaged only a few seconds earlier. Robbie is attentive. He makes no attempt to reach out toward the bell toy, but his hands go through the pantomime of grasping.

Here we see that the bell sound from his oldest and most intimate bed toy does not yet elicit a gesture of reach or search. The bell sound is still linked to his own actions; he "causes" the sound through his manual contact and manipulation of the toy. He cannot yet conceive of the objectivity of the toy through the sound which he has not "caused."

But in this example and a number of others during this period, we see that following tactile contact the bell sound activates the hands; the hand goes through a pantomime of grasping, which tells us again that bell sound and bell-in-hand are slowly uniting.

3. On sound cue alone

Age: 0;8.8

The examiner presents Robbie with one of his own toys, the musical dog. Without giving Robbie prior tactile contact with the toy, the music is started. Robbie makes groping gestures with both hands, but there is no intentional reaching or search. In random movement of his hand he makes accidental contact with the toy animal. He immediately grasps it and brings it to his mouth.

Here, for the first time in our observations, we have an isolated instance in which the sound of the object alone activates the hands in a groping gesture. There is not yet purposeful search or reach, but the hand behavior tells us that the sound of the familiar toy and a tactile-motor memory of the toy are beginning to converge. Here, there was no antecedent tactile experience with the toy dog. Yet, for nearly two months this remains our only example of a specific hand behavior on sound cue without prior tactile contact.

We have demonstrated that, for Robbie, at this stage sound alone does not yet confer substantiality upon the object. There is no gesture of search or reach even when the object is a familiar toy. However, we cannot attribute this behavior to absence of vision alone. Once again we have an interesting parallel in the behavior of the sighted child of eight months as recorded by Piaget (1936). In a typical example Piaget hides Lucienne's rattle under the coverlet and makes it sound. Lucienne looks in the right direction, examines the coverlet, but makes no attempt to raise it. Sound alone does not confer substantiality upon the object when it disappears from the visual field of the sighted child. This is a conceptual problem for the child of this age, sighted as well as blind.

The sighted child, however, has an enormous advantage in building the concept. As early as the second month in Piaget's samples, the child coordinates sound and vision, he searches with his eyes for the source of sound, and there soon develops an expectation that sound will evoke a visual experience. The sound of mother's voice and the visual experience of mother will be united. By the third month the sighted infant is practiced in localizing sound.

At eight months Robbie has just begun to orient his head to the source of sound, but in the absence of vision he cannot locate the source of sound with any degree of accuracy, and he cannot, of course, locate an object on sound cue alone. In order to place an object on sound cue alone, in order to reach for and recover an object on sound cue, he will need a concept of the object in space. And he will need to build the concept without the visual experiences that organize and synthesize sense experience for the sighted child.

Robbie will need to construct an object's trajectory in space without having *seen* movement. He must come to believe that an object can undergo various displacements in space that are independent of his own activity and his own manipulations, and that it remains the same object. But what is movement to a blind child? He can only discover movement through analogues of his own motor and kinesthetic experience which ties the discovery of objective phenomena to his body image in ways that can imperil the construction of an object concept. This is an intellectual feat for the blind infant. Some blind babies never find the route and we see in certain deviant children a developmental arrest which, by all signs, reveals a failure to differentiate self and not-self, an inability to go beyond the self and construct a world of objects.

4. No stimulus for the initiation of the creeping pattern

The inability to reach on sound cue retards the development of locomotion during this period. As early as nine months Robbie has demonstrated postural readiness for creeping, supporting himself well on hands and knees, bridging, rocking back and forth. But in Robbie's case, as in the case of the infant Toni reported in the New Orleans study, the creeping pattern cannot be initiated in the absence of an external stimulus for reaching. In the case of the sighted child the visual stimulus provides incentives for reaching, and the reach propels the child forward. The blind child typically comes to an impasse at the point where there is postural readiness for creeping. Many blind babies do not creep at all, and developmental data for blind infants show a lag of one year in establishing independent locomotion.

In the following sequences we are attempting to find experimentally whether an attractive object, sound-making or soundless, can provide incentives for reaching while Robbie is supporting himself on hands and knees.

Age: 0;9.8

(a) Robbie is on the floor, supporting himself on hands and knees, rocking and inching forward. Now he elevates his trunk and bridges on hands and feet. Someone brings his musical dog to him, touches his hand to it, removes it a few inches from his extended hand, well within his reach. He makes no attempt to reach for it.

(b) Robbie is again on hands and knees, rocking back and forth. His squeaky hammer is given to him. He mouths it. Now he loses it and somehow propels himself backwards. He does not reach in the place where he lost contact with it, but makes swiping motions of his hand in an area a few inches from the object. He makes no further search. Now he reverts to a passive prone position on the rug, face down, quite immobile.

Age: 0;10.10

(a) Robbie is on hands and knees, rocking. The squeaky hammer is placed a few inches from Robbie's elbow and squeaked by the examiner. No gesture of search or reach.

(b) Following (a) the examiner brings the toy in contact with Robbie's hand, removes it, and places it within easy grasp for Robbie. Robbie elevates himself, is poised in a bridging posture, elevates one leg for a few seconds, and maintains this three-point posture with beautiful balance. In moving his hand he actually makes contact with his toy but makes no effort to retrieve it. He continues rocking, actually moves back from the object.

(c) Robbie is given a large patent-leather handbag to play with on the floor. He moves to hands and knees and the bag is moved directly in front of him. The examiner taps the bag to give him a cue. Robbie reaches both hands forward and makes contact with the purse.

(d) Following (c), while Robbie is rocking, bridging on hands and toes, the examiner gives him contact with the handbag. There is no reach. The examiner alternately touches the bag to Robbie's hand and moves it a few inches in front of him. Robbie makes no attempt to reach for the bag. (The examiner during this sequence is seated on the floor, parallel to Robbie's position, and there are no directional cues from the position of the examiner.)

It is interesting that even though Robbie has demonstrated reach for the tactile object since thirty-four weeks, he behaves as if this were a new problem for him when he is on hands and knees. This is not a problem of maintaining his balance on hands and knees because he has demonstrated for us that he can use one hand freely and maintain his balance and can even maintain balance on one leg and two hands. We have the impression that this problem has to do with the blind child's "space." In the circumscribed space of the crib, the play table, the playpen, he can believe that an object can be found through one or another of his search patterns; but on the floor he behaves once again as he did at twenty-four weeks when lost objects were swallowed up in a void. Until he can creep, the floor and room space cannot be mapped by him. But until he can locate and pursue objects, he will not be able to creep!

In the examples cited we see that on hands and knees he does not employ search patterns that he has already learned and demonstrated. On tactile cues he does not pursue the object with his hand. He does not search in the direction of the examiner. When he himself loses the squeaky hammer, he does not search for it in the place where he lost it but makes swiping motions with his hand a few inches away. There is also a problem of relativity involved for him. When he loses the hammer and somehow propels himself backward, he cannot make the necessary correction based on his movement backward and the object's position.

In one of the ten-month examples he reaches for the patent-leather handbag when the examiner taps it to give him a cue. He has had prior tactile contact with the bag when he was playing with it the moment before. The bulk of the bag made contact virtually inescapable under these circumstances if Robbie reached out. It remains the only sample we have during this period of reaching for an object while on hands and knees.

Clearly he needs time to transfer the search behavior from one plane and one kind of space to another plane and a new unmapped space. But search on tactile cue alone is a highly unsatisfactory method for the recovery of lost objects in unlimited space. Until Robbie can place objects on sound cue he will have no directional cues for search that can lead him into creeping.

5. Toward convergence of the two schemas

In the following sequence, we have good samples of Robbie's search patterns at 0;10.10 and the convergence of the tactile and auditory schemas.

Age: 0;10.10

(a) Robbie is seated in his little chair. The examiner rings the bell without giving Robbie prior tactile contact with it. Robbie rocks back and forth. The hands are immobile. No gesture of search or reach.

(b) Following (a) the examiner brings Robbie's hands to the bell. Robbie grasps it at the handle, pulls it away from the examiner, and rings it himself. As the right hand rings the bell the left hand goes through the pantomime of ringing. Now Robbie transfers the bell to the left hand, rings it, explores the rim, and appears to be exploring the interior of the bell with his finger.

(c) Following (b) the examiner removes the bell, brings the bell very briefly in touch with Robbie's fingers, and moves it about six inches from Robbie's hand at this moment. Robbie now begins to make a tentative search in the area where he last encountered the bell on touch. (The bell is actually a few inches away from this place.) Robbie now moves the fingers across the board a few inches until he makes contact with the bell, accidentally pushes it further across the tray; now with his finger and thumb around the bottom, he lifts it, clasps it by the handle, and begins ringing the bell in his right hand. Again the left hand goes through the pantomime of ringing. He transfers the bell back and forth between both hands, examining the rim of the bell, and appears to be examining the clapper too.

(d) Following (c) the examiner attempts to remove the bell. Robbie is holding fast to it and the arm is extended toward the examiner as it resists the attempts of the examiner to remove the object. The examiner removes the bell from Robbie's hand and places it on the tray. Robbie begins a search, again in the area where he last encountered it. He does not find it, withdraws his hand, does not pursue the search, begins rocking in his chair.

(e) Following (d) the examiner rings the bell, touches it briefly to Robbie's hand, and places it on the tray. When Robbie hears the bell, his hands move slowly toward the bell and he grasps it.

(f) The examiner removes the bell, touches Robbie's hand to it, places it on the tray close to Robbie's hand. Robbie reaches in the area where his hand was touched and recovers the bell. Robbie rings the bell, now holding it in both hands; again begins to re-explore the interior of the bell with much interest.

(g) Following (f) Robbie drops the bell on the right side of the tray. He fingers the air briefly in the place where he lost it, but when he does not recover it, makes no further search.

In (a) when Robbie hears the bell without having prior tactile contact with it the hands remain still, there is no gesture of search or reach. But now in (b) and throughout this sequence we see a new kind of investment in the bell and active search following loss.

In (b), (d), and (f) he examines the bell's interior and exterior surface, ringing it, transferring it from one hand to the other. He grabs it from the examiner's hand in (b), resists the examiner's attempts to remove the bell in (d). His exploration and manipulation of the bell tell us that he is interested in the qualities of the bell, that there is now an investment in the bell as an object. It is a thing which has qualities of its own, independent of his own activity.

This investment of the bell with qualities has correlates in Robbie's behavior toward the bell in his search. Following loss of the object his reach is intentional, his pursuit of the bell is purposeful and his search patterns demonstrate that he has some belief that the object can be rediscovered. His search in (c), (d), and (f) is in the area where he last had tactile contact with the bell, which means, of course, that the object is still conceived as if it had only one position in space. When he is unsuccessful in finding the object in this position, he does not pursue his search, although in (f) he makes accidental contact with the object as his hands move across the tray. When he himself drops the bell in (f), he fingers the air in the place where he last had contact with it, then gives up his search. The trajectory of a falling object cannot yet be reconstructed by him through any cues available to him at this point. Until sound can be utilized to construct an object's movements in space he cannot have the experience of "movement" as an objective phenomenon.

In this ten-month-old sequence, however, we see Robbie begin ning to place an object on sound cue. In (a) following brief tactile contact with the bell, he does not direct his search to the place where he last had tactile contact with it, but searches in the area where the bell *sound* was heard. He recovers the object.

At the same time he showed a parallel development in his behavior toward persons:

Age: 0;10.10

Robbie is supine on the floor. The examiner is talking to him. Robbie raises both hands to the examiner's face, feels it, touches it, and at the same time begins to kick his legs with excitement.

This reach toward "the human source of sound" is demonstrated to us for the first time in the same session in which Robbie locates and reaches for the bell through its sound. Robbie's exploration of the examiner's face is not a new behavior in itself; we have demonstrations as early as seven months when Robbie explored his father's face while sitting on his lap. But in this instance Robbie is clearly reacting to the voice of the examiner, he is not in tactual contact with him, and he reaches for the face in response to sound.

It should be mentioned, too, that in all of our testing the examiner talked with Robbie during the test and usually spent time playing with Robbie and talking with him at the beginning of each session. This was the first time in our observations that Robbie reached for the examiner at the sound of his voice. We have no earlier examples of his reach for either of the parents upon hearing their voices.

We cannot generalize further from this experience in the observational situation. It is entirely possible that this behavior toward human objects, particularly the parents, had appeared earlier than the time of our observation and was already beginning to emerge as a generalization to inanimate objects, such as the bell, at the time we saw it. We lost the opportunity to study the evolution of this behavior because the summer vacation schedule gave us only one observational session, August 13, the month preceding the 0;10.10 observation on September 15. We are able to say only that all of our own observations up to September 15 had shown that there was no *reach* for the human object, parents or investigators, in response to voice alone. The behavior elicited by the sound of the human voice was "attentiveness," orientation of the head toward the source of sound, smiling in recognition. There was no manifest anxiety at the sound of the stranger's voice, but typically Robbie would become very quiet and cease activity when he first heard the voices of strangers.

The location of bell and person on sound cue is an important transitional behavior at this point, but we note that the search for the bell was still dependent upon an antecedent tactile experience which granted it substantiality. The reach for the examiner on voice cue was independent of a tactile experience of the examiner and may be considered a more advanced behavior.

FORTY-NINE WEEKS

Robbie at eleven months begins to reach for and recover objects on sound cue alone. Two days after this demonstration he begins to creep in pursuit of sound-making objects.

Age: 0;11.0

(a) The examiner rings the bell in front of Robbie (without giving him prior tactile contact with it). Robbie extends his right hand directly to the bell and retrieves it. He then spontaneously rings the bell with the right hand and the left hand goes through the motions of bell ringing.

(b) The examiner bangs the tin cup on the table. Robbie at first makes no attempt to reach for it. The cup is banged again. He reaches out and retrieves it.

Age: 0;11.2

Robbie's mother reports that Robbie has begun to creep.

Age: 0;11.21

Robbie is on hands and knees during the observational session. The bell is rung by the examiner about three feet away from Robbie's position. Robbie creeps toward the bell in a purposeful movement, retrieves the bell with his left hand, rolls over on his back, bell held in hands, and kicks his feet joyfully.

One month later we see Robbie pursuing objects through creeping, using minimal sound cues. His mother is proud and mildly exasperated. She cannot hide things from him, she says. When she tries to get her sewing basket out of his reach, he discovers it in each new place. Both parents wonder if Robbie can see, after all. (We know he cannot, but arrange for another ophthalmological examination at their request. The original diagnosis is confirmed.)

To test Robbie's pursuit on sound cue we improvise a test that parallels mother's sewing basket "experiment."

Age: 1;0.19

(a) Robbie is playing with a large cardboard box on the rug. He is fingering it and exploring it. We then slide it across the rug to a new position. Robbie immediately locates it and creeps to it.

(b) The examiner then picks up the box and moves it carefully to another position, giving barely audible cues. This time Robbie does not search and we realize that the camera motor, which has just been started, is masking sound for him. We turn off the camera and record his behavior in note form.

(c) The examiner lifts up the box carefully, sets it down a few feet from the place where Robbie last had contact with it. The only sound heard by the investigators was the faint scratching of the lid of the cardboard box as it abraded another surface of the box in coming to rest on the rug. Robbie immediately crawled to the box and retrieved it.

(d) The experiment is repeated with two other locations. Robbie retrieves the box each time, using minimal sound cues as the box makes contact with the rug.

From the parents' reports we learn at this visit that Robbie creeps to the television set, turns it off and on. When the heater comes on (there are floor grills) he is attracted to the sound of air moving, goes in search of the radiator and puts his hand over the grill to feel the heat. When his mother is cooking, Robbie is attracted by the kitchen sounds and smells and creeps into the kitchen. During five weeks of creeping he has learned the map of his small home, can easily find his way about.

SUMMARY

Our findings with regard to the role of sound in the search behavior of Robbie are representative of findings in the study of four infants blind from birth. In Robbie's case we regard the following points as significant for further study of ego formation in the child who is totally blind from birth.

1. In the absence of vision the coordination of prehension and hearing appears as a late achievement in the last quarter of the first year. In the sighted child visual search for the source of sound is demonstrated under two months of age. The sighted child makes a purposeful reach for an object "on sight" between five and six months of age. There are no equivalents in a blind baby's behavior toward a sound object. Orientation to the source of sound did not appear in Robbie's case until seven months. Intentional reach on sound cue alone did not appear until eleven months of age.

2. Search is initiated for the tactile object beginning at seven months in Robbie's case. On sound cue alone there is no behavior of search or reaching, until eleven months of age. Confronted with the sound of familiar toys the child behaves as if there were "nothing there," from which we can conclude that sound alone does not confer substantiality upon the object at earlier stages.

3. Search on sound cue alone is finally linked to the achievement of a stage in the development of the object concept. When Robbie at eleven months makes a sure reach for objects on sound cue alone, he also demonstrates that he attributes the beginnings of permanence to objects, that he can believe that the object is "out there," external to himself, has properties of its own.

These findings, we believe, are significant for the study of ego formation in the blind infant and promise some insights into the role of vision in facilitating and insuring the autonomous functions of the ego. Apart from the unique problems of the blind infant in establishing preobject and object relations (now speaking of the libidinal object), the adaptive problems of the first year are made infinitely complex by the difficulties in utilizing sound and tactile experiences in constructing an object world. We can demonstrate, in the case of Robbie and in other cases known to us, that sound is not an equivalent of vision in search, in reaching, in attaining an object. Where vision unites the sound and tactile qualities of objects in early experience, the tactile and auditory properties of the same object remain discrete experiences for the blind child until late in the first year. The experience of "something out there" must occur before a child can endow a thing with objective qualities. Vision insures that the thing presented as a picture, the thing grasped, and the thing heard will bring about identity of an object. Vision facilitates the encounter of the hands with the thing "out there," and with practice produces the sure reach for the object that will later lead to the construction of an object concept. Vision enables the child to construct the invisible displacements of an object between the ages of eight and twenty months, and to believe in the permanence of objects independent of his perceptual experience.

But for the blind child "something out there" is a chance encounter for most of his first year. An accidental swipe of the hand may bring him in contact with an object. An object lost is an object swallowed up in a void. Even the human object, when attachment is demonstrable, is ephemeral for most of the first year, and remains at the disposal of need and magic far beyond the time that sighted children have achieved object constancy (in psychoanalytic terms). Robbie did not extend his arms in reach for a human object much earlier than he did for a treasured toy—a puzzle which remains unexplained in our studies of other babies at this stage of our investigation. And because tactile experience alone cannot serve the construction of an object concept, the blind child is dependent upon acoustical tracing and his own mobility to augment tactile experience in the discovery of the object world. But sound will not inform him until late in the first year. And mobility, ironically, is dependent upon the incentive of a sound stimulus for reaching. In all these ways the early ego development of the blind child is imperiled. We are beginning to understand the clinical picture of the deviant blind child who remains arrested at the level of mouth centeredness and nondifferentiation. The blind child who finds the adaptive solutions —and Robbie is one of them—must take a long and treacherous detour to the discovery of the object world.

BIBLIOGRAPHY

Burlingham, D. (1964), Hearing and Its Role in the Development of the Blind. *This Annual*, 19:95-112.
Fraiberg, S. & Freedman, D. A. (1964), Studies in the Ego Development of the Congenitally Blind Child. *This Annual*, 19:113-169.
Piaget, J. (1936), *The Origins of Intelligence in Children*. New York: International Universities Press, 1952.
—— (1937), *The Construction of Reality in the Child*. New York: Basic Books, 1954.
Wills, D. (1964), The Role of Sound in the Development of a Young Child (unpublished).

GENITAL SELF-DISCOVERY DURING A BOY'S SECOND YEAR

A Follow-up

JAMES A. KLEEMAN, M.D.

Observations of a boy's discovery of his penis and the nature of his genital self-stimulation during the first year of life were recently reported (Kleeman, 1965). It was noted that relatively few such data are available in the psychoanalytic literature. Comparable data from the second year of life are even sparser. For this reason observations of this child (William) during his second year are presented here. They illustrate several points of general interest: (1) the first *significant* awareness of the testicles and scrotal sac; (2) certain precursors of castration anxiety; (3) the gradual unfolding of acquaintance with this body area; (4) the quality of male genital self-stimulation during this period; and (5) the apparent beginning mental registration of self representations of this aspect of the body image. In addition, these observations demonstrate at least one point of specific interest: William's pregnancy fantasies late in the second year, an identification in conjunction with his perception of his mother's pregnancy. The conclusions are less speculative than might be expected at this age because of William's advanced language facility.

OBSERVATIONS

Observation 1 (1;2 + 8):[1] In his bath William tugged several times at his foreskin. His mother identified the part for him, "That's your penis, Billy." At that he patted his genitalia with the palm of his

---

Assistant Clinical Professor, Department of Psychiatry, Yale University, New Haven, Connecticut.

[1] Only highly condensed samples are selected from the large number of recorded observations. Observations during William's thirteenth and fourteenth months were summarized in the previous paper and are not repeated.

hand and a minute afterward repeated the patting a second time. A little later his mother tested him with the question: "Where is your penis, Billy?" He tugged at his foreskin in response.

Observation 2 (1;3 + 0): During the course of a bath he tugged at his penis several times without glancing at his genitalia and without much apparent stimulation.

Throughout William's fifteenth month there was a definite decrease in his touching and looking at his penis. During many baths he did neither. Mrs. W. believed he now really knew of the existence of his penis; therefore he no longer needed to check it visually and tactilely as often as he had done in the previous months.

At fifteen months William had the outer appearance of a robust, active, healthy, attractive boy, though inwardly he was still frequently distressed by his gastrointestinal sensitivity, manifested by abdominal tenseness, gas, apparent cramping with crying, and disturbed sleep whenever his extremely limited diet of banana, milk products, a few cereals, and two baby fruits was expanded. He was still nursing once a day at bedtime. William had a sleep problem related to his stomach difficulty; a parent needed to go to him for comforting or diaper change one night in two. He also had repeated upper respiratory infections and teething discomfort (he had four upper and two lower teeth).

William was doing well in his gross and fine motor skills. For example, he would insert a stick into the hole of a Cheerio and lift it to his mouth to eat it; he walked and ran effectively (walked upstairs alone holding the banister or the hand of an adult), and fed himself with a spoon; he was fascinated with various mechanical devices. He was socially responsive and deeply devoted to his mother, but he could tolerate separation from her for short periods without difficulty. He was advanced in communication, language, and concept formation. For example, he comprehended the concept of "light" whether it be a street light, a ceiling light, an automobile tail-light even unlighted, or a wall light switch; after Mrs. W. taught him that the point of a safety pin was "sharp," he demonstrated to her that a pencil point and his own fingernail were "sharp." He loved books, turned the pages himself, looked at them, "talked" about them, and liked to be read to.

Very little cleanliness training had been instituted. William occasionally sat on a "toidey" at his mother's suggestion when she thought he was about to urinate. He enjoyed sitting there, but did not yet seem to know where his urine came from and did not urinate in the "toidey." Thumb-sucking wth a soft diaper pressed against his face was his main lulling behavior, occurring only when he was tired. Genital self-stimulation was not used for this purpose.

Observation 3 (1;3 + 6): There was no genital self-stimulation in the bath. He was reclining as his mother dried him in her lap. His genitals were more exposed to him than usual. He tugged at his foreskin several times, accompanied, on this occasion, by a vocalized "aaah" with each tug (as though he were acknowledging a sensation in his penis from the tugging). He tugged a few more times and quickly had a 3+ erection.[2]

This observation clearly demonstrates erection from genital self-stimulation and suggests an increased conscious awareness of the sensation.

Observation 4 (1;3 + 15): Twice in the previous week William showed interest in his penis during the bath. He would lean over to look as he stood, and would reach for his penis, tugging at the foreskin.

Mrs. W. believed that there was a distinct change in his stimulating behavior. Earlier, he reached for his penis as if it seemed interesting as an object or part of himself. After he had touched it, a sensation resulted. Now, apparently more aware of its presence, he seemed to reach in order to *create* a sensation.

Observation 5 (1;3 + 18): At the beginning of the bath William stood with a 3+ erection. His mother felt sure he needed to urinate. She asked William if he wished to "make peepee" on the toilet. He replied with an unequivocal "No," which he repeated when the question was asked again. After about a minute and a half, while he played with a bucket, there was a spontaneous detumescence (2+) without urination. He was washed, the water drained out, and he sat on the rubber mat with a 3+ erection. He had not touched or looked at his penis up to this time, despite erection throughout the bath. As his mother helped him categorize other body parts and objects, she asked: "Where is your penis?" He knew the meaning of the word

---

[2] An approximate grading of the degree of penile erection was recorded: 0 for no erection, 1+ for slight, 2+ for moderate, and 3+ for full erection.

and immediately began to lean over to try to see it. Because of his pendulous belly he had to push up with his feet to view it. He held his penis between his thumb and forefinger and squeezed it. He looked at it part of the time, and continued stimulating it by squeezing and tugging in a fashion suggesting that he was creating a sensation which was definitely pleasurable. This lasted about forty-five seconds and had a masturbatory character. He let go for half a minute. He repeated squeezing and pulling. He rubbed it between his thumb and fingers. This lasted thirty seconds; then he got out of the tub.

This observation illustrates his self-awareness in this area, the increasingly masturbatory character of his genital self-stimulation at times, and the definite association of the word *penis* with his organ.

Observation 6 (1;3 + 20): Several times this day when his diapers were changed, William squeezed his legs together and each time had a 3+ erection. On one occasion immediately following the squeezing of his thighs, causing the erection, he squeezed his mother's forearm with his fingers and then took her finger in his mouth and bit it (it appeared more like a "love bite," a discharge of some sexual excitement rather than anger).

The genital stimulation by thigh pressure, the squeezing of mother's arm, and the biting of her finger had a modal quality in common—an autoerotic excitement which was partially discharged toward his love object. This meaning was also deduced from other observations made at this time; in addition, they demonstrated: (1) a growing awareness of himself; (2) more masturbatory quality to his genital self-stimulation; (3) erection arising almost regularly in response to thigh pressure or manual self-stimulation of the genitalia; (4) greater individuation in his development; and (5) more clear-cut love for his mother as a distinct and separate person.

At the age of fifteen months and twenty-one days complete weaning, the omission of the night breast feeding, was begun.

Observation 7 (1;3 + 23): The mother was holding William in her lap. He put his hands on her fully clothed chest and ran them downward in a way that indicated a consciousness of her form as his hands moved over her breasts. Later in the day William was playing on the floor. Mrs. W. leaned over, and she found William staring down her blouse as an older male might.

It is difficult to decide whether to attach any great significance to this and similar observations. William's visual and tactile cognizance of his mother and her body paralleled his increased knowledge of his own. He had just given up nursing at the breast, at a late age for babies in his social group. His mother frequently observed that *looking* was very important to William, and in my earlier report (1965) I noted the extent to which he used this sensory modality to explore his genitals in the first months of the second year. *Active looking* would seem to be more a male sexual characteristic than female one, and we possibly may here be encountering early forms of this activity.

Observation 8 (1;4 + 5): During the past ten days William touched his penis more frequently. His increased comprehension of it was evident in his often touching it without simultaneously looking at it. At almost every diaper change, he reached for his penis. He seemed to know it was there and to realize it felt good to touch it. On the previous day, after Mrs. W. had put on his diapers, William slipped his hand down to his genitalia inside the diaper. This was a new behavior. Today he repeated this. At one point his mother kissed his foot. Immediately, he patted his genital area (over diapers and rubber pants) and said: "Oooh, oooh." His mother felt this could mean "kiss me here as you did on my foot" or "it feels good here," i.e., kissing his foot makes his genital area feel good.

At sixteen and a half months William touched his genitals in order to stimulate them, without having to look each time. His self image had reached the point where he now referred to himself by name.

Observation 9 (1;4 + 17): In the bath William was standing and started to urinate. For the first time he looked down and watched himself urinating, with some evidence of pride.

Observation 10 (1;4 + 18): Sitting in his crib after his bath with just an undershirt on and no diaper, William discovered a new game as his mother stepped out of the room momentarily. By "sucking in" his belly he could both see his penis and cause it to bob up and touch a plastic bottle resting in his lap. He apparently enjoyed the activity and the sensation and repeated it a number of times. He laughed as he repeated it, then touched his penis with his hand, "talked" about it, and giggled as he did. He next picked up the plastic bottle and pressed it against his penis. He also experimented with a paper cup in his bed, putting the cup over his penis and testicles. He removed it and again covered the genitalia with it (almost a peek-a-boo equivalent). After doing this several times, he handed the cup to his mother and said, "Back!" (He wished to stop, and she should put the cup away.)

Several times when the mother changed his diaper containing a bowel movement, he started to put his hand to the diaper area, and she gently forbade it. As a result, an association was established, and several times when there were no feces in the diaper, he started to put his hand toward his penis, said "Oooh," and inhibited the complete motion.[3] Subsequently William was helped to differentiate that it was all right to touch his penis but not put his hand in the bowel movement.

Observation 11 (1;4 + 23): In the bath William carried on active and rather absorbed manipulations and stimulation of his genitals for approximately five minutes. This resulted in a 3+ erection, which had been occurring frequently but not invariably with less concentrated stimulation. He lifted the penis upward, rolled the testicles and scrotum up toward the penis, squeezed the scrotum and penis together, and tugged on the foreskin and the glans. He was "talking" and chortling as he stimulated himself. Clearly this directed behavior brought him localized sensation and pleasure. There was no evidence of an orgasm.

Later during the night he awoke crying. When his mother went to him and changed his soaked diapers, he again had a full erection (3+). William squeezed his thighs together and "sucked in" his abdomen in a way suggesting an effort to stimulate the genitals. He was "speaking of it" as he did, and goose pimples appeared on his thighs. That these did not represent an orgasm is supported by the fact that the erection did not recede as the goose pimples disappeared.

This was the most prolonged and absorbed genital self-stimulation yet observed and could be called masturbation.

Observation 12 (1;4 + 26): Apropos of his recent more vigorous and active tugging on his genitals, William on this day was pulling on his penis and said, "Off, off!" His mother quietly explained it was his penis, and it didn't come off.

---

[3] Ernst Kris (at a seminar) has pointed out that some degree of castration threat during cleanliness training is experienced even by children of "enlightened" parents (who do not forbid masturbation or genital touching), because of the proximity of the genitals to the anus.

This behavior—possibly an early precursor of castration anxiety (William showed no anxiety as he said, "Off, off")—was developmentally related to his general approach to protuberances, tops and caps of boxes, cans, and bottles, which come off and are put back on. It suggests that the mental self representation of his penis was still rudimentary and not yet an integrated part of his body image. There was at this time beginning gender differentiation. Looking at a magazine with his mother, he distinguished a "boy" or "man" from a "durl," usually correctly.

Observation 13 (1;4 + 28): William was standing in the tub as water ran in from the faucet. By holding his pelvis forward, he was able to use the stream of water to stimulate his penis, which was fully erect (3+). This was repeated in the bath the following day and was associated with erection (2+).

Observation 14 (1;5 + 4): At this time William was stimulating his genitals frequently and actively not only in the bath, but almost every time his diaper was changed, he would reach for his genitalia and stimulate himself. His mother each night put white salve on his perianal-scrotal area to prevent diaper rash from feces. This night when she did, his penis became erect (2+); he giggled and reached for it.

Observation 15 (1;5 + 9): During this period his putting his hand to his genitals was more prominent and frequent during diaper changes than during baths. His tugging on his penis and saying "off" continued, but was now done as a joke. He did this in his mother's presence; she would jest back, "Oh, Billy, you know your penis doesn't come off," and he laughed and repeated the "game." This behavior coincided in time with his having a few bowel movements on the toilet; thus he experienced a "body part" becoming separated from him and being flushed away, an experience which was associated with some apparent anxiety.

Observation 16 (1;5 + 14): During a diaper change William picked up a safety pin and tested the sharpness of the point on the skin over his testicles.

Observation 17 (1;5 + 17): Several times recently William treated his penis like a separate object, not only by saying "off" but by anthropomorphizing it—"feeding" it a cracker as he now did his stuffed dog and his toes. Again Mrs. W. and he made a joke of it as she would say: "Oh, your penis doesn't eat crackers." He would laugh and do it again.

Observation 18 (1;5 + 25): Four days previously he urinated in his small toilet for the first time and again made a bowel movement in it. This day he urinated in the bath, though he did not seem aware of having done so.

Observation 19 (1;5 + 28): On the previous day William had seen his father urinate and watched the process intently with great interest. He pointed to his father's penis, started to touch it, but instead commented on the bubbles in the toilet bowl. Mr. W. identified the penis with the word, which William could already say. On this day as his clothes were being changed, William tugged on his penis and muttered, "Boken." It was not clear whether this was related to his recent learning of the word, which he also applied to door latches, etc., resulted from a comparison with his father, or was part of the game which then followed: he continued to tug on his penis, saying, "Off." It was no longer an anxiety-free joke with his mother as she reassured him that it would not come off. He now showed mild concern about it, and in addition pursued his anthropomorphizing of his penis, offering it cookies and drinks of water.

In his bath at the end of the day he was standing and bent way over, looking at his genitals. He pushed the penis aside and pointed to his scrotum and testicles, uttering "Oooh, oooh" with concern. When his mother named them, "Those are your ballies," he repeated, "Ballies," and seemed relieved.

The same day when his diaper was being changed and his genitals were being powdered after a bowel movement, he giggled and said "more." He obviously enjoyed the stimulation, but it was not clear whether he felt more pleasure than, for example, when his abdomen was tickled. Still lying on the changing table, William put his stuffed dog down to his genitals. His mother asked, "What are you doing?" William answered, "Peebis" (penis). His mother inquired further, "What else is there?" William replied, "Ballies" and then "Peek." He did peek, talked of something else, and mentioned "Daddy." Mother made the connection for him, "Whom do you know who has a penis?" William: "Daddy." Mother: "Who else?" William: "Mommy." His mother explained that he and daddy did, but mommy did not.

This observation captures the moment at which William actually discovered his scrotum and testicles. Though he had previously touched and stimulated them many times, on this occasion there was a new element: a fuller awareness which contained mingled puzzlement, surprise, and some concern.

At eighteen months William was large for his age and well coordinated. His gross and fine motor skills continued to be good; he liked tools (screwdrivers, wrenches, hammers), was an active explorer, and remained mechanically inclined. He had a ravenous appetite, but his diet was still quite restricted, although gradually less so. He drank milk well from a cup, which he handled himself. His language development, thought processes, and concept formation continued to be advanced. He had a vocabulary of over 150 words, most of which he used spontaneously, spoke with simple sentences, and used possessives.

Bowel and urinary training was still at the beginning stages. William occasionally made a bowel movement or urinated in the infant toilet. He now associated urinating with his penis and the penis with the presence of his father (when his father came to his changing table, William would often start to speak about his penis, which he called "peebis," "pedis," "peemis," or "penis"). There was greater absorption in pleasure in his genital self-stimulation. He had learned to *seek* pleasure through such stimulation but did not use it as a means of comfort or relief from frustration.

While William developed much autonomy and individuation, he needed his mother when he suffered from the stomach distress, which still contributed to a sleep problem. He showed affectionate behavior with a small doll and his stuffed dog. The latter and a cotton blanket and diaper were his most treasured bed companions. He greatly enjoyed being read to, could fill in many words of the stories, and showed the beginnings of fantasy play. He opened doors, ran from his mother in a teasing way, and tried to climb out of his crib (which Mrs. W. was able to discourage for a few months). He sucked his thumb while he sniffed at his diaper at sleeptime. Despite the casualness of the toilet training he showed an organized orderliness and cleanliness. He tended to grasp the essence of situations without preoccupation with minor details.

Observation 20 (1;6 + 3): The combination of William's awareness of his penis and his mastery of the word resulted in his mentioning his penis almost every time his diaper was changed. He talked of its existence even under the diaper. The naming was not always accompanied by touching.

Observation 21 (1;6 + 6): William's mother lightly pinched his buttocks and asked, "What is mommy pinching?" William replied, "Penis" (as though everything below the belt and above the knees were called penis).

This observation illustrates the fluctuations in the accuracy of the self representations. One day he clearly knew this body part and at other times he did not.

Observation 22 (1;6 + 8): In the bath William, apparently needing to urinate, had a full erection (3+). He looked at his genitals and "sucked in" his abdomen which caused his erect penis to point straight up. He liked this and repeated the "sucking in" a number of times. The erection fluctuated during the bath and again was 3+ as he sat in the tub with the water running out. He had just been scolded for splashing excessively and reached with both hands to his penis without gazing at it and rather vigorously squeezed the glans and body for a full two minutes. He pulled the foreskin over the glans and back from it. The intensity and duration of the self-stimulation were unusual. He never did urinate. After he stopped the stimulation, the tumescence receded to 0 to 1+ within a minute.

Observation 23 (1;6 + 17): William had learned well that his mother did not like him to put his hand into a bowel movement. When his diaper containing feces was being changed, he put his hand in the vicinity of his genitalia and the movement and asked, "Touch?" His mother replied, "Wait a minute until I've cleaned you up." After she had, he asked again, "Touch?" She said, "Yes"; he touched his penis with his finger, and that was all. His whole focus was on touching rather than on stimulating himself.

Observation 24 (1;6 + 29): Several times recently when William called his mother to his crib during the night, she found his diapers quite wet and changed him. As she took off the wet diapers, he had a full erection (3+); he then stretched his legs, squeezed his genitalia with his thighs, showing a lot of excitement. On this occasion he raised his right knee, put his right hand on it, and said, "Pedis."

Since he was fairly well able to differentiate between his knee and penis at this time, the occurrence suggested that some sensation from the genitalia was experienced up the leg and in the knee.

Observation 25 (1;7 + 1): After a quiescent period of several weeks William again showed a fair amount of interest in his genitals and stimulated himself moderately. Several times at diaper changing he put his "doggie" (still his favorite inanimate companion) down to his genitals. Today when he did, he squeezed the "doggie" there several times between his thighs, without verbal comment. He had a partial erection.

Several times the following was observed: After he was undressed for his bath, William would sit on the floor stimulating his penis with his fingers. It quickly became fully erect and he tugged on his penis with excitement of considerable intensity. He would bob his erect penis up and down with his fingers. The degree of absorption in self-stimulation was still such that he could be readily distracted. Whenever his mother said it was time for his bath or nap, he turned to his mother at once.

Certainly this kind of genital self-stimulation was more masturbatory than anything observed during the first year.

His willingness to use the "toidey" had waned in recent weeks. Occasionally he wished to sit on it, but even less often urinated in it. Frequently he looked at and touched and stroked his penis as he sat on the "toidey." It would quickly become erect from such stimulation, and he would sometimes spontaneously say "Peemis" as he rubbed it.

Observation 26 (1;7 + 7): William had a fair degree of urinary control at this time, though he did not consistently exercise it. He could sit on his "toidey," let out some urine, stop, announce "more peepee," let out more, declare "baby peepee" (a little bit), and urinate again.

Observation 27 (1;7 + 10): On his changing table William playfully pulled off a sock and announced: "Off sock." He then tugged on a toe and added with a laugh, "Off toe." Mrs. W. kiddingly instructed: "Toes don't come off."

The experimentation with body parts and body coverings and what comes off and what does not showed many variations during the mastery of this stage of reality testing.

As Anna Freud (1965) suggested, this behavior is a sample of the prolonged play which ultimately leads to the differentiation of the self and object representations. At this stage the "not-I" and the "I" and what comprised the self still involved many ambiguities.

Observation 28 (1;7 + 13): Three times this day William made a very active approach to his genitals with his hand, once during a diaper change and twice while walking nude, before and after his bath. He grabbed his penis and scrotum together, put his fingers under the scrotum, lifted the penis and scrotum up, and with his thumb repeatedly pushed the end of the penis in. No marked erection resulted. The whole activity would go on intensely for twenty to thirty seconds at a time. There was also some tugging on the penis itself.

The pushing inward of the penis represented additional exploration which was correlated with his current pleasurable interest in pushing buttons of all kinds—doorbells, electric switches, etc.

Observation 29 (1;7 + 17): William continued to prefer urinating in his diapers or in the bath rather than on the toilet. As was frequent, tonight in the bath he had a 3+ erection without touching his penis, and urinated standing up. This was quickly followed by detumescence. Often he urinated sitting in the bath as warm water entered the tub.

Observation 30 (1;7 + 18): Sitting in a swimsuit, William stimulated his nonerect penis through the cloth with his forefinger. He continued the stroking movements until he had a 3+ erection. After approximately a minute the stroking decreased, and his attention was directed elsewhere.

Observation 31 (1;7 + 20): William discussed his parents' double bed with his mother, checking who slept where. He insisted that the place beside the mother was his place, not his father's.

This incident was characteristic of a variety of behavior indicating early oedipal feelings. He greatly enjoyed "possessing" his mother's body, climbing over her when she rested, kissing her, running his hands over her clothes. There was a clear-cut increase in these activities when his father was not present. Mrs. W. did not forbid such behavior, but often distracted William to prevent his becoming too excited.

Observation 32 (1;7 + 26): William had been urinating less often in the bath. Tonight he had a 3+ erection in the tub. He was sitting, contracting his abdominal wall inward, which caused his penis to bob upward. On one such "bob up" he started to urinate and "shot himself in the face." He was not much affected by it and became interested in his mother's rinsing his face with water. During the preceding days the masturbatory type of genital self-stimulation had been observed less frequently, but on the few occasions when it was, he tugged very vigorously on his penis for a few seconds.

Observation 33 (1;8 + 2): William's conscious intention to urinate in the bath rather than on the toilet was now more definite. When his dry diaper was removed prior to his bath, he was asked if he would like "to make peepee in the toilet." He emphatically answered "No, in the bath!" and he did.

At twenty and one half months William's cognitive development had proceeded to the point at which he comprehended his own name more fully. He regularly used "mine" or "Billy's book" or in listing family members who carried out a particular activity, he gave his own name with the others.

Observation 34 (1;8 + 25): When William's mother removed his diaper prior to his bath, his penis was 3+ erect. She asked whether he would like to make "peepee" in the toilet. He answered clearly and without hesitation: "No, in the baff." Mother: "Where do big boys make peepee?" William: "In the toidet." Mother: "Do you want to be a big boy?" William: "Yeth." Mother: "Do you want to make peepee in the toilet?" William: "No! In the baff," and again he did.

For some weeks he himself suggested going to the toilet. He requested a magazine which he "read," turning the pages one by one and commenting on the pictures as he sat on the toilet. Rarely did he defecate or urinate there. It was a stalling device used most often prior to a nap or bedtime.

He appeared to be rather proud when he urinated in the tub, often put his hand or finger in the stream, and sometimes, before urinating, thrust his erect penis into the stream of water entering the tub from the faucet. This seemed moderately enjoyable. While Mrs. W. did not shame him for this behavior, she repeatedly suggested it was better to urinate in the toilet. She drained the tub, letting in fresh water after he voided, thus indicating that children did not bathe in urine water.

Observation 35 (1;9 + 0): At twenty-one months William's awareness of his scrotum and testicles became more definite. Before his bath, he was sitting nude on the floor. Looking down at his genitalia, he pointed to his scrotal sac and asked: "Dat is?" His mother replied, "Those are your ballies." He then named them: 'Ballies."

Observation 36 (1;9 + 3): Today William watched his mother empty his bowel movement from the diaper into the toilet. The feces were brownish and ball-shaped. When she flushed the toilet, William commented: "Billy's other penis down the toidet." His mother explained very carefully: "Billy's penis and ballies are right here [she had already put on fresh diapers and pointed to the genital area through them] and *they don't come off!*" On the previous day, while sitting on the toilet, he had leaned over, pointed to his scrotal sac and testicles, and asked: "Dis is?" His mother had explained: "Those are your ballies."

In this observation it is not clear whether "other penis" means "penis" or "testicle" to William. His confusion of his bowel movement with his penis or testes contributes to an early form or precursor of castration anxiety and is reminiscent of Bell's description (1964) of confusion of testicles and bowel movements in somewhat older boys. She postulates a precursor testicular castration anxiety preceding a penile castration anxiety.

Observation 37 (1;9 + 4): William today called his penis a "BM" when his diaper was off. His mother bantered with him and said, "You know that is your penis, not a BM."[4]

At this time William usually could identify his penis and other visible body parts correctly by name (see Observation 38). It was not clear whether this error was due to a fluctuation in the gradual differentiation of the self representations or to a minor regression

---

[4] Because the Observations are of necessity condensed and selective, some readers may infer that Mrs. W.'s focusing on William's genital and anal anatomy and functioning was excessive and seductive. Admittedly the dividing line between what is too little or too much is a delicate one. In general, Mrs. W.'s combination of psychological sophistication, sensitive observation, empathy with the small child's need to talk frankly without pretense or shame, her assessment of his anxiety level, her interest in educating, whetting curiosity, and anticipating the boy's next developmental readiness (which included cognitive advance and potentiality to be overstimulated) resulted in a reasonable balance for William.

resulting from the anxiety experience of the previous day (Observation 36).

Observation 38 (1;9 + 9): William was examining his nude body in his mother's presence. He tugged at the nipple of one of his breasts and asked: "Dat is?" Mother: "That is your breastie." He then pulled at his other nipple and asked the same question. Next he indicated his umbilicus and queried: "Dat is?" His mother replied, "That is your belly button." William then pointed to his penis and said, "Dat is my penis!"

Observation 39 (1;9 + 13): At diaper changing before bed William grabbed his penis in a stimulating way three separate times, developing a 2+ erection, and then squeezed his genitalia between his thighs. Mrs. W. reported that this rough masturbatory-looking behavior was not typical. She noted his rectum moving, expelling gas, and thought his clutching the genital area might be associated with intestinal distress rather than just pleasure or play.

At twenty-one and a half months genital self-stimulation occurred from time to time (see Observation 40) but was not prominent and did not seem an important source of autoerotic comfort or pleasure. His thumb-sucking with a soft diaper against the snout area still fulfilled that need much more extensively.

Observation 40 (1;9 + 15): In the early morning William's father changed his wet diaper, and William rubbed his penis five or six times with his hand, which resulted in a beginning erection, starting from 0 and increasing to 2+. This seemed to involve slight to moderate pleasure. His father asked: "What is that?" William answered, "Billy's penis." He then shifted his hand to his scrotum and questioned: "Dat is?" His father replied: "Those are Billy's ballies." When the dry diaper was put on him, William's attention shifted to his right foot. With a laugh he spontaneously exclaimed, "Billy's piggies." His father said, "Those are Billy's toes." William joked further, insisting with a big chuckle, "Billy's piggies!"

This observation illustrates a gradient of self representation at this age. William had a fairly clear mental picture of his penis, to the degree that he himself could spontaneously or in response to a question identify it by name as his own. His mental representation of his scrotum was less clear and less advanced so that he asked his

ather what it was as he had on several occasions in the previous two
weeks. The representations of his toes were more organized than
either those of his penis or scrotum in that he not only knew they
were his toes, but he could joke about them and call them his
'piggies." He knew not only his own toes but also those of his
parents and dolls.

Observation 41 (1;9 + 17): During the past ten days on a number
of occasions when William's diaper containing a bowel movement
was changed, William reached for his penis and gave evidence of
concern whether it was still there. Each time his mother would
assure him that his bowel movement came out, but his penis and
ballies did not come off.

William's association of shedding his bowel movement and losing
his genitalia, each representing the loss of a body part, is another
instance of an early form of castration fear.

Observation 42 (1;9 + 20): William had a 1+ erection before
entering the bathtub. He refused an invitation to urinate in the
toilet. In the bath he showed a 2+ erection without any external
genital stimulation and began to urinate standing up, facing his
mother and father, who was there at this time. He watched the
stream with fascination and pride. After the first burst, he tried to
put his hand in the urine jet, touching it only slightly. Detumescence
to 0 occurred within ninety seconds of his completing the micturition. He made no approach to his genitalia but played in the water.
Someone mentioned his having "made peepee." This stimulus directed his attention to his penis. He squeezed the corona with a lot
of force and said, "Billy's penis." He moved his fingers to the scrotal
area, and asked: "Dat is?" His mother returned the question, "What
is it?" He laughed and replied, "Billy's ballies." He again pressed
the corona between his right fingers, directing the meatus upward.
He put his left forefinger to the meatus to examine it. William then
tugged on the loose skin of his penis, pulling it laterally. All this
stimulation resulted in a 2+ erection. "Crazy Foam" (a moldable
soap) diverted him. In the bath he did not touch his genitals, but
while sitting in his mother's lap and being dried, William made
three separate and vigorous approaches to his penis. During the first
he squeezed the corona very hard, making the meatus open. He inquired, "Dat is?" His mother explained, "That is the hole your
peepee comes out." He squeezed additionally and tugged at the loose
skin. Each of these active stimulations of the corona and loose skin

resulted in erection, which then faded between times. He seemed
interested in the feeling resulting from such mauling (such forcefu
handling might well have created pain had someone other than he
himself done it), but he was also exploring the meatus, which opened
and closed as he pressed and released.

This observation is of special interest because for the first time
William focused his attention on the meatus. In my perusal of the
relevant literature I have not found a reference to the timing of a
boy's first awareness of this anatomical detail. It is also worthy of
comment that William had recently (this observation was an exception) not been putting his hand in the urine stream. Rather he often
cleared away objects in the way of the intended spurt (as he sat in
the tub) when he felt the urine coming and proudly watched it
shoot. There was an early exhibitionistic aspect to it. He obviously
liked himself very much in this regard. At this stage of his life it was
all pride—no shame.

Observation 43 (1;9 + 22): In the bath William again focused
on the meatus and asked about it. He also actively stimulated his
penis by holding the loose skin in the thumb and forefinger of both
hands moving the skin forward and backward over the glans, resulting in an erection. This genital self-stimulation resembled the
masturbation of an older boy.

Observation 44 (1;9 + 27): In saying a nursery rhyme, "Sing a
Song of Sixpence," William jokingly supplied some of his own end-
ings. For "the queen is in the parlor eating milk and honey" he
substituted *the baby* for "milk and honey." (Mrs. W. was in the fifth
month of a new pregnancy, and William had been told that his
mother had a baby in her belly.) Later he referred to "my baby." His
mother asked, "Where is your baby?" expecting him to designate
one of two dolls he had. Instead he patted his epigastrium and ut-
tered, "In Billy's belly."

This pregnancy fantasy in a twenty-two-month-old boy is a vivid
example of the fluctuating identifications the preoedipal child can
experience. In the following two months William often expressed
the pregnancy fantasy, but just as often *he was a baby*, regressing in
terms of crawling, using an affected "baby talk" and a babyish sound
through his teeth, and suggesting his mother get him a bottle (never

arried out).[5] In addition, when she referred to him as a boy at such moment, he corrected her, "I am not a boy; I am a baby."

On several occasions during this period William explored and sked questions about his scrotum and testicles, his meatus, and his oreskin. Although he often actively stimulated his penis, this activity hould not be characterized as genuine masturbation because it acked self-absorption and because it involved a cognitive process in he sense that he was thinking about what he was doing, studying, questioning, and recording, not just experiencing the pleasurable ensation.

Observation 45 (1;10 + 10): William's self-stimulation in the path resulted in the most intense excitement observed during the wo years, but did not reach orgastic intensity. He was quite absorbed in rubbing his penis for a short period and really seemed to njoy himself. He had a full erection and was again interested in the meatus; he pointed to it and acted pleased with it. In addition to queezing his penis, he tried with both hands to pull the foreskin over the glans, but the degree of erection made this impossible.

Earlier in the day at a diaper changing he announced to his mother, "Billy made a BM." When his mother removed the diaper nd found none, she said, "You didn't make a BM." William insisted, "Yes, I did." His mother tested, "Where is Billy's BM?" Without looking down, he took hold of his penis. His mother explained, "You know that is Billy's penis." She supported his trunk so that he ould see his genital area and asked again, "Where is Billy's BM?" He was then looking at his genitals and pointed to his testicles, "Dat is Billy's BM."

William continued to confuse bowel movements and his genitals, especially the scrotal organs. He showed another distortion of his mage of himself in repeatedly elaborating his pregnancy fantasy.

Observation 46 (1;10 + 15): The family had recently discussed "the baby in mommy's belly." William again said he had a baby in his belly. When his mother asked him what the baby did, he announced, "The baby eats milk and peas and walks around." He then demonstrated with a wide-based strut how the baby walks. Mrs. W.

[5] His request for a bottle was a creation of his imagination and originated in seeing ther "babies" with bottles because he was weaned directly to a cup and had not had bottle since he was a small infant.

remonstrated, "In your belly, Billy?" He insisted, "Yes, mommy, i does."

Observation 47 (1;10 + 22): On this day William told his mother "Billy is a girlie." Mother: "Billy is a boy. Billy isn't a girl." William "Oh, yes, Billy *is* a girlie; eat the girlie's toe." He held up his too for his mother to pretend to nibble it. His mother went on, "Billy has a penis. Girls don't have a penis. Billy is a boy. Is Betsy a girl?" (Betsy was a little girl relative whom William knew well.) William "Yes." Mother: "Does she have a penis?" William: "No, Billy has a penis *and* Billy is a girlie. Put the girlie's shoe on."

At this point William experimented with being a girl, but was not willing to give up his male genitals to that end. William evinced an unusual degree of self-awareness, especially body awareness and sexual role differentiation, but this observation illustrates the young child's simultaneous acceptance of the reality principle and his resistance to it (Jacobson, 1964, p. 111).

Observation 48 (1;10 + 23): As William's diaper was being changed, he was kicking his mother's belly, and the following conversation ensued. Mother: "Don't hurt the baby." William patted his mother's bosom and claimed, "Billy no want to hurt the baby." Mother: "You know the baby's in my belly; that's not my belly What is it?" William: "Finger." Mother: "No!" William: "Penis." Mother: "What is it?" William: "Breastie, breastie hanging down." The mother, struck by the train of thought and description, asked "What hangs down on Billy?" William: "Billy's penis. Girlies have a penis?" Mother: "You know girls don't have a penis."

This confirmation of the breast-penis equation from the mouth of a twenty-three-month-old child was supported by a number of other observations. It should be noted that a few days earlier William had seen his mother undressed for the first time. His curiosity had focused on her breasts rather than on her genital area.

At about the same time (twenty-two and a half months) William exhibited a type of behavior that can be interpreted as another precursor of castration anxiety. When his temperature was taken rectally (an unusual event) at the time of a mild respiratory infection he grabbed his genitalia and looked at them as though he needed to check if they were all right. Similar "checkups" often occurred during a diaper change following a bowel movement.

Observation 49 (1;11 + 14): Mrs. W. noted that recently William had been playing with his scrotum when his diapers were changed and had discovered the testicles. He did not seem to handle the scrotum when the testicles were retracted. On this occasion when his wet diapers were removed, he had an erection. He handled his penis and scrotum. In his mother's words: "He asked to 'peek' at himself, which he often has done after a BM, as though to see if he lost anything—I think he believes his testicles are a BM; I raised his buttocks to let him peek. This time the testicles were very prominent in the sac and were pulled by gravity to hang toward him. He seemed to see them, and he squeezed them and focused on them. After that he focused on his penis. He asked to go on the toidey, sat fifteen minutes but didn't urinate."

At twenty-three and a half months William began to show more anxiety, of the separation type, manifested by crankiness, demandingness, disturbed sleep with frequent calling "Mommy, mommy," and crying when his mother went out for errands without him. The specific source of this upsurge of anxiety was not clear, but seemed to be associated with the following factors: (1) the baby growing in "mommy's belly" (William crawled some, talked about the baby, and often wanted to be *the* baby); (2) his parents had been away on an overnight trip which seemed the acute stimulus for the anxiety; (3) his mother's increased fatigue, body awkwardness, and lessened patience in conjunction with the progressing pregnancy; (4) his confusing bowel movements with testicles and concern about loss (as mentioned above, he often needed to check his genitalia after making a bowel movement); (5) new motor skills—he had discovered how to climb out of his crib, which, combined with a burst of aggressive energy, kept him fired up day and night. That early forms of castration anxiety were mingled with separation anxiety was suggested by the following:

Observation 50 (1;11 + 20): Lying on the changing table, William said, quite unrelated to anything previously spoken, "Mommy, don't sing dat song any more!" Mother: "What song?" William: "Cut off their tails with a carving knife." Mother: "You mean Three Blind Mice?" William: "Yesth. Don't sing that song." A little while later, William: "Sing that song." The mother did not.

Mrs. W. actually had sung this song only a few times and not at all for several weeks. She found that telling him she loved him, that she would not go away and would not stop loving him when the new baby came seemed to lower his anxiety noticeably.

At two years William was a vigorous, muscular, but not chubby boy. Although the gastrointestinal disturbance had improved, it still was a problem and continued to contribute to his sleep difficulty. He would wake at 4, 5, or 6 A.M. almost daily.[6] He acquired new motor skills: on his second birthday he went ice skating for the first time. On double runners he was able to "skate" (moving his feet followed by a glide) unaided, and with few falls, after about fifteen minutes. Verbal communication continued to be advanced. He differentiated past, present, and future tenses, used conjunctions such as *so that,* utilized subject pronouns (he, she, I, you, we), object pronouns (me, him, her, you), and a variety of prepositions, adjectives, participles, and adverbs. He identified five or six colors, distinguished right from left usually correctly, counted to six, and showed great interest in books and magazines.

Occasionally he would ask to sit on his toilet but rarely urinated in it. He could control his urination, as evidenced in his bath, where he continued to urinate almost daily. However, the rest of the time micturition and defecation were performed in his diapers. A degree of stubbornness, not previously prominent, was emerging. The burst of autonomy, noted at twenty-three and a half months, was expressed in such behavior as insisting on putting himself to bed at night. Whereas earlier he had wanted an elaborate routine of back patting, storytelling, and drinks of water prior to sleep, he now said goodnight to his mother outside his room, closed his own bedroom door, and climbed into his high-sided crib alone. The heightened independence coincided with signs of greater separation anxiety at other times. His increased individuation was a source of both pride and some fear. At times it contributed to a tendency to regression. For example, he repeatedly insisted that he be referred to as a baby, not a boy, as if he needed to be cared for, lest he "run away with himself."

He sucked his thumb when tired. His genital self-stimulation was sporadic; his diapers were off relatively little in the course of a day. Before, during, and after his daily bath was the longest period. Perhaps one day in seven he would stimulate himself intensely; three

6 Anna Freud (1965, p. 157) mentioned the universality of sleep problems during the second year.

ays in the week he might explore or stimulate his genitals slightly ɔ moderately and the other three days direct very little attention ɔ them. At times he could be quite seductive. On several occasions t this age he suggested that his mother squeeze his penis (she esponded by distracting him to other pursuits).

William at two was a friendly child capable of strong emotions nd attachments. He was quite responsive to people he knew and trangers, and especially affectionate with babies. He was very fond ·f his mother and would seek *her* at moments of stress. Though less ntense and sensuous, his relationship with his father was close and epresented fun and activity. There were various indications of a rowing fantasy life. He exhibited some oedipal feelings, at times vishing exclusive possession of his mother and displaying some ivalry with his father. There were also clear-cut identifications with is father.

By twenty-five months his need to regress to the "baby" role was reatly reduced,[7] and this was also the time at which he first spoke ɔf his (and others') penis and "ballies" as a unit, apparently seeing hem associated together rather than unrelated.

DISCUSSION

This study, describing a boy's sequential interest in his genitalia ɪnd related developmental and maturational events in his second ·ear, coupled with comparable data from his first year (Kleeman, 1965), utilizes the developmental line approach (Anna Freud, 1963, 1965). It is limited by covering only the first two years, but we are ɪble to follow the line starting from (1) the mother's care of the nfant's body through (2) the child's accidental touching of his gen-talia, (3) experiencing a pleasant sensation as a result of manipula-ɔion, to (4) the point at which he actually seeks his genitals in order ɔ obtain a sensation, which ultimately leads to (5) unmistakable nasturbation in the oedipal period. Or we can pursue the line of the mental representation of this body area from (1) the point where the ɪnfant's and the mother's parts are not clearly differentiated from

---

[7] Interestingly, a major factor in his relinquishing the regression seemed to be cer-ɔain restrictions that were imposed on his hyperactivity. Apparently, the restraint low-ɔred his anxiety about his autonomy.

each other, through (2) early memory traces from sensations in the penis, (3) to memory schemata comprising visual and tactile perceptions as well as sensations from the genitalia, leading to (4) the registration of the penis as an object, a period during which there exist confusion about its separateness (it is fed crackers like a distinct being, and is seen as detachable like a bowel movement), (5) a stage where it is clearly experienced as part of the self ("Dat is *my* penis!") and identified with a word and a personal possessive, to (6) a level at which the penis is not only part of the body image but also highly prized and recorded mentally in association with the scrotum and testicles, an organ capable of great pleasurable feeling, and the function of urination.

The concept of developmental lines permits a much more comprehensive view of behavior, such as genital self-stimulation, than is realized by attempting to understand it within the confines of a single psychoanalytic metapsychological viewpoint or concept. For example, Spitz and Wolf (1949) examine infantile genital self-stimulation in terms of *autoerotism*.

Discovery of the Scrotum and Testicles

Bell (1961) states that male infants often encounter their scrotum manually before the penis. This statement implies that the discovery of the scrotum often precedes that of the penis. The observations of William do not confirm this implication. In my earlier report (1965), I quoted Halverson, who mentioned a fifteen-week-old infant grasping his penis and scrotum, but I also emphasized that the random contact described by Bell and Halverson is very different from a significant awareness of the penis and scrotal organs. William discovered his penis at eight months, he explored and mentally represented it over a period of months, and called it by name after seventeen months. In contrast, the acquisition of meaningful knowledge of the scrotum and testicles proceeded in the following sequence: (1) Sporadic and rather undifferentiated touching and grasping of the scrotum occurred in the first year, starting at ten months eighteen days; especially during the eleventh month, William handled the penis and scrotum together (Kleeman, 1965). (2) A more specific focus on the scrotum, amounting to discovery, was seen at seventeen and a half and eighteen months (Observations 16 and 19). (3) More precise "discovery" took place at twenty-one months when he asked, "Dat is?" several times (Observations 35, 36, 40). (4) At twenty-one and a half months he could name the organs "ballies" (Observation 42). (5) At twenty-three and a half months he differentiated the testicles within the scrotum (Observation 49). (6) By twenty-five months William conceptualized the penis and scrotal organs as a totality.

We might expect awareness of the scrotal organs to come later than awareness and understanding of the penis for several reasons: (1) the more anterior position and greater accessibility and visibility of the penis; (2) the heightened pleasurable sensitivity and erectile capacity of the penis; (3) the focus resulting from the urinary function; (4) the tendency of parents to name and draw attention to the penis prior to the scrotal area; (5) the closeness of the scrotum to the anus and the similarity of its appearance to feces increase the likelihood that the scrotum will be included in the fecal aversion.

Progression of Self Representations

Although many theoretical papers deal with the development of the inner world including the self representations (especially Jacobson and Hartmann, who introduced the term), there exist few *clinical* contributions describing their origins. Approaching the study of William's genital self-stimulation in terms of developmental lines yields insight into the way in which elements of the self representations are laid down. William's advanced language capacity facilitated this. Although William's early knowledge of his body, fostered by his mother's verbal teaching, illustrates the importance of secondary-process symbols (language) for the laying down of mental representations, as Novey (1961) has correctly noted, the most primitive object representations are largely affective. Many authors have stressed that the earliest self representations are of the body self. Greenacre (1958), e.g., discussed the significance of the face and genital areas in the establishment of the body self and the contribution that the development of body image makes to the sense of identity.

The observations of William in temporal sequence give a picture of the increasing clarity of the mental image of the different genital organs. Striking are the fluctuations and regressions: at one point a mental representation seems definitely established and at the next it appears blurred. At nine months no mental representation of the genitalia could yet be discerned by the observer. At ten months nine days William had to check whether his penis was still there after he had previously examined it (cf. Loewenstein, 1950). At eleven months eight days he stimulated himself with *intent*, from which I infer considerable advance in memorial capacity. The firmer establishment of this faculty was seen at fifteen and a half months. Gender differentiation began to appear at sixteen and a half months. William then had enough of a mental concept of his penis so that he no longer needed to look each time he wished to stimulate it; yet the representation of this body part was still rudimentary in that he could tug on it, uttering "off, off," as he did with a toe or a sock. While William partly understood the meaning of the word "penis" by fourteen and a half months, he began to use it correctly at seventeen and a half months, although occasionally he would also call his buttocks "penis." By twenty months he expressed his conscious intent to urinate in the bathtub, knowing definitely the role of his penis in doing it. Two weeks later he used personal possessives in relation to his penis and called himself by name, but at twenty-one months he could slip into calling his penis a BM.

At many specific times gradients of the self representations could be distinguished. For example, at twenty-one and a half months he identified his toes more definitely than his penis or scrotum and his penis was more precisely represented than the latter (Observation 40); he knew his penis better than his nipples or umbilicus (Observation 38).

It is also noteworthy that the fuzziness of self representations can contribute to symbolic equations. In a number of observations (see 36, 37, 45), William confused his penis with feces (i.e., he misidentified the words), or his scrotal organs with feces (see 45), or associated his penis with his mother's breasts (see 48) (cf. Kleeman, 1965, p 243).

Pregnancy Fantasies Based on Identification

William's fantasy that he had a "baby in his belly" started late in the twenty-second month, extended throughout the duration of the observations (to the twenty-fifth month), and represented an identification with his pregnant mother. This pregnancy fantasy is of interest because it occurred at an earlier age than any reported in the

terature and because in the case of William it can be related to
ther aspects of his sexual behavior and libido development. In the
sychoanalytic literature Little Hans's fantasy of having a baby is
robably best known (1909). Little Hans was four and three quarters
hen he related most of these fantasies and was at least three when
e was stimulated to have them (his sister was born when he was
iree and a half). This clearly places him in the oedipal period, at
hich time such fantasies are obviously more complex than they were
i the case of William. Jacobson (1950) studied the wish for a child
i boys and made several points that are applicable to William. His
tterances also strikingly confirm Van de Leeuw's (1958) and Rose's
1961) contention, arrived at by analytic reconstruction, that the
iale's early wish for a baby may have an active and omnipotent
ither than a definitely feminine character. William's wish to become
girl *in addition* to remaining a boy (Observation 47) is comparable,
i that his identification with the active, omnipotent, baby-producing,
reoedipal mother is something *added* to being a boy, not a substi-
ite for it. Numerous studies have established that the boy's early
lentifications are with the mother or her substitute. While the rami-
cations of William's identifications are beyond the scope of this
aper, it must be stressed that his pregnancy fantasy was only one of
iany fantasy and real ways in which he identified with his mother
ie sewed, cleaned, "cooked" elaborate dishes and meals, etc.); it was
nly one manifestation of his identification and only one of multiple
intasy roles with which he experimented (milkman, baby, girlie,
usband, daddy, builder, gasoline man, doctor, tractor driver, etc.).

he Developmental Line toward Masturbation

Analysts are familiar with the meaning of *infantile sexuality* as
escribed in the *Three Essays* (Freud, 1905). Unfortunately, the same
rm is also used in the more restricted sense to describe manifesta-
ons of genital sexual behavior in infancy or early childhood. The
ime lack of precision is involved in the usage of *masturbation*.
ornstein (1953) gives the usual psychoanalytic definition: "We
efine masturbation as autoerotic manipulations of the genital as
ell as of other erogenous zones. By erogenous zones we understand
i portion of skin or mucous membrane in which stimuli produce
feeling of pleasure of definite quality' " (p. 65). This definition is so

broad that it is of limited usefulness in studying the genesis of genital sexual behavior. Although the development of William's libido in all its forms of expression is of interest, I shall confine my discussion in this section to masturbation, which I shall define in my own way (closer to Kinsey's view, 1948, p. 498) to insure a more careful description of William's behavior. The term *masturbation* is limited to (1) the genital zone and includes (2) the quality of self-absorption, (3) consciously intended self-arousal, (4) with mounting excitement, and (5) a climax type of rhythm (though not necessarily resulting in orgasm) rather than lulling, (6) where seeking pleasure predominates over exploring and acquiring knowledge.

Using this definition I shall discuss the degree of masturbatory quality in William's genital self-stimulation during the second year. The literature contains three different types of relevant statements: (1) "Genital masturbation subsides in the course of the second year" (Bornstein, 1953, p. 67). (2) During the second half of the second year and especially during the third year, genital feelings gradually increase (Greenacre, 1958, p. 617). (3) "In a general way, one might say that some genital play should be expected in the infant by the end of the first year of life. In the toddler or the preschool child, a transition from genital play to masturbation is to be expected, the details of which have not yet been investigated either quantitatively or qualitatively" (Spitz, 1962, p. 298). The data on William do not support Bornstein's conclusion. Actually, Freud (1905, p. 189) without systematically observing young children suggested that the earliest genital self-stimulation can either disappear for an interval or progress to masturbation. Spitz, with a wide experience in infant observation acknowledges our ignorance in this area. We need careful observations of a number of children to determine the individual variations. The information about William is only a beginning. In the first quarter of the second year there was greater consciousness of penile sensation, greater deliberateness in the stimulation, and an observable increase in genital sensitivity especially beginning in the fifteenth month.

Observations 11, 22, 25, 43, and especially 45, are illustrative of the intermittent genital self-stimulations which were transitional between the largely exploratory behavior of the first year and the more definitely masturbatory stimulation of the oedipal years. These episodes were more masturbatory in character than anything seen in the first year and yet did not completely coincide with masturbation as defined above; they were intermingled with much exploratory and reality-testing stimulation and quiescent periods. Observation 45 included behavior most closely resembling an orgasm but was unconvincing in that regard. No other orgasm was observed.

A multitude of data demonstrated the association of reflex erection with a need to urinate and detumescence following micturition. Tumescence as a result of genital tactile stimulation was also more frequent than in the first year.

Other Libidinal Manifestations

In the second year several behavioral derivatives of the libidinal drive were of special interest: (1) early scoptophilia (Observation 7); (2) exhibitionism and its associated affect, pride (Observations 9, 42); and (3) early signs of oedipal feelings appearing from nineteen and a half months on (Observation 31). These are usually reported as appearing later, although Ruth Mack Brunswick (1940) declares, without much further elaboration: "In the boy, the preoedipal mother attachment is apparently of much shorter duration than in the girl, merging very early into the Oedipus complex" (p. 296).

Precursors of Castration Anxiety

Data of William offer a basis for comparison with Bell's report (1961) on precursors of castration anxiety.

The observations of William which illustrate prephallic sources of the later oedipal castration anxiety can be recapitulated as follows: (1) At one year (Kleeman, 1965) William was experimenting with putting on a snap-on top of a bottle and removing it repeatedly. (2) This aspect of reality testing—with regard to what is detachable and what is not—was then applied to his genitalia in a "peek-a-boo" game with a paper cup at sixteen and a half months and to his penis as he tugged and said, "Off, off" at seventeen months as well as to toes and socks. (3) Soon afterward he made a couple of bowel movements in his small toilet and showed some anxiety. (4) At seventeen months twenty-five days he first urinated in his bath. (5) Three days later he referred to his penis as broken, which might have been related to seeing his father's genitals that day and comparing himself unfavorably. This coincided in time with his discovery of the scrotal sac and testicles, which were identified for him.[8] This discovery was accompanied by some apprehension, so that from then on the "off" game was connected with anxiety. (6) At nineteen months William had fair urinary control but definitely preferred urinating in the bath rather than in his toilet. During the remainder of the second year he rarely sat on his toilet and even less often defecated or urinated there. He did not explain his preference for urinating in the tub; it seemed a combination of pride and pleasure in watching himself urinate and anxiety about the toilet. (7) Clearly categorizing for him his scrotal organs did not modify his insistence on urinating in the bath. (8) William labeled feces from his diaper his "other penis" as they were flushed down the toilet.[9] (9) During the rest of the second year William clearly demonstrated that he sometimes confused his penis with feces, his testicles with feces, and rectal sensations from defecation or temperature taking with fear of loss of testes and penis. (10) William's anxiety about a nursery rhyme with a mutilation theme occurred in the absence of any known outside threat.[10]

In comparing Bell's material (1964) with the observation of William it must be noted that William was somewhat younger than the age group she described. While Bell referred to the period from two to four years, her case material actually consists only of boys aged two and a half and older.

The observations of William confirm Bell's main thesis that the common innervation of sphincter ani, scrotal sac, testes, cremasteric muscle, and penis results in a confusion of sensations causing an association of testicular loss with fecal loss. Bell emphasizes that during the pregenital period *the testicles* and *scrotal sac* play a precursor role to that of the penis in the development of castration anxiety.

---

[8] Whereas the directed self-stimulation of the genitalia, including the testes and sac (Observation 11), *could* be designated "discovery," I am reserving this designation for the time when he singled out the scrotal organs and inquired about them (Observation 19).

[9] One can only speculate whether the reasons are an unclarity of the mental representation, an uncertainty of language, a heightened level of anxiety resulting in an ego regression affecting language or representation or both.

[10] See Freud (1909): "Any one who, in analysing adults, has become convinced of the invariable presence of the castration complex, will of course find difficulty in ascribing its origin to a chance threat—of a kind which is not, after all, of such universal occurrence; he will be driven to assume that children construct this danger for themselves out of the slightest hints, which will never be wanting" (p. 8, n. 2).

The observations reported here amply corroborate the importance of the scrotal sac and testes in the genesis of this anxiety, but they *simultaneously* demonstrate the importance of the penis in its origins. William interchangeably confused testes *and* penis with feces, and his fear of the toilet involved defecation *and* urination. Identifying his testes for him and certifying their safety along with the inviolability of his penis did not lure William back to the toilet from his diapers and bath. The data on William do not support Bell's construct of an anal-testicular amalgam (omitting the phallus), nor did they suggest a specific testicular phase in psychosexual development. A fused visual image of testes and fecal mass dropping into the toilet (Bell, 1964) did not seem to play a significant role in William's aversion to the toilet. However, there was considerable evidence that the visual similarity of the scrotal organs and fecal balls perceived under other conditions (Observation 45) created a confusion of identity.[11]

In two of her papers (1961, 1964) Bell speculates that the little boy's awareness of his testicular motility (plus the association with fecal movement) might be one of the roots of the proverbial mechanical interests of boys. This may be so, but I think it is worth pointing out that William's mechanical bent was already apparent at nine months, long before he had any real cognizance of testicular movement.

I have very few data bearing on Bell's hypothesis that the motility of the testes[12] and their potential disappearance from view contribute to castration anxiety. Two items are worth describing: (1) William

[11] I had the opportunity to observe a two-year-old girl who, watching her male sibling of two months being diapered, pointed to his scrotum and said he had made a bowel movement. Her mother reported that this misidentification continued for several months. Only *repeated* explanations about his scrotal organs dispelled this notion. Moreover, the error was always unidirectional, i.e., the scrotum was always called a bowel movement, but a bowel movement was never called scrotum.

[12] Anita Bell stressed the importance of kinesthetic sensations arising from the reflex retraction of the testes associated with anal closure, fear, cold, anger, and sexual arousal. From her study of little boys she concluded that these kinesthetic sensations contribute significantly to genital exploration, fear of the toilet, and other behavior. I have not emphasized this because I have tried to limit myself to what could be directly observed. There is no way of ascertaining how much awareness William had of kinesthetic sensations arising from testicular movement. Certainly a number of observations (e.g., 45, 49), and his need to check his genitalia after a bowel movement, raise the possibility that he experienced the retraction and responded to it, but his responses could also be explained in other ways.

did not seem to handle his scrotum when the testicles were retracted (Observation 49). He therefore differentiated them in relation to their movability. (2) At twenty-five months William injured his right thumb (his sucking thumb) requiring a bandage that completely covered the thumb. Though William complained that he would have nothing to suck, he was able to "be brave" despite pain and anxiety about the injury because of the comforting of his mother's care and the promise he could suck again when his loved thumb was healed. However, during the night he awoke crying. Half-asleep and evincing some anxiety, he gave as a clue, "I can't see my thumb" (he had a night light permitting some visibility in the room). His mother, appraising the source of his discomfort, offered to remove the big bandage and substitute a Band-aid, permitting him to see the end of his thumb. When this was done, a big smile of relief appeared on his face, and he returned to sleep. In this instance, the inability to visualize directly a body part patently created anxiety.

The observations of William contribute an additional element to our knowledge of the roots of castration anxiety. Freud (1909),[13] Loewenstein (1950), Bell (1961), and others have traced the oral and anal precursors of castration anxiety. Loewenstein described an observation of a ten-month-old boy who experimented to determine whether his penis would stay with his body when he crawled away. Loewenstein stated his belief that this represented a model upon which later castration anxiety is formed. William demonstrated the further elaboration of this type of reality testing from about ten to nineteen months by his repeated investigations of caps and tops, body parts, and coverings in his relentless search for the detachable and the nondetachable, the "I" and the "not-I." This can be observed at somewhat varying ages in all normal children and represents an additional maturational component (in Lipin's [1963] terms, "maturational" drive representative) of the sources of castration anxiety.

---

13 I am grateful to Edith Jacobson for reminding me that Abraham promulgated "anal castration fear" as a forerunner of genital castration fear. For example, Abraham (1920) stated, "Psycho-analysis, however, has shown that the child in this early psychosexual period of development considers its faeces as a part of its own body. The process of identification further establishes a close relation between the ideas 'faeces' and 'penis'. The boy's anxiety regarding the loss of his penis is based on this assimilation of the two ideas. He is afraid that his penis may be detached from his body in the same way as his faeces are" (p. 343). See also Freud (1918, p. 84).

Another contributing factor, which was not overlooked by Freud, is the anxiety associated with separation from the love object. Since the second year is crucial in the individuation-separation phase (Mahler and Furer, 1963) of the child, the concomitant anxiety adds its part to later castration anxiety.

Conclusions

Longitudinal observations of a normal boy during his second year revealed the following findings with regard to the developmental line of genital exploration and self-stimulation:

1. Genital self-stimulation during the second year showed a gradual progression with discontinuities from the largely exploratory behavior of the first year toward behavior having a clearly masturbatory quality in the oedipal years.

2. I found the traditional psychoanalytic definition of masturbation too general to capture the details of infant behavior. My definition emphasized primarily consciously sought pleasure rather than exploration, self-absorption not readily distracted, mounting excitement, with an orgastic rather than soothing rhythm. If masturbation is viewed in this way, one can state that, in the case of William, it still occurred infrequently during the second year but definitely more often than in the first year.

3. There was no genital excitement that could be labeled an orgasm in this period.

4. Erections resulting from genital tactile stimulation and tumescences arising reflexly from the need to urinate followed by detumescence after micturition were both more frequently seen in the second year than in the first.

5. During this period several component instinctual drives were in evidence; e.g., scoptophilia, exhibitionism, with its associated affect, pride, and early manifestations of oedipal feelings.

6. Meaningful knowledge of the scrotal sac and testicles appeared later than a comparable awareness of the penis, the precise "discovery" of the scrotal organs occurring at twenty-one months.

7. Finding and exploring the meatus urinarius took place at twenty-one and a half months.

8. This child's advanced language facility afforded an unusual

opportunity to gain some insight into the structuring of the self representations, particularly their gradual progression, interrupted by fluctuations and regressions, and to discern gradients of clarity of representation of different body parts. Indistinct differentiations of mental representations contribute to the well-known symbolic equations of feces = penis or testicles and breast = penis.

9. William's pregnancy fantasy was an identification with the active, all-powerful, baby-producing mother, an *addition* to being male, not a substitution. It represented only one aspect of his many identifications with his mother and was one facet of his fantasy role playing.

10. In addition to the better known roots of castration anxiety inherent in birth, oral deprivation, and daily loss of feces, William demonstrated an anal-genital confusion of sensation which resulted in anxiety about the genitals related to the loss of feces. William alternately associated and confused penis and feces and scrotal organs and feces, and did not exhibit primarily the testicular-anal misunderstandings which Bell stressed. Likewise, he showed a visual jumbling of scrotal and fecal percepts, though largely independent of sitting on the toilet. There was suggestive evidence that motility of the testicles can contribute to castration anxiety as Bell claimed.

11. Two other maturational factors also predispose to later castration anxiety. These are (a) the prolonged reality testing involved in differentiating between the "I" and the "not-I" and between the detachable and the nondetachable, and (b) the separation anxiety centering around the love object in the individuation-separation phase.

Summary

A longitudinal or developmental line approach to the study of the genital exploration and self-stimulation of a normal boy during his second year permits correlation of these specific observations with other developmental and maturational data to elucidate: (1) the progression from first-year genital self-stimulation toward oedipal masturbation; (2) the boy's gradual acquisition of knowledge about the penis, scrotal sac, testicles, and meatus urinarius; (3) the fluctuating emergence of the mental representations of self and object, especially as they pertain to this important body area; ambiguity of representation seemed to contribute to symbolic equations of breast = penis and feces = penis or testicles; (4) precursors of castration anxiety; (5) early fantasies related to his identification with his mother's pregnancy; and (6) vignettes of other aspects of infantile sexuality (libidinal) such as exhibitionism (with its related affect, pride), looking (scoptophilia), and oedipal feelings. This child's verbal facility permitted the collection of more nonspeculative data than are usually obtainable at this age.

BIBLIOGRAPHY

Abraham, K. (1920), Manifestations of the Female Castration Complex. *Selected Papers on Psycho-Analysis.* London: Hogarth Press, 1927, pp. 339-369.

Bell, A. (1961), Some Observations on the Role of the Scrotal Sac and Testicles. *J. Amer. Psa. Assn.,* 9:261-286.

—— (1964), Bowel Training Difficulties in Boys: Prephallic and Phallic Considerations. *J. Amer. Acad. Child Psychiat.,* 3:577-590.

—— (1965), The Significance of Scrotal Sac and Testicles for the Prepuberty Male. *Psa. Quart.,* 34:182-206.

Bornstein, B. (1953), Masturbation in the Latency Period. *This Annual,* 8:65-78.

Brunswick, R. M. (1940), The Preoedipal Phase of the Libido Development. *Psa. Quart.,* 9:293-319.

Freud, A. (1963), The Concept of Developmental Lines. *This Annual,* 18:245-265.

—— (1965), *Normality and Pathology in Childhood: Assessments of Development.* New York: International Universities Press.

Freud, S. (1905), Three Essays on the Theory of Sexuality. *Standard Edition,* 7:125-245. London: Hogarth Press, 1953.

—— (1909), Analysis of a Phobia in a Five-year-old Boy. *Standard Edition,* 10:5-147. London: Hogarth Press, 1955.

—— (1918), From the History of an Infantile Neurosis. *Standard Edition,* 17:3-123. London: Hogarth Press, 1955.

—— (1923), The Infantile Genital Organization. *Standard Edition,* 19:141-145. London: Hogarth Press, 1961.

Greenacre, P. (1958), Early Physical Determinants in the Development of the Sense of Identity. *J. Amer. Psa. Assn.,* 6:612-627.

Halverson, H. M. (1940), Genital and Sphincter Behavior of the Male Infant. *J. Genet. Psychol.,* 56:95-136.

Hartmann, H. (1950), Comments on the Psychoanalytic Theory of the Ego. *This Annual,* 5:74-96.

Jacobson, E. (1950), Development of the Wish for a Child in Boys. *This Annual,* 5:139-152.

—— (1964), *The Self and the Object World.* New York: International Universities Press.

Kinsey, A., Pomeroy, W., & Martin, C. (1948), *Sexual Behavior in the Human Male.* Philadelphia: Saunders.

Kleeman, J. A. (1965), A Boy Discovers His Penis. *This Annual,* 20:239-266.

Lipin, T. (1963), The Repetition Compulsion and 'Maturational' Drive-Representatives. *Int. J. Psa.,* 44:389-406.

Loewenstein, R. M. (1950), Conflict and Autonomous Ego Development during the Phallic Phase. *This Annual,* 5:47-52.

Mahler, M. & Furer, M. (1963), Certain Aspects of the Separation-Individuation Phase. *Psa. Quart.*, 32:1-14.

Novey, S. (1958), The Meaning of the Concept of the Mental Representation of Objects. *Psa. Quart.*, 27:57-79.

—— (1961), Further Considerations on Affect Theory in Psycho-Analysis. *Int. J. Psa.*, 42:21-31.

Rose, G. J. (1961), Pregenital Aspects of Pregnancy Fantasies. *Int. J. Psa.*, 42:544-549.

Spitz, R. A. (1952), Authority and Masturbation: Some Remarks on a Bibliographical Investigation. *Psa. Quart.*, 21:490-527.

—— (1962), Autoerotism Re-Examined. *This Annual*, 17:283-315.

—— & Wolf, K. M. (1949), Autoerotism: Some Empirical Findings and Hypotheses on Three of Its Manifestations in the First Year of Life. *This Annual*, 3/4:85-120.

Van der Leeuw, P. J. (1958), The Preoedipal Phase of the Male. *This Annual*, 13:352-374.

SLEEP AND ITS DISTURBANCES APPROACHED DEVELOPMENTALLY

HUMBERTO NAGERA, M.D.

Survey of the Literature on Sleep and Its Disturbances in the First Year of Life

In 1955 Margaret S. Mahler introduced a panel on sleep disturbances in children with the statement "that research in child development and child analysis, just as in physiology, affords little knowledge of the normal patterns of the sleep cycle or of its individual variations at various ages. She emphasized that except for pavor nocturnus and sleep phobias we do not know . . . whether we are dealing with *disturbances* of sleep or variations of the sleep pattern" (see Friend, 1956, pp. 514-515).

Although the amount of research on sleep has vastly increased since this statement was made, the study of the sleep patterns of infants has remained a comparatively neglected field. As a consequence we still know relatively little about the sleep disturbances of children, especially in the first year of life.

Although the product of one individual author who remains responsible for its form and content, this paper represents a characteristic example of team research as carried out in the Hampstead Child-Therapy Course and Clinic. The relevant *clinical data* were extracted from the files of several departments of the Clinic, notably the Well-Baby Clinic, the Diagnostic Department, and the Index. Help with the *revision of literature* and Section II was given by Mrs. Marion Burgner, a qualified child therapist who also assumed responsibility for Section III. Ample opportunity for informed *discussion* of the subject was offered within the program of the Clinical Concept Research Group, whose members are: H. Nagera (chairman), Anna Freud (consultant); S. Baker, E. Barley, M. Burgner, A. Colonna, E. Dansky, R. Putzel, P. Radford, M. Hodgson, G. Jones (qualified psychoanalysts, child therapists, and students). Special aspects of the literature were helpfully reviewed by Dr. M. MacMillan (post-Doctoral Fellow in Child Psychiatry, Baylor University College of Medicine, Houston, Texas), a visiting member of the Clinical Concept Research Group.

This paper forms part of a Research Project entitled "Assessment of Pathology in Childhood," Part II, which is conducted at the Hampstead Child-Therapy Course and Clinic, London. This project is financed by the National Institute of Mental Health, Washington, D.C., Grant No. 05683-0405.

In the same panel Samual A. Guttman noted the difficulties in establishing whether or not an infant is asleep because the criteria such as responsiveness to noise or vibration as well as movement and posture are exceedingly complex. Gregory Rochlin made the same point and mentioned the existence of similar observational difficulties even in the case of older children.

Recent advances in our knowledge of sleep have solved some of these problems. With the help of EEG studies, it is now possible to establish accurately and quickly not only whether a child or adult is sleeping but also at which stage of the sleep cycle the person is. Nevertheless, more information is needed about the earliest periods of life. At that time the infant's nervous system is far from a finished product and still requires a long extrauterine period for its maturation. In view of this immaturity, it is not possible to draw too many inferences from the work on adults, whose central nervous system is a fully developed organ.

These early developmental stages are, for analysts, a particularly obscure period about which we can talk only in rather general terms. The different conceptualizations of these early phases are not only patchy and incomplete but frequently contradictory and sometimes even untenable. I believe that this state of affairs is a necessary stage in the development of our knowledge. I mention it here for two reasons: first, to highlight the difficulties involved in the study of sleep and its disturbances during the first year of life. Since we assume that development proceeds on the basis of a complex interaction between specific innate givens and environmental, experiential factors, we must evaluate not only the child but also the role of the mother and other specific environmental influences. Secondly, I believe that analysts in order to gain a better understanding of these stages must continue to give due weight to the many valuable contributions made by scientists in related disciplines. This coordination of findings[1] is essential, especially in view of the fact that direct observation and reconstruction—the only tools available to the analyst—have obvious limitations in their application to the earliest phases of development.

[1] A good example of this procedure is Sanford Gifford's (1960) investigation of the infant's sleep-wakefulness pattern, which is viewed in terms of analytic theory, observational material, and Kleitman and Engelmann's findings (1953).

With regard to the infant's sleep pattern many authors agree that significant changes occur in the third month of life, but there is no agreement on whether this change is due partly to "learning" or determined fully by biological factors. In view of these changes and their relation to physical and psychological maturational advances taking place at different points during the first year of life, I shall present the relevant material in chronological order.

THE FIRST THREE MONTHS

Analysts differ somewhat in their assumptions concerning the degree of ego development present at birth, the newborn's capacity to experience stimuli of an external or internal nature, his ability to process and integrate them, and the level at which biopsychological integration and meaningful experiences take place. Yet these are essential considerations for a better understanding of the influences which the mother's handling and other environmental factors have on the normal or abnormal development of the child. In order to characterize the functional state of the mental apparatus of the newborn it is important to refer to Kleitman's (1939) very significant statement: "We are accustomed to think of ourselves as being awake and something must be done to make us sleep. It is actually the other way round. We begin asleep and thereafter have interruptions of sleep by wakefulness" (p. 212). This statement has been corroborated by a number of electroencephalographic studies. For example, Walter's (1953) EEG studies revealed that infancy is characterized by a pattern of delta waves, which in the adult are found only in states of somnolence. The delta waves become less prominent on some occasions, e.g., when the child is attentive, usually around the second or third month of life. This state of alertness coincides with the appearance of alpha waves in the electroencephalographic record; that is, when the "twilight state" of the newborn (Ribble, 1943) begins to give way to a sharper demarcation between sleep and mental activity. These findings are relevant to any formulations of the mental processes taking place in the first few weeks and later stages of life. (I shall later formulate some tentative hypotheses based on these findings.)

In the panel previously referred to Rochlin stated that many "inferences drawn from observed behavior of the infant do have a natural tendency to be anthropomorphic and homuncular. The highly organized performance of the baby at the breast may not be so much an index of its cerebral-cortical activity as has been supposed, but may be that avenue of behavior through which a primitive, psychic, homeostatic state is arrived at by gratification of relatively simple visceral needs which have a distinctly temporal character" (see Friend, 1956, p. 517).

Whatever view of the early stages one is inclined to hold, all authors agree on the fact that there is constant maturation and development of a physical and psychological nature and that this process reaches, in terms of the sleep-wakefulness rhythm, an acme around the third month of life. The newborn starts with a polycyclic type of existence, in which sleep is punctuated by irregular periods of wakefulness determined or regulated by his basic needs, especially by hunger. From this pattern the newborn moves into what Kleitman (1939) calls the "monocyclic type of existence" seen in older children and adults. He says: "one of the first *learned* performances is sleeping through the night by skipping one feeding, and the gradual lengthening of the daytime period of wakefulness."[2]

Sanford Gifford (1960) utilized Kleitman and Engelmann's observations of the sleep characteristics of a group of nineteen normal infants from the third to the twenty-sixth week of life. He interpreted their statistical data "as indicating three developmental phases, approximately corresponding to hypothetical phases of ego development" (p. 38). These three developmental phases are: (1) an undifferentiated phase (from birth to the third week); (2) precursors of ego functioning (from the third to the twelfth or fourteenth week); (3) the beginning of object relations (from the twelfth or fourteenth to the twenty-sixth week).

Gifford states that "the development of the ego and the sleep-wakefulness pattern are both determined by an interrelationship between the infant's genetic pattern of neurophysiological maturation and his mother's characteristic mode of response to his biological and emotional needs. This continuous interaction between constitutional equipment and maternal responsiveness is a unitary process of psychophysiological adaptation, at a time when the infant's mani-

[2] Quoted by Gifford (1960, p. 32).

fest behavior, homeostatic patterns, and precursors of ego structure are still undifferentiated" (p. 34).

From Birth to the Third Week

Gifford (1960) characterizes the sleeping patterns of the "undifferentiated phase" (from birth to the third week) as "Seemingly random, irregular intervals of sleep and waking that follow an innate rhythm of hunger, awakening, motor excitation, feeding and sleep, unrelated to external events or the 24-hour calendar day" (p. 21). Toward the end of the third week, one can observe an adaptation of the sleep-wakefulness pattern to the periodicity of day and night. Gifford considers this adaptation to be one of the earliest precursors of ego functioning; it appears earlier than, for example, the smiling response and purposeful finger sucking. His view is that "an innate biological tendency [is being] progressively influenced by the environment as the infant's perceptual apparatus matures. A random, disorganized pattern undergoes a systematic modification that is mediated through the infant's relationship with his mother, beginning before the development of accurate distance perception or awareness of the mother as a differentiated object" (p. 13). In support of his thesis Gifford quotes Brazelton, a pediatrician who in a personal communication expressed the opinion "that after the third week the infant's innate tendencies, his activity level, responsiveness to the environment or ease in being satisfied by feeding, begin to reflect his mother's attitudes, to show the influence of her fears and anxieties, as when a relatively stable and easily satisfied baby becomes discontented and overactive" (p. 23).

This statement raises the question how early the influence of the mother, in emotional and psychological terms, shows itself in the child's specific reactions. It is clear that babies react to their mothers' handling in one way or another from the very beginning of life, but what remains unclear is the level at which that response occurs. In this context, it is important to remind ourselves of Rochlin's statement that our observations of babies often are anthropomorphic and homuncular so that we tend to interpret the baby's reactions to environmental stimuli and maternal handling as taking place on a much higher level of complexity and integration than is possible in the early stages.

Although I agree with Gifford's view that the sleep pattern undergoes a systematic modification through the relationship with the mother, I have some doubts about considering the sleep pattern as disorganized and random as he describes it during the first three weeks of life. These doubts are based on observations made over twenty years ago in the Hampstead War Nurseries where charts on the sleeping patterns of a number of children of different ages were kept. One of them is a record of the sleep-wakefulness pattern of baby Joseph from the second to the thirtieth day of life. This graph[3] shows from the very beginning a clearly defined pattern which subsequently developed in the directions outlined by Gifford and others. From the third day onward there is a clear and consistent pattern of more prolonged and continuous sleep during the night period than during the daytime. Joseph slept approximately between the periods of 6 P.M. and 7.30 A.M., although during that period of time he used to wake up spontaneously three times for the first nine days. He was usually awake less than an half hour at a time. Beginning on the eleventh and twelfth day of his life he woke up two or three times during the evening period, usually for a short while, until nearly the end of the thirty-day period of observation, when in the last four evenings he started to wake only twice each evening. The daytime pattern of sleep during the whole month shows three sleeping periods, two generally of longer duration and the third a brief one. Toward the second half of the first month of observation the periods of wakefulness in the daytime noticeably increased.

As can be seen from the chart, the child slept almost continuously day and night only during the second, third, and fourth day of his life, but even then the evening periods of sleep were longer and less broken than those during the day. Since there was a very significant change in the general rhythm of almost continuous sleep on the fifth day, I wonder whether the pattern observed during the initial three to five days is not an artifact introduced by the trauma of birth.

It can be argued that at the Hampstead War Nurseries Joseph was living in a group and that his pattern of sleep-wakefulness clearly shows the influence of this condition. This is of course quite possible. For this reason, as well as others, I stress the need for further research

[3] The graphs were prepared at the Hampstead War Nurseries by Sophie and Gertrude Dann.

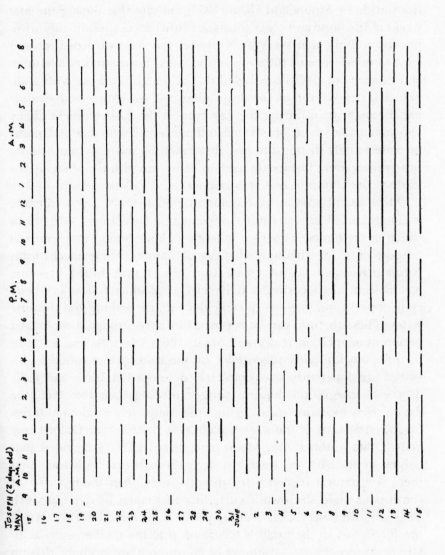

on the sleep patterns in early infancy. On the other hand, the observations made by Moore and Ucko (1957) indicate that during the first weeks of life noise and other forms of disturbances (presumably within certain limits that the War Nurseries may have exceeded) do not tend to interfere with the sleep of the baby. Furthermore, Kleitman and Engelmann (1953) concluded that although there are wide individual variations, the infant sleeps more and for longer peirods during the night than during the day even in the earliest weeks. They also noted that these observable differences betwen day and night increase rapidly during the first three months and only much more slowly thereafter. These data seem to be in line with the observations made at the Hampstead War Nurseries.[4]

More recent studies have demonstrated that the sleep schedule is closely linked to many other physiological regulatory mechanisms which in the human organism follow a 24-hour period that seems to be geared to the rhythmic changes of nature. These mechanisms regulate rise and fall of temperature, heart rate, blood pressure, metabolism, adrenocortical activity, etc., all of which follow a 24-hour cycle of peaks and lows which coincides with the waking and sleeping states. These rhythms can be reversed but only through a prolonged period of adaptation (Luce and Segal, 1966). Nevertheless, some of the physiological and endocrinological mechanisms and functions involved are apparently not completely developed at birth and their degree of integration requires further investigation. However, the data already available speak against the completely random and disorganized pattern of the sleep-wakefulness rhythm that Gifford suggests. Other authors, e.g., Moore and Ucko (1957), concluded that babies do not have to "learn" to sleep through the night but "that there is a natural tendency for infants to lengthen their period of continuous night sleep while curtailing that taken by day" (p. 341). Yet their own observations seem to point in the direction that certain specific factors in the infant's relationship to the mother may facilitate or hinder the establishment of an appropriate sleeping rhythm

[4] Parmelee et al. (1964) studied the sleep patterns of forty-six infants from birth through the sixteenth week. The infants slept an average of 16.32 hours daily during the first week and 14.87 hours by the sixteenth week. The average longest period of sleep per day was 4.08 hours during the first week and 7.67 hours in the twelfth week. The average longest period of wakefulness per day was 2.39 hours in the first week and 3.11 hours in the twelfth week.

during the evening. Moore and Ucko also found that a number of the factors generally assumed to influence or interfere with the sleep rhythm of babies do not seem to be operative before the third month of life.

From the Third to the Twelfth or Fourteenth Week

In the second phase described by Gifford (1960), that of "precursors of ego functioning," there is a sharp decrease in the hours of sleep during daytime and in the frequency of night feedings and a proportional increase in the hours of night sleep. Thus the number of total hours of sleep remains similar, while at the same time a more organized sleep-wakefulness rhythm develops. To Gifford, "This configuration suggests an integrated process of adaptation to the 24-hour cycle, more complex and organized than reflex responses to crude external stimuli can account for. The 'physiological' basis for this process is the maturation of the perceptual apparatus, perhaps constitutionally determined, and its psychological or 'learned' basis is the result of a developing emotional interrelationship between the infant and his mother. An alternative explanation, that the evolution of the sleep rhythm is entirely the result of neurophysiological maturation, fails to account for sleep disturbances before the third month when the mother-child relationship is disturbed, as in Rank and Mcnaughtons atypical child [1950], or in the frequent lesser disturbances that occur in normal and neurotic families. If a disturbed maternal relationship can interfere with the development of the sleep-wakefulness pattern, it may be assumed that a relatively normal relationship can exert a favorable influence" (p. 25).

On this point there still exists some controversy. Moore and Ucko (1957) concluded that babies do not have to "learn" to sleep through the night. They state: "What we have called the 'settling' process, a form of learning at the level of biological adaptation, requires no consciously directed training by the parents" (p. 347). Luce and Segal (1966) concluded that "the mounting evidence suggests that the twenty-four hour rhythm is a reality, ticked off by the central nervous system, and that a baby begins to sleep through the night, not because his parents train him but because his brain has sufficiently matured" (p. 55). Parmelee et al. (1964) assert that the development of the sleep pattern "is a normal phenomenon of neurological maturation and rather independent of training and feeding efforts" (p. 582). On the other hand, Oswald (1966) assumes that the "recurrence of inactivity every twenty-four hours constitutes a rhythm which the body has 'learned' through experience" (p. 10). He believes, as does Kleitman, that babies acquire or learn (through the pressures of social life, etc.) the 24-hour rhythm.

Whereas Gifford assumes that an important modification of the previously random and disorganized pattern of the first three weeks takes place, our observations do not support this early disorganized pattern. On the other hand, our charts indicate a reduction of the sleeping time during daytime and a more continuous sleeping period in the evening.

I also question Gifford's use of atypical children to draw conclusions concerning normal development. His argument, that his view can explain the frequent minor sleeping disturbances observed in babies of normal and neurotic parents, is sharply contradicted by the findings reported by Moore and Ucko. Their study of 200 babies from birth onward shows that there are grounds to question many of the generally accepted assumptions about the influence of parental handling (under reasonable conditions, that is, excluding instances of extreme mishandling) on the "so-called" sleep disturbances in babies *before the third month of life*. These authors established empirically that the age of thirteen weeks is a turning point in the process of adjustment to sleeping through the night.[5] They designate the point at which this change takes place as the "age of settling" and refer to the developments that lead to the change observed by the thirteenth week as the "settling" process.

Several other findings of the Moore and Ucko study are of special interest. The sexes show no significant differences in the age of the first "settling" (at the thirteenth week). However, if the whole year is considered, it is apparent that boys wake significantly more often than girls and that these tendencies are already present, though not statistically significant, in the waking scores for the first three months. This finding is also in agreement with Kleitman's observations al-

[5] Moore and Ucko define sleeping through the night as undisturbed sleep between 12 A.M. and 5 A.M. in the morning. Although this interval may be considered to be arbitrary, the substantial body of their observations and conclusions is nevertheless of interest.

though Moore and Ucko cover slightly different spans of time in the life of the children observed.

Moore and Ucko also studied the effect of illness on sleep during the first three months of life, that is, before the age of settling; they concluded that illnesses seem to have no lasting effect on the night sleep during this period, although ill health may cause a few broken nights. The sleep pattern was resumed as soon as the acute phase of the illness was over.[6]

Analysts have postulated a connection between sucking and sleep. Moore and Ucko's findings also suggest such an interrelationship which deserves further study.[7]

Their observations also indicate that before the age of three months, i.e., before the age of settling, seasonal changes in light and temperature show no relationship to the age of settling.[8]

Sharing a room and noise had no demonstrable effect on the "settling age"; the authors in fact thought that it was remarkable "how easily those babies that sleep in the living room would go to sleep with the whole family present making no special effort to be quiet" (p. 338). They refer to Irwin and Weiss (1934) whose studies have shown that continuous fairly strong stimuli—visual, auditory or cutaneous—have an inhibitory effect, at least on the newborn infant.

[6] This finding was in sharp contrast to their findings with regard to the effect of illness on the sleep rhythm during the later part of the first year of life. At that time illness can induce sleep disturbances that may last several months.

[7] One of my patients has a baby, aged seven and a half weeks, who at five weeks already slept through the night. This baby is allowed as much sucking time as he desires. His last feeding, consisting of the breast first and then a bottle, is usually taken between 9 and 10 P.M., whereupon he falls asleep until 5 A.M. in the morning. Then again he has the breast and a bottle. This baby is fed on demand and the mother allows him to suck at the breast for any length of time, even when her milk is finished.

[8] In the adult sleep-rhythm disturbances have been observed when the 24-hour periodicity of day and night disappears, e.g., in northern Scandinavia and among Arctic explorers (see Gifford, 1960).

My own children moved from a country in which there are no significant seasonal changes between day and night to England where at the peak of the summer it is still daylight until 10 P.M. When we moved the children, three and four years old, objected for some time to going to sleep at their usual hour (between 7 and 7.30 P.M.) on the basis that it was still daylight. The opposite was never observed; that is, in winter when it was dark by 3.30 P.M., they were never ready for bed before their usual time.

Anna Freud observed at the Hampstead War Nurseries that when double summer-time was introduced, there were great difficulties in getting the children to sleep in daylight.

Further Moore and Ucko found that a change of cot or sleeping room did not produce any noticeable effect on a large number of infants under three months, whereas *from the third month* on such changes frequently produced temporary disturbances.

On the other hand, they noticed that minimal changes in routine, such as shifting the bath time from morning to evening, proved helpful in "settling" some of the babies, while in other cases a temporary change such as a holiday upset a previously good sleeper. Generally, however, they found that this type of upset tends to pass easily when it occurs before the third month of life, while at a later age it can be the starting point of prolonged difficulties.

The child's position in the family was significant in terms of the age of settling, but the significance started only with the third child and not with the first two. Moore and Ucko concluded that the mother's experience of having had *two* children is more important than her age or education, which were not significant. The third child usually settles better.

The age of weaning from the breast showed no relationship either to the settling age or to the tendency to wake during the first three months. Breast- and bottle-fed babies behaved similarly. Moore and Ucko state that "actual weaning had a settling effect on sleeping in at least a dozen cases. In no case did weaning from the breast before three months, however sudden, lead to increased waking (we are not here considering other effects of weaning)" (p. 339). Flexibility or lack of it in respect to feeding times (demand versus clock feeding) showed no special relationship to the "age of settling"; the three groups classed as "demand fed," "clock fed," and "latitude allowed," contained approximately the same number of settlers and nonsettlers and children with high and low waking scores. Certain children, however, benefited (in terms of settling) from a more reasonable adaptation of the timing of feeding in contrast to an early one that had proved too rigid.

Moore and Ucko found that *for most children an adequate amount of interplay with the mother is an important factor conducive to the establishment of an appropriate sleep rhythm.* They referred to this form of contact as "excess nursing time," that is, a measure of the time given by the mother to the baby for contact and play over and above what he may need for feeding. The babies who received the least excess nursing time had the greatest tendency to wake, and those who received an excessive amount were the next most wakeful group, while those who had ten to twenty minutes in addition to the feeding time settled best. The mothers in the third group, it seems to me, had the best functional adaptation to their children. In *Early Childhood Disturbances, the Infantile Neurosis, and the Adulthood Disturbances* (1966), I emphasized that the mother's role in furthering the development of the child consists not only in satisfying his more fundamental needs and protecting him from unnecessary or harmful stimulation but in providing diverse types of stimulation which facilitates the development of specific ego functions.

I am inclined to think that before the third month of life the mother's stimulation, or lack of it, affects the infant's ego development in toto and that the result of this can be observed in the delayed appearance of the smiling response, the "age of settling," motor skills and coordination, etc. I do not mean to imply that certain specific forms of stimulation preferred or neglected by mothers may not further or hinder the maturational processes of certain ego apparatuses and functions in preference to others, but I mean to say that a minimum general form of stimulation is necessary for harmonious development. There is sufficient evidence from studies of neglected and institutionalized children to warrant the assumption that extremely disturbed mothers, who cannot provide this basic minimum of overall stimulation and comfort to their babies, or who overexcite them, affect far more of the child's ego progress than just the "age of settling." This will be just one of several areas affected.

Finally, Moore and Ucko found an important relationship between night waking and the circumstances of birth. For example, asphyxia at birth was encountered in forty infants (according to the obstetric records), nineteen of whom (47 percent) failed to settle by three months, compared with only 28 percent of nonasphyxiated infants. The asphyxiated group continued to display a greater tendency to wake throughout the year. (The authors point out that the diagnosis of neonatal asphyxia is a somewhat subjective matter and that these records have to be considered with caution.) They quote Preston who also found that children who have suffered a mild degree of anoxia during (child) birth show a permanent tendency to hyperactivity and overresponsiveness, with much crying and disturbed feeding and sleep in infancy, while those with a greater depth of anoxia show serious apathy.

Birth weight, weight at three months, and weight increment over this period were not related either to age of settling or to waking scores for this period.

Discussing the "age of settling" and sleep disturbances during the first three months of life Moore and Ucko were surprised by the large number of babies who adhered to the norm, especially in view of the fact that more than one adverse factor was present in children who slept throughout the night. In their final assessment Moore and Ucko list the factors associated with continued waking during the first three months and the failure to settle: (1) *lack of wisdom in the parents:* insufficient nursing by the mother due to lack of time or inclination; excess of anxious oversolicitous mothering; erratic behavior due to fecklessness or ambivalence to the child; rigid controlling attitudes leading to the imposition of unsuitable regimes; (2) *some cause within the child:* asphyxia or other birth trauma, constitutional sensitiveness, etc. The interaction of these numerous factors is so complex that, in the opinion of these authors, it is seldom possible to say definitely that the failure to sleep is due to any one particular cause.

Some Hypothetical Correlations between EEG Findings and Psychoanalytic Observations

Many of the surprising findings of Moore and Ucko are perhaps more easily understood if we keep in mind that the electroencephalographic pattern characteristic for most of the first three months of life —the delta waves—corresponds to a state of somnolence in the adult. In view of this fact it is possible that during this early stage of development the impact of some maternal attitudes on the child has been overestimated, while that of other environmental factors has been neglected. This statement is in no way intended to minimize the significance of the mother-child interaction from the very beginning of the infant's life. However, this statement is intended to specify the nature of this interaction. At first the mother acts as an organizer and stimulator of maturational processes (of a physical and psychological nature) which steer development into appropriate channels and at the same time open the way to later different types of interactions.

Furthermore, as has been pointed out, the functional condition of the infant's brain with its delta waves resembles that of the adult in the somnolent states in the adult. The delta waves disappear only at moments when the child is attentive in a special way by the second or third month, at which point the functional capacity is heightened and the alpha waves appear. The stimuli that cause the infant to emerge from the somnolent state can be assumed to be increased internal needs or discomfort, at which point the mother will come to him. The communication between mother and child thus takes place during a stage of heightened alertness and functional capacity. It is plausible that the baby's experiences under these functional conditions are more significant and that the contacts of baby and mother at such points (when the alpha waves displace the delta pattern) facilitate not only ego development but also a beginning awareness of the object.[9]

It is perhaps not without significance that the institutionalized baby will miss this opportunity of contact with another human being at the times when he is in a state of functional alertness. These occasional states of alertness during the first few weeks of life usually charm mothers who respond intensely and in kind to the child, as all those who have had the opportunity to observe babies and their mothers will confirm. I believe that this interaction has a chain effect: such states of alertness tend to arise more frequently when the child is responded to; the mother's response leads to increased alertness and to the wish for more contact. Conversely the lack of response to these early occasional states of alertness in the institutionalized child may well contribute to, and perhaps determine, his

[9] Oswald (1966) remarked that "the alpha rhythm is an indication that the brain is functioning at one particular level of efficiency, alertness or 'vigilance'. . . . When the alpha rhythm is lost in drowsiness, the brain is functioning at a lower level of effectiveness" (p. 21). He also refers to the experiments of two American psychologists, Emmons and Simon, who tested the commercial "sleep-learning" claims. They played tape-recorded answers to questions while the subjects were asleep and also took EEG records. They conclude that we do not learn while asleep (slow waves and spindles). However, the authors found that in the morning answers played while alpha rhythm was present (the subjects were not sleeping at this point) were recalled easily, whereas those played while the alpha rhythm was waning often were not recallable.

later withdrawn attitude, lack of alertness and interest, and even fear of contact which Spitz and others have described so well.

On the other hand, many ministrations of the mother take place when the functional condition of the baby's brain is of the somnolent type (delta waves pattern); therefore, their impact on the infant must be of a different quality. At such points things happen to him when he is not as alloplastically orientated as in the previous state. Nevertheless, the ministrations of the mother under such conditions still provide him with a wide range of new sensory stimulation, contributing to the functional awakening and development of different ego apparatuses and, at the beginning, more especially the perceptual one. Through these ministrations the mother also provides a good deal of the necessary and basic conditions of minimum comfort and well-being, without which ego development cannot proceed normally.

It seems too that by the second and third month, specific aspects of the mother's behavior, certain types of stimulation and play will have an arousing capacity similar to that of internal needs. The careful study and interpretation of electroencephalographic findings in neonates and their correlation with psychoanalytic observations may help to clarify both the essential needs of the child and the role of the mother as a stimulating agent for further development. As mentioned, the observations on neglected and institutionalized children have demonstrated the damage done to the child resulting from the lack of the necessary stimulation; significantly this damage becomes more evident from the third month on. Other observations seem to point to the fact that there is an "ideal" amount of stimulation which has the most beneficial effects. Not only lack of stimulation but also excessive amounts of it interfere with the child's well-being, as has been pointed out earlier with regard to sleep. Provence and Lipton (1962) state that the infants in the institution they studied slept longer hours and with fewer interruptions than babies reared in families. They received similar reports from the foster mothers of children coming from institutional settings. The foster mothers felt that for several weeks the children slept for excessive periods of time. Furthermore, a reduction in the total hours of sleep accompanied the general improvement in the child's development as a response to the improvement in the nurturing care.

At the very early stages of development the infant's response to the mother and to the environmental handling should be understood in the above context and not as a specific symptomatic emotional and psychological response of a complexity that is possible only at a somewhat later stage when the child's ego development and object relations have reached the appropriate levels. Anthropomorphic and homuncular interpretations are thus avoided.

FROM THE THIRD MONTH ONWARD

Kleitman described the important changes in the sleep-wakefulness rhythm of the baby that take place around the twelfth week. These changes correspond to the "age of settling" as defined by Moore and Ucko in the thirteenth week. Thereafter the development of the child's ego proceeds at a faster rate. As shown above, many of the factors that did not significantly influence the "age of settling" and the sleep patterns before the third month trigger more or less serious sleep disturbances after the third month. All authors agree that from this time on, many such factors are increasingly capable of having this effect.

From the Twelfth or Fourteenth Week to the Twenty-sixth Week

Gifford describes the "third phase" of development in terms of the beginning of object relations. The early stages of this phase are in a continuum of development with the last stages of the previous one (Gifford's second phase of early ego development) since many of the achievements begin to appear at the very end of it and will proceed further during this third phase. Some of the landmarks of development appear at this point for the first time, e.g., the hand-mouth coordination.

With regard to the development of the sleep-wakefulness pattern Gifford quotes Kleitman who emphasized the importance of perceptual maturation in the adaptation of the waking state to the activities of the daytime. This maturation and development of the perceptual apparatuses and processes provide the infant with new sensory experiences and objects of interest in his immediate surroundings. Gifford and others consider the period between the twelfth to the twenty-sixth week as one when rapid advances in perceptual integration take place. The infant becomes increasingly aware of his surroundings and begins to communicate visually with his mother.

Among other advances in ego development Gifford refers to the smiling response (which appears around the tenth to twelfth week) and
the development of the hand-mouth coordination, which, according
to Hoffer (1949), usually does not take place intentionally before the
twelfth week and is well established between the twelfth and sixteenth week. As Gifford points out, the exact chronological relationship between the smiling response, the hand-mouth coordination,
and the change in the child's sleep pattern around the twelfth week
has never been systematically studied and the possible interaction
between these factors has not been established. In any event, as Gifford states, "the infant's capacity for purposeful self-gratification by
bringing the hand to the mouth, according to Hoffer [1949], contributes to the organization of the ego, by defining its surfaces, parts,
and functions. This capacity for self-gratification increases his independence from his mother's feedings and enables him to sleep
through the night . . . [there is] a reduction in the number of night
feedings, from over three to about one at the twelfth week" (pp. 31-
32).

Rochlin also expressed the view that there seems to be a correlation between structural maturation and sleep-wakefulness behavior.
He thought that as the child grows, his needs become more insistent
and the periods of wakefulness increase (see Friend, 1956).

Gifford quotes Gesell who described "the period between the
sixteenth and twenty-fourth week as one of rapid organization within the central nervous system, with the loss of the tonic-neck reflex,
the development of occular fixation and the 'recognition' of familiar
faces and sounds" (p. 32).

The sleeping time during the day continues to decrease, while
the frequency of night feedings and hours of night sleep remain
unchanged, thus reducing total sleep by slightly more than one hour.
There are well-defined morning and afternoon naps, with the longer
period of unbroken sleep between 8 P.M. and 8 A.M.[10] Thereafter a
mean ten hours of sleep during the night remains more or less constant during childhood since any reduction in the total sleeping time
is due to the disappearance of daytime naps.

[10] Our own charts from the Hampstead War Nurseries confirm Kleitman's observations, in spite of the fact that our children, unlike those observed by Kleitman, were
living in a communal environment.

Moore and Ucko (1957) point out that during this period about half of the infants who settled at the appropriate time revert to night waking. They quote Shepherd who emphasized the large number of new causes for night waking in the period between six and nine months.

Our own observations at the Hampstead Clinic confirm these findings. Among the many factors capable of triggering disturbances of sleep, particularly after the third month of life, are: changes of environment; the mother's tension, depression or ambivalence to the child; seriously disturbed marital relationship; a new pregnancy; separations, etc. As we have mentioned earlier, their effect on the very young child is not necessarily a direct one, but may be due to the impact of such events on the mother in whom they elicit anxiety, tension, anger, depressive reactions, guilt, shame, etc., that interfere with the previously more satisfactory relationship to and care of her baby.

Perhaps even more striking is the fact that some of the disturbances initiated in this way remain with the child for many years, as the following example will illustrate.[11] This example further shows how some of the factors referred to above trigger off a disturbance of sleep or make it worse. It should also be noted that the form in which the disturbance manifests itself can change at different points according to the new dimensions introduced by the new stages of the child's development and the nature of the underlying conflicts of which the original disturbance has become the vehicle.

I. F. was first seen at the Well Baby Clinic *at 9 months.* The mother's general tenseness and her ambivalence to the baby girl were observed; tension was also seen in the baby who trembled and wriggled. The relationship between mother and child was obviously disturbed and battles took place in several areas.

At 10½ months: Difficulties in falling asleep were noted; the child cried unless Mrs. F. sat with I. until she fell asleep; this had started when the family stayed with the maternal grandmother but continued after they returned home.

At 15½ months: I. still needed her mother to stay in the room until she fell asleep.

11 I am grateful to Dr. Stross and the staff of the Well Baby Clinic for making available their observations.

At 20 months: I. tended to awake after one or two hours of sleep demanding company.

At 25 months: The child must have mother sit with her for as long as two hours before falling asleep. The father no longer can settle her, whereas previously I. had been more responsive to him than to the mother. She tends to wake frequently during the night and takes a long time to settle. She cries desperately when she is left alone.

From the Twenty-sixth Week Onward

During this period development generally proceeds as rapidly as during the previous phase. More and more factors of increasing complexity can operate as possible sources of interference with sleep or development in general.

Hirschberg (1957) described some of the parental anxieties that frequently accompany the sleep disturbances of children. He found that sleep disturbances in the very young infant (up to one year) frequently affect the mother's narcissism. As a result she will be fearful, make excessive efforts to change, or feel utterly helpless, hopeless, and defeated. Mothers frequently associate their care and acceptance of the infant with his sleep patterns, feeling that if they truly accepted the baby, he would sleep well; or that if they really enjoyed feeding and gratifying the child, he would sleep well. When the infant does not sleep properly, some mothers tend to feel unworthy, doubt their capacity as mothers, and become more ambivalent to the child and to motherhood in general. Hirschberg occasionally found mothers who wanted their infants to sleep uninterruptedly and who reacted with anger and annoyance when the children were awake and demanded food, warmth, and care. These mothers tried to avoid any relationship with the child by having him sleep.

Other mothers regarded the young infant as a part of their own bodies, worried about the effect of the sleep problem on the health of the child, and at a preconscious level feared for his bodily integrity, which unconsciously implied his death; or they experienced strong oral-sadistic impulses as unconscious threats of disintegration and death of their own selves. Still other mothers equated the child's sleep disturbance with oral deprivation, some of them having at the same time unconscious fears of "being swallowed" by the babies.

It is inevitable that these fantasies influence the mother's response to her child.

SLEEP DISTURBANCES IN THE SECOND YEAR OF LIFE

A detailed consideration of the relevant literature and reports on sleep disturbances in this age group impresses the reader with a certain imbalance in approach: while several writers describe gross disturbances of sleep such as nightmares, pavor nocturnus, somnambulism, and extreme anxiety dreams, the well-established fact that virtually every parent anticipates some form of sleep interference after the first year of life is often given scant acknowledgment in the literature. While it is obviously important to survey the etiology and course of the more severe disturbances, I shall consider difficulties and disturbances around sleep in this age group principally from the viewpoint that such malfunctioning is only one of many possible expressions of infantile anxiety. This "infantile anxiety" may arise from conflicts of a neurotic nature, but it may also be an expression of developmental imbalances in the personality. For this latter group I reserve the term *developmental disturbances*[12] which can manifest themselves in many ways, one of them being "sleep disturbances."

Gesell and Ilg (1943), on the basis of their behavioral studies, consider the reluctance to go to sleep as well as night waking developmental features of the age group fifteen to thirty months. Anna Freud's (1965) references may be understood as an extension of this viewpoint to encompass the psychoanalytic approach to child development:

> However carefully and successfully an infant's sleeping habits and arrangements have been handled in the first year of life, difficulties with sleep, or with the ease of falling asleep, intervene almost without exception in the second year. . . . falling asleep is no longer a purely physical affair as the almost automatic response to a body need in an undifferentiated individual, in whom ego and id, self and object world are not yet separated off from each other. With the strengthening of the child's object ties and of his involvement in the happenings of the external world, with-

12 For a detailed exposition of the early developmental disturbances, developmental conflicts, etc., see Nagera (1966).

drawal of libido and of ego interests to the self becomes a prerequisite for sleep. This is not always accomplished without difficulty, and the anxiety aroused by the process makes the toddler cling all the more tenaciously to his wakefulness. . . . These [symptomatic manifestations of the state of wakefulness] again disappear spontaneously when the child's object relationships become more secure and less ambivalent, and when his ego becomes stabilized sufficiently to permit regression to the undifferentiated, narcissistic state necessary for sleep [pp. 157-158].

During the second year of life the physical maturation of the central nervous system continues and will be fairly complete toward the end of this period. Only then does the child reach that level and degree of maturation of the organic structures of his central nervous system which most other mammals possess at birth. Only at this point do the *physical structures underlying* the mental apparatus reach the level of completeness and maturity which is necessary for the normal functioning of the mental apparatus in the human. This completeness, however, refers only to the basic organic structures; in functional terms there are great differences between the child and the adult. To fill the functional gap between the two requires a long and arduous process of experiencing, learning, exposure to the most diverse sources of physical and psychological stimulation, opening new functional pathways of an ever-increasing complexity (for which the structures are now getting ready). We have sufficient evidence to postulate that the mother and her stimulation are necessary for the normal maturation of the central nervous system of the child, side by side with the natural and innate physical forces tending toward the physical maturational completeness of this system. Similarly we know that the mother is essential for the awakening of the functional capacities of this structure.[13]

Sleep disturbances (as well as other disturbances) cannot be properly understood without paying due regard to the peculiarities of the developmental stage. In this way we learn what factors in the child's personality favor or contribute to the sleeping difficulties which are so characteristic for this period and which have to be considered a

[13] This is an extremely complex process which we do not yet understand. Suffice it to say that the mother exerts an influence, directly and indirectly, on the development of the child's ego apparatuses and drives, both of which run parallel and interact with each other (Nagera, 1963).

developmental disturbance. Anna Maenchen suggested this approach in 1955.[14]

Among the different factors that need to be considered is the degree of ego development reached, i.e., the child's capacity to understand the happenings in the world around him, the level of his thought processes, the existence of an early capacity for internalization, the capacity to bind and deal with anxiety, etc. In addition, we must assess the child's drive development and its influence on his ego processes and object relations. Similarly, we have to consider the fact that in the second year of life there normally exists a relative imbalance between these three lines of development and that this imbalance is bound to provoke certain types of responses in the child when he is confronted with certain experiences.

With regard to object relations, there has been a gradual development from the stage of need satisfaction to that of object constancy. Because of this development (itself the result of complicated maturational advances) it is no longer the child's "needs" and the object's need-fulfilling functions that are all important. The object, independently of its need-fulfilling aspects, has become the child's primary concern. Obviously, the transition from the phase of need satisfaction to object constancy is a very slow and gradual process which starts in the third or fourth month, gains further impetus during the second half of the first year, and reaches its full development during the second year of life. In most cases it is already well established toward the end of the first half of the second year.

At this point most of the child's interest is concentrated in the mother, a situation of the greatest significance for the evaluation of the child's reactions. On the other hand and in spite of this unique tie to his mother, the child takes notice of and relates to other persons in the family, especially when these persons make efforts to earn the toddler's sympathy. In this way, father, grandparents, older siblings, and others become part of the toddler's enlarged world. It has perhaps not been sufficiently realized that these other relations take place only under the shadow of the relationship with the mother. The two-year-old child will spend much time playing with the grand-

14 I am grateful to Dr. Maenchen for allowing me to examine the unpublished paper "Sleep Disturbances and Ego Developments." For an abstract of this paper, see Friend (1956).

parents away from the mother (if they take the trouble to come down to his level and appeal to his interest), secure in his knowledge that the mother is around the house though not necessarily in sight. This behavior may suggest the child's independence from his mother. However, if she were to leave the house, the child would demand to go with her and refuse to play with the grandparents; and if he is left behind he will break down in tears and anxiety.

Similarly there are certain times and activities that belong exclusively in the context of the relationship to the mother. At these points the toddler demands his mother and will not accept a substitute—not even those persons to whom he has a good relationship at other times. It is due to this special type and quality of the cathexis attached to the mother that the toddler finds it difficult to settle down to sleep. He is very reluctant to relinquish contact with this precious object. This explains his constant demands for the mother to lie down with him, hold his hand, sit beside his bed, read him yet another story, etc. The presence of the mother is required not only at bedtime but also when the child wakes from his sleep, when he is unwell, has hurt himself, or is frightened, etc. On all these occasions the child demands his mother. In fact, fathers, grandparents, and other relatives are shocked by his rejection, by his extreme distress and despair if the mother is not available, and by their complete inability to soothe and comfort him. This reaction is a direct consequence of the developmental stage the child has reached in his object relations. His reaction is further clarified if we examine it against the background of ego development in order to see what the latter can do to cope with the experience.

From our observations we have to conclude that especially during the first half of the second year there is little the ego can offer. When the child is distressed and anxious, the ego is still easily put out of action and cannot make use of the scarce resources available. Earlier during this period the ego still lacks the capacity to distinguish between absence and complete disappearance or to link absence with the subsequent return of the object. A child at this age has no concept of time. From his egocentric position he cannot understand that the mother is not there when he requires her presence (a feeling justified by his previous experience since normally the mother has been available to him); he has not developed the capacity to delay his affective response, to pause and consider the meaning of, and the reasons for the mother's absence. Because of his limited capacity to comprehend and draw inferences, the child's ego, especially when under the stress of anxiety, can do little to master the experience and the automatic affective response that follows it.

Yet, only a few months later when the ego has developed further, the child's response is of a very different nature. The link between the mother going out and her return has established itself, his experiences have been broadened, and his thought processes have matured further. His ego is then in a much better position to deal with the problem. Thus we have observed children who in the first part of the second year of life, were overwhelmed by the mother's absence, but in the second part of the same year were able to cope with it by ego means.

In one of the cases I have in mind, the child woke up during the evening and went searching for the mother. His grandmother told him that mummy had gone out but had left the message for him that she was going to be back soon. The little boy turned around and walked to his bed, repeating to himself two or three times, "Mummy will be back soon," adding, "Mummy went to cinema." He fell asleep again without any difficulty or distress. He could now master the meaning of her absence as his own explanatory addition to the mother's message "went to the cinema" shows. It is of interest not only that he could bind the anxiety which otherwise might have arisen by means of meaningful thought processes, but also that at this stage "cinema" was for him a place where mother went occasionally and from which she returned soon. He did not really know the concrete meaning of "cinema." As is well known, the ego's capacity to tolerate anxiety and to bind it by means of thought processes increases markedly during the second year because language, though still limited, makes important contributions (A. Katan, 1961).

Another child started to say "mummy holidays" whenever the mother was absent. This simple mental link greatly helped the child to cope with the mother's absence because this link had a concrete meaning to him—mummy was not gone or lost forever but away for a short period and would come back. With the help of this associative link, his ego was able to bind the anxiety.

In view of the fact that the toddler's ego becomes increasingly

able to cope with the anxiety engendered by the mother's absence
it is necessary to emphasize this especially vulnerable and critical
period in the early part of the second year of life. This period, usually
of short duration, is characterized by the high cathexis of the object
at a time when ego development is still limited. Special efforts must
be made not to expose the child to negative experiences during it
The child has for developmental reasons no tolerance for the absence
of the object. This is feared per se. But added to this is the fact that
when the child is confronted with the mother's absence, his automatic response is an anxiety state which may reach overwhelming
proportions. Repeated traumas of this type cannot fail to have serious
consequences for his later development, quite apart from the fact
that they may lay the basis for later sleep disturbances as in a case
reported by Anna Freud (1966). This child developed a sleeping disturbance at two and a half years. The parents led a very secluded life
and had never left the infant until that age. They arranged to go out
expecting that the child would not even wake up, but she did wake
found a stranger, and reacted with a screaming attack. From that
moment on the child clung to her mother and had many difficulties
in settling at sleep time. Anna Freud once suggested to the parents
that they play games of hide and seek with the child, but this proved
impossible because the child went into a panic each time a parent
disappeared. The following years were very painful for the child
and the parents. At latency the picture changed and the child reacted
with excessive independence and a great deal of hostility to the
parents.

These considerations apply to all "separations" during the day
or at night. They are of particular significance at nightime when the
ego is in a regressed state.

Similarly, other types of sleep disturbances at this period are
largely dependent on the developmental stage reached by the ego
Children in this group are occasionally overexcited and stimulated
by the parents. This creates states of inner tension to a degree that
the primitive ego cannot cope with or bind. Something similar may
happen if the child has been exposed to overexciting or frightening
experiences during the day. Furthermore, such experiences may lead
to disturbing dreams. At this early stage the child's ego is frequently
not yet able to distinguish between dreams and reality and may

therefore express fears about going to bed and sleep. Luce and Segal (1966) quote the sympathetic comment of a child psychiatrist concerning this problem: "If you went to sleep one night and found a tiger in your bed, would you want to go back? True, the tiger is not in the bed before sleep, yet the child knows that when he closes his eyes it may return to pounce upon him" (p. 23). Even exciting positive experiences during the day may lead to broken sleep. This happened in one of my children who was then eighteen months old. He woke up from a dream in the middle of the night looking for a horse he had seen in the living room of the house. He was most upset when he did not find the horse. The overexcitement about the horse was a residue of his actual experiences during the day preceding the dream. Naturally with the increase in ego development and the establishment of a clear-cut distinction between dreams and reality this type of developmental disturbance will disappear.

This view is at some variance with that of Mack (1965) who assigns a symbolic and highly conflictive content to the child's "nightmare" in the first half of the second year; such content implies a degree of structuralization and a use of dream work which are more commensurate with a somewhat later stage of development (beginning approximately at eighteen months). As Freud (1901) has shown, a common element in childen's dreams is that they are "simple and undisguised wish-fulfilments" (p. 644). Another characteristic of such dreams is "their connection with daytime life. The wishes which are fulfilled in them are carried over from daytime and as a rule from the day before, and in waking life they have been accompanied by intense emotion. Nothing unimportant or indifferent, or nothing which would strike a child as such, finds its way into the content of their dreams" (p. 645). These comments suggest a more appropriate explanation of dreams occurring from approximately twelve to eighteen months: that they contain either a direct wish fulfillment or an expression of more archaic fears and anxieties which were evoked by relatively commonplace daytime events and which were not adequately assimilated into the child's experience at the time they occurred.

The type of interference with the ease of falling asleep due to increasing ego development, which nevertheless is not yet sufficient to master many of the situations confronting it, is already apparent in some children from the thirteenth month on and increases during the second year. The sleep pattern charts of children at the Hampstead War Nurseries show this clearly. Anna Freud (1966) referred to similar experience in her experimental nursery in Vienna. She noted that before the thirteenth month many children fell asleep spontaneously almost any place they were and needed to be carried to their cots, while afterward the pattern changed and the children tossed and turned in their cots for a long time before going off to sleep. She thought that this change in sleep pattern had to do with ego development.

As Margaret Mahler appositely put it: "precisely the most cherished and relatively farthest advanced partial function of the individual ego may be the one which is most vulnerable and therefore the troublemaker. To guard the integrity of functions in the organs which execute them, the child is reluctant to go to sleep, or awakens" (see Friend, 1956, p. 519).

Some children in this age group (second year) resort to obsessionallike arrangements before going to sleep. These "rituals" are the result of specific interactions between ego and drives and are especially pronounced when the move into the anal-sadistic stage coincides with advanced ego development and a tendency to internalize early toilet-training demands. These obsessionallike arrangements are an expression of the anal-sadistic conflicts and the defense activity directed against them, as well as the child's strong ambivalent feelings toward the objects that interfere with his anal pleasures. Some of these children fight falling asleep or wake up from sleep because of the fear of not having control over their sphincters. As Selma Fraiberg (1950) stated, "The conflicts of the anal period play an important role in symptoms of sleep disturbances. . . . When pleasure in soiling must be relinquished for fear of loss of the mother's love the conflicting tendencies may produce another type of anxiety dream which results in interruption of sleep. Here the fear of soiling in sleep breaks through. In two such cases [described in the paper] it was seen that the wish to soil was manifest in the dream . . . but fear of loss of the mother exerted a more potent influence at the critical moment, so that the wish-fulfilling function of the dream failed and anxiety broke through, resulting in the interruption of sleep" (p. 308).

Anxiety over loss of sphincter control and the fear of gratifying forbidden instinctual wishes need not be expressed through dreams. For example, the following account of a child, C. A., who attended our Mother-Toddler Group and Nursery School contains material which encompasses both the child's fear of loss of control (early superego concern) and her anxiety over separation from mother and loss of mother's love (which was expressed in attempts to keep mother up during the night).

When C. was fourteen months old, her mother returned to work and C. was looked after during the day by an *au pair* girl. "C.'s toilet training entailed tremendous struggles. When she was two years old and completely untrained, the grandmother and the helper tried to train her, expressing their disgust at C.'s inability to conform. C. described motions as 'gusting' but resisted the pot for seven months. During the latter part of this period she would withhold her stools for several days. At two and a half years C. attempted bladder and bowel control during the day. Three months later she demanded to be put to bed without her nappies. When this was granted, she developed a sleep disturbance and demanded her mother's attention for hours. When C. was left alone she busied herself with washing the floor in the bathroom and the bedroom, running back and forth to the bathroom to get the pot and empty it. She became very preoccupied with scissors and cut her doll's hair, her pretty hair ribbons, and her clothes, and expressed her usual wish to be a boy while fighting with her elder brother. When she gave up withholding her motions, she started spitting fights with her brother instead." C. thus appeared to react aggressively to her mother's absence and the imposed toilet training. As she relinquished the symptom of withholding her motions, she expressed sequentially the conflict over her penis envy and over her competitive relationship with her brother.

Another relevant case was described by Berta Bornstein (1931). This child's extreme fear of lying down was understood as fear of falling asleep and dreaming, which was determined by fear of loss of sphincter control and of soiling the bed while asleep. Similarly, in a mother guidance case seen over several months at the Hampstead Clinic, a three-year-old boy would call out for his mother several times during the night saying he wished to urinate. When his mother came to him, he appeared tense and anxious, but usually passed only a few drops of urine. When the mother was encouraged to take a more lenient attitude to the occasional wet bed, the boy became less anxious, the calling out diminished, and his sleep improved.

It should be noted that such obsessionallike reactions as described above can also be observed in a different group of children, who are characterized by slow ego development. In spite of the external similarities, the obsessionallike reactions of these children are the result of primitive ego anxieties which lead to a need for uniformity, for exact repetition of every step in the sleep arrangements. These rituals are related to the ego's primitive fear of change and of the unknown. In a minority of cases they are the first signs of what will later prove to be an atypical ego. In still others they indicate a special type of imbalance between the levels of ego development and object relations, and more specifically a different quality of the object relationships. At the beginning of the toddler stage normal children can and do take on trust a great deal from their objects. On the basis of this relation most of the normal ego fears of this phase are automatically alleviated and controlled by the mere presence or reassurance of the object. The primitive ego fears of the other children, however, are not reduced by such reassurances because this automatic trust is lacking and as a result they have a very disturbed presleep period.

In the sleep disturbances described so far I have stressed their developmental background. That is to say, most of them are manifestations of developmental interference rather than the result of conflicts of a neurotic nature. An exception are those disturbances which are due to early internalization of parental demands, for example, with regard to toilet training.

In still another group of cases, the so-called disturbed sleep of children between the first and the second year of life started, for example, when the family returned from a holiday during which the child was allowed to sleep with his mother or parents. On his return the child, naturally enough, refuses to sleep in his own bed. Here again there are no neurotic reasons for the difficulty, the child is only trying to cling to the gratification afforded by sleeping with the parents in terms of skin erotism, warmth, security, etc., gratifications which are in no way conflictive to him at this point in his development. A significant number of so-called sleep disturbances of this period belong in this group.

According to Hirschberg (1957), the parental anxieties about the one- to three-year-old "are concerned with the separation and loss meanings involved in the sleep disturbance, and the aggressive attack implied, and are associated with problems in the parent-child relationships" (p. 138). The records of the Hampstead Clinic show that many factors which precipitated sleep disturbances during the first year of life—the mother's tension, depression, ambivalence; unsatisfactory marital relationships—continue to be a significant influence during the second year, while many others now become operative, e.g., the birth of siblings, hospitalizations of mother or child, the father's absence, etc.

The above considerations indicate that the normal physiological process of sleep begins to be interfered with as the development of the mind gains momentum and is increasingly influenced by mental activities and conflicts. Sleep, furthermore, now takes on a diversity of psychological meanings. All these psychological factors can interfere with the physiological process as effectively as—at times more effectively than—the purely physical disturbances of the body.

Analyses of children under five at the Hampstead Clinic have clearly demonstrated that sleep, at first merely vulnerable in infancy, assumes the specific coloring of each successive libidinal phase and can gradually become a major area of neurotic conflict. In many of the children who began analysis at ages of two and a half to three years, the sleep disturbances began either in the first or early in the second year of life, continued into the anal and phallic phases. They were overdetermined and were an expression of the phase-specific libidinal and aggressive impulses and anxieties.

SLEEP DISTURBANCES IN THE THREE- TO FIVE-YEAR-OLD

Children in this age group are confronted with the phallic-oedipal conflicts and have to deal with the resultant infantile neurosis. Melitta Sperling (1955) remarked that "The occurrence of mild and transient sleep disturbances during the oedipal phase can be considered a typical feature of childhood in our culture. The severer disturbances of this phase, however, especially the acute exacerbations leading to persisting sleeplessness, are pathologic phenomena indicative of serious emotional disorder" (p. 359). This statement has been amply borne out by the children who have been referred to the Hampstead Clinic: it is quite rare to find a child in this age group who is not experiencing some difficulty over sleep, whether it be tardiness in falling asleep, night waking, anxiety dreams, projective fears of ghosts and wild animals, inability to sleep alone, desire to share the parental bed, sleep phobia, ritual behavior at bedtime, etc. In our experience, however, such sleep difficulties frequently do not represent the central core of the neurotic conflict and are offshoots of the symptom formation proper.

Anna Maenchen (see Friend, 1956) expressed the opinion that the sleep disturbances in the oedipal and postoedipal stages of development are essentially the same as those of adults, a point of view with which I agree.

In the majority of children aged one to three years, and particularly in those under two and a half years, a disturbance of sleep can most usefully be viewed as a developmental disturbance which either will show spontaneous remission or will improve with more appropriate environmental handling. To some extent this statement is still true with regard to children aged three to five. Perusal of our Clinic treatment records discloses, however, that a *consistent* disturbance of sleep is to be understood as a symptom (frequently one of several) resulting from internalized neurotic conflicts and that this symptom cannot be dealt with solely by manipulation of the environment. A more fundamental change in the child's functioning will be effected only by analytic treatment.

Even in this age group, however, there are some "disturbances" which still appear to be based largely on the maternal handling of the child. For example, I have at present a girl, J.H., in analytic treatment who was referred at the age of two and a half because of stammering and a lavatory phobia. Mrs. H., in her interviews with me, continued to express concern about the child's wakefulness at bedtime and about her screaming and insistent demands to join her parents downstairs. Whenever we discuss this situation, it becomes quite apparent, both to mother and therapist, that the child's difficulty in remaining in her bed is intimately connected with the mother's inability to be firm with J. as well as with the mother's underlying wish to have J. present downstairs with her husband and herself. It should not, of course, be overlooked that the mother's handling in this regard coincides with the girl's own desire to participate in the parents' activities and with J.'s oedipal wishes to separate the parents.

I have previously referred to children who showed an early vulnerability of sleep which assumed neurotic proportions when they moved into the anal and phallic phases of libidinal development. The analytic material of all these children was indexed (Sandler, 1962), and the statements listed on some of the index cards are particularly relevant to this study. The following example clearly demonstrates that a sleeping disturbance can be an admixture of the child's own anxiety and neurotic conflict and be determined by inadequate parental handling.

A. Z. began treatment at the age of two and a half. I quote from material indexed eight months later. "The referral letter described A.'s symptom simply as difficulty in sleeping. This was amplified by the mother as meaning that he would not go to sleep at the proper time and would waken most nights several times. He was usually taken into the parents' bed, where he thrashed about and kept his parents awake. At the beginning of treatment he slept in the same bedroom as the parents. This problem was dealt with in two ways, first, by interpretation of Tony's fear that the mother might go away while he slept, his wish to separate the parents, and his wish to join their exciting intercourse; secondly, by encouraging the mother to provide another bedroom for him and relieving her anxiety about him. He moved into a bedroom of his own and after a few nights of broken sleep, he slept the whole night through from 6.30 P.M. to 6 A.M.—the first time since he was an infant. Thereafter the pattern varied from time to time. Sometimes he slept all night through, sometimes he awoke during the night. When he awoke, however, the sound of either parent's voice was sufficient to allow him to go back to sleep. During the last month or two prior to indexing his sleep has been sound and there appears to be no difficulty now."

Hirschberg (1957) makes the point that "with the three to five year old, the parents are less consciously aware of their attitudes which are involved in the sleep disturbance since these attitudes are related to [their own] Oedipal anxieties, parent-child competitiveness, and aggressive-castrative wishes on the parents' part" (p. 138).

Based on his investigation of forty cases of sleep disturbances studied over a two-year period, Hirschberg maintains that parents tend to view their children's difficulties in terms of specific reality fears rather than as disturbances in drive development and in the children's object relationships to the parents. Our clinical data (both diagnostic and analytic) certainly indicate that parents become increasingly unable to cope with symptoms connected with sleep as the child moves into the phallic phase of libidinal development. Among the factors that may determine the difficulties and induce the parents to seek external psychiatric help are, as Hirschberg postulates: the parents' own unresolved oedipal conflicts and ambivalence to the child; impairment of important areas of ego functioning, particularly cognitive processes which normally show acceleration at this time (in this area one must consider not only the physiological effects of consistent lack of sleep, such as apathy, listlessness, irritability, but also the contamination by neurotic conflict); impairment (frequently sadomasochistic involvement) of the child's relations to his parents and, as a consequence, impairment of his ability to move into the wider world of social relationships.

I have previously stressed that a vulnerability of sleep in infancy can grow into a neurotic conflict and assume the coloring of each phase of libidinal development. While Melitta Sperling (1949) puts the onset of oedipal wishes somewhat earlier than we would be inclined to do, her statement is relevant to our own findings: "Even if toilet training is conducted in an understanding manner, in our culture it represents a frustrating experience to the child who has to give up satisfaction of anal-sadistic impulses and also repress the aggressive impulses which may arise as a reaction to toilet training if it is carried out in a forceful manner. From the ages of two to five, these repressed aggressive impulses are intensified greatly by the addition of repressed sexual impulses of the oedipal phase. Even in the most favorable setting, every child at this age lives through a period of emotional frustration which leads to repression of sexual and aggressive (sadistic) impulses. Under normal circumstances, that is, if repression comes about gradually and not too abruptly, the child is able to pass through this phase without obvious manifestations. If, however, in addition to this, other traumatic experiences are added, particularly sexual overexposure and overstimulation arrival of a sibling (who is favored by the mother), operation, severe masturbation threats, and similar frustrations, the increased aggressive impulses will be reflected, mostly in disturbed sleep" (p. 33).

This adhesiveness of the sleep disturbance symptom is nicely illustrated in the following example of a girl, G. H., who was taken into analytic treatment at the age of two years eight months. The index was prepared two years later. In her case we see clearly the evolution of a sleep disturbance beginning at eleven months which by the time she was three years old contains a complex symptom formation.

On referral, G. H. could never sleep alone, even with sedation, but awoke crying and got into the parents' bed.

This continued into the second year of treatment, with symptom-free intervals from three to four months, and was seen to express her conflicts on various libidinal levels:

1. The wish to possess mother and displace father. This was a bid for mother's protection from father's physically exciting activity.

2. The desire to possess the mother in the negative oedipal phase and to be mother's sexual partner. She played going to sleep, then awakening and jumping onto the therapist's (mother's) lap, while the father was somewhere nearby. For the most part these instances occurred in regression from the positive oedipal wish.

3. The wish to keep the mother safe, after having observed the primal scene in which she conceived the mother as hurt.

4. The wish to separate the parents to prevent their having another baby. This was connected with the fear of being replaced by another baby; and the oedipal wish to be the one to make the baby: "She wants to be the one to make babies."

Interpretations of fears and conflicts gradually led to diminution of the symptom, and by the eighth month she was sleeping alone. Exacerbations arose after G. witnessed sexual intercourse and the anxiety caused by the above conflict continued.

However, the persistence of the symptom was due mainly to the parents' use of the symptom; they acted out their own sexual inadequacies via the child. As soon as they were firm in their demand that the child sleep in her own bed, G. complied and the symptom disappeared.

Another determinant of G.'s difficulty in falling asleep was fear of retaliation for her aggressive impulses. These were expressed on several libidinal levels: against the brother's penis; against either mother or father both in the positive and negative oedipal position. The aggressive impulses dramatically broke through in relation to the therapist as well. G. bit the therapist as a phallic attack expressed in oral terms. She felt ill. After an interpretation of her outside aggressive impulses, she appeared sleepy. She repeatedly forced her eyes open to see whether the therapist was near before she fell asleep.

This symptom completely cleared after an interpretation of the aggressive impulses arising from the oedipal strivings. Another requirement was that mother not collude with this symptom, i.e., that she not invite it in the service of maintaining her masochistic defense. The mother would berate the child because she was so tired and had so much work to do, but she assumed that she would not go to sleep alone. When the mother insisted, the child immediately complied.[15]

In another child, D. B., we see the cumulative and encompassing effect of a sleep disturbance. D. attended the Hampstead Well Baby Clinic from the age of ten weeks. Although the pediatrician recorded that sleep began to be a problem toward the end of his first year, Mrs. B. dates the onset of the real problem just before D.'s second birthday when Mrs. B. was depressed, unhappy in her marriage, and formed an extramarital attachment. By the time he started treatment at the age of three, he refused to sleep alone and involved the whole family in shifts from bed to bed; he was also unable to separate from his mother during the day even for a short period. When he was two and three quarter years old, a sister was born and her birth added to D.'s problems (cf. Melitta Sperling's remarks above) in that she became another rival for mother's attention; the therapist who treated D. considered it likely that the mother's pregnancy, together with her depression and consequent withdrawal at the time, contributed to the consolidation of the boy's sleep disturbance. What follows is a summary of the various meanings of D.'s sleeping disturbance as they were understood in treatment (the index was prepared one year and ten months after therapy began.)

D. was referred because of his refusal to go to sleep at night without his mother's presence, which started in his second year. It sometimes took up to three hours to get him to sleep. If she tried to leave him before he was asleep, he got up and followed her around. He woke again during the night, and could not sleep again unless he was taken into the parents' bed, or one of them came to sleep in his room. Often having got one parent sleeping in his room, he would again get up and go and wake the other, from fear of the consequences of separating the parents. He was anxious and fright-

15 The parents' contribution to G.'s sleep disturbance will be discussed later.

ened when left alone, but would become overexcited when his father or mother was with him.

This disturbance was found in treatment to be overdetermined. It arose originally as a part of his reaction to his mother's emotional and physical absences, which aroused intense hostile and aggressive fantasies, so that D. then needed her presence as a reassurance that she was unharmed. It was intensified when D. began to move into the phallic-oedipal phase, and then represented also an acting out of his wish to separate the parents and control their sexual activities. It was enhanced and prolonged by the seductive atmosphere of the home, where the parents made little attempt to conceal their turbulent marital relationship and their extramarital affairs. Finally, the disturbance was one manifestation of D.'s need to use his parents as external ego supports in controlling his own instinctual impulses.

After two years of intensive treatment D.'s sleep disturbance was resolved.

At the oedipal stage the fear of going to bed or the difficulty in falling asleep may be due to masturbation conflicts. The following extract from an index card of a girl, H. J., who began treatment at the age of five, illustrates this. Toward the end of the first year of her analysis she refused to go to bed because "sleep was dirty." When the therapist linked this with H.'s guilt over masturbation, she replied: "It is even right" and followed this by expressing a wish to see how father goes to sleep and to sleep with him, corrected to: "with mummy and daddy."

At the time of referral the mother reported that H. occasionally woke up screaming. Often H. was able to recall the terrifying dream from which she woke, e.g., that a thief wanted to take something. Her dreams during the course of her analysis mostly reflected her penis envy and her oedipal strivings, libidinal and aggressive.

Disturbing dreams with an oedipal content are of course frequently noted in children of this age group in treatment at the Hampstead Clinic.

Melitta Sperling (1949) thinks that sleep disturbances at this stage may be more frequent among boys than girls because of its relation to castration fear. Our impression is that there are no great differences between boys and girls in this respect.

SLEEPING DISTURBANCES OF THE LATENCY PERIOD

At around five years of age and with the resolution of the phallic-oedipal conflict children begin to move into the latency period. The sleeping disturbances of latency resemble those of the adult, as was the case with the sleep disturbances in the oedipal period. They can be the expression of all sorts of underlying psychopathology and cover the whole range of conflicts to which human nature is exposed.

In the latency period sleep difficulties may manifest themselves for the first time or a previously existing sleep disturbance may disappear or be expressed in a different form. Very frequently at this stage the conflicts around masturbation move into the foreground. They are sometimes associated with unresolved phallic-oedipal conflicts and phallic-oedipal fantasies of the most diverse nature; they are thus frequently found at the basis of a large number of symptoms, rituals, and behavioral manifestations which usually occur during the period immediately preceding sleep. Their performance becomes a necessary and unavoidable precondition of falling asleep. Although other forms of disturbances such as nightmares, somnambulism, and even pavor nocturnus can occur during latency, there is in general a shift of emphasis to the presleep arrangements with a marked diminution of the tendency to go into the parental bedroom and to ask for the company of one of the parents, so typical of the three to five year period. On the other hand, earlier sleep disturbances frequently disappear in the latency period. This is usually due to a combination of several factors, some of which are the result of developmental advances while others are based on cultural patterns and attitudes.

Naturally, many of the sleep disturbances in the preceding phase resulted from the intensity of the phallic-oedipal phase-specific conflicts. And where the sleep disturbance has existed earlier, the phallic-oedipal conflicts usually made a distinct contribution to this disturbance. With the onset of latency and the satisfactory resolution of the phallic-oedipal conflicts, a number of sleep disturbances (as well as other disturbances) tend to disappear. During a normal latency period there is a marked reduction in the activity and intensity of the drives, a situation that frequently changes the internal balance of the personality and the forces involved in conflicts in ways that permit their resolution or at least favor better adaptations. Apart from the fact that there is less pressure from the drives, further ego development takes place. The ego is now in a better position than before to cope more satisfactorily with the drives and reality.

In addition, the ego is now capable of using new and more efficient defense mechanisms.

Similarly, these changes in the drive and ego organization contribute to the important advances in the child's object relationships. Previously the child was almost completely involved with and dependent on the parents. Now he can take a number of steps away from this intense and exclusive tie. He gains some independence, and much of the cathexes previously invested in the parents are now redirected toward the community of peers.

When the child leaves behind the normal and unavoidable stage of his infantile neurosis, we can expect him to leave behind all the symptomatic manifestations that were the direct expression of the conflicts of that phase, including those concerning sleep. In favorable cases, minor disturbances of earlier phases are brought under more satisfactory control. Obviously qualitative and quantitative factors play an important role in the final outcome of these developmental processes.

Unfortunately in a large number of cases, these qualitative and quantitative factors are such that a satisfactory outcome of the infantile neurosis and a reasonably normal latency period are not possible. When this is the case, the sleep disturbances (as well as others) will find their way into latency, adolescence, and adulthood. Naturally, each period makes a specific contribution to the personality and the nature of the conflicts as well as to the variations in the form in which symptoms are expressed.

Another favorable contribution to the possible solution of the sleep disturbances comes from the side of the environment in the form of a cultural attitude. As the child enters the latency period, the parents begin to show some flexibility in their handling of the child's sleeping arrangements. He is usually no longer "put to bed" but is given a certain leeway. This implies that to some degree the child increasingly assumes responsibility about his going to bed. This allows him to establish his own adaptive ceremonials during the presleep period (what Fenichel [1945] calls the "secondary measures"). Anna Freud once remarked that the young child has fewer coping mechanisms allowed to him, not more sleeping disturbances.

The following case taken from the files at the Clinic illustrates the multiplicity of conflicts that can find expression in an extremely disturbed presleep period as well as in the innumerable obsessional rituals and arrangements that were required by this seriously disturbed girl. Because of the severity of the disturbance the behavior observed is a caricature of what in lesser degrees is quite generally present.

J. M., twelve and a half years old when treatment began, had among other symptoms numerous rituals and compulsive actions that she was forced to perform at bedtime before she was able to settle down to sleep. Thus, for example, the window curtains had to be arranged to have a fold in the middle. She had to make sure that the arm of the chair did not touch the table and was separated from it by a space of one inch; the tablecloth had to be placed exactly on the middle of the table; the pillow had to be placed exactly in the middle of the bed; the books had to be arranged in a certain manner; other objects had to be placed in such a way that they would not fall to the floor during the evening making noises that would frighten and waken her. Similarly, two clocks in her room had to be kept at a certain distance from each other so that they would not make too much noise during the night and wake her, a preoccupation that was accompanied by an intense fear that one of the clocks might stop altogether, in which case she felt it would be impossible for her to sleep for weeks.

All these manifestations were the condensed expression at anal and phallic-oedipal levels of her libidinal and aggressive conflicts and were due to the contamination of anal fantasies, intercourse fantasies, primal scene fantasies, aggressive impulses, conflicts around masturbation, penis envy, castration fantasies.

When J. was a baby she constantly fell asleep in the middle of her feedings and had to be tickled or slapped to wake her to continue feeding. The mother stated that J. had no special sleeping disturbance in early infancy. If she woke at that time she would talk to herself for some time without disturbing the parents. At around three years anything new upset her and the special ceremonials began to appear. The routines always had to be followed in exactly the same way. By latency at sleeptime she demanded that the curtains be drawn exactly the same amount, and the parents noticed that she was afraid of new shadows.

During latency many children develop the habit of reading before falling asleep as a defense against engaging in various fantasies (very frequently of an erotic nature) and in order to avoid the impulse to masturbate.

I treated an extreme case of this type where the disturbance grew more severe and continued into adulthood. During the latency period this boy began to read compulsively in bed to avoid engaging in fantasies which usually led to his playing with his penis. In later life he developed the severe obsessional neurosis that brought him to treatment. At this time a large number of obsessional rituals had to be performed before he was ready to go to bed. Once in bed he had to read compulsively the daily newspaper from the first page to the last one, including advertisements and everything else. Usually he fell asleep at some point during the process of reading the newspaper and before he was able to finish reading every bit of it. Consequently the following night he was forced to start reading the newspaper (of the previous day) where he had interrupted it before he could proceed to the paper of the day. There were times when he was several days behind in his reading. This incongruous behavior served the useful purpose of having several old newspapers to read through on those days when the wish to masturbate and the concomitant anxiety were stronger and kept him awake for a longer period of time than was usual. On such occasions he caught up with reading the old newspapers, managed to get exhausted and fell asleep. The specific aim of this compulsive behavior was made patently clear by the fact that on the rare occasions when he succumbed to the temptation to masturbate in bed he had no need to read the newspapers that evening but went straight off to sleep.

The following case of a latency girl, P. C., six and a half years old at the beginning of treatment, shows how a sleeping disturbance that started at one and a half years was used for the expression of phallic-oedipal conflicts during that phase. It further shows how an unsatisfactory resolution of the infantile neurosis perpetuated the symptom into the latency period. P. C. started to wake three to four times every night at the age of eighteen months. She then shouted for her parents to come and rub ointment on her itching skin or went into the parents' bedroom to wake them. In treatment the analyst could interpret the oedipal fantasies behind this behavior; that is, her curiosity about what the parents were doing together in bed as well as her wish to interfere with it; and the sexual gratification she derived from having the parents, especially the father, rub the ointment on her body. The symptom cleared up; P. now had undisturbed nights for the first time in her life.

It should be noted that in this case the interpretation of the oedipal content was sufficient to clear up the symptom, although the sleeping disturbance had been present long before it could have had any phallic-oedipal significance. As we have seen, sleeping disturbances that begin early in life and persist serve different purposes and have different contents and meanings at different times. I believe that in this case and many similar ones the interpretation of the later and more significant layers of content was sufficient (in therapeutic terms) because earlier the "symptom" had no specific psychological content, in terms of a "neurotic conflict" situation, and acquired significant content only during the phallic-oedipal phase. At first the "symptom" appeared in conjunction with the skin complaints and was *retained* because the child's skin erotism was gratified, a gratification that at that particular stage of her development was not necessarily conflictive (as it became later when the phallic-oedipal fantasies were attached to it).

This observation and similar ones make it clear that some of the earlier "sleeping disturbances" are not always due to compromise formations arising from specific neurotic conflict situations but are attributable to factors of a completely different nature. Although in their outward manifestations there are no apparent differences between the earlier and later disturbances, there are very significant metapsychological differences which account for the later vicissitudes of these different "symptoms."[16] We further believe that many of the nonconflictive determinants of the early disturbances disappear as development progresses. If the symptom is nevertheless retained, it is due to the psychological conflicts that may have attached themselves to it in the meantime. For this reason the interpretation of the current psychological conflict rather than the genesis of the symptom is sufficient in therapeutic terms. This is in sharp contrast to those cases in which the disturbance of sleep likewise appears at an early age but is the result of specific "neurotic conflict" situations, for example, the fear of wetting or soiling during sleep when the child has already internalized the wish to be clean and dry. In this type of case interpretation of the phallic-oedipal content alone will usually not suffice to clear the symptom, although it may bring a

16 It is clear that to refer to all these different types of phenomena as a "symptom" is not quite appropriate and has only descriptive meaning.

measure of relief and generally improve the sleep disturbance. Since the phallic-oedipal significance was superimposed on a symptom resulting from conflicts at an earlier level, the symptom cannot be resolved without interpretation of the anal-sadistic impulses and the wish to wet and soil.

Finally, some of the conflicts that appear during the phallic-oedipal stage may find an even more forceful expression during a disturbed latency period. This happens, for example, with regard to conflicts around aggression which at this stage are frequently seen in children who have not resolved their infantile neuroses. These aggressive conflicts lead to massive fear of separation from the mother and can create a particularly difficult situation when the mother has to go out during the evenings, but they are operative even if the mother stays at home. The following example illustrates this situation.

J. R. had suffered from a disturbed sleep since the age of three and a half years. By the time she was nine years of age these difficulties had greatly increased. Her behavior at that time clearly indicated the nature of the underlying conflicts. After she went to bed she felt compelled to come downstairs to kiss her mother and reassure her that she loved her. When the mother had to go out at night, whether alone or with the father, J. showed a great deal of anxiety, asking compulsively, "Will you be all right?" She insisted that her mother wake her up on her return in order to reassure herself that the mother was safely back.

A similar situation exists in those cases in which the child has a sadistic conception of the sexual relationships between the parents that has been reinforced by early primal scene observations and by an unsatisfactory hostile relationship between the parents. In several latency children seen at the Clinic the unconscious fear that the father will harm or kill the mother was the prime motive of their need to sleep in the parents' bed or to separate them during the evening.

GENERAL CONSIDERATIONS

As we have seen, from the second year of life on sleep becomes an increasingly more vulnerable area. When we examined a large number of the files from our Diagnostic Department, we were surprised by the high frequency of references to difficulties around sleep. In some cases the sleep disturbances were present at the time of referral and were one of the reasons for referral; more frequently they had been present in the past or were considered a minor complaint among the more important ones. It is self-evident that "sleeping disturbance" is no more than a descriptive term covering many different types of underlying psychopathology the specific nature of which must be determined in each case.

A no less striking situation exists in the adult if we consider the amount of ritualized behavior that most human beings go through before settling down for sleep. Luce and Segal (1966) state that "however inconspicuous, almost everybody performs some rituals embodying unspoken and perhaps unrecognized feelings, and without these rituals it is hard to sleep. It may be the ceremony of bedtime ablutions, washing, bathing, brushing teeth. It may be the dog's walk, locking the house, turning on night lights—or something more bizarre" (p. 29). They refer to Charles Dickens's habit of rearranging the furniture of hotel bedrooms in which he stayed; he would push the bed around until its head pointed north according to his compass; the rationale behind this peculiar behavior was that he wanted to benefit from certain magnetic currents. Similarly, Winston Churchill during a Big Three conference in 1953 insisted on having twin beds in his room, sleeping part of the night in one bed and the rest in the other. Fenichel (1945) considers impairment of the function of sleep one of the most frequent neurotic manifestations, to be found in almost every neurosis.

There is no doubt that in the process of socialization and civilization we have sacrificed much of what in earlier times may have been the patterns of sleep, assuming that these patterns were then determined largely by the needs of human nature and not as nowadays by social conventions, fashions, and the progress of civilization. Luce and Segal (1966) point out that the neat bedclothing and nightdress of today are recent innovations, while previously the sleeper wound himself into a shroud of linen. They also state that beds came into general use throughout Europe only in the ninth century, while the private bedroom was an innovation of the fifteenth century and is not yet the norm of mankind in general. As they say: "A child who is reluctant to be left alone for sleep, who insists on leaving his door open and having a light, may be showing an impulse for protection and comfort that was more readily satisfied during past eras, and today among the less privileged" (p. 25).

Anna Freud (1966) pointed to the difficulties of studying "need patterns" with regard to sleep because social conventions interfere with them from the beginning of life. On the one hand, the infant is "put to sleep" and in this way patterns are imposed. On the other hand, it is not "natural" for the infant to sleep under the conditions imposed—alone and between cold sheets. The human baby is perhaps the only creature (among mammals) who sleeps alone without any skin contact and natural warmth. Present cultural conditions may disregard important aspects of sleep which more closely approximate "natural" conditions. Anna Freud recalled a patient who, in describing how he went to sleep as a child surrounded by his toy animals, said that he was probably trying to re-create a litter. She further remarked on Aichhorn's description of the sleeping patterns in his home for dissocial boys. The first thing many of these boys did was to rip the sheets off the beds in order to sleep in contact with the rough blankets, which may be an indication of the importance of skin contact.

Anna Freud considered it of special importance to assess the degree to which the disturbances of sleep are due to the handling of the child and how much comes from within the child as the symptomatic expression of specific conflict situations. At one point in life every child wants to stay up but is put to sleep. Conversely, there are many occasions in life when a person may want to sleep but is forced to stay up. The same is true with regard to the time of waking. The young child wakes up early; then the child begins to attend school and with it begin the difficulties in waking. She pointed out that while we have feeding on demand for children, we do not have sleeping on demand.

One cannot help being reminded here of the role played by "transitional objects" (Winnicott, 1953). Our attention has been attracted by a limited number of observations in which the mother lies with the child for a short while as part of the process of putting him to sleep. These children have never shown any interest in or need for a transitional object, but we cannot say whether this is true in all cases or is just a chance observation.

Some of the cases studied at Hampstead have shown that the sleep problem of the child is sometimes the expression of the psychopathology of one or both parents. In such cases the child's symptom belongs in the context of the family disturbance. I have earlier described the case of a little girl, G. H., whose sleep disturbance was multiply determined by inner factors at different developmental stages. Here I want to describe how her "family milieu" helped to create and maintain her symptoms.

Mrs. H. was seen weekly in mother guidance. Shortly thereafter the father was taken into psychoanalytic treatment (under the Hampstead Clinic program of simultaneous analysis). We soon discovered that the older brother, P., also suffered, among other things, from some disturbances of sleep; he frequently woke up during the night and would then roam around the house for long periods of time.[17]

From the analysis of the father we learned that although the marriage was not completely unsatisfactory, he experienced no sexual satisfaction for which he blamed his wife. He described his wife as a very compulsive woman who had to finish a multitude of house cleaning chores before she was able to go to bed. These severe compulsive needs of the wife oscillated, being worse at some times and slightly better at others. As a result she was never in bed before 12 o'clock at night, by which time Mr. H. had been overcome by sleep. He asserted that this situation ruined his sexual life. He would argue with his wife to persuade her to come to bed early and leave some of the completely unnecessary chores for the next day, but she could not do this. Mr. H.'s complaints about the difficulties introduced into their sexual life by his wife's disturbances were certainly true, but these complaints simultaneously served the function of a useful rationalization by means of which he could hide his own inner difficulties. As his analysis progressed, it was found that he was riddled with fantasies of being damaged and of having a small damaged penis. Earlier in his life he had had occasional difficulties with his potency which further strengthened his fears. He felt he was an unsatisfactory sexual partner and that he was incapable of satisfying a woman sexually. Unconsciously, this was the real reason for his wife's avoidance of sexual intercourse with him. Mrs. H. was seen in weekly interviews throughout the period of the child's treatment. From her material it was clear that there was a great deal of reality in Mr. H.'s complaints. Her compulsive behavior had as one of its aims the avoidance of sexual intercourse. She too unconsciously very much welcomed the sleeping disturbances of the children because they made it nearly

17 This child was studied by our Diagnostic Department.

impossible to have a regular sexual life with her husband. As far as the father was concerned, the sleep disturbances of both children and especially that of the little girl, although a conscious motive of complaint (as another source of interference with his marital sexual life), were a most welcome and unconsciously encouraged symptom that helped him to avoid being exposed to what he feared most—his lack of virility. Because of these fears much of his sexuality found an outlet in a number of unconscious fantasies in which he was very potent sexually with women who were small in size (his wife was in fact a very small woman) and with little girls. The discovery of these fantasies in analysis terrified and depressed Mr. H. who had been in the habit of getting into bed with his little girl when, because of her disturbed sleep, she called one or the other parent. At the time of the diagnostic evaluation of G. H. it had already been noted that her father was in the habit of overexciting her at bedtime and that his behavior acted as a seduction and greatly contributed to her inability to fall asleep and to sleep through the night. Furthermore, partly as a result of his homosexual conflicts and partly as a defense against the incestuous wishes for his daughter, Mr. H. was in the habit of getting into bed with his slightly older son completely naked, behavior that must have contributed to the boy's sleeping difficulties as well. A further determinant of the child's sleep disturbances, especially that of the little girl, was the fact that the father had an unconscious need to expose the children to primal scene observations as he himself had been exposed in childhood, events of which he retained a vivid recollection. I have earlier pointed out the repercussions which witnessing the primal scene had in the inner life and fantasies of the little girl. At the beginning of his treatment Mr. H. expressed surprise at the frequency with which the little girl woke up and walked into the parents' room while they were having intercourse. He was for some time completely unaware that this was usually not accidental. He often managed to wake her up by making excessive noise, etc. It was striking that P. frequently roamed about the house while the parents had intercourse, but he never came into the parents' bedroom.

It can be seen that different unconscious needs, fantasies, and conflicts in each of the parents and the conflicts in their relationship to each other have all contributed to the onset and the establishment of the disturbances of sleep in these children. Each parent's psychopathology as well as that existing in their marital relationship required the maintainance of the children's symptoms as significant elements and safety valves for the parents' equilibrium.

It seems probable that disturbances of sleep in children are particularly suitable vehicles for the expression of parental difficulties of a most diverse nature. They add themselves to whatever contributions come from the conflicts of the child himself at the different developmental stages.

In a number of our cases the sleep disturbances of the child have become the battleground on which the parents express the aggression and tension that really belong in the context of their unhappy marital relationship. The child's sleeping difficulties often exacerbate weaknesses that exist in the marital relationship, e.g., when the mother who is usually the most affected by it finds herself faced with a chronic shortness of sleep or when the husband resents having his sleep disturbed or refuses to take his share in coping with the situation. In one case the mother unconsciously favored the maintenance of the symptom in the child because it gave her an opportunity to express hostile feelings to her husband. The hostility had its roots in an unhappy marital situation about which she did not feel able to complain. She could use her husband's refusal to share the burden of coping with the child during the night to express much of her bottled-up resentment. On a conscious level she strongly wished that the child's sleep return to normal both for her own sake and because of her awareness of the increasing deterioration of the relationship with her husband. In this respect it must be taken into consideration that fathers usually escape the unpleasantness of their children's disturbances by being away at work; however, having their sleep interfered with is something they can hardly ignore or escape from.

Since the disturbance in these cases must be considered a "family disturbance," the child therapist is forced to ask himself whether individual treatment can substantially influence the disturbance. If he suspects intense parental involvement in the child's symptom, the only answer to the problem probably is simultaneous analysis. It is feasible, on the other hand, that as the child develops further and gains some independence from the parents, he may find means of disengaging himself from this interaction. The child described by Jenny Waelder-Hall (1935) seems to indicate that this may be possible, at least in those cases where the parental contribution has not been too excessive. Longitudinal and follow-up studies of this type of problem will clarify some of these issues—the dependence on parental psychopathology, the possibility of detachment as the personality grows, etc.—but the fact that most adults require special (though mostly unconscious) arrangements and preparations before going to sleep points in the direction that inevitably significant contributions to the later personality come from multiple areas. This fact also leads back to a point made earlier: by now we may have departed from what at one time were more "natural" conditions of sleep in early infancy to such an extent that hardly anyone really escapes unharmed.

In a number of our cases the child's disturbed sleep (which served an essential function in the parent's psychopathology) disappeared when the mother was able to be firm and to correct her attitudes and expectations of the child with regard to sleep, with the help of the child's therapist, her own treatment, or mother guidance. These observations seem to point to the fact that some sleep disturbances are "service symptoms"—that is, they serve a function in the child's external relations; in spite of their apparent severity, these symptoms are essentially not compromise formations resulting from conflicts in the child. Once the child accepts the imposition of the "service symptoms," however, the latter is utilized for the expression of the different developmental and neurotic conflicts that the child may be dealing with at any given time. It must be noted that there are important metapsychological and prognostic differences between sleep disturbances having a "service function" and those resulting from a compromise formation of internal and internalized conflicts in the child. In the cases in which the symptom has not been suggested, provoked, or somehow superimposed on the child's personality, nothing short of analytic treatment of the child will do away with the disturbance. Anna Freud (1965) pointed to another reason why parents contribute to the maintenance of the child's sleep disturbance: "Parents may also play a part in maintaining a child's disturbance. Some of the . . . sleeping rituals are kept up by the child only in collusion with the mother. Owing to her dreading the child's anxiety attacks as much as the child does himself, the other participates actively in keeping up defenses, precautions, etc., and thereby camouflages the extent of the child's illness" (pp. 47-48).

It is evident that the tolerance of different parents to having their sleep disturbed by the child's difficulties varies greatly, and what constitutes an intolerable upset for some is not even mentioned by others as a problem. This reaction is significant not only for the child's sleep disturbance itself, but also for how it will affect the mother-child relationship in general. An unsettled mother-child relationship may in turn affect other developmental conflicts and other areas of the child's personality. The therapist must therefore abandon whatever concept of "norm" he himself may have with regard to sleeping patterns and assess each problem on its own merits: how much physical and psychic stress is experienced by the child, the mother, and other members of the family; and what is the threshold of tolerance for disturbed sleep in each family unit.

In this paper, I have traced the vicissitudes and different forms of expression that the sleeping disturbances acquire according to the degree of ego development, the level of object relationships, and the different developmental stages and conflicts that the child must go through. I noted that during the latency period, partly because of the increasing liberty given to the child to make his own sleeping arrangements, many of the earlier symptoms disappear or are replaced by special arrangements specific to and characteristic of each individual. This process of adaptation sometimes continues in adolescence and adulthood resulting in a further reduction of the earlier symptomatic manifestations. However, not all persons find these happy solutions; in many instances, early disturbances persist and are still manifest in adulthood. In these cases the nature and intensity of the conflicts do not permit of such adaptive solutions referred to above.

One of my adult patients is a good example of this type of case. The patient began analytic treatment at the age of thirty. He complained of anxiety states, faulty potency, and a large number of conversion and psychosomatic symptoms, for which no physical causes had been found in repeated medical checkups. Although he did not complain of sleep difficulties it soon was apparent that sleep was a disturbed area as well. The patient was a bachelor who lived alone. At bedtime he was haunted by fantasies that somebody was hiding in the dark of his flat ready to attack him. He frequently searched the place to reassure himself that there was nobody in the room, but in spite of the search he remained uneasy and anxious and was in no way reassured. Whenever his anxiety became too intense, he took a sleeping pill. In the treatment there soon appeared other fantasies and behavioral manifestations relating to his sleep difficulties. The nature of his work required him to travel a great deal and to sleep in hotels and quite often to stay at the homes of friends or business associates. On all these occasions, and especially when he was a guest in a family, he had to make a number of elaborate arrangements before settling to sleep. He locked his door and placed chairs and other objects behind it and blocked the different approaches from the door to his bed. This behavior was based on a fantasy that the host had every intention of attacking him during the night. His elaborate arrangements would ensure his waking up (through the noise of falling objects) if anybody entered his room or approached his bed. Curiously enough, in spite of his fear (which he consciously recognized as irrational), once he had finished the arrangements described he would take some sleeping pills. During treatment it became clear that the precautions and symptoms reached a peak when his host had an attractive wife who aroused him sexually.

Two different sets of impulses determined this behavior. The first one was his wish to kill the husband and take possession of the wife. This wish was defended against by means of projection: his host had murderous designs on him. The second group of fantasies concerned his fear of sexually assaulting his host's wife in an extremely sadistic way. To protect both himself and them in case he should do this while asleep, he made certain that if he were to take a step out of bed he would wake up. He had to make sure that he could not possibly leave the room. He believed he had had one or two episodes of somnambulism in his early childhood which further increased his fear of his actions during sleep.

These disturbances of sleep had started in his early infancy and had never completely disappeared. A necessary precondition of his falling asleep as a very small child had been his chewing a special piece of cloth which his mother attached to his blanket and which was renewed every two weeks when the previous one was destroyed. After the birth of his sister when he was four years old he became afraid of the dark, a fear which was intensified when he was ten or eleven. He feared that somebody was about to attack him. He traced this fear of the dark to a memory of the age of five: he woke up once and saw an old woman beside his bed sitting in the dark. He was terrified but turned his back on this figure pretending he was asleep. He believed the old woman might have been his grandmother who was living in the house at the time and with whom he had a special relationship. He always liked her and used to play with her breasts a great deal, which apparently he was allowed to do. The anxiety he experienced then turned out to be the result of a displaced oedipal fantasy (from the parents to the grandparents). His grandmother had come to him in the evening "abandoning" the grandfather, and he feared that the latter would come and attack him for the seduction of his wife (that the wife of his host might come to him during the evening was an ever-present fantasy of his.) Furthermore, while he was in treatment he visited his parents for a short holiday after he had been away from home for several years. To his surprise he had to take the same precautions and had the same irrational fear that his father would come to kill him during the night.

The intensity of the unresolved oedipal conflicts which were reinforced by massive conflicts with his strong aggressive and sadistic impulses, made it impossible for this patient to deal with his early difficulties by simple ritualized arrangements (the "secondary measures" of Fenichel). It is of interest that this patient regularly fell asleep during the sessions whenever his aggressive feelings to the analyst went beyond a certain point.[18] By falling asleep he protected the analyst from his conscious death wishes and possible aggressive attacks; on the other hand, if he were to attack the analyst in his sleep, he could not be held responsible for it.[19]

Similarly, whenever a girl friend spent an evening in his flat he felt greatly distressed and suffered from insomnia motivated by the fear of what he could do to her in his sleep. To ensure that nothing could happen he always took some sleeping tablets.

According to our observations, there are many persons who because of their fear of aggressive impulses, take pills to ensure that they will be immobilized during the night. In this way they assure themselves that they can control the feared impulses during sleep.

Turning to the classification and definition of sleep disturbances, we encounter some difficulties. The developmental approach followed in this paper has a number of advantages, but in some respects it is not sufficient, especially for the study of older children and adults. It should be complemented by a consideration of the specific phase of the sleep process that is affected:

1. Disturbances in the presleep stage, of which many instances were given, the severe obsessional rituals being an extreme example. Sleep phobias should also be considered and the nature of the specific fear must be determined. Is it the state of sleep itself, the room, the bed, nightmares, etc.?

[18] Simmel (1942) also referred to the sleep disturbances arising from important conflicts around aggression.

[19] Davison (1945) remarks, "the anxiety which produces insomnia in one individual [and we may add even in the same individual at different times] may be responsible for somnolence in another because he fears that if awakened he will be incapable of resisting the temptation to carry out his powerful incestuous masturbatory or aggressive wishes in reality" (p. 485).

2. Disturbances in the falling asleep period (see Varendock, 1921).

3. Disturbances of the sleeping period, including:
   (a) certain types of dreams;
   (b) talking during sleep, general restlessness, etc.;
   (c) night waking, which might imply simple waking during the night with quick return to sleep or hours of delay, anxiety, and agitation;
   (d) nightmares;
   (e) night terrors (pavor nocturnus);
   (f) sleep walking;
   (g) some fuguelike states, in which even crimes have been committed.

4. Disturbances of the waking-up period, including early waking, incapacity to wake, and perhaps hypersomnia that may well require a category of its own.

In this respect it is necessary to mention that the generally assumed relationship between dreaming and sleep talking, sleepwalking, enuresis, teeth grinding, etc., has been disproved by recent and conclusive research. As Fisher (1965) points out, these phenomena do not take place during the REM periods (characteristic of the dreaming periods) but they occur mostly during the NREM periods of sleep. Furthermore, it has been demonstrated that mental activity during sleep is not restricted to the dreaming period. A discussion of these aspects and of the effects of sleep deprivation and dream deprivation, as demonstrated by Fisher and Dement (1963) and West et al. (1962), is unfortunately beyond the scope of this paper.[20]

Finally, I briefly want to note the similarities between some actual neuroses in adults and those sleep disturbances in very young children which are due to overstimulation or seduction of the child. In the actual neurosis of adults a sleep disturbance may be a prominent symptom, which has arisen from a state of inner tension built up as the result of insufficient drive discharge (not infrequently of libidinal impulses). In the first case, the inner tension is due to the lack of

[20] For an excellent summary of the research on sleep deprivation and many other aspects of sleep and dreams in general, see Luce, Segal, and McGinty (1965). The relationship between dream research and psychoanalytic theory has been studied by Trosman (1963) and Fisher (1965).

satisfactory outlets either because of unfavorable environmental circumstances or because of other reasons. In the second case, the seduction or overstimulation arouses a degree of excitation for which the child lacks the appropriate channels of discharge due to his limited physical and psychological maturity. Furthermore, he still lacks the ego functions necessary to bind this amount of excitation.

BIBLIOGRAPHY

Bornstein, B. (1931), Phobia in a Two-and-a-half-year-old Child. *Psa. Quart.*, 4:93-119, 1935.

Davison, C. (1945), Psychological and Psychodynamic Aspects of Disturbances in the Sleep Mechanism. *Psa. Quart.*, 14:478-497.

Fenichel, O. (1945), *The Psychoanalytic Theory of Neurosis.* New York: Norton.

Fisher, C. (1965), Psychoanalytic Implications of Recent Research on Sleep and Dreaming. *J. Amer. Psa. Assn.*, 13:197-303.

—— & Dement, W. (1963), Studies on the Psychopathology of Sleep and Dreams. *Amer. J. Psychiat.*, 119:1160.

Fraiberg, S. (1950), On the Sleep Disturbances of Childhood. *This Annual*, 5:285-309.

Freud, A. (1965), *Normality and Pathology in Childhood.* New York: International Universities Press.

—— (1966), Personal communication.

Freud, S. (1901), On Dreams. *Standard Edition*, 5:629-686. London: Hogarth Press, 1953.

Friend, M. R., rep. (1956), Panel on Sleep Disturbances in Children. *J. Amer. Psa. Assn.*, 4:514-525.

Gesell, A. & Ilg, F. L. (1943), *Infant and Child in the Culture of Today.* New York: Harper.

Gifford, S. (1960), Sleep, Time and the Early Ego. *J. Amer. Psa. Assn.*, 8:5-42.

Hirschberg, J. C. (1957), Parental Anxieties Accompanying Sleep Disturbance in Young Children. *Bull. Menninger Clin.*, 21:129-139.

Hoffer, W. (1949), Mouth, Hand and Ego-Integration. *This Annual*, 3/4:49-56.

Irwin, O. C. & Weiss, LaB. A. (1934), The Effect of Darkness on the Activity of Newborn Infants. *Studies in Infant Behavior I. University of Iowa Studies, Study in Child Welfare*, 9:163-175.

Katan, A. (1961), Some Thoughts about the Role of Verbalization in Early Childhood. *This Annual*, 16:184-188.

Kleitman, N. (1939), *Sleep and Wakefulness.* Chicago: University of Chicago Press, 1963.

—— & Englemann, T. G. (1953), Sleep Characteristics of Infants. *J. Appl. Physiol.*, 6:269-282.

Luce, G. G. & Segal, J. (1966), *Sleep.* New York: Coward-McCann.

—— —— & McGinty, D. (1965), *Current Research on Sleep and Dreams.* Public Health Service Publication No. 1389. Washington, D.C.: U.S. Government Printing Office.

Mack, J. (1965), Children's Nightmares. *Int. J. Psa.*, 46:403-428.

Moore, T. & Ucko, L. E. (1957), Night Waking in Early Infancy. *Arch. Dis. Childhd.*, 32:333-342.

Nagera, H. (1963), The Developmental Profile. *This Annual*, 18:511-540.

—— (1966), *Early Childhood Disturbances, the Infantile Neurosis, and the Adulthood Disturbances [The Psychoanalytic Study of the Child, Monogr. 2].* New York: International Universities Press.

Oswald, I. (1966), *Sleep.* London: Penguin Books.

Parmelee, A. H., Wenner, W. H., & Schulz, H. R. (1964), Infant Sleep Patterns from Birth to 16 Weeks of Age. *J. Ped.*, 65:576-582.

Provence, S. & Lipton, R. C. (1962), *Infants in Institutions*. New York: International Universities Press.

Rank, B. & Macnaughton, D. (1950), A Clinical Contribution to Early Ego Development. *This Annual*, 5:53-65.

Ribble, M. A. (1943), *The Rights of Infants*. New York: Columbia University Press.

Sandler, J. (1962), The Hampstead Index as an Instrument of Psycho-Analytic Research. *Int. J. Psa.*, 43:287-291.

Simmel, E. (1942), In: Symposium on Neurotic Disturbances of Sleep. *Yearbook of Psychoanalysis*, 1:194-201. New York: International Universities Press, 1945.

Sperling, M. (1949), Neurotic Sleep Disturbances in Children. *Nerv. Child*, 8:28-46.

—— (1955), Etiology and Treatment of Sleep Disturbances in Children. *Psa. Quart.*, 24:358-368.

Trosman, H. (1963), Dream Research and the Psychoanalytic Theory of Dreams. *Arch. Gen. Psychiat.*, 9:9-18.

Varendock, J. (1921), *The Psychology of Day-Dreams*. London: Allen & Unwin.

Waelder-Hall, J. (1935), The Analysis of a Case of Night Terror. *This Annual*, 2:189-228, 1946.

Walter, W. G. (1953), Electroencephalographic Development of Children: In. *Discussions on Child Development*, ed. J. M. Tanner & B. Inhelder. New York: International Universities Press.

West, L. J., Janszen, H. H., Lester, B. K., & Cornelisoon, F. S., Jr. (1962), The Psychosis of Sleep Deprivation. *Ann. N.Y. Acad. Sci.*, 96:66-70.

Winnicott, D. W. (1953), Transitional Objects and Transitional Phenomena. *Int. J. Psa.*, 34:89-97.

FREUD'S CONTRIBUTION TO LANGUAGE THEORY

LILI E. PELLER†

From the eighteenth century until recently the dominant view of language as presented in textbooks of psychology was that its origin and main function lay in its being an instrument of social control, man's main vehicle of communication. Human language was seen as a further development, a "higher" branch of animal communication but not categorically different from it. Karl Bühler (1934) stressed the fact that a study of the child's acquisition of language will yield the most valuable clues to mankind's acquisition of it.

Recently other views, some old, some new, have come to the fore. Language is seen as a requisite for conceptualized thought (Cassirer, 1944); the structure and vocabulary of specific language types are considered of primary importance in shaping the thinking of an ethnic group (Whorf, 1956); language is regarded as a vocal actualization of man's tendency to see realities symbolically (Sapir, 1933). Communication is one of the basic functions of language.

It is, of course, generally known that the term "symbol" has a specific meaning in psychoanalysis. It refers to the affect-loaded, partly unconscious, *primordial* symbols that are central to our understanding of mental disorders and of creative thought, dreams, parapraxes, jokes, etc. Freud, Ferenczi, Jones, O. Rank, Sachs, Silberer, and others all used it in this way. However, in general usage and in language theory "symbol" has a very broad meaning: a symbol is primarily a conceptual tool. It represents, brings to the mind, something that is a "mere idea" and as such has no other physical properties, or something that transcends the sensory data given here and now.

Presented at the Fall Meeting of the American Psychoanalytic Association, New York, December, 1964.

A superficial study of Freud may leave the impression that he ignored the existence of symbols in that broad sense, i.e., of *cognitive* symbols. Nothing could be further from the truth. Freud's "verbal sign" ("word remnant") obviously has a symbolic function; it is a symbol in the general sense. Many everyday symbols carry an affective charge in addition to their cognitive significance. Many primordial symbols are universally ("naturally") understood. They transcend the understanding of language.

Freud's early study of the functions of consciousness led him to views about language which, to the best of my knowledge, anticipated those of later thinkers. His references are brief, indeed fragmentary, yet they hit upon essentials. They are unknown for a number of reasons, one of them being that they are cast in different terms.

Therefore, I shall briefly comment on Freudian terms and on some key linguistic concepts before I come to my main topic. Many of Freud's propositions departed radically from those generally accepted, yet he hardly ever entered into polemics.[1] Instead he simply avoided terms which implied assumptions he regarded as no longer tenable. For instance, the term "libidinal object" was introduced by him in order to undo the contemporary belief that sexual strivings of necessity attach themselves to a person of appropriate age and opposite sex. A "libidinal object" may very well be such a person, but it can also be somebody of the same sex; it can be oneself, a body part, a thing or—an idea. Furthermore, while a "beloved person" is generally treated in about the same way throughout the relationship, the libidinal object is—during the successive phases of individual development or during life's vicissitudes—experienced and treated in radically different ways.

For the new science of psychoanalysis, Freud sought to avoid such terms as *Geist, Seele* (mind, soul) and instead introduced the neutral "mental apparatus."[2] He shunned expressions like "reasoning" (judging, meditating, cogitating) and spoke simply of "mental acts." The deliberate simplicity of this terminology is obvious. We

[1] Dr. L. Jekels once told me that Freud also advised his disciples not to waste time and energy in polemics.

[2] Here I am at variance with Arlow and Brenner (1964). According to them, "mental apparatus" refers to a particular group of processes, to a part of the contents of the mind, mind being the more inclusive term.

have a muscular appartus carrying out muscular acts, and we have a mental apparatus carrying out mental acts.[3] And of mental acts there are *two* basic types. Again striving for the least pretentious terms, Freud introduced *numerals* to denote them. He spoke of mental acts (functions, processes) which are either on the *primary* or on the *secondary* level. These terms are not content oriented. Not being definitive, they do not hamper further modifications of the concepts. (The irony is that today the terms primary and secondary are far from being simple.) Primary processes are called so for two reasons: they come earlier and they are more primitive (1900). They are governed by affects, while secondary processes also take cognizance of reality.

In linguistics we speak of *signs, signals,* and *symbols.* I shall use "sign" as the umbrella concept, comprising both signals and symbols. In our daily life we seldom wait for the full impact of an event but respond to its signals. To give simple examples: dark clouds signal rain; when a car slows down on the highway, red lights shine up in its tail fins. Here we have one *natural* and one *artificial* (conventional) signal. Both inform us about impending events and tell us how to act, to behave, now or in the very near future. Higher animals, too, respond to a wide variety of signals. A grazing deer sniffs the air or stands motionless to detect the faintest rustle of leaves "signaling" a hunter. Obviously animals may surpass us in the detection of particular signals and in the speed of their motor response. Although animals also respond to artificial signals, the other kind of signs, namely, symbols, are not part of their world, of their *Umwelt* (self-world) in Jakob von Uexküll's sense (1934). A symbol represents something that transcends the physical data given to us *hic et nunc.* It may represent—and thus make manageable (or permit us to make public)—something that has no other sensory qualities. Here I have referred primarily to a symbol in the general sense, to a conceptual symbol.

A symbol in the psychoanalytic sense refers to an image carrying an affect that in the deepest strata belongs to something else. According to Ferenczi (1912): "Only such things (or ideas) are symbols

---

[3] *"Psychischer Apparat"* in German. However, "psychic" carries other connotations in English. The customary "mental" neglects affects. The abbreviation "psy" may be the most appropriate usage. However, in this study I shall use the customary term.

in the sense of psycho-analysis as are invested in consciousness with a logically inexplicable and unfounded affect . . . which . . . they owe . . . to *unconscious* identification with another thing (or idea), to which the surplus of affect really belongs" (p. 277).

Psychoanalytic (or *primordial* symbols, as I propose to call them) and conceptual symbols may be far apart, but they are not categorically different. I have introduced (1962) yet another term, *protosymbol*, to refer to the young child's not differentiating clearly between symbol and symbolized. Many times his interest goes to things which he seemingly confuses with body parts, functions, products, or persons. A transitional object, for instance, is something that stands midway between a protosymbol and a psychoanalytic symbol. The intense affect that the infant directs toward it belongs in its fullness to his mother and to his own body self. Hence, it is typical for the child to lose the transitional object when his relationship to his mother is profoundly shaken.

Freud's comments about language can be found in his earliest and latest writings (1891, 1895, 1900, 1911, 1913, 1915, 1923, 1933, 1939, 1940). In a way, all references to primary and secondary processes deal implicitly with the functions of language. Freud's brief scattered comments on the relationships between thought processes, consciousness, and verbal signs (language) should be culled from his work so that they can be related to one another and to the more recent studies in the field. Hartmann's comment (1956) about the long latency of many Freudian ideas comes to mind. The different terminology partly explains the delay, but another reason is probably more important: Freud's later work assigns to consciousness a position of secondary importance, while his comments on language seem to stress the fact that consciousness plays—via language—a decisive role in shaping mental acts.[4] Yet this supposed contradiction is hardly an actual one. By clarifying the specific functions that consciousness performs, we obviously also deepen our insight into the consequences of its absence. Here are several of Freud's main references to language in their chronological order.

---

[4] Edelheit (1964) states: "I should like to speak of the ego as a vocal-auditory organization—both a generator of vocal utterances (speech) and, reciprocally, a differentiated structure whose features are critically determined by vocal utterances and its derivatives."

In two remarkable passages, Freud outlined, in 1900, the functioning of the mental apparatus in its relation to language:

. . . [this apparatus] is capable in waking life of receiving excitations from two directions. In the first place, it can receive excitations from the periphery of the whole apparatus, the perceptual system; and in addition to this, it can receive excitations of pleasure [*Lust*] and unpleasure [*Unlust*], which prove to be almost the only psychical quality attaching to transpositions of energy in the inside of the apparatus. All other processes in the ψ-systems, including the *Pcs.*, are lacking in any psychical quality and so cannot be objects of consciousness, except in so far as they bring pleasure or unpleasure to perception. We are thus driven to conclude that *these releases of pleasure and unpleasure automatically regulate the course of cathectic processes*. But, in order to make more delicately adjusted performances possible, it later became necessary to make the course of ideas less dependent upon the presence or absence of unpleasure. For this purpose the *Pcs.* system needed to have qualities of its own which could attract consciousness; and it seems highly probable that it obtained them by linking the preconscious processes with the mnemic system of linguistic symbols, a system which was not without quality. By means of the qualities of that system, consciousness, which had hitherto been a sense organ for perceptions alone, also became a sense organ for a portion of our thought-processes. Now, therefore, there are, as it were, *two* sensory surfaces, one directed towards perception and the other towards the preconscious thought-processes [p. 574].

The new surface (the new organ of perception) has a highly specific function: it registers those thought processes that are coupled with verbal signs.

The second passage deals with the same facts, but the emphasis and the metaphors are altered. Freud speaks of the creation of a new series of qualities or attributes leading to "a new process of regulation which constitutes the superiority of men over animals" (p. 617). He states the reasons why this new series of qualities arose. On the one hand, mental functions as such have no sensory properties (i.e., they cannot be heard, seen, or touched); on the other hand, affects accompanying thought must be kept within narrow limits lest they disturb its course. How, then, can mental processes reach consciousness? He answers: by becoming linked with word memories, with verbal signs.[5]

I have some comments on these passages. To state in 1900 that human beings had something that animals did not possess, not even to a lesser degree, must have taken considerable courage. This was, after all, the century in which the concept of discontinuity between man and beast had been most forcibly and spectacularly challenged.

The problem of the *origin* of language has long been an arena for speculation. Freud might have felt that the tools for tackling this problem of human evolution were not yet at hand, or that its solution was not mandatory at this juncture, and thus he went straight to the *function* which language serves, bridging the gap in our knowledge with a bluntly teleological phrase: "it later became necessary" (p. 574).

He returned to problems of thinking and language in 1911. The explanatory concept of fluid and bound cathexis was amplified and thinking was defined as a kind of trial action, requiring expenditure of less energy than would actions of our striated muscles. He also expanded his earlier idea: those mental processes that deal not with mere pictorial representations (memory images) of sensory data, ikons in today's terminology, but with *relations* between them were originally unconscious. Only by becoming linked with verbal signs did they obtain qualities which then could reach consciousness.

Once again I recommend comparing my version with a verbatim translation of the same paragraph. To describe the process of thinking as a kind of trial action is in line with Freud's endeavor to use the least pretentious terms and similes. Moreover, this simile is very fruitful. Not only does a trial action require less energy; it is characteristic that everything that occurs in a trial action can be reversed, undone.[6] That an action executed merely in "thought" is not final can of course also be a tremendous danger. For creatures living in the midst of constant emergencies, it would be more often than not a severe, potentially fatal drawback. Those who are not surrounded

---

[5] My summary of these and subsequent statements is considerably simplified and the original text should be consulted.

[6] A similar thought has been expressed by Craik (1952): "If the organism carries a 'small-scale model' of external reality and of its own possible actions in its head, it is able to try out various alternatives, conclude with the best of them, react to future situations before they arise" (p. 61).

by predators, however, become free to explore a wider range of possibilities. They can—without anxiety—try many more combinations: whatever has been "done" in thought can be undone. In this and in some other respects I consider play to be the prestage or matrix of thought. In play, too, almost every move can be reversed.

In "The Unconscious" (1915), Freud discussed the functions of language more extensively than in any of his earlier or later studies. He examines the peculiarities of schizophrenic language and thought and amplifies what he said earlier about primary and secondary processes. Nonanalytic psychology distinguishes between the simple and rather concrete thought processes of animals and the "higher" mental acts of man, and some writers have seen in Freud's distinction between primary and secondary processes a parallel to these two forms of thought. This view I cannot share. Both processes as characterized in psychoanalysis are quite distant from the mental processes of animals; both rely on symbols, although on different kinds of symbols: the role of primordial symbols for primary processes is similar to the role of conceptual symbols for secondary processes.

In the same study Freud introduces another topic: the conscious representation of an object can be regarded as consisting of the representation of a thing (*Sachvorstellung*) to which has been added the representation of the word. It is the joining of these two—thing and word—that creates the representation of the object. In short: thing representation plus word representation equals object presentation. This may seem to be a novel and difficult idea, but only because we often use "thing" and "object" as synonyms, which they are not. Actually, it is a restatement of Freud's earlier views: a mental function which carries no affect can reach our awareness only by becoming linked with a verbal sign. This addition of a verbal sign constitutes a hypercathexis: "It is these hypercathexes, we may suppose, that bring about a higher psychical organization and make it possible for the primary process to be succeeded by the secondary process . . ." (p. 202).

In 1900, Freud had differentiated between the act of mentally *representing* something (*vorstellen*) and the act of *relating* such representations. Now he indicates the importance of relations:[7] they

---

[7] "Relations" refer to any and all connections, functions between representations of things; relations establish facts, abstractions, groupings, generalizations.

and not the images of sensory data constitute the decisive part of our thought processes.[8]

He returned to this topic in 1923. In addition to verbal signs, indeed, prior to them, there exist visual memory traces which can be linked by thought processes. Some people seem to have a preference for them. Yet, by and large, such images can bring to consciousness only the sensory *materials* of thought, not the relations between them. Visual or other sensory expressions for relations do not exist. Thus thinking in images produces at best a very incomplete awareness. It remains closer to unconscious processes than does thinking in verbal signs. No doubt, it is both ontogenetically and phylogenetically older.[9]

Freud then deals with the question: how can something be remembered? How can it once again become conscious? This is his reply: "it dawns upon us like a new discovery that only something which has once been a *Cs.* perception can become conscious, and that anything arising from within (apart from feelings) that seeks to become conscious must try to transform itself into external perceptions: this becomes possible by means of memory-traces" (p. 20).

No doubt, experiences of the preverbal phase exert a far-reaching influence upon our character, and actual experience in analysis shows that the earliest preverbal memories tend to reappear in dreams, symptoms, moods, and affects, but seldom and only with great difficulty can they be cast into verbal form. They remain forever shadowlike, unconvincing. Of course, events that occurred in the child's preverbal phase may have been later recounted to him by a parent or a relative and the child may confuse the memory of the anecdote he was told with the actual experience. We also need to remember that the verbal phase starts with the understanding of language, not with its use. Between the two there may be quite a time gap.

[8] "But most of our interests center upon events, rather than upon things in static spatial relations. Causal connections, activities, time, and change are what we want most of all to conceive and communicate. And to this end pictures are poorly suited. We resort, therefore, to the more powerful, supple, and adaptable symbolism of language. . . . The trick of naming relations instead of illustrating them gives language a tremendous scope; one word can thus take care of a situation that would require a whole sheet of drawings to depict it." This quotation is from S. Langer (1942, pp. 71-72), on whose clear distinctions I have drawn to a large extent.

[9] Of course, some formal relations can be crudely indicated by images (this happens in dreams), and motor activities can be pantomimed.

Freud's statement (1923) may refer to the complete and distinct clarity with which verbal signs endow our experience. In the foregoing studies he had based the need for verbal signs upon two different factors. Verbal signs are introduced in order (a) to *replace* affects, or (b) to bestow sensory attributes upon thought *relations*, thereby enabling them to reach consciousness. And later, he added that relations—not imagery of *any* kind—are the characteristic of thinking.

However, Freud not only elaborated his earlier views and added to them, he also revised one point. In 1915, Freud had declared verbal signs to be indispensable for thinking on the secondary level, but in his last work (1940) he modified his earlier view: "It would not be correct, however, to think that connection with the mnemic residues of speech is a necessary precondition of the preconscious state. On the contrary, that state is independent of a connection with them, though the presence of that connection makes it safe to infer the preconscious nature of a process" (p. 162).

This revision cuts deep.[10] Verbal signs remain a reliable indication that a process takes place on the secondary level, but they are no longer regarded as indispensable. The formation of an idea and putting this idea into inner language are not *one* but *two* distinct processes. We may assume that secondary processes have a widely varying admixture of verbal signs, which may be faint or distinct, auditory, visual, or kinesthetic. In Freud's formulation: "The preconscious state, characterized on the one hand by having access to consciousness and on the other hand by its connection with the speech-residues, is nevertheless something peculiar, the nature of which is *not exhausted by these two characteristics*" (p. 162; my italics). But if the presence of verbal signs is not mandatory, we are left with the question: what *is* the essential feature of thought processes on the secondary level? Freud stated the question but left it unanswered. In his writings Freud discussed primary processes extensively, but he referred only occasionally to processes on the secondary level. Would it nevertheless be possible to pinpoint *the*

[10] Without it we might find ourselves thrown back to a position resembling the theories of J. S. Mill who postulated an identity between correct thought and correct language. Students of psychoanalysis and language conceptualize the relations between language and thought in different ways. Balkányi (1964) distinguishes verbalization—putting something into inner language—from the process of speech.

essential features of secondary processes by first enumerating the characteristics of primary processes and then stating their direct opposite? While such a procedure may not necessarily yield correct results, it is worth attempting.

In the *New Introductory Lectures* (1933), Freud tells us quite forcefully that primary mental acts lack the framework of time and space which philosophers regard as the essential prerequisite for all thought. That the dimension of time has no validity for the processes in the unconscious had been stated by him repeatedly before. In 1900 and again in 1915 he had pointed out that primary acts are basically isolated from one another. They enjoy a high degree of mutual independence. It is this isolation that results, among other things, in the fact—so bizarre to our conscious thinking—that incompatible opposites may stand side by side without disturbing each other. In still other contexts, we are told that for primary processes external reality is nonexistent; they know only inner reality. In a footnote added to "The Unconscious" Strachey states: "Mentions of the 'timelessness' of the unconscious will be found scattered throughout Freud's writings" (p. 187).

By the direct and complete reversal of these findings, we arrive at the following characteristic of *secondary* mental processes: they take place in a *framework of time and space*—and, we may add—of *causality*. They follow the laws of grammar, syntax, and logic. Secondary mental processes relate to external reality. Secondary mental acts are *coherent*. And here we realize that we are back on very familiar ground: the ego's synthetic or organizing function reigns for secondary processes (Nunberg, 1930).

By this indirect procedure, we may, after all, have struck upon the distinctive feature of secondary mental acts: they occur within a stable multiple framework *the conception of which is predicated upon language*. It is for this reason that they can be so easily cast into verbal signs. And verbal signs, i.e., words, enable us to make mental acts public, to project them into the future or to retrace them step by step, to compare them with physical reality and with the thoughts of others, to distinguish the possible from the actual.[11]

---

[11] "The psychic concatenation, or the establishing of the unity of context, is due to the synthetic function of the ego; we are thus faced with a general principle that may well deserve to be re-emphasized" (Kris, 1950, p. 308).

When Freud first mentions verbal signs he refers primarily to the fact that they endow mental processes with attributes, i.e., sensory attributes which render them "perceivable." This is similar to the way in which a thyroid metastasis becomes perceptible to the Geiger counter: i.e., by becoming linked with a *substance* that registers with the electronic device. Or, in order to study certain features of the blood circulation, we inject methylene blue into the arteries of a rabbit. In either case the added substance does not change the process we are observing; it merely temporarily links this process with something that can register with our senses. But verbal signs have a different function: they change the basic character of mental acts. Or more correctly: the addition of verbal signs is indicative of a basic change. Freud's later formulation (1915) makes this quite clear: "becoming conscious is no mere act of perception, but is probably also a *hypercathexis,* a further advance in the psychical organization" (p. 194).[12]

A person's mental acts can take place on the secondary level only insofar as he recognizes and accepts the framework of *time, space,* and *causality.* The laws of ordered (disciplined) thinking are predicated upon this framework. These laws in turn can be conceived and integrated only by someone who has developed the "second surface of perception." In sum: for conceptual thought verbal signs must be *available* to the mental apparatus. By no means do they have to accompany each step of a mental act. Words are not tags added to precreated images; they may serve as labels, but that is not their principal function.

Freud commented on the role of language only in relation to our thought processes; he did not deal with communication. However, in today's discussion this essential function of language cannot be left out. Animals living in groups communicate with one another effectively, with the help of signals, employing various sense modalities—hearing, sight, smell, and touch. Some even have coded signals —that is, signals with a standardized meaning (see, e.g., the studies

---

[12] "Freud found that in the transition from the unconscious to the preconcious state, a cathexis of verbal presentations is added to the thing-cathexis . . . [and later] the fixing of verbal symbols is in the development of the child linked with concept formation and represents one main road toward objectivation" (Hartmann, 1951, pp. 149-150).

on communication among bees and ants by von Frisch [1927] and Schneirla [1946]).

Human beings also communicate with one another by means outside the realm of symbolic language. Just what comes under the heading "communication"? Spitz (1957) tells us: "We will call communication any perceivable change of behavior, be it intentional or not, directed or not, with the help of which one or several persons can influence the perception, the feelings, the emotions, the thoughts or the actions of one or several persons, be that influence intended or not" (p. 3).

In the worthy attempt to avoid a narrow definition (i.e., "communication equals language"), Spitz seems to have gone too far. I consider it communication when the mood, affect, or thought of one person reaches another person, influencing his thought or affect. A communication may be conscious or not, addressed (directed) or not, current (face to face) or recorded (mediated over spatial or temporal distance).[13]

The foremost means of direct communication are speech, facial and body expression, gesture, pantomime. Vocalization of any kind and tactual contacts can also serve communication. Recorded (i.e., mediated) communication can use various sensory modalities. Usually there is a *sender* and a *receiver*. However, a broad definition should also include those marginal instances in which there is only a sender or only a receiver; e.g., the recording of a thought without making it public (making it potentially public) or the erroneous assumption that the behavior of another person expresses an affect or thought. There is only a sender in the former case, while there is only a receiver in the latter. In addition, there is self-communication, the case in which sender and receiver are one and the same person.

Spitz's definition does not cover all these instances, but it includes other interactions which I do not consider communication. Another person's action, his "perceivable change of behavior" may influence my behavior in a mechanical way, i.e., without conveying any affect or thought of his. For instance, in a crowd somebody

13 "Communication is a complex phenomenon that appears in different forms wherever there is social structure whether in human or animal society. In human beings communication is supplemented by language and speech and becomes the more subtle and delicate an instrument" (Beres, 1957, p. 421).

pushes me and I am perfectly aware that he did not do it deliberately and is unaware of it. In this case his behavior does influence my actions, and it may indeed cause strong feelings—yet he did not communicate with me. Spitz's definition minimizes the human element. The defunct author of a book, or of an orally transmitted song or riddle, or of a sculpture or a painting, still communicates with us. Indeed, human existence is unthinkable without this kind of communication.[14]

A disturbed mother may take care of her baby in a competent way —she goes through the processes of feeding, cleaning, dressing— without any attempt to communicate with the infant. There is plenty of "perceivable changes of behavior" on her part; yet there is no communication. Spitz himself has contributed excellent studies of this phenomenon and its dire consequences. Direct communication relies mostly "on changes of behavior"; yet these are not indispensable, while the knowledge that "the other" has feeling and thought is. The patient who remains silent for a few minutes communicates something else to us than when he prolongs the silence for a longer time, and the same is, of course, true for the person who stares at us for a short time or a long period. The *absence* of a change of behavior can indeed be communicative.

Loewenstein (1956) says about unconscious communication: "Certainly we do not underestimate the importance of the immediate understanding of the unconscious between two people, of the intuitive grasping of non-verbal forms of emotional expressions" (p. 466).

One more point: there is little doubt that for most of us communication with others is needed not only for social give and take, but to preserve the integrity of secondary-process thinking. Recent studies on sensory deprivation have shown that hallucination takes over when there is no sensory input (Heron et al., 1953; Lilly, 1961). It is safe to assume that even with sensory input but without com-

[14] As a definition of "social interaction" the statement by Spitz may be more acceptable. The *Columbia Encyclopedia* (1950) gives this definition of communication: "the transfer of thoughts and messages, as contrasted with transportation, the transfer of goods and persons. The basic forms of communication are by signs (sight) and by sounds (hearing). The reduction of communication to writing was a fundamental step in the evolution of society for, besides being useful in situations where speech is not possible, it permits the preservation of communication, or records, from the past."

munication with anyone, secondary processes are likely to deteriorate. Restriction of self-communication (no pen and paper) will accelerate the decay. Defoe's Robinson Crusoe starts a diary before he takes care of other urgent needs.

Today the conceptual organization of experience is considered to be the primary function of language. Freud's views on language were in sharp contrast to those dominant in his own time; that may explain why they were ignored. Today they are unknown partly on account of the terms he used. This is a loss because his hypotheses about primordial symbols and instinctual drives, about conscious-ness and language are relevant to modern linguistics. The ability to use conceptual symbols is preceded by and can scarcely be seen as in-dependent of the propensity to understand symbols and to form them in the psychoanalytic sense (primordial symbols). The acquisition of language activates the child's latent ability to bestow conceptual order on his experience. This development changes the child's whole existence; it is by no means restricted to his intellectual growth. Anna Freud (1936) has expressed this forcefully and lucidly: "We recall that in psychoanalytic metapsychology, the association of affects and drive processes with verbal signs is stated to be the first and most important step in the direction of the mastery of instinctual drives. . . . The attempt to take hold of the drive processes by link-ing them with verbal signs which can be dealt with in consciousness is one of the most general, earliest and most necessary accomplish-ments of the human ego. We regard it as an indispensable component of the ego, not as one among its activities" (p. 178; my translation).

In other words, the ego does not gradually learn to use symbolic language; symbolic language is one of its constituents. In a recent study A. Katan (1961) indicated that emotionally disturbed children whose ability to express their feelings was severely limited could be helped by fostering this ability.

An animal has instincts and can be taught to restrain them by a system of reward and punishments. These may be either gross or subtle; in any case, they are external agents. A human being is not only differently endowed; he also goes through phases that are radi-cally different from the phases of animal development. Rewards and punishments play their part, but they are not the *essential agents of the child's changes*. It is the acquisition of symbolic language that makes possible the metamorphosis of the manifestations of drives and the burgeoning of human mental life. Language brings a tremendous enrichment to all inner life, to the affects we experience as well as to our thought processes. The acquisition of language is in turn predicated upon earlier emotional developments. All cognitive growth is based upon earlier steps in the sphere of affects. The following points may have been expressed before; however, for me, they represent new facets, arrived at by combining recent findings about language with those indicated by Freud. Academic psychology stresses how much language widens our knowledge of the external world. Now we add that language deepens greatly our awareness and knowledge of our inner world and that the two developments are interdependent. The tool of language enables us to take a position of distance from our own physical and mental acts. Of course, the clarity of self-awareness differs greatly for different people and for the same person at different times. Language gives us both a distance from and a new intimacy with our own selves. Because language permits us to make mental processes public it also enables us to keep them private. And the defense mechanism of repression is predicated upon language.

Language enables us to "step out of our skin," to see ourselves as it were from the outside. Thus it is language that makes it possible for us to put ourselves into somebody else's place. The infant comes to differentiate between self and nonself in a gradual way. With the acquisition of language this distinction becomes far more clear-cut. This view in turn implies that there are strata of the personality for which this distinction is not valid.

Once the child has entered the language world, his store of information about the world around him grows by leaps and bounds —not because the acuity of his sensory organs or his memory span increases so much but because language makes possible the conceptual organization of what he sees and hears.

Freud stressed that initially we tend to *deny the existence* of something we do not like. Later we become able to conceive of its existence, even though it gives us displeasure. There are other somewhat similar developments. The young child acts as if things that he cannot perceive at the moment, upon which he cannot act with his sensory or motor apparatus, have *ceased to exist* (Piaget, 1957).

By developing an attitude of trust in his mother and by practical experience the child gradually learns that something that is absent or hidden *can* return. He begins to live in a world where there is *object constancy* (Hartmann, 1952). This decisive step in the child's object relations and in his cognitive growth is predicated upon antecedent emotional development. But it is language that makes this step far more reliable and distinct: if something is not here now, we may nevertheless be in a position to know—through the coordinate system of verbal signs—how far away in space and time it is. We may even establish if, how, and when it will be here again. In Freud's terminology: the mental representation of a sensory datum —the thing representation—now has the hypercathexis of the word representation.[15]

The developments which issue in early object constancy do not depend upon language. On the other hand—and this is my proposition—the oedipal situation is unattainable without language. The genital arousal, the awakening of possessiveness, of jealousy and hostility, are, of course, not language bound; but the oedipal fantasies and ambitions, the broad spectrum of oedipal wishes are.

Gradually we come to realize how decisively language influences the expression of drives and is influenced by them. One more comment: language appears as the most distinctive human achievement. Yet this does not imply that the gulf between the preverbal human infant and the offspring of the other primates is smaller than the gulf between the human adult and the adults of the other primates (Peller, 1962).

According to Kris (1950), formulations in terms which permit differentiations in degrees, in shading, are preferable to formulations in terms of extremes. Yet in presenting the functioning of the mental apparatus the concept of two types of mental activities seems indispensable. It is a theoretical rather than a practical distinction because both types take part in most mental activities. Even in dreams and in the manifestations of neurosis secondary processes are not absent. Moreover, the decision which type an act belongs to is at times very difficult.

15 "Indeed, the use of language permits human beings to give actuality even to events that are remote in time and space, and yet to distinguish them from those which exist here and now" (Loewenstein, 1956, p. 466).

Freud's insight into the functions of language came in these steps: first he realized that language, "verbal signs," endowed mental acts with qualities that made it possible to perceive them, to make them public and manipulate them. Later he postulated that language had a far greater scope—it made possible, indeed, it brought into being "a higher psychic organization" which from then on could partly replace the earlier organization. Finally, he postulated that this did not imply the linkage of every mental act with a verbal sign.

Recent theoretical formulations (Hartmann, 1953; Arlow and Brenner, 1964; Beres, 1957) stress that the structural point of view adds far more to the understanding of dynamics than the descriptive fact of consciousness or its absence. It seems that by a completely different route, emphasizing very different aspects of mental processes, I have come to a similar finding: verbal signs are the decisive acquisition of mankind not because they aggrandize the potential territory of consciousness but because they make possible a radically different organization of our mental apparatus.

I am well aware of the incompleteness and the shortcomings of my presentation. Today's formulations have a good chance of appearing crude and trivial tomorrow. Perhaps we are still bypassing essentials, but that should not be a reason to hold back what we can state. Language does two things of very unequal consequence: it labels sensory data and by this adding of another physical property—i.e., the name—makes them more definite and stable. And language is our main tool in the construction of a symbolically organized universe. Words are both—signals as well as symbolizers. In the former capacity they are additions to something pre-existent. In the latter capacity they take part in the creation of what they symbolize.[16]

And one more speculative thought. Freud (1900) asserts that unconscious wishes are always active (p. 577). In another context (p. 567) he says that nothing but a wish can set our mental apparatus

---

[16] Hartmann (1953), discussing the disturbances of language in schizophrenia, also refers to the general functions of language. Language provides signals for communication (a function which is not restricted to humans), while symbolic language is "designatory." He continues: "I am speaking of words meaning something, pointing to something, stating something—that function by which . . . language, besides adding verbal to thing representation, is also that function by which the former is made to signify the latter (p. 189).

at work. And in still another place (p. 537) he states that all psychical activity starting either from outer or inner stimuli ends in innervations. I suggest this reformulation: *our mental apparatus is active all the time*. Most of this activity is unconscious. An arising wish gives it direction, effectiveness, and may bring it to consciousness. Only a part of our mental activity becomes conscious and *only a part* of either kind (conscious or unconscious) leads into acts that are open to sensory inspection: to talking, doing, or intentional perceiving. Another part remains without visible, palpable results. This brings me to my last point.

The function of language which interested Freud was the added consciousness (awareness) it could bestow on mental acts. From here we can go on a short excursion into theoretical biology. It is customary to differentiate between lower and higher phyla by the early absence and the later growing ability to learn by experience. Instinctive acts of, say, insects were formerly viewed as absolutely rigid; today students of animal behavior concede that there is a limited plasticity. A spider follows a sequence of acts in catching its prey; a moth has a certain chain of acts in finding and preparing a place where it will deposit its eggs, disguise the spot, etc. If the experimenter interrupts this sequence and then permits the animal to return to it, the insect will not continue from where it left off—it will start again from the beginning. This can be repeated until the animal gives up altogether. In contrast, the members of the higher phyla are said to "learn," i.e., to observe environmental conditions and to adapt their behavior to them. Feedback modifies their behavior. They learn from previous experience.

I would like to express the same facts with a slightly changed emphasis. The awareness of lower animals of the effects which their own actions have upon the environment is very limited. This may account for the narrow limits within which they can change their actions. In contrast, the higher animals are able to see, hear, feel or smell *what their actions* do to the environment and to modify them accordingly. The ability of higher animals to learn, to profit by experience, is a function of their ability to observe the impact of their own acts upon their environment.

Man's specific asset is his ability to "observe" the impact of his motor acts *and* of his mental acts as well. We can say that the source of his superior power to modify his environment derives from his ability to evaluate, to gauge, to change his doings *before* they have any visible effects. We arrive at this paradox: man is capable of carrying out complex acts which are—for the time being or forever —*completely inconsequential for his physical environment*. This ability is the matrix of his power to modify his physical environment profoundly, to construct and destroy on a far greater scale than any other animal.

BIBLIOGRAPHY

Arlow, J. A. & Brenner, C. (1964), *Psychoanalytic Concepts and the Structural Theory*. New York: International Universities Press.

Balkányi, C. (1964), On Verbalization. *Int. J. Psa.*, 45:64-74.

Beres, D. (1957), Communication in Psychoanalysis and in the Creative Process: A Parallel. *J. Amer. Psa. Assn.*, 5:408-423.

Bühler, K. (1934), *Sprachtheorie*. Jena: Fischer.

Cassirer, E. (1944), *Essay on Man*. New Haven: Yale University Press.

Craik, K. J. W. (1952), *The Nature of Explanation*. Cambridge: University Press.

Edelheit, H. (1964), Speech and Psychic Structure: The Vocal-Auditory Organization of the Ego. Unpublished manuscript.

Ferenczi, S. (1912), The Ontogenesis of Symbols. *Sex in Psychoanalysis*. New York: Basic Books, 1950, pp. 276-281.

Freud, A. (1936), *The Ego and the Mechanisms of Defense*. New York: International Universities Press, 1946.

Freud, S. (1891), *On Aphasia*. New York: International Universities Press, 1953.

—— (1895), Project for a Scientific Psychology. *Origins of Psychoanalysis*. New York: Basic Books, 1954, pp. 347-445.

—— (1900), The Interpretation of Dreams. *Standard Edition*, 4 & 5. London: Hogarth Press, 1953.

—— (1911), Formulations on the Two Principles of Mental Functioning. *Standard Edition*, 12:213-226. London: Hogarth Press, 1958.

—— (1913), Totem and Taboo. *Standard Edition*, 13:1-161. London: Hogarth Press, 1955.

—— (1915), The Unconscious. *Standard Edition*, 14:159-215. London: Hogarth Press, 1957.

—— (1923), The Ego and the Id. *Standard Edition*, 19:3-66. London: Hogarth Press, 1961.

—— (1933), New Introductory Lectures on Psycho-Analysis. *Standard Edition*, 22:3-182. London: Hogarth Press, 1964.

—— (1939), Moses and Monotheism. *Standard Edition*, 23:3-137. London: Hogarth Press, 1964.

—— (1940), An Outline of Psycho-Analysis. *Standard Edition*, 23:141-207. London: Hogarth Press, 1964.

Hartmann, H. (1951), Technical Implications of Ego Psychology. *Essays on Ego Psychology*. New York: International Universities Press, 1964, pp. 142-154.

—— (1952), The Mutual Influences in the Development of Ego and Id. *This Annual*, 7:9-30.

—— (1953), Contribution to the Metapsychology of Schizophrenia. *Essays on Ego Psychology*. New York: International Universities Press, 1964, pp. 182-206.

—— (1956), The Development of the Ego Concept in Freud's Work. *Int. J. Psa.,* 37: 425-438.

Heron, W., Bexton, W. H., & Hebb, D. O. (1953), Cognitive Effects of a Decreased Variation to the Sensory Environment. *Amer. Psychologist,* 8:366-372.

Katan, A. (1961), Some Thoughts about the Role of Verbalization in Early Childhood. *This Annual,* 16:184-188.

Kris, E. (1950), On Preconscious Mental Processes. *Psychoanalytic Explorations in Art.* New York: International Universities Press. 1952, pp. 303-318.

Langer, S. K. (1942), *Philosophy in a New Key.* Cambridge: Harvard University Press; New York: Mentor Books, 1951.

Lilly, J. C. (1961), Symposium on Sensory Deprivation. In: *Sensory Deprivation.* Cambridge: Harvard Univ. Press.

Loewenstein, R. M. (1956), Some Remarks on the Role of Speech in Psycho-Analytic Technique. *Int. J. Psa.,* 37:460-468.

Nunberg, H. (1930), The Synthetic Function of the Ego. *Practice and Theory of Psychoanalysis.* New York: International Universities Press, 1960, pp. 120-136.

Peller, L. E. (1962), Language and Development. In: *Early Childhood Education,* ed. P. B. Neubauer. Springfield: Thomas, 1965.

Piaget, J. (1957), The Child and Modern Physics. *Sci. American,* 196:46-51.

Sapir, E. (1933), *Selected Writings of Edward Sapir in Language, Culture, and Personality.* Berkeley: University of California Press, 1964.

Schneirla, T. C. (1946), Ant Learning as a Problem in Comparative Psychology. In: *Twentieth Century Psychology,* ed. P. Harriman. New York: Philosophical Library, pp. 276-305.

Spitz, R. A. (1957), *No and Yes.* New York: International Universities Press.

von Frisch, K. (1927), *Aus dem Leben der Bienen.* Berlin: Springer.

von Uexküll, J. (1934), A Stroll through the World of Animals and Men. In: *Instinctive Behavior,* ed. & tr. C. H. Schiller. New York: International Universities Press, 1957, pp. 5-80.

Whorf, B. L. (1956), *Language, Thought and Reality.* New York: Wiley & M.I.T. Press.

AN OBSERVATION AND COMMENTS ON THE DEVELOPMENT OF MEMORY

HELEN SCHUR, M.D.

Psychoanalytic and academic psychology have long been interested in perception and memory and their development. It is now assumed that perception and memory are functions of autonomous apparatuses, and that the development of these functions depends on the maturation of those apparatuses in interaction with the environment.

Freud postulated early that "all impressions are preserved, not only in the same form in which they were first received, but also in all the forms which they have adopted in their further developments" (1901, p. 275, n.). Freud (1918) used this hypothesis in his interpretation of the "wolves dream." He postulated that the memory trace of a primal-scene observation which, according to reconstruction in the analysis of the Wolf Man, had occurred at the age of one and a half (when the boy could not yet grasp the meaning of his perception) subsequently acquired a dynamic impact through superimposed memory traces laid down in the interval. On another occasion Freud stated: "while he [a child] is not yet credited with possessing an understanding or a memory . . . the possibility cannot be rejected that he will be able to understand and react to the impression in *retrospect* (1916-1917, p. 369).

This postulate, that the subsequent recall of a memory trace of visual perception may carry with it information of a higher order of abstraction, has thus far remained hypothetical. This is not surprising. An assumption of this kind, based as it is on reconstruction, is open to certain doubts. Longitudinal studies have elucidated, e.g., the "birth" of a screen memory (Kennedy, 1950), but they are not geared

---

Clinical Instructor in Child Psychiatry, Downstate Medical Center, Brooklyn, New York.

to studying the recall of a perception after a long interval. Extensive observational and experimental studies of perception and memory have dealt mainly with the maturation and ongoing development of these functions in certain age groups. Nonetheless, Gestalt psychologists such as Bartlett (1932) have arrived at hypotheses similar to those of Freud.

The event described below may contribute to the confirmation of such hypotheses.[1]

Derek, aged eighteen months, driving with his father on a Sunday, passed a roadside stand where they stopped to buy some cider. At that time Derek's vocabulary was still limited, and his parents were making it a point to teach him only names of categories (e.g., "car" for all moving vehicles rather than "bus," "truck," "tractor") in order not to confuse him.

A year later, during the cider season, the family by chance stopped at the same roadstand. By then Derek's vocabulary had markedly increased, and his parents were now calling each object by its specific name.

Looking around at the roadside stand Derek asked his father: "Where is the red tractor?" His father, not knowing just what Derek was referring to, questioned the owner of the stand who replied: "Yes, there was a tractor here last year next to the stand, but it was blue. You can see it in the shed in the backyard." An inspection of the tractor revealed that the upper part was indeed blue, but the lower part, including the wheels, was red. The red portion exceeded the height of the little boy, so that while an adult would receive an impression primarily of blueness, a small child would have a dominant impression of redness.

Discussion

This set of observations covers two situations which are accurately dated. I shall first formulate my assumptions concerning the meaning of these observations, and then attempt to correlate these assumptions with the hypotheses of psychoanalytic and academic psychology.

1. The memory trace of the first perception (at eighteen months) was laid down as a visual image of a complex Gestalt.

[1] I am indebted to Dr. Allan Milofsky for the details of this observation.

2. The recall of the memory trace (at thirty months) was probably enhanced by the absence of an element (the tractor) of the total Gestalt which had attracted special attention cathexis at the time of registration.

3. The child's question: "Where is the red tractor?" was expressed in terms of a higher level of abstraction than that characteristic of the original memory trace.

4. I therefore conclude that the recall included information acquired in the interval between the original perception and its recall.

We must assume that the memory trace of the first percept included, in addition to the roadstand, a vehicle, its form, position, and color. Any assumption about the character of the registered and stored memory of the first perception (eighteen months) must take into consideration the theoretical and observational facts gathered by psychoanalytic and academic psychology which indicate that perception and memory traces, at age one and a half, encompass (a) a complex Gestalt, which is (b) predominantly visual in nature. Freud's first conceptualizations of perception and memory were formulated in neurophysiological terms and appeared primarily in the "Project" (1895), Chapter VII of *The Interpretation of Dreams* (1900), and "A Note upon the 'Mystic Writing-Pad' " (1925a). I shall limit myself to some of the most pertinent statements from these works. In the last-mentioned paper Freud says:

> . . . our mental apparatus . . . has an unlimited receptive capacity for new perceptions and nevertheless lays down permanent—even though *not unalterable*—memory-traces of them. As long ago as in 1900 I gave expression in *The Interpretation of Dreams* [p. 540] to a suspicion that this unusual capacity was to be divided between two different systems (or organs of the mental apparatus). According to this view, we possess a system *Pcpt.-Cs.*, which receives perceptions but retains no permanent trace of them, so that it can react like a clean sheet to every new perception; while the permanent traces of the excitations which have been received are preserved in 'mnemic systems' lying behind the perceptual system [1925a, p. 228; my italics].

The more extensive formulation in *The Interpretation of Dreams* had been as follows:

It is a familiar fact that we retain permanently something more than the mere *content* of the perceptions which impinge upon the system *Pcpt*. Our perceptions are linked with one another in our memory—first and foremost according to simultaneity of occurrence. We speak of this fact as 'association'. It is clear, then, that, if the *Pcpt*. system has no memory whatever, it cannot retain any associative traces; the separate *Pcpt*. elements would be intolerably obstructed in performing their function if the remnant of an earlier connection were to exercise an influence upon a fresh perception. We must therefore assume the basis of association lies in the mnemic systems. Association would thus consist in the fact that, as a result of a diminution in resistances and of the laying down of facilitating paths, an excitation is transmitted from a given *Mnem*. element more readily to one *Mnem*. element than to another.

Closer consideration will show the necessity for supposing the existence not of one but of several such *Mnem*. elements, in which one and the same excitation, transmitted by the *Pcpt*. elements, leaves a variety of different permanent records. The first of these *Mnem*. systems will naturally contain the record of association in respect to *simultaneity in time;* while the same perceptual material will be arranged in the latter systems in respect to other kinds of coincidence, so that one of these later systems, for instance, will record relations of similarity, and so on with the others [1900, pp. 538-539].

An important elaboration may be found in Freud's paper entitled "Negation" (1925b).

The reproduction of a perception as a presentation is not always a faithful one; it may be modified by omissions, or changed by the merging of various elements. In that case reality-testing has to ascertain how far such distortions go [p. 238].

Freud's other assumptions about the early development of perception and memory were based, in part, on reconstructions in analysis, where the emphasis was on the recall of forgotten (repressed) memories. Some of the hypotheses were linked with theories of the development of the mental apparatus. Freud (1900) assumed that early perception and memory were closely linked with drive (need) gratification and the objects providing such gratification. In a different context (1923, p. 20) he also distinguished between memory images and perceptual images, and between memories based on sensory perception and those memory traces which included verbal residues.

Lewy and Rapaport (1944), elaborating on this point, postulated (a) that the memory image is a more complex unit "which probably contains all the qualities a perception acquires when it becomes embodied into the individual's psychic life," and (b) that the "perceptual image" is really a "sensory image" (p. 26).

If perception and memory are viewed in terms of ego psychology and autonomous development (Hartmann, 1939), the emphasis is shifted to different aspects. Perception and memory are then viewed as functioning with regard to the *whole* environment, animate and inanimate, and *interests* which draw attention cathexis become more independent of immediate drive gratification. However, at an early stage of memory organization "there do not yet exist discrete and well-delineated 'objects' or 'ideas,' but only 'diffuse' ones. In the language of developmental psychology: the concepts are syncretic" (Rapaport, 1951, p. 694).

Freud's formulation concerning the laying down of memory traces and associations implied that this process of registration was a complex one. Rapaport (1942) and Klein (1966) indicate that memory encompasses several concepts such as stimulation, perception, apperception, understanding, coding, short-term and long-term registration, organization according to schemata, and so forth. These authors point out that investigators consider perception and registration to be *active* rather than passive processes of the mind.

According to Werner (1940), percepts are at first diffusely organized and homogeneous, with each constituent part containing some of the quality of the whole, which suggests to him a partial explanation of the so-called "mechanical" or "associative" memory of children (pp. 113-114). Werner asserts that "On the higher levels of mental organization the image is distinctly differentiated from the percept. . . . Imagined objects are our own inner products, and are felt to be controlled by and dependent on the activity of the ego" (p. 143). On the other hand, there exists between the level of "the objectively conditioned percept and the completely ingenerate image" an intermediate stage, i.e., eidetic imagery, which, according to Jaensch, possesses characteristics of both the percept and the true image. Werner believes that if Jaensch's findings are substantiated more fully, "we may then assume that a primordial functional unity exists in the sensory and imaginative fields, and that out of this undifferentiated function arise the true memory and fantasy image (the knowing of an inner world) in contradistinction to objective perception (the knowing of an outer world)" (p. 145).

Other authors made several points relevant to my discussion. Klüver (1933) points out the dependence of the eidetic imagery on the "interest" or "set" of the subject. Katona (1940) asserts that the meaning, the whole character of the percept, leaves "structural traces" which must be distinguished qualitatively from "individual traces" left by specific items. Müller-Freienfels (1913) noted the subjective selection active in the process of registration. Gordon (1937) states that neither percepts nor memory images are merely photographic records, the material of both being transformed according to the interests of the experiencing subject.[2]

In summary, these authors emphasize (a) the predominantly visual character of early registration; (b) the importance of a Gestalt of the percepts and its registration; and (c) the selectivity of perception and registration which is influenced by special "interests."

This selectivity has also been shown to exist in adults through Fisher's work on subliminal perception (1956, 1960). The neurophysiological substrate for this selectivity has been delineated in the studies of Granit (1955).

Piaget's concepts concerning perception have been outlined by Flavell (1963) as follows:

> . . . for Piaget, *perception* covers a narrower, more restricted range of behaviors than it does for most. . . . perception is both developmentally subordinate and structurally inferior to intelligence as a class of adaptation. . . . perception arises developmentally, not as an autonomous mode of adaptation in its own right, but as a kind of dependent subsystem within the larger context of an evolving sensory-motor intelligence. . . . early perceptions have 'meaning' to the infant only through the mediation of the sensory-motor schemas of which they form a part [p. 232].
>
> Perceptual development simply appears to Piaget to be a more continuous, qualitative-versus-quantitative affair than is the case for its intellectual counterpart [p. 234].

In line with his exclusive emphasis on sensori-motor intelligence, Piaget explicitly disagrees with Freud's concept of the drive organiza-

2 See also Rapaport (1940, pp. 122-124).

tion of memory. He also neglects the importance of "interests" (valences) which are inherent in the memory concepts of ego and Gestalt psychology.

According to Piaget (1945), "There are no memories of early childhood for the excellent reason that at that stage there was no evocative mechanism capable of organising them. Recognition memory in no way implies a capacity for evocation, which presupposes mental images, interiorised language, and the beginnings of conceptual intelligence. The memory of the two or three year old child is still a medley of made-up stories and exact but chaotic reconstructions, organised memory developing only with the progress of intelligence as a whole" (p. 187).

Finally, of special importance to my topic is Bartlett's (1932) formulation that incoming impulses are organized by and integrated with previous ones and that they do not persist as isolated traces.

In Derek's case I have assumed that his recall of the original perception was enhanced by the absence of an element of the total Gestalt which had attracted special attention cathexis. This assumption follows the model used by Freud in formulating the concept "wish," first applied to the memory trace of a need (drive) gratification.

> An essential component of this experience of satisfaction is a particular perception (that of nourishment, in our example) the mnemic image of which remains associated thenceforward with the memory trace of the excitation produced by the need. As a result of the link that has thus been established, next time this need arises a psychical impulse will at once emerge which will seek to re-cathect the mnemic image of the perception and to re-evoke the perception itself, that is to say, to re-establish the situation of the original satisfaction. An impulse of this kind is what we call a wish; the reappearance of the perception is the fulfilment of the wish. . . . Thus the aim of this first physical activity was to produce a 'perceptual identity' [i.e., something perceptually identical with the 'experience of satisfaction']—a repetition of the perception which was linked with the satisfaction of the need [1900, pp. 565-566].

With the maturation and development of psychic structure, wishes and the need to recathect the perception of a situation of satisfaction extend to ever-widening experiences, involving various percepts not directly linked with drive gratification. When Derek first perceived the tractor, he was already interested in cars, as are most boys of that age, and played with various vehicles while pretending to be a driver. We may therefore safely assume that the tractor, a big vehicle, had attracted special attention. The question: "Where is the red tractor?" indicated a wish to recathect the entire Gestalt and a recognition that an essential element of this Gestalt was missing. The fact that Derek's recall was put in the form of a question is also understandable if we follow Freud's reasoning (1925b) that: "all presentations originate from perceptions and are repetitions of them. . . . The first and immediate aim, therefore, of reality-testing is, not to *find* an object in real perception which corresponds to the one presented, but to *refind* such an object, to convince oneself that it is still there" (pp. 237-238).

The fact that children have the faculty of recalling many details of a memory Gestalt as well as the need to have the experience embodied in this memory repeated in every detail has also been emphasized, in particular by Werner, who states that "any phenomenon known in terms of qualities-of-the-whole, rather than in terms of strictly articulated qualities, is apt to be perceived by the young child as undergoing a complete change, even if no more than minor details in the situation are altered" (p. 128).

E. and G. Scupin (1907), in writing about their child aged one year ten months comment: "Custom is law for him, and he repudiates any inconsistencies" (quoted by Werner, 1940, p. 131).

In contrast to Freud's assumption that the gratification of a wish involves the need to recathect a specific memory, Werner assumes that "From the child's standpoint no one of these elements need be more essential than any other, since all of them contribute to the characteristic coloration, or tone, of the situation totality. Such a 'whole-structure' tends to a rigid traditionalism, since any element that is changed or left out may completely transform the total situation to which the child is adjusted" (pp. 130-131).

However, there is no inherent contradiction between the tendency to a *general* "traditionalism," in Werner's terminology, and the assumption that simultaneously and more and more independently a hypercathexis of certain elements of the Gestalt will develop.

All observers agree that at the age of eighteen months, perception and memory are of a global, syncretic character. As applied to the observations reported here, this means that Derek, at eighteen months, was well aware of such generalized terms as car, big car, little car. Children of this age are often able to point out an object when they are told its name, but they cannot yet name such objects themselves, because they lack the ability to coordinate the visual representation with the verbal representation. While they may at an early age learn to discriminate among colors insofar as their perceptions are linked with physical and emotional reactions,[3] they continue to show confusion in linking the verbal representation with the visual representation of certain colors up to the age of six years (Werner, 1940, p. 98).

As far as Derek is concerned, his vocabulary was limited at the age of eighteen months, and did not include a term as specific as "tractor." Neither was he able to name colors. However, as a result of the maturation and development which had taken place during the year following the first observation, Derek's vocabulary had greatly increased by the time of the recall, his mode of speech had developed to the point where he was using sentences, spoke in terms of "I" and "you," was well aware of certain abstractions, and could distinguish and name various vehicles and many colors.

CONCLUSION

The fact that Derek's recall included information of a higher level of abstraction than that involved in the original perception is self-evident and requires no discussion.

The importance of this observation for the theory of memory registration is enhanced by the fact that the two perceptions were separated by a one-year interval during which time no further visits to or discussions of the roadstand had occurred. Hence the added information which Derek displayed in his question—the category of the vehicle (tractor) and its color (red)—must have originated from percepts and information acquired from other sources in the

---

[3] Werner reports experiments in which six-month-old children learned to react to differently colored milk bottles, and a three-month-old infant looked for varying lengths of time at each of two differently colored skeins held simultaneously before his eyes (1940, pp. 99-100).

course of that year. Moreover, the incident occurred in the presence of an observer aware of its theoretical significance. Both of these fortunate circumstances contribute to the validity of the observation as a confirmation of Freud's hypothesis that recall of a memory trace of a visual perception may include information of a higher order of abstraction, acquired subsequently to the original perception.

However, such confirmation does not provide us with an explanation of how the mental apparatus performs this task. In other words, we are confronted here with the problem of structure formation or learning. It is in this area that psychology and neurophysiology are most successfully striving to find some common ground.

We might simply assume that additional information—in this instance a cognition (tractor; red)—was superimposed upon and integrated with the original memory microstructure. Such a rather naïve assumption would underestimate the potentialities of the substrate of the mental apparatus—the central nervous system.

Freud's hypothesis, expressed first in the "Project" (1895) and later in other works (1900, 1911, 1920, 1925a, 1925b), presupposes the formation of many additional memory traces (or, as we would now call them, "memory structures"), linked to each other by associations based on "similarities." Such "similarities" include various levels of need gratification (instinctual needs, ego interests), "perceptual identity," identity of word and content representation, and so forth. We must assume that all additional information is available not just for one memory trace (in my example, the added information "tractor" and "red" would not be limited to the specific roadstand-tractor memory trace) but for an indeterminate number of memory traces.

Modern neurophysiology is bringing us closer to an understanding for the method of transmitting such information. The work of synaptic transmission done by Sir John Eccles is of particular importance in this area.

Electron microscopy has shown not only that each nerve cell has hundreds of connections with other nerve cells, but that it transmits and receives information as well. This process is performed by means of special extensions that deliver a squirt of a transmitter substance. Any given nerve cell may fire an impulse or inhibit an impulse or reverse its direction (Eccles, 1965).

Although this statement does not explain how a memory is stored, it points to the mechanism by which any registered and stored impression can at any time combine partly or wholly with other impressions.

It is my conviction that incidents such as the one described occur frequently, and I hope that further observations, perhaps stimulated by this one, will eventually lead to a fuller psychological understanding not only of memory structure formation but of its entire neurophysiological basis as well.

BIBLIOGRAPHY

Bartlett, F. C. (1932), *Remembering: A Study in Experimental and Social Psychology.* Cambridge: University Press.

Eccles, J. (1965), The Synapse. *Sci. Amer.*, 212:56-66.

Fisher, C. (1956), Dreams, Images, and Perception: A Study of Unconscious-Preconscious Relationships. *J. Amer. Psa. Assn.*, 4:5-48.

—— (1960), Introduction to *Preconscious Stimulation in Dreams, Associations, and Images [Psychological Issues, 2, Monogr. 7].* New York: International Universities Press.

Flavell, J. (1963), *The Developmental Psychology of Jean Piaget.* Princeton: Van Nostrand.

Freud, S. (1895), Project for a Scientific Psychology. *The Origins of Psychoanalysis.* New York: Basic Books, 1954.

—— (1900), The Interpretation of Dreams. *Standard Edition,* 4 & 5. London: Hogarth Press, 1953.

—— (1901), The Psychopathology of Everyday Life. *Standard Edition,* 6. London: Hogarth Press, 1960.

—— (1911), Psycho-Analytical Notes on an Autobiographical Account of a Case of Paranoia. *Standard Edition,* 12:3-82. London: Hogarth Press, 1958.

—— (1916-1917), Introductory Lectures on Psycho-Analysis. *Standard Edition,* 15 & 16. London: Hogarth Press, 1963.

—— (1918), From the History of an Infantile Neurosis. *Standard Edition,* 17:3-123. London: Hogarth Press, 1955.

—— (1920), Beyond the Pleasure Principle. *Standard Edition,* 18:3-64. London: Hogarth Press, 1955.

—— (1923), The Ego and the Id. *Standard Edition,* 19:3-66. London: Hogarth Press, 1961.

—— (1925a), A Note upon the 'Mystic Writing-Pad.' *Standard Edition,* 19:227-232. London: Hogarth Press, 1961.

—— (1925b), Negation. *Standard Edition,* 19:235-239. London: Hogarth Press, 1961.

Gordon, K. (1937), Memory Viewed as Imagination. *J. Gen. Psychol.,* 17:113-124.

Granit, R. (1955), *Receptors and Sensory Perceptions.* New Haven: Yale University Press.

Hartmann, H. (1939), *Ego Psychology and the Problem of Adaptation.* New York: International Universities Press, 1958.

Katona, G. (1940), *Organizing and Memorizing: Studies in the Psychology of Learning and Teaching.* New York: Columbia University Press.

Kennedy, H. E. (1950), Cover Memories in Formation. *This Annual,* 5:275-285.

Klein, G. S. (1966), The Several Sides of Memory. In: *Psychoanalysis: A General Psy-*

chology, ed. R. M. Loewenstein, L. Newman, M. Schur, & A. J. Solnit. New York: International Universities Press, pp. 377-389.

Klüver, H. (1933), Eidetic Imagery. In: *A Handbook of Child Psychology*, ed. C. Murchison. Worcester: Clark University Press, pp. 699-722.

Lewy, E. & Rapaport, D. (1944), The Psychoanalytic Concept of Memory. *Psa. Quart.*, 13:16-42.

Müller-Freienfels, R. (1913), Der Einfluss der Gefühle und motorischen Faktoren auf Assoziation und Denken. *Arch. ges. Psychol.*, 27:381-430.

Piaget, J. (1945), *Play, Dreams and Imitation in Childhood*. New York: Norton, 1951.

Rapaport, D. (1942), *Emotions and Memory*. New York: International Universities Press, 1950.

—— (1951), *Organization and Pathology of Thought*. New York: Columbia University Press.

Werner, H. (1940), *Comparative Psychology of Mental Development*. New York: International Universities Press, 1957.

DIAGNOSTIC PROFILES

A DIAGNOSTIC PROFILE OF
PSYCHOPATHOLOGY IN A LATENCY CHILD

DALE R. MEERS

Foreword by Reginald S. Lourie, M.D.

The child presented in the Diagnostic Profile that follows has suffered from a seizure disorder for at least six years. This Profile is *not* intended as a differential assessment of an organic as contrasted with a hysterical dysfunction. The child continues under independent neurological supervision during his ongoing psychotherapeutic treatment.

The purposes of this paper would *not* be served if it were considered as an extension of the discussion of organic versus psychogenic etiology of epileptic or seizure disorders. However, at the present stage of the child's treatment (and continuing diagnostic assessment), it is essential to consider the nature of the convulsive disorder as it affected the boy's defense organization, ego capacities, and neurotic solutions to conflict. It is hoped that the treatment will clarify whether, or to what degree, neurosis has made use of a convulsive potential. If hysterical features were to emerge during treatment, if psychotherapy were to disclose a hysterical etiology (which might accompany an organic predisposition), such questions might eventually be examined in the light of analytic documentation.

Clinical experience has consistently underscored the desirability of psychotherapeutic help for many of the patients suffering from emotionally enhanced seizure disorders. In the present case, the

The author is a Research Associate at Children's Hospital, Washington, D.C., a guest lecturer and research student with the Baltimore Psychoanalytic Institute; he was formerly a research assistant and a student of the Hampstead Child-Therapy Clinic, London, where he received his training in child analysis.

Dr. Lourie is Director, Department of Psychiatry, Children's Hospital of the District of Columbia.

psychopathological symptomatology might be ascribed, ultimately, to an organic seizure condition and a concomitant intolerance in the ego organization. The structure of both symptomatology and pathogenic defense organization, as evidenced in the following Profile, make it clear that the *form* of the disorder is that of a childhood neurosis which has moved toward encapsulation in a character disorder. That the origins of psychopathology may have roots in an organic impairment is hardly an irrelevant question. Quite the contrary. If true, organic dysfunction is an even stronger reason for psychotherapeutic intervention to help the child cope with atypical neurological dysfunction that complicates and burdens an overtaxed child who adapts by psychopathological means.

The merit of the Diagnostic Profile derives from the clarity of a conceptual biopsy, an ordering of symptoms and developmental data that are both complex and otherwise obscure in the wealth of usual historical and analytic detail. As an *illustration* of the utility of the Profile for the incisive assessment of complexities of childhood disorders, the following paper is a helpful clinical contribution, as is the Profile itself.

R. S. L.

THE RESEARCH ORIGINS OF THE PROFILE

There are four papers that form an indispensable background to the present paper and the use of the Profile in general. A summary of these papers would be an exhaustive commentary on psychoanalysis—and would also do gross disservice to theoretical and clinical formulations that are already concise and renowned for their clarity. The first of these is Anna Freud's classic "Indications for Child Analysis" (1945) in which she stressed the need for a change in emphasis from clinical considerations of manifest childhood symptomatology to an assessment of the impediments to the child's/maturational progression. In that paper Anna Freud also discussed the appropriateness and timing, the essential need for diagnostic justification of psychoanalytic intervention in the child's life.

In "Assessment of Childhood Disturbances" (1962), Anna Freud continued and extended a number of formulations and considerations that lend themselves to effective diagnosis, based on the integrated structure of a psychoanalytic "profile of development." A major subsection of the Profile was given more detailed explication in the following year with the publication of Anna Freud's "The Concept of Developmental Lines" (1963). These "lines" provide a specific frame of reference in the assessment of the complex differences, processes, and phases that (may) help differentiate relative normality from varied pathogenic manifestations in childhood.

Clinical and observational data have established that regressions or transient symptoms in particular phases (and ages) of childhood are not essentially pathogenic and that fixations are not unequivocal. Moreover, some expressions of evident and established childhood pathology (which indicate an inadequate resolution of childhood conflict) may be "bypassed" without impeding the mainstream of maturational forces available to the young ego. In Freud's (1916-1917) famous analogy, the question of fixation then involves assessing whether the maturational army had need to leave a regiment to guard against insurrection, or whether a patrol squad sufficed. The concept of "developmental lines" offers a particularly helpful and rewarding conceptual approach with which to evaluate the relative degrees of fixation, regression, or progression in the diagnostic exploration.

The "developmental lines" contain virtues that are not revealed at first blush. There is the explicit need for a diagnostic appraisal of the "age adequacy" of behaviors, defenses, etc. "Age adequacy" could be misunderstood as a static concept, particularly when behaviors (and their modes) reflect strong social and cultural pressures that facilitate (or impede) given drives or modes of their expression (e.g., in the expression of aggression or libidinal forms of gratification). The evaluation of the "age adequacy" of behaviors, i.e., in the context of "developmental lines," permits a bypassing of social and cultural preconceptions or misconceptions of "normalcy" and "pathology." The Profile requires a structured consideration of the ubiquitous processes of biology and psychology operating in all infants and their maturation. *Whatever* the direction or impact of social or cultural stress (manifest in parental-environmental nurture) on the infant and child, a "line of development" exists and permits assessment of its characteristics in that context. Among these universal "lines" are those that lead toward body independence, e.g., from suckling to rational eating, from wetting and soiling to bladder and bowel control, from irresponsibility to responsibility in body management, etc. (A. Freud, 1963, 1965).

In discussing the use and development of the Profile, Nagera (1963) extended the rationale of its structure while providing the first published illustration. The adequacy of diagnosis is obviously not to be measured in the completion of subsections of a formula or Profile. Yet the inception and developmental structuring of the Profile, via prolonged diagnostic research at Hampstead, have "built in" a progression of considerations leading from developmental data to increasingly specific theoretical, metapsychological formulations of explicit diagnostic significance.

The problems of differential diagnosis of childhood disorders are obviously not resolved by the Profile, which is essentially a conceptual tool that can be used with varying degrees of adequacy, depending on the experience of the diagnostician. The Profile does, however, provide for a "fail-safe" (in the vernacular of the day) to the degree that the diagnostician must relate his clinical observations back to the structure of psychoanalytic, developmental metatheory. As Anna Freud has underscored in her most recent work, *Normality and Pathology in Childhood* (1965), the assessment of childhood disturbances continues to be complicated because, among other reasons, we know so little of "normal" variations of maturation.

It is of importance to restate the Hampstead staff's caution, in this regard, that the Profile was developed from the study of psychoneurotic conflicts of childhood, vis-à-vis (what is known of) "normal" ego-drive development. As a diagnostic research tool, the Profile has undergone significant internal modifications. It has been considered less a "finished product" than an experimental research tool designed for specific types of assessment.[1] The Profile's utility for assessments of other forms of pathology has been extended to adult neuroses (A. Freud, H. Nagera, and W. E. Freud, 1965), the study of impulse disorders (Michaels and Stiver, 1965), atypical and borderline children (Thomas et al., 1966), etc. Its value for teaching, with reference

[1] My own (limited) familiarity with Hampstead's Profile work derives from attending Diagnostic and Profile Research Committee Meetings during my last two years of training there.

to both analytic diagnosis and conceptualization, seems to have very rich but still undocumented or unexplored possibilities.

Nagera's clinical elaboration, in the first published case presentation (1963), is authoritative and representative of the succinct character of Profiles at the Hampstead Clinic. The relative scantness, however, of his published clinical material in the body of a conventional Profile is misleading because there is no indication of the wealth of data available to the diagnostician. It may be helpful to note the convention and practice at Hampstead, viz., that extended data derived from diagnostic interviews of parent and child, projective and psychometric reports, school reports, etc., are used as the explicit base for the skeletal "profile." Since all research staff review precirculated diagnostic data in their entirety, the Profile itself can then be kept succinct and dispense with extensive documentations.

In settings other than Hampstead, and particularly for research publication, the scantness of data in the body of the Profile (i.e., presented *without* extended documentation) poses a problem of credibility. The need to extend the internal documentation of the Profile, i.e., in other settings, had been anticipated by the principal investigators.[2] The present extended paper is somewhat of an experiment as to the degree of documentation necessary to insure the adequacy of diagnostic credibility. The wealth of data in the case that follows is somewhat unusual, i.e., for a first Profile of a child. While it draws on two months of twice weekly treatment, it still remains evident that a considerable amount of relevant data is lacking—and in fact may be unobtainable without the depth provided by analytic treatment.

This broaches the additional research value of the Profile in the area of diagnosis and systematic investigations of the etiology of psychopathology, related defense organization, etc. As Nagera (1963) has noted, such research in London has included the diagnostic *reassessment* of a child during or on completion of analytic treatment. The comparisons of second and third Profiles of the same child, over varying periods of time, provide for increasing accuracy and corrections

[2] I am particularly indebted to Dr. H. Nagera (London), one of Hampstead Clinic's principal investigators, for his many helpful suggestions on the first draft of this paper and for his comments on the historical development of Profile research.

Special thanks are also due to Dr. J. Waelder-Hall for the opportunity of presenting this paper at the postgraduate child analytic seminar (Baltimore Institute).

of diagnosis via the depth of data provided in the child's analysis. Heinicke (1965) has made use of the Profile to research questions of effectiveness of treatment, etc. In the present assessment, two considerations led to the use of the Profile: (1) the great complexities of differential diagnosis in a latency age boy with both manifest neurological and psychopathognomonic symptomatology, and (2) the potentialities for research, i.e., if the child concerned should enter analytic treatment.

Gottschalk (1956) noted a particular diagnostic difficulty where in "certain types of paroxysmal activity, variously called 'psychic equivalent seizures,' 'affective epilepsy' . . . and so forth, it may become impossible to differentiate between epileptic experiences (and behavior) and nonepileptic experiences (and behavior). This is especially likely to be so when the presumed seizure activity involves complicated and highly integrated patterns of behavior and psychologic processes" (p. 352). The present Profile has attempted this type of differentiating assessment; it also led to the child's start in analytic treatment. The research value of the Profile necessitates second and third (if possible) reassessments. The publication of such extended documented material poses two problems: one expository; and the second, that of protection of the patient's anonymity. These considerations have led to some essential nonclinical distortions, which, hopefully, will not unduly complicate the reporting of future diagnostic reassessments of this case.

Diagnostic Profile

Ian F.

Age: 11 years 6 months (at start of treatment)

Sources of Information:

Psychiatric interview, Dr. A., Date: Current
Social history, Miss B., Date: Current
School history, Miss B., Telephone report, Date: Current
Intelligence test reports, Dr. C., Date: Current
                              Dr. D., Date: 5 years earlier
Neurological notes, Dr. E., Consultation records covering two years.
Psychotherapeutic treatment notes and interviews with parents, author's records.

I. REASONS FOR REFERRAL

Ian's parents have been concerned about his well-being since the age of eighteen months when he was hospitalized with a convulsive episode that lasted three hours. Subsequently, between the ages of four and five years, Ian's aggression and behavioral difficulties were sufficiently trying that he was referred for psychiatric evaluation. At age six and a half (following the death of a sister, Gwen) Ian had his first psychomotor seizure. While neurological examinations and EEGs were negative, the clinical picture was classically that of a petit mal attack and he was started on anticonvulsants. At about age nine, Ian developed facial and neck twitches or tics accompanied by nauseous stomach sensations. These were considered neurological corroboration of the diagnosis of psychomotor seizures, and Ian's anticonvulsant medication was subsequently experimentally modified and increased to date.

During the year preceding this referral, Ian's school grades dropped markedly. Moreover, he became increasingly provocative and aggressive with peers and negativistic and rebellious with his parents, particularly his mother. The neurologist concluded that such increase in aggression might have accompanied an increase in medication.

The crucial determinant of the parents' decision to seek psychotherapeutic help was this increase in Ian's negativism and aggression, accompanied by the mother's despair that she could no longer cope with her son. In addition, the parents also feared that Ian's emotional difficulties were ruining his academic opportunities in one of the city's best schools. The parents were intelligent and insightful in their conclusions that whatever the intrinsic, organic or neurological nature of the boy's difficulties, he needed psychotherapeutic treatment. They had become increasingly aware of their son's impairment and distortion of his "self image," particularly evident in his repeated, perhaps manipulative, "I can't help it, after all I'm sick in the head." It is also clear that the parents were concerned about the possibility that organic damage might be progressive and that it could lead to psychosis. A referring psychiatrist had added to the parents' concern by his suggestion that the seizures might be hysterical and that the mother might have the greater need for therapeutic treatment.

II. Description of the Child

Ian is a rather handsome and impressive boy who is tall and well built for his age. He has raven black hair, a dark complexion, and is the more striking for the unexpected blue of his eyes. Ian stands in slightly exaggerated erectness, as if in awareness that someone might be looking at him. His rather handsome appearance is marred by an expression that is often "suspicious" and perhaps sullen; yet Ian can also relax into a gracious and warm smile when secure. In his initial treatment interviews, Ian's tics were constantly evident. His efforts to disguise them were frequently more bizzare than the tics themselves, e.g., strange movements of the head, twisting or poking at his eyebrows, etc.

It is apparent that Ian shares his parents' attitudes toward dress and personal grooming. He has come to his sessions from school, usually dressed in well-pressed slacks, clean shirt, a Windsor knot in his tie, well-polished shoes, etc. At other times, when coming from home, his garb may be casual, but in such instances his sweaters and trousers are in excellent taste and quality, suggesting a familiarity with the best of men's shops. Ian is also impressive and immediately so, for his precocious and pleasantly direct attitude in relating to adults (e.g., schoolmasters, psychiatrists, his therapist, etc.). Ian seems to expect that he should know and should be held responsible for his behavior. In this he seems consciously to anticipate adult evaluation and criticism; his expectation of adverse judgment is evident in his guilt reactions and self-recriminations (e.g., in not studying, in misbehaving, etc.). One senses a measure of insincerity in the boy's confessions, as if he had discovered a technical means of circumventing adult punishment by pseudo self-castigation.

III. Family Background and Personal History

The father's family has enjoyed relative wealth, impeccable repute, and considerable status as owners of extended estates in the English midlands. Mr. F. recalls his parents as being infinitely gentle, kind, and mutually tolerant. His father in particular was considered by the family as *not* second in place to the angels. Mr. F.'s only brother seems of some significance to this history because of his indirect impact on Ian, of which more will be said later.

Mr. F. was graduated from Oxford before World War II, following which he worked a short time on the family's estates. Abandoning this position, apparently precipitously, he secured temporary employment at an Austrian ski lodge. Thereafter, Mr. F. returned to graduate school where he studied philosophy. During his graduate college years, Mr. F. met and married Ian's mother. The sequence of subsequent events is not clear, but it appears that Mr. F. also taught at Oxford, served in World War II as a lieutenant in Navy intelligence, and at some point began his work with a government ministry where his activities were secret to the family, and by inference were exciting and dangerous. Mr. F.'s past and present work schedule has been predictable only for its irregularity; i.e., the family expects that he will be called away from home at night or for days on end. His present position has permitted a greater degree of stability.

Mr. F.'s appearance is distinguished, not least by his 6'4" height and the consonance of his excellent physical proportions. He has handsome, though somewhat "pretty" features, set off by a shock of hair as black as his son's. In manner, the father appears reserved but quietly interested and alert. He is an intellectually insightful person who has long suffered from migraines and more recently from an acute depressive episode. On this occasion, approximately two years preceding this referral, Mr. F. entered psychotherapy which both he and his wife agree was of considerable help to him. From his therapy, Mr. F. notes that he dramatically identified with his own father who has always considerably influenced his life. As a result Mr. F. feels he has led an "as if" existence in which he "played at being in school," "played at marriage," "played at having an occupation," etc. He has agreed with his wife's accusations that he is and always has been far too passive. Mr. F. also noted that he felt he was different from others in his own incapacity to love with affection and intensity. He has always fought clear of emotions of any sort, e.g., consciously exercising self-controls even when viewing an emotional film or play. Mr. F. states that in years past he has had only two alternatives in coping with his son: (1) by mimicking his own father's gentle, superior, and benevolent attitudes; or (2) by treating his son as another adult. Mr. F. felt that his own therapy left him somewhat freer in his relationship with his son, in permitting greater expression of both fondness for Ian but also of legitimate annoyances and grievances.

Since Mrs. F. is most volatile and explosive, Mr. F. has been motivated over the years to intervene intellectually between mother and
son, trying to mitigate the mother's apparent severity and discipline.
Because of his own emotional isolation, Mr. F. could rarely give Ian
much affection and had hoped that his wife, on Mr. F.'s urging,
could recompense the boy in this way.

The father's depressive episode may relate to the death of his own
father at that time. The paternal grandmother is still alive and family
correspondence seems regular. There is no known family history of
psychopathology or neurological disorder. The paternal uncle warrants comment because Ian links his own intensity to the time when
this man's wife melodramatically deserted. The aunt absconded with
her two sons, secretly taking them to France by airplane without
warning either the children or her husband of her intent. She is
castigated in the family as an evil woman who deserted for the only
and express purpose of "catching a millionaire" (which she did). The
elder son of that marriage, Ian's cousin, developed a stutter at that
time; Ian notes feelings of murderous rage whenever he is reminded
of his aunt by stutterers whom he hears today.

The father's contribution to Ian's misbehavior should be illustrated. During Mr. F.'s momentary absence, Ian burned pages of a
school book in the family study in front of his mother (who had been
reading there). When she intervened with both anger and anxiety,
Ian wrestled with his mother, threw her to the floor, and when she
just lay there he snarled, "Well! Have you given up on me again?"
When the mother allowed herself tears (for the second time in her
life in front of Ian), the boy contemptuously kicked her where she
lay and walked out of the room. Mrs. F. was furious, outraged, and
frightened. After her husband's return, she waited until her temper
was under control and then told him of the event. The father was
very angry and ordered Ian to his room where Mr. F. then remained
to talk with the boy. Thereafter the father returned to Mrs. F., full
of admiration for Ian's "keen insight." Ian had told his father he felt
apologetic, yet he knew he would do it again (this was insight!). Ian
was concerned about his mother's forgiveness, and the father told Ian
that when Christ was asked how many times He would forgive, He
replied not only forty times over, but as much more again if necessary. Mrs. F. wanted understanding and protection for herself, not a

comparison with or a fate similar to that of Christ. But she listened to her husband's unimpeachable Christianity and was eventually won over to the view that it was her responsibility to go to her troubled son and both forgive and kiss him so that he could sleep untroubled that night. Such incidents suggest a mutually unconscious collusion of father and son in which Ian perpetuates some of the aggression that the father denies in himself.

The mother's background sounds as explosive as the father's seems serene. The maternal grandmother in particular is eternally present, both in fact and in fantasy. She is described as a controlling, insidiously devouring woman who takes and holds everything she can. There is one maternal uncle, a source of continuing shame and humiliation. He is described by Ian's mother as a "professional psychopath," a drunkard, drug addict, a troublemaker, etc. He reputedly never "escaped" mother and the latter nominally continues to pursue, and in reality occasionally secures, the uncle's temporary psychiatric institutionalization. Mrs. F.'s aversion to (and fear of) psychiatry is identified with her experience with one of her brother's psychiatrists. Mrs. F.'s protestations that she had nothing to do with her brother's illness are sufficiently excessive to be suspect. One is immediately impressed with some sense of unconscious guilt as well as with her concern for this brother. The uncle's importance to Ian is of long standing, both because of the boy's incipient fear that he may have inherited some genetic defect and secondarily because of the mother's invidious and continued comparisons. She has harassed Ian over the years, telling him that he would be just as incompetent, incapable, or in need of institutional care, i.e., if Ian did not do as mother instructed. The mother is somewhat abashed in such self-reporting, but it is abundantly clear that she has felt that such "shock tactics" would be one of the only real ways of deterring her son from misbehavior. She does not recognize the fact that such comparisons serve only to frighten Ian and provide him with rationalizations.

It is known that the maternal grandmother lived in London when Ian was a toddler and that she occasionally cared for him then. Later she lived in the family's home for several years where, from Mrs. F.'s point of view, the grandmother was a constant source of chaos in the family. It is of interest to note that the increase in Ian's hostility and aggression at home coincided with the mother's insistence that the grandmother move and find residence elsewhere. Ian indicates that he likes his grandmother very much, but separately notes to his mother that he needs help to protect himself from her excessive needs for hugs and kisses.

Mrs. F. is very tall, and is as attractive and equivalently well proportioned as her husband. She is invariably smartly dressed, well groomed, and her appearance is strikingly handsome, though not "feminine." Mrs. F. describes herself with nominal amusement as emotional, explosive, and strong-willed. (Her family and Ian's therapist would rather agree.) She also describes herself as most loving and interested in her husband and son, implying by this an ambivalent, erotic intensity. She feels that she is unsure of her maternal capacities and is consequently manipulable by innuendoes that might touch on her adequacy in this area, where she feels sensitive and guilty. Mrs. F. also feels that her husband is much more intelligent than she is and that she should follow his advice even when she is emotionally in profound disagreement. She bitterly resents her husband's "inability to be active and masculine," particularly in family matters where discipline or control of Ian has been important (from this statement one can draw a clear inference about their sexual relationship). Whatever difficulties may exist between the parents, they leave the impression of a fundamental and mutual respect, with an apparent reciprocity in their individual psychopathology which binds rather than divides them.

Sexuality was openly and excessively discussed in the house, in the "liberal and progressive" mood of the times. There have been, for example, detailed discussions of the approaches for intercourse in the matings of Ian's white rats. His surviving sister, Fiona, discusses her beaus' sensual overtures to her with the mother, but in Ian's presence. The mother has confronted Ian on the question of whether he masturbates, etc. The father has occasionally showered with his son, and Ian has felt free to walk into the bathroom of the parents, regardless of whether his mother or his father is there. This may be the more important since the parents have noted Ian's precocious move into puberty, evident in the boy's pubic hair and genitals. The father has insisted, as earlier noted, that the mother give more physical, intimate loving to the boy than she would prefer. She has accommodated in such matters, nominally only under duress.

The violence and intensity of feelings in the home, particularly between mother and son, will be noted elsewhere. The mother's temper, as well as Ian's, has precipitated innumerable quarrels over everything in the gamut of possible mother-child difficulties. While verbal discipline is common, isolation is more so. Physical discipline has included forcibly washing Ian's mouth out with soap, hitting him on the head with a broom handle, hitting him in the face, etc. This picture of violence within the family is deceptive, however. The violence is more impulsive than studied. Outside the home, the mother presents a most poised, socially presentable, and smart appearance. She is indeed an attractive person who seems to enjoy meeting others, going to teas, taking art lessons, etc. In other than family matters, the mother's poise and keen interest, her slightly caustic humor, are undoubtedly social assets that make her a well-accepted guest and friend.

Siblings: The F.'s first daughter, Fiona, is nine years Ian's senior. During her college years, she worked in biological and psychological sciences and seems to have a spurious knowledge of Ian's early neurological difficulties. Fiona is presently professionally employed and lives semi-independently in the family's house. Fiona's influence on her parents seems to be considerable; e.g., she apparently gives psychological direction or instruction to her parents. Little is known of her significance to Ian's early years or to his present life. So far as is known, Fiona has suffered from no psychological or neurological disorder.

The second child born to the family was another daughter, Gwen. When Gwen was eighteen months old, Mr. F. was assigned to Greece and the family moved to Athens. Shortly after their arrival there, Gwen suffered from encephalitis and was hospitalized with a convulsive seizure. Her subsequent slow development resulted in extended neurological examinations. Gwen had suffered brain damage and was left permanently mentally retarded. By the time of Mrs. F.'s next pregnancy (with Ian), Gwen was sent to an institution (the family having returned to London). The sister did not return home again, and Ian knew of her only as his sick sister who had to live in an institution because she was "sick in the head." Only at Gwen's death, when Ian was six years ten months of age, did he ever see her, i.e., when she was returned home for her funeral. Ian was described as having been most upset, sorrowful, feeling tricked by his parents that he had not had the opportunity of seeing his sister in life (when in fact she had not been far from home). It should be further noted that Gwen had always been openly considered the mother's most loved and special child, though physically absent. Whatever ambivalence the mother must have felt for this damaged daughter, any rejection or disavowal seemed encapsulated by an overcathexis and restitutive undoing.

Friends: Parents, schoolteachers, and Ian agree that he has no intimate friends, yet that he has reasonably good peripheral relationships. There is apparently one boy slightly younger and much smaller than Ian whom he likes best. Little is known of their common interests or activities. At school, Ian is characteristically shy, reserved, indeed embarrassed if asked procedural questions by his teachers. Yet Ian is not rejected or teased for his shyness, though the mother reports considerable fighting with school peers during the previous year. The teacher does not confirm this, but rather thinks the parents have preconceived feelings and err in oversimplifying Ian's difficulties. Ian indicates that his size and athletic skills make him a much-desired participant in team sports; e.g., Ian is one of two boys who have been given special consent to play with the older ones in the school's regular competitive football matches. Ian's success at team sports is not matched by any direct friendships away from the structured and supervised team companionship. His occasional visits to the homes of acquaintances brought requests that he be permitted to stay overnight. Ian has never been successful in this because of his sleep disturbance (not a referral symptom); Ian becomes extremely unhappy and anxious because he cannot fall asleep away from home. Few boys call on Ian and still fewer ask him back for a second time.

Personal history: It is to be recalled that the parents decided to institutionalize Gwen when the mother became pregnant with Ian. Since she was the mother's favorite, it can be surmised that the pregnancy with Ian was not an unmixed blessing. Mrs. F. was troubled by indigestion and nausea; her delivery, however, was short and uncomplicated. Ian weighed seven pounds at birth and appeared to be a healthy and normal infant. He was described as a fussy baby in that he spat up considerably, though he ate well. He was not breast-fed. Troubles with formula occurred between ten and twelve and a half weeks; he had continual diarrhea, which stopped with a changeover to skim milk. Bottle feedings were gradually replaced with a cup at age six months. Nothing is recalled as to his teething. There are no feeding disturbances, and there were no indications of maternal discomfort in Mrs. F.'s indirect allusions to orality, e.g., that the boy continued sucking his thumb until the age of two.

It is not without significance to Ian's oral needs, however, that the mother reported that Ian had difficulties which she described as related to sleep. Ian was left to "scream himself blue with rage." When, at the suggestion of others, Ian was brought down with the other children or adults and held, the mother reports (without insight) how surprisingly pleasant the child could then be. One may conjecture here as to the mother's early attitudes and fears regarding her infant son: she described him not as having been unhappy, but as having been "in a rage." It is quite clear, by inference, that the mother describes herself as unresponsive to her son's earliest infantile needs, and as expecting her son to be hostile and aggressive.

Ian is further described as having been a very active and determined infant and toddler, with early developmental achievements, e.g., walking at nine months and walking independently on the stairs by fifteen months. By age eighteen months, the boy was already memorizing and reciting nursery rhymes. The mother recalls with curiosity and surprise her own failure to capitalize on Ian's obvious intellectual precocity as a means of preparing him for the dramatic changes that then occurred in his life at that age.

At age eighteen months, Ian was left for a week with his maternal grandmother while the parents packed and made their farewells in preparation for yet another assignment in Greece. Ian rejoined his parents when they boarded ship in a milieu that was anything but "home," a situation which must have been fraught with all the additional tensions occasioned by the confusions aboard ship and the proprioceptive discomforts induced by a sea voyage. The parents found Ian inseparable, crying, and screaming if they tried to leave him alone, e.g., for dinner. Moreover, he would not nap and refused to sleep away from the parents at night. It is not clear whether the parents attempted to use phenobarbital at this time, as they did later. By the end of the voyage, separation anxiety had not abated and sleep had become a chronic problem, with Ian keeping the parents up progressively later until two, three, or four o'clock in the morning.

In Athens, housing was difficult and the father's assignment took him away almost immediately. At their hotel, Ian gorged on food and finally and most pleasantly (to the parents) went to sleep. This left the parents with the impression that they could have one quiet meal together before the father left. Leaving a "do not disturb" sign on the door, the parents left the sleeping infant and dined at leisure. On their return, they found several frightened and very worried maids in the hall outside the door from which came the sound of Ian's voice screaming in panic. The maids, who feared to trespass, reported that the screaming had continued for some thirty to forty minutes. The mother recalled that when she entered the room it seemed impossible to her that one small child could have vomited so much. She felt intuitively that this situation was all too much, hor-rifically, like the time years before when her daughter had fallen ill (also at age eighteen months and also in the same city). The mother rushed Ian to the hospital. En route, Ian began to have a seizure that continued for three hours. The mother indicates that the convulsions were not controlled by medication and that her son was kept on the critical list in the hospital for the next two days. The hospital in-vestigation of the convulsion indicated that the boy had no fever; neurological examinations and EEG were also negative. The mother's account is not clear, but it appears that following discharge Ian was returned to the hospital for outpatient examinations on at least two occasions. Attempts were made to use phenobarbital to facilitate repeated EEGs, and these precipitated acute panic reactions ("he was given enough to knock out a horse and it didn't faze him"). Attempts to examine Ian were apparently traumatic to both mother and child. Yet Mrs. F. later indicated to Ian's neurologist that the boy was kept on phenobarbital until the following year. There are no known sequelae to this episode.

While still in Athens, before the age of three, Ian was hospital-ized for a tonsillectomy. However real or distorted, Ian recalls this as having been done under local anesthesia and insists that he recalls the surgeon dropping his tonsils in a wastebasket while his mother left the room in anxiety. It is of significance that Ian developed a devouring interest in dinosaurs, a thorough knowledge of their classification, and a preoccupation with them that was so intense as to concern his later nursery school teachers. It should also be noted that Ian had kept a "transitional object" throughout these years. It was abandoned in Greece, when his mother refused to take his "filthy blanket" back to London. The family returned there when Ian was three (during treatment it was learned that Ian still, episodically, demands his mother's silk scarf as a precondition to sleep). The return voyage to London was also problematic and difficult, with abortive attempts to quiet Ian's anxiety and excitation with phenobarbital. Little more is known of the boy's next year, during which time the family resettled in London.

The mother recalls little of Ian's habit and toilet training. She suggests that she was less demanding of him than she was of his sisters, and that he "may have been a bit delayed" in bowel control, becoming clean between the ages of eighteen and twenty-four months. Given the "normal negativism" and independence of this phase of development, and given the mother's present, demonstrable rage reaction to Ian for even looking disagreeable or in disagreement with her, one can only surmise that the mother's memory of toilet training has been expurgated. Ian, at this late date, remembers surprisingly more than is typical. At age four to five years, he reports that he was frequently constipated and afraid of letting go. On one particular occasion his mother insisted on giving him two tablespoons of castor oil. Ian lost his control completely and felt terribly ashamed. He has since concluded that his early constipation must have derived from his fear, viz., that if he ever relaxed, he would lose control and all his feces or insides would come out. He also recalls and describes with precision his mother's using enemas on him. (The mother separately volunteered that she did not think she had ever given the boy an enema. One may question whether this is the mother's repression, or whether there are anal, sexualized fantasies of the child involved here.)

At about age five, Ian was physically abused by an older boy in his neighborhood, who repeatedly picked on him. The parents were concerned that Ian had provoked such attacks (and there is an inference of sexual assault suggested by Ian in his psychiatric interview; i.e., Ian described masturbation as that which little boys are forced to do by bigger, older ones who take them off alone). Details are limited, but it appears that from the age of five, Ian persistently attacked his own peers. There are also reports that at the same age he was in various types of trouble with his parents and that he may have been a firesetter as well.

As a consequence, Ian was referred for psychiatric diagnostic evaluation at five and a half years. He was tested by a Dr. D., who administered both projective and psychometric tests. The latter indicated a high intellectual potential, with a Binet (L) I.Q. of 136. Ian was grossly fearful of aggressive impulses and dangers. His castration anxiety was exceptionally open, with the boy holding his hands over his penis during much of the examination, yet somehow finding it possible both to unzip his trousers and to unbuckle them so that he had to ask for help from the examining psychologist at the end of the session (counterphobic?). Mrs. F. remembers some of Ian's interview, particularly his "three wishes." Ian had wanted a new mother, a toilet tank, and something else the mother could not recall. Ian was given the toilet tank for his backyard, but not psychotherapy. The installation of the toilet tank is recalled by both mother and Ian as giving rise to considerable amusement and pleasure, with the neighborhood children as frequent visitors who came to play with it and Ian. In line with this interest, Ian also became a precocious reader and owned an encyclopedia set of his own. His keenest interest was in the study of waterworks, internal plumbing, etc. (such interest has continued to date, but at a vastly more sophisticated level; Ian now studies "water hydraulics").

As previously noted, Ian's sister Gwen died when he was six years ten months of age. He saw her for the first and last time at the funeral. Some two weeks later, as Mrs. F. recalls, she was sitting at dinner and asking Ian his multiplication homework—when he had his first psychomotor seizure. The mother gives a very graphic description of her son's behavior, a classical neurological picture of a petit mal seizure. During the following two years, Ian apparently had six or seven similar seizures. The neurological examinations that followed included some four or five EEG's, all negative with the exception of one that seemed a bit "suspicious." Increases and changes in medication were followed by initial abatement in the seizures, which invariably returned shortly afterward. Medication was progressively increased over many months with dosages of Meberal, and eventual substitution of this by Mysoline, always accompanied with dosages of Dilantin. Ian's present dosage is 1000 mg. Mysoline, plus 200 mg. Dilantin taken thrice daily.

With the change in medication there may have been a modification of seizures or their manifestation, e.g., the first appearance of his tics. It is clear that Ian began to develop more extended difficulties with his sleeping during this time and that he became more explosive and more provocatively difficult with his parents. The neurologist expressed concern that medication might be responsible for the explosiveness, but could see no relationship to the sleep disorder. It should also be noted that Ian was undergoing orthodontic treatment during these times and there was concern that massive doses of Dilantin might adversely affect his gums. Ian also suffered from a diaphragmatic hernia, diagnosed about age nine and a half, and surgical correction remained a continued threat. Eventually Ian was hospitalized at age ten and the hernia was corrected under a general anesthetic, but without surgery (via oral, esophagal probe).

The family is Anglican and Ian is a very religious child, which he partly exploits in asking for parental (if not Divine) absolution. At the mother's persuasion, Ian had continued a childhood practice of sharing his confessions of the bad things he had done during the day, i.e., until age eleven. The parents had been concerned that Ian should not have to feel guilty. Ian seems to exploit his parents' sensitivity by using his "confessional" maneuver to manipulate his parents, knowing that if he "confesses" he will not be punished, i.e., directly. But it is also evident that the parents have been frustrated and angered by this behavior, and have punished the boy indirectly for different, otherwise acceptable behavior. Ian evidences the normal range of conventional moral values for a boy his age. At school and at others' homes, Ian's reaction formations seem well maintained; he appears honest, compliant to the interests and needs of others, cooperative, respectful of others, sympathetic, etc.

The dramatic difference in Ian's attitudes and regressive values is evident only at home. The aberrant nature of his misbehavior and particularly his open aggression impressed the parents as evidence of gross psychological disturbance. Detailed information of the mother's interactions, her seductive attitudes, and her provocations need to be assessed, however. To illustrate, Ian made a snide comment concerning his sister and the mother involuntarily slapped his face. Hurt, humiliated, and angry, Ian ran up the stairs shouting choice and unkind things at his mother. At the top of the stairs, Ian paused to pick up his baseball, turned and gestured as if he would throw the ball at his mother. At this juncture, she smiled and sarcastically suggested that Ian throw it; and with this she turned her back and started to walk away. Ian, in fact, threw the ball and hit his mother. The pain was apparently considerable and the mother found herself in tears, something that she had never permitted herself in front of the boy. Ian was shocked and dismayed by his mother's behavior, begged her forgiveness, and was a model child for a short while thereafter. Whatever the mother's ambivalence to her son, whatever her seductions, the degree of Ian's provocations cannot be minimized: Ian is a constant tease, and a not-too-humorous, rather sadistic mimic.

With the increased behavioral difficulties at age ten, Ian's parents asked for a psychiatric re-evaluation. While psychotherapy was recommended, and the question was raised as to the mother's need for therapeutic help, the consulting psychiatrist did not have sufficient time free to accept Ian. Further modifications and increases in medication were made that summer on a neurological basis, with Ian's seizures again diminishing, particularly at a time when he was separated from his parents and spending his vacation on one of the family's estates. While his seizures abated, Ian reportedly threatened a kindly adult with violence and was involved in many provocative disputes with an older boy. These incidents seemed important since the inference was that Ian provoked in such a manner that it was he who would be punished. Ian ran away from the family estate, hiking and hitchhiking some 30 to 40 miles to rejoin his parents. The seizures re-emerged at home and the last psychiatric referral was made to Dr. A., and then to me.

Ian was initially resistant to treatment, e.g., forgetting to leave school in time for his appointments, being "disturbed with school matters" and running away from school instead of coming to treatment, etc. During the first two weeks of therapy (he was seen twice), Ian acted out considerably; e.g., mutual, nude exhibitionism with a neighbor boy, smashing a window at home, threatening his father with a prized saber, etc. Treatment was then increased to two appointments per week; the immediate result was complete cessation of acting out at home. Ian has since come to his treatment sessions with verve and enthusiasm. He has viewed his treatment as an introspective "detective story" in which he searches his experiences and memories for clues to the origins of his difficulties, for pieces of his own jigsaw puzzle. Ian has displaced some of his provocative teasing of his mother into his treatment sessions, where he enjoys and now openly delights in intellectual torture of his therapist. But Ian is also able to look at himself somewhat intellectually, lamenting his lack of friends, his humiliation in his sleep disorder, and considerably enjoying the ready acceptance he has found in his therapist. Treatment is of interest and acceptable, i.e., so long as this does not reach too far or come too close to Ian's most sensitive areas (e.g., feelings of humiliation, worries over toilet matters, questions of his sanity, etc.).

IV. POSSIBLE SIGNIFICANT ENVIRONMENTAL INFLUENCES

Ian's neurologist, a most experienced specialist in childhood disorders, was unequivocal in his conclusions that this boy suffered from an organic convulsive disorder, petit mal in nature and idiopathic in origin. What had struck me, however, was the fact that Ian had never been seen by the neurologist during a seizure and that the clinical description of such seizures had been largely provided by the mother. What is also suspected, but not clear, is the degree of Ian's suggestibility, his readiness or potentiality for physical expression of maternal suggestion of his illness.

It may well be that Ian's seizure condition derives solely from an organic dysfunction. But Freud's comments seem of particular interest in the diagnostic assessment, viz., that it is "quite right to distinguish between an organic and an 'affective' epilepsy. The practical significance of this is that a person who suffers from the first kind has a disease of the brain, while a person who suffers from the second kind is a neurotic. In the first case his mental life is subjected to an alien disturbance from without, in the second case the disturbance is an expression of his mental life itself" (1928, p. 181).

The neurological evaluation and diagnosis cannot be improved on. Yet it would seem desirable to consider Ian's developmental history with a view to assessing alternative psychogenic contributions to his seizures. Whether organic or psychogenic (or possibly a combination of these), there are a number of "significant environmental influences" (1) which may have lowered a neurological-psychological seizure threshold, or (2) which have predisposed the ego organization toward hysterical discharge processes and interrelated psychopathological defense organization. Whatever theoretical orientation might be emphasized, the same basic environmental influences seem relevant:

1. The mother's early (and continuing) incapacity to respond to her son's needs as an infant, e.g., letting him scream "until blue in the face." The mother's projection of her own aggressive expectations seems paralleled, in this respect, by her intolerance of passivity and her need to provoke aggressive responses in her son.

2. Separation from the parents at age eighteen months for one week, followed by the immediate loss of the home environment, and consequent disequilibrium aboard ship (separation anxiety seems specific and related to sleep disturbances).

3. Accumulative fatigue and anxiety during the ship's voyage; plus excitation due to the ship voyage, sharing of parents' bedroom, change of language, etc.

4. Acute anxiety attack in hotel, with screaming, vomiting, etc., in absence of parents. Possible cyanotic asphyxia from screaming and consequent aspiration of vomitus (?) with consequent convulsion.

5. Hospitalization of Ian, with further separation, acute anxiety of both child and mother (in the absence of the father).

6. Attempts at both massive medication with phenobarbital and electroencephalographic examination; consequent manic-hyperactive response.

7. Tonsillectomy at age two and a half, same hospital (?), local anesthesia (?).

8. Further exacerbation of separation fears with change in home, environment, ship voyage, return to London; acute anxiety reactions and panic; attempts to quiet him with phenobarbital on board ship; age three.

9. Impact of mysterious, exciting, and dangerous implications of father's occupation and nighttime absences.

10. Parental attitudes are particularly suspect. There is an impression that they feared Ian's convulsion in infancy might have left him damaged, like his sister. Parental overindulgence at present suggests possible overindulgence in infancy so that age-appropriate

expectations were inconsistently demanded. The mother also expected her son to be similar to her "professionally psychopathic" brother and has long viewed Ian as potentially defective, e.g., in his lack of control of rages. One suspects that the mother compensated for her ambivalent aggression by inconsistent, restitutive overindulgence. This is consonant with the tentative view of her needs for anal-sadistic battles, evident in her own comments that she cannot "keep her hands off of her son, either in anger or affection."

11. The physical attacks on Ian at age four or five appear to be symptomatic (because of provocations) rather than precipitating causal experiences. Yet it is possible that the child experienced a sadistic or sexual attack. Ian's account of anal assault by the mother during his phases of constipation could be true or might represent fantasies relating to anal-sadistic sexual wishes.

12. The sister Gwen existed as a phantom, an ideal, best-loved child who was absent *and* "sick in the head." The potentialities for identification with the sick or dead sister are facilitated by the actual facts, and by the family folklore of the remarkable coincidence in which Ian suffered his infant convulsion at the same age and the same place as the dead Gwen. It hardly seems fortuitous that Ian's first seizure occurred within two weeks of his sister's death and his first and only view of her.

13. Hospital and medical examinations, electroencephalographic investigations, and the various pharmaceutical medications have all been environmental interventions and probable stresses. The significant ages would appear to be eighteen months, three years, six and a half years, and rather continuously since then. Ian seems to have handled his later neurological and medical examinations comfortably, but it is evident from his treatment that he fears that he is "brain damaged" and potentially insane, a boy whom the best doctors and the best medications have been unable to cure.

14. The date of diagnosis of Ian's diaphragmatic hernia is not clear. One wonders if this is coincidental with the increase in the boy's seizures two years ago.

15. Equally obscure are the inferences that Ian's paternal grandfather died two years ago, that the father suffered a concomitant and prolonged depression, and that the maternal grandmother was rejected from the family household.

V. Assessment of Development

A. *Drive Development*

1. *Libido*

(a) *With regard to phase development*

There seems no question that Ian has reached the phallic stage of psychosexual development and has made tenuous advances into latency. Phenomenologically, the latter is evident in Ian's relatively adequate academic competence, his active and interested participation and skill in particular group sports, his capacity to relate (under structured circumstances) and take at least minimal pleasure in some age-adequate activities with peers and adults other than his parents.

Such progression, however, is not secure and Ian's capabilities remain partly dependent on his being reassured via the supervision of adults. Ian's schoolwork also breaks down, sometimes completely, when the mother insists on supervising his homework. He is more successful when he isolates his schoolwork and arranges to remain in school in the afternoons to continue studies under the more benign supervision of a teacher.

The tenuousness of Ian's freedom from oedipal, sexual and aggressive drives is clear, even to the mother who notes her son's unusual interest in her and feels his provocations have an odd aura of sensual sadism. One clearly sees the existence of libidinal fixations in the anal phase in Ian's beginning references to toilet problems, his difficulties over enemas and constipation, and more particularly in the ease of regression in which he provokes and fights with his mother (as a love battle).

The evidence of oral fixations is not clear. The history notes an early yet transient feeding difficulty. More suspect are the reports that the child was left to scream in times of need. Ian presently attributes his having orthodonture treatment to self-damage caused by prolonged thumb sucking, i.e., until age two years. There is a long history of oral, medical interventions and it should also be recalled that the vomiting at age eighteen months preceded the first convulsion. If there is a hysterical contribution to Ian's seizures, then the boy's oral and labial tics and mouthings, plus his nauseous stomach feelings, should be questioned as derivatives of oral fixations. It is equally clear that the more dramatic oral traumata occurred during or after the anal phase of development. Whether such oral assaults were experienced or understood as a consequence of anal retribution (upwardly displaced) or whether they may have reinforced a more primitive oral fixation is anything but clear.

Ian's characterological and defense organization, however, is predominantly anal. His history of continuing interest in waterworks, toilets, etc., indicates the existence of excremental sexual fantasies, and permits the inference of fixation, and perhaps regression, from phallic to anal expression of libidinal phase dominance.

(b) *With regard to libido distribution*

(i) *Cathexis of self:* While Ian is not hypochondriacal, his seizure condition has greatly contributed to an intense self cathexis, both of his body and his psychological self-awareness, self-judgment, etc. Despite this high cathexis of the self, it does not seem positive or pleasurable. He makes high demands of himself, e.g., that he should be well dressed, scholastically superior, etc., yet he obtains little gratification from his successes. On the contrary, Ian gives the impression not only that he feels he is organically defective or damaged, but also that his standards (introjects) are so perfectionistic that whatever the adequacy of his real-life performance, it is never quite good enough to leave him pleased or secure with himself.

(ii) *Cathexis of objects:* Ian's cathexis of his objects is relatively normal, i.e., it shows no evidence of borderline or psychotic processes. There is a neurotic, psychopathological unevenness of cathexis, however, since Ian views his objects as potentially dangerous or threatening to him. There is an intense ambivalent cathexis of objects, particularly during his regressions, which are markedly reminiscent of the toddler stage of development; e.g., he expects his parents to accept his violent aggression not only without objection, but with love and forgiveness.

2. *Aggression*

(a) *Quantity of aggressive expression*

Ian appears to have a relatively normal endowment of aggressive drives, but his history suggests an abnormal degree of reactive aggression from infancy onward. This could relate to the mother's ambivalence and need to stimulate aggressive, masculine responses (which she finds so lacking in her husband). Both the developmental and the current history are replete with incidents in which the mother helps to perpetuate ongoing, sadomasochistic battles over even the most incidental of matters. Ian's experiences at age four or five when he attacked his peers has the sound of an abreactive, passive-into-active defense in which he enacted on others what he had experienced himself (the attacks on him by the older boy). Yet this behavior is also described by the parents as having been provocative. In this sense, Ian's very early behavior fits a general pattern of sadomasochistic provocations which may have continued from infancy onward.

While Ian's aggressive outbursts have the appearance of quantitative abnormality, one might better view these outbursts in terms of imbalance in that aggressive fury is defended against in most social situations, yet is afforded too frequent, too prolonged expression at home (where the father remains Ian's apologist). Ian notes, for example, that by the age of five he was quite prepared to set fires in ashtrays, throw over chairs, throw knives on the floor, all as manipulations to insure that his mother would return home from a cocktail party when he was in a fury and wanted her.

At noted earlier, in structured situations such as football games, his aggression is effectively directed. It is only at home that Ian has "let himself go" and demonstrated his negativistic fury in fierce and vulgar arguments, in physical battles with his mother, etc. His relationships outside of the home have remained relatively free of such outbursts, although during the previous summer there were indications that Ian's fears and aggression might be carried over into other areas of his life as well.

(b) Quality of aggressive expression

Ian mimics his parents' attitudes when he speaks of his "violent feelings." While using a vocabulary of violence, he speaks with a bland and sometimes humorous affect. It is not clear whether Ian parrots and makes jokes of his parents' expectations that he should feel terribly upset and aggressive over incidents which might otherwise seem trivial in everyday life. At other times, he speaks almost melodramatically of his evil deeds and attacks (e.g., of running his father through with a saber) when in fact the incident was more one of Ian's fantasy and *not* one of action. While such behavior has the appearance of a "breakthrough," as if it were psychotic, it gave the clinical impression of a contrived dramatization and a perverse reversal of values, which could be related to parental acting out. In illustration, the father tends to see all of Ian's misbehavior as expected and forgiven from its inception, even his breaking of windows, throwing the mother to the floor, etc. The mother, in dramatic contrast, seems to see any small indication of teasing or refusal as tantamount to rebellion against established authority. Ian's *modes* of expression of aggression are as unbalanced as the quantitative expression. In fact, he has been unexpectedly violent over relatively trivial matters. On the other hand, he has accepted inappropriate discipline of himself as being logical and desirable. One is left with the confused impression that, for this boy, aggression in any form may at one time be devastatingly horrible and at another time have little significance because it will be excused no matter how inappropriate.

(c) *Direction of aggressive expressions*

There is lack of aggressive reaction toward persons who have in reality actually deprived, hurt, or demeaned Ian. He rarely permits himself to express openly or appropriately a legitimate grievance or annoyance. Yet he berates himself at such times for his horrible tempers and anger, which in fact have not been expressed. It is not surprising to find that Ian is devoutly religious and prays to God for help with his rages (and also melodramatically and manipulatively exhibits his religiosity to his parents). It is clear that Ian provokes people in such a way that they are bound to direct aggression toward him. His excitement, evident in treatment, suggests a masochistic overdetermination. When Ian does express aggression directly, it is usually inappropriate, disproportionate in its intensity, and more often directed toward his mother (as a scapegoat?).

Freud (1928) believed that hysterical convulsive disorders involved a massive turning of aggression against the self. Bartemeier (1932, 1943), discussing and extending Freud's views on the hysterical features of convulsive disorders, noted that the superego may use an existing tendency to seizures as a means of directing aggression against the self. Ian's seizures could represent such a turning of aggression against the self, but this cannot be documented at this time.

B. Ego and Superego Development

1. Ego Apparatus

Ian's ego apparatus (his endowment of physiological and sensory equipment facilitating ego functioning) seems to be intact. If his seizure condition has an organic basis, one would hypothesize transient and perhaps global impairments of the entire ego apparatus. Yet studies such as those of Peterson et al. (1950) suggest that patients with hysterical convulsive disorders have full recall under hypnosis for events occurring during the time of the seizure. Whatever the etiology of Ian's seizures, they do not seem to have affected his basic progression and relatively normal development.

2. Ego Functions

Ian has been tested on both the Stanford-Binet and the WISC, at ages five and eleven. In both instances, his performance was at the superior level. Until a year and a half ago, his school performance was most adequate in a competitive setting with high standards. The impairment of intellectual ego functions seems to be of psychoneurotic origin and his difficulties in this area seem to be affected especially by his mother's concerns.

Ego functions such as control of motility, integration and synthesis, may be impaired by Ian's seizure potential. It is noteworthy, however, that he has never injured himself physically during a seizure and (so far as is known) that he has never been observed having a seizure other than in the presence of his parents. (However, see also Section 4, Secondary Interference.)

3. Defenses

Ian's relative honesty, cleanliness, pity, and compassion, etc., are clearly and firmly established. One would consider them well-established reaction formations if it were not for the fact that Ian seems to derive little or no *pleasure* from the gratification of these opposite-drive tendencies. One may conjecture that Ian cannot tolerate or find pleasure in himself (excessive standards or extreme punitiveness of the superego?) or that the urgency of the unconscious aggression is so demanding and unsublimated that he pays a constant, defensive price in keeping alien aggressive impulses in check.

Projection of aggression is in pathological evidence, with Ian misconstruing unstructured or ambiguous situations (or comments) as evidence of anger and potential rejection of him (e.g., by teachers, friends, therapist, etc.).

Ian "panics" when he is unable to sleep away from home; he fears that something will happen if everyone else in the house goes to sleep before him. He is afraid he might die from accumulative fatigue when he is unable to sleep; his environment seems alive with aggressive and hostile undercurrents. Treatment suggests that there is an excited malice in the boy's midnight interruptions of his parents' sleep, in his telephone calls asking them to bring him home when he is unable to sleep at a friend's house. While the behavioral characteristics of Ian's sleep disturbance support the mother's conviction that it originated at eighteen months (in connection with separation anxiety), Ian's fantasies that mothers kill fathers and abandon them (for millionaires) suggest that the sleep disturbance also incorporates a projection of the boy's own anger and death wishes toward his father. One should also consider that the mother may be explosively aggressive, that she may reinforce Ian's fears of an extremely aggressive world. Such factors provide Ian with a rationalization for the appropriateness and intensity of his own feelings, thereby masking both Ian's provocations and the indigenous base of his own projections. On the other hand, Ian's extrafamilial school milieu is quite benign; yet Ian carries his own internalized, defensive attitudes into his peer relationships, which are independent of the reality of his problems with his parents.

Denial of affect and *intellectualization* are two defenses that seem to be characteristic modes of Ian's coping with everyday matters. He rarely permits himself to experience age-adequate feelings in an appropriate manner. He functions as a rather "feelingless" young man who intellectualizes and reviews his behavior from a psychological distance. While Ian's use of defensive intellectualization has the appearance of a precocious adolescent reaction, it seems developmentally related to his parents' extensive intellectual expectations of their son; i.e., they treat him as if he were an adult. There are also indications of obsessive ruminations that possibly reinforce introspective intellectualization, as a means of controlling drive activity.

Regression is another characteristic defense, which is particularly in evidence at home, under stress. In public, Ian functions rather well, e.g., at school or when adult friends are visiting his home. He successfully avoids and withdraws (with phobic characteristics of anxiety if he cannot avoid painful situations), and retreats physically to his home where he may then regress emotionally to anal-sadistic behavior. In this, he is petulant, demanding, torturing; and he expects complete acceptance from his parents no matter what he has done. Fearing even worse behavior, the parents have accepted, if not reinforced, such regressive and infantile behavior.

Identification with the aggressor is clear in Ian's mimicking and provoking of his mother, his therapist, etc. His behavior seems to have a degree of conscious purposefulness when he denigrates and cynically exploits or exhibits his parents' shortcomings by adopting inappropriate behavior which they have in fact exhibited to him. Ian's misbehavior is a parody of his mother's lack of control, and with it he mimics and cynically exploits her guilt.

Ian's earliest history also supports the view that aggressive identification may be syntonic (and not altogether defensive), e.g., as an effective mode of coercing his parents to give him care and attention. His ability to identify has been effectively used in learning by anticipatory trial actions.

Ian's defenses are not characteristic of his age, and the lack of joy or self-confidence suggests that sublimations are possible only to a limited degree. His defense organization does not seem adequate to the task of coping with excessive aggressive and sexual conflicts (partially influenced and exacerbated by provocations and seductions of the parents). The two characteristics of turning aggression against the self and identification with the aggressor may relate to a masochistic, sexual conflict, but this is obviously speculative.

4. Secondary Interference with Ego Functions

Ian's reality testing, e.g., of the benign or malignant nature of situations or people, is significantly impaired, and in this respect there is clear evidence of interference with ego functioning.

Ian's school performance was transiently impaired at about age five, when he was said to have been obsessionally concerned with dinosaurs. Academic functioning, however, remained relatively free thereafter until about age ten, and since then it has varied considerably and dramatically. Cognitive functions, as demonstrable via psychometric tests, remain relatively free. Ian's intellectual capacities seem impaired predominantly via the mother's concern or interventions. Preliminary exploration of Ian's underlying fantasies (in treatment) suggests that full exploitation of intelligence is impaired by a fear of success and an inhibition of exhibitionism. Ian fantasies, for example, that he is a genius whose success could be so overwhelming that either he would devastate his competitors, or they would be so fantastically jealous, envious, and hostile that they would murder him for his success. Ian's fantasy life fits in with Sperling's theoretical formulations of petit mal in children. In discussing psychogenic headaches, petit mal and epilepsy, Sperling (1953) suggests that "*petit mal* is interpreted as an instant cutting off from functioning of those parts of the mind which serve the perception and execution of stimuli from within and without, because perception of certain stimuli would lead to an explosive reaction endangering the life of the patient and that of the people in the environment" (p. 252).

C. *Development of Total Personality (Lines of Development and Mastery of Tasks or Age-adequate Responses)*

   1. *From Dependency to Emotional Self-Reliance and Adult Object Relationships*

Ian appears to be having a very difficult time consolidating himself in latency (Stage 6). There is much evidence of attempts to establish mutual and reciprocal relationships with a select group of boyfriends and responsive teachers. Such relationships are not secure and may break down when Ian meets with frustrations that are amenable to misconstruction, e.g., when an acquaintance fails to telephone, when there is a relevant criticism of schoolwork, etc.

Not unrelated is Ian's difficulty in maintaining his academic work, particularly when his mother tries to help him. The most dramatic disturbance of object relationships is Ian's incapacity to cope with his parents. The intensity of the battles between parents and child is sufficiently dramatic to obscure the more fundamental fact that Ian has been unable to establish age-adequate and conflict-free relationships outside of the family.

While Ian has been described by his parents as a self-reliant, emotionally self-contained and independent boy, the developmental history documents other features as well. Separation anxiety, clinging, and inability to separate were manifest at eighteen months and thereafter. The use of a transitional object, "the filthy blanket," cannot be unrelated to Ian's present, though occasional, need for his mother's silk scarf as a prerequisite to going to sleep. Similarly, Ian's inability to sleep away from home, his fear of being the first to go to sleep, his self-isolation from peers, all reflect on his dependence.

2. *Toward Body Independence*

(a) *From suckling to rational eating:* Ian's earliest history is equivocal but suggestive of inconsistent oral gratifications and complications. Historically later oral traumas have been noted. Whatever battles may have evolved in the family's eating patterns or traditions, it appears that Ian's attitudes toward food and eating have now approximated those of the parents and are age-adequate. He seems free from notable food fads, battles over meals, and readily and appropriately can eat away from home, seemingly at any time or place. This may overstate the case, since Ian is also most egocentric and can hardly envision that he should eat at any time or place that he might dislike. In the selective, benign environments in which he is cared for, covert oral problems could readily be disguised. However, it appears that Ian has moved relatively completely into rational eating that is uncontaminated by psychological conflict.

(b) *From wetting and soiling to bladder and bowel control:* Ian became dry and clean at about age two. So far as is known, there have been no regressions (encopresis or enuresis) when he was ill, emotionally upset, and during or after seizures. His attitude toward cleanliness, neatness, etc., seems Spartan. It is not surprising to find Ian volunteering the information that it was appropriate for his mother to have washed his mouth with soap when he first used "dirty words." Whatever developmental battles may have occurred in the line toward independent bladder and bowel control, it is evident that these controls are both secure and age-adequate.

(c) *From irresponsibility to body management:* The history of Ian's precocious motor abilities and his aggressive, nominal independence are consistent with his present capacities. Ian seems completely responsible and fully capable of his own body management, including responsibility for intake of medications. If there is anything unusual, it is in the excessive independence rather than in the failure to take responsibility for body management.

(d) *From egocentricity to companionship:* When conditions are favorable, Ian seems to relate well and to accept the mutual needs and interests of other children. He is unable, however, to do this under stress, e.g., in groups lacking adult supervision, when visiting away from home, etc. It is clear that Ian relates to other children at least as temporary helpmates in sustained activities such as group sports and occasionally on an individual basis in play. Ian's treatment material suggests a yearning for peer relationships and a sorrow that he cannot maintain friendships. He is somewhat aware of the reactions of other children to his own joking provocations. It is also clear that he has a capacity to identify with other children as "objects in their own right," as persons whose feelings and wishes he would like to acknowledge and would like to respect. The parents' and Ian's reports suggest that he began a more secure step in his social relationships about a year and a half previously. This evidence indicates that Ian had reached Stage 4 on this line of development, however tentatively, and that his present inability to accept or reach out for companionship and friendship derives from a neurotic interference.

(e) *From the body to the toy and from play to work:* Assessments of this developmental line take into consideration the earliest cathexis of the infant's body, the extension of cathexis to the mother and to inanimate objects such as "transitional objects." Stage 3 describes the toddler who may cuddle and maltreat symbolic objects with a full range of expression of his ambivalence toward them. In Ian's case, one is impressed by the fact that his episodic regressions are to this stage of development. However, I hesitate to use the term "regression" because his developmental history clearly indicates that such behavior has persisted from early infancy onward. Ian's use of his mother's scarf, however, is not syntonic and gives rise to shame. This need does seem regressive and is consonant with developmental fixations in a very early stage at which "transitional objects" are cathected as an extension of the mother.

Ian's toys, his hobbies, and his physical activities in sports are aggressive and phallic in nature and are used to express and work through transient fantasies. He has extensive sets of toy soldiers and battle equipment, and in his play with them he usually identifies with the Nazi and Russian armies, identifications which are consonant with other manifestations of his sadomasochistic and aggressive impulses (which are not adequately neutralized). His pleasure in and capacity for task completion and problem solution show a clear, however tenuous, move into Phase 5. As noted earlier, Ian is dissatisfied with his capacities to function adequately and is hypercritical of his performance. He leaves the impression that he is grossly insecure as to his capability in functioning, therefore turns to his objects for reassurance, and when this is lacking, regresses to earlier stages under stress.

Many of Ian's achievements seem based on counterphobic dynamics, e.g., his study of water hydraulics, the collection of sabers and guns, etc. He has obviously mastered the drive controls and achievements necessary for such activities, but the autonomy of such secondary ego functions is not well established and he seems to lack an adequate degree of neutralization and sublimation, both prerequisites for the ability to progress from play to work.

3. Assessment of Correspondence between Developmental Lines

There is a high degree of consistency in an overall evaluation of the different developmental lines. On the side of ego development, there is a uniform and marked precocity and early achievement beyond age-adequacy and expectations. But equally consistently, one finds Ian unable to make use of his excellent endowment and ego skills. He is not satisfied with himself; he shows an inadequate capacity to separate from his parents; a limited capacity to maintain age-adequate relationships with peers; and a marked restriction in the progression from play to work.

VI. REGRESSION AND FIXATION POINTS

The early developmental history, though ambiguous, suggests that Ian received inconsistent care in relation to his early oral needs.

The history of oral traumas, dating back to eighteen months, continues through the latency period. Since the child's early years were symptom-free, the degree of orality implicit in Ian's psychomotor seizures may in fact have stemmed from retrospective trauma, or may otherwise reflect an upward displacement of anal and phallic fears of damage.

The mother's known attitudes to and intolerance of aggressive activity or "insolent disregard" of her wishes must be considered along with the fragmentary evidence of early fixations. It is particularly striking that the mother fails to remember her son's habit training when Ian so vividly recalls his extended troubles with constipation, laxatives, and enemas. It is clear that Ian was precociously active and aggressive, presumably before the advent of habit training. Given his particular assertiveness of independence, along with the normal negativism of the average toddler, one can only conjecture on difficulties of toilet and cleanliness training. Dominant defenses and character traits suggest anal fixations, which were perpetuated into phallic and (fragmentary) latency development. Both the neurologist and Ian's therapist have noticed the interesting and continuing fact that the boy's aggressive outbursts become more extensive and frequent when he is *less* subject to seizures. This permits the inference, as one possibility, that the psychomotor seizures are a regressive, primitive psychophysiological response which occurs when anal-sadistic behavior is checked. Whether Ian's symptomatic mouth movements, tics, and nauseous stomach feelings reflect early oral fixations or are merely a concomitant of primitive psychophysiological reactions is quite unclear.

The mother's comments on Ian's phallic development are largely negative; i.e., she does not remember exhibitionistic, protective attitudes; competitive play initiated by Ian with his father; genital masturbation, etc. Yet the psychological evaluation of Ian at five years six months is striking in its emphasis on the boy's phallic anxieties. At that time, the boy's projective materials were predominantly concerned with aggression and castration fears. Ian's concern for a toilet tank could reflect regressive anal preoccupations; or, if considered along with his extended interest in waterworks, it might be better understood as reflecting his concern about phallic potency. We know from the father that he asked, if not seduced, his wife to

indulge the boy in intimate and caressing body care. Ian's continuing sadomasochistic, highly exciting and sexualized aggression with
his mother indicates an anal-sadistic manifestation of phallic drive
development.

In the attempt to assess the question of regression, one should
recall that the first psychomotor seizure occurred in the middle of
Ian's sixth year, shortly after he saw his dead sister. It will be recalled that she was the mother's favorite child who was "sick in the
head." I suspect that this trauma may have precipitated further
regressive tendencies at the very time Ian was making peripheral
and tenuous movements into latency.

VII. Dynamic and Structural Assessments (Conflicts)

A. External Conflicts

This section of the Profile is customarily used for much younger
children, i.e., prior to the internalization of conflicts. Some of Ian's
behavior is sufficiently bizarre or aberrant to indicate that only
limited or inadequate introjections (in terms of superego formation)
may exist. In view of the open and regressive conflicts within the
family, some of Ian's reactions have the quality of external conflicts
with the parents. From the parents' point of view, these are external
conflicts because the boy is "psychopathic," without conscience.

B. Internalized Conflicts

Ian has deliberately broken windows in front of his parents,
"deliberately worked himself into rages," melodramatically threatened his father with a sword, etc. All such behavior has been described as if it were nonconflictual and did not induce anxiety or
guilt. These features led the parents to compare Ian with Mrs. F.'s
"psychopathic" and often-institutionalized brother. Ian's behavior in
treatment has illustrated, in minimal fashion, some of the characteristics the parents have alluded to, i.e., his slyness and manipulative provocations. Ian adds further support to this impression by
purporting that he does things because he wants to be bad; i.e., he
wishes me to believe that he is consciously controlling and directing
his temper tantrums (which is highly questionable).

When this type of behavior is juxtaposed with the developmental history of Ian's provocative attacks on older and larger boys and on his mother, one is left with a different impression, viz., that Ian feels impelled to precipitate trauma, which he is eternally expecting and fearing. The boy's aplomb after such incidents has the quality of a ritualized, parentally induced attempt to intellectualize or rationalize, to find reasons for behaviors and rages that are otherwise inexplicable. This is further complicated by Ian's unconscious sadism which colors his attacks. In this respect, he is aware of a partial truth, viz., that he does want to hurt, ravage, and revenge himself upon his parents.

The superego is fully structuralized, but is archaic in its sadism and intensity. The evidence for this statement is derived from several sources. Ian's reaction formations, his religious orientation and fears, the general adequacy of his moral values and standards, all are maintained independent of his parents or setting. Moreover, his depressed moods, his constant self-devaluation and sadistically cruel innuendoes as to self-damage and inadequacy indicate that aggression has been turned against the self (via the superego). The apparent lack of guilt in Ian may be explicable in terms of the parents' behavior; viz., their solicitation of Ian to confess his misdeeds so that they could mitigate his guilt. One suspects an externalization of the superego, in which the parents either absolve or punish him so that Ian escapes responsibility, anxiety, and guilt.

The developmental history is consistent with the view that structuralization occurred early, and self-control, via introjection, was an early and dramatic necessity for a child who seemed to have felt overwhelming concern both for his own rages and those of the environment.

C. Internal Conflicts

Ian has been a vigorously active child since birth. Whatever passive drive endowment he may have, it is little evident today, except perhaps in his symptom formation, e.g., in his dependent inability to separate from his parents at night. Ian's controlled activity has the hallmark of a defense against passivity and indicates a pathological resolution of his passive-active tendencies. Such attitudes are relatively age-adequate. The pathological implications derive from the developmental history and the clear evidence that this boy has warded off passivity since earliest childhood.

His masculine-feminine conflicts are of a similar nature. Ian is a most "masculine" boy who permits himself few behavioral characteristics that might imply anything "girlish." He acknowledges that he sometimes cries to himself in despair and anger, but he considers this to be a bit "babyish" and not feminine. Ian's inability to sleep in the home and bedroom of school friends could reflect a defense against passive, feminine tendencies. While his father is a passive-appearing and gentle man, he is also as dynamically coiled and powerful as a steel spring. Ian emulates his father's silent superiority and strength, and shares with him a rather pious but implicitly contemptuous attitude toward girls and women. This attitude is age-adequate for Ian, and the pathological implications are inferred only from the implacability of defense.

VIII. Assessment of Some General Characteristics

A. *Frustration Tolerance*

The mother has always believed that Ian had little tolerance for frustration and cites his earliest screaming "until blue in the face" in illustration. While the dynamics of that particular parent-child interaction is suspect (e.g., the mother's intolerance of passivity), the history does suggest an early developmental impasse in which Ian did not have a gradual and easy introduction to frustrations that were within his capacities to cope. The mother seems to have been consistently unable to respond appropriately in gauging the child's capacities at each developmental level and she seems to have permitted excessive frustrations and then overindulged in compensation. Ian has developed a view according to which his tempers are all rages, his hungers are all famines, his loves are all passions, etc. He seems, unrealistically, to judge his needs as potentially overwhelming. Yet this overstates the problem, since Ian has established that he functions reasonably well in a benign atmosphere away from the parents. Moreover, the parents have also strongly suspected that Ian's tempers and allusions to his seizures may have a highly melodramatic undercurrent, and be used by him as a manipulative control of them.

It will be recalled that the father, in particular, has expected Ian to act like an adult, and Ian seems to have adopted this attitude with regard to his own behavior, particularly when he is away from home. Ian shows an age-adequate degree of frustration tolerance in postponing direct gratification, e.g., in deferring free play for hard and continuous practice in football games; saving pocket money for deferred plans in weeks to come; etc.

Frustration and anxiety tolerance are not always easy to distinguish. Moreover, Ian's frustration tolerance may have a masochistic quality, and some of his frustrations and suffering may be unnecessary. The boy seems to obtain a measure of self-esteem regulation in a stoic ideal of being strong and tough (perhaps like his father). He has coped most adequately in the area of his physical illnesses requiring many neurological examinations, orthodonture treatment, hospitalization and correction of hernia, etc. There is little question that he can and does cope with many more frustrations than most boys his age. His inability to cope in other areas and his "babyish" reactions to hurt and frustration have a regressive and neurotic coloring that is dramatic for its contrast with his otherwise excellent adequacy.

B. *Sublimation Potential*

Where Ian's psychopathology does not distort his perception, where the environment is benign, his progress seems to have been fairly constantly progressive. He has clearly demonstrated his capacity for displacement of drive energies, and his learning capacity is relatively free of id invasions. His work, however, seems relatively joyless; and his humor, when it emerges, is more often sadistic (practical jokes). His activities are controlled, competent, and "neutralized." Ian is capable of directing a considerable degree of psychological effort to secondary-process activity, but much of this leaves the impression of defensive activity.

The conceptual distinction between sublimation and the defense of displacement is not an easy one to make, particularly with the limited evidence available in the case of Ian. As Anna Freud (1948) has noted, when viewed from the side of the id, sublimation involves a displacement of sexual and aggressive energies to noninstinctual aims and implicitly involves a loss of pleasure. She also notes, how-

ever, that sublimation "brings great gains: the flow of instinctive
energy into socially adapted behaviour widens the scope of the child's
interests, transforms otherwise dull and uninteresting tasks into
interesting and fascinating pursuits, and—as every teacher can observe—thereby improves the child's ability to work and play and
quickens his intelligence" (p. 28). Robert Waelder (1964), commenting on Anna Freud's formulation, has noted that "all later papers by
various authors emphasize merely the desexualization of the drive
without noticing the concomitant sexualization of the respective ego
activity. Thus, sublimation appears in these later publications as a
net gain from the point of view of the ego; actually, the implicit
sexualization of the ego entails the danger that the ego activity in
question may be embroiled in the conflict to which the drive has
been subject. The ego is somewhat in the position of a nation that
has called on another nation for help—an action which may have its
immediate rewards but also its perils; the ego has marshaled the
mighty support of an instinctual drive, but that is not always a
comfortable ally to have."

Ian's sublimation potential seems constantly threatened by con-
taminations of aggressive and sexual drives which he cannot adequately displace. This is evident in the boy's recurrent difficulties
with schoolwork, in his need to isolate himself in social relationships,
in his preoccupations with intellectual processes intimately connected with instinctual conflicts.

C. Overall Attitude to Anxiety

Both the parents and Ian indicate that he suffers and experiences
little anxiety. The only indication that Ian might have such feelings
concerns his abortive attempts to stay overnight in the homes of
friends. He (blandly) told me that he was "panic-stricken." Yet his
description of thoughts, feelings, and behavior during such occasions leaves doubt that he actually suffers much anxiety, as contrasted
to that described by other patients. Rather, one gains the impression that Ian has scant tolerance for anxiety and defends himself
phobically against any circumstance or situation in which anxiety
might arise. He has been free to withdraw from most anxiety-pro-
ducing situations, returning to his home and parents. There is some
evidence that he resorts to obsessional rumination to handle anxiety

when either self-esteem or physical circumstance has limited the possibility of physical withdrawal. In his regressions to tantrum behavior at home, Ian does *not* give the impression of a child whose ego is completely wanting in intrinsic strength to cope with anxiety, but rather that his compliant and perhaps seductive environment has indulged him to such an extent that he has had little reason to cope with anxiety by means of internal resources.

D. *Progressive Forces versus Regressive Tendencies*

Ian's aggressive and defiant behavior at home, which brought him to treatment, has been seen by the parents as a regressive trend. Preliminary indications from the boy's treatment, however, indicate clearly that Ian had begun to withdraw from his mother's seductive and aggressive demands that he share his intimate secrets with her, that he confess, etc. He knew very well that his deviant tantrum behavior maneuvered his parents into a psychiatric referral for him. In a restrictive sense, such deviant behavior then constitutes a "progressive tendency," a use of acting out to precipiate outside intervention in a developmental impasse. This view is supported by Ian's enthusiastic response to his treatment. He has been quite concerned about his "babyishness," his inability to stay away from home. He has been even more concerned that he might be "mad" and beyond help. He is a hurt and lonely boy in search of better solutions. His regressive tendencies and family battles have been a way of life, providing both excitement and pleasure, yet this has not been totally syntonic for Ian. Large for his age, Ian is growing rapidly and already showing secondary sexual characteristics. His pubertal growth and concomitant sexual drive activity may facilitate progressive movement. But there is little question that Ian's psychopathology is most pronounced and that his defense organization is maladaptive and regressive.

IX. DIAGNOSIS

The openness of Ian's aggression with his mother is understood as a peculiar derivative of his fixations, his neurotic conflict, and the mother's seductiveness. There is no evidence of atypical, borderline or psychotic impairment. While there is evidence of possible organic complications, this does not imply a destructive, degenerative process that affects mental growth. One is impressed with the fact that Ian has a lot to cope with, both because of his fear of organic damage and because of the constant reality that he might have a seizure and that he must take anticonvulsant medications.

What seems to have been a psychoneurotic behavioral disorder of essentially oedipal nature has now settled into a less easily recognizable symptomatology. Ian's intense and sexualized tie to his mother (in particular) indicates a faulty resolution of his oedipal conflict. Ian's move into age-adequate latency is obviously hindered by his powerfully ambivalent ties to his mother; in addition, a secondary complication derives from his archaic superego which denies Ian pleasure in his achievements and demands punishments that infantilize and damage him. One also suspects that he has identified with the brain-damaged sister. Ian's infantile neurosis seems to be in the process of becoming encapsulated in a character disorder, in which there is ego-syntonic phobic avoidance of anxiety- or frustration-producing situations. The externalization of responsibility (superego) and the parents' readiness to justify and rationalize Ian's deviant behavior (as due to organic damage) have facilitated a beginning character structure that has the hallmarks of a delinquent or impulse disorder.

Psychotherapy has now continued for three months, with two sessions per week. Ian has settled into a secure and reasonably effective therapeutic relationship. His behavior in school and his academic performance are temporarily undisturbed, probably because he now studies in the school building, thereby neutralizing the mother's interventions. Ian's tics have (temporarily?) disappeared. Behavioral difficulties at home have markedly diminished but gradually begin to invade the treatment situation, where Ian likes to provoke, test, tease, etc. As one would expect, the emergence of these transference reactions has drained much of Ian's· neurotic impulses to act out at home. The treatment problem becomes one of determining whether twice weekly treatment can control the development of negative transference aspects and permit sufficient intellectual insight so that at least some defensive readaptation might be accomplished. It seems highly questionable that the neurotic problem can be adequately worked through in nonintensive treatment, which provides only a very limited possibility to break the circularity of parent-child excesses of overstimulation. At best, one would antici- pate that progressive maturational forces (alone with nonanalytic treatment) might facilitate more effective encapsulation of the neu- rotic process.

Analysis would be the treatment of choice. Ian seems highly motivated and accessible to therapy. In considering analysis, his ob- sessive, ruminative insightfulness constitutes a resistance to treat- ment, but taken in conjunction with his excellent intelligence it is also an advantage.

The timing of this referral was not ill-advised. Ian presented the picture of a boy who was almost prepared to abandon his limited relationships with peers and the social standards which he had pre- viously maintained effectively. For Ian, the danger seems to have been the extension of sadomasochistic battles with his parents to other relationships and the acceptance of such behavior as normal (epileptic), and approximating the behavior of his "psychopathic uncle."

The seizure condition and continuing heavy medication have undoubtedly put additional stress on Ian's strained resources. How- ever, his difficulties do not date from his first seizure episode or from the increases in his medication. Rather, the developmental history gives clear clues as to the inception of difficulties, i.e., separation anxiety, with a persistent developmental impasse in the parent-child relationship. Even if medication could alleviate further seizures, the diagnostic picture is that of an encapsulated psychopathological de- bility which impairs the child's psychological functioning and poten- tials for emotional, sexual, and social development.

However clear the neurological diagnosis, the presenting symp- toms are not incompatible (given the developmental history) with a hysterical exacerbation (if not hysterical origin) of a latent neuro- logical dysfunction (Gottschalk, 1956). In this regard, one is re- minded of Freud's observation that a patient's susceptibility to specific modes of tension discharge might well be based on prior illness that would lay down certain psychophysiological patterns. The introductory months of psychotherapy have made it clear that Ian is exceedingly concerned about his "damage." In this regard, whatever the boy's "seizure potential" may be, he suffers from a sense of damage and a feeling of incapacity which has caused long-standing anxiety and is now an integral part of his neurotic problem.

BIBLIOGRAPHY

Bartemeier, L. H. (1932), Some Observations of Convulsive Disorders in Children. *Amer. J. Orthopsychiat.,* 2:260-267.
—— (1943), Concerning the Psychogenesis of Convulsive Disorders. *Psa. Quart.,* 12: 330-337.
Freud, A. (1945), Indications for Child Analysis. *This Annual,* 1:127-149.
—— (1948), Sublimation as a Factor in Upbringing. *Health Educ. J.,* 6(3):25-29.
—— (1962), Assessment of Childhood Disturbances. *This Annual,* 17:149-158.
—— (1963), The Concept of Developmental Lines. *This Annual,* 18:245-265.
—— (1965), *Normality and Pathology in Childhood.* New York: International Universities Press.
—— Nagera, H., & Freud, W. E. (1965), Metapsychological Assessment of the Adult Personality. *This Annual,* 19:196-221.
Freud, S. (1916-1917), Introductory Lectures on Psycho-Analysis. *Standard Edition,* 16. London: Hogarth Press, 1963.
—— (1928), Dostoevsky and Parricide. *Standard Edition,* 21:175-196. London: Hogarth Press, 1961.
Gottschalk, L. A. (1956), The Relationship of Psychologic State and Epileptic Activity. *This Annual,* 11:352-380.
Heinicke, C. M., et al. (1965), Frequency of Psychotherapeutic Session as a Factor Affecting the Child's Developmental Status. *This Annual,* 19:42-97.
Michaels, J. J. & Stiver, I. P. (1965), The Impulsive Psychopathic Character According to the Diagnostic Profile. *This Annual,* 20:124-141.
Nagera, H. (1963), The Developmental Profile: Notes on Some Practical Considerations Regarding Its Use. *This Annual,* 18:511-540.
Peterson, D., Sumner, J., & Jones, G. (1950), Role of Hypnosis in Differentiation of Epileptic from Convulsive-Like Seizures. *Amer. J. Psychiat.,* 107:428-433.
Sperling, M. (1953), Psychodynamics and Treatment of Petit Mal in Children. *Int. J. Psa.,* 34:248-252.
Thomas, R., et al. (1966), Comments on Some Aspects of Self and Object Representation in a Group of Psychotic Children: An Application of Anna Freud's Diagnostic Profile. *This Annual,* 21:527-580.
Waelder, R. (1964), Personal Communication.

COMMENTS ON SOME ASPECTS OF SELF AND OBJECT REPRESENTATION IN A GROUP OF PSYCHOTIC CHILDREN

An Application of Anna Freud's Diagnostic Profile

RUTH THOMAS

in collaboration with

Rose Edgcumbe, Hanna Kennedy, Maria Kawenoka,
and Lilian Weitzner

The four children whose analyses and profiles form the basic material for the following discussion were chosen from a large group of atypical children resident in the High Wick Hospital where care and study are devoted exclusively to this type of child.[1] After a period of residential care these children (ranging in age from seven to ten years) were considered to have developed sufficiently to be amenable to a modified form of analytic therapy. In addition to being able to walk, dress, feed themselves, and perform highly co-ordinated activities, they had acquired a degree of verbal ability sufficient to insure some basis for verbal communication.

They had in common an extreme primitiveness of instinctual behavior and very uneven ego development, which precluded the diagnosis of mental defect. The various descriptions of such children in the psychiatric literature indicate that we are far from under-

The material used has been collected at the Hampstead Child-Therapy Clinic, a therapeutic and research center financed by the following foundations: The Field Foundation, Inc., New York; The Anna Freud Foundation, New York; The Estate of Flora Haas, New York; The Old Dominion Foundation, U.S.A.; The Psychoanalytic Research and Development Fund, Inc., New York; and the National Institute of Mental Health, Bethesda, Maryland.

1 High Wick is a hospital under the National Health Service, and is under the general and psychiatric direction of Dr. George Stroh. To Dr. Stroh, Dr. Tischler, and the staff of the hospital we are heavily indebted for information and detailed observations outside the scope of the analyses.

standing the contribution of organic, genetic, dynamic, and environmental factors to their disturbances.

GENERAL COMMENTS ON DIAGNOSIS

The diagnosis of childhood psychosis is made on the basis of: (1) highly unusual or bizarre behavior; (2) speech disturbance indicative of confusion of thought or thought disorder; (3) grossly disordered relationship to people. Furthermore, when these abnormalities are present, their frequency and intensity warrant the diagnosis of psychosis; they readily differentiate it from neurosis. Three discernible groups can be identified under the heading of psychosis:

1. *Early infantile autism* (to which none of the four children belong) is characterized, usually, by absence of speech, and when speech is present, it has a specifically automatic quality. There is extreme withdrawal and preoccupation with sameness (repetitive manneristic activity).

2. *Childhood schizophrenia,* a term which is here not used as synonymous with either "psychosis" or "autism," but which denotes a syndrome not unlike schizophrenia in later life, with periods of marked regression, withdrawal, and thought disorder. (Lucille belongs in this group.)

3. *Traumatic psychosis.* Children in this group (Basil, Norma, Stanley) have suffered psychological traumata of such frequency and severity that their experiences can reasonably be understood to be of primary importance in the causation of their disturbance. In this sense, these children can readily be differentiated from the autistic child, whose basic perceptual defect causes experiences of everyday life to assume the quality of trauma, and who defends himself against this by complete withdrawal. Other features that seem to be characteristic of the "traumatic" psychosis are excessive demandingness and relative absence of pleasurable experiences.

The children have been grouped together in a single research unit at Hampstead although they show a diverse adaptive potential and divergent learning achievements. They are identical in retaining archaic, grossly pathological ego attitudes which dominate their primitive capacity for object relations and preclude the maturation of feeling states which have meaning for the child and are recognizable by others. This paper focuses on what these children have in common—i.e., a level of primitivity and immaturity which persists and remains largely intractable—although in other respects they have diverse characteristics which preclude their classification into a single pathological entity.

We do not feel that we have broken new ground in our analytic approach to these children. Our results show only partial success in two of the four cases. Our discussions, doubts, and dilemmas concerning the modified analytic approach we deemed appropriate at the time we undertook treatment have been described previously (Kut Rosenfeld and Sprince, 1965).

In what follows we present a brief description of the children's histories and symptomatology; to these we have added a survey of the areas in which analysis with our present techniques was effective. Three cases have been terminated because we felt that they could not be further influenced by our present techniques; the fourth, Basil, still continues in analysis and we have recently begun to approach his deepest pathology by more flexible attempts to reconstruct his earliest years. In his material appeared some indirect clues to which we feel we have been insufficiently alerted. Our openness to this new approach is largely a result of writing this paper and is in part due to a closer study of the work of D. W. Winnicott. The limited treatment results do not affect the validity of the observations, though the contributions of the various genetic factors to the disturbances of each child have been only slightly clarified as a result of our work.

Basil was a thin, hyperactive, mulatto child with closely cropped curly hair and light brown skin. His bearing demanded attention at all times; he was extremely alert, spoke precisely, giving accurate descriptions, but usually with a flat voice and affectless facial expression. He was placed in residential care in his seventh year, following the final breakup of the marriage between his middle-class white Jewish mother and his Jamaican Negro father. He was found to be unmanageable in this residential center and was eventually hospitalized at High Wick at the age of seven years two months. He began treatment at the Hampstead Clinic when he was nine and a half years old and is now almost fourteen.

At eight years, tested with the Revised Stanford-Binet Scale, Basil scored an I.Q. of 100; at thirteen, tested with the Wechsler Intelligence Scale for Children (WISC), he showed an I.Q. of 118 on the verbal scale and 97 on the performance scale, with an I.Q. of 109 on the full scale. The most prominent features were the extreme scatter of scores on the subtests and the marked differences between the verbal and performance results. Basil was unable to find a logical and reasonable solution to tests that had an emotional and interpersonal impact. His perception of situations was distorted and his pseudo affects were apparent. The psychologist was left with the impression that Basil had a mask or cloak of normality which would be vulnerable if he encountered emotional demands. It was felt unwise and inappropriate to undertake an EEG for this reason.[2]

Basil was absorbed in a fantasy world, isolated from other children, and showed no affection. He often threatened to bite or strangle his younger sister. His behavior varied from rigid overcontrol to complete breakdown of control with acute and unbearable anxiety attacks. Primitive play with urine and feces evoked no shame in him, and he spent much time in isolated play devoted mostly to digging holes. The bizarreness of his fantasies was apparent in his notions of the body. "Why does my nurse not turn her head right round, so that I could use it as a wheel? Why can't I squeeze your breast and get all the spaghetti out?" He was demanding and fastidious about food. He made frequent use of neologisms and concrete thinking. There was some compulsive head jerking and smelling of objects. He sadistically manipulated other children to act out his aggressive fantasies, while he withdrew to avoid retribution.

Much of Basil's early family life had been stormy, chaotic, and traumatic enough to account for his deviant ego development. He was a premature baby, weighed only 4 pounds at birth, although his delivery was normal and he was never in an incubator. His mother alternated between turning all her affection and care on him and depressive withdrawal from him. From earliest infancy until the beginning of treatment he had periodically shared his mother's bed and had experienced her embraces and her excitement as highly seductive.

In the hospital his attachment to three staff members represented separate aspects of these frustrating infantile experiences. From one

---

[2] Dr. David Buick of High Wick Hospital undertook the testing of all children, and Dr. George Stroh was responsible for the diagnostic findings.

he would accept a caretaking role, and apply to her for help in his activities or general assistance; from another he demanded erotic gratification in the form of body contact and sexual gratification; and a third he overwhelmed with tormenting and teasing manifestations which she found almost unbearable. During his sojourn at High Wick, he longed ardently for his mother's visits and had idealized expectations of gratification which broke down with each real encounter. Their meetings were either stormy and upsetting to both or involved each in marked overcontrol, giving an unreal quality to their relationship. He strenuously avoided initiating an erotic contact with his mother always fearing a rebuff. The analytic work revealed that he usually sought erotic contact with others when he felt particularly unloved and unwanted by his mother, and that the crucial and damaging experience for him had been not the actual or fantasied seduction by his mother but the repeated experience of loss of a close and intimate relationship that was entailed in his experiences of being subsequently "pushed out of her bed."

Throughout his early childhood there were intense quarrels and violent scenes between his parents, often resulting in his father staying away for prolonged periods, or his mother leaving the home with Basil, frequent moves to new houses, and placement in day nurseries and nursery schools, all situations which he was unable to master and react to adaptively. In the analysis it emerged that Basil had interpreted the many observations of parental quarrels and fights, as well as the final separation of his parents, as mother pushing father out and not letting him return. In this way, he was identified with his father, suffering or anticipating the same fate. He brought many vivid memories of being confined to a cot while witnessing parental fights; he felt excluded, shut out, and isolated. Later, these experiences crystallized into fears of being abandoned, deserted, and forgotten.

There was, of course, also material indicating his conflict over loyalty, his being forced to take his mother's side in the conflict; his fear of his own violent and aggressive wishes, which would make him attack his mother as his father had done and lead to loss of love and abandonment; and his masochistic involvement, which made him wish for father's role of victim. In all these memories and reconstructions two features always emerged: the fact of being immobilized, either physcially restrained or panic-stricken and "frozen"; and the painful realization of being left out and "forgotten." The former became the basis for massive sexualization of anxiety, and the latter led to a lifelong attempt to defend himself against the pain of feeling unloved and unlovable.

The most traumatic event of his life leading to massive ego

regression occurred in his sixth year. The birth of his sister, when he was four and a half years, temporarily improved the marital relationship, but for Basil it entailed yet another separation from his mother and forcibly reaffirmed again his precarious position in maintaining his mother's love and affection. At first, he attempted completely to deny his sister's existence, later he became violently jealous and aggressive toward her. The mother's third pregnancy two years later led to the father's final desertion. In desperation, Mrs. B. sought refuge with the paternal grandparents in Jamaica. After a nightmarish journey in which Mrs. B., near term, traveled alone with her two children across stormy seas, they found only horrible, squalid conditions, and grandparents who were severely rigid and brutal guardians. Basil was left with them for some weeks while his mother traveled to the city awaiting her confinement. His two-year-old sister was left with other relatives, but for Basil it looked as if his mother was taking her and leaving him behind, and later returning with two children. On her return she found Basil like a "terrified animal." He had been beaten, starved, and restricted; he crawled on all fours, wetted and soiled.

He remembered many painful experiences in Jamaica. The analytic material revealed his great distress over not knowing his parents' whereabouts and his gradually mounting hopelessness of ever seeing them again. At first, he made attempts to run away and search for them; later he gave up all hope. His isolation, loneliness, and sadness were accentuated by the frequent punishments of being locked up all day alone in a room, and the thoughtless or deliberately cruel attitude of his guardians who would not even allow him to keep his mother's letters. The other children in the family were hostile and antagonistic toward the intruder and took delight in taunting him about his mother never returning again. This he took as confirmation of his own fear and doubt.

Basil's memories of his early life consisted of a series of frightening and painful events with the ever-recurring theme of "feeling all deserted, feeling all alone, and waiting and waiting for something or someone who never comes."

The main experiences of loss in his life at different periods, together with the cumulative fantasies with which he imbued them, were worked through extensively and in great detail. This work gave a marked impetus to his ability to attend normal school and reach secondary school entrance standard. He now travels alone in London and meets unexpected situations sensibly and without acute anxiety. He is living at home with his mother and siblings and is moderately adjusted. Nevertheless, the core of his personality with its focus on irremediable loss and emptiness remains untouched. He has some intellectual understanding of and regret for the emotional impact his unreasoning demands make on people, and to a great extent he is able to control himself to meet their expectations. He has hardly ever talked about good experiences or indicated that he has such memories as well. Yet we know that he was not an unloved baby. At times, he was the center of his mother's whole life and on occasions he even replaced her sexual object. In many ways his mother overestimated his achievements, particularly his artistic productions by calling him her "Leonardo." The father, too, when present, took great interest in his development, and played and talked to him, although he often did so on a level above the child's functioning.

The analysis is now oriented to the "false self" (Winnicott, 1960a), which his accomplishments may well represent, as distinct from the real self, which the emotional demands of both parents kept from developing. It may still be possible to clarify his problem further if we can gain a deeper understanding of the primitive introjective processes to which his immature ego may have resorted in his attempts to cope with the intense feelings with which he was surrounded, and of which he was sometimes the focus, but which were not geared to his needs. In the father's relation to him, there was a demand for precocious learning; in the mother's, for precocious feeling; intermittently he was dropped altogether from a relationship. He has recently become aware of the intense hatred which his mother feels for him, though he has still much to learn of its history. We still have to determine the extent to which the damage he has suffered is reversible.

Stanley was a first child born when his father was abroad. Even after the father's return he had little contact with the child. During Stanley's first year the family lived with indulgent grandparents whose handling is said to have contrasted strongly with the admittedly strict and critical attitude of both parents. Stanley's highly phobic mother did not impress workers with any spontaneous warmth, and both parents felt gravely threatened by Stanley's disturbance.

Stanley was a full-term baby and was bottle-fed from the beginning because his mother's milk was insufficient. He sucked well and is supposed to have thrived. It is not easy to form a picture of his babyhood. He is said to have woken crying most nights until he was two years old; he delighted in teasing his mother and would scratch and tear wallpaper. (At the same time, both parents had the impression of relative normality until the birth of David, when Stanley was three.) He sat up at nine months, walked at eighteen months, and was clean and dry at three years. His speech development was

slow and he began to talk only at three years. He did not like to
be held and showed no signs of affection. After David's birth,
Stanley began to follow the parents around and would not sit down.
The circumstances of the birth were unusual: the father delivered
the baby at home in the absence of a midwife. Stanley was unpre-
pared for David's arrival and for the first time in his life was looked
after exclusively by his father. During labor, the father was forced
to leave Stanley alone in his high chair, where he was very quiet.

The severity of Stanley's disturbance struck the parents when
at the age of five he was expelled from school as unmanageable. A
child guidance report at this time described him as hyperactive, often
talking to himself, repeating unintelligible phrases, living in a fantasy world, and unable to relate to other children. When he was
admitted to High Wick at six, he was very anxious; he talked only
in shouts; there was much blinking, spitting, and drooling; he used
many neologisms; and he was afraid of physical contact with adults.

Stanley was able to complete an intelligence test only at the end
of treatment (when he was nine years nine months old). By then, his
I.Q. on the WISC was 110 (verbal), 116 (performance), 109 (full
scale). In comparison with an earlier testing there was an increase
of 23 points in the verbal I.Q., and of 11 points in the full scale I.Q.

When at age seven and a half Stanley came to treatment, the
confusion of pronouns was no longer in evidence, but his need for
neologisms and word distortions soon came to the fore. However,
the main initial impression was that of a tremendously anxious
child. His anxiety proved to be severe both with regard to intensity
and spread. Stanley had innumerable fears and was easily overwhelmed by them.

Stanley was in treatment for over two and a half years. His material, reflecting the fragmented way in which his ego functioned,
was often disjointed. He communicated by actions, which frequently
were provocative and aggressive. There was, however, one theme
which kept returning and on which much work was done—the trauma
of his brother's birth and the fears of the birth of yet another sibling. The prevailing anxiety was undoubtedly that of being immobilized and unable to reach his mother. This was complicated by
Stanley's feeling that as his father came and went from the kitchen
to the bedroom, boiling kettles and using scissors, murderous attacks on the mother were in process. His wish to investigate was
acted out in the Clinic in excited running from one room to another.
At this point, he became highly interested in things electrical and
preoccupied with getting electrical shocks. Nevertheless, he developed great skill in handling electrical appliances, had a large assort-
ment of electrical power points, plugs, and batteries, and would

think out innumerable combinations of these. His inventiveness was often striking. The noise made by his apparatus was of great concern to him and so was its movement. If he managed to set an assembly in motion, he was greatly excited. Some working through of the birth experience was possible, but it was limited by the fear his memories aroused in him, exacerbating his intense castration anxiety. His object relations remained at a strongly sadistic level. The absence of basic tenderness indicated a partial arrest at the level of very early part-object relationships, an arrest which the analysis was unable to touch.

One of Stanley's most prominent fears was that of being abandoned by his parents. Placement at High Wick appeared to be its immediate cause, but underneath it were painful memories of helplessness, loneliness, and exposure to frightening, incomprehensible events. His way of coping with this fear was to reject his love objects. He could be helped to the extent of recognizing some love for his parents, but his need to provoke rejection remained strong and led to a premature termination of treatment. However, Stanley had improved sufficiently to be moved from High Wick to a boarding school for neurotically disturbed children.

When *Norma* came to High Wick at the age of four years and eight months she looked like a two-year-old. She spent most of her first months rocking on all fours and moaning. She did not speak and usually refused solid food. She made a primitive relationship with her housemother, first adopted a creeping gait like a small disabled animal, then began to walk and after six months to speak. She has made steady progress in speech though it was still somewhat retarded and bizarre. She had an aortic systolic murmur loudest medially of the apex. EEG and X-ray were normal. There was a hypochromic anemia, which responded readily to oral administration of iron, and recurrent eczema, first evident during treatment.

Norma was an unwanted child and her mother is said to have attempted abortion. The parents were unmarried and led a stormy, unstable life. The delivery was normal. The mother found the idea of breast feeding repulsive, and all the children were bottle-fed. Norma took the bottle well and never refused feedings.

When Norma was four months old, her mother became pregnant again, attempted suicide, and the pregnancy was terminated. The mother was depressed for at least the first year of Norma's life; she did not want to be bothered with the baby, but somehow managed to feed and change her. Norma cried a lot and was given a bottle whenever she cried, for whatever reason. She was mostly left to hold the bottle herself. Various attempts were made to give her solid foods, but Norma consistently refused them, would not allow a spoon into her mouth, and would not swallow. Her mother returned to bottle feeding for the sake of peace, and this continued until Norma was four and a half years old.

The mother remembered little about Norma's infancy. There was apparently little attempt to play, and no babbling or other sounds apart from crying and yelling. Norma sat at four months, stood at about one year, and walked at about fifteen months, without previously crawling. But she preferred to stand rocking from foot to foot in one favorite corner, from which she disliked being moved. She was frightened when she was taken out of the house. She would not approach people and pushed them away when they approached her; she screamed and struggled when she was picked up. She would not sit on her mother's lap, and resisted or rejected anything her mother tried to do to or for her. Toilet training was attempted at age two, but abandoned as hopeless.

An examination at two and a half years revealed no physical abnormalities. When Norma was three and a half she went to a day nursery. She gradually lost her fear of leaving the house and began to run about more normally instead of standing and rocking. The nursery eventually managed to get her to eat solids, when she was four and a half. She began to make sounds, but there were still no words. She often had tantrums and screamed a lot. Gradually she understood and obeyed commands given in a casual voice, but resisted anything said abruptly. Norma's development was erratic, with alternating periods of progress and regression, which made her mother despondent. When Norma was referred to High Wick her mother was relieved and openly expressed her hostility for the child. For the last three years the parents have not visited or shown any interest in her.

Norma's psychotic behavior became increasingly apparent as her speech developed and her motility improved. Treatment was commenced at the age of seven and discontinued four years later. In the early years of treatment, aggression was manifested in unpredictable outbursts of diffuse destructiveness directed at anything within reach, including herself. In the course of treatment aggression became more specifically object-directed and was often traceable to frustration, disappointment, or anxiety. These affects were sometimes aroused by external circumstances, but more often by the failure of objects and herself to do away with her internal sensations of tension and discomfort.

For Norma, the most distressing and intolerable aspects of her disturbance were her inability to deal with physical and mental sensations of tension and unpleasure and her striking paucity of pleasurable experiences. She seemed, indeed, to seek unpleasure rather than pleasure, centering attention on her anxieties and worries, only rarely appearing happy. In the course of treatment, she acquired some slight capacity to remember past pleasures and anticipate future ones, and to use these to exclude feelings of unpleasure from consciousness. But she could do this only in periods of optimal functioning. Under stress she became unable to seek, remember, or anticipate pleasure.

When Norma entered treatment, body boundaries were firmly established so that she could differentiate self from objects, but objects were sometimes confused with each other. Other related differentiations had not occurred. She could not distinguish between physical and mental states, so that psychic pain and unpleasure tended to be experienced in terms of hurts and ailments, a tendency reinforced by her physical condition. She could not distinguish between her own feelings and those of her objects and believed their feelings to be identical with her own. These differentiations began to appear during treatment, but they were always precarious.

From indiscriminate use of all available objects Norma moved to definite preferences on the basis of the object's capacity to fulfill the roles of need satisfier or auxiliary ego; eventually she began to discriminate between objects on the basis of function, e.g., between therapist and housemother. At first, people were often viewed as dangerous, at best harmless. For years her projected aggression interfered with all moves toward new objects and turned even a beloved object into a focus of terror. She slowly began to develop limited trust and the wish to be fed and to enjoy her food. Her need to provoke the repetition of rejection was always paramount. Her communications moved slowly from primary-process thinking to an unstable use of secondary process; she had organized memory though never of pleasant experiences.

Norma's aggressive attacks stemmed mostly from her fears of being deserted and left homeless. She felt she had damaged herself and destroyed her penis and that without one she could never be acceptable. Her wish for a penis led to endless attempts to find substitutes in long hair, high heels, and body attachments, and to much curiosity not only about external body protuberances but about internal organs as well. She finally acquired an extraordinary though distorted knowledge of physiological processes. While all attempts to deal with her penis envy proved abortive, her preoccupation with the inner states of her body led directly to her feeling of emptiness. Her therapist's main concern, therefore, became that of establishing herself as a trusted object who could support and supplement Norma's inadequate attempts at defense against her greedy and destructive wishes to engulf her objects.

Norma developed new ways of displacing aggression onto toys and of substituting less dangerous forms of attack, e.g., squirting water instead of scratching. She would also withdraw from situations which aroused anxiety; and when she had failed to control herself, she externalized her destructiveness onto creatures she invented. Having torn her dress she explained, "A birdie pecked it." Later, she invented a jumper-caughter—a creature who caught and tore her dress—laughing mischievously as she elaborated about "glove-caughters" and "sock-caughters."

There were some indications of reaction formation and primitive identifications: as she cared for her dolls she said she wanted to be a housemother to look after them.

Much of Norma's anxiety was contained in her "worry words," about which she complained bitterly because she could not get them out of her mind and felt constantly forced to say them, so that they punctuated her conversation and interfered with her thinking. These worry words changed frequently and could sometimes be traced to an anxiety-provoking situation; e.g., "dolly" became a worry word after a refusal to let her have another child's doll. Usually the word and the anxiety soon became detached from the original context, and even if the therapist succeeded in discovering and verbalizing the original anxiety, this did not dispel it. On the contrary, it seemed that Norma's worry words were used to encapsulate and make manageable incipient panic attacks which threatened to overwhelm her. These mostly derived from comparatively harmless events to which she had attached terrifying fantasies. Reconstruction of the original situation served only to revive the panic and the ego's experience of being overwhelmed, and in no way mitigated the fantasy content.

Norma's reparative efforts increased concurrently with the recovery of a degree of internal control. She used vast quantities of tape, sticking plaster, glue, staples, and string in "mending" and strengthening toys. But if these materials ran out, as they often did due to her extravagance, she would be thrown into a state of panic (Winnicott, 1960b).

On the whole, Norma disliked ordinary toys because they were too fragile, preferring to make things for herself. She revealed an extraordinary creativity and ability to manipulate unlikely materials. For example, she could make weird but convincing people and animals out of bits of plastic stuck together with tape. In time she began to use this ability to overcome disappointment at the refusal of toys belonging to other children; e.g., she envied Stanley his possession of a guitar, and made herself one out of tins, tape, and elastic bands. In these activities Norma demonstrated her fear of her own omnipotent destructiveness—in her endless search for indestructible toys and materials. She rejected paper, cardboard, plasticine, and cloth because they could be torn or squashed. She usually settled for tin and plastic, with wire, tape, and sticking plaster to fix them together. But there were days when she rejected one thing after another, accompanying her frantic search with wails of "But it might break." She endlessly asked repetitive questions about how strong things were and thought up circumstances in which they might break.

The therapist attempted to supply Norma with the ego functions she lacked, to anticipate, delay, and control actions. The child not only used her therapist for this purpose but took over some of these functions for short periods as if she herself had developed them. Finally, it was possible to approach Norma's feelings of emptiness and their psychic content and to elucidate her confusion between penis and breast. In the context of her eating problems, she expressed the idea that animals have udders to give milk to their babies, while humans have only milk bottles. Then she remembered that ladies have breasts, but patted her genital to show where. She then pointed to the proximity of genitals and udders in animals. Shortly thereafter it was possible to reconstruct the young child fumbling for the propped bottle which forever escaped her.

While much further work was done to support her defective ego functioning, it finally became apparent that these gains were not cumulative. It seemed that Norma made progress on the basis of some inner belief that she would achieve her satisfaction and fullness if she imitated the thought processes and verbal formulations offered her by the therapist. This process did not lead, as it can in the normal child, to autonomous ego functioning which persists in the face of frustration and dissatisfaction. It was at such points that her forward steps revealed their "as if" quality, and there was a massive retreat into miserable and destructive behavior which could not be dealt with.

Norma was tested on the WISC shortly before termination and achieved a prorated verbal I.Q. of 85, which was considered to be a reliable estimate. Her ability to cooperate was limited, and her efforts to involve the tester in her confused inner states resulted after several attempts in only a partial test score. Norma is still enuretic at night. She has attended the High Wick School and can read, write, count, and do simple sums. She can do her own laundry and will help prepare meals and wash up and do housework adequately as long as she is able to contain herself emotionally.

Lucille began treatment at the age of seven years three months. Tall and slender, she was an attractive blonde child, with blue eyes, which frequently had a vacant, dreamy, unfocused expression. In contrast, her movements were direct, purposive, determined, and markedly agile. She usually looked clean, but even when she wore skirts, her appearance lacked feminine softness, probably because of her wiry build. Usually isolated from other children, she could be found alone preoccupied with making a mess with sand and water, eating it, or cleaning it away. Her play was accompanied by a constant monologue, directed to herself or the doll in a scolding, admonishing tone, or describing her intent in the play. At these times her voice was deep in pitch, forceful, loud, quite different from the tone she used for communication. Although she frequently appeared to be oblivious of activities or events about her, she was in fact very perceptive and alert to almost all that occurred on the hospital grounds. She was obsessively preoccupied with hammers and brushes, which represented people.

Lucille was a first and only child (two subsequent pregnancies ended in stillbirths), born to an intelligent, quiet, withdrawn, working-class couple. There was evidence to suggest that they both warded off depression with difficulty. Excessive cleanliness was a feature of the mother's personality. After a difficult delivery without any birthcry, Lucille developed inhalation pneumonia followed by bilateral atelectasis. For the first few days Lucille vomited every feed; later she was a lazy feeder and did not suck easily. She did not sit up until ten months of age. At the same time she was very active bouncing up and down and able to undo the straps of her harness. She learned to walk at about sixteen months, but her motility was uncertain until the age of two and a half years. At four years Lucille's speech was a repetitive, incomprehensible jargon and at seven and a half years it was still abbreviated, telescoped (with reversal of you-I pronouns), and represented condensation of desires, thoughts or broken memories. She became dry but not clean at about fifteen months. Later on she became constipated and passed a motion only after days of irritability ending in violent tantrums. This condition persisted with intermittent, more normal periods until after treatment began. We know that she sat on the pot for long periods and her mother used suppositories. Extremely low frustration tolerance and panic states were expressed in tempers in which she attacked herself as well as others.

All these difficulties with the child made the mother "feel inadequate," and from the latter part of the first year of life the parents gradually became aware that something was wrong.

At five and a half years Lucille was hospitalized for neurological examinations and EEG, which was performed both waking and asleep under Seconal. The findings suggested a local lesion in the left occipital area, without any signs of a gross lesion. X-ray revealed a mild degree of asymmetry of the vault of the skull only, the right frontal bone was more prominent than the left. The relevance of these findings to her mental state was doubtful. There was a marked psychotic overlay. Continued hospitalization was recommended. Psychological tests administered at five and a half years yielded an I.Q. of 71 on the Stanford-Binet Scale and an I.Q. of 89 on the WISC.

In the first year of treatment primary-process thinking was extant; crude instinctual drives, both libidinal and aggressive, were expressed directly in speech, body language or function, and play activity. Her material revealed that she had been traumatized by the primal scene, and that she had a severe touching problem arising from anal masturbation, followed by soiling and playing with her feces. The touching prohibition extended to a variety of things and bodily functions, which were damaging because they were dirty. She attempted to reproduce these activities which were "allowed" to the parents in displaced fashion which always precipitated disasters. It appeared that Lucille was dominated by a basic sexual fantasy of danger, freely moving from danger in the present to danger in the past. Causality and time, two concepts vital to the development of ego boundaries, were lacking. Treatment helped her to distinguish between the inner and outer factors contributing to stressful events, to sort out cause and effect, and to anticipate unpleasant experiences, and deal with them in more adaptive ways.

At eight and a half years she was given a toy tortoise with which she remained preoccupied for a long time. Identification with animals was a prominent feature in Lucille's treatment; she often gobbled up cat food and other inedibles, prior to gross destructive attacks on animals. The gift of the tortoise occurred in the second year of treatment at a time when she was extremely depressed following the death of another child cared for by the same housemother. Lucille's despair was increased by the housemother's depressive reaction and inability to turn her attention to Lucille. The tortoise to which she clung, symbolized for her a roof over her head, a permanent and safe place to retreat to. It also epitomized the oneness with her object which she despaired of finding and also her magical wish for self-sufficiency. The failure of her present relationship with her housemother provoked feelings of intense emptiness, helplessness, loss of identity, and a need to preserve the object by incorporation. However, it is doubtful whether this child was ever able to internalize a satisfying object representation; therefore she remained dependent on the external object or its symbol as a replacement. In Lucille's case there never developed the reciprocal relationship between mother and child so essential to provide the affective experience necessary for development (Spitz, 1957).

In Lucille's early life, a cat had indeed been the recipient of her mother's spontaneous attention and affection. The mother remarked: "I felt more for my cat than I was able to feel for Lucille." The "sibling's" death at the hospital now confirmed Lucille's jealous destructiveness and recalled events not long past when she had killed small animals as if they had been the cat who she felt displaced her and received her mother's affection. More recently she was fascinated by a housemother's tortoise protecting itself from attack by withdrawing into its shell, which also provided a home.

Her aggression was constantly provoked by the feeling of not being adequate and loved for herself, and she defended against this anxiety by greedy demandingness and gobbling. She fended off loneliness and emptiness by an attempt to create body fullness, both through eating and anal retention. Later, she demanded eardrops (suppositories) to dissolve the hard, painful wax. It would seem that the infantile, archaic sensory modalities were still highly cathected.

At the time of the rival child's death, despite her intense suffering, Lucille finally organized herself to function, to tidy up, and to engage in constructive activity. She responded more to the personal situations of other children and the housemother. Internally, however, she was even more alone, for she identified only with the ordering aspect of the therapist. Without libidinization, the control she evidenced was insecure and undependable, and she became self-destructive.

The level of object relations moved during treatment in the direction of establishing a symbioticlike attachment with efforts to avoid, rather than incur, pain. At this stage, the you-I confusion decreased, and she began to use the you-I pronouns correctly. The therapist was the gratifier of drives, but, more importantly, she became that part of the ego that sorted out and integrated past and current perceptions of repeated traumatic experiences. The relationship was not libidinized and the therapist did not become a unified, consistent object.

As an alternative to this process, Lucille endowed her chosen objects with sexual and aggressive intent or conceived them like herself as lifeless and "dead." To get the object, she had to be dead, like the missed child, a fantasy which she verbalized. In defense against this anxiety, she requested enemas or tried to fill herself up with grass. She pushed her arm through a window in her need to achieve somatic discharge, precipitate punishment, and achieve a sense of aliveness.

As treatment progressed she perceived her own defects and her inability to identify with more capable children. She thought there was something physically wrong with her head, and, as in the past, saw herself cast out by the housemother as the fecal, smearing child. She requested that the object function as a protector, but the basic model was that of being eaten up. She denied the destructive aspect when she asked if her housemother would swallow her so that she would be in her tummy and then come out again in bowel movements.

Her object relations remained unaltered at the end of treatment and when treatment had to be discontinued, she became totally regressed and withdrawn.

THE PURPOSE OF THE PROFILE

The treatment of these children was undertaken at the Hampstead Clinic by trained child therapists under my general direction and supervision. Problems of transport made it possible to see the children only four times weekly. The therapists submitted weekly reports on each child and attempted a more integrated summary of their work at two-monthly intervals. A comprehensive report on each child was submitted at the end of two years of treatment. These reports were read and discussed by Anna Freud and myself as they appeared, and the longer comprehensive reports were read and discussed at general clinic meetings. They were also discussed by the Study Group for Borderline Children whose members have used this case material together with other material available on borderline children attending the Clinic for different studies. This material has also been discussed by the Profile Group.

The aim of the Profile is to present a comprehensive metapsychological picture of a child in which the analyst's thought processes are broken up into their component parts. Profiles can be drawn up at various junctures, at the preliminary diagnostic stage, during analysis, and after the end of analysis, or as a follow-up. "At the diagnostic stage the profile for each case should be initiated by the referral symptoms of the child, his description, his family background and history, and an enumeration of the possibly significant environmental influences. From these it proceeds to the internal picture of the child which contains information about the *structure* of his personality; the *dynamic* interplay within the structure; some *economic* factors concerning drive activity and the relative strength of id and ego forces; his adaptation to reality; and some genetic assumptions (to be verified during and after treatment)" (Anna Freud, 1962, p. 151; see also 1963, 1965).

Our attempts to use the Profile for the clarification of the problem presented by borderline children led to two findings. On the one hand, the Profile enabled us to highlight aspects of the children's chaotic development and reaction to treatment. On the other hand, the apparently more significant characteristics also appeared in a wide variety of other diagnostic categories in which the disturbance arose in the earliest infantile period. These characteristics therefore did not differentiate between a gross disturbance such as our children manifest and other severe disturbances with arrested development where the children nevertheless show greater adaptive capacity and lack psychotic features.

We have, therefore, studied manifestations of behavior and functioning which seem significant for the group and for which the Profile does not yet make provision or does so only by implication which we now attempt to define. The aim of this report is to indicate our attempts to modify the Profile where it has not proved a fine enough sieve to differentiate between the degree of disturbance we are studying and lesser disturbances which are better understood. We have chosen for discussion only those aspects of the Profile on which our work has recently concentrated for their potentiality in understanding these peculiar difficulties and which have an overriding significance for our chlidren. It is hoped that such understanding may eventually contribute to a clearer discrimination of the processes of earliest ego growth and the factors on which this depends.

Aspects of the Profile Selected for Discussion

A. FAMILY BACKGROUND AND PERSONAL HISTORY (Profile Point III[3])

1. Only two of our cases show evidence of gross disturbance in one or both parents, though none of them would qualify as normal. In a third the mother reports her outstanding inability to relate to this particular child from birth, though the mother herself is not a

---

[3] Points A and B of our Profile headings and their immediate subheadings represent the original plan of the Profile, while the subheadings "Cathexis of Self" and "Cathexis of Objects" represent modifications deemed necessary for the description of the group of children under discussion.

grossly disturbed person. While the parents of the fourth child are highly anxious and have debilitating neurotic symptoms, their social adaptation is constructive and well within the norm for the population.

2. All children showed early feeding disturbances and derivatives of these persist.

3. Speech was uniformly delayed in all children, and all continue to show some disturbance of this function.

4. Two of the children are reported to have shown an abnormal degree of erratic and aimless activity early in life and this has persisted to a large extent; in a third, these manifestations developed later, a fourth was a constant rocker well beyond the period when this activity usually subsides. Three of the children had a history of sleep disturbances and excessive crying fits from an early age, unduly prolonged beyond infancy.

5. History and analysis reveal that the children were exposed to potentially damaging experiences at a very early age. While the traumatophilic features of this type of child are well known, the experiences referred to do not permit the inference that they were initially self-engendered.

6. They all are now in a hospital because their families were unable or unwilling to cope with their unmanageable behavior.

At present we are not in a position to assess the importance of any one of these features, or to suggest that singly or together they may account for the peculiar and far-reaching character of these children's disturbances. The comparative data do, however, highlight one factor. In the histories of more normal children we are used to finding a dynamic interrelatedness in a succession of symptoms, one giving place to another with the growing age and maturity of the child. For example, in neurotic children an early disturbance in feeding or habit training may clear up totally and be replaced by a learning inhibition or a school phobia. Phobias arising in the phallic phase may be directed to a changing series of situations as one phobic object is replaced by another. This does not happen in these children. The intractable survival of erratic and aimless behavior and the persistence of early feeding and sleeping disturbances are manifestations which may come to have some etiological significance when they are better understood.

B. ASSESSMENT OF DEVELOPMENT *(*Profile Point V)

1. DRIVE DEVELOPMENT WITH REGARD TO PHASE DOMINANCE[4]

The presenting picture is an overlapping of phases with oral, anal, and phallic manifestations and no evidence of latency. The bulk of libido is active in primitive forms at the oral and anal stages. Its quantitative distribution is difficult to evaluate in the present state of our knowledge. Crudely impulsive oral manifestations in action and fantasy are common in this group, though finger sucking is absent; the object relations of all four children are partly tied to this phase by fantasies of incorporation and primitive identificatory mechanisms. Unintegrated phallic manifestations exist in all cases, without phallic dominance, and without the appropriate developments in ego and object relations. In only one case, Basil, is there an area of structured ego functioning akin to what we expect at the phallic stage. Nevertheless, in this child the archaic ego attitudes seem to have persisted from a very early age; they are isolated to some degree from his structured development but intensively color all his feeling attitudes. While there is some evidence that instinctual development is open to influence by the process of analysis, the general picture is one of arrested libidinal development.

While this picture can be found in a great number and variety of unrelated disturbances, the degree of arrest and its intense and unremitting character are outstanding in our cases.

2. DEVELOPMENT WITH REGARD TO DISTRIBUTION OF LIBIDO AND AGGRESSION

a. *Cathexis of Self*

(1) *The self as a body*

In children who move unpredictably back and forth between various levels of maturity, it is not possible to draw clear-cut lines of development between the self as a psychic entity built on a firmly demarcated body image with recognizable experiences of pleasure

---

[4] In Anna Freud's Profile the development and distribution of libido and aggression are treated separately. In applying the Profile to psychotic children, we have not separated libido and aggression because to do so would suggest a greater degree of differentiation than is apparent from our observation.

and pain, and more archaic forms of body experience which we have learned to attribute to the developing infant. In following the transitions of our children's self experiences we encountered the following confusions:

1. A confusion of inner emotional states with body fullness or emptiness.

Lucille described another child in these terms: "She's got motions in her; that makes her happy." Lucille also envied children who were given suppositories or enemas for the same reason that in this way they achieved fullness. When she felt lonely and neglected, she ate dirt and plasticine. Basil constantly craved for food supplies and measured his feeling of well-being by the supplies available. He was anxious about defecating because: "You never know when you sit on that hole what will happen. Everything may fall out and you'd find yourself being a skeleton with nothing but a bit of skin holding you together." Urinating, bleeding, and even crying were experienced in terms of breaking apart. His concern over losing part of himself by coughing or sneezing reached a climax in a session when he had a bad cold. He spent the whole hour trying to ascertain whether it was safer to blow out the mucus through the nose than to pull it up and keep it, and which way would secure replacement. This fear extended to his genitals. "If you are a daddy and don't want to make a baby, can you save the seed? What happens if you lose it somewhere?" While these confusions are often found in the fantasies of adult neurotic patients, the latter are highly developed formations in contrast to those of our children which appear to reflect early developmental stages and belong to the pleasure-pain series. In the adult neurotic, feelings of fullness and emptiness frequently denote pregnancy fantasies, and fears of loss of body content are related to the threat of castration. These children's experiences and their meaning can be differentiated from the more mature fantasies of the adult neurotic only on the basis of the contexts in which they emerge and the level of interpretation to which the child responds. For example, only when Lucille's feelings of fullness and Basil's fear for his viscera and genitalia were interpreted as reflecting the loss of an object did the children accept the therapist's understanding. While the possibility is still left open that these expressions were overdetermined, several years of analysis intervened without their more extended meanings appearing to have any validity for the children.

2. A confusion of inner emotional states with peripheral sensations.

When Norma felt content she described herself as having a "tender and delicate face." She thought her therapist had "different kinds of worries, nice tender ones." When she was angry she had to whisper because her therapist "had tender and delicate ears." Her angry feelings were constantly confused with a noisy impact on her "delicate ears." She sometimes felt she had square ears. Round ears were soft and delicate, square ears were painful and belonged with angry feelings. Once when she was afraid of being cross during an anticipated visit, she asked for a swimming cap to protect her hair. In this context the cap was to prevent her having feelings which were experienced as a hurting head. Once she repudiated the need for a therapist in these words: "Don't want feeling doctor. Want dentist. Don't talk about feelings. Talk about teeth, upper teeth, lower teeth, baby teeth." Anger was often experienced as a splinter in her throat. Uncomfortable feelings of being to blame were described thus: "They make me feel not so pretty, a buzzing in the head."

When Norma was upset or disliked something for its emotional impact, she referred, quite out of context, to its sensory and not to its emotional qualities. "No-like puppet-panda. It has rough edge. What panda eats? Neck too rough, hurts my finger." She showed the hurt finger and then had an itchy toe. She connected these hurts with the bites of a crocodile whose "bumps" intrigued her. "Why it have bumps on skin? Who made teeth, will teeth bite? Ladies have bumps. They have brown spots [breast aureoles]."

In two additional confusions *the integrating attempts at defense* against states of disintegration are more evident.

3. A confusion of the state of well-being with the possession of symbolic bodily attachments.

In spite of the apparent relation of this material to phallic anxieties, interpretation at this level resulted only in an endless proliferation of fantasy, while interpretation at the level of the child's need to replenish "bodily emptiness" brought about some resolution, though only temporarily.

Norma tried to attach rubber tubes to her genitalia and fitted flippers to her feet. She made herself breast appendages and added high heels to her shoes. She made a complete study of the entrails of birds and (by inquiry) of humans, to persuade herself that she was not empty inside. Ultimately it became clear that she equated these appendages with the functioning of a constantly replenishing breast. It was possible to reconstruct early feeding situations in which her bottle was propped and she constantly lost contact with the nipple. At this point she gave up her use of body appendages.

4. A confusion of the state of well-being with the possession of a symbolic object which could be kept within the body orbit by vision.

Basil made the transition from the Clinic to the waiting car which conveyed him to and from treatment by placing a box of chocolates in the back window of the car so that it could be seen from the treatment room, and in reverse by placing notices in the Clinic windows which could be seen from the car. These devices helped him to retain a feeling of self without "falling apart" as he moved between car and Clinic.

Relatively normal children also utilize symbolic objects in their attempts to defend against anxiety caused by loss of their objects. The degree of their anxiety usually indicates the intensity of a highly ambivalent object relationship. To Basil, however, the therapist appeared not as a person but rather like a known experience which acted, for the period of her presence, as a skin holding him together and preventing him from breaking to pieces. What he feared was a complex of *bodily* sensations which felt like breaking to pieces physically, because the holding-together-therapist experience or alternately the holding-together-car experience was lacking. However we may conceive of the dynamics of this situation, it must be distinguished from the normal child's experience of defense against an imminent *affective* state linked with a whole object relationship.

These confusions seem to arise in a futile attempt to organize organic and peripheral sensations into an abiding sense of a bodily self. They significantly lack the experience of emotional states with specific *quality* as we know them, and are characterized by an intense, diffuse form of excitement. Basil expressed this as follows: "I feel like electricity inside. What I need is a fuse box to give me warning before I get too excited and wild. Getting excited is like breaking in two."

Norma also drew attention to the exaggerated *quantity* of her inner states. "Not hurt much—little hurt not hurt." It would be possible to deduce that the quantitative element and its overwhelming, unorganized character as well as its quality as excitement are responsible for the sense of "hurt" in all the children.

It is not possible to link this diffuse state with a particular level of instinctual need. Excitement at the various instinctual levels seems to manifest itself at the *more integrated* levels of the children's functioning.[5] But the diffuse state is accompanied by the most intense and ungovernable anxiety and gives rise to aggressive reactions of great magnitude. Some children feel threatened with bodily disintegration, some are driven to wandering, some to killing animals, some to violent attacks on themselves or others; the person attacked may be an uninvolved person.

There is evidence that these outbreaks follow ineffectual attempts to obliterate feelings. Norma, for instance, often wished she were dead, which to her meant not to have any feelings. But the feeling of being dead was also unpleasant. This primitive mechanism of obliteration could be traced more clearly when greater maturity of feeling was evident following some analytic intervention. Norma treated more normal feelings of anxiety and depression as if they were foreign bodies which could be shaken out of her system. She was then given to standing on her head to rid herself of them. Only much later when Norma could recognize the value of the human object were we able to observe these primitive reactions give place to recognizable defense mechanisms.

Lucille could say at a later stage in her analysis when her housemother left the hospital, "We'll talk about anyone but not Miss B. She's not nasty but we won't talk about her."

There is evidence that the child's perception of emotional states is replaced by the perception of organic and peripheral sensations and represents a partial arrest at a primitive form of pre-emotional experience. This primitive state is superseded only when a certain level of object cathexis and ego development has been reached. As a result

---

5 All the children masturbate, some anally; none make use of finger sucking. We are reminded that autoplastic modes of discharge are influential in maintaining whatever psychic unity the child may have achieved (Anna Freud, 1954, p. 61). The absence of finger sucking may be a significant diagnostic feature in pinpointing the absence of a basic form of object relationship without which normal integration cannot be achieved.

of this development the experience of excitement is tamed and can then assume the function of a signal of anticipated instinctual activity.[6]

When first encountered prior to analytic intervention the sensory experiences described seem to bypass the existence of the human object. It is as if the children were unaware that satisfaction had anything to do with the human person and as if the feeling experiences that would be appropriate in this respect were unknown to them. In Mahler's term (1952) they operate at a stage of primary body narcissism.[7]

[6] ". . . in comparison with unconscious ideas there is the important difference [between unconscious affect and unconscious idea] that unconscious ideas continue to exist after repression as actual structures in the system Ucs., whereas all that corresponds in that system to unconscious affects is a potential beginning which is prevented from developing. Strictly speaking, then, and although no fault can be found with the linguistic usage, there are no unconscious affects as there are unconscious ideas. But there may very well be in the system Ucs. affective structures which, like others, become conscious. The whole difference arises from the fact that ideas are cathexes—basically of memory-traces—whilst affects and emotions correspond to processes of discharge, the final manifestations of which are perceived as feelings. In the present state of our knowledge of affects and emotions we cannot express this difference more clearly" (Freud, 1915, p. 178, our italics). The "affective structures" to which Freud refers may have some correspondence to built-in systems regulating organic and peripheral discharge. These systems may antedate the period at which the oral erotic zone is dominant and may act as an overflow system of discharge even after that zone has been established. They appear to continue to characterize the psychotic child's experience of affect and may belong to the undifferentiated id-ego described by Hartmann (1952). In discussing this footnote, Anna Freud pointed to the need to consider the question: under what conditions does the child return to experiencing affect in terms of bodily sensation after having already achieved the capacity for normal and appropriate affect.

[7] "The newborn and young infant gradually must be brought out of this tendency toward vegetative splanchnic regression, out of the tendency to lapse into this exhausted, semistuporous state, into an increased sensory awareness of, and contact with, his environment (Greenacre, 1946; Spitz, 1947). In terms of energy or libidinal cathexis this means that a progressive displacement of energy quanitities from the inside of the body (particularly from the abdominal organs toward the periphery of the body) has to occur so that the perceptual conscious system, as Freud calls the surface of the body, the peripheral rind of the ego, containing the sense organs, may receive cathexis. The turning from predominantly proprioceptive awareness to increased sensory awareness of the outer world occurs through the medium of affective rapport with the mother. The baby's libido position thus proceeds from the stage of fetal narcissism to primary body narcissism, a stage in which representation of the mother's body plays a large part" (Mahler, 1952, p. 287). In the children we describe, both the visceral cavity and the sensory surface would appear to have retained an archaic form of cathexis which in the earliest stage of the analysis seemed in no way connected with the felt need for an object. They solicited the caretaking functions of the adults to deal with their disturbance in an adventitious way, if at all, much as they might ask for a minor cut to be bound up.

The children do not have internally consistent object relations at any one time, and they unpredictably move back and forward between different stages of object orientation (see "Cathexis of Objects"). There is, however, a considerable uniformity in their *more archaic* states which appear side by side with some disparity in their ability to take up more advanced positions. What is abundantly clear is that at this point they all seek and can verbalize a demand for a state of homeostatic equilibrium which is felt as deriving from different sources at different times.

The following sources seem to approach but not fulfill the desired state of balance (fullness): (1) soothing sensory stimulation; (2) primitive instinctual gratification at all pregenital levels; (3) the continuous presence of the object who, the child expects, will be totally responsible for instinctual gratification and control and for the elimination of undue excitement.

Basil stated: "I don't want a therapist. I want someone there all the time. I want to be *looked at* all the time."[8] Norma expressed this wish in terms of being a baby monkey clinging always to the body of a mother. At times of intense excitement she would say: "Hold me I am so bad." We have called this *the stage of the object as auxiliary ego*. Provided the object fulfills the child's conditions, there is almost no recognition of the object's identity. Even her physical appearance is readily mistaken (see "Cathexis of Objects"). Basil always asked for his "therapy" on arrival, not his therapist. When told of an impending absence, he would say: "Then who will give me my therapy?"

The children's attempt to maintain a state of mental equilibrium is doomed to failure, because this attempt is based on an archaic model of feeling which is out of harmony with their more advanced instinctual and physical development and their uneven ego states. Instinctual pleasure is necessarily transitory and is in these children insufficiently reinforced by pleasant memories of past gratification and the assurance of future ones. The model, however, seems to presuppose the activation of memory traces involving some good experi-

---

8 This statement recalls to the observer—though not to the child—the role of the mother as watcher and executor of the child's wishes when the child becomes capable of locomotion (see Spitz, 1957). At this and earlier phases the child may conceive of the situation as being held together by the mother's look.

ence with an object. With growing frequency and for lengthening periods they become aware of this in analysis.

Norma once linked the "dead" feeling with the absence of an object. She described a dead bird she had found as follows: "Dead Mummy bird. No baby. The baby all finished, 1962. Dead Mummy bird, 1962." On a later occasion she had been able to maintain her sense of well-being for some days, but it vanished as soon as she experienced some disappointment in her therapist. She described the change in this way: "Now my baby [herself] all dead. All the magic gone." In the course of treatment she moved from collecting transitory and unconnected symbolic objects which were inevitably lost, to amassing a large collection of silver paper which she used sparingly and with discrimination so that she would always have some for future use. As treatment progressed there was an increasingly spontaneous and continuous recognition of the value of the human object and the specific emotional states generated by loss. However, an unusually great or unexpected threat of loss could always revive the diffuse manic type of excitement with its threat of disintegration and total loss of control. In Basil's case we have become sure only now that his sense of physical emptiness can be replaced by feelings for an object, or by states of feeling with a recognizably normal quality, which are capable of reinforcing his self-love. On separating from his mother on an occasion when they had both been pleased with his adjustment at home, he said, "Today, I would not have cried even if she had not given me any chocolate. I thought it was the chocolate last week I missed but it was not."

While all the children achieved a small vocabulary for describing feeling states, we were cautious in judging this new facility as representing a true change in emotional experience because of their easy adoption of adult patter.

We have confined this account to the descriptive level. In two of our cases, treatment failed to enable the children permanently to obtain greater specificity and more varied quality in their emotional states. Moreover (except in the case of Basil, who is known to have developed more mature instinctual and ego positions), we do not know why object cathexis has been kept at so low a level. We have few definitive clues to whether the primitive way of experiencing emotions arose in a retreat from the object because of pain and frustration, and if so, why it was so total. Spitz (1945, 1957), in his observations of hospitalized babies aged nine months to one year and a half, records the manifest unpleasure which they evidenced at the human approach and the rotating avoidance movements of the head which this engendered. Spitz specifically connects this rejecting reaction with a dislike of rising tension intruding on a pathological state of lethargy. The institutionalized children described by Provence and Lipton (1962) ultimately failed to avail themselves of the object only with regard to some aspects of care. For example, they did not expect help where the normal child would do so. In Provence's children this feature sometimes proved irreversible. We still know too little about the irreversibility of early damage due to defective care. Our own material is too scant to answer the question whether our children's gross ego disturbance is inborn or acquired.

(2) *Psychic image of the self*

While disturbances of body feeling took priority in the children's cathexis of self at the commencement of analysis, the self also existed as a psychic representation in which other features derived from a variety of instinctual and ego states emerged. While these features varied from the magical to the more or less reality-syntonic, they contributed to the small degree of self-esteem which the children maintained.

(i) Elements Deriving from Fantasies of a Primary Narcissistic Character

The ability to verbalize feelings of omnipotent self-importance arising in fantasies of *magical action* appeared in the most developed of our cases and was absent in others. We are inclined to attach some benign prognostic value to this aspect.

In treatment Basil felt he should never wait. The car should be waiting for him, the road clear, and the therapist on the doorstep to receive him. Fog and traffic jams were experienced as personal affronts and reacted to by an increase of omnipotent thinking. "I felt like opening that door, stepping right out and turning myself into a giant and pushing all that traffic out of the way." He planned to write letters of complaint to the bus companies and often did.

When Stanley opened the Clinic door and saw the sun shining

he felt he had brought this about. He also felt it specially shone for him. "Every time we come into therapy, the sun shines." Stanley maintained some self-esteem through the bravura with which he brandished aggressive and libidinized *words,* in a meaningless and omnipotent way. These words had a demoralizing effect on adults and children alike and when other children adopted them, Stanley's self-esteem was increased.

In Norma's psychopathology, a masochistic self-blame for all the catastrophes which occurred in the hospital was an outstanding feature. She constantly ruminated about her imagined part in causing illness and used this "worry" to present herself as needing care from her objects. The most intractable aspect of this feature was embedded in masochistic self-love generated by her belief in the magic of her aggressive *thoughts.*

Basil came back from a holiday saying everything had been fine. After he had expatiated on this for some time, his therapist said she had some doubts because he was involuntarily shaking his head, which, she said, must be a *magic gesture* to keep him feeling good and happy. Basil replied, "But it helps me," adding that his mother had been ill and he had met her new boyfriend. The head-shake immediately diminished to a token, and finally disappeared some weeks later. *Magical wishes* at one time dominated Basil's view of himself. He referred to himself as the most popular boy in High Wick and drew attention to himself everywhere without discrimination.

(ii) Elements Deriving from Objects

All the children maintain what sense of well-being they can by demanding constant tokens or gifts from their objects. This is an endless and disappointing process, bringing only transitory satisfaction.

It was important to Basil that he should collect as many things as possible to put in his locker. When the locker was full, he felt "full." It was best when the things were quite new and intact. He locked them away so that no one should damage them or even touch them. He would finger them himself with satisfaction and show them off to others. He collected books but neither read nor used them himself. The mere quantity and newness were sufficient. He kept his bike, a birthday gift from his mother, locked away while he competed for the use of the hospital bike, which he would joyously crash into the fence; he never did this with his own bike.

Norma emphasized that the indiscriminate and valueless things she collected from her objects kept her "safe." Unlike Basil, she kept them only for short periods. Her growing ability to retain the good memory of the giver could be measured by the time it took to lose or destroy them.

Stanley collected valueless objects with the aim of having more and more.

All the children collected words from their special caretakers, often with little understanding of their meaning. These collections were subject to considerable flux and were tenuously dependent on the child's growing object relations. It was often possible to trace the current importance of a human object to Norma by her temporary selection of words.

In the early stage of his analysis, Basil asked his therapist for a cash register. This gift brought enduring and exceptional bliss. To him, it represented all he desired of a love object: it was a machine and thus entirely under his control; it could be locked away and was therefore always available; it lent itself to living out in concrete symbolic form his wish for continuous oral supplies. Since the contents could be used over and over again, the danger of loss of content was eliminated. The extent to which his well-being depended on it became apparent when he labeled his locker "Basil, with cash register." Basil went through a stage of hoarding pocket money, thus giving himself "fullness" and safety. Much later he employed his pocket money to buy objects which he protected and made use of and which he was willing to share.

Lucille was for a long time preoccupied with the gift of a toy tortoise. This symbolized to her (by transitory identification) a roof over her head which would be permanent and a safe place of retreat. It expressed her wish for magical self-sufficiency as well as her sense of unrelatedness and also epitomized the oneness with her object which she despaired of finding.[9]

---

[9] In a discussion, Anna Freud suggested that the stages in cathexis of self and objects made explicit in this paper in order to capture the particular qualities of psychotic functioning might be retained in the Profile and be assessed in all children. While in psychotic children, these archaic phenomena have a rigidity and gross inappropriateness to age, in other disturbances they manifest themselves in a more fluid and transient

(iii) Elements Deriving from Ego Activity

(a) *Modification of behavior.* While all the children appeared to mature in response to the opportunity for object cathexis afforded them, the tenacity with which they adhered to their accomplishments was uncertain. After a period of analysis these appeared to be rigidly tied to the wish to please and thus retain the object through conformity to its wishes. Their achievements had little cathexis in their own right, and their retention was therefore subject to the extreme vicissitudes of the children's object relations, the nature and level of which changed unpredictably.

At a time of great depression, Lucille could tidy up at the end of the hour when help was not forthcoming from the therapist, at the same time reminding herself that she could not have the object with her always. Her activity, however, had the quality of a performance she was demanding of herself out of fear of loss of the object's care and attention. Her identification with the ordering aspect of the object appeared libidinally incomplete—a barren imitativeness.[10]

Norma was cross with her nurse, shut herself in her bedroom, soiled her bed, and smeared the walls deliberately. While she showed anxiety about this when she came to therapy, the fear of disapproval and not shame was the outstanding emotion.

It sometimes appeared that the children had occasional insight into this discrepancy in their make-up.

When Norma had been particularly provocative and was later prepared to be more compliant, she would cover her face with a mask and ask how pretty she was now.

When conformity was established it tended to be a blind conformity in which the adult's demand was in no way mitigated by the child's ability to judge time and circumstance.

Basil's mother was cross because he came home in winter without his scarf. Basil now insists on wearing a scarf when going home, no

---

fashion. The extent to which they have been retained in the personality or returned to at a later age should facilitate quantitative and qualitative comparisons and sharpen the differential diagnostic features between types of disturbance. Blind children also collect seemingly valueless articles and these collections appear to be aimed at raising their self-esteem. The collection of words is also a feature of the adolescent's attempt to obtain oneness with his objects.

[10] We are, however, reminded of a remark which Ferenczi is reported to have made: that all morality begins in an act of hypocrisy. This could with justification be amended to all sublimations begin in such an act.

matter what the weather. "My mother will be cross," he says to any protest.

Sometimes one had the impression that as a result of behavioral modification the children were for long times more anxious and lonely and not more self-esteeming or self-sufficient.

Norma, whose aim is to be adopted by her aunt, exerts the most painful self-control in the period prior to her visit and is ridden with anxiety and fear of being unable to please. Her efforts produce greater certainty in the adults that she will be able to behave well, but they produce no such certainty in her and relatively little pleasure. On the other hand she has recently "lit up" when her therapist has been genuinely able to praise her.

It has become a feature of therapeutic technique to show the children from time to time their advances and encourage their pleasure in this. Basil and Stanley both became able to take stock of their development and gain a measure of self-esteem. However, it is doubtful whether in either child this improvement would altogether outlast a failure in the support they are afforded by their special objects.

(b) *Maturation of skills.* While the ability to learn and perfect new skills varied, the children had certain features in common which at their age were unusual.

They showed an unusual degree of selectiveness as to the person with whom they would exercise these skills; this selectivity is normally observed in the second year of life and again later in the latency child's division of home and school activities which he keeps apart.[11]

Lucille would make things only with her therapist and her teacher. The libidinal aspect of the process seemed to be confined to the presence and participation of the object and did not adhere to the process itself.

On the other hand, the content of the construction was often

---

11 Anna Freud noted, in a discussion, that these children represent an extreme version of the general dependence of learning on the presence of a love object. However, in this group there is a massive discarding of learned skills in the face of object loss, more basic and excessive than in younger children and in depressed patients. In Lucille, the loss of her therapist precipitated the loss of the moderate gains of the analysis which were never recovered.

used to add a libidinal element which the child experienced as missing in the object relationship.

In a period of depression, Lucille insisted that the therapist make for her a tiny swimming boat with a baby figure in it, which gave her real pleasure and filled out her empty relationships.

The vicissitudes of the object relationship were reflected in the fluctuation of effort directed toward the skilled activity.

On her return from holiday to High Wick Norma attempted to ride a bicycle and wanted to learn to skate. This was clearly an attempt to recapture her High Wick objects and keep them with her and when this did not succeed she attempted to destroy her bicycle and the word "bicycle" became phobic.

There is often a short and unusually productive period following a setback in Norma's relationships. When her housemother left, she made her first attempts to read and write which were very successful. This lasted only a few weeks, however. Recently she said: "When I feel bad, I work so as to feel better. I am in a rush to learn to grow up."

The attempt to displace libidinal cathexis in the direction of sublimation is made all the time and with some success, but far from age-adequately. It is not clear whether more than one feature in the psychopathology contributes to this. It is a peculiar quality of the children's object relationships that they continue to exist at many levels simultaneously and that the tendency to total withdrawal is never completely absent (see "Cathexis of Objects"). We may postulate a special quality of the libido, an adhesiveness or inability to give up primitive libidinal positions, whether for reasons familiar to us in connection with the concept of fixation points, or because of some quantitative lack in the libido itself or a constitutional imbalance between libidinal and aggressive drives. We would then have to postulate a pathology of the drives which impedes ego development and reality orientation.

On the other hand, Loewald (1951) describes how the child's attitude to reality and his ability to build boundaries between his inner and outer world bear the imprint of the stages of his relation to his object. While the primary narcissistic identity with the mother constitutes a libidinal motive force for the ego's striving to progressive differentiation and unification of reality, it is also the source of a threat to perpetuate and re-establish this position and engulf the emerging ego into its primary narcissistic unity, "the unstructured nothingness of identity of 'ego' and 'reality' " (p. 17). Hartmann (1956) states: "The transition from 'egocentric' thinking to recognizing the relativity of qualities depends on the insight into the relativity of the 'me' " (p. 42).

Basil, the most advanced of the children has still clearly stopped short of this phase of development. His housemother reports on a journey to the Clinic: "Basil was reading a book, so I was talking to Norma. She was going on about her worries with words. I said they didn't worry me as I had too much to think about. Basil looked up and said, 'Yes, you think about me don't you.' "

We might also postulate that the extreme difficulty these children have in displacing libido in the direction of sublimations and in maintaining them is evidence of a primary deficiency in the ego, an ego which is unable to lend its energies to maintain the positions the children constantly begin to take up and just as constantly fall back from.

Norma appears to verbalize some such feeling when she says, "Wind me up [like a clockwork toy] so that I go," and, "I am in a rush to learn to grow up." Sometimes Norma also seems to be paralyzed by the effort she makes toward reality orientation.[12]

Our observations suggest that in these children growth occurs under great stress, proceeds slowly, and that they experience much less pleasure in their accomplishments than normal children do. While their self-esteem owes a little to their growing skills, the

12 In a discussion, Anna Freud suggested that such eagerness to reach a higher point of development at a time when ego control was not adequate to the achievement was analogous to a child vainly trying to establish urinary control for the sake of the object when he is not physiologically equipped to do so. In our children, however, the search for homeostasis through the use of and cooperation with the object, not object love in itself, is the prior and more pervading need. Martin James raised the possibility that a very early experience of being dissociated from the mother might be a relevant factor. He was reminded of those mothers who did not respond to the infant's needs but rather encouraged the infant to perform in a way that would satisfy their own needs— a situation which sets up a dystonic experience for the baby, interrupts the mutuality of the mother-child relationship, and prematurely emphasizes for the baby his separateness from his environment. Joseph Sandler stressed the distinction between behavior aimed at reducing and discharging instinctual tension and that geared to securing well-being from the object. In these children the instinctual side was secondary to the ego's need to attain and preserve feelings of safety and integration afforded by the presence of the object. It was not a true libidinal cathexis of the object.

limited nature of these skills is also the source of great anxiety and disappointment. When they suffer the additional stress of object deprivation, constructive activities disappear and the cathexis of the self diminishes.

At a time when her therapist was absent because of a prolonged illness Norma appeared dressed in a towel the former had left behind. Asked who she was, she replied, "Nobody." Whenever anyone left her, she assumed a transitory identity by wearing portions of their clothing.

At present the following hypothesis seems most valid to us: the fulfillment of ego potential for which the children strive unavailingly and which they lose so readily may depend on a primitive stage of mother-child relatedness which for unknown reasons was never achieved. Without this, the libidinization of ego functions and their consequent maturation does not take place. In Basil's case, there was considerable achievement, manifesting itself in an age-adequate scholastic competency. Nevertheless, the original maternal unrelatedness, which may have been less in degree than in our other cases, persists in his insatiable emptiness and sense of persecution whenever he experiences normal frustrations. Our uncertainty about the adequacy of our analytic techniques still leaves open the problem whether the damage sustained is reversible. We might expect different degrees of reversibility in different cases of early damage.

(c) *The ideal self.* At the onset of treatment the children show no evidence of any wish *to be* something different from what they are. The emphasis is altogether on *having* something which they endow with the power of altering their uncomfortable states of psychic tension. This varies from the need for special food (Basil) or presents of token objects with symbolic value to permanent attention from the desired object for purposes of maintaining homeostasis and instinctual equilibrium. The emphasis throughout is on the attempt to find means of dissipating internal states of discomfort.

The wish *to become* other than they are emerges in all the children during treatment. While the wish to retain an object as a constant source of supply comes into existence at an early stage in treatment, the fact that the object can be retained in memory is the child's first introduction to the need for change in his own internal functioning as the only solution to his problems. Gradually he voices the need to live in an ordinary home with a permanent object; with this emerges the wish to be normal, expressed differently by each child. They all become *intellectually* quite clear that this involves the ability to control behavior without distraction from their chaotic emotions.

The ability *to anticipate* a state of well-being, however vaguely defined, is at first not related to *intentionality* in which self-direction is a governing force. It is rather related to being given something or possessing something or having something done to them in a way which will produce a magical result. This attitude, characteristic of the stage preceding structuralization, implies that change can be initiated only by an outside agency.

Norma still wishes to reach her ideal by *magical means*. She frequently asks to be "wound up" like a clockwork toy, so that she will "go."

Basil at first felt that living at home would magically endow him with normality. However, when he visited his home, his chaotic behavior made the family and him equally unhappy. Only much later did he set himself the aims of self-control and maintenance of unaggressive behavior, and then became very critical of those who could not live up to this standard. It is still doubtful whether he has established a libidinal cathexis of these ideas for their own sake as distinct from the advantages which they buy, namely, praise and an assured welcome.

Stanley's ideal is attached to the wish to attend a "normal" school, a wish that is overdetermined. "To have a normal school" is partly a residue of the need to possess a talisman as an aid to instinctual equilibrium. It has also some of the qualities of a phallic idea; at the same time it acts as a defense against his oedipal fears which manifest themselves on visits home. Nevertheless, this ideal contains elements of the wish to become different and thus motivates his growing self-control, though the latter is not yet adequately cathected. A short comparative study of his development in this respect is of great interest. At the onset of treatment Stanley could not tolerate any mention of "when you were little." This seemed to have the effect of undermining his present abilities and to expose him to regression. It acted like a threat to his self-regard in the present as if the words would magically reduce him to "littleness." But recently when he asked for some string to take home as a memento of his therapist, she refused, saying, "Now you can remember me." Stanley agreed, saying, "Do you remember when I used to make timetables to remember you?" He referred to a much earlier time of great emotional upset when he despaired at the end of each session of ever seeing the therapist again and marked off the intervening time on a chart, in an endeavor to combat his feeling that the absent object no longer existed. The stabilization of his object representation was now clearly linked with the stabilization of self boundaries and the ability to contemplate changes in the self without the fear of dissolution. These changes would therefore appear to have laid a foundation for encompassing *a time concept* in relation to the self. This development must be central to the ability of maintaining distance from the self as a changing or growing entity without experiencing a threat of dissolution, and would therefore lend momentum to the growth of the capacity to make and tolerate judgments about the self. It is apparently an important step in the abandonment of primary-process thinking. This development must be a necessary first step in the process to which Hartmann (1956) refers as achievement of "the relativity of 'me.'" This seems to be an area in which the libidinal cathexis of the object and the cathexis of ego functions are closely interrelated.[13]

13 Anna Freud noted that the phenomena under discussion represented an area in which the move from primary- to secondary-process thinking could be studied. Behind Stanley's belief in the magic of words was his fear of any reference to a past self and this thought was of the order of a dream representation which depicts a time of being little as an image of someone *now* little. Joseph Sandler added that Stanley's later development showed a growing capacity for thinking in relative terms. This dimension, also described by Piaget, appeared to involve a move from an egocentric mode, operating on a "here and now" basis which precluded the possibility of imagining a different self, to a stage where the child could step outside himself and view himself in relation to his objects and his environment. The authors noted that the step from egocentricity initiated in Stanley and others a tolerance for the revival of memories and anticipatory thinking about future states. (On the other hand, Basil's ready translation of words into concrete things was a mode of thinking which interfered with his capacity to view himself from a distance.) It was generally agreed that the hierarchy in the development of various functions and their interdependence was a vital consideration for further study. The variability of functioning in our children gives the impression that a function might be available in one activity and not in another and, conversely, that a defect in one function might disturb other functions in a particular area of operation but not have such effect in other areas. Anna Freud noted that the egocentricity and the concrete use of words were part of the primary process. The question she posed was: what are the specific features of the move from primary- to secondary-process functioning; and with regard to the present discussion, when does a child learn to use words in a

The reverse of this process, the loss of cathexis of ego functioning, could be studied in Norma at a late stage in treatment when she was threatened with the loss of her therapist.

Norma became afraid she would get "lost" on the long journey to Hampstead. Since she was driven by a hospital attendant she was clearly referring to a sense of inner "lostness." As she talked about how she could tell people where she lived and ask for help, and wondered how dumb people managed who could not speak, the threat of overall loss of ego functions was clear.

The decathexis of elementary ego functioning was often the prelude to a deeper withdrawal of libido which threatened the body self.

Norma was pleased to be thought sensible enough to visit the village hairdresser for the first time. She had also achieved a dry bed and was praised for this. However, she wanted the nurse to stay and talk to her and when this was not possible and she was left alone, she pulled out two front teeth and showed the blood-stained bed to the nurse on her return. The teeth were not loose and she must have exerted considerable force in this attack on herself.

The sequence would appear to be that the child felt threatened with homeostatic failure through impending withdrawal of libidinal cathexis of ego functions and of the self image, and demanded the presence of the object to hold her together. A refusal led to a cathexis of ego functions and body image with undiluted aggression, and a temporary loss of boundary between self and object.

The instability of the cathectic processes and their unpredictability can be judged by two observations almost contemporaneous with the above, but in complete contrast to them.

At one stage of treatment Norma began to verbalize the discrepancy between what she was and what she would like to be. She said: "I don't like myself because myself is not as nice as other people's." In a recent anxiety state she said, "I shall go to my room and leave the 'moany' Norma there." Here she manifested an intentionality that was directed as much to pleasing herself as to pleasing others.

---

nonmagical way and to see himself in relation to objects. She felt that the individual features of the primary process are probably lost at different times; it was her impression that the magical use of words was abandoned before the egocentric attitude was given up.

Norma rode her bicyle so far ahead of her housemother that the latter was disturbed. "When we came to the town, Norma managed everything so well that I relaxed. She picked up on this in my tone of voice and said 'Now you like me again.'" Norma was able to maintain her ego functioning in a difficult situation and for some considerable time, in spite of her feeling that the object was failing her.

In so far as the children have learned to tolerate a deferred wish to become something different and to anticipate and work for its fulfillment on the basis of seeing the need for internal change as a precondition of gratification, their stage of ideal formation approximates that of the child between three and five years of age. Hartmann (1939) underlines the importance of anticipation in the development of the reality principle and secondary-process thinking. However, the capacity of our children to abstract and maintain libidinization of the ideal is so limited that their strongest efforts toward control and direction have a precarious and tentative quality. Even so primitive an ideal formation, however, can act as a temporary organizing element in the psyche and an elementary source of integration of short duration.

So far our observations seem to suggest that there is a capacity for ego development which is not being consistently used. We are not able to say what the limits of this capacity are; indeed, our evidence covers only the most primitive forms of development and in minimal quantities. The maintenance of this development may well require more complex ego functioning of which the children show no evidence. We are used to observing a similar unstable cathexis of ego processes in very young children.

Our observations also suggest that to the extent to which we are able to influence object cathexis in a positive fashion, this minimal ego development can be discerned, but not necessarily maintained.

b. *Cathexis of Objects* (Profile Point Vb)

The very varied states of object relatedness which we shall describe should be considered a course over which the children move in two directions, i.e., progressively and regressively. The direction in which they will move at any one moment is quite unpredictable. The initial more primitive stages were more obvious before treatment and appeared later with less frequency and for shorter periods, and the

later stages which emerged in the course of treatment were sometimes held to more tenaciously. At later stages it was possible to trace
the reasons for regression in terms of a frustrating experience, anticipated or undergone, at other points there seemed to be a fluctuation
of defense for unknown reasons, leading to the reinvestment of more
primitive positions.

(1) *The tendency toward dissolution in the object*

The precariousness of body boundaries appeared most frequently
in children who approached the object for physical comfort and
almost immediately withdrew in panic. At times neither Norma nor
Lucille could stay in the treatment room close to the therapist but
withdrew to the garden. The child seated herself on a mat as if to
define her own limits, and the therapist sat near. Confusion of the
I-you pronouns appeared in most children, and in Norma and Lucille
the *confusion of psychic identity* with that of the object was a massive
one.

At a time of great anxiety Lucille used to feed her therapist with
a spoon, simultaneously opening and shutting her own mouth.

Norma would ask to be fed with candy from her therapist's
mouth, in the mouth-to-mouth position.

Norma asked for a tiny doll to be taped to her hand. When this
was done, she burst into tears as the concrete manifestation of the
fantasy undermined its reality and she tore the doll off.

At times of severe strain when Norma felt she was "Nobody," she
dressed in a towel belonging to the therapist.

These manifestations differ from the role play of normal children
in that any interference precipitated an anxiety attack and a state of
confusion. There appeared to be a partial fusion of self and object
images; this fusion was paramount in the maintenance of the child's
equilibrium, but was also perceived as a danger.

(2) *Symbolization of the object in the inanimate and the non-human*

We refer here to the intensive investment of a thing with a quality
of relationship normally confined to a person. The attachment
appears to be to a *function or functions of the thing* which, because
it represents human functioning as it exists or as the child desires or

imagines it, appears for a time to create a profound feeling that we expect to see only in relation to the human object. At its most primitive level the particular thing invested differs from the transitional object in that it gives no immediate sensuous gratification, such as is given to the child who is attached to a piece of shawl or an article of mother's clothing; it is not cuddly and it does not smell.

Spitz (1957) states: "As we have shown by experiments, no distinction is made [by the three-month-old child] between animate and inanimate surround as long as both possess certain primitive Gestalt attributes" (p. 122).

The totally inhuman Gestalt of our children's symbolic objects may therefore mark them out as representing traces of a very early phase of not-I representation. At the slightly more mature level of their personalities which seems to coexist, it may be part of a defensive maneuver to avoid the sensuous element in objects which threaten the stability of their primitive self images.

Basil's cash register was used for its indefinite capacity to feed and be fed into, to control and be controlled by, for the idea of gratificatory functioning, but not for immediate sensory gratification. It related primarily to homeostasis.

In fact, the symbolic object seems at times to be explicitly chosen because it is incapable of directly stimulating feeling of a sensory type. At other times the emphasis appears to be on its incapacity to suffer damage and become the object of aggression.

Although humanlike toys were available, Lucille for a long time used blocks and beads to symbolize people. She remarked, "These things have no feelings." What could be involved here is the residue of the most primitive not-me, inanimately conceived, "holding-mother" necessary for homeostasis. In normal children, this element does not appear so markedly in their earliest toy selection, although it may be thought to appear in the baby's play with spoons and other functional hard objects. It is usually not noticed because of the preference for the sensuous soft object where the sensory gratification of the "holding-object" has become a markedly discriminated feature, invested with value. Our children's disinterest in and aversion to such soft toys may mean that the inanimate, "holding-object" world has to be established as a necessary foundation for attachment to the sensorily gratifying and finally libidinized object world. Their tendency to touch and fondle live human creatures is always tentative and slight. Either the children lack the development to value this type of gratification or they defend against it by some form of obliteration. There is a further possibility that the toy which is not sensuously gratifying represents a memory image of the dissociated, ungratifying mother. Our material does not allow us to do more than formulate these hypotheses.

It would be important to differentiate in this area the dynamics of the normal developmental displacements involved in the move to the transitional object and ultimately to the toy (infancy) and the hobby (latency and postlatency). The normal advance through play with material having human characteristics or relationships (dolls) to hobby activities involving identification with a functioning human object is an attempt at partial, not total decathexis of earlier satisfactory forms of object relationship. In this respect our children differ significantly from normal children, and this difference probably is at the basis of our doubts concerning the stability of our children's play accomplishments; these have a compulsive, repetitive quality even when they embrace quite marked skills, and appear to have some of the quality of hobbies.

When Lucille's housemother gave her two teddies, Lucille said, "Jean did not know that you wanted a metal tortoise that can't be broken."

Basil played with the window for hours, and then said, "Do you like the window more than me?"

There is no doubt that these objects are cathected at the expense of cathecting humans.

Norma asked for a little object to take with her to keep her safe, "Something that would not break or crumple if washed or tear or get dirty." She selected a little tin bowl but was afraid it might get dented if banged.

Even when the cathexis of the human object was central, it was still in the nature of a cathexis of functioning. The children initially reacted to the treatment and to Clinic personnel in terms of a person's function and not to the person herself. The emphasis was not on the object as libidinal provider.

At the time of the cash register, Basil still asked for his therapy and not his therapist. When Basil had been coming to the Clinic for several months, needing a drink one day in the absence of the receptionist who dispenses the drinks, he turned to a very dissimilar therapist and said, "Is she the orange-juice lady?"

When Lucille's treatment had to stop, it was the treatment not the therapist for which she grieved.

More nearly related to the transitional object, though still lacking in sensuality, is the symbolization of the human part or appendage, used as a substitute for the human object.

Lucille's fantasies often referred to people such as Mr. Leg, Mr. Trouser, Mr. Mouth, giving the impression that such external aspects were all she had been able or willing to encompass.

The idea that people were like things was implicit in Norma's comment on the death of a child: "Why could she not be mended?" The same notion was carried over to her self image when in periods of depletion of self cathexes, she asked to be wound up like a clockwork toy. She still saw herself as made up of pipes like a drainage system. "You pour water in and wee comes out. You need a plumber to unblock you and clear the blockage."

In its primitiveness, this stage has some affinity with Provence and Lipton's institutionalized babies who cathected the bottle before the human object. This statement is certainly an oversimplification, and consideration must be given to the fact that our observations were made when the child was in the company of an adult of whom he was perceptively aware and whom he must have minimally cathected. Nevertheless, our children have an overriding preference for the inanimate and impersonal, which differs fundamentally from the usual displacement of cathexis from the human to the inanimate object. The difference is apparent in the emphasis on safety as distinct from comfort and gratification. The anxiety appears to concern survival.[14]

[14] In assembling our material on this aspect of the children's object relations, we were impressed by the parallel it offered to Tausk's theoretical formulations concerning the origin of the "influencing machine" in adult schizophrenics (1919). His major premise is that the ultimate delusion was preceded much earlier, possibly in childhood, by states (not noticed by observers) in which changes in self and object representation were experienced, rationalized, and otherwise defended against. Tausk's formulation is given an almost slow-motion exemplification by our children. The "estrangement" from the whole body or from a specific organ arising from the perception of its libidinization is exemplified in the cases we have quoted (see, for instance, Norma and Lucille). Subsequent persecution by the "thing" world was shown by Norma (see below), though the defensive mechanisms involved were not identical with Tausk's adult cases. In fact,

The cathexis of the inanimate object represents a retreat from the human object or a fixation at the stage of the most primitive human relatedness; the "thing" elicits no sensuous feeling and its cathexis may sometimes represent a part-way defensive stage in the process of becoming "numb" or "dead," i.e., in the process of emotional obliteration. In Norma, this was most apparent; interest in an inanimate object always coincided with the emergence of a somatic symptom, and was a prelude to the state to be next described, in which the object world was conceived as wantonly depriving and destructive. It would appear, therefore, that there is a secondary anxiety—secondary, that is, to the fear of annihilation—that concerns the dominance of the child's destructiveness toward the human object who fails to meet the child's needs. The retreat to an inanimate world is difficult to maintain, and the double defense of obliteration and somatization finally proves inadequate in the face of internal pressures. The result may be a violent aggressive attack which represents renewed contact with a revitalized but unbearable world.

(3) *Perception of the object world as hostile*

As a result of analysis, the children's need for the object was revived, but they also became demanding and insatiable. Hartmann, Kris, and Loewenstein (1946) describe the young child's normal development in terms of a widening series of satisfactions which begin with sensory and instinctual gratification, embrace satisfactions from the object relationship, and increasingly include satisfaction from his own activities. The absence of satisfaction as distinct from zonal pleasure was a marked feature of the children we are describ-

---

all the children were preoccupied with a machine and its makeup in some specific and compulsive way, but the degree of pathology was often veiled by the fact that these were children at play. Norma constructed a cardboard phonograph which operated by string, and Stanley became expert at electrical wiring. The frustrations involved in these activities gave a veneer of realism to the underlying persecutory feelings. The positive aspects of the mechanical thing were also usually evident. The machine and the thing represented an estrangement from self and object representations, linked together by the process of identificatory thinking (see below). Important changes in instinct theory formulated by Freud in the year immediately following the publication of Tausk's paper and the development of psychoanalytic ego psychology in the intervening years invalidate Tausk's premature explanation of these phenomena. Moreover, while ego regression from established positions of maturity can clearly be seen as deriving from instinctual regression in adult schizophrenics, age-adequate ego functioning has never been established in our children.

ing. For a very long time we had no evidence that they could experience satisfaction. They very rarely expressed pleasure and then only momentarily. When they admit satisfaction now, it is often in a reminiscent mood where the events referred to are in the past.

Lucille said, "You once let me sleep at the other house. Do it again. Take me to tea, get me a koala bear, buy me a cardigan" (all past gratifications).

But even this type of reminiscence is rare. The children remember their deprivations infinitely more than their satisfactions.

Norma said, "When I am feeling bad, I can't remember any nice things at all."

The most outstanding need for the object is as a provider of more and more things which promise satisfaction. When provided, they prove inadequate and for the most part harmful in the child's view.

Norma's demandingness at one point started again. She wanted to invade the other rooms, to equip herself with innumerable objects which were now "necessary." However, each was discarded as too vulnerable, and she started a moaning complaint because "they" did not provide differently. In this context, "they" referred to the unknown makers of objects, not the known people who provided them more immediately. "Why do they make needles that prick? Or airtoys that break? Why don't they put a solid stopper on glue pots? Why rubber? Rubber reminds me of airtoys and balloons that prick and go empty." She could not bring her airtoy to the Clinic because there were too many scissors to prick it. Plastic which was provided reminded her of paper which tore. At this point she threw away her precious collection of silver paper and asked: "Why did you get it for me?" She attempted to make an airtoy with tape and plastic, but the air escaped and it emptied. Finally, she turned on the therapist and asked: "Why don't you get me something interesting?" It was as if the whole inanimate world now lacked the power to afford pleasure. At this point Norma's thoughts ran to clockwork toys that go when they are wound up, humans that have inside works like lungs and a heart that ticks, and from time to time she asked to be wound up. Although she had maintained herself at a higher level for several months, Norma and her therapist appeared to be helpless observers of the dissolution of her inner world.

Stanley's therapist wrote to him when he was ill, saying what a nuisance he had diarrhea. Stanley's reaction was: "Why you say it? It is a silly word. If you write it, it makes me say it. Why you say I am a nuisance? Don't write me letters."

When Basil rang his therapist and she was absent, he later asked, "Did you not answer because you knew it was me?"

Basil does not believe that his siblings were also placed in an institution. He complained: "Perhaps they are at home while I am here." His mother does not lie to him.

Stanley said, "This is more than I can stand. Why does everything go wrong with my life and not with my brothers?"

Stanley asked, "Why am I left-handed? Why me?"

It is the overall appearance of being in a bad world that is so outstanding a feature and which amounts to a total depletion of satisfaction and at times of pleasure, except for the more primitive autoerotic ones.

The anxieties aroused in the context of killing and being killed were maximal at times of illness. On at least one occasion the endeavor to deal with this anxiety gave rise to a hallucinatory experience.

Lucille's therapist visited her when she was ill in bed. Lucille became immediately out of control and screamed for her to leave. She later compared this experience with that of taking LSD, which she had once been given.

In the neurotic child, "the hostility of the world" can be understood as the result of projection arising in the context of destructive wishes in a state of gross dissatisfaction. However, the mechanism in our children appears rather to be an uncontrollable externalization brought about by the tenuousness of boundaries between the self and the external world. Moreover, while projection is effective in maintaining a libidinal position, this mechanism of externalization may again result in entirely emptying the self of feeling. Its aftermath may be a series of anxiety attacks which lead to chaotic functioning of catastrophic dimensions, and continue for days on end, often followed by a period of placid functioning.

The wish to be devoid of feeling carries with it the obliteration in memory of the immediately provoking situation which becomes unusually difficult to ascertain. It is a feature of the children's analytic development that this technical problem lessened and a temporary change in their ego capacity to maintain the relationship between feeling and precipitating event ensued; their new capacity to communicate this link decreased for a time the outbreak of anxiety attacks.

(4) *The object as auxiliary ego*

At earlier stages of our contact with the children the feelings of emptiness and depletion were massive and the object was needed to ensure that an identity was retained. At later stages the prevailing fear was to be overwhelmed by instinctual impulses rendering the ego helpless against desires to attack and kill. The children's fear of being unable to protect themselves or their objects against destruction was realistic and had to be constantly guarded against.

The fear of total helplessness was at its worst when change of any type was imminent. This situation provoked the most archaic defenses.

Prior to going to camp, Lucille made plans to meet the unknown situation. Finally, she bedded herself down on the floor of the treatment room, saying, "I in camp." Her last defense was always to take to bed as a safe place where she would be protected and could indulge in autoerotic activities.

This imminent helplessness could be studied as the children waited to be called into the consulting room and as they waited to be collected after treatment. The waiting period was minimal, usually a matter of minutes, but precipitated great anxiety, often complete lack of control, and sometimes destructiveness.

At first nothing helped Basil if the therapist or the attendant collecting him was not with him in the waiting room. Chaotic functioning would break out in an instant. Even when the therapist was present, Basil was difficult to control, the prevailing anxiety being that no one would come and he would be abandoned. Later, the therapist's presence reassured him. Still later, he was able to reassure himself by envisaging where the attendant would be. "I did not panic because I knew she would now be coming up the hill."

The nature of the help demanded was the practical one of controlling outbursts due to anxiety, but it had to have the quality of omnipotence. "Help me, stop my worries, stop me hurting." The magic was assumed to reside in the adult and was beyond the power of the child.

Following her attacks on animals and children, Norma feared to repeat these events and said, "Please help me." Following a failure of her parents to visit, Norma made houses for beetles, but in installing them they were inevitably killed. She then placed the hands of the clock at three and at seven, three being the time of her session and seven her bedtime (safe times).

The interrelation of the various forms of object orientation we have just described offers a considerable challenge to our understanding. It is clear that the instinctual forces involved are mediated by a primitive ego organization, about which we know comparatively little. Moreover, the likelihood is that the ego is not only primitive in the area of object relations but also defective in some unknown way. It is clear that the main mechanism is not projection, as it would be in other types of object disturbance to which we are accustomed. According to our observations, the sequence of experiences is as follows: the world becomes dead through a failure to find the object at the level of psychic need; the child also feels dead; the world and the self then become replete with an undiluted form of terror which is dangerous to the self and the objects. But in the aggressive outburst, both child and object come alive again. A primitive need to survive plays an inescapable part in the sequence.

The trend away from the object and the far-reaching obliteration of feeling also seem to derive from an anxiety concerning survival.

(5) *Safe object relations maintained by identificatory thinking*

Alice Balint (1943) describes a process whereby the very young child transforms a strange and consequently frightening world into one that is familiar and enjoyable—identificatory thought,[15] a process which is employed for the purpose of avoiding what is unpleasant and obtaining what is pleasurable. In this type of thinking, the primitive pleasure ego plays a greater part than in objective thinking. The basis of the earliest identifications is not resemblance

[15] The term as used by Alice Balint has no relation to the mechanism of identification; in a discussion Anna Freud suggested a more apt description: that the child maintains a primitive state of animistic thinking.

to the object but the manner in which the object enters into relation with the child's instincts. Identificatory thinking forms a bridge to the external world and to object relations. Alice Balint postulates that "we are able to know the external world only as something akin to the ego [in our terminology, self]" (p. 320).

Much of our children's relation to the anxiety-provoking aspects of the world is expressed in terms of this type of thought. They deal similarly with the anxiety-provoking aspects of their own experience, seeking through an animistic link with their objects to give acceptable meaning to what otherwise lacks it.

Thus, Stanley's therapist wrote: "Ever since I have known Stanley he has envisaged a unity of feeling and experience between us. He would ask if I had washed my hair when he had washed his; if I had been to the barber when he went; if I was upset because his housemother left; even whether I was jealous because the curtains were higher than he. He resented all proofs of my separate existence. When I took out a handkerchief, he asked why, because he didn't have a cold. When I commented on his father being a policeman, he asked, 'Is your's one too?' "

Basil constantly asked about the adult's tastes; he was distressed and felt rejected when they did not coincide with his. To him, this appeared as if he was unliked. He commented: "It is good if people want to be like you, because it means they like you."

Much of the children's use of language, which gives an inaccurate view of their advancement, can be understood as a superficial identity with their close objects. The aim of the general parroting of words and phrases is to keep this safe link with the adult. It is often difficult to know how much the children understand words they use and how much is imitative repetition.

Concerning his dislike of his new escort, Stanley commented: "That's because I'm not used to her. What does used mean?"

In the context of her own sadness, Lucille always repeated explanations her therapist had given her. Their meaning was less important to her than the fact that they were the words the therapist would use in this context. For example: "Don't be disappointed if you can't have it"; "You don't need two crocodiles"; "Jean's sad about Joy dying. She'd be sad if you died." She reminded herself that she could not have the therapist to herself and tidied up as the therapist would wish her to. At the same time she seemed to be more alone suggesting that this identificatory link with the therapist's rational and ordering aspect was in some way libidinally incomplete. It had the quality of a performance she demanded of herself, but it did not lead to a state of satisfaction.

The following examples indicate a more advanced stage where the children hover, as it were, between the world of egocentric thinking and true awareness of the object. Perceptual discrimination is available in problematic situations, but belief in it is uncertain. Hence action is still conflicted.

Norma reported, "I saw a man walking under a bridge and he wasn't frightened." Bridges are frightening to Norma, but this observation surprised rather than reassured her.

When a housemother was upset, Norma commented, "Poor Mrs. M., are you sad? Shall I break something for you?" On this occasion Norma ended up by spontaneously helping to dry the dishes as a consoling action, but she was clearly uncertain which line to take.

(6) *Ambivalent object relations, with development of defense mechanisms*

In the course of treatment, the ability to retain the object as both loved and hated developed in varying degrees in different children. It was always precarious and the degree of the regression from it differed from child to child. On the whole, the trend was toward maintaining this state of orientation; for a time the ego functioning on which it hinged could be increasingly depended on, though only in limited areas.

Sometimes Norma expressed her ambivalence by alternately being tender and cross, at times hitting the therapist while using a caressing voice. This state was reminiscent of a year-old baby. At other times she manifested some distance from her aggression with changed modes of adapting herself to it. She said: "I saw a little girl with a bicycle and was jealous. It worried me and I had to run away." When the therapist asked where to, she replied: "In here to you." She would cross the road to avoid difficult experiences but usually told the therapist about them with a clear ability to define her conflict.

Basil, who used to fight his way through his weekends at home and was overcome with jealousy and demandingness, now says (and acts upon it!), "If there is any quarreling, I shall take a book and go to my room."

Occasionally a child developed empathy with the deprived object in areas strictly limited by his own experience of deprivation.

Norma was always upset by the traffic jam at the roundabout on her journey to the Clinic. One morning she said, "Poor lorry driver when he held up." She was also sorry for girls who have no penises and for boys who cannot have babies as girls do.

Gratitude for and pleasure in what was done for them began to emerge, if uncertainly.

Norma took pleasure in what the therapist gave her and said, "You nice to me." She then began to make presents for other people.

Important objects were more clearly discriminated: the child noted not only their appearance and functions but also their individual qualities and characteristics which he was ready to understand and react to.

Basil said: "I don't tell my housemother about anything nasty. I tell you the nasty things because you can help me."

"Why is my mummy so impatient and cross? She never used to be. When I do something for her, why does she always ask more and more from me?"

Acceptance of the object's sensory and emotional states led to transitory attempts to protect them.

Norma asked, "Shall we close the window if you cold?" When she wanted a gift at the store and the therapist was short of money, Norma was concerned whether the therapist would have enough to buy a pineapple for herself as well.

When his therapist had eye trouble, Stanley asked, "Shall I put you to bed?"

Norma's frequent visits to the lavatory on walks were disconcerting to her therapist and caused some resentment in shopkeepers. Gradually Norma learned to anticipate her problem and to avoid the unpleasantness.

The ability to contain aggression by expressing it verbally in critical statements based on reality and even to indulge in a macabre type of humor about it emerged surprisingly often.

Basil and Stanley now consider the effect of their own behavior on their parents and with growing accuracy are capable of discriminating between those aspects which they have induced and those for which they have no responsibility.

Norma after an argument with her housemother said the next morning: "Bloody God! Twilley's not dead yet." She then went into a variety of descriptions of how Twilley could die. She might stick a knife in her. Asked if this would work, her housemother replied, "Would you like to try?" Norma burst into laughter and said: "You teasing me." Norma now speaks of her own death in the same macabre way. She does not feel certain whether she will have a cross on her grave. This bizarre and unfeeling speech has to be compared with the terror of dissolution for its positive aspects to be apparent. The child's continuing fear of being overwhelmed by aggression is only too clear. However, Basil's recent statement, "What's the good of being good if it doesn't lead anywhere," has a ring of normality about it.

SUMMARY

We have confined this report to our observations on the self and object representations of a group of four children in analysis. Our attempt to systematize these has of necessity made use of formulations which derive from our understanding of the earliest stages of ego development. The distribution of instinctual forces in self and object representations is in these children mediated in part by a primitive ego organization which utilizes archaic modes of functioning and which nevertheless shows some small capacity for development under the stress of a modified analytic process, though not always predictably and only for limited periods of time.

We may formulate the following unstable advances:

1. The synthesis of body states into recognizable feeling states which from being meaningless and tormentingly detrimental to homeostasis, now take on the significance of signals of need.

2. The gradual acceptance of a priority of cathexis of the human person as a satisfier of need.

3. Some rudimentary acceptance of a reciprocal feeling relationship with the human object (observed in the development of limited empathy, gratitude, protectiveness, and the wish to give). Neverthe-

less, this advance still seemed to be carried out in the face of a severe arrest in the area of self and object relationships, in which, for long periods, feeling states were in abeyance or defended against and in which preoccupation with the inanimate was an unusual feature. When for internal reasons, these defensive activities failed, there appeared a trend toward animistic thinking with the denial of differences between child and adult.

In Norma and Lucille, this arrest seemed to affect their whole ability to relate. In Stanley and Basil, a larger area of their personalities seemed capable of operating independently of this arrest, though the disparity between the two levels was always grossly evident and remained so.

Being in analysis which involved a close and continuous opportunity to relate has undoubtedly helped the children to communicate and made possible the detailed observations we have recorded. Without the analytic contact, the children could not have verbalized their inner states so clearly and intensively. Nevertheless, we are aware that our clinical approach influenced scarcely more than the uppermost neurotic features of these children's disturbances. In Basil and Stanley, their social awareness and to some degree their ability to conform have advanced, but there has been no advance in the level of their most basic object relationships. In adolescence this may well prove disastrous. We are considering whether a different clinical approach aimed at reconstructing the failure of early environmental holding might be more effective in cases such as theirs.

Norma and Lucille came to us at a much lower level of integration. We do not yet know whether this could have been influenced by a different technique. The experience of the staff of High Wick, where the children receive constant intensive care from a single object, and where allowances for regression in a permissive environment are made, does not lend support to the idea that the children would improve merely by devoted care given over a prolonged period of time. Our findings as set out in this paper suggest that the arrest in development involves in all cases a failure in relating at the most primitive ego levels prior to structuralization. However, our data do not permit us to determine whether this failure is due to an innate lack of potentiality or neurological defect or to a deficit in the earliest "holding environment."

BIBLIOGRAPHY

Balint, A. (1943), Identification. *The Yearbook of Psychoanalysis,* 1:317-338. New York: International Universities Press, 1945.

Freud, A. (1954), In: Problems of Infantile Neurosis. *This Annual,* 9:16-71.

—— (1962), Assessment of Childhood Disturbances. *This Annual,* 17:149-158.

—— (1963), The Concept of Developmental Lines. *This Annual,* 18:245-265.

—— (1965), *Normality and Pathology in Childhood: Assessments of Development.* New York: International Universities Press.

Freud, S. (1915), The Unconscious. *Standard Edition,* 14:159-215. London: Hogarth Press, 1957.

Greenacre, P. (1946), The Biologic Economy of Birth. *This Annual,* 1:31-52.

Hartmann, H. (1939), *Ego Psychology and the Problem of Adaptation.* New York: International Universities Press, 1958.

—— (1952), The Mutual Influences in the Development of Ego and Id. *This Annual,* 7:9-30.

—— (1956), Notes on the Reality Principle. *This Annual,* 11:31-53.

—— Kris, E., & Loewenstein, R. M. (1946), Comments on the Formation of Psychic Structure. *This Annual,* 2:11-38.

Kut Rosenfeld, S. & Sprince, M. P. (1965), Some Thoughts on the Technical Handling of Borderline Children. *This Annual,* 20:495-517.

Loewald, H. W. (1951), Ego and Reality. *Int. J. Psa.,* 32:10-18.

Mahler, M. S. (1952), On Child Psychosis and Schizophrenia: Autistic and Symbiotic Infantile Psychosis. *This Annual,* 7:286-305.

Provence, S. & Lipton, R. C. (1962), *Children in Institutions.* New York: International Universities Press.

Spitz, R. A. (1945), Hospitalism. *This Annual,* 1:53-74.

—— (1947), Anaclitic Depression. *This Annual,* 2:313-342.

—— (1955), The Primal Cavity: A Contribution to the Genesis of Perception and Its Role for Psychoanalytic Theory. *This Annual,* 10:215-240.

—— (1957), *No and Yes: On the Genesis of Human Communication.* New York: International Universities Press.

Tausk, V. (1919), On the Origin of the "Influencing Machine" in Schizophrenia. In: *The Psychoanalytic Reader,* ed. R. Fliess. New York: International Universities Press, 1948, pp. 52-85.

Winnicott, D. W. (1953), Transitional Objects and Transitional Phenomena. *Collected Papers.* New York: Basic Books, 1958, pp. 229-242.

—— (1960a), Ego Distortion in Terms of True and False Self. *The Maturational Processes and the Facilitating Environment.* New York: International Universities Press, 1965, pp. 140-152.

—— (1960b), String: A Technique of Communication. *The Maturational Processes and the Facilitating Environment.* New York: International Universities Press, 1965, pp. 153-157.

PATHOBIOGRAPHY

THE ORIGIN OF *THE TURN OF THE SCREW*

M. KATAN, M.D.

Several years have elapsed since I wrote my "Causerie" (1962). I had received a request to discuss *The Turn of the Screw*. Not only the book but also the author himself was unknown to me. I accepted the challenge and, with no further information to guide me, arrived at the conclusion that the story was a description of a crucial phase of James's oedipal development. The analysis did not offer much difficulty, and the result was an elaborate construction, containing James's traumatic infantile experiences and their influence upon his later development.

At the end of my "Causerie" I promised to examine James's autobiography in order to obtain corroborations of my interpretations.

In order to delineate the extent of this task, I shall review my construction, which covers a number of successive phases. First, there were primal scene observations by the young Henry James and another sibling. The witnessing of these scenes had aroused the children to such a degree that sexual play resulted between them. Next, their mother got the notion that something very undesirable was going on between the two, and she tried to force the truth out of the children. This action on the mother's part had a deleterious effect upon the children as well as upon her husband.

The father, as I have deduced, felt quite helpless in this unprecedented situation and was probably also frightened by his wife's domineering attitude. He therefore left the handling of the children solely to her. Thus the children, upset by the mother's relentless prodding and receiving no support from the father to counterbalance the mother's harmful attitude, were indeed very badly off. The story pictures a disturbed latency, but the origin of this disturbance lies, of course, farther back. I drew the conclusion that the little Henry, at about the age of five, felt a strong resistance to assuming the masculine role. At the onset of his adolescence he had the same problem to struggle with, and at this time it led to a severe outbreak of castration anxiety. The mother's influence retained the upper hand of whatever example the father may have set. The result was a turning away, in adult life, from any direct sexual contact with another person. Henry James became a bachelor.

This group of successive interpretations can be divided into three parts: (1) The constructions concerning the events in Henry James's childhood form the basis of this group. (2) Next, we have to consider the parents' attitudes. The actions of the parents and of the children are completely interwoven, and therefore the parents' attitudes cannot be separated from the childhood events. However, we may assume that the parents will have shown some of the same characteristics even under less crucial circumstances. Thus it occurs to me that the parents' attitudes are more open to examination than one might at first expect. (3) Similarly, we may distinguish my interpretations of Henry James's ego development from those in the preceding subdivisions.

It would be most convincing if the first group of constructions (the group centering around the primal scene observations) could be corroborated. However, my search for this type of material has proved unsuccessful. The autobiographical data contain no evidence that Henry James ever observed sexual intercourse, nor is there any hint of his having performed a forbidden sexual act with another child. It would be rather naïve on our part if our method of corroboration were to rely solely upon obtaining direct confirmations of our constructions.

Our task will have to assume a much wider scope. As I see it, the task is twofold. First of all, it is essential to scrutinize thoroughly my method of dealing with the story. For only if this method is based upon sound psychoanalytic principles can we expect the results to reveal the truth. The second part of our task requires more explanation. The analysis of a novel will succeed in harvesting a rich crop of biographical data about its author only if the story itself has emerged directly from the author's most intimate thoughts. We, the analysts, cannot feel satisfied unless we find objective proof for the existence of such a relationship.

MY METHOD OF INTERPRETATION

If one is sensitive to criticism, one should never publish a paper of the type of my "Causerie." To conceive of a novel as a dreamlike fantasy pertaining to the personal past of the author is to risk one's reputation. When one has the audacity to continue with an analysis of the story, it is practically synonymous with sacrificing one's head. The strange aspect of the whole affair is that these deadly criticisms are fully predictable. One's paper is an intellectual exercise based upon speculations and fantasies! As if such an opinion did not make further criticism superfluous, one must be prepared for what one is going to hear next. Verification of the results is impossible, and, after all, such a paper lacks scientific value! Thus *"der langen Rede kurzer Sinn"*[1]—the gist is that the paper becomes an intellectual exercise void of any significance.

There is a strong psychological reason for this predictability. My paper is of such a kind that the chances for pitfalls are many. Thus the critic is on the safe side; he plays, so to say, the percentage point by declaring that the whole thing is worthless. Nevertheless, in the interests of the critic himself, one could wish that he possessed greater ability to differentiate between interpretation and speculation. In that case, he might be able to deliver constructive instead of merely destructive criticism.

As an example that negative criticism can be advantageous, I want to point to the opinion of Leon Edel, the well-known and competent biographer of Henry James. Edel (1949) pronounces the· following judgment: "what James set himself to do in his ghostly stories was to create such nightmares for his reader. 'Make him *think* evil, make him think it for himself, and you are released from weak specifications,' James wrote. This was his formula for 'The Turn of the Screw,' and the critics who have been explaining this story for more than half a century have, in reality, been telling us their own nightmares" (p. vii).

Edel takes James's words at their face value. It is as if the meaning of *The Turn of the Screw* is revealed by James's efforts to induce the reader to think evil for himself. Although Edel has applied analysis to Henry James's personality, and even to "The Turn of the Screw," he is still adamant in his opinion about the attempts made by others to unravel the story. From the little I have read of these faintly

---

[1] Literally: "In brief, the meaning of the long talk" (Schiller). I am indebted to Dr. Heinz Hartmann for pointing out to me that Schiller—and not Goethe, as I had thought—was the author of this well-known epigram.

analytically tinted attempts, I must admit Edel is correct in this regard.

But does Edel's pronouncement have a general value? Is his judgment also applicable to my attempt at interpretation? If Edel's opinion really had an overall validity, not only would the analysis of *The Turn of the Screw* be impossible but the analysis of patients as such would become simply a chimera. For there is not a single analysis in which the patient's resistance does not set a trap for the analyst, a trap frequently far more complicated and tricky than the one James tried to set for his reader.

It is clear that James tried to create anxiety in his reader by appealing to childhood fears, the memory of which was no longer conscious. Thus James tried to revive his own old anxieties in his reader. He hoped that, as a result, a regressive process would be started in the reader and that through this process the old frightening ideas, by an increase of their energetic charge, would come to life again.

Edel, a man of letters, not being acquainted with the intricacies of daily analytic practice, was led to believe, by James's conscious efforts to fool the reader, that an analysis of *The Turn of the Screw* was not possible. In my "Causerie" I pointed to James's wish to create anxiety in the reader and I deduced that in this way James was trying to discharge his own anxiety. He was here applying a common defense mechanism.

This deduction leads immediately to another one. The same story through which James tried to arouse his reader's anxiety reflects the tale of his own woes. Accordingly, *The Turn of the Screw* becomes for us an autobiographical, although distorted account of James's childhood. By interpreting the defensive aspect of the story, we not only avoid being trapped by James's intent, but we have also created an opportunity to analyze the ghost story itself.

The haunting, supernatural character of the story was the main tool through which James hoped to instill anxiety in the reader. This antirealistic feature served another purpose as well. It was the source of information for the governess about what went on between the children. We set ourselves the task of divesting this part of the story of its supernatural character. By skillfully playing the instrument of the supernatural, James hid the simple fact that in one way or another the mother had gotten an inkling that something bad was occurring between the two children.

Here a critic—of course solely an offspring of my imagination—asks to be heard. "Up to this point you have done nothing else except repeat the wisecracks of your 'Causerie' and have not provided the slightest evidence that your method or your conclusions are correct. You have even made things worse. For you deal with James as if he were your patient. After pretending that you have eliminated his resistances, you think that a lot of new material is now available for interpretation. It may be very little, but I have read at least enough about analysis to know that treatment hinges on the transference. This phenomenon is, of course, absent in the author's story. Finally, therefore, I have an objective reason for declaring that your interpretations are worthless!"

Laying aside my critic's first remarks—for it is my intent to prove only the correctness of my method of interpretation, not its results—I shall focus on his last point. I start with a question. What if the same material had been presented to me by a patient? Let us assume that the patient had a nightmare similar to James's story and that he gave associations comparable to the author's information. Would my interpretations then have led to the same conclusions?

When I started my discussion of *The Turn of the Screw,* I emphasized that my approach would be no different from the one I use in an analysis. Of course, between the two situations conspicuous differences exist. I have just remarked that James, at the time he wrote his novel, for reasons still obscure at the moment, must have been emotionally upset. His state of mind betrayed clearly that a regression had taken place. Childhood experiences and fantasies were revived and threatened to throw his thinking off balance. In order to regain mastery over his difficulties, he wrote a book through which he attempted to discharge his anxiety onto his reader. It is necessary for me to cope with this mode of contact with his reader if I am to succeed in writing an analytic biography.

In analytic treatment a different process takes place. The patient submits himself to the treatment in order to be cured, and this attitude becomes the basis for his relationship with the analyst. During the course of treatment, this relationship becomes much more complicated. Material appears which is relevant not to the present but to the past, especially to the patient's childhood. As a result, a role is ascribed to the analyst which in reality has nothing to do with him; it is a role that was played by other persons when the patient was still a child. Thus we observe the occurrence of transference phenomena as an intricate part of the treatment. The past becomes reflected in the present. By analyzing these transference phenomena, we obtain important insight into what happened during the patient's personality development in childhood, when the foundation was laid for his later symptoms. Accordingly, the transference may constitute a very favorable factor; it becomes the principal means by which the patient's wish to be cured can be fulfilled.

Again the patience of my imaginary critic is exhausted. He tells me he does not want to be drawn into a theoretical discussion about the similarities and differences between transference in an analysis, on the one hand, and the relationship which the author is aiming to establish with his reader, on the other. My critic is quite scornful and reproaches me by saying I am using a trick to lure him into a maze of analytic concepts, among which he does not feel at home. In short, he accuses me of trying to hide my defeat behind a smoke screen of theoretical digressions. He insists that I bring corroborations of my constructions or else keep quiet.

Here another critic—more analytically inclined than the first one, but still not convinced by my explanations—wants urgently to express his opinion: "I think I have understood very well your method of reasoning. The author brings his infantile material because, among other things, he wants to arouse anxiety in his reader; the patient may offer the same sort of ideas to his analyst on the basis of his transference. I expect you were going to say, if our friend had not interrupted you, that whatever the motivation for communication might have been, once the material is brought, the motivation does not matter any more. For now this material provides an opportunity for interpretation." And my new critic continues: "I don't even ask for objective corroboration of the constructions relating to the author's childhood. After all, in regular analysis, such corroboration frequently cannot be found either. I am told that something else takes the place of objective proof. In analysis, patient and analyst build together, in their mutual exchange of thoughts, a model that represents the personality development of the patient. Missing links

are discovered, and, in the long-lasting and slowly advancing treatment, insight is acquired about how the symptoms were formed. In
this working-through process the patient will see his development
from early childhood up to the present day. This understanding of
himself does not take place without a great many emotional reactions.
I have heard that this difficult struggle for clarification brings with
it, for patient and analyst alike, a feeling of being on the right path.
I, for my part, would be quite satisfied if you could produce something which might be comparable to the process I have just tried to
describe and which would give rise to a similar feeling of correctness
about your biographical endeavors."

Relieved to find such a helpful and well-informed critic, I now
take over. Really, this second critic has taken the words out of my
mouth. What else did I have in mind than just such a procedure, as
pointed out by this critic?

In the beginning, only isolated parts of James's ghostly tale became understandable. Gradually the interpretations increased, and
then—a big step forward—I discovered that these interpretations,
which at first were only separate elements, appeared to be in harmony
with one another. Progressively more and more things fell into place,
and finally I was able to present an overall construction of the various
states of the ego as it passed through a turbulent childhood period. Is
not this, I want to ask, a description of working at the model of the
author's ego?

Of course, in analytic biography, in contradistinction to analytic
treatment, this working at the model is a one-sided affair. The
author's share of participation is of necessity lacking, but we may try
to replace it with something of comparable value.

Our benevolent critic has just told us that the need for objective
corroboration is not felt so much in analytic treatment. After all, the
outside world is completely excluded from the discussion. The
patient, in the daily routine of close cooperation with his analyst,
brings sufficient evidence to show that the constructions really pertain to forgotten events.

It is completely different with analytic biography. From the very
beginning, the public has been invited in by the author. The one
who wants to analyze the author's work starts out as a reader himself.
The analyst therefore is one of the crowd; through the act of analysis

he has become the self-appointed representative of the public. This role, however, does not remain unchallenged; others have the right —yes, even the obligation—to insist that he put his cards on the table. To deserve to be their representative, he must provide corroborating evidence.

Since the collaboration of the author is missing, we are left with the task of acquiring the author's information in a different way. We must try to get hold of biographical data pertinent to the results of our analytic endeavors.

When I started out using Henry James's story as a source of biographical information, I was not at all aware that I was thereby obligated to adhere to very strict rules, rules which to a certain extent are even comparable to those valid in psychoanalytic treatment. Contemplating these rules, it very soon becomes clear that there is nothing strange about them. They boil down to the maintenance, under all circumstances, of an unwavering analytic attitude. In the long run, this attitude will lead to an optimum of understanding.

Freud (1912) remarked that in conducting analysis the analyst places his mind in a state of "evenly suspended attention." One may call this a topographical regression in the service of the analysis. The analyst's mind is then in the same state as the patient's. In this way the analyst is able to use his own mind as a sensitive instrument which will react to the patient's associations. Accordingly, the basis is formed for the analyst's understanding of the patient. The analyst has to be sufficiently detached not to permit speculations and fantasies to come instead of interpretations. In that case the analyst would be serving his own narcissistic interests rather than the interests of the patient.

My analytic approach to *The Turn of the Screw* was, of course, the same as I try to maintain in a therapeutic analysis.

The next question is: what steps are necessary for the maintenance of the analytic attitude? For these steps must provide the optimum of insight. One cannot determine these steps prior to the acquisition of insight into the problems contained in the story. Therefore these steps will depend upon the novel's structure. Behind this structure the personality of the author lies hidden.

After these preliminary deliberations, we are better equipped to shed further light upon James's attempt to discharge actively onto the reader the anxiety that James had originally experienced passively. Why these experiences, dating from childhood, threatened to overwhelm him during that particular period of his life I am not yet ready to discuss. Through this process of discharge, his ego tried to gain control over these traumatic events. The ego used its artistic talents as a tool to accomplish this task. The author, by establishing contact with his reader, succeeded in breaking down an isolation which otherwise the ego probably would have been forced to use in its defense against the demands arising from the id.

Let us have a closer look at James's process of discharging his anxiety. In order to frighten his readers, James made use of his own anxiety-arousing childhood experiences. He was forced to do this, for otherwise he would have had no effect at all upon the reader.

This requirement places the ego in a position far from enviable. The ego has to be simultaneously both enemy and friend of these threatening experiences. To be their enemy requires the keeping of the defense against them intact; i.e., the ego has to keep these threatening experiences repressed. To be their friend, on the other hand, requires that the ego relinquish its repression and enter into an alliance with these threatening experiences. What actually happens is already known to us, but metapsychological considerations compel me to tell it again. By creating a nightmarish story intended to frighten the reader, the author has indeed made it possible for his ego to form such an alliance with what is warded off. Does this mean that his ego is now exposed to the danger of being overwhelmed by a return of the repressed infantile events? In the "Causerie" I reasoned that "James, in order to create the proper atmosphere for a ghost story and even more in order to deny the autobiographical origin, created a very complicated chain of events to explain how the story became known" (p. 478). By disavowing the fact that he is referring to his own childhood, James found it possible to speak of the dangers of the past without having to experience anxiety. The author has, so to say, passed on his anxiety to the reader. Again quoting from the "Causerie": "Since he had never found a proper solution for it [his terror], he did not want his reader to find a solution, either" (p. 477).

In a story which leans so heavily upon dream techniques as this one, the boundary between ego and id is no longer sharply demarcated. As a result of the eased relations between ego and id, an avenue is created through which a part of the pent-up energy can be discharged. Here the story has an advantage over the dream. For the main function of the dream is an attempt to protect sleep, a function which seems to be irreconcilable with the process of discharge.

James's artistic endeavors to restore the balance in his mind gave rise to secondary gains, and these gains are not to be weighed lightly. Fame and substantial monetary rewards are sources of satisfaction which add to the relief of the ego. A number of times James remarked that *The Turn of the Screw* was a potboiler, as if he wanted people to believe that he had written this story solely to make money. James, it is true, in complete contrast to his father, never lost sight of his financial interests. By pushing this monetary aspect into the foreground, James tried to disguise the fact that he was engaged in mastering a conflict of vast psychological dimensions.

We may ask whether the author's work can be considered to have therapeutic value. By changing passive into active, the ego is trying to gain control over the trauma created by the early experiences. The discharge of anxiety, the satisfaction connected with the ego's creative activity, the narcissistic rewards, the sublimation, and, last but not least, the ability to give direct expression, limited though it may be, to pent-up energies which have been warded off, all together contribute to achieving the goal of regaining an equilibrium. Yet, praiseworthy as the author's labor may be, the result cannot be compared with the results of a successful analysis. The difference is this: whereas the author is striving for a controlled conflict, an analysis aims at a dissolved conflict.

It has not become clear, at least not up to this point, whether James was conscious that in a disguised way he was portraying his own past.[2]

Let me return now to the maintenance of the analytic attitude. This attitude has to be adjusted to the fact that we are dealing with a novel. The analysis has to advance without the presence of a transference situation. No immediate corroborating proof of the correctness of the interpretation is possible, and, as far as the analyst is concerned, he is working without a therapeutic aim.

[2] See my discussion of "The Figure in the Carpet" (to be published).

The steps which must be taken in obedience to the analytic attitude are so interwoven with the structure of the novel that I can be very brief in dealing with them. In their chronological order they are as follows: (1) I made an initial interpretation that James was attempting to discharge his anxiety onto the reader. (2) This interpretation led to the conclusion that James was portraying his own childhood. (3) I then made an interpretation of the story. I pictured the ego as trying to achieve its aims by making use of what was warded off. The unconscious could now be detected. Thus an opportunity was offered to study the components which constituted the conflicts. The story became interpretable. (4) As a result, we were able to gain insight into James's psychogenic development. We could pursue the formation of his ego in its main stages from the oedipal level up to adulthood.

Indeed, the maintenance of the analytic attitude during the interpretive procedure of *The Turn of the Screw* bears similarities to the execution of a therapeutic analysis. One may think of a patient who wards off his anxieties by great aggressiveness toward others. The analyst will try to induce this patient to experience the anxiety which he has previously warded off. In the transference situation the patient relives his past. Analysis of the ego defenses diminishes his resistance to the repressed. This is the step necessary for making the unconscious conscious. In this process the ego regains the strength required for improvement. Analyst and patient, in close cooperation, build together a model of the psychogenic development of the patient. From this shared labor, corroborating evidence arises and becomes in turn a stimulus for further insight.

But again, in order not to be misunderstood, I want to emphasize that, notwithstanding certain similarities, vast differences exist between the two procedures I have just summed up.

So far I have been silent about another feature resulting from adherence to the analytic attitude. In my analysis of *The Turn of the Screw* I did not make use of any material that was not present in the novel, with the exception of a single fact. On the basis of the fact that Flora, Miles, the governess, and the bachelor all shared the same fantasy, I concluded that these four persons not only represented the different persons taking part in James's childhood events but also portrayed states of James's ego at four different stages of development.

In making this interpretation, I applied my knowledge that James was a bachelor.

In retrospect, how much better it would have been if I had not known this fact! The possibility escaped me that I could then have reasoned in the following way: "My conclusion that the four persons reveal the narcissistic aspect of the story, namely, that they picture four different stages of the author's ego development, leads me to assume that the author remained a bachelor." This interpretation would have relied solely on the previous interpretation about the narcissistic aspect of the story. It would have demonstrated the analytic value of a sound construction, which in turn would have opened up the situation for further conclusions. As it was, my use of factual knowledge spoiled my chance.

In the therapeutic analysis of an adult patient we do not, as a rule, make use of material not acquired from the patient. In the analysis of *The Turn of the Screw* no such therapeutic consideration forbade the application of facts that were not present in the novel. For me, however, there are two good reasons for also maintaining the analytic rule when analyzing a novel or a case history like that of Schreber, etc.

I have already started to explain my principal reason. Knowledge obtained from outside sources, not present in the text, will blunt the sharp edges of sensitivity necessary for the interpretation. Consequently this knowledge will drive a wedge into my trend of thought which the author has stirred up. Second, adherence to the text is an excellent way to prevent drifting off into beautiful speculations and fantasies.

Thus, in analytic biography as well as in therapeutic analysis, I refrain from using material that has not come to me directly.

Finally, I want to stress a difference, between the analysis of a novel and the analysis of a patient, in the opportunity to make interpretations. The book is always available; whenever one wants to, one can look at the text. In contrast, the analytic session is gone when it is ended. It happens quite often that the analyst knows the correct interpretation just when the patient has left the session. It is a pity—and still it must be admitted—that the opportunity to give an interpretation does not always return. We analysts smart from the remembrance of missed interpretations.

Compared to the analyst, the biographer has it easy. The opportunity to meditate about his subject is practically timeless. He has the advantage of not being bothered by any therapeutic responsibility.

I have spent a lot of time defending my method of operation. But whatever turn I have taken, I have been faced with the necessity of providing a confirmation of my conclusion that *The Turn of the Screw* is based upon Henry James's childhood experiences. A nightmare or its equivalent must have served as an example, and *The Turn of the Screw* dwells upon the cause of this example. We have searched in vain for an immediate confirmation of our constructions of early childhood events. But even if we were able to detect such an event behind one or another screen memory, it would be a method of verifying one construction by making another. Even a less severe critic than the critics with whom I am supposed to deal would never let this one pass by!

Finally, we will also have to find corroborating evidence of the correctness of the construction of the model of Henry James's psychogenic development. In short, it has to be proved that my "Causerie" was not simply the brain child of my own wild imagination.

During the entire course of my deliberations I have kept an eye on my critic. I have seen how he could hardly contain himself. The breaking point has been reached. Although he mutters more than he clearly pronounces the words, I nevertheless am able to hear him distinctly. "For more than half an hour I have listened to this fellow, and he is still just where he started. He is using his so-called constructions to prove the correctness of his method. I am even inclined to assume that he wants to convince us that his method in turn may serve as evidence of the validity of his constructions. All I want to say is that he is going around in circles. First, no corroboration of the infantile material was possible. Now, at the end, we hear that a corroboration is essential. I repeat what I have already said in the beginning. I can see clearly through his game. His constructions are nothing more than a bunch of speculations based upon facts which he grabs out of thin air."

I don't have to answer. My benevolent critic has already started to speak. Directing himself toward my opponent, he replies: "I too came here to criticize, but time and again I discovered some sense in what the speaker had to say. I admit he has not yet convinced me, for his corroborating proofs are still missing. Indeed, his constructions are in tune with his analytic attitude. One cannot reproach him for feeling sufficiently encouraged by the results of his interpretations to use these results for further penetration into the personality of Henry James. Thus, method and constructions grew together, from the very beginning, into a strong unity. One cannot find fault with that. After all, the speaker announced at the end of his "Causerie" that further discussion would follow, and he has kept his word. Thus he became his own critic before anyone from outside could assume this role. In his discussion he again tried to separate constructions and method, the latter being derived from the maintenance of the analytic attitude. As far as speculations are concerned, there are none. These deductions were always in tune with the flow of thought in the story itself. He especially has opened my eyes to what he means by wanting to verify his deduction that *The Turn of the Screw* is intimately related to James's childhood experiences. If the speaker succeeds in providing evidence of the correctness of his conclusion, he will have brought his entire study of the novel within the realm of scientific research. Then, indeed, his constructions will be of the same order as those obtained in regular analysis. Of course, he might have made mistakes, but mistakes also occur in any other comparable research. Furthermore, if enough evidence can be found to show that the structure of the model of James's psychogenic development is acceptable, we might consider this a proof that his constructions about James's childhood cannot be very far off. For the development of this model was based upon these constructions concerning the oedipal period. I don't know whether I have made any impression upon our friend who, in every circumstance, has his 'no' ready, in answer to whatever the speaker says. In the meantime I have become impatient myself. After all, where are your corroborations?"

Indeed, I get the hint that I ought not to wait any longer to come forward with what I consider to be the childhood origin of James's *The Turn of the Screw*.

THE CHILDHOOD ORIGIN OF *The Turn of the Screw*

In *A Small Boy and Others* James recalls "the most appalling yet most admirable nightmare" of his life (p. 347). One summer night, when he was already an adult, he dreamed that the door of a room which he had been defending against an intruder had opened, whereupon he found himself in "sudden pursuit . . . of a just dimly-descried figure that retreated in terror before my rush and dash" out of the room. Lightning revealed the scene of the pursuit. It was the Gallerie d'Apollon, part of the Louvre, the museum that he had visited for the first time when he was twelve (p. 348). The theme of "so to speak of turning the tables . . . on a ghost" James, according to his own statement, applied in another story, "The Jolly Corner." In this story the nightmare is reversed. Spencer Brydon, the chief character, instead of being attacked by the intruder and then gaining the upper hand, as in the dream, challenges the ghost to appear and ends up being overwhelmed by this apparition.

At this point I do not want to attach any interpretation to either the nightmare or the story. I want to stress only that it was not at all foreign to James, as we can see from "The Jolly Corner," to build a story around one of his nightmares.

The theme of "so to speak of turning the tables . . . on a ghost" reminds us that in *The Turn of the Screw* James had already applied the same mechanism. At the end of Chapter 9 the governess meets Peter Quint on the stairs.

It was the dead silence of our long gaze at such close quarters that gave the whole horror, huge as it was, its only note of the unnatural. If I had met a murderer in such a place and at such an hour, we still at least would have spoken. Something would have passed, in life, between us; if nothing had passed one of us would have moved. The moment was so prolonged that it would have taken but little more to make me doubt if even *I* were in life. I can't express what followed it save by saying that the silence itself— which was indeed in a manner an attestation of my strength— became the element into which I saw the figure disappear; in which I definitely saw it turn as I might have seen the low wretch to which it had once belonged turn on receipt of an order, and pass, with my eyes on the villainous back that no hunch could have more disfigured, straight down the staircase and into the darkness in which the next bend was lost [p. 61].

[A few pages further (p. 64), The governess] took noiseless turns in the passage and even pushed as far as to where I had met Quint. But I never met him there again; and I may as well say at once that I on no other occasion saw him in the house.

Although the governess had been unable to make the ghost disappear for good, she at least had been forceful enough to ban him from the house. In my opinion, the quoted material depicts the governess's state of mind. She had succeeded in separating her "sinful" thoughts about the bachelor from the contents of the house, namely, her feelings for the children. This demonstrable connection supports my impression, stated in the "Causerie," that James was certainly relying upon memories of his nightmares when he composed *The Turn of the Screw*.

We would do well to keep in mind that we know only about a single nightmare; neither in *A Small Boy and Others* nor in James's voluminous notes is any other nightmare recorded. Moreover, the content of this recorded nightmare does not at all resemble the principal theme of *The Turn of the Screw*. Let us distinguish between the dream mechanism and the dream content. We conclude that James made use of the mechanism of the nightmare in his little novel (*The Turn of the Screw*); however, the source of the content of this story remains a mystery to us. Fortunately the thread which we thought we possessed when we pointed to James's application of the dream mechanism in *The Turn of the Screw* does not have to be broken off. The first chapter of *A Small Boy and Others* contains sufficient evidence of the source of James's little novel.

This is a remarkable chapter. Superficially, it might seem to be the haphazard chatter of an old man. Upon closer acquaintance with this material, however, this first impression completely vanishes. As we peer beneath the surface of this first chapter, we see it could very well have been the first analytic hour of a patient who is telling the analyst about his childhood. It is not an orderly summing up of a series of events, in the fashion of realistic thinking, but the rambling words of a patient who in this first hour—in conveying an important part of his life—is already letting himself be guided by free associations.

When Henry James's brother William (born in January, 1842) died in 1910, William's widow asked James to write a book in honor of her deceased husband. At first Henry James was willing to follow his sister-in-law's suggestion; the final outcome, however, was radically different. James began the first chapter by saying his own life had been so intertwined with his brother's (William was fifteen months older) that he could best write about his brother by giving his book a more or less autobiographical form. It is clear that we are already confronted here with an analytic problem of the first order, the discussion of which will have to wait until we are much further along. These early years of life were spent in various places. Henry James was born in April, 1843 in New York City. His parents were well off through inheritance. Shortly after his birth the parents went with their two little sons to Europe, from where they returned when Henry was about two years old. The family then lived for a few years in Albany in order to be near the paternal grandmother, who was a widow. When Henry was four years old, the family moved back to New York City, where they remained until he was twelve. At that time they again left for Europe, where they stayed for five years.[3]

In this first chapter James dwells on the memories of people and of houses, and also on the memories of feelings very largely associated with these houses. The early images are subject "to a soft confusion —which is somehow consecrated, none the less, and out of which, with its shade of contributory truth, some sort of scene insists on glancing" (p. 11). These images revolved principally around what James called "our infantile Albany," that is, from the age of two until four. As we shall come to understand, the confusion disappeared when latency was reached.

> [James speaks of] long summer afternoons—occasions tasting of ample leisure, still bookless, yet beginning to be bedless, or crib-less; tasting of accessible garden peaches in a liberal backward territory that was still almost part of a country town; tasting of many-sized uncles, aunts, cousins, of strange legendary domestics, inveterately but archaically Irish, and whose familiar remarks and "criticism of life" were handed down, as well as of dim family ramifications and local allusions—mystifications always— that flowered into anecdote as into small hard plums; tasting above all of a big much-shaded savoury house in which a softly- sighing widowed grandmother, Catherine Barber by birth, whose attitude was a resigned consciousness of complications and accre- tions, dispensed an hospitality seemingly as joyless as it was cer- tainly boundless. What she *liked,* dear gentle lady of many cares

[3] Although not mentioned by James, the following will complete the family picture. After Henry, three more children were born: Garth Wilkinson ("Wilky," 1845-1883), Robertson ("Bob," 1846-1910), and Alice (1848-1892). "From 1847 until they left for Europe in 1855, the family occupied a house at 58 West Fourteenth Street, New York" (Dupee, 1956, p. 602).

and anxieties, was the "fiction of the day." [The authors of these novels "are forgotten now," but these books] used to drive her away to quiet corners whence her figure comes back to me bent forward on a table with the book held out at a distance and a tall single candle placed, apparently not at all to her discomfort, in that age of sparer and braver habits, straight between the page and her eyes. . . .

I had reached my sixteenth year when she died, and as my only remembered grandparent she touches the chord of attachment to a particular vibration. She represented for us in our generation the only English blood—that of both her own parents— flowing in our veins; I confess that out of that association, for reasons and reasons, I feel her image most beneficently bend. We were, as to three parts, of two other stocks; and I recall how from far back I reflected—for I see I must have been always reflecting —that, mixed as such a mixture, our Scotch with our Irish, might be, it had had still a grace to borrow from the third infusion or dimension. If I could freely have chosen moreover it was precisely from my father's mother that, fond votary of the finest faith in the vivifying and characterising force of mothers, I should have wished to borrow it; even while conscious that Catherine Barber's own people had drawn breath in American air for at least two generations before her. [According to Dupee (1956), James was wrong. This grandmother was not of English but of Irish descent.] . . .

The sweet taste of Albany probably lurked most in its being our admired antithesis to New York; it was holiday, whereas New York was home; . . . [James next speaks of "our father's friend from an early time, R. W. Emerson," who gave his blessing to the "lately-born" William. James remembers "the great and urbane Emerson's occasional presence" in the house on Fourteenth Street, which the family occupied until they left for Europe the second time.]

[Henry James's interest returns to his very first perceptions. The scene is the Dutch House in Albany, where Miss Bayou kept school. His brother William,] occupying a place in the world to which I couldn't at all aspire, [was] already seated at his task when the attempt to drag me crying and kicking to the first hour of my education failed on the threshold of the Dutch House. . . . [Henry's "retreat shrieking" from that schoolhouse] was to leave him [William] once for all already there an embodied demonstration of the possible. . . ." [It was as if William] had gained such an advance of me in his sixteen months' experience of the world before mine began that I never for all the time of childhood and youth in the least caught up with him or overtook him. He was always round the corner and out of sight, coming back into view but at his hours of extremest ease. We were never in the same schoolroom, in the same game, scarce even in step together or in the same phase at the same time; when our phases overlapped, that is, it was only for a moment—he was clean out before I had got well in. How far he had really at any moment dashed forward it is not for me now to attempt to say; what comes to me is that I at least hung inveterately and woefully back, and that this relation alike to our interests and to each other seemed proper and pre-appointed. I lose myself in wonder at the loose ways, the strange process of waste, through which nature and fortune may deal on occasion with those whose faculty for application is all and only in their imagination and their sensibility. There may be during those bewildered and brooding years so little for them to "show" that I liken the individual dunce—as he so often must appear—to some commercial traveler who has lost the key to his packed case of samples and can but pass for a fool while other exhibitions go forward.

I achieve withal a dim remembrance of my final submission, though it is the faintest ghost of an impression and consists but of the bright blur of a dame's schoolroom, a mere medium for small piping shuffling sound and suffered heat, as well as for the wistfulness produced by "glimmering squares" that were fitfully screened, though not to any revival of cheer, by a huge swaying, yet dominant object. This dominant object, the shepherdess of the flock, was Miss Bayou or Bayhoo. . . . [Her "temple of learn-ing" faced his grandmother's house.]

[There are memories of streets; for instance, Steuben Street,] as steep even to the very essence of adventure, with a summit, and still more with a nethermost and riskiest incline, very far away. [And there is "the other house" where the family stayed, which was] much smaller than my grandmother's, conveniently near it and within sight; which was pinkish-red picked out with white, whereas my grandmother's was greyish-brown and very grave, and which must have stood back a little from the street, as I seem even now to swing, or at least to perch, on a relaxed gate of approach that was conceived to work by an iron chain weighted with a big ball; all under a spreading tree again and with the high, oh so high white stone steps (mustn't they have been mar-ble?) and fan-lighted door of the pinkish-red front behind me. I lose myself in ravishment before the marble and the pink. There were other houses too—one of them the occasion of the first "paid" visit that struggles with my twilight of social consciousness; a call with my father, conveying me presumably for fond exhibi-tion (since if my powers were not exhibitional my appearance and my long fair curls, of which I distinctly remember the lachrymose sacrifice, suppositiously were), on one of our aunts, the youngest of his three sisters. . . . [This last house was on Elk Street,] the name itself vaguely portentous, as through beasts of the forest not yet wholly exorcised [pp. 4-12].

Let us turn now to the description covering the latency period.

The confusion clears, however, though the softness remains, when, ceasing to press too far backward, I meet the ampler light of conscious and educated little returns to the place; for the education of New York, enjoyed up to my twelfth year, failed to blight its romantic appeal. The images I really distinguish flush through the maturer medium, but with the sense of them only the more wondrous. The other house, the house of my parents' limited early sojourn, becomes that of those of our cousins, numerous at that time, who pre-eminently figured for us; the various brood presided over by my father's second sister, Catherine James, who had married at a very early age Captain Robert Temple, U.S.A. Both these parents were to die young, and their children, six in number, the two eldest boys, were very markedly to people our preliminary scene; this being true in particular of three of them, the sharply differing brothers and the second sister, Mary Temple, radiant and rare, extinguished in her first youth, but after having made an impression on many persons, and on ourselves not least, which was to become in the harmonious circle, for all time, matter of sacred legend and reference, of associated piety. Those and others with them were the numerous dawnings on which in many cases the deepening and final darknesses were so soon to follow: our father's family was to offer such a chronicle of early deaths, arrested careers, broken promises, orphaned children. It sounds cold-blooded, but part of the charm of our grandmother's house for us—or I should perhaps but speak for myself—was in its being so much and so sociably a nurseried and playroomed orphanage. The children of her lost daughters and daughters-in-law overflowed there, mainly as girls; on whom the surviving sons-in-law and sons occasionally and most trustingly looked in. Parentally bereft cousins were somehow more thrilling than parentally provided ones; and most thrilling when, in the odd fashion of that time, they were sent to school in New York as a preliminary to their being sent to school in Europe. They spent scraps of holidays with us in Fourteenth Street, and I think my first childish conception of the enviable lot, formed amid these associations, was to be so little fathered or mothered, so little sunk in the short range, that the romance of life seemed to lie in some constant improvisation, by vague overhovering authorities, of new situations and horizons. We were intensely domesticated, yet for the very reason perhaps that we felt our young bonds easy; and they were *so* easy compared to other small plights of which we had stray glimpses that my first assured conception of true richness was that we should be sent separately off among cold or even cruel aliens in order to be there thrillingly homesick. Homesickness was a luxury I remember craving from the tenderest age—a luxury of which I was unnaturally, or at last prosaically, deprived. Our motherless cousin Augustus Barker came up from Albany to the Institution Charlier—unless it was, as I suspect, a still earlier specimen, with a name that fades from me, of that type of French establishment for boys which then and for years after so incongruously flourished in New York; and though he professed a complete satisfaction wtih pleasures tasted in our innocent society I felt that he was engaged in a brave and strenuous adventure while we but hugged the comparatively safe shore [pp. 13-15].

I have quoted extensively from this first chapter—and yet, in my opinion, still not enough—in order to examine the sources of *The Turn of the Screw*. What does James's romantic daydream about life have to offer us that will increase our understanding? We are seduced by curiosity into taking a quick look, although only a more profound examination of the material quoted can bring us deeper insight.

James's "first childish conception of the enviable lot" of his parentally bereft cousins "was to be so little fathered or mothered." This sentence shows clearly that he wished his own parents were dead, too, and that vague overhovering authorities had taken over. This situation is the common denominator of both the daydream and the story. In *The Turn of the Screw* the vague overhovering authority of the bachelor, the children's legal guardian, had dwindled practically to nothingness. The bachelor did not want to be bothered and accordingly delegated his task to a young, inexperienced girl. Certainly this girl does not fit the term of "a vague overhovering authority." What the bachelor lacked, this young girl had in abundance. She interfered continually in the lives of the children.

Thus the task of guiding the children rested solely on the shoulders of the young governess, who had to fight the persisting evil influence of those previously responsible for the upbringing of Miles and Flora. The ghosts of Miss Jessel and Peter Quint kept the fire burning which they had started while still alive. The outcome of this struggle between the opposing forces, with its ever-changing aspects, leads to the "constant improvisation . . . of new situations and horizons," thus constituting "the romance of life" for Miles and Flora. The "luxury" of which young Henry "was unnaturally, or at least prosaically deprived" was being sent off separately "under cruel aliens" in order to be "thrillingly homesick." To be removed from his parents and siblings was only an attenuated version of his wish that his family would be dead. Miles may not have felt that he was being subjected to treatment by a cruel alien, but Flora does get this feeling. She accuses the governess of being cruel and wants nothing more to do with her (Chapter 20). One has to admit that the two children in the story were "engaged in a brave and strenuous adventure," whereas in reality the James children "hugged the comparatively safe shore."

Although my severe critic might say about me that a child's hand is quickly filled, I, for my part, think that for a first reconnaissance the result is very satisfactory. *The Turn of the Screw* is based upon Henry James's daydream. In this daydream lies the corroboration of the autobiographical nature of the story. Thus my interpretation that James tried to frighten his readers by exposing them to his own childhood experiences is correct. According to my benevolent critic (see above), my entire study of the novel has now been brought within the realm of scientific research. As a result, James's latency fantasy gains in importance. For a deeper understanding of *The Turn of the Screw* it will be necessary to submit this fantasy to a closer examination.

THE ROMANCE OF LIFE

According to a statement made by Dupee, we may conclude that James wrote the first chapter of *A Small Boy and Others* during the fall of 1911.[4] Only a few years earlier, Freud had written two short articles dealing with this same subject (1908, 1909). I assume that James was completely unaware of these two publications.[5]

[4] Dupee (1956), in his Introduction to James's autobiography, quotes the author's secretary, Theodora Bosanquet. At James's request, when he returned to London for the winter of 1911-1912, she found rooms for him in Chelsea, and the two of them went briskly to work on his projected memoirs.

[5] At least it is unknown to me whether or not Henry James was acquainted with Freud's work. It is true that William James had made a deep impression on Freud when the two men took a walk together on the occasion of Freud's visit to Clark

The translators of Freud's first article ("Der Dichter und das Phantasieren") changed this title to "Creative Writers and Day-Dreaming" (1908), thereby robbing it of its poetical overtones. Freud stresses that the writer derives the contents of his writings from his fantasies and that childhood memories usually play a role in these fantasies. The other article of Freud's is about "Family Romances" (1909). In the most common form of this romance, the child does not believe that his parents are really his; rather, he is of much higher birth, is descended from royalty, etc. The fantasy expresses the child's dissatisfaction with his parents as he sees them in the present, compared with the high esteem in which he held them in the past. Various analysts in recent years have stressed the importance of such fantasies and have elucidated their meaning (H. Deutsch, 1930; E. Kris, 1952; Greenacre, 1958; Frosch, 1959; Meyer, 1964).

Let us examine James's romantic daydream. It is remarkable that James's selection of a name for this daydream comes so close to the one chosen by Freud. In other respects it seems that the "romance of life" differs structurally from the family romance. James's daydream does not contain anything that points to the past, when the child regarded his parents as omnipotent. Thus, at first glance, this chronological split in the parental images, the insignificance of the parents' present role measured against their past radiance, does not occur in James's daydream.

We know that the manifest content of James's "romance of life" revolves around homesickness. In the previous section I concluded that his fantasy of being separated from his family in order to feel homesick was an attenuated version of a death wish against all the members of his family. James tries to make us believe that the attraction of the example of his parentally bereft cousins had caused his craving for homesickness. At this point the question arises whether this sequence is correct.

University (Worcester, Massachusetts) in 1909. However, this fact does not permit us to presume that William might have informed his brother about Freud's work. Even if Henry James had read anything of Freud's (at that time), I still doubt whether he would have liked it. Although James was an inveterate analyst of himself—*The Turn of the Screw* is an excellent example of this self-analysis—I suspect that James would have shied away from any closer contact with psychoanalysis. Freud developed a method which might work as a sort of mental X-ray machine, making the invisible visible. If I am not mistaken, Henry James would have been horrified at the thought that in this way his unconscious might be revealed.

Let us engage in some figuring. James remembers craving for homesickness from "the tenderest age." This suggests that his craving began very early. The attractive example was set by his Temple cousins and by Gussy Barker. Captain Temple had married a sister of Henry James's father. Captain and Mrs. Temple both died of tuberculosis in the year 1854. Henry was then eleven years old. This many years far surpasses the mark up to which it is permissible to speak of "the tenderest age."

The situation is different, however, as far as his cousin Augustus Barker is concerned. The mother of the latter (the eldest sister of Henry's father) had not "survived" the birth of Augustus in 1842. Thus Gussy Barker was somewhat older than Henry and had since birth been deprived of his mother. Nevertheless, it can be proved that either Henry did not know Gussy at "the tenderest age" or that, if he did know him at that period, this cousin had not yet cast his spell of charm over Henry. Henry's grandmother, during a stay in the neighborhood of New York (Henry would then have been about ten years old), had arranged a visit to Sing-Sing "for the befriending of juvenile Gussy" (p. 177). On that occasion Gussy, who was there at a "military" school, made this enviable impression of richness upon Henry (p. 173). After the Sing-Sing episode, Gussy visited the James family in New York on Sundays and holidays (p. 187). I shall return to this material to examine it in more detail. However, the little I have quoted is sufficient to show that certainly Henry was not influenced by Gussy before Henry had passed the critical point of "the tenderest age." In short, the origin of Henry's craving for homesickness dates back to a time when he had not yet made contact with his orphaned cousins.

If it was not the example set by his parentally bereft cousins, what then was essential to make him feel "thrillingly homesick"? It must have been a spontaneous wish of Henry's to be removed from his parents as well as from his siblings. We have to add that such a removal conceals the wish that all the members of his family would be dead. The answer is right at hand. This wish expresses his rebellion against being too much "fathered" or "mothered," a condition which led to his intense "domestication." But why would this wish also include his siblings? Henry must not have liked having an older brother nor welcomed the arrival of his juniors.

Thus, in my opinion, Henry's craving for homesickness must have started rather early in life. Initially it may have been more or less dormant, awakened only under certain circumstances—for instance, when he felt jealous of one of the others. It was the observation of his privileged cousins that set ablaze his craving for homesickness. In them he discovered that his existing death wishes were realizable!

We recognize that Henry's death wishes constituted the root of his romantic fantasy about life. Are they the only root? Does not love also play a part in his "romance"? For a romance without love is unthinkable. Let us therefore have another look at the basic fantasy, "my first assured conception of true richness was that we should be sent separately off among cold or even cruel aliens in order to be there thrillingly homesick." The coldness or even cruelty to which he would be submitted under such circumstances would become the stimulus to experiencing a longing for his parents and siblings. It is evident that hostility and love are simultaneously present in James's romance of life. For all practical purposes we may paraphrase our conclusion by saying that ambivalent feelings are the origin of James's spectacular daydream. Hidden behind this fantasy is the thought, "If everybody were dead, it would be possible for me to experience my love for them."

Perhaps here somebody will object by asking, "Is this really ambivalence? Is this hostility not a prerequisite for feeling love as well? Does it not mean that the one is built upon the presence of the other, whereas in true ambivalence both feelings are simultaneously present without one being the cause of the other?"

This objection leads to a new conclusion. James's wording of his daydream is a rationalization of the fact that if he wants to feel positively toward his relatives, he also has to accept his negative feelings. The opposite is true, too. When his negative feelings are conscious, he has to admit his positive feelings as well. A further conclusion presents itself. During latency Henry James either felt ambivalent or had no feelings at all toward his relatives; at least separate feelings of love or hate were probably experienced only in very specific situations when there were strong reality reasons for being thankful or angry.

A consideration of these various conclusions results in the impression that Henry James had a disturbed latency period. In order to experience *spontaneous* feelings, it was necessary for him to withdraw into his fantasy world. There, in his daydreams, he could give full rein to his ambivalence. The antidote to this tendency to withdraw must have lain especially in his contacts with his "privileged orphan-cousins," who offered him an opportunity for identification.

It is now time to study another detail of Henry James's "romance of life." Why did the imagined foster parents have to be "cold or even cruel aliens"? It is obvious that James's ambivalence is endowed with a masochistic feature, a combination which is certainly not unknown to analysts.

One could think of many possibilities which might be responsible for this wish to be treated coldly. One, he might feel guilty as a reaction to his hostility. However, such a reaction would not explain why this cold and cruel attitude constituted a source from which he derived pleasurable feelings. Two, do these cold aliens perhaps represent some harsh teacher or nursemaid? What might such a person have done to him to be accorded a major role in his romantic fantasy? A third and most important possibility occurs to me. Could it be that Henry conceived of certain aspects of the parental method of "extensive domestication" as being cold or even cruel? Next, that notwithstanding his negative attitude toward this method, he still received a secret pleasure from it? We may even be dealing with a combination of these various possibilities. Yet, at the moment we lack the knowledge that could confirm any or all of these possibilities.

Thus we have put the detail of the cold or even cruel aliens into the limelight of our consideration. Early in our discussion we developed the idea that James's "romance of life" was structurally different from Freud's concept of the "family romance." We found that there was no chronological split detectable between parental images formed during two different phases of development. The split was more on one level between "vague overhovering authorities" or "cold and cruel aliens," on the one hand, and dead or locally absent parents, on the other.

Under the influence of our latest theoretical ponderings, we may ask whether this chronological split is not also present in James's fantasy. If it was true that the "cold and cruel aliens" represented an early aspect of the parental images when they enforced a special method of domestication upon the child, then a new way of looking at the romance of life would be opened. The masochistic experience connected with the cold or even cruel attitude of the parents in the past would still be preferable to the present unexciting contact with his parents. If we take this possibility into account, we cannot deny there is a chance that James's daydream is structurally more closely related to Freud's concept of the family romance than we had at first supposed. In both fantasies the past gains in importance, compared with the present. However, there is a difference. Whereas in Freud's concept of the family romance an "Olympic father figure" (Green-acre, 1958) or, in general, omnipotent parents occupy the scene of early life, in James's daydream the feature of coldness or even cruelty of the parents at the time when he was very young is emphasized.

So far we have tried to probe more deeply into James's romance of life without turning to the infantile material from which it un-doubtedly stemmed. I want to remind you of my previous remark that this first chapter of *A Small Boy and Others* is comparable to the beginning hour of a patient's analysis. Reviewing the infantile material contained in this first chapter, we are greatly surprised by what we find—or, more correctly, by what we don't find. We discover that the importance of what is memorized is far overshadowed by the absence of anything that we might reasonably expect to be present. There is not a trace of the central figure of the first years of life. His mother is not mentioned at all—not with a single word. If we did not possess his complaint, stemming from latency, that he was too much "fathered" or "mothered," we would never know from this first chapter that Henry James had a mother who was living.

It is perhaps better to start with what James remembers. It will probably make his silence surrounding his mother even more con-spicuous. The three persons who primarily draw his attention are his grandmother, his brother William, and his father. Of the three, his grandmother fares best. To her he devotes the most tender descrip-tion, and it lacks the ambivalence which so strongly colors the pic-tures of the two others.

This "dear gentle lady" is his "only remembered grandparent." We are conscious that there is a lot written between the lines, the hidden meaning of which will be revealed if we subject James's description to a close scrutiny (see above). Under her touch, the chord of his attachment had come into a "particular vibration." Her English descent—he was convinced she was English—had contributed a great deal to his feeling of attachment. He recalled "from far back" having reflected about "the grace" borrowed from this English infusion. Accordingly, this grace is something very special, for which one would look in vain if one tried to find it in connection with the Scotch or Irish blood components of his ancestry. Of what this grace consisted let us try to discover by examining a peculiar sentence, the meaning of which is to me very obscure if not totally confusing. Therefore I repeat the sentence in its entirety: "If I could freely have chosen moreover it was precisely from my father's mother that, fond votary of the finest faith in the vivifying and characterising force of mothers, I should have wished to borrow it; even while conscious that Catherine Barber's [his grandmother's] own people had drawn breath in American air for at least two generations before her." His paternal grandfather was of Irish Protestant stock; his mother was of mixed Scotch-Irish descent.

What James previously called "the grace" is clearly "the vivifying and characterising force of mothers," which his grandmother had in abundance. His ideal of motherhood comprises the elements of this force. It is confusing to me that James wants to borrow "this fond votary of the finest faith" in this force. A woman in whom these highest qualities of motherhood can be found might inspire in others this devoted faith in these qualities, but she herself does not possess this faith. This is the crux of the problem of obscurity surrounding this sentence. It dawns upon me that James purposely omitted some important material that would make the entire sentence intelligible. This newly acquired insight causes me to wonder further why James placed so much emphasis upon his grandmother's English descent. It is as if he had started a comparison but then stopped in the middle of it. The second member of this comparison he withholds from us. Suddenly this consideration sheds light upon the cause of the obscurity, and finally the problem is solved. It is obvious that James quite intentionally keeps us uninformed about somebody who is not of English blood and therefore does not possess those qualities which he so greatly admires in his grandmother. His mother's blood was mixed Scotch and Irish; consequently she could not show this special grace. The full meaning of this enigmatic sentence now penetrates into our consciousness. If James could have chosen freely, he would have adorned his own mother with this "vivifying and characterising force," for then she would have instilled in him this "fond votary of the finest faith" in her, which obviously he had never been able to develop.

At this point we are again reminded of the technique of the dream. We find an element of confusion at the point where the ego would have to confess something of a very disagreeable nature. The ego either does not want to lift its repression or downright refuses to tell what is already conscious to it. Obviously, in contrast to James's paternal grandmother, his own mother did not inspire in him any devout faith in her motherly characteristics. He does not want to confess openly that his mother lacked those features of attractiveness which his grandmother possessed to such a high degree.

It is evident that Henry James's mother lacked the warmth he craved. We may even venture a guess that in his early childhood Henry accused her of sometimes being "cold or even cruel." Thus, through this statement, I have stressed a similarity between James's mother and the "cold or even cruel aliens" of his romance of life. I shall return to this point later.

What James's "softly-sighing widowed grandmother" really liked were her books. She would withdraw to quiet corners to read. Young Henry, presumably as soon as he could read, followed her example. In 1911, at the age of sixty-eight, Henry James recalled these years "at our infantile Albany" as being "still bookless, yet beginning to be bedless or cribless." Does this recollection not testify, if somewhat humorously, that the old man wondered whether he had ever been without a book? In this connection let me cite a remark from Edel's biography of Henry James, *The Untried Years* (1953): "We are indebted to T. S. Perry for a significant glimpse of Henry at Newport. '. . . When we got to the house and the rest of us were chattering, Henry James sat on the window-seat reading Leslie's *Life of Constable* with a certain air of remoteness' " (p. 64). This "glimpse" of Henry James reminds me of the picture of his grandmother as he brought her to life for us! Certainly the portrayal of her as an avid reader, withdrawing to quiet corners, must have made a lasting impression upon him.

"It sounds coldblooded, but part of the charm of our grandmother's house for us—or I should perhaps but speak for myself—

was in its being so much and so sociably a nurseried and playroomed orphanage." Thus another attractive aspect of his grandmother is revealed. She becomes "the vague overhovering authority" who guides this enviable lot of orphaned cousins in Albany. This is, of course, a far step from "the cold or even cruel aliens" who would take care of young Henry if, as in his fantasies, he were removed from his parents.

It occurs to me that still another aspect of his grandmother is left "unsaid" in this first chapter. Why did Henry's parents want to live near her after their return from Europe? Was it simply because they had been separated from her for such a long time? Or were there perhaps other reasons why the father wanted to be close to this "gentle lady"? At least I can think of a few reasons that might have kept the father away from Albany. James's father was a cripple, having lost a leg when he was thirteen. "Through a grave accident in early life country walks on rough roads were, in spite of his great constitutional soundness, tedious and charmless to him; he liked on the other hand the peopled pavement, the thought of which made him restless when away" (p. 73). Albany, to use James's own words, was still "a country town" (p. 4). Therefore its pavement could not have held any great attraction for his father. Moreover, his father was an intellectual, finding spiritual food in his contact with outstanding contemporaries. If there were any intellectuals at all in Albany, certainly there were very few of them. It can hardly be imagined that the politicians who gathered in this state capital would have provided the father with sufficient compensation.

My conclusion is that Henry's grandmother must have exerted an extremely strong attraction upon her son in order to lure him away from the advantages offered by New York.

Henry James's father did not have an easy childhood. Old William James tried to rule his son with an iron hand, in accordance with the principles of a joyless Calvinism. It must have been very difficult for Henry's father to shake off the shackles of Old William's constricting influence and to gain some independence of his own. The elder Henry James (young Henry's father), while in England with his family, went through a crisis. One afternoon he experienced a sudden anxiety attack, which within a short time caused him to feel like "a helpless infant." It took quite some time for him to recover his balance. A befriending lady advised him to seek support in the teachings of Swedenborg, and this he did.

In my opinion, it is very plausible that the elder Henry James, for these various reasons, should want to live close to his mother upon his return to his homeland. His father had then been dead for approximately thirteen years, and the elder Henry James no longer had to fear his presence. Is it not natural that a man who in a crisis regresses so quickly to the state of "a helpless infant" should look to his mother for help, especially to a mother portrayed as she was by her grandson? To come to the point, did Henry, at the tender age between two and four, witness a mother-son relationship of a warmth such as he was never to experience with his own mother?

Next in line, among the persons mentioned in the first chapter, is Henry's brother William. Although Henry James does his utmost to convince us that William's genius was already detectable in early youth, Henry's ambivalence toward his elder brother cannot remain concealed. William stood first, not only in order of birth but also in intellectual prowess. The text is unmistakable. So well has James stressed his envy, his rebellion, and his final submission that the analyst would have nothing to add to it were it not for some wistful thoughts on the part of Henry. In comparison with William, all that Henry had of his own that was worthwhile to exhibit were his qualities of imagination and sensibility. Certainly he was unfit to display any of these qualities during "those bewildered and brooding years."

All this led Henry to a painful contemplation. In the eyes of others he must have appeared to be a dunce, and he draws a further comparison with "a commercial traveler who has lost the key to his packed case of samples and can but pass for a fool while other exhibitions go forward." These bitter ideas about himself express only too well how impotent he must have felt in comparison with William. A self-awareness of failing in masculinity could not remain hidden!

This same feeling of failure is vocal also in his description of a social call with his father upon one of his aunts. Henry suspects that his father wants to exhibit him, not of course for any intellectual powers, but for his appearance and his long fair curls. I do not hesitate to translate this description as a complaint that he was shown for his girlish features—his father could not brag about Henry's masculine powers, as he did about William's. In this we may read a reproachful attitude toward his father, who does not try to conceal but on the contrary exposes Henry's feminine traits. The next step is still worse. When Henry's long hair is finally cut, he does not experience this as a relief, a loss at least of a detestable mark; rather, it becomes a tearful sacrifice, a sure sign that at this time his femininity has become a defense. Here I want to be plainly understood. I do not say that Henry's masculinity was destroyed. The "lachrymose sacrifice" points to the fact that the display of masculinity was likely to cause anxiety, a reaction which could be prevented by embracing a more feminine attitude. At the same time this reaction indicates that Henry does not regard his father as an object of masculine identification.

The other persons mentioned in this first chapter of *A Small Boy and Others* cannot have had much influence upon Henry James's development. Emerson is named because he gave his blessing to William when he was born—another thing to be envious of!

The aunt to whom Henry paid his first visit when his father wanted to show him off is mentioned in this chapter for another reason. A series of associations are presented, Elk Street, etc., the Capitol of Albany, which "loomed, familiar yet impressive, at the end of almost any Albany vista of reference," and finally the association "that our uncle, our aunt's husband, was a son of Mr. Martin van Buren, and that *he* was the President" (p. 13). It was as if Henry was impressed by the status of his uncle, a sign of looking up to a father figure; this feature we miss in his description of his own father.

From the first chapter I have also quoted some remarks about taste, adventure, etc. There is a seemingly endless sentence (p. 4) in which tasting is repeated four times—tasting of ample leisure, tasting of garden peaches, tasting of many-sized uncles, etc., and finally tasting above all of a much-shaded savoury house in which Henry's grandmother lived. In another sentence "the sweet taste of Albany" makes this town like "holiday" (p. 7). The tasting of the peaches is the only somatic and certainly primary taste; the others are of a more figurative nature but still derived from the primary one. This is not the only time James speaks of peaches. One paragraph begins: "I keep picking out at hazard those passages of our earliest age that help to reconstruct for me even by tiny touches the experience of our parents, any shade of which seems somehow to signify" (p. 69). Via many disgressions he arrives at "some vast succulent cornucopia. . . . Where is that fruitage now, where in particular are the peaches *d'antan?*" (p. 70). From hereon, as one may easily imagine, the fruit is all over the page—bushels of peaches, "peaches big and peaches small, peaches white and peaches yellow . . . every garden, almost every bush and the very boys' pockets grew them" (p. 71). How they were cut up and eaten with cream, how they were "domestically 'brandied' " to last for the rest of the year, etc., is all very important. James's decription ends with the remnants, "the note of the rejected and scattered fragments, the memory of the slippery skins and rinds and kernels with which the old dislocated flags were bestrown, is itself endeared to me and contributes a further pictorial grace. We ate everything in those days by the bushel and the barrel, as from stores that were infinite; we handled watermelons as freely as cocoanuts, and the amount of stomach-ache involved was negligible in the general Eden-like consciousness" (p. 71).

Such is James's description of the child's garden of Eden. Adam was thrown out of Paradise because he ate the apple. The fate of young Henry was not very different from that of the mythical Adam. Henry cannot forget his childhood paradise and sings its praises. Not of his mother's breast, for only very rarely is breast feeding recalled. His praise is for the cornucopia of his youth, a time which is gone forever. In his adult life there are but few peaches left, and those that are cannot stand comparison with the ones of his childhood! It was the only happy time of togetherness with his mother! What remains of all this beauty? Slippery skins and rinds and kernels and an eventual stomachache and dirtied flagstones. Where did the time go when the diapers caught all the debris, and the food the mother offered kept the bowels in a steady motion? After all, the oral intake, unless coughed up, always ends at the excremental openings! But, as we gather from these last sentences of Henry James's, his early childhood was an idealized period!

One might raise the objection that this period of indulging in peaches obviously came some years after the period of breast feeding. It may be that the peach-time coincided with seeing a younger sibling at his mother's breast. The jealousy aroused was counterbalanced by the happy awareness of "I, too, was once in paradise." The abundance of the peaches may even have led to the soothing consideration: that was the period when not only one child was the recipient but when there was enough for everybody.

There was a time when Steuben Street in the child's mind was "as steep even to the very essence of adventure." A child's fantasy has no limits; any observation suffices to become the scene of daring activity. We encounter the same mood in the associations around Elk Street, "the name itself vaguely portentous, as through beasts of the forest not yet wholly exorcised. . . ." But we know that very soon the time would come for young Henry when anxiety would overpower him and prohibit any deed of rebellious bravery. His final submission, i.e., his acknowledgment of his brother's superiority, came all too quickly. As far as the not yet wholly exorcised beasts of the forest are concerned, they had to adjust themselves to a very limited domain where they might behave under the sweet delusion that they still were undauntedly free. "Intensive domestication" confined them to a reservation where they could experience their "romance of life."

There are memories of houses, presumably connected with the persons who lived in them or with Henry's experiences in these houses. For instance, his revolt against his brother, who was "already seated at his task when the attempt to drag me crying and kicking to the first hour of my education failed on the threshold of the Dutch House in Albany after the fashion I have glanced at in a collection of other pages than these (just as I remember to have once borrowed a hint from our grandmother's 'interior' in a work of imagination)" (p. 9). James admits that these impressions, so very important to the little child, are later used by him in his work. These childhood impressions, mind you, have contributed to shaping his "romance of life."

The feeling of swinging "on a relaxed gate, or at least to perch," is still with him at the age of sixty-eight. The excitement supposedly connected with these feelings in childhood is forgotten in his later years, unless some recollection lives on in the symbolic meaning of "an iron chain weighted with a big ball," the mechanism by which the gate closed. Machinelike instruments are usually phallic symbols. James loses himself "in ravishment before the marble and the pink," as if a touch of artistic appreciation was already present in that childhood period.

At the beginning of our examination of the infantile material, we were struck by the absence of even the slightest mention of his mother, as if she were eradicated completely. Usually our analytic patients know something about their relation with their mothers; for instance, the mother's attitude about what they should and should not eat. Or we hear of the mother's interest in the children's excremental functions. Henry James does not report anything that points to little accidents that might arouse the mother's displeasure. Or our patients tell us how they were occupied with thoughts about the difference between the sexes, or with the overall important question about where children come from, or with fantasies about what the parents do together. Or they remember how jealous they were, as children, when somebody else was favored by the mother. It is especially conspicuous that the younger children in the James family are not alluded to at all in this first chapter. During his first six years of life Henry must have noticed three times the change in his mother's body caused by pregnancy. Every time this happened, a new baby enlarged the family circle. Moreover, each time he was exposed to the sight of the baby being fed. All these impressions he erased from the screen. This entire period around his mother is enveloped in a cloak of silence.

Do the results of our examination of the other infantile material throw any light on the meaning of this silence? We made a profound discovery when we saw that behind Henry James's praise of his grandmother's special qualities lay hidden an accusation against his mother: she was cold. Being too much "mothered," too intensively domesticated, betrays that she was too demanding. But we also detected a strong positive aspect in his mother. In his earliest year he must have greatly enjoyed a togetherness with her when he was at the breast. However, our imagination tells us—and really not much of this function is required—that for the same reasons he must have felt upset, angry and jealous when he saw the privilege of getting the breast passed on to a younger sibling. These observations—and he must have gathered quite a few of them—undoubtedly strengthened his idea, already present for other reasons, that his mother was cold.

His elder brother William, through his superior qualities, aroused Henry's jealousy, and we may conclude from the example in which his father plays a role that the latter did nothing to mitigate this jealousy. Unknowingly, his father, just like his mother, contributed to the increase of this feeling.

It is true that Henry James may have known satisfaction during his oral phase, but the anal phase that followed was of quite a different nature. The known facts, in combination with a great many experiences that are unknown, lead us to conclude that a fixation of certain anal traits must have occurred. How else was it possible for his latency fantasy to show such strong ambivalence? Between latency and the anal phase lies the oedipal period. About this period particularly, James is remarkably silent. We receive only a glimmer of an existing oedipus complex in relation to a rather remote person. Henry's uncle is the son of *the* American father figure, the President of the United States. In my opinion, this strong ambivalence in latency contains a hint as to why James in later life failed to show much evidence of possessing a sufficiently strong genital urge. Obviously the latter urge, to a great extent through regression, was kept on an anal level.

Through our examination of the material remembered by Henry James, we have been able to fill in a few spots in the blank surrounding his mother. And this leads to a better understanding of why Henry James might have tried as hard as possible to eradicate the picture of his mother in his early years. His death wish is the reason for his omission of her. Through our previous analysis of one obscure sentence, we have discovered an element of confusion covering the place where otherwise an accusation against his mother would have been revealed. Similarly, he spreads a blank over what is too painful to express. This blank and the accompanying confusion are signs that strong and painful emotional processes are involved. The blank is one of deathly silence. The Dutch and the German languages have a more apt expression for it. James has "silenced his mother to death."

THE RELATION BETWEEN "THE ROMANCE OF LIFE" AND *The Turn of the Screw*

Our thorough examination of James's "romance of life" revealed many complaints. His mother was too cold, his father exhibited him only for his feminine appearance, his elder brother far outshone him, and he was jealous of his younger siblings because they had inherited the privileges which he was forced to surrender. His latency fantasy clearly shows his dissatisfaction with his parents, who have too "intensively domesticated" him. On closer scrutiny, we see that the homesickness he craved in his fantasy was based upon an outspoken ambivalence. He would be better off if they all—parents and children alike—were dead. In those circumstances he would at least be able to feel love for them.

However, we still remain completely uninformed about his oedipus complex. We have not discovered any competitive struggle with his father for the love of his mother. The dense fog hanging over this important phase of life has not been lifted at all.

Where does this short review bring us in relation to *The Turn of the Screw*? This little novel is based upon James's latency fantasy. I had hoped that my scrutiny of the "Romance of Life" would make its connection with the ghost story much clearer. True, the results of my study of the daydream may not be in any way contradictory to my interpretations of *The Turn of the Screw*, but this is the very least I would have expected to find. I had hoped to be far more successful!

My disappointment causes me to come back to *The Turn of the Screw*. Did I overlook something? Especially did I fail to make sufficient use of the untitled chapter which precedes the story? This chapter contains the reason for telling the story in the first place. A Mr. Griffin had told a tale about "an appearance, of a dreadful kind, to a little boy sleeping in the room with his mother and waking her up in the terror of it; waking her not to dissipate his dread and soothe him to sleep again, but to encounter also, herself, before she had succeeded in doing so, the same sight that had shaken him" (p. 1).

Griffin's story stimulated Douglas, one of the listeners, to tell a similar story. He possessed a manuscript in which his sister's governess had noted down an adventure of hers, even more gruesome, involving two children. Forty years ago Douglas had met this governess when he came home for the vacation following his second year at college. During the vacation he fell in love with this woman, who was ten years his senior. This love for a woman much older must have affected him profoundly: for the rest of his life he remained a bachelor. She had told him her gruesome adventure, which until that time she had kept hidden. Twenty years later, before she died, she sent him the pages in question.

The evening of his promise to read the story as soon as the written account could be sent to him, "he had broken a thickness of ice, the formation of many a winter; had had his reasons for a long silence" (p. 2).

These facts I did not properly evaluate in my "Causerie." Consequently it escaped me that the introduction contains the subject which is the leitmotiv of *The Turn of the Screw*. This subject is the joining of the mother in her child's terror. The story suggests that the apparition seen by the child must have struck a responsive chord in the mother, for it creates in her the same frightening perception.

This shared experience of mother and child I used in my earlier paper as a proof that my first impression of the story was correct: James was trying to communicate a nightmare to his reader. Somewhat later I discussed the fact that, for a mystery story, the first page revealed too much. There should have been no hint in the story that a nightmare, or at least a nightmarish fantasy, was the source of the story.

In stressing this point, I missed my chance to obtain a firmer grip on the structure of the story. To the reader it is completely irrelevant whether or not James's story reveals at the outset that it is derived from a nightmare. The betrayal of the origin of the narrative is not important at all; many readers, to be sure, have noticed the nightmarish quality without being able to take the next step which would lead to a better understanding. Thus the story remains to them a mystery! This proves that James had enough tricks at his disposal to keep the reader from making an important deduction: James was trying to discharge his anxiety onto the reader by means of a veiled autobiographical confession. To me, the analyst, it seems unbelievable that for so many years this simple deduction has escaped James's readers as well as his biographers.

Instead of belaboring an irrelevant issue, I should have paid more attention to the supernatural element in Griffin's contribution. I shall now try to rectify my oversight.

A child sharing the same room with his mother has a nightmare. This is a very common occurrence. Any child analyst can give numerous examples of this kind. The bedroom situation, the close proximity of the mother, etc., make a strong appeal to the child's oedipal wishes. He reacts to his aroused sexuality with a nightmare. We know, however, that the story is not as simple as all that.

At this point in my "Causerie" I failed to "click." I remained insensitive to the importance of the message contained in what seems to be the mother's extrasensory perception. For the emphasis is no longer on what the child has seen. On the contrary, the mother's observation forces itself into the center of the story. Therefore the narrative is compelled to revolve around what the mother has seen. Thus Griffin's story outlines the plan according to which *The Turn of the Screw* will develop. This "ghostly tale" continues where Griffin left off.

We should firmly keep in mind the difference between Griffin's "programmatic" dream event and *The Turn of the Screw*. First of all, there is *un changement de décors*. The actions no longer take place in the world of dreams; they now occur as events in daily life. Second, the story is more complicated because not one child but two children are involved. Third, it is not the mother who tells about her miraculous observation of her child's nightmare. An inexperienced twenty-year-old governess, the youngest daughter of a country parson, is the narrator. Nevertheless, we may say that the example given in the introduction serves as a prelude to the events in *The Turn of the Screw;* these events are built on the same last.

The complication of having two children involved makes it possible for these two (Flora and Miles) to act out their primal scene observations. It does not matter whether these observations have been made by only one child or by both children. If by only one child, through the communication of his knowledge to the other, the same effect results as if both children were present.

These considerations convince us all the more that Griffin's contribution contains the key to a better understanding of *The Turn of the Screw*.

I have not yet dealt with what should be the main factor of comparison. In Griffin's story, the mother wakes up "to encounter also, herself . . . the same sight that had shaken him [her child]." In *The Turn of the Screw* the governess meets the ghost of Peter Quint before she is aware that the children, too, have been in contact with the ghost. One of the attractions of the story is that James purposely leaves it indefinite whether or not the children have shared the governess's supernatural observations. Psychologically, however, not the slightest doubt remains about this point. The children, through

their symbolic play and their conspicuous show of deniallike behavior, betray that they are in tune with the governess's observations
and thoughts. Nevertheless, in *The Turn of the Screw* the emphasis
falls upon the mental processes of the governess.

Is the same true of Griffin's story? Does the mother, too, make her
supernatural observation more independently of the child's than
Griffin's story seems to indicate? Let us try to solve this problem by
posing another question. Does the mother perhaps dream what the
child has seen in his nightmare? After all, the mother's state of mind
cannot be too far apart from the child's state of mind if she experiences the same apparition as the child does. I know very well the
objection that will be raised. If this was a dream that the mother
had, it implies that she would be asleep. We have read that the child
wakes her up. These two facts are irreconcilable with each other. This
"impasse" is exactly what offers me the solution. A mother dreams
that her child, who is sharing the room with her, wakes her up because he has a nightmare. However, she does not really wake up, for
the dream continues. She sees the same apparition that the child has
just seen! Thus, in a dream, she experiences the waking up from
sleep and continues to dream about what has caused the interruption
to her sleep. Freud (1900) called this phenomenon, as one can easily
understand, "a dream within a dream."

At this point a sudden association occurs. I remember that Henry
James was acquainted with this phenomenon. I want to remind you
of his "most appalling yet most admirable nightmare of my life." A
"just dimly-descried figure" had tried to enter his room, but in the
next moment "retreated in terror before my rush and dash. . . ." Let
me quote the crucial sentence: "The lucidity, not to say the sub-
limity, of the crisis had consisted of the great thought that I, in my
appalled state, was probably still more appalling than the awful
agent, creature or presence, whatever he was, whom I had guessed,
in the suddenest wild start from sleep, the sleep within my sleep, to
be making for my place of rest" (p. 348). James's guess comes as an
afterthought, added to the already fixed memory of the dream. Yet
this addition is the core of the dream. The creature making for his
place of rest wakes him up within the dream, *"the sleep within my
sleep."* James had this dream long before he wrote *The Turn of the
Screw.* We may assume that very probably he never thought of this
meaningful detail when he conceived of Griffin's "ghostly" introduc-

tion. Especially he would not have been aware that he was turning "the sleep within my sleep" phenomenon into a supernatural experience. James wrote this confabulation guided by his unconscious. Is it not remarkable that at the same time when James, during a period of years in the 1890s, was in the throes of a conflict which he finally shaped into his poetical creation, Freud in Vienna was conceptualizing his scientific masterpiece, *The Interpretation of Dreams?* In this dream book Freud brilliantly explained the phenomenon which occupied the minds of both men. Freud pointed to "the play within the play," as it occurs in *Hamlet.* In the play, Hamlet engages a troup of actors to perform a drama in which the truth is revealed. His father was slain by his brother, who then married Hamlet's mother. Thus "the play within the play," "the dream within the dream," "the sleep within my sleep," all stress that the manifest content of the primary dream has occurred in reality. Henry James, unbeknown to himself, is in the illustrious company of Shakespeare and Freud!

I return to *The Turn of the Screw.* Griffin's tale, notwithstanding its antirealistic character—or perhaps we can better say by virtue of its antirealistic character—points compellingly to the truth. To stick to James's own wording, a sleep within his sleep, veiled by something supernatural, supports my claim that what is described in the ensuing story is an account of what actually happened to the author in his childhood.

The Turn of the Screw stems from "the romance of life" as well as from "a dream within a dream." These two phenomena are not contradictory. Unconscious processes led to both. Henry James must have had many a dream, many an "appalling" and far from "admirable" nightmare, and hence unrecorded, all of these dreams and nightmares caused by his infantile conflicts.

It is conspicuous how my evaluation of Griffin's tale has changed. Instead of this tale being a weak spot, as I thought at first, I end up by calling it a stroke of genius on the part of James. The supernatural event hides again what the dream within a dream would have stressed so clearly. This change is part of James's attempt to frighten his public. It reflects his problem of how to reveal the truth without admitting that he is exhibiting his own past. Thus Griffin's tale adds to the structural strength of the story. It forms the true psychological backbone of *The Turn of the Screw.*

I feel encouraged to make further use of the introductory chapter in *The Turn of the Screw*. In Griffin's story, a mother is in the center; in *The Turn of the Screw*, the governess has acquired this place. What better proof than this sequence to substantiate my claim that the governess stands for the mother, that according to my analysis she will exhibit some of those unpleasant characteristics of James's mother, characteristics which were very painful for him to admit?

This likeness James wants to hide by describing his governess-mother as a twenty-year-old unmarried girl. How well James has succeeded in keeping his readers off the right track!

Simultaneously, however, he gives free rein to his criticism of his mother. How could more scorn be evoked than by comparing one's mother with a twenty-year-old girl who has no understanding of children? James's mother is so obsessed with ferreting out the truth that she is completely insensitive to what the effect may be upon her children. Namely, through her relentless prodding she harms her children by exciting them, instead of calming them! She is so headstrong that she even keeps her husband from interfering in the children's behalf. Little wonder that young Henry became convinced how cold or even cruel his mother could be!

In the "Causerie" I pointed out that Miles's conflicts arise from the oedipal situation. We find the oedipal character exceptionally well stressed in the introductory chapter, which James did not number, as if he wanted to keep it separate from the story that followed. Yet there are many bridges between this introductory chapter and *The Turn of the Screw*. Douglas fell in love with a woman who was ten years his senior. This same woman, approximately ten years earlier, had been "swept off her feet" by the bachelor of Harley Street. What was the age difference between this woman and the distinguished gentleman? "He had been left, by the death of their parents in India, guardian to a small nephew and a small niece, children of a younger, a military brother, whom he had lost two years before" (p. 6). The bachelor must have been at least one or two years older than his younger brother. We are not told whether this brother immediately followed him or whether other siblings came in between. When would this brother have married? In Victorian England men of this station usually did not wed too early. Even so, let us assume that the brother was only twenty and that a year passed before his first child was born. In the novel Miles is ten years old.

This calculation places the age of the bachelor at thirty-two, as the lowest limit, with the possibility that he was much older.

The boy Miles, who loved the governess, was ten years younger than she was. The same age difference is true for Douglas, who continues the love that Miles began. The boy and the young man are successively in love with a girl ten years older, a mother figure. This girl, in turn, has been in love with a much older man, a father figure. Indeed, every fact points to strong oedipal ties on the part of everyone concerned.

We, the readers, gain the impression that the governess was a woman whose motherly feelings were saturated with an instinctual need to find out. All in all, we conclude that she had a tendency to dominate her husband and children alike.

Listen how differently Douglas, now an old man, speaks about this same woman, with whom he fell in love when he was twenty. "She was a most charming person. . . . She was the most agreeable woman I've ever known in her position; she would have been worthy of any whatever" (p. 3). We are left to decide for ourselves whether he meant worthy of any position or worthy of any man. Very probably it is both. Our impressions of the governess, and of Douglas's praise of her, are antipodal. Could it be that James, once he became an adult, as Douglas is portrayed in the story, felt much more tenderly inclined toward his mother than he had as a child?

In *The Turn of the Screw* a great deal of emphasis falls upon the oedipal situation and its ensuing dangers. May I remind you of my conclusion, previously expressed, that James's ego was not strong enough to find a solution through which his masculine urge could have a chance to be dominant. On the other hand, the first chapter of James's autobiography, which covers a large part of the beginning of James's life until well into latency, is silent about any oedipal material. This difference between story and autobiography is too conspicuous to let pass unnoticed. *The story fills in that part which is left open in James's autobiographical account. Story and autobiography supplement each other.*

The phenomenon of the dream within the dream emphasizes, as it is applied to *The Turn of the Screw*, that the childhood events really happened. Thus, in my opinion, the autobiographical nature of the story is beyond all doubt. But be that as it may, this fact does not prove that my various interpretations are correct. At this point, therefore, it is necessary to make a provisional balance of the present results. Can I corroborate my previous conclusions (1962) about Henry James's parents?

Let us first consider his mother. We turn to the autobiography. The conspicuous absence of any information about Henry's mother in the infantile material appears to be based upon his hatred for her. His death wish is not put into words but is expressed in his silence about her; as the saying goes, borrowed from my native Dutch, he has silenced her to death. His mother did not possess the warmth which his parental grandmother spread around her; his mother was cold or even cruel. Yet his hatred was combined with an equally strong love. This ambivalence was predominant in latency and gave rise to a craving for homesickness.

My study of the novel revealed the following. The relentless prodding by the governess—who stands for Henry's mother—in order to ferret out the truth had a deleterious influence upon the children; it inordinately excited them. Flora revolted, accusing the governess of being cruel. The governess's method of dealing with Miles made too strong an appeal to his incestuous wishes. He died. I ascribed the cause of Miles's death to his overwhelming castration anxiety resulting from these wishes. Thus I deduced that the upbringing by Henry's mother was to a large extent responsible for the fact that James's masculine strivings could never assume sufficient dominance in later life.

The conclusions gained from the novel are most of the time far more detailed than those derived from the autobiographical data. I am very pleased that the two sets of conclusions concur so well; indeed, the result is better than I had hoped for.

Next, I want to see whether my constructions about James's father can be confirmed. It became clear from the autobiography that his father did not encourage young Henry's masculine characteristics. On the contrary, the father showed the boy off for his feminine traits, especially his long fair curls. When James described the angelic appearance of Miles and Flora, he must have been thinking of himself at an early age. Henry had the nickname of "the angel" (Edel, 1953, p. 66; 1962, p. 136); we may assume that this name was applicable not only to his mental attitude but also to his physical appearance. Indeed, in his sparse autobiographical remarks about his father in the early part of Henry's life, I do not find any evidence that his father provided a preoedipal basis for the development of a strong positive oedipus complex.

The Turn of the Screw completes this impression by concentrating on the events which led to the disturbed course of this complex. In a crucial period the father failed to offer his son any possibility for a competitive struggle with him for the mother's love. On the contrary, the father withdrew, leaving the boy unprotected against his mother's exciting influence—a most unfortunate outcome! For now Henry lacked the opportunity to identify with a masculine father. Thus Henry James was unable to develop his masculinity because of what his mother did to him and what his father failed to do for him.

In James's strong emphasis in his novel upon the withdrawal of the bachelor (= his father), we may read a hidden death wish toward his father. "As long as you don't protect me against my mother, who arouses such unbearable castration anxiety in me, you might as well be dead." Henry's father, in his own childhood, suffered so much from his father's harshness that he erred in the opposite direction when it came to bringing up his own sons.

I have already touched upon another reason why Henry probably could not regard his father as a strong man. His father was missing a leg. This conspicuous difference from all other men must have attracted the child's attention very early in life. When, in addition, Henry did not find much evidence to the contrary in the father's mental attitude, the father must have appeared in the child's eyes not only different from but also inferior to other men. This is a point to which I shall certainly want to return later.

With regard to Henry's relationship to his parents as it becomes clear from the autobiographical data, let us consider why I failed to arrive at this conclusion in the "Causerie." I have in mind James's outspoken ambivalence toward both parents. In the novel the parents are dead. The substitute parents James split into the sexual couple, who were also dead, and the living bachelor and the governess. My interpretation was that James had thus removed the parents from any connection with sexual matters. The removal of the parents made it possible to deny any direct observation of parental intercourse or fantasies about the primal scene.

Not only are the parents dead, but their substitutes, Peter Quint and Miss Jessel, share the same fate. I should have asked, why so much emphasis upon death? When I mentioned death in connection with primal scene observations, I should have taken the next step, too. The chain of these observations—the boy becoming too excited sexually, the ego reacting with strong castration anxiety, and finally the wish developing that the parents would be dead, for then the ego could again become quiescent—should not have escaped me.

I should have been more alert in another respect as well. The combination of shortcomings in the method of upbringing by both bachelor and governess spoke loudly. As a result, this method failed to safeguard Miles's masculinity, and I should at least have thought of the possibility that through this failure James's genital urge might have regressed to an anal fixation. For there is certainly reason to believe that Henry's anal phase met interference from his mother. A mother so strongly possessed with the idea of forcing the truth out of her children might very well also strive to exert a similar control over their excremental functions. A fixation on an anal level is then usually the result. When next the genital urge encounters strong obstacles, the ego, as a defensive measure, finds it relatively easy to bring the genital urge to regression.

My remarks about why I did not draw certain conclusions in the "Causerie" are, of course, the result of hindsight, when everything becomes much easier. Nevertheless, these belated remarks are valuable in showing that this ghostly tale hints at the same facts which I could demonstrate rather easily in the autobiographical material.

Our discussion of the parents finished, it is now the children's turn to be examined. Both parents in the story are dead. The father had been a military man. Miles and Flora are of the same order as the enviable lot of parentally bereft cousins. Both parents of the Temple cousins died in 1854; their father was also a military man, a captain. Thus Miles and Flora are the English version of the American Temple cousins.

Here one might interject that there were six Temple cousins. Two boys and Minnie were the three among these cousins who were specially preferred by Henry. Why, then, would Henry James use only two cousins as examples? The answer is rather simple. The author, because he had acted out as a child with only one other sibling, needed only two children for his story. It might also be asked, why did James choose a boy and a girl? Why, for instance, not two boys? Again, it was because a boy and a girl best fulfilled the author's purposes. We remember that Flora had to represent, among other things, young Henry's feminine traits. At least, that was my conclusion at the time. Now I feel able to corroborate this interpretation. The father exhibited young Henry for his feminine appearance, and Henry was reluctant to give this up, as evidenced by the tearful sacrifice of his curls.

It is very interesting that Henry, when he reached adulthood, should be attracted to Minnie Temple. It was a feeling which he shared with many other young men. Yet, in my opinion, Henry's feelings were aroused for different reasons than the feelings which steered other young men in Minnie's direction. The autobiography mentions that young Henry's attraction was already present in latency. From *The Turn of the Screw* we may deduct the nature of his attraction to Minnie at that early period. In Minnie he found the externalization of his own feminine traits, foreshadowing his adult feelings for Minnie. I doubt whether Henry could free himself from the type of influence that she exerted upon him in latency. This will be a point to think about when I discuss this later period.

I want to remind you that not only the Temple children but also his cousin Gussy Barker made a lasting impression upon Henry. It was not one of the Temple boys but Gussy Barker who, during his short life, continued to have an influence upon Henry James. Gussy Barker was killed in action during the Civil War at the age of twenty-one.

There was another cousin, Marie James (1841-1906), who, although not belonging to the enviable lot of parentally bereft cousins, left an indelible mark in Henry's memories. It must have been in 1854 when his father took the eleven-year-old Henry with him to visit his sister, Mrs. Temple, who was then deathly ill at the home of his brother, Augustus James. Henry's uncle (Augustus James) had ordered Marie to go to bed. The latter, "in a visible commotion," fled into her mother's arms, "a protest and an appeal in short which drew from my aunt the simple phrase that was from that moment so preposterously to 'count' for me. 'Come now, my dear; don't make a scene—I *insist* on your not making a scene!' " The impression on young Henry was "epoch-making." He expended a lot of thought on it, as evidenced by this summing up: "The mark had been made for me and the door flung open; the passage, gathering up *all* the elements of the troubled time, had been itself a scene, quite enough of one, and I had become aware with it of a rich accession of possibilities" (pp. 185-186).

Certainly Henry James grasped one of these possibilities when he described the scene Flora made when the governess attempted to confront her with Miss Jessel's ghost. And it was not the only scene she made. Later, when Flora was alone with Mrs. Grose, she used "really shocking" language in talking about her tormentor, the governess. "It's beyond everything, for a young lady; and I can't think wherever she must have picked up . . ." (p. 117).

I cannot resist expressing my suspicion—in the "Causerie" I already touched upon this subject—that young Henry, the angel, must have gathered quite a profane vocabulary for himself. If he had opened the floodgates of his speech, he might have amazed a number of people, who would have wondered where he picked it up.

My suspicion seems to be contradicted by William's statement, "*I* play with boys who curse and swear," on the occasion when Henry offered William his company on a planned excursion (p. 260). Henry's contemplative remark, "It wasn't that I mightn't have been drawn to the boys in question, but that I simply wasn't qualified" (p. 260), leaves the question open. Let us not forget that Miles was expelled from school because he had said things—the nature of which never was made clear—to other boys. Only under special circumstances might Henry have revealed his carefully hidden knowledge, if indeed he had not lost it through repression.

Speaking of the children in *The Turn of the Screw,* I want to stress another of my failures in understanding the situation. In the "Causerie" I ventured the opinion that James in his "attempt to disguise the underlying events . . . may have distorted the ages of the children as well" (p. 477). The story is of two latency children, eight and ten years old. My figuring led me to think that the traumatic events "took place before and around the time when he [James] was about five years old" (p. 478). I could not reconcile these two facts and failed to find the solution. How easy the next step would have been! The events which occurred around the age of five formed the basis for his latency fantasy!

But let us change the subject and turn our attention to the lovable Mrs. Grose. She was only a menial hand, who could neither read nor write, but she made up for these shortcomings by her love for the children. I remarked that the person of Mrs. Grose was necessary in order to identify the ghosts for the governess. She herself did not see any apparitions; she had no forbidden wishes to ward off in that manner. Do you want a proof of her warm feelings? When the governess tried to confront Flora with the ghostly appearance of Miss Jessel, Mrs. Grose came to the support of the child. "She isn't there, little lady, and nobody's there—and you never see nothing, my sweet!" And so on. At that particular moment Mrs. Grose showed quite a different attitude from that of the governess. Where did we meet a similar difference? We know where. Henry James was thinking of his dear old grandmother when he created Mrs. Grose. In some respects the latter became practically the opposite of the gentle old lady. James took away her books, her glasses, and her candlelight. He even transformed her into an analphabetic. But for all he left out, he retained her abundant warmth. We feel quite comfortable after this last discovery. We find ourselves face to face with the charm of the grandmother's "playroomed orphanage"! *The Turn of the Screw* re-creates perfectly the external situation which represented the realization of James's already existing romantic fantasies about life.

Mrs. Grose excepted, women do not fare well in *The Turn of the Screw*. Take the introductory chapter, in which Douglas promises to read his story if everyone will stay. " '*I* will—and *I* will!' cried the ladies whose departure had been fixed." But when the evening arrived, these ladies were gone. "But that only made his little final auditory more compact and *select,* kept it, round the hearth, subject to a common thrill" (p. 5; my italics). James's attitude is fittingly described by a line from *My Fair Lady:* "Don't let a woman into your life."

At last my critic has refound his voice. His beginning words contain a surprise. "When you made a connection between *The Turn of the Screw* and James's 'romance of life,' I began to have for the first time some appreciation for your idea. Although the evidence was flimsy, there was some truth in what you said. This is the reason why I kept silent so long, all the time waiting to give you a chance to bring more material to substantiate your findings. But I waited in vain. Soon you fell back into your old habits, and especially I did not like the way you dealt with the biographical material. Instead of leaving this material unchanged so that it could be used as a solid background against which your constructions could be measured, you started to apply your highly questionable method to the autobiographical data themselves. Thus you thoroughly destroyed the yardstick needed to procure evidence for establishing that your interpretations had a certain degree of validity. Still I did not object. However, in the last part of your presentation you have gone from bad to worse. You have not kept the analysis of the story separate from the analysis of the autobiography, but have mixed the two analyses up so that I can no longer make head or tail out of them. Not only have you 'enriched' the autobiography with your findings from *The Turn of the Screw,* you have done the opposite as well. According to a previous remark of yours, the knowledge that James was a bachelor dulled your sensitivity—the sensitivity necessary for interpretations. Therefore you concluded that the analysis of the story should not make use of material obtained from other sources. It seems that you now ignore completely what you once preached yourself. It boils down to this. You now defend the thesis that autobiography and novel supplement each other, whereas at first you wanted no interference from the autobiographical information."

My critic is finally ready with his accusation. "I have the feeling that you have abandoned your original point of view because it became advantageous to you to bend two different sets of conclusions toward each other. You are trying to impress people with the result, in the hope that they won't notice your change of attitude. Either your first or your second point of view is wrong. They cannot both be correct."

This is quite an accusation. I am glad to receive help from my benevolent critic, who in the meantime has become highly amused. "It seems that you pick out something to praise in order to become more firmly opposed to everything else. As for your attack on our speaker's attempt to analyze the autobiographical material as well, I, on the contrary, very much approve of it. It is a necessary procedure if one wants to compare the interpretation of the novel with the autobiographical facts. The analysis of the story acknowledges the unconscious. Therefore one has to do the same with the autobiographical data, for otherwise the two members of the comparison would be unevenly matched.

"The analytic method cannot be tested by procedures that are not based upon analytic thinking. If the analysis of the two different sources of information, namely, autobiography and novel, leads to the same results, this outcome has to be respected. It proves that the novel is indeed autobiographical in nature. Simultaneously the results speak for the correctness of the analytic method; in other words, the analytic method has to prove its own correctness."

Here my benevolent critic pauses for a while. I am already considering whether it would not be better to enter the discussion when suddenly he resumes his speech with a very vigorous attack upon my first critic. "You want, above all, to be destructively critical and you were already enjoying your triumph when you discovered that the speaker had resorted to a trick: he silently dropped a viewpoint which could no longer be of advantage to him. I want to show that, contrary to your opinion, the two different viewpoints are not irreconcilable at all. I shall try to do this, for I believe I have fully understood the speaker's method. He first tried to explain *The Turn of the Screw* by using only the text. The fact that Henry James remained a bachelor could have been deduced from the text; I agree with the speaker that to be already informed of this single fact before any interpretation about it was made, was a definite disadvantage. Next, the autobiography had to be analytically examined. When it became clear that novel and autobiography concurred so well, a new step could be taken. The increased insight made it possible also to analyze the introductory part of *The Turn of the Screw,* which until that moment still remained obscure. But once the material of autobiography and ghost story had been analytically exhausted separately, still further clarification could be obtained by using autobiographical data to throw light upon certain details in *The Turn of the Screw,* and vice versa, namely, to use conclusions gained from the novel to fill in the gaps where the autobiography failed to supply information. Thus there is no contradiction at all. What you [the skeptical critic] call two irreconcilable viewpoints may be regarded as a development in the method. The extended method not only served to bring new facts to light but also succeeded in correcting certain mistakes."

My benevolent critic's (and also my) opponent shakes his head in disbelief. "I thought I had such an excellent point when I discovered the contradiction between the previous and the present method of interpretation. You insist that the latter is the logical extension of the first." Meditatively he continues, "I am afraid analysis is not for me."

I feel sorry for the downcast fellow, although I know, as soon as he sees fit, he will again try to throw me off balance with a disparaging remark. I want to cheer him up and tell him some of the opinions of James's biographer, Leon Edel. On various occasions Edel emphasized the impossibility of analyzing *The Turn of the Screw*, but he nevertheless unwittingly supplied proofs corroborating my interpretations. For instance, when Henry James's nephew (William's eldest son) inquired why his uncle said so little about his mother, James answered, "Oh! my dear Boy—that memory is too sacred" (Edel, 1953, p. 48). As the Dutch say, blood crawls where it cannot go. The memory may be too sacred, but the warded-off still finds ways to break through. The silence occasioned by James's consideration for his mother's memory is simultaneously used by the warded off to express a death wish toward his mother. The feeling of sacredness hides his ambivalence.

Or listen to this quotation from Edel (1953). Speaking of mothers in James's novels, Edel concludes: "Fear of women and worship of women: the love theme plays itself out in striking fashion throughout Henry James's work" (p. 55). Fear of women arises from the one valency of his ambivalence; worship of women, from the other.

And here is a more recent opinion: "What is less understandable is his inveterate choice of women [that is, the women with whom James had social contact] who were strong, domineering and had in them also a streak of *hardness, sometimes even of cruelty*. These women probably appealed to him because rich qualities were distinctly familiar: Mary James had been quite as hard, firm, sovereign, but more desirous. Indeed during all the years of his childhood he had learned how to make himself agreeable to such a woman" (Edel, 1962, p. 356; my italics).

Our explanation of the reason why Henry James chose the company of this type of woman differs analytically from Edel's explanation. We remember Henry's "first assured conception of true richness was that we should be sent separately off among cold or even cruel aliens in order to be there thrillingly homesick."

As an adult, James left the United States to settle in a foreign country. He was not "sent off," as the fantasy expressed it, but acted of his own free will. Among his conscious motivations for leaving his homeland we would probably look in vain for a craving for homesickness. Nevertheless, the women whom he contacted, according to Edel, were domineering, hard, and sometimes even cruel. The analyst would conclude that James's choice was still influenced by his latency fantasy. He was reacting to the same ambivalent feelings which in latency gave rise to his craving for homesickness. He felt simultaneously hostile toward and attracted to this type of woman, who represented his mother of the anal period. Thus Edel's conclusion unexpectedly offers us the opportunity to discover that James was acting out his childhood fantasy when he made his decision to live outside the United States.

The origin of *The Turn of the Screw* needs further discussion, but I think we are already justified in drawing the following conclusion. According to all indications of the "provisional balance," our analysis of *The Turn of the Screw* is here to stay.

BIBLIOGRAPHY

Deutsch, H. (1930), Zur Genese des Familienromans. *Int. Z. Psa.*, 16:249-253.
Dupee, F. W. (1956), *Henry James, Autobiography*, ed. with an Introduction by F. W. Dupee. New York: Criterion Books.
Edel, L. (1949), Introduction to *Ghostly Tales of Henry James*. New York: Grosset & Dunlap, 1963.
—— (1953), *Henry James, 1843-1870: The Untried Years*. Philadelphia: Lippincott.
—— (1962), *Henry James: The Conquest of London*. Philadelphia: Lippincott.
Freud, S. (1900), The Interpretation of Dreams. *Standard Edition*, 4 & 5. London: Hogarth Press, 1953.
—— (1908), Creative Writers and Day-Dreaming. *Standard Edition*, 9:141-153. London: Hogarth Press, 1959.
—— (1909), Family Romances. *Standard Edition*, 9:235-241. London: Hogarth Press, 1959.
—— (1912), Recommendations to Physicians Practising Psycho-Analysis. *Standard Edition*, 12:109-120. London: Hogarth Press, 1958.
Frosch, J. (1959), Transference Derivatives of the Family Romance. *J. Amer. Psa. Assn.*, 7:503-522.
Greenacre, P. (1958), The Family Romance of the Artist. *This Annual*, 13:9-43.
James, H. (1898), *The Turn of the Screw*. New York: Modern Library, 1930.
—— (1908), The Jolly Corner. *Ghostly Tales*. New York: Grosset & Dunlap, 1963.
—— (1913), *A Small Boy and Others*. New York: Scribner, 1941.
Katan, M. (1962), A Causerie on Henry James's "The Turn of the Screw." *This Annual*, 17:473-493.
Kris, E. (1952), *Psychoanalytic Explorations in Art*. New York: International Universities Press.
Meyer, B. C. (1964), Psychoanalytic Studies on Joseph Conrad: I. The Family Romance. *J. Amer. Psa. Assn.*, 12:32-58.

CONTENTS OF VOLUMES I–XX

D